# Media Literacy

## THIRD EDITION

# W. James Potter

*University of California at Santa Barbara*

**SAGE** Publications
Thousand Oaks ▪ London ▪ New Delhi

*For information:*

Sage Publications, Inc.
2455 Teller Road
Thousand Oaks, California 91320
E-mail: order@sagepub.com

Sage Publications Ltd.
1 Oliver's Yard
55 City Road
London EC1Y 1SP
United Kingdom

Sage Publications India Pvt. Ltd.
B-42, Panchsheel Enclave
Post Box 4109
New Delhi 110 017 India

Printed in the United States of America.

*Library of Congress Cataloging-in-Publication Data*

Potter, W. James.
Media literacy / W. James Potter.— 3rd ed.
    p. cm.
Includes bibliographical references and index.
ISBN 1-4129-0989-9 (pbk. : alk paper)
   1. Media literacy. I. Title.
P96.M4P68 2005
302.23—dc22                                                    2004024119

This book is printed on acid-free paper.

05   06   07   08   09   10   9   8   7   6   5   4   3   2   1

| | |
|---|---|
| *Acquisitions Editor:* | Margaret H. Seawell |
| *Editorial Assistant:* | Jill Meyers |
| *Production Editor:* | Tracy Alpern |
| *Copy Editor:* | Gillian Dickens |
| *Typesetter:* | C&M Digitals (P) Ltd. |
| *Indexer:* | Will Ragsdale |
| *Cover Designer:* | Michelle Lee Kenny |

# Contents

# Preface

Most of us think we are fairly media literate. We know the names of a great many television shows, films, magazines, books, and song titles. We recognize the names and faces of celebrities. We know how to read. We can easily follow plots in movies and television shows. We understand what flashbacks mean, and we know enough to get scared when the soft background music builds to a shattering crescendo as a character steps into danger. We might even be skilled at playing games on a computer and programming a VCR. Clearly, we know how to expose ourselves to the media, we know how to absorb information from them, and we know how to be entertained by them.

Are we media literate? Yes, of course. We have acquired a great deal of information and developed remarkable skills. The abilities to speak a language, read, understand photographs, and follow narratives are achievements that we too often take for granted.

We should not overlook what we have accomplished. However, it is also important to acknowledge that we all can be much more media literate. Your level of media literacy now is probably the same as it was when you first became a teenager. Since that time, your information base has grown enormously about some types of media messages, such as popular songs, movies, TV shows, video games, and Internet sites. However, your information base is not likely to have grown much in other areas—about how messages are produced and programmed, who controls the media, the economics of the industry, and how the media exert subtle effects on you and society. Thus, your continuing level of media literacy allows you to do many things with the media. However, what you do not know about the media keeps you in a state of ignorance that allows the media to do many things to you without you realizing it.

The more you are aware of how the media operate and how they affect you, the more you gain control over those effects, and the more you will separate yourself from typical media users who have turned over a great deal of their lives to the media without realizing it. By "turning over a great deal of their lives to the media," I mean more than time and money, although both of those are considerable. I also mean that most people have allowed the media to program them. The media have programmed their exposure habits. The media have programmed the way they look at the world by setting their expectations for relationships, attractiveness, success, celebrity, health, newsworthy events, problems, and solutions. At relatively low levels of media literacy, people know enough about how to access media messages but not enough to be able to protect themselves from the subtle, yet constant, shaping of perceptions about life. Once the media have gradually defined what life means for people, those people's behaviors, attitudes, and emotions will fall in line with those definitions. Ascending to higher levels of media literacy gives people the ability to gradually undo the media definitions and erase those "lines of code" that the media have programmed into our minds and replace the media programming with ideas of our own. This book is written to show you what it means to operate at a higher level of media literacy and thereby gain more power to use the media to achieve your own goals rather than letting the media use you to achieve their goals.

This book is composed of a core of 21 chapters that are organized into six parts: Foundations, Knowledge Structures of Media Content, Knowledge Structures of Media Industries, Knowledge Structures of Media Effects, Increasing Media Literacy, and Issues in Media Literacy. The four chapters in the Foundations section ask you to confront the following question: Should I work on developing my knowledge about the media? In Chapter 1, I show you why developing media literacy is such an important thing to do. Chapter 2 presents a range in thinking about what media literacy is and builds to a definition that I use throughout this book. In Chapter 3, I show the model of media literacy that organizes all the information in the book. Chapter 4 explains how higher degrees of media literacy can be developed. It shows that certain skills of media literacy grow on their own during childhood along several dimensions: cognitive, emotional, and moral. Growth can still take place during adulthood, but we must work at it in specific ways.

Part II contains four chapters that focus on media content and help you build your knowledge structures about the content of the media. Chapter 5 introduces the idea of content and presents the major characteristic of all media content—what I call "one-step remove" reality. Then, Chapter 6 focuses on entertainment content, Chapter 7 on news content, and Chapter 8 on advertising content.

The four chapters in Part III deal with important concepts that you can use to build your knowledge structures about the media industries. Chapter 9 helps you see the media industries from a historical perspective. Using a life cycle structure, it shows what is behind the innovation and development of the media industries. An economic perspective is used in Chapter 10 to show the business foundations of the industries. Chapter 11 shows patterns of ownership and control of the mass media companies. Chapter 12 takes a marketing perspective as the nature of the audience is presented through the eyes of industry decision makers. The topics laid out in these four media industry chapters are illustrated in Appendix A, where each of the mass media is profiled.

The three chapters in Part IV deal with the effects of the media. Chapter 13 will help you expand your vision about what constitutes a media effect. Effects are both long term as well as immediate. Although they can influence our behavior, they also have profound influences on us cognitively, affectively, emotionally, and physiologically. And they have positive as well as negative effects. Appendix B provides a list of immediate and long-term effects. The question of how the effects processes work on us is explored in Chapter 14. Those processes are hardly ever simple or direct. More often, the media work in concert with many other factors that each serve to increase the probability that an effect may occur. When we take a broader perspective on effects, we can more accurately assess the influence of the media in our lives. This also puts us in a much better position to manage the effects of the media.

In Chapter 15, the influence of media is examined in terms of changes on the fundamental institutions of politics, family, religion, and society. The media, especially television, have forever altered the way these institutions function. Those media-generated changes on institutions affect all of us as individuals.

Part V begins with a chapter that illustrates why a broad knowledge about the real world is as important as a thorough knowledge about the media industries. Real-world knowledge helps us check to see if the media are presenting a balanced picture of society. Although this chapter cannot present a full inventory of the real-world knowledge a person needs, it presents some examples (such as in the areas of crime, the legal system, and government) to illustrate how real-world knowledge is often at odds with the media picture.

The next two chapters lay out some key strategies for improving literacy. Chapter 17 focuses on how you can become more media literate by synthesizing the findings in the previous 16 chapters to help you develop a lifelong media literacy plan. Chapter 18 presents ways you can help others build their media literacy.

In Part VI, I present three chapters that allow you to use the skills and knowledge structures you have developed up to that point. Chapter 19 examines how the media have changed sports in this country, Chapter 20 provides an analysis of violence in the media, and Chapter 21 examines privacy and piracy in today's digitized media environment. These three issues were chosen for special examination because each has generated some strong opinions. However, public opinion is frequently based on faulty reasoning, so these issues will give you a chance to examine your own opinions and analyze the degree to which they are based on accurate information and inference.

# How to Get the Most Out of This Book

When you read each of these chapters, think in terms of developing your knowledge structures. Begin with the thesis statement, which is the "key idea" of that chapter. Then look at the outline at the beginning of the chapter. Outlines will show you the major branches and each branch's supporting ideas. Then read the text while continually asking yourself the following: How does this new information fit in with what I already know? And how can I use this? After your first reading, close the book and see how much you can recall. Can you remember only an assortment of facts, or can you envision an organized knowledge structure?

This book has a self-help tone to it as it presents guidance and practical exercises to help you achieve higher levels of media literacy. Do not get caught in the trap of thinking that it is sufficient to memorize the facts in each chapter and then stop thinking about the material. Simply memorizing facts will not help you increase your media literacy much. Instead, you need to internalize the information by drawing it into your own experiences. Continually ask yourself, "Can I find an example of this in my own life?" and "How can I apply this when I deal with the media?" The exercises at the end of each chapter will help you get started with this. The more you think through the exercises and the more you develop new exercises for yourself, the more you will be internalizing the information and thus making it more a natural part of the way you think. For example, in the chapter on broadening your perspective on media effects, I present a four-dimensional scheme. If you simply memorize this scheme, it may help you a bit on a test, but memorization alone won't help you become a more acute observer of media effects. To develop such acuity, you need to use the scheme to guide your observations of behaviors, emotional manifestations, utterances of opinions, and the like. The more you practice spotting and naming these effects, the more you will be internalizing the information and learning a useful tool to keep with you the rest of your life. Thus, the concepts are presented as tools to help you achieve more awareness in your everyday life.

In summary, the purpose of this book is to help you develop strong knowledge structures about the media. Will the book provide you with all the information you need? No. That would require too much information to fit into one book; you will need to continue reading. At the end of most chapters, I suggest several books for further reading on the topic of that chapter. Although some of those books are fairly technical, most of them are easy to read and very interesting.

## How to Get the Most Out of Teaching With This Book

For educators adopting the book, an Instructor's Resources CD is available. You will notice that this CD, unlike other instructor's resources, does not include a long list of objective questions that you could draw upon to create exams. Because my approach to media literacy does not focus on the skill of memorizing, I feel that testing student knowledge with true-false, multiple choice, or fill in the blank questions sends the wrong message to students about knowledge.

The CD is organized into three parts. Part I includes diagnostic tools. The section begins with a questionnaire that I have used as a quiz to diagnose where students' individual levels of knowledge stand as they enter my course. This quiz not only helps me get students thinking reflexively but also provides me with a picture of what students know and do not know at the outset of their journey to media literacy. In addition to this quiz, Part I includes the related answer key and some guidelines for scoring the quiz. Part I goes on to expand upon the idea of knowledge styles, which is introduced in Chapter 4 of the text. The section includes a second diagnostic test and answer key to help determine the dominant knowledge styles in your class. Knowing what styles dominate in your course will help further clarify the challenge you have in teaching these students to become more media literate.

Part II of the CD presents general guides. First, there is a Guide for Writing Exercises, and this is followed by the Guide for Evaluating Student Knowledge and Skills. One of the principles to effectively teaching media literacy is keeping students involved, and this is best done, in part, by continually employing learning exercises. There are many exercises in the text at the end of the chapters. However, you may want to develop your own exercises to supplement or substitute for those in the text. These guides will help you do just that. I also present some guidelines for writing essay questions to test how students build their knowledge structures, sharpen their thinking skills, internalize information, and craft stronger personal opinions. After doing this, I discuss ways of assessing student performance using such questions.

Part III contains chapter guides for each of the text's 18 numbered chapters and the issue chapters. Each of these chapter guides begins with the outline from the front of the chapter, then presents a list of important points to emphasize in classroom presentations. Finally, I suggest particular exercises you might want to try, in addition to what I present in the text itself.

# To Conclude

This book is an introduction. It is designed to show you the big picture so you can get started efficiently on increasing your own media literacy. It is important to get started now. The world is rapidly changing because of VCRs, computers, the Internet, and other media channels that are substantially revising the way the media industries do business and the way we receive messages.

I hope you will have fun reading this book. And I hope it will expose you to new perspectives from which you can perceive much more about the media. If it does, you will be gaining new insights about your old habits and interpretations. If this happens, I hope you will share your new insights and "war stories" with me. Much of this book has been written to reflect some of the problems and insights my students have had in the media literacy courses I have taught. I have learned much from them. I'd like to learn even more from you. So let me know what you think and send me a message at wjpotter@comm.ucsb.edu.

See you on the journey!

# Acknowledgments

This book project has traveled a very long distance from its beginnings as an idea in the mid-1990s. Since then I have had the privilege of using various versions of the book with hundreds of students at Florida State University, Stanford University, and the University of California at Santa Barbara. These students helped me form the idea into a useful book for a broad range of undergraduates and refine the material through two subsequent editions. I thank them for every question, every puzzled look, and every smile of satisfaction from an insight gained.

I thank the many reviewers whom SAGE called on to critique the text in each edition. Some contacted me directly; others chose to remain anonymous. In all cases their comments were valuable. The reviewers include:

Michael Bartanen, Pacific Lutheran University

Ralph Beliveau, University of Oklahoma

William Christ, Trinity University

John Dillon, Murray State University

W. A. Dorman, California State University, Sacramento

Deborah Dunn, Westmont College

Ivy Glennon, University of Illinois at Urbana-Champaign

Tim Meyer, University of Wisconsin, Green Bay

Timothy J. Moreland, Catawba College

Joy F. Morrison, University of Alaska

Richard M. Perloff, Cleveland State University

Brian Steffen, Simpson College

I am grateful for the support of numerous SAGE staff. Margaret Seawell, Executive Editor, is the consummate professional you wish everyone could be. Her early excitement over the proposal made me believe that I could write this book, and her steadfast commitment to the project over the years has seen the book into its third edition. In the Production Department, Astrid Virding skillfully took the first edition from manuscript to bound book, as did Claudia Hoffman on the second edition and Tracy Alpern on the third. They made it look easy, though there must have been days when it was anything but. I also want to thank Ben Badger in Marketing and Gina Fenwick and Heidi Axcell in Sales for their enthusiastic support of the new edition.

If you like this book, then I share the credit of success with all the people I mentioned above. If you find a mistake, a shortcoming, or a misinterpretation, then it is my fault for not fully assimilating all the high-quality help I have been privileged to experience.

# FOUNDATIONS

# Why Increase Media Literacy?

*Key Idea:* We put our minds on "automatic pilot" to protect ourselves from the flood of media messages we constantly encounter. The danger with this automatic processing of messages is that it allows the media to condition our thought processes.

**Message Saturation**
**The Default Model of Automaticity**
**Traps**
   Trap 1: Information Fatigue
   Trap 2: False Feeling of Being Informed
   Trap 3: False Sense of Control
   Trap 4: Faulty Beliefs
**Need for Media Literacy**
**Conclusion**
**Further Reading**

When you go to a supermarket and buy, let's say, 25 items, how many decisions have you made? The temptation is to say 25 decisions because you needed to have made a decision to buy each of your 25 items. But what about all the items you *decided not to buy?* The average supermarket today has about 30,000 items on its shelves. So you actually made 30,000 decisions in the relatively short time you were in the supermarket—25 decisions to buy a product and 29,975 decisions not to buy a product.

How is it possible to be so fast and efficient in decision making? The answer is that you have automatic routines in your brain that direct you to filter out almost all products and focus on a small, manageable set of products. This makes it possible for you to shop efficiently and not spend all week in the supermarket.

There is a great advantage of using automatic routines. However, there is also a serious disadvantage to using automatic routines—we can become too focused on efficiency and lose sight of why we go shopping. Perhaps you are very health conscious. Had you been less concerned with efficiency, you would have read the labels on more products to make better selections. For example, not all low-fat products have the same fat content; not all products with vitamins added have the same vitamins or the same proportions. Or perhaps you are very price conscious. Had you been less concerned with efficiency, you would have looked more carefully at the unit pricing and might have gotten more value for the money you spent.

# Message Saturation

Our culture is a grand supermarket of media messages. Those messages are everywhere whether we realize it or not, except that there are far more messages in our culture than there are products in any supermarket. This proliferation of messages comes to us through the mass media (see Table 1.1). For example, this year in the United States alone, there will be almost 65,000 book titles published, and each of these is available in public libraries or through online bookstores for a relatively modest price. Furthermore, books are only one channel of information. Throughout the world, radio stations send out 65.5 million hours of original programming each year, and television adds another 48 million hours. In this country alone, the seven major film studios have an additional 169,500 television programs in their archives.

With personal computers, we have access to even more information than ever when we connect to the Internet. The Internet gives us access to about 3,000 newspapers (Kawamoto, 2003). Also, the World Wide Web offers access to about 2.5 billion documents. These are the publicly available pages, referred to as the surface web. There is also what is called the deep web, which consists of pages that require memberships, fees, or are otherwise private. This deep web has been estimated to be 400 to 550 times the size of the surface web (Lyman & Varian, 2003).

The information problem has shifted from one of gaining access to one of protecting ourselves from too much. Until about two centuries ago, the majority of the population could not read, and even if it could, there were few books available. In the early 1300s, the Sorbonne Library in Paris contained only 1,338 books and yet was thought to be the largest library in Europe. Only elites had access to those books. Today, there are many libraries with more than 8 million books, and they lend out their books to millions of

**Table 1.1**  Information Vehicles

| Medium | United States | World |
|---|---|---|
| Books (titles per year) | 64,711 | 968,735 |
| Radio stations | 13,261 | 47,776 |
| TV broadcast stations | 1,686 | 21,264 |
| Newspapers | 2,386 | 22,643 |
| Mass-market periodicals | 20,000 | 80,000 |
| Scholarly journals | 10,500 | 40,000 |
| Newsletters | 10,000 | 40,000 |
| Archived office pages | $3 \times 10^9$ | $7.5 \times 10^9$ |

SOURCE: Lyman and Varian (2003).

people every year. With literacy rates high and the availability of public libraries in every city and almost every small town, access to books, magazines, newspapers, and audiovisual materials of all kinds is no problem.

Not only is information easily available to almost anyone today, but information also keeps getting produced at an ever increasing rate. More information has been generated since you were born than the sum total of all information throughout all recorded history up until the time of your birth. Half of all the scientists who have ever lived are alive today and producing information. Also, the number of people in this country who identify themselves as artists increased from 737,000 in 1970 to 2.2 million in 2000, the number of musicians grew from 100,000 in 1970 to 187,000 in 2001, and the number of authors quadrupled to 128,000 (Kiger, 2004). These artists, musicians, and authors are pumping even more messages through our media channels everyday.

Researchers estimated that in the year 2002 alone, there were 5 exabytes of information produced worldwide (Lyman & Varian, 2003). How much information is this? A byte is a unit of information storage. A kilobyte is 1,000 bytes or the information contained in two typed pages or a low-resolution photograph. A megabyte is a million bytes, which is the information in a small novel or 6 seconds of a high-fi recording. A gigabyte is 1 billion bytes. A terabyte is 1,000 gigabytes, a petabyte is 1,000 terabytes, and an exabyte is 1,000 petabytes. To put 5 exabytes in perspective, the 19 million books and other materials in the U.S. Library of Congress, if digitized, would take up about 10 terabytes of information. This means that the amount of information produced in 2002 alone is 500,000 times the amount of all the holdings in the Library of Congress. As if that is not scary enough, Lyman and Varian (2003) estimate that the rate of growth of information increases at 30% each year. This means that in 2005, the amount of new information produced *in that one year alone* will be 10 exabytes or about 1 million times as much information currently in the Library of Congress.

The information problem is no longer about how to get access. The much more pressing problem is how to keep up with all the information. For example, if you were to try to read only the new books published this year, you would have to read a book every 8 minutes for 24 hours each day with no breaks over the entire year. All that effort would be needed just to keep up with the new titles published in only the United States! You would have no time left to read any of the other 66 million book titles in existence worldwide (Lyman & Varian, 2003). Also, the world produces about 31 million hours of original TV programming each year (Lyman & Varian, 2003). If you wanted to watch all the television programming broadcast in this year alone, it would take you about 35 centuries—if you took no breaks!

We live in an environment that is far different from any environment humans have ever experienced before. And the environment changes at an ever increasing pace. This is due to the accelerating generation of information and the sharing of that information through the increasing number of media channels and the heavy traffic of media vehicles traversing those channels. Messages are being delivered to everyone, everywhere, constantly. We are all saturated with information, and each year the media are more aggressive in seeking our attention.

We have long since reached a saturation point; it is a hopeless expectation to keep up with information. There is now so much information that the information problem has shifted from one of access, to one of trying to keep up, to one of avoidance.

How can we protect ourselves? We can stop buying and reading books. We can cut back on our subscriptions to magazines and stop newspaper delivery. We can reduce our time searching for particular messages in radio, television, and the Internet. But exposures will still occur because the media are aggressive and will create hundreds of opportunities each day to grab our attention. We cannot avoid all media messages unless we physically remove ourselves from our culture. But then we lose the opportunity to experience all the good things about the media. What can we do? Instead of physically removing ourselves from the culture, we psychologically remove ourselves. This means that we place our brains on automatic pilot so that our minds filter out almost all the messages bombarding us.

# The Default Model of Automaticity

To keep ourselves sane in the information-saturated culture, we program our minds to filter out almost all messages automatically. Psychologists refer to this automatic processing of information as *automaticity*. Automaticity is a state where our minds operate without any conscious effort from us. Thus, we can perform even complicated tasks routinely without even thinking about them. For example, typing is a relatively complicated task, but after we learn to type, we do it automatically. Think about your experience in first learning to type. You had to think of the individual letters in each word, think about which key controlled which letter, and then command a finger to press the correct key. It took you a long time to type out a word. But with practice, you are able to type out paragraphs without thinking much about which finger needs to strike which key in which order. Now when you type, you enter the state of automaticity where well-developed habits guide your actions without requiring you to think about them.

Although automaticity is a very efficient state for filtering *out* almost all media messages, there are times when we want to filter *in* a message; that is, we want to pay attention to it rather than ignore it. So the state of automaticity has "triggers" programmed into it so that when a particular kind of message is in the environment, our attention is triggered. To illustrate this, imagine yourself driving in your car with the radio playing while you are talking to your friend. Your attention is on the conversation with your friend, and your mind is automatically filtering out the music playing from the radio. But then your favorite song starts playing, and your attention to the music is triggered. You are likely to interrupt your conversation and shift your attention to the music.

An important question for media literacy is, Who or what programs your triggers? Naturally, you program some of your triggers. When we are aware of particular motives and goals for entertainment or information, we can easily program our triggers. You make your favorite song a trigger. Your favorite actors are triggers; when you scan through the newspaper, quickly skipping over most stories, the name or picture of your favorite actor appears, and this triggers your attention, so you slow down and read the story.

When we have specific goals or needs for certain kinds of messages, it is easy to program our triggers. But a great deal of the time, media exposure is done mindlessly; that is, we are not really sure what we want so we have no goals as we flip through a magazine, have the radio playing in the background, or "veg" out in front of the television set. At times like these, the media program your triggers. They use programming strategies to condition you into habitual exposure states and then reinforce those habits. The longer you stay in the mindless state of automaticity, the more power the media have at conditioning you to stay in that state, where they can continue to program the triggers. Therefore, the problem with following the default model (see Figure 1.1) is that we do not think about what

**Figure 1.1**    The Default Model

our triggers are, and we do not care. We float along day after day, being exposed to some information, and feel we are being informed. We are being exposed to exciting images and feel we are being entertained. We are being exposed to problems with easy solutions that we can buy in stores and feel we have control over our lives. These superficial, programmed feelings keep us pleasantly in the state of automaticity. We lose the opportunity to exercise a high degree of control over our lives. We lose the opportunity to satisfy our innate needs rather than the media-programmed needs. We lose the opportunity to construct meaning for ourselves and achieve goals that are truly our own.

# Traps

The state of automaticity is a wonderful tool protecting us from being overwhelmed by the flood of messages. But this state has traps that can hold us back from achieving our own goals. These traps divert our attention from the disadvantages of being in the state of automaticity. They give us a false sense of well-being, but the longer we are caught in these traps, the more susceptible we are to negative effects of the media. I will illuminate four of the more dangerous traps in this section.

## Trap 1: Information Fatigue

The media present so many messages and aggressively compete for our attention that we have no choice but to retreat into the state of automaticity. It is natural to feel fatigued by all the information and want to avoid it. But we must also realize that many messages in that flood could be very valuable to us. There is information that we need to live a better life— information about nutrition, exercise, avoiding dangerous behaviors, building relationships with other people, and finding a means to support ourselves in a rewarding manner. There are messages we need to expand our experience beyond our everyday lives—messages about other kinds of people, places, times, feelings, and accomplishments. We must get beyond the fatigue and get energized in the search for information we need and want.

If we cannot get beyond the fatigue, then we stay in the state of automaticity and have the same narrow set of experiences over and over. Thus, we automatically watch a few kinds of TV shows and listen to only one kind of popular music and read one kind of magazine. We have no energy to explore any of the wide spectra outside our little groove, and that is a trap. The longer we stay in this trap, the feeling of fatigue is reinforced, and it becomes harder and harder to find the energy to explore other kinds of messages. The media get more powerful in programming our triggers to keep us in the same habitual exposure patterns. We lose interest in programming our own triggers. Over time, our experience gets more and more narrow, and eventually we lose the ability to break out of these heavily reinforced routines.

## Trap 2: False Feeling of Being Informed

Because our culture bombards us with so much information, we think we are informed. We are marinating in information; how could we not be absorbing a great deal of information?

The problem is not with the *amount* of information. The problem is with the *variety* and *type* of information. When we stay in the state of automaticity, the variety of information gets more constrained. We stay in a narrow groove of messages while the media program us to stay with the same kind of exposure over and over.

As for the type of information, the state of automaticity is a mindless state, so when we are presented messages, we simply accept the surface meanings. Media messages are typically constructed to be slick and superficial; that is, rarely do messages trigger people to engage their minds and dig deeper. Instead, media messages appear easy to understand, and thus people are satisfied when they are exposed to the surface meaning. To illustrate, think of television news programs. For example, CNN is a major news organization with reporters all over the globe and with a huge news hole of 24 hours a day, 7 days each week. With all of these resources, CNN could offer messages that are really in-depth and reveal the complex nature of the major issues in our economy, political system, and culture. But CNN does not use its considerable resources to do this. Instead, it presents very short, superficial stories over and over again all day and night. CNN, as well as other news presentation services, has chosen repetition of stories over depth of stories. Rarely is there any depth in reporting, even on the many complex issues that demand it. Instead, we are presented with a short 90-second story if it is important or a 30-second story if it is not a "major" story.

For many people, however, watching 30 minutes of news each night provides them with a feeling that they are staying informed of all the important issues of the day. About half the adult population also reads a newspaper every day, and this exposure serves to further reinforce in them the feeling that they are informed. But the stories in the typical newspaper are the same stories that are on the television news. Although print stories are longer than television stories, they do not provide significantly more depth in their reporting.

## Trap 3: False Sense of Control

Most of the new technological developments with the mass media channels give us, the audience, the potential for more control over our exposures. But the irony is that as we are offered greater control, we exercise less and less control. That is, we feel overwhelmed by all the messages available and default to more time—not less—in the state of automaticity, where the media message providers exercise their control over us.

To illustrate the greater potential for control by us, think about how the newer media deliver their messages compared with the way the older media deliver messages. With print, which is the oldest of the mass media, consumers have had almost all the control over exposures. Books could not expose themselves to consumers; we have to take the initiative to go out to a store or a library. Magazines and newspapers are a bit more intrusive because they are delivered to our doors, but we need to subscribe for this to happen. Also, with all forms of print, we control the exposure sequencing and pace. We could begin reading a magazine with any story, read the stories in any order, and read the stories as fast or as slow as we wanted. Thus, with the print media, we exert a relatively high degree of control with all the important exposure decisions: whether to be exposed, which stories to read and in which order, the timing of the exposure, and the pace of the exposure.

With the arrival of electronic media, new forms of control were established that contrasted with print media. In the 1920s, radio was introduced, and people began to lose some of their control over the media exposure. Of course, radio requires that someone turn on a radio receiver for information to flow, but once the audio is in the environment, everyone is exposed. In this way, radio is more intrusive than print. Also, radio controls the timing, sequence, and pacing of the messages. If you want to listen to a particular show, you have to tune in when the program is broadcast. You have to listen to the messages in the order they are broadcasted. Radio producers also gained control of the interruptions (for ads) and when to suspend the story (as in serialized stories). Of course, some magazines present serialized stories, but an audience member could wait for all issues to be published and then read them all at once; this was not possible with serialized radio dramas. Radio, then television, trained us to structure our lives around certain times when their shows were broadcast; they trained us to tolerate interruptions for commercial messages, and they trained us to develop weekly habits of exposure.

Over time, some technological innovations have been made available to give people the potential for more control over media exposures. For example, tape recorders and MP3 players enable people to rearrange audio messages through editing; also, people can control the playback time. VCRs do the same for video. And computer software seems to give people more control over searching for information (Web browsers and search engines). But to use these technologies, we have to expend more effort. It also requires us to scan more messages to make our decisions about what to record or use, and this serves to increase our exposures. Therefore, most people stay with their media-shaped habits of exposure most of the time. Also, these technologies have hidden features that serve to reduce our control while making it appear that they are increasing our control. For example, Internet service providers (ISPs) and search engines make people feel that they are in control of their Internet searches, but these devices constrain people's access. ISPs have links to favored Web sites while excluding others. Search engines cannot possibly access more than a small percentage of Web pages, so the decisions concerning which pages to access lies at least as much with the search engine company as it does with the user.

We are at a time when the amount of messages bombarding us is at an all-time high, and it continues to grow. The providers of those messages are at a high point in being able to control our knowledge, our attitudes, and our behaviors. However, at the same time, we have more potential now than ever before to control our own exposures and their effects on us, but sadly, few people recognize this potential. Most people are either too fatigued by the onslaught of messages to confront it consciously. Or people who do want to confront the problem and gain control for themselves are not sure about what to do.

## Trap 4: Faulty Beliefs

The information-saturated environment and our response to it leaves us vulnerable to faulty beliefs. Either we will accept the beliefs presented to us in the media, or we will construct our own beliefs, which tend to be faulty if we rely on the superficial and spotty information we absorb during automatic exposures.

A fruitful place to observe faulty beliefs in the general population is to examine the results of public opinion polls. Often, these polls will ask people about issues that would seem to be very important. However, when we look at the patterns of public beliefs, we can see that many people are not really well versed about these seemingly important issues. We can see that these beliefs are clearly faulty because they either are not accurate reflections of reality or are logically inconsistent.

In public opinion polls about crime, only 17% of people think crime is a big problem in their own community, whereas 83% of Americans think crime is a big problem in society (Whitman & Loftus, 1996). People think this way because most do not experience crime in their own lives and therefore do not think it is a big problem where they live. However, they are convinced that it is a big problem in society. Where could the public get such an idea? From the media's fixation on deviance in the news. Also the news media prefer to present *sensationalized* events rather than *typical* events. So when a crime is reported, it is usually a violent crime, following the news ethic of "if it bleeds, it leads." Watching evening newscasts with their highlighting of crime and violence leads us to infer that there must be a high rate of crime and that most of it is violent assaults. But in reality, less than 20% of all crime is violent. More than 80% of all crime is property crime, with the victim not even present (U.S. Bureau of the Census, 2000). Furthermore, the rate for violent crime has been declining in this country since the mid-1980s, yet very few people are aware of this decline (Whitman & Loftus, 1996). Instead, most people believe that violent crime is increasing because they continually see crime stories and gory images in the media. They have fashioned their opinions on sensationalized events, and this type of information provides no useful basis to infer an accurate picture about crime.

In a wide range of public opinion polls, we find that people not only exaggerate the problems with crime but also overestimate the problems with health care, education, religion, and family—believing that they are all serious, growing problems. For example, with health care, 90% of adults think that the health care system is in crisis, but at the same time, almost 90% feel that their health care is of good quality. About 63% of people think other people's doctors are too interested in making money, but only 20% think their own doctor is too interested in making money. As for education, 64% give the nation's schools a grade of C or D, but at the same time, 66% give their public school a grade of A or B. As for religion, 65% say that religion is losing its influence on American life, whereas 62% said religion is becoming a stronger influence in own their lives. As for responsibility, almost 90% believe that a major problem with society is that people don't live up to their commitments, but more than 75% say they meet their commitments to families, kids, and employers. Nearly half of the population believes it is impossible for most families to achieve the American Dream, whereas 63% believe they have achieved or are close to the American Dream. And 40% to 50% think the nation is currently moving in the wrong direction, but 88% of Americans think their own lives and families are moving in the right direction (Whitman, 1996).

Most people think that the media, especially television, have a very strong effect on other people. They have an unrealistic opinion that the media cause other people to behave violently. Some believe that if you allow PSAs (public service announcements) on TV about using condoms, children will learn that it is permissible and even a good thing to have sex. This is clearly an overestimation. At the same time, people *under*estimate the influence the media have on them. When they are asked if they think the media have any effect on them personally, 88% say no. These people argue that the media are primarily channels of entertainment and diversion, so they have no negative effect on them. The people who believe this say that they have watched thousands of hours of crime shows and have never shot anyone or robbed a bank. Although this may be true, this argument does not fully support the claim that the media have no effect on them; this argument is based on the false premise that the media only trigger high-profile, negative, behavioral effects that are easy to recognize. But there are many more types of effects, such as giving people the false impression that crime is a more serious problem than it really is or that most crime is violent.

There is a faulty belief in this country that television is to blame for the educational system not being very good. The media often present reports about how poorly this nation's youth do on learning compared to youth in other countries. For example, the Third International Mathematics and Science Study, which is administered to eighth graders in 41 countries, revealed that American students rank 28th in math and 17th in science in the world ("The Learning Lag," 1996). The 1998 National Assessment of Educational Progress, administered nationally by a group established by Congress, reported that one third of high school seniors lack even a basic understanding of how the American government is run, and only 26% of seniors were considered well versed enough in civics to make reasonable, well-informed choices during elections (McQueen, 1999). The National Assessment of Educational Progress (NAEP) reports that only about one quarter of American schoolchildren have achieved the proficiency standard in writing (Wildavsky, 1999). Reports such as this lead critics to complain that children in this country watch too much television. However, the same report says that students in Japan rank 3rd on both tests, although they watch as much television as do American kids, but this bit of information is rarely reported.

Many conscientious parents have accepted the belief that it is bad for their young children to watch television. They believe that TV somehow will make their children's minds lazy, reduce their creativity, and turn them into lethargic entertainment junkies. If this happens, children will not value achievement and will not do well in school.

This belief is faulty because it blames the media, not the child or the parent, for poor academic performance. It also focuses only on the negative effect and gives the media no credit for potentially positive effects.

This is an important issue, but again it is not a simple one. When we look carefully at the research evidence, we can see that the typically reported finding is wrong and that when we look more carefully, there are several effects happening simultaneously (see Potter, 1987a). For example, the typically reported finding is that television viewing is negatively related to academic achievement. And there is a fair amount of research that reports this conclusion. What makes this faulty is that this relationship is explained better by something else—IQ. School achievement is overwhelmingly related to IQ. Also, children with lower IQs watch more television. So it is IQ that accounts for lower achievement and higher television viewing. Research analyses that take a child's IQ into account find that there is no overall negative relationship; instead, there is a much more interesting pattern. The negative relationship does not show up until the child's viewing has passed the threshold of 30 hours per week. Beyond that 30-hour point, the more television children watch, the lower their academic achievement, and that effect gets stronger with the more hours they watch beyond that threshold. This means that academic achievement goes down only after television viewing starts to cut into study time and sleep. But there is no negative effect for less than 30 hours of viewing per week. In fact, at the lowest levels of television viewing, there is actually a positive effect; that is, a child who watches none or only a few hours a week is likely to do less well academically than a child who watches a moderate (around 12 to 15 hours per week). Thus, the pattern is as follows: Children who are deprived of the source of information that television provides do less well in school than children who watch a moderate amount of television; however, when a child gets to the point where the amount of television viewing cuts into needed study time, academic performance goes down.

When we pose the question, "What effect does viewing television have on a child's academic performance?" we could give the simple, popular answer: There is a negative effect. But now you can see that this answer is too simple—it is simpleminded. It is also misleading because it reinforces the limited belief that media effects are negative and polarized and that the media are to blame. This conclusion is not so simple as to lend itself easily to a short sound byte or flashy image, so it is not likely to be presented in the mass media.

The reason faulty beliefs are such a dangerous trap is because they are self-reinforcing. By this, I mean that as people are continually exposed to faulty information, they feel even more secure that their faulty beliefs are accurate. They feel less and less motivation to challenge them. When someone points out that the information on which their beliefs are based is faulty, they do not accept this criticism because they are so sure that they are correct. Thus, over time, they are not only less likely to examine their beliefs but also less tolerant of other beliefs having the possibility of being correct.

# Need for Media Literacy

We encounter almost all media messages in a state of automaticity—that is, mindless acceptance—when we are not interested in investing the effort for conscious attention, much less the effort to analyze and evaluate the messages and to find more information to construct more accurate interpretations. We cannot eliminate the need for this state of automaticity because it is an essential tool that helps us avoid being overwhelmed by the flood of messages from the media. However, we can do two things to work with this tool and become more media literate.

First, we can reduce the time we spend in the state of automaticity. We do this by planning to expose ourselves to messages that are different from what we habitually do. This expands our experience with media messages. It also requires us to think about these new messages; that is, we cannot take them for granted. New types of messages, as well as messages on new topics, force us to confront the unknown and to work a bit to make sense of this new information. As we work on trying to make sense of the messages, we stay away from the mindless state of automaticity.

Second, we can try to program our triggers. In doing this, we need to be guided by our own goals rather than let the media set our goals for us.

# Conclusion

We cannot physically avoid the glut of information that aggressively seeks our attention in our culture. Instead, we protect ourselves by psychologically avoiding almost all of the messages in the flood of information. We do this by keeping our minds on automatic pilot most of the time. This automaticity allows us to avoid almost all messages and to do so efficiently.

Automaticity, however, comes with a price. We allow the media to condition us while we are in this automatic state. The media condition us to habitual exposure patterns to the messages they want exposure for. This increases the risk that we will miss many of the messages that might have value for us. The media also condition us to accept unchallenged the meaning they present in their messages. This increases the risk we will accept faulty meaning.

Taking control is what media literacy is all about. Becoming more media literate gives you a much clearer perspective to see the border between your real world and the world manufactured by the media. When you are media literate, you have clear maps to help you navigate better in the media world so that you can get to those experiences and information you want without becoming distracted by those things that are harmful to you. You are able to build the life that *you* want rather than letting the media build the life *they* want for you.

Those who fail to develop their literacy of the media will get swept along in a tide of messages. They will have a false sense that they know what is going on in the world simply because they are exposed to so much information. Everette Dennis, who is the executive director of The Freedom Forum Media Studies Center at Columbia University in New York and vice president of The Freedom in Arlington, Virginia, refers to media illiteracy as "potentially as damaging and poisonous to the human spirit as contaminated water and food is to our physical well-being" (Dennis, 1993, p. 4). The metaphor of pollution is an apt one. The media industries provide us with many products that we desire—products that are good for us—but these same media industries are also producing harmful by-products and dumping them into our culture. If we are not literate, we don't know the difference, and we consume the bad with the good.

This book will show you how you can become more media literate. It presents a plan of action for you. If you work hard at executing this plan, you will develop your media literacy to a much higher degree. You will acquire a great deal of information about media content, the industries, and their effects on us as individuals and on society. But developing a high degree of media literacy requires more than knowledge; it also requires the development of skills. The more you develop your skills, the more levels of meaning you will be able to perceive in the media. By the end of this book, you should have a highly developed set of skills that will help you elaborate the beginning knowledge structures presented in the heart of this book.

# Further Reading

Lyman, P., & Varian, H. R. (2003, October 27). *How much information? 2003.* Retrieved May 14, 2004, from http://www.sims.berkeley.edu/research/projects/how-much-info-2003/

A research team at the UC Berkeley School of Information Managements and Systems has analyzed the world's media and constructed estimates for how much information is produced each year. This is a very ambitious project that presents startling results about the amount of information available.

Wurman, R. S. (1989). *Information anxiety.* New York: Doubleday. (356 pages)

Although this book is now more than 15 years old, its intriguing ideas about how much information has invaded our culture and how that flood is affecting us are still compelling. The author has written it in a nonlinear manner so that the chapters and even the paragraphs can be read in any order.

# CHAPTER 2

# Defining Media Literacy

Harry and Ann are discussing their relationship over lunch on campus.

"Harry, you never pay attention to what I say!"

"How can you say that? We spend almost all day together everyday and you are constantly talking," Harry replies. "I hear what you say."

"Maybe, but you don't understand what I say."

"Yes, I do. I know a lot about you. I know the names of all your brothers and sisters, and where you went to high school, and your favorite color and . . ."

Ann interrupts, "Those are facts about me. They are not me! You don't seem to know me."

"I know the meaning of every word you say. I don't need a dictionary!"

"There is more to meaning than the definitions of the words I use!"

# Key Distinctions

In everyday language, we commonly use terms such as *information, attention, knowing,* and *understanding.* But sometimes—perhaps often—we have a different meaning for a term than the person with whom we are talking. This creates problems with communication. To avoid that type of problem in this book, I need to make it clear what my meaning is for some key terms—the most important of which is *media literacy,* because there are many definitions floating around for this term. But before I define *media literacy,* I need to define some key terms that are foundational to my definition of media literacy. So I begin this chapter by defining some key terms organized by five contrasts. First, I make a distinction between media and mass media. Second, there is an important difference between information and knowledge. Third, exposure is different from attention. Fourth, there is the difference between automaticity and mindfulness. And fifth, there is a difference between meaning matching and meaning construction.

## Media and Mass Media

The media are the technological means of disseminating messages. They are usually categorized as being print (newspapers, books, magazines) or electronic (radio, CDs, film, television, Internet).

There are two kinds of media: mass and nonmass. This distinction has very little to do with the size of the audience—although that is how most people approach defining *mass.* Nor does it have much to do with the experience the audience has when receiving the messages, although this was the main criterion for defining a mass audience for a long time. Instead, mass has to do with the motives of the sender. To be a mass medium, the sender's main intention is to condition audiences into a ritualistic mode of exposure; that is, mass media are much less interested in coaxing people into one exposure than they are in trying to get people into a position where they will regularly be exposed to their messages.

Nonmass media use the same channels as mass media. For example, if you watch a broadcast television show on your TV set, you are being exposed to mass media; if you watch a videotape of your birthday party on the same TV set, you are being exposed to nonmass media. If you read an e-mail from your friend, this is nonmass media; if you read an e-mail from your Internet service provider (such as AOL) that has been sent to all subscribers, this is mass media exposure. If you read a letter to the editor in your local newspaper, this is mass media exposure. If you read a letter from your local editor telling you that she has decided to hire you as a reporter, this is nonmass media.

Mass media condition audiences by making their messages very easy to understand (thus keeping mental costs low for the audience) while delivering a big payoff (thus increasing value to the audience). When costs are low and value is high, audience members will regard the exposure as an efficient use of their time, and this perceived efficiency will make people want to continue the exposure. When audiences keep coming back for more exposures, the media have conditioned a loyal audience that they can rent out to advertisers.

The mass media create vehicles as the means of delivering their messages through a medium to an intended audience. For example, newspaper is a medium; the *New York Times* and the *Wall Street Journal* are vehicles. Television is a medium; *Friends,* the evening news, and the *Sopranos* are vehicles. These are all successful vehicles because they each reach a special kind of intended audience on a regular basis and have conditioned their audiences to continually seek exposure to the messages delivered by those vehicles.

## Information and Knowledge

In everyday language, the terms *information* and *knowledge* are often used as synonyms, but in this book, they have meanings very different from one another. Information is piecemeal and transitory, whereas knowledge is structured, organized, and of more enduring significance. Information resides in the messages, whereas knowledge resides in a person's mind. Information gives something to the person to interpret, whereas knowledge reflects that which is already been interpreted by the person.

Information is composed of facts. Facts by themselves are not knowledge any more than a pile of lumber is a house. Knowledge requires structure to provide context and thereby exhibit meaning. Think of messages as the raw materials and skills as the tools you use to do something with the raw materials. That "something" is in the service of attaining the goal of pulling the information out of the messages and turning that information into knowledge, that is, to reconstruct the information so that it will contribute to our knowledge structures. A characteristic of higher media literacy is the ability and habit of transforming information into knowledge structures.

While I'm on the topic of distinguishing information from knowledge, I also need to define a few terms related to the idea of information: *message, factual information,* and *social information.* Messages are those instruments that deliver information to us. Information is the content of those messages. Messages can be delivered in many different media—television, radio, CDs, video games, books, newspapers, magazines, Web sites, conversations, lectures, concerts, signs along the streets, labels on the products we buy, and so on. They can be large (an entire Hollywood movie) or small (one utterance by one character in a movie).

Messages are composed of two kinds of information: factual and social. A fact is something raw, unprocessed, and context free. For example, when you watch the news and hear messages about terrorism, those messages are composed of facts, such as the following: *The World Trade Center in New York City was destroyed on September 11, 2001. On that day, the United States declared war on terrorism. The person suspected of planning the attack on the World Trade Center was Osama bin Laden.* These statements are facts. Facts are discrete bits of information, such as names (of people, places, characters, etc.), definitions of terms, formula, lists, and the like.

Social information is composed of accepted beliefs that cannot be verified by authorities in the same way factual information can be. This is not to say that social information is less valuable or less real to people. Social information is composed of techniques that people learn from observing social interactions. Examples of social information are rules about how to dress, talk, and act to be considered attractive, smart, athletic, hip, and so forth.

The mass media present three general types of messages: news, entertainment, and ads. At base, the mass media's *primary* purpose for producing and distributing all messages is to construct audiences to generate revenue. The three types of messages differ in their *secondary* purposes to the mass media. With news messages, the intention of the mass media is to evoke in audience members a sense that they are being informed. With entertainment messages, the intention of the mass media is to evoke in audience members a sense that they are having pleasant emotional experiences, particularly of laughter, character attraction, or vicarious fear. With advertising messages, the intention of the mass media is to stimulate in companies paying for the advertising a sense that those ad messages are changing target audiences in terms of their cognitions, attitudes, and/or behaviors.

The mass media over time have blended two or more of their secondary intentions to achieve their primary purpose better. This has had the result of making it more difficult for audience members to understand the nature of the messages. For example, there are messages referred to as docudramas, which are based on actual happenings in real life (from the news) but have been fictionalized to increase their entertainment value. Thus, audiences are given a sense that they are accruing more value from a single message—that is, receiving information about the real world plus being entertained. Also, there are messages referred to as infomercials, which use a news show or informational talk show type of format but are paid advertising messages. Thus, audiences are given the sense that they are accruing valuable, objective information on a problem for which they are given an easy and compelling means to solve.

There are also genres of messages. For example, within the set of television entertainment messages, there are comedies, dramas, sports, news/information, cartoons, and music. Each has its subgenres. For example, within dramas, there are crime dramas, action/adventure dramas, family dramas, and continuing dramas.

## Exposure and Attention

In everyday language, *exposure* is a term that is often used synonymously with the term *attention*, but with media literacy, we must draw an important distinction between the two terms. Exposure refers to being in the physical proximity to a media message, such that a person is in contact with that message. Attention is a conscious awareness of the message. Thus, attention is encompassed within the idea of exposure; that is, a person cannot attend to a message without being exposed to it. However, exposure is broader than attention because people could be exposed to a message without attending to it. For example, some students like to study with the radio on in the background. Their attention is on their books and notes. The sounds coming from the radio are creating exposure, but the students may not be paying attention to those sounds. Then the students' favorite song starts playing. This triggers them to pay attention to the song, and they start singing along with the song. When the song is over, they switch back into automatic processing and stop paying attention to the ads and other songs coming from the radio.

## Automaticity and Mindfulness

This distinction refers to the degree of awareness in the processing of information. Automaticity refers to cognitive activity that occurs outside of consciousness; that is, it is mindlessness (Fiske & Taylor, 1991, p. 283). Mindlessness is a state where a person is not especially alert, thoughtful, or creative. Although the person is awake (not unconscious as if asleep or in a coma), the person is not active in thinking through decisions; instead, the person's mind is on automatic pilot, where it executes habitual routines with very little mental effort. Typically, automatic processing occurs without intention, without involving conscious awareness, and without interfering with other mental activity (Posner & Snyder, 1975).

For most people, driving a car is an automatic task. When we first learn to drive, however, it can be an overwhelming cognitive experience. But after lots of practice, we do not need to think consciously about all the hand motions we make when we get in the car, turn it on, and get it moving. We do not think consciously about all the visual information we process that guides us to drive safely and arrive at our destination accurately. People who drive to work each day rarely remember any of the details or hundreds of decisions they made on a particular commute. When we know a routine very well, we no longer pay attention to individual components of the routine; we accomplish a wide variety of encoding tasks without much bothering our intentional, voluntary, effortful, conscious selves.

The state of automaticity is the opposite of the state of mindfulness. In the automatic state, we are operating on automatic pilot; that is, our minds are automatically following preprogrammed routines. In contrast, mindfulness is a state where we are aware of what we are doing, we monitor our options, and we think about the decisions as we make them.

There are also times when we are concentrating on one task while automatically filtering out all other stimuli around us. When this happens, it is usually the background media messages that are being filtered out. For example, when students are studying, they often have the television, radio, or stereo playing in the background. Although these background messages can be distracting, often they are not because students automatically filter them out. In a study of high school students, Pool, Koolstra, and van der Voort (2003) found that studying is usually unaffected by background exposure to media; that is, having the TV or music playing in the background did not affect either the amount of time they spent on homework or the quality of their performance. However, when the background became foreground, such as while watching a soap opera, the studying got interrupted and students' performance suffered. This is evidence of automatic processing that takes place during a good deal of media exposure.

It is not uncommon for people to use the media for background noise. Almost half (46%) the time people watch TV in their homes, they are also engaging in nonviewing activities. Children talk, play, and eat, and adults read and do chores (Schmitt, Woolf, & Anderson, 2003).

## Meaning Matching and Meaning Construction

This distinction between meaning matching and meaning construction is a major one for media literacy. With meaning matching, meaning is assumed to reside outside the person in an authority, such as a teacher, an expert, a dictionary, a textbook, or the like. The task for the person is to find those meanings and memorize them. Parents and the educational institution are primarily responsible for housing the authoritative information and sharing it with the next generation. The media are also a major source of information, and for many people, the media have attained the status of an authoritative source, so people accept the meanings presented there.

Meaning matching is essentially a task that can be accomplished well automatically once we have acquired some basic competencies, such as reading. Meaning construction, in contrast, is a much more challenging task. Meaning construction is a process wherein we must do things to the messages we filter in and create meaning for ourselves. The things we do to messages require the skills of analysis and evaluation for screening messages consciously. Then, when information is screened in, we must use other skills such as induction, deduction, grouping, and synthesis to incorporate the new information with our existing knowledge structures to construct our meaning.

Many meanings can be constructed from any media message; furthermore, there are many ways to go about constructing that meaning. Thus, we cannot learn a complete set of rules to accomplish this task; instead, we need to be guided by our own information goals, and we need to use well-developed skills to creatively construct a path to reach our goals.

The two processes of meaning matching and meaning construction are not discrete; they are intertwined. To construct meaning, we first have to recognize symbols and understand the sense in which those symbols are being used in the message. Thus, the meaning-matching process is more fundamental because the product of the meaning-matching process then is imported into the meaning-construction process.

To understand how this distinction is important for media literacy, we must focus on how people regard a task of information processing. Figure 2.1 shows that both processes are continua, and they each can be plotted on a larger continuum of how people regard the task. On the left side are tasks that are fairly routine; that is, they are very familiar and can be performed with high accuracy and little effort. An example would be reading simple sentences and being able to recognize words and their designated meaning. On the right side are tasks that are idiosyncratic; that is, they have never been encountered before and are unusual. There are no standard rules that can be learned to complete these tasks. They must be solved in a creative manner. In the middle of the continuum, the two process of meaning matching and meaning making overlap. There are some information-processing tasks for which people have automatic routines that match meaning to messages, but these tasks also offer the opportunity for people to apply skills and construct their own meaning. For example, when watching a news program, many people will simply accept the information as presented; they are so used to seeing the same types of stories told in the same way, with the same sources of information and the same graphics, that they process the stories with their meaning-matching competencies. However, other people may actively analyze stories for missing information, make evaluations about which facts presented are not accurate, group the new information with what they already have in their existing knowledge structures, and synthesize a new opinion about the topic being covered. Thus, the same message in a news program can be treated as either a meaning-matching or a meaning-construction task. This is a key area of opportunity for being more media literate. The more you choose to confront this task as a meaning construction task, the more you will need to think about the message, the more you will need to apply skills, the more you will be controlling the process, and therefore the more likely you will arrive at a creative and personal meaning for the message.

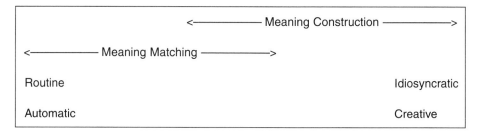

**Figure 2.1**    Meaning Matching and Meaning Construction

Notice that the meaning-matching task is not a point on the routine-idiosyncratic continuum; meaning matching is a continuum of challenges. Although some of the challenges can be met in a relatively automatic manner, others require more effort. These more challenging meaning-matching tasks are in instances when symbol recognition is not yet learned well or when a symbol is ambiguous. Also, a symbol may have more than one meaning, so a person has the additional task—beyond recognizing a symbol and associating its definition—of selecting among the definitions to chose the one most appropriate given the context. Notice too that the meaning-construction task occupies a range on the routine-idiosyncratic continuum. Some meaning constructions require more effort and creativity than others.

Finally, notice that there is an overlap between the two processes. There are many tasks of information processing where people regard the task as one of meaning matching and try to find an automatic association of a message with a definition when they would be better off making the effort to treat the task as one of meaning construction. Taking this easy route serves to keep people at a low level of media literacy. There are times when we should not accept the media-presented meaning, even though it is easier and more efficient to do this. Instead, we should expend the extra effort and construct our own meaning.

# Defining Media Literacy

In the minds of many people, the term *literacy* is most associated with the print media, so it means the ability to read (Scribner & Cole, 1981; Sinatra, 1986). Some people expand the term to *visual literacy* as they think about other media such as film and television (Goodwin & Whannel, 1990; Messaris, 1994). Other writers have used the term *computer literacy* (Adams & Hamm, 1989). *Reading literacy, visual literacy,* and *computer literacy* are not synonyms for *media literacy;* instead, they are merely components. *Media* literacy includes all these specialized abilities as well as something more. If we don't know how to read, we cannot get much out of the print media. If we have trouble understanding visual and narrative conventions, we cannot get much out of television or film. And if we cannot use a computer, we are cut off from what is growing into the most important medium.

Media literacy is more than these specialized abilities. It is something more general. The definition of media literacy is as follows:

Media literacy is a set of perspectives that we actively use to expose ourselves to the media to interpret the meaning of the messages we encounter. We build our perspectives from knowledge structures. To build our knowledge structures, we need tools and raw material. These tools are our skills. The raw material is information from the media and from the real world. Active use means that we are aware of the messages and are consciously interacting with them.

What is a perspective? Let's illustrate this with an analogy. Let's say you wanted to learn about Earth. You could build a 100-foot-tall tower, climb up to the top, and use that as your perspective to study Earth. That would give you a good perspective that would not be blocked by trees so that you could see for perhaps several miles in any direction. If your tower were in a forest, you would conclude that Earth is covered with trees. But if your tower were in a suburban neighborhood, you would conclude that Earth is covered with houses, roads, and shopping centers. If your tower were inside the New Orleans Superdome stadium, you would conclude something quite different. Each of these perspectives on Earth would give you a very different set of perceptions. None of these perspectives is better than any other. The key to understanding Earth is to build lots of these towers so you have many different perspectives to enlarge your understanding about what Earth is. And not all of these towers need to be 100 feet tall. Some should be very short so that you can better see what is happening between the blades of grass in a lawn. And others should be hundreds of miles away from the surface so that you can tell that Earth is a sphere and that there are large weather formations constantly churning around the globe.

Media literacy is a multidimensional concept with many interesting facets. Therefore, we need to view it from many different perspectives to appreciate all it has to offer.

# Key Characteristics

To illuminate this idea of media literacy further, I need to describe two of its most important characteristics.

## Media Literacy Is a Continuum, Not a Category

Media literacy is not a category—like a box—where either you are in the category or you are not. For example, either you are a high school graduate or you are not; either you are an American citizen or you are not. In contrast, media literacy is best regarded as a continuum—like a thermometer—where there are degrees.

We all occupy some position on the media literacy continuum. There is no point below which we could say that someone has no literacy, and there is no point at the high end where we can say that someone is fully literate—there is always room for improvement.

People are positioned along that continuum based on the strength of their overall perspective on the media. The strength of a person's perspective is based on the number and quality of knowledge structures. And the quality of knowledge structures is based on the level of a person's skills and experiences. Because people vary substantially on skills and experiences, they will vary on the number and quality of their knowledge structures. Hence, there will be a great variation of media literacy across people.

People operating at lower levels of media literacy have weak and limited perspectives on the media. They have smaller, more superficial, and less organized knowledge structures, which provide an inadequate perspective to use in interpreting the meaning of a media message. These people are also habitually reluctant or unwilling to use their skills, which remain underdeveloped and therefore more difficult to employ successfully.

## Media Literacy Is Multidimensional

When we think of information, we typically think of sets of facts such as from a textbook, a newspaper, or a magazine article. But this is only one type of information—cognitive. Media literacy requires that we acquire information and build knowledge in more than just the cognitive dimension but also to consider information from emotional, aesthetic, and moral dimensions. Each of these four dimensions focuses on a different domain of understanding. The cognitive domain refers to factual information—dates, names, definitions, and the like. Think of cognitive information as that which resides in the brain.

The emotional domain contains information about feelings, such as love, hate, anger, happiness, and frustration. Think of emotional information as that which lives in the heart—feelings of happy times, moments of fear, instances of embarrassment. Some people have very little ability to experience an emotion during exposure to the media, whereas others are very sensitive to cues that generate all sorts of feelings in them. For example, we all have the ability to perceive rage, fear, lust, hate, and other strong emotions. Producers use easy-to-recognize symbols to trigger these, so they do not require a high degree of literacy to perceive and understand. But some of us are much better than others at perceiving the more subtle emotions such as ambivalence, confusion, wariness, and so on. Crafting messages about these emotions requires more production skill from writers, directors, and actors. Perceiving these subtle emotions accurately requires a higher degree of literacy from the audience.

The aesthetic domain contains information about how to produce messages. This information gives us the basis for making judgments about who are great writers, photographers, actors, dancers, choreographers, singers, musicians, composers, directors, and other kinds of artists. It also helps us make judgments about other products of creative craftsmanship, such as editing, lighting, set designing, costuming, sound recording, layout, and so forth. This appreciation skill is very important to some scholars (Messaris, 1994; Silverblatt, 1995; Wulff, 1997). For example, Messaris (1994) argues that viewers who are visually literate should have an awareness of artistry and visual manipulation. By this, he means an awareness about the processes by which meaning is created through the visual media. What is expected of sophisticated viewers is some degree of self-consciousness about their role as interpreters. This includes the ability to detect artifice (in staged behavior and editing) and to spot authorial presence (style of the producer/director).

Think of aesthetic information as that which resides in our eyes and ears. Some of us have a good ear for dialog or musical composition. Some of us have a good eye for lighting, photographic composition, or movement. The more information we have from this aesthetic domain, the finer discriminations we can make between a great actress and a very good one, between a great song that will endure and a currently popular "flash in the pan," between a film director's best and very best work, between art and artificiality.

The moral domain contains information about values. Think of moral information as that which resides in your conscience or your soul. This type of information provides us with the basis for making judgments about right and wrong. When we see characters make decisions in a story, we judge them on a moral dimension, that is, the characters' goodness or evilness. The more detailed and refined our moral information is, the more deeply we can perceive the values underlying messages in the media and the more sophisticated and reasoned are our judgments about those values. It takes a highly media-literate person to perceive moral themes well. You must be able to think past individual characters to focus your meaning making at the overall narrative level. You are able to separate characters from their actions—you might not like a particular character, but you like his or her actions in terms of fitting in with (or reinforcing) your values. You do not focus your viewing on only one character's point of view but try to empathize with many characters so you can vicariously experience the consequences of their actions throughout the course of the narrative.

Strong knowledge structures contain information from all four of these domains. If one type of information is missing, the knowledge structure is weakened. For example, you may be able to be highly analytical when you watch a movie and quote lots of facts about the history of the genre, the director's point of view, and the underlying theme. But if you cannot evoke an emotional reaction, you are simply going through a dry, academic exercise.

When you have strong knowledge structures that contain information from all four domains, then you can move the focus of deficiencies off yourself and onto the media messages. For example, with strong knowledge structures, you might find yourself hating a movie for manipulating your emotions but really admiring the artistry of the director. Or you might greatly admire the moral position of a book but feel that the author was not a good writer because he was not able to evoke any strong emotions. Whereas if your knowledge structures are weak, you will be much less likely to spot deficiencies in the messages because the deficiencies are so prevalent within yourself.

# Purpose of Media Literacy

The purpose of media literacy is to empower individuals to control media programming. When I use the term *programming* in this sense, I do not mean television programs or media messages. An individual by himself or herself will not have much influence on altering how the mass media craft their messages. An individual will never be able to exercise much control over what gets offered to the public. However, a person can learn to exert a great deal of control over the way one's mind gets programmed. Thus, the purpose of media literacy is to show people how to shift control from the media to themselves. This is what I mean when I say that the purpose of media literacy is to help people control media programming.

The first step in shifting control away from the media to the individual is for individuals to understand how the media program them. This programming by the media continually takes place in a two-phase cycle that repeats over and over again. One of these phases of the cycle is the constraining of choices, and the second phase is the reinforcing of experience.

## Constraining Choices

The media have programmed us to believe that we are being offered many choices, but the range of choices is greatly limited. Although there appear to be differences across the choices of messages, those differences are minor compared to the similarities. For example, situation comedies on television each have a different cast of characters and a different setting. But all situation comedies share an enormous number of characteristics, such as that they are all 30 minutes long, all have frequent breaks for ads, all must have a joke every few seconds, all present some conflict that is resolved within the 30 minutes, almost all have a laugh track, the types of characters are relatively consistent across shows, and all have static characters (i.e., they do not change from episode to episode).

Let's consider another example—magazines. Let's say you go to a bookstore to buy a magazine. Although there are about 10,000 magazines published in this country, the bookstore is likely to have only about 300 on its magazine shelves. You don't want to have to scan through all 300 magazines, so you rely on your automatic filtering to narrow your choice down to about a dozen magazines that you have found interesting in the past— that is, the media have conditioned you to like these magazines. Your choice is then to buy 1 or 2 from this smaller list of 12. Do you have a choice? Yes, of course. But see how the media—first through the bookstore buyer, then through media conditioning—have narrowed your choice down to 12; in other words, the decision you made was determined 99.88% by factors other than you. The media have programmed you to think that you have choices when in fact the degree of choice is greatly limited. It is rather like a parent laying out two pairs of dress pants—one black and the other dark blue—for their 4-year-old son and giving him the total power to choose what he is to wear today. Whether you regard this as a real choice depends on how much you know about the real range of options. If the boy knows about jeans, cargo pants, skater shorts, bathing trunks, and football pants, then he will not think the two dress pants is much of a choice. But what if he only knows about dark dress pants? In this case, he believes he does have a big choice between black and dark blue.

This constraining of choices would be less dangerous if there were a balance of choices across the potential range of audience interests. But the constraints are constructed by the media businesses to achieve their own economic objectives; that is, they provide only those services that they feel will generate the greatest revenues while keeping their expenses as low as possible. Of course, revenue is associated with audience size, so people do have an influence on what messages get offered. However, it is not as simple as saying that the largest audiences will command the messages. This is because audiences are not the only source of revenue for the media; with some media, the message providers are also a source of revenue. For example, cable television companies charge cable networks for carrying their signals, and they charge subscribers for access to these signals. There are two sources of revenue. Let's say a cable company finds that it has an open slot on its channel menu and is considering whether to schedule Channel X or Channel Y. The cable company knows that demand for cable Channel X among its subscribers is very high but that the provider of cable Channel X is not willing to pay to get on the cable company's menu. And let's say that demand for cable Channel Y among subscribers is low but that the provider of cable Channel Y is willing to pay a good deal of money to get on the cable company's menu. In this case, it is likely that the cable company will fill the open slot with Channel Y to make more money, even though the demand is much higher among subscribers for the other service. Then, over time, people are conditioned to like Channel Y because they get used to it and forget about Channel X.

## Reinforcing Experience

Your exposure patterns have been gradually programmed over the course of your past experiences with the media. As long as those experiences have been satisfactory and free of negative emotions of frustration or disgust, those exposures have been reinforced. You keep going back to the same kinds of messages, trusting that you will have a satisfactory experience once again like you had in the past. It is easy to slip into the state of automaticity and trust that your default choices are acceptable. Over time, habits get stronger, and it becomes much more difficult to try something new.

There are many things you can do to reduce the influence of media programming on you. This book will show you how to do this in the upcoming chapters. Suffice it to say that at this point, your most powerful strategies in reducing the influence of media programming are to increase self-awareness of your goals, strengthen your information-processing skills, and carefully build your own knowledge structures rather than accepting the surface meaning repeatedly presented by the media. When you follow these strategies, you will be much more powerful in programming your own triggers as well as enjoying a higher proportion of mindful exposure at the expense of automaticity.

# Conclusion

This chapter defines many key terms relevant to the understanding of media literacy. These definitions were organized by five contrasts. First, I made a distinction between *media* and *mass media*. Second, there is an important difference between *information* and *knowledge*. Third, *exposure* is different from *attention*. Fourth, there is the difference between *automaticity* and *mindfulness*. And fifth, there is a difference between *meaning matching* and *meaning construction*.

The chapter then presents a definition of media literacy. That definition presents media literacy as a perspective from which we expose ourselves to the media and interpret the meaning of the messages we encounter. We build our perspective from knowledge structures. It is not a category; there are degrees of media literacy. It is multidimensional, with development taking place cognitively, emotionally, aesthetically, and morally.

Finally, the chapter shows you that the purpose of attaining higher degrees of media literacy is to gain more control over programming how you interact with the media messages and construct your own meaning from them. This book is designed to elaborate on this definition and to help you build strategies to increase your own media literacy.

# Further Reading

Adams, D., & Hamm, M. (2001). *Literacy in a multimedia age.* Norwood, MA: Christopher-Gordon. (199 pages, including glossary and index)

Coming from an educational technology background, the authors argue that media literacy needs to include media analysis, multimedia production, collaborative inquiry, and networking technologies. They present many practical ideas to help teachers guide their students to learn how to get the most out of messages in all forms of media.

Alvarado, M. & Boyd-Barrett, O. (Eds.). (1992). *Media education: An introduction.* London: British Film Institute. (450 pages with index)

This edited volume contains 63 short essays organized into four sections: development and traditions of the subject of media education, key aspects of media education, analyzing classroom performance, and practical issues of practice, in-service training, strategies, and media education across the curriculum. All the contributors are British, and the attention is on how media education should be incorporated into the curriculum to educate people between the ages of 4 and 18.

Aufderheide, P. (1993). *Media literacy: A report of the national leadership conference on media literacy.* Washington, DC: The Aspen Institute. (37 pages)

This is a report of a meeting held in December 1992 of several dozen Americans concerned about the need for media literacy to be taught in the nation's public schools. They derived the following definition of media literacy: It is "the ability of a citizen to access, analyze, and produce information for specific outcomes" (p. v). They recommended that "emphases in media literacy training range widely, including informed citizenship, aesthetic appreciation and expression, social advocacy, self-esteem, and consumer competence" (p. 1).

Brown, J. A. (1991). *Television "critical viewing skills" education: Major media literacy projects in the United States and selected countries.* Hillsdale, NJ: Lawrence Erlbaum. (371 pages, including index)

Brown tries to inventory the range of systematic projects that have developed integrated curricula and long-range projects in media education with an emphasis on television. His audience is educators who are trying to design and implement their own media education projects at all levels: grade and high school, college, and adult education, as well as in local, regional, and even national interest groups.

Buckingham, D. (Ed.). (1990). *Watching media learning: Making sense of media education.* New York: Falmer. (234 pages with index)

This is an edited book of 10 chapters dealing with various aspects of media education in Britain. The main questions addressed are as follows: What do students already know about the media? How have students learned what they already know? What should students know about the media?

DeGaetano, G., & Bander, K. (1996). *Screen smarts: A family guide to media literacy.* Boston: Houghton Mifflin. (206 pages with appendices and index)

Written by two teachers, this is a book for parents who are concerned about what their children are learning (or not learning) from television. They observe that "we are taught how to read and write, but we are not taught about visual images—how they work, how they affect us, and how we can use them for our purposes" (p. xv). The book is full of practical suggestions and exercises for parents and children. There are in-depth treatments of media violence, advertising, stereotypes, and news and talk shows.

Goodwin, A., & Whannel, G. (Eds.). (1990). *Understanding television.* New York: Routledge. (192 pages with index)

This contains 12 chapters primarily by British cultural scholars who teach about television to college students. These essays comprise a text that the authors use to introduce their students to the history, social context, and textual interpretation of television.

Gordon, D. R. (1971). *The new literacy.* Toronto: University of Toronto Press. (190 pages with index)

Gordon argues that the three Rs are no longer sufficient for literacy in the new media environment. But in this rather McLuhanesque book with its changing type faces, odd graphics, and use of white space, he raises issues more than he provides prescriptions or definitions.

Hart, A. (Ed.). (1998). *Teaching the media: International perspectives.* Mahwah, NJ: Lawrence Erlbaum. (208 pages including indexes)

This edited volume includes eight chapters. The authors explore classroom practices of media education in English-speaking countries around the world. The variety of approaches presented reveals how different countries and educational systems deal with their cultural values when setting goals and devoting resources to helping their children deal with the media.

Hedley, C. N., Antonacci, P., & Rabinowitz, M. (Eds.). (1995). *Thinking and literacy: The mind at work*. Mahwah, NJ: Lawrence Erlbaum. (314 pages, including indexes)

This edited volume includes 17 chapters organized into four sections: theoretical views of cognitive processing and literacy, literacy learning, creating contexts for thinking and literacy, and strategies for thinking and learning. Most authors write from a cognitive psychological perspective as they explain what is known about how the human mind works and how that understanding can be used to construct educational experiences.

Johnson, L. L. (2001). *Media, education, and change.* New York: Lang. (182 pages with index and appendices)

Written from a postmodernist perspective, this book examines the core concepts of contemporary media literacy education. The author reports on her observations and interviews with teachers during a 15-week course to train them in basic video production. She draws conclusions about those teachers' experiences in their classrooms and their perspectives on students, learning, and media.

Kubey, R. (Ed.). (1997). *Media literacy in the information age: Current perspectives.* New Brunswick, NJ: Transaction. (484 pages with indexes)

This is an edited book with 21 chapters organized into five sections: where we've been and where we're going, theoretical and conceptual perspectives, international perspectives, curricular and research perspectives, and perspectives on computer, information, and "museum" literacy. The goal of the essays is to broaden ways of thinking about the nature of literacy.

Masterman, L. (1985). *Teaching the media.* London: Comedia. (341 pages, including annotated bibliography and appendices)

Written for teachers of media, this book addresses the following questions: Why teach about the media? What are the best ways to teach about the media? Why are media texts the way they are? It seeks to present a set of general principles for teaching about any mass medium.

McLaren, P., Hammer, R., Sholle, D., & Reilly, S. S. (Eds.). (1995). *Rethinking media literacy: A critical pedagogy of representation.* New York: Lang. (259 pages)

This is an edited book of seven chapters by different college professors, concluding with an interview with the four editors on the topic of strategies for media literacy. The chapters are critical of the media and argue for activism.

Messaris, P. (1994). *Visual "literacy": Image, mind, and reality.* Boulder, CO: Westview. (208 pages)

Paul Messaris, a communications professor at the University of Pennsylvania, argues against some commonly held assumptions about visual literacy. For example, he rejects the popular notion among many scholars that there can be no objective standards to judge the reality of visual images. He says that there are generic cognitive skills that people apply when they experience the pictorial media. His notion of training people to be media literate focuses on helping viewers detect unrealistic visual manipulation.

Metallinos, N. (Ed.). (1994). *Verbo-visual literacy: Understanding and applying new educational communication media technologies*. Montreal, Canada: 3Dmt Research and Information Center. (276 pages)

These 38 chapters are from a symposium of the International Visual Literacy Association. They focus on suggestions about how best to use the emerging new technologies to foster verbal and visual literacy.

Silverblatt, A. (1995). *Media literacy: Keys to interpreting media messages*. Westport, CT: Praeger. (340 pages, including index)

This is a mass media book that presents some chapters with information about what is needed as far as knowledge about the media. It has the feel of a textbook for an introductory-level course with its use of photographs and exercises for students to undertake. The first section of the book, called "Keys to Interpreting Media Messages," lays out a method of critically analyzing the process, context, framework, and production values of the mass media. The second section, called "Media Formats," presents exercises to show students how to analyze print journalism, advertising, and American political communications. The third section—the smallest at under 40 pages—briefly raises some critical issues such as violence in the media, children, social change, and global communications.

Sinatra, R. (1986). *Visual literacy connections to thinking, reading and writing*. Springfield, IL: Charles C Thomas. (307 pages with indexes and appendices)

Richard Sinatra, a professor in human services and counseling at St. John's University, argues that visual literacy is primary to more developed forms of literacy such as oral language literacy and written language literacy. Many of the arguments in this book are rather technical. For example, he provides an in-depth treatment of the topic of how the human brain processes verbal and visual information.

Tyner, K. (1998). *Literacy in a digital world: Teaching and learning in the age of information*. Mahwah, NJ: Lawrence Erlbaum. (291 pages with indexes and appendix)

Using an historical approach, Tyner examines how new communication technologies are accepted as well as resisted over time. She also looks at how media education has responded to changes in technologies. She argues there are multiple literacies—visual, informational, and media.

Unsworth, L. (2001). *Teaching multiliteracies across the curriculum: Changing contexts of text and image in classroom practice*. Philadelphia: Open University Press. (306 pages, including index)

The author trains primary and secondary school teachers in Australia. He argues that teachers need to build from traditional literacy, which is print, to the many other literacies across the curriculum.

# CHAPTER 3

# The Media Literacy Model

Knowledge Structures
Personal Locus
Competencies and Skills
Information-Processing Tasks
Conclusion
Further Reading

As we learned in the first chapter, we are flooded with messages from the media. We cannot possibly pay attention to all of them or even to a majority of them; we must screen out most of them. To help us do this screening with the least amount of mental effort, we use a default form of processing the messages; that is, we stay in a state of automaticity. While we are in this state, we automatically screen out messages without thinking about the process until a particular message triggers our attention.

There are some serious disadvantages to this default model, as you saw in the previous chapter. To avoid experiencing these disadvantages, we need to get in the habit of using another model of encountering messages—the media literacy model. Learning to use this model requires more effort than simply staying with the default model. But this effort will be worth it because it will help us gain much more control over our exposure habits and the way meaning is constructed in our everyday lives.

The media literacy model (see Figure 3.1) emphasizes four major factors. At the foundation is the factor of knowledge structures. The combination of knowledge structures feeds information into the second factor, which is the personal locus. This is where decisions about information processing are motivated. The third factor is a person's set of

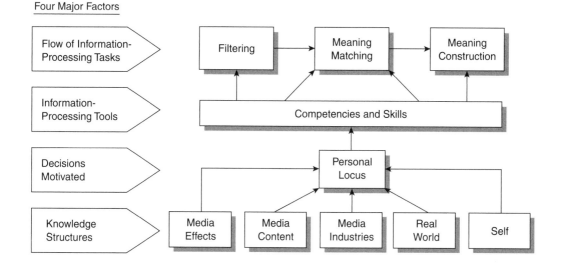

**Figure 3.1**    The Cognitive Model of Media Literacy

competencies and skills, which are the information-processing tools. And the fourth factor is the flow of information-processing tasks. The four factors work together interactively in a system. Let's examine each of these four factors in more detail.

# Knowledge Structures

The foundation of building media literacy is a set of five strong knowledge structures. The foundational knowledge structures are media effects, media content, media industries, the real world, and the self. With knowledge in these five areas, people are much more aware during the information-processing tasks and are therefore more able to make better decisions about seeking out information, working with that information, and constructing meaning from it that will be useful to serve their own goals. The information that makes these awarenesses possible resides in knowledge structures.

Knowledge structures are sets of organized information in a person's memory. Knowledge structures do not occur spontaneously; they must be built with care and precision. They are not just a pile of facts; they are made by carefully crafting pieces of information into an overall design. To perform such a task, we rely on a set of skills. These skills are the tools. We use these tools to mine through the large piles of facts, so that we can uncover the particular facts we need and brush away the rest. Once we have selected the facts we need, we shape those facts into information and carefully fit those pieces of information into their proper places in a structure. The structure helps us see the patterns. We use these patterns as maps to tell us where to get more information and also where to go to retrieve information we have previously crafted into our knowledge structure.

Information is the essential ingredient in knowledge structures. But not all information is equally useful to building a knowledge structure. Some information is rather superficial, such as the names of television shows or the melodies of popular music. If all a person has is the recognition of surface information such as lyrics to television show theme songs, names of characters and actors, settings for shows, and the like, he or she is operating a low level of media literacy because this type of information addresses only the question of "what." The more useful information comes in the form of the answers to the questions of "how" and "why." But remember that you first need to know something about the "what" before you can delve deeper into the questions of how and why.

People who have had a wider range of experiences in the real world have a broader base from which to appreciate and analyze media messages. For example, those who have helped someone run for political office can understand and analyze press coverage of political campaigns to a greater depth than those who have not had any real-world experience with political campaigns. People who have played sports will be able to appreciate the athletic accomplishments they see on television to a greater depth than those who have not physically tested themselves on those challenges. People who have had a wide range of relationships and family experiences will have a higher degree of understanding and more in-depth emotional reactions to those portrayals in the media.

Knowledge structures provide the context we use when trying to make sense of new media messages. The more knowledge structures we have, the more confident we can be in making sense of a wide range of messages. For example, you may have a very large, well-developed knowledge structure about popular music. You may know the names of all the popular musical groups (as well as all of their members and managers), all their songs, the dates of those songs, which awards each group has earned, and what the critics have said about every song. If you have all of this information well organized so that you can recall any of it at a moment's notice, you have a well-developed knowledge structure about popular music. If some people, for example, were to claim that there were only three members of the Backstreet Boys, you would argue with them and have complete confidence that they were wrong and you were right. Your knowledge structure about popular music prevents you from being misled. Are you media literate? Within the small corner of the media world where popular music resides, you are. But if this were the only knowledge structure you had developed, you would have little understanding of the content produced by the other media. You would have difficulty understanding trends about who owns and controls the media, how the media have developed over time, why certain kinds of content are never seen while other types are continually repeated, and what effects that content may be having on you. With many highly developed knowledge structures, you could understand the entire span of media issues and therefore be able to "see the big picture" about why the media are the way they are.

# Personal Locus

*Personal locus* is a term that refers to that which governs the information-processing tasks. It also shapes meaning matching and meaning construction.

The personal locus is composed of goals and drives. The goals shape the information-processing tasks by determining what gets filtered in and what gets ignored. The more you are aware of your goals, the more you can direct the process of information seeking. And the stronger your drives for information are, the more effort you will expend to attain your goals. However, when the locus is weak (you are not aware of particular goals and your drive energy is low), you will default to media control; that is, you allow the media to exercise a high degree of control over exposures and information processing.

The more you know about this locus and the more you make conscious decisions to shape it, the more you can control the process. The more you pay conscious attention to your locus, the more you control the process of information acquisition and usage. The more you engage your locus, the more you will be increasing your media literacy.

Being media literate, however, does not mean that the locus is always fully engaged. This is an impossible task because no one can maintain that high a degree of concentration continuously. Media literacy is a process, not a product. Therefore, becoming more media literate means that a person uses the locus more (thus less time with mindless exposures) and uses it more actively.

The locus operates in two modes: conscious and unconscious. When the locus operates in the conscious mode, you are aware of options and can exercise your will in making decisions. In contrast, when the locus operates in the unconscious mode, the decisions are made outside of your awareness and control. In both modes, knowledge structures can get formed and elaborated. However, when you are consciously using your locus, you are in control of the information processing and meaning making, but when your locus is operating in the unconscious mode, the media exert their most powerful effect. The locus is in the unconscious mode when we follow the default model and are in a state of automaticity.

# Competencies and Skills

After the personal locus provides the plan and the drive energy, tools are needed to execute the plan. Those tools are competencies and skills. Competencies are the tools people have acquired to help them interact with the media and to access information in the messages. Competencies are learned early in life, then applied automatically. Competencies are relatively dichotomous; that is, either people are able to do something or they are not able. For example, either people know how to recognize a word and match its meaning to a memorized meaning or they do not. Having competencies does not make one media literate, but lacking these competencies prevents one from being media literate because this deficiency prevents a person from accessing particular kinds of information. For example, people who do not have a basic reading competency cannot access printed material. This will greatly limit what they can build into their knowledge structures. This will also suppress the drive states in the locus; people who cannot read will have very low motivation to expose themselves to printed information.

Skills, in contrast, are tools that people develop through practice. Skill ability is not dichotomous; instead, there is a wide range of ability on skills. On any given skill, some people have little ability, whereas other people have enormous ability. Also, skills are like muscles. Without practice, skills become weaker. With practice and exercise, they grow stronger. When the personal locus has strong drive states for using skills, those skills have a much greater chance of developing to stronger levels.

The skills most relevant to media literacy are analysis, evaluation, grouping, induction, deduction, synthesis, and abstraction (see Figure 3.2). These skills are rarely used in an automatic fashion; instead, they require conscious effort, even when a person has a high ability on them.

To illustrate this distinction between competency and skills, think of "reading" as it is taught in elementary school. Children learn to recognize symbols that are words. They learn how to vocalize those symbols and how to fit those symbols together into sentences. These are competencies. By the time people have reached secondary grades, it is assumed that they have reading competency, yet they still practice reading. At these more advanced grades, however, reading is regarded less as a competency and more as a skill. Students

---

1. Analysis—breaking down a message into meaningful elements

2. Evaluation—judging the value of an element; the judgment is made by comparing the element to some standard.

3. Grouping—determining which elements are alike in some way; determining which elements are different in some way

4. Induction—inferring a pattern across a small set of elements, then generalizing the pattern to all elements in the set

5. Deduction—using general principles to explain particulars

6. Synthesis—assembling elements into a new structure

7. Abstracting—creating a brief, clear, and accurate description capturing the essence of a message in a smaller number of words than the message itself

---

**Figure 3.2**    The Seven Skills of Media Literacy

focus on how to get more meaning out of paragraphs and stories. For example, when teachers ask students to read aloud in elementary school, it is to check students' competencies at word recognition and pronunciation. But when teachers ask students read aloud in high school, it is to check students' skill at reading for meaning and expression.

Media literacy is much more concerned with addressing improvement of skills rather than the attainment of competencies. Although competencies are relatively high, 20% of the adult population in this country cannot read. This is a large percentage when we think of the educational system failing to teach one in five people the basic competency of reading; these people are having their exposure to media messages severely limited, and it is important that we have advocates for reading literacy to work on shrink this percentage. However, the larger concern is with the other 80% of the adult population who has the basic competencies but may be lacking the level of skills needed to be media literate. Skills are the tools we use to construct our knowledge structures. Skill development is what really can make a large difference in a person moving from low to high media literacy. People who have weak skills will not be able to do much with the information they encounter. They will ignore good information and fixate on inaccurate or bad information. They will organize information poorly, thus creating weak and faulty knowledge structures. In the worst case, people with weak skills will try to avoid thinking about information altogether and become passive; the active information providers—such as advertisers and entertainers—will become the constructors of people's knowledge structures and will take control over of how people see the world.

Skills and competencies work together in a continual cyclical process. With certain information-processing tasks, some skills or competencies may be more important than others. For example, with the task of filtering, the skills of analysis and evaluation are most important. With the task of meaning matching, the competencies are most important. And with the task of meaning construction, the skills of grouping, induction, deduction, synthesis, and abstracting are most important. However, the value of the individual skills and competencies varies by particular challenges presented by different types of messages.

# Information-Processing Tasks

The three information-processing tasks are filtering, meaning matching, and meaning construction (see Figure 3.3). These tasks are ordered in a sequence of information processing. First, we encounter a message and are faced with the task of deciding whether to filter the message out (ignore it) or filter it in (process it). If we decide to filter it in, then we must make sense of it, that is, recognize the symbols and match our learned definitions for the symbols. Next, we need to construct the meaning of the message.

The processing of information begins with the task of filtering. How can we make good decisions about filtering messages in a way that, on one hand, protects us from the negative effects of being overwhelmed or from having our minds shaped by forces outside

<u>Filtering Message</u>

*Task*:    To make decisions about which messages to filter out (ignore) and which to
         filter in (pay attention to)

*Goal*:    To attend to only those messages that have the highest utility and avoid
         all others

*Focus*:   Messages in the environment

<u>Meaning Matching</u>

*Task*:    To use basic competencies to recognize symbols and locate definitions for each

*Goal*:    To efficiently access previously learned meanings

*Focus*:   Symbols in messages

<u>Meaning Construction</u>

*Task*:    To use skills in order to move beyond meaning matching and construct
         meaning for one's self to get more out of a message

*Goal*:    To interpret messages from more than one perspective as a means of
         identifying the range of meaning options, then choosing one or synthesizing
         across several

*Focus:*   One's own knowledge structures

**Figure 3.3**     Summary of Three Tasks of Information Processing

our control and, on the other hand, helps us take advantage of the positive effects? And furthermore, how can we achieve this in a relatively efficient manner?

Once we have filtered in messages, we need to determine their meaning. Meaning matching requires basic competencies to recognize elements in the message and access our memory to find out which meaning we have learned is associated with that element. This is a relatively automatic task. Increasing media literacy requires that we not stop with this task but that we move on to meaning construction. If we simply accept the surface meaning from the media messages and do not construct meaning for ourselves, we are in danger of negative effects. Some of these effects are relatively minor, but many are more profound and change the way we think about reality, truth, and ourselves. Ignoring the problem makes it worse because the messages will continue to aggressively invade our subconscious and shape our fundamental values as well as the way we think.

Media messages are not always the way they seem. There are often many layers of meanings. The more that people are aware of the layers of meaning in messages, the more they can control the selection of which meanings they want. The constant exposure to media messages influences the way we think about the world and ourselves. It influences our beliefs about crime, education, religion, families, and the world in general. If our exposure is mostly passive, then the mundane details in those messages exert their effect without our awareness. From this massive base of misleading or inaccurate images, we infer our beliefs about the world.

Some people perform these information-processing tasks better than others and are therefore more media literate than other people. Each of these tasks relies on a different set of skills. The more developed one's set of skills is, the more media literate one is. Each task relies on knowledge structures. The more developed one's knowledge structures are, the more media literate one is.

# Conclusion

Media literacy works in contrast to the default model of processing media information. The media literacy model features four major factors: knowledge structures, personal locus, competencies and skills, and the flow of information-processing tasks. Each of these factors works interactively in a system.

Processing of information can take place either consciously or unconsciously. With conscious processing, the individual is aware of goals, exercises careful selection of information, and is able to exert a relatively high degree of control. With unconscious processing, the individual is unaware of the schema-driven automatic processing and therefore is not able to exercise any degree of control over the process. Media literacy requires that individuals spend more time and effort with conscious processing.

Media literacy is a broad perspective. It is not limited to reading or to any other single skill. Media-literate people are able to see much more in a given message. They are more aware of the levels of meaning. This enhances understanding. They are more in charge of the process of meaning making and selection. This enhances control. They are much more likely to get what they want from the messages. This enhances appreciation. Thus, people operating at higher levels of media literacy fulfill the goals of higher understanding, control, and appreciation.

At the foundation of media literacy is a set of five well-developed knowledge structures. We build these knowledge structures by using our skills to select information. Then we assemble those selections into meaningful designs. These knowledge structures inform our locus and provide context for the information-processing tasks.

# Further Reading

Potter, W. J. (2005). *Becoming a strategic thinker.* Upper Saddle River, NJ: Prentice Hall. (183 pages, including index)

This book focuses on eight skills essential for success in higher education. These are essentially the skills needed for media literacy in the information-processing tasks of filtering and meaning construction.

# CHAPTER 4

# Developing Media Literacy

**Key Idea:** Media literacy must be developed gradually over time. It cannot simply be suddenly switched on.

Two fathers are proudly discussing how smart their children are. One of the fathers says, "Robert, my 5-year-old, already knows how to read."

"So does my 4-year-old Jeremy," says the other father.

"When I say Robert can read, I don't mean simple preschool books. I mean he can read books that my older children read in the fourth and fifth grade."

"Jeremy reads at a sixth-grade level."

"Is that so? Well, Robert reads the newspaper—every night, and we discuss the news. He really understands everything."

"We had to get Jeremy a subscription to the *New York Times*. He just pestered us so."

"Well, Robert saved up his own money and bought his own subscriptions to *The Atlantic Monthly* and *Forbes*."

"That's great! Then your Robert must have read the article that my Jeremy had published in *The Atlantic Monthly*—it was only a short article but then Jeremy is only 4 years old."

Sometimes proud parents exaggerate their children's level of development. Proud parents believe that their children can understand and produce much more than they really can. Sometimes adults overestimate their own abilities, especially concerning media literacy. Being an adult does not guarantee that you are highly media literate.

The development of higher levels of media literacy relies on four factors. They are maturation, natural abilities, experience, and active application of skills. The more you understand these four factors, the more you can control the development of your own level of media literacy.

# Maturation

Maturation is the first, and most fundamental, of the four factors responsible for developing media literacy. This factor is especially important during childhood, and this is why children are often treated as a special group when it comes to the media. Our abilities increase from when we are infants through adolescence. This is obvious physically; that is, as we age from infancy, we are able to run faster, jump higher, and lift heavier objects.

We also mature cognitively. When we are very young, our minds are not developed enough to allow for an understanding of abstract thoughts, such as required by mathematical reasoning, for example. A task of reasoning (such as multiplying four times five) is very difficult for us when we are 4 years old but very easy for us a few short years later. We also mature emotionally (Goleman, 1995) and morally (Kohlberg, 1981). As we reach higher levels of maturation cognitively, emotionally, and morally, we are able to perceive more in the media messages.

Think of maturation as a series of gates along the path to higher media literacy. When we encounter one of these gates, we must wait behind it until we mature to a certain level, then the gate opens and we can proceed. There are a series cognitive gates, emotional gates, and moral gates. These gates occur every few years throughout childhood and hold us back in the early stages of media literacy. For example, most humans are not capable of acquiring the skill of reading until they are beyond the age of 4 or 5 because their minds have not matured to a point where such learning is possible. Trying to teach reading to 2-year-olds is very frustrating. No matter how hard you work as a teacher or how hard the children work to learn, they will not get much out of this effort because their minds have not matured enough to handle this task. But once a child's mind matures to the point where he or she can use those skills, the practice of reading begins to pay off.

Let's take a closer look at how people develop multidimensionally—cognitively, emotionally, and morally.

## Cognitive Development

The most influential thinker on the topic of cognitive maturation during childhood has been the Swiss psychologist Jean Piaget. From years of research, Piaget has found that a child's mind matures from birth to about 12 years of age, during which time it goes through several identifiable stages (Smith & Cowie, 1988). Until age 2, children are in the sensori-motor stage and then advance to the preoperational stage from 2 to 7 years of age. Then they progress to the concrete operational stage, and by age 12, they move into the formal operational stage, where they are regarded as having matured cognitively into adulthood. In each of these stages, children's minds mature to a point where they can accomplish a new set of cognitive tasks. For example, in the concrete operational stage (ages 7–12), children are able to organize objects into series. If you try to teach this skill to a child of age 3, you will fail—no matter how organized and clear your lessons are. Another skill that is developed throughout childhood is conservation, which is the ability to realize that certain attributes of an object are constant, even though that object is transformed in appearance (Pulaski, 1980). For example, ask a child to make two balls of clay exactly the same size. Then roll one of them out into a long, thin shape like a snake, and ask the child which of the two pieces of clay is bigger. Children will say the snake is bigger than the ball because the snake is longer. The child does not have the ability to understand that the same amount of clay has been conserved; only the shape (not the quantity) has been changed. Children's minds have matured enough to understand the idea of conservation by the time they reach about age 7.

### Infants and Toddlers

Children begin paying attention to the TV screen as early as 6 months of age (Hollenbeck & Slaby, 1979), and by age 3, many children have developed regular patterns of viewing of about an hour or two per day (Huston et al., 1983). Their viewing is primarily exploratory. This means that they are looking for individual events that stand out because of certain motions, color, music, sound effects, or unusual voices. They look for action, not dialog. They have great difficulty in understanding that individual events are ordered into plots, that characters have motives that influence the action, and that characters change as a result of what happens in the plot (Wartella, 1981). The reason for this is that young children have not developed a very sophisticated understanding of narratives. Until they learn more of the principles of narrative progression, they will have difficulty making sense out of stories longer than a minute or two (Meadowcroft & Reeves, 1989).

## Younger Children

By about age 4, children are spending less time in the exploratory mode and more time in a search mode. This means that children begin developing an agenda of what to look for; their attention does not simply bounce haphazardly around from one high-profile action to another. By kindergarten, a continuous story line holds their attention. They focus their attention on formal features in making their decisions about what is important in the shows. For example, they interpret that a laugh track signals that a program is a comedy.

Also by age 4, children begin trying to distinguish between ads and programs. At first this is difficult, until they develop the skills of perceptual discrimination. During this trial-and-error learning, children either express confusion about the difference or use superficial perceptual or affective cues as the basis for the distinction. With practice, they become more facile at separating ads from program content.

Children must also acquire the knowledge that ads are paid messages that are designed to get them to buy something—or make them ask their parents to buy something. Only 10% of children 5 to 7 years of age have a clear understanding of the profit-seeking motives of commercials; 55% are totally unaware of the nature of ads and believe commercials are purely for entertainment. For example, Wilson and Weiss (1992) found that compared to older children (ages 7–11), younger children (ages 4–6) were less able to recognize an ad for a particular toy and comprehend its intent when it was shown in a cartoon program, even when the product "spokesperson" was a character from a different cartoon program.

Disclaimers placed before ads to alert children to the fact that the program is being interrupted and an ad is about to be shown do not generally work well with children younger than age 7 because they do not fully understand what an ad is. However, when disclaimers are in both the audio and video tracks, children are better able to perceive them. Also, when disclaimers are reworded into the language of children, their comprehension dramatically increases.

By the second or third grade, most children have overcome their difficulty distinguishing between programs and commercials. With the combination of cognitive maturation, experience, and active application of critical skills, children really understand the nature and purpose of ads. This understanding leads to a drop in attention to the ads. Furthermore, attention is inversely related to the knowledge and experience necessary for critically evaluating them. By the fourth grade, children have developed a critical and skeptical attitude toward advertising. They are also cynical about the credibility of commercials and begin feeling that they have been lied to in an effort by the advertiser to get them to buy products that are not as desirable as the commercials' portrayal.

Recall of brand names and product attributes increases with age, especially between kindergarten and third grade. Simplified wording significantly affects comprehension and recall. But even with older children, there is still some difficulty in understanding certain types of claims such as superlative, comparative, and parity claims. For example, a parity claim is something like, "Buy Brand X because it is as good as the Brand Y." Children are confused by this type of claim if they don't use Brand Y. Also, children get confused about how Brands X and Y can be so similar, unless the ad clearly shows the similarity across brands on the product attributes that are most important to children.

## *Older Children*

By ages 8 to 10, most children have developed a good understanding of fictional plots, how motives of characters influence plot points, and how characters change as a result of what happens to them. Children of this age are not limited to understanding characters on only their physical traits but can also infer personality characteristics. Also, they can distinguish among characters along more dimensions.

By ages 10 to 12, children have a well-developed idea of the economic nature of TV, that is, its profit-making motive. And most children this age and older are very skeptical of ads. However, this skepticism is usually limited to their experience with products. For example, the skepticism is high with ads for familiar toys. Presumably, they have had real-world experiences with these toys and have learned that the ads contain exaggerated claims. However, children are much less skeptical of ads for medical or nutritional products; understandably, they have much less technical knowledge about these products and have less of a basis for skepticism.

## **Emotional Development**

Media messages can arouse emotions in people of all ages. Emotions do not need to be learned in the sense that we learn to recognize words to read. Instead, emotions are hardwired into our brains (Goleman, 1995). Regardless of the culture in which we are raised, we all can recognize in ourselves and others the basic emotions of anger, sadness, fear, enjoyment, love, surprise, disgust, and shame.

We develop higher levels of emotional literacy by gaining experience with emotions and by paying close attention to our feelings as we interact with the media. As we gain greater experience with emotions, we are able to make finer discriminations. For example, we are all familiar with anger because that is one of the basic emotions. But it takes experience with this emotion to be able to tell the difference between hatred, outrage, fury, wrath, animosity, hostility, resentment, indignation, acrimony, annoyance, irritability, and exasperation.

A lack of cognitive development can be a barrier to appropriate emotional reactions to media messages. For example, very young children cannot follow the interconnected elements in a continuing plot; instead, they focus on individual elements. Therefore, they cannot understand suspense, and without such an understanding, they cannot become emotionally aroused as the suspense builds. So a child's ability to have an emotional reaction to the media messages is low not because of a lack of ability to feel emotions but because of a lack of ability to understand what is happening as certain narratives unfold.

By adolescence, children have reached cognitive maturity, and all the gates are open to a full understanding of all kinds of narratives. But some adolescents and adults still do not have much of an emotional reaction to media stories. Some people can be very highly developed cognitively but very undeveloped emotionally. Goleman (1995) argues that a person's emotional intelligence interacts with IQ:

> We have two brains, two minds—and two different kinds of intelligence: rational and emotional. How we do in life is determined by both—it is not just IQ, but emotional intelligence that matters. Indeed, intellect cannot work at its best without emotional intelligence. (p. 28)

In summary, emotional literacy is tied to cognitive development. Children who cannot read or follow visual narratives will have their emotional reactions limited to reactions of microelements in messages. As people mature to a point of mastering the low-order skills, there is still a range of emotional abilities. Some people are better able to "read" emotions in themselves and others by having a higher degree of empathy and a greater self-awareness. In contrast, people with a lower level of literacy are not able to experience emotions vicariously through characters, and they may be desensitized to many emotions by constant exposure to superficial treatments of news stories and formulaic fictional plots.

## Moral Development

We also develop along a moral dimension. We are not born with a moral code or a sensitivity to what is right and wrong. We must learn these as young children, and children learn these things in stages. Like Piaget, Lawrence Kohlberg has studied the development of children. While Piaget was concerned with cognitive development, Kohlberg focused on moral development. He suggested that there are three levels of moral development: preconventional, conventional, and postconventional. The centerpiece is *conventional*, which stands for fair, honest, concerned, and well regarded—characteristics of the typically good person (Kohlberg, 1966, 1981).

The preconventional stage begins at about age 2 and runs to about age 7 or 8. This is when the child is dependent on authority, and inner controls are weak. Young children depend on their parents and other adults to tell them what is right and to filter the world for them. The child's conscience is external; that is, the children must be told by others what is right. This stage has two substages.

*Substage 1:* Children are motivated to avoid punishment, and this guides their reasoning. They do not distinguish between accidents and intentional behaviors. So if a child spills milk or steals a cookie and both are punished, both are regarded as equally bad.

*Substage 2:* The child is guided by self-satisfaction, as expressed in the following attitude: You do me a favor and I'll do you one. What brings pleasure to the child is felt as a reward.

During the conventional stage, children develop a conscience for themselves as they internalize what is right and wrong. They distinguish between truth and lies. However, the threat of punishment is still a strong motivator.

*Substage 3:* The child is motivated to get the approval of others such as peers, parents, and other people. This is the "good-boy, good-girl" orientation.

*Substage 4:* The motivation shifts to a sense of duty. The child becomes concerned with avoiding harming others and avoiding bringing dishonor to one's self. There is an orientation toward law and order. Many people stop developing at this point, and this is the highest level they ever exhibit.

The postconventional stage can begin as early as middle adolescence, when some people are able to transcend conventional notions of right and wrong. They tend to focus on fundamental principles. This requires the ability to think abstractly and therefore recognize the ideals behind society's laws. Thus, the stages in this level are characterized by a sense that being socially conscious is more important than adhering to legal principles.

*Substage 5:* In this stage, there is a focus on the social contract. Individuals agree to do certain things even if they do not agree with them. In return, those individuals get to live in a society where things run harmoniously. Correct action is defined by terms of general rights, usually with legalistic or utilitarian underpinnings that are agreed on by society.

*Substage 6:* The person is motivated to make ethical decisions according to one's own conscience. The focus is on universal principles of justice and respect for human dignity. The rules of society are integrated with one's conscience in the creation of a person's hierarchy of moral values. Thus, there are times when the demands of society are most important, but at other times, the dictates of one's conscience must be obeyed. To an individual at this stage, external punishments are much less important than the internal feeling of being right.

Kohlberg's stages are not fixed steps that everyone follows in sequence. People can move around among the steps, given particular problems and moods. However, each stage is very different, and they are hierarchically ordered such that the more evolved person is likely to operate most often at higher levels.

Gilligan (1993) has extended the ideas of Kohlberg by arguing that there is a gender difference in moral development. Men more typically base their moral judgments on rights and rules, whereas women tend to think in terms of care and cooperation. So in a conflict situation, women are likely to try to preserve relationships. Men will search for a moral rule and try to apply it.

Let's examine these stages with a media example. Bobby is a young child in a family where the television is used as a babysitter. Bobby watches a great deal of television unsupervised; there is no parent or authority figure to help him process the messages or to show him alternatives to what is portrayed in the media world. Therefore, his moral development during the preconventional stages is shaped by the themes in the television messages, mainly cartoons, action/adventure shows, and situation comedies. From his steady exposure to these types of shows and values, Bobby is likely to learn the following moral lessons: Aggression (both physical and verbal) is an acceptable and successful way to solve problems; with a little hard work, everyone can be successful, that is, be wealthy, powerful, and famous; family relationships are full of conflict and deceit, but everyone still loves each other; and romantic relationships are exciting but superficial and temporary.

As Bobby moves into the conventional stages, much of his behavior will be governed by these moral lessons. He feels that the best way to get approval from others is to be funny, live dangerously, and have lots of peer relationships filled with conflict—that is the active, interesting life.

Finally, as Bobby reaches late adolescence and confronts the postconventional stages, he should begin asking questions such as the following: How can I live my life so as to benefit society in general? How can I resolve moral dilemmas so that I don't decide on a purely selfish basis? Given Bobby's moral development and the lessons learned, it is unlikely that he will be interested by these postconventional questions. It is probable that he will stay at the conventional stage and continue to make moral decisions based on the principles he learned while watching TV as a preschooler.

After reading this section on maturation, it is tempting to think that once we have completed childhood, we have matured to the point cognitively, emotionally, and morally that there are no barriers to high media literacy. But this is not true. There is one more barrier, and that is you. Once the maturation "gates" are open, people have the potential to move on to higher levels, but not everyone does. Some people are held back due to weak natural abilities. Others are held back due to lack of motivation, and still others are held back due to lack of guidance in knowing what to do to become more media literate. There is more than simple maturation to developing high levels of media literacy.

We can increase our awareness of moral issues in the media. All media messages have moral implications. These are easy to spot in some documentaries, news stories, or fictional stories that portray difficult choices people must make. But when we look at cartoons, game shows, or sports, it can be harder to understand that these kinds of shows also have moral implications. We need to be sensitive to the characters revealed in the people portrayed. We need to look at the implications of the decisions those characters make and judge whether the story is fair in showing them. And we need to dig below the surface action and infer the themes in the stories as well as the values of the industry that produces them.

## Natural Abilities

Once we have finished childhood and passed through all the developmental gates, our abilities are no longer being held back by lack of maturation. But this does not mean that we all end up in adolescence with equal abilities. Some of us have more highly developed abilities in certain areas compared to other people. Some of these differences in abilities can be explained as certain people being more gifted than others; that is, certain people have been born with more ability than others. To an extent, this is an accurate explanation. However, this does not mean that people who take their natural abilities for granted will always have an advantage, nor does it mean that weak ability cannot be strengthened with practice. When we practice our natural abilities, they get stronger and more valuable to us.

Our natural abilities are suggestive rather than definitive. To illustrate what I mean by this, let's take a physical example of running. When you are young, you may find yourself racing your playmates and almost always winning. People think of you as a fast runner. This is a natural ability that suggests that you could be a successful athlete. But if you don't practice running or join a track team, your natural ability remains suggestive—you might become a successful athlete, but you might not. If you work on this natural ability and try to develop it to its fullest, you grow it and reach your suggested potential. So running fast in preschool does not define you as a successful athlete, but it does suggest that you have potential. Conversely, if you are slow and always lose running contests, you likely have little natural ability at running. But this need not define you as slow. You can learn how to run races; you can build up your leg muscles and lungs; you can use good equipment. All these things can increase your running ability over what was suggested by the outcome of your first races. All of this practice is not likely enough to overcome a very low level of natural ability so that you could become an Olympic athlete and set world records. But neither will this low level of natural ability at running doom you to always finish last. There is a good degree of elasticity in any natural ability; that is, there is the possibility to get stronger with practice, and there is also the possibility to get weaker with neglect.

There are seven natural abilities that are most related to media literacy. Four of these are cognitive abilities—field independency, crystalline intelligence, fluid intelligence, and conceptual differentiation. The remaining three are emotional abilities—emotional intelligence, tolerance for ambiguity, and nonimpulsiveness.

## Field Independency

Perhaps the most important ability related to media literacy is field independency. Think of field independency as your natural ability to distinguish between the signal and the noise in any message. The noise is the chaos of symbols and images. The signal is the information that emerges from the chaos. People who are highly field independent are able to sort quickly through the field to identify the elements of importance and ignore the distracting elements. In contrast, people who are more field dependent get stuck in the field of chaos—seeing all the details but missing the patterns and the "big picture," which is the signal (Witkin & Goodenough, 1977).

For example, when watching a story during a television news show, field-independent people will be able to identify the key information of the who, what, when, where, and why of the story. They will quickly sort through what is said, the graphics, and the visuals to focus on the essence of the event being covered. People who are field dependent will perceive the same key elements in the story but will also pay an equal amount of attention to the background elements of how the news anchors are dressed, their hairstyles, their makeup, the color of the graphics, and so on. To the field-dependent person, all of these elements are of fairly equal importance, so they are as likely to remember the trivial as they are to remember the main points of the story. This is not to say that field-dependent people retain more information because they pay attention to more; on the contrary, field-dependent people retain less information because the information is not organized well and is likely to contain as much noise (peripheral and tangential elements) as signal (elements about the main idea).

Let's try one more example of this concept. Have you ever had to read a long novel and gotten so lost about 100 pages into it that you had to quit in frustration? You may have felt that just when the author was getting the story going with one set of characters, he or she would switch to a different setting at a different time with a totally new set of characters. This may have been happening every few pages! There were too many characters talking about too many different things. You were overwhelmed by all the detail and could not make sense of the overall story. This indicates that the novelist was making demands on you to be much more field independent than you could be as you read his or her novel. If you had been more field independent, you would have been able to see through all the details and recognize a thematic pattern of some sort, then use that thematic pattern as a tool to sort through all the details about characters, settings, time, dialog, and action to direct your attention efficiently to those elements that were most important. We live in a culture that is highly saturated with media messages. Much of this is noise; that is, it does not provide us with the information or emotional reactions we want. The sheer bulk of all the information makes it more difficult to sort the important from the trivial, so many of us do not bother to sort. Instead, we default to a passive state as we float along in this stream of messages. The advantage of this automatic processing is that it screens out the noise, but the disadvantage is that it screens out the signal too. When we are more field independent, we can better program our attention triggers to pick up on the signal while still filtering out the noise. The signal tells us what are the significant patterns and themes in our culture. We need to see past the thousands of details in order to recognize the big picture that tells us what our world really is.

## Crystalline Intelligence

It is helpful to make a distinction between two types of intelligence: crystalline and fluid. Both types of intelligence are important for media literacy.

Crystalline intelligence is the ability to memorize facts. Highly developed crystalline intelligence gives us the facility to absorb the images, definitions, opinions, and agendas of others. With most adults, crystallized intelligence seems to increase throughout the life span, although at a decreasing rate in later years (Sternberg & Berg, 1987). This means that as adults get older, they do better on tests requiring factual knowledge of their world, such as vocabulary and general information. In general, older people can more easily add new information to existing knowledge structures and more easily retrieve that information from those knowledge structures they use most often. When you have a well-developed knowledge structure on a topic, it is easy to sort through new information as you are exposed to it, compare the new information to what you already have in your knowledge structure, and make a determination whether the new information is useful to remember. If the new information is worthwhile to remember, it is easy to catalog it in a way that it is easy to recall later. However, if you are exposed to a message on a brand-new topic (one for which you do not have a knowledge structure), it is difficult to process that new information. To test this, pick a topic that is of equal interest to you and your parents (your neighborhood, your family, politics, sports, etc.) and then see how much detail your parents remember compared to you.

People strong in crystalline intelligence are good at what is called vertical thinking. Vertical thinking is systematic, logical thinking that proceeds step by step in an orderly progression. This is the type of thinking we need in order to learn the introductory information on any topic. We need to be systematic when we are trying to learn basic arithmetic, spelling, and dates in history. People high in crystalline intelligence are likely to have a more extensive list of competencies because they have memorized a much larger set of symbols and their denoted meanings.

## Fluid Intelligence

The other type of intelligence is fluid, which is the ability to be creative, make leaps of insight, and perceive things in a fresh and novel manner. Fluid intelligence increases in early adulthood but then decreases. This means that there is a decrease in our ability to use abstract symbols, manipulate words and numbers, recognize analogies, and complete number series.

People strong in fluid intelligence are good at what is called lateral thinking. Lateral thinking, in contrast, does not proceed step by step in the usual vertical manner. Instead, when confronted with a problem, the lateral thinker jumps to a new and quite arbitrary position, then works backwards and tries to construct a logical path between this new position and the starting point. Lateral thinkers tend to arrive at a solution to a problem that other thinkers, who are locked into a lock-step form of thinking, would never arrive at. Lateral thinkers are more intuitive and creative. They reject the standard beginning points to solving problems and instead begin with an intuitive guess, a brainstorming of ideas, or a proposed solution "out of the blue."

Few people have a natural aptitude for lateral thinking. Those who have such aptitude use it often. Many inventors and scientists usually produce a string of new ideas, not just one. For example, Thomas Edison invented so many things that by the end of his life, he had more than 1,300 patents in the areas of the telegraph, telephone, phonograph, movie camera, and projectors. This suggests that there is a capacity for generating new ideas that is better developed in some people than in others. This capacity does not seem to be related to sheer intelligence but more to a particular way of thinking. There are smart and not so smart lateral thinkers, just like there are smart and not so smart vertical thinkers.

There are advantages and disadvantages to both forms of thinking. Vertical thinkers tend to do best at solving traditional problems for which the solutions can be learned. However, when their traditional methods of solving problems break down and they reach a dead-end, they are stuck and have nowhere to go. In contrast, lateral thinkers can often be flighty and may come up with many unique ideas; however, none of those ideas may work or be feasible ways of solving a problem. When others are stuck at a dead-end of thinking, it is the lateral thinkers who break through the barriers. People who are good at both and who know when to try each approach are, of course, the most successful problem solvers.

Being strong on both these abilities helps with increasing one's level of media literacy. Highly developed crystalline intelligence gives us the facility to absorb the images, definitions, opinions, and agendas of others. This helps us a great deal in the meaning-matching task because we are likely to have acquired a large set of accurate matches of symbols and meanings. Highly developed fluid intelligence gives us the facility to challenge what we see on the surface, to look deeper and broader, and to recognize new patterns. This helps us a great deal in the meaning construction task because we are able to move beyond the surface meaning and construct meanings that are more useful for our own purposes.

## Conceptual Differentiation

This refers to how people group and classify things. People who classify objects into a large number of mutually exclusive categories exhibit a high degree of conceptual differentiation (Gardner, 1968). In contrast, people who use a small number of categories have a low degree of conceptual differentiation.

Related to the number of categories is category width (Bruner, Goodnow, & Austin, 1956). People who have few categories to classify something usually have broad categories so as to contain all types of messages. For example, if a person only has three categories for all media messages (news, ads, and entertainment), then each of these categories must contain a wide variety of things. In contrast, someone who has a great many categories would be dividing media messages into thinner slices (breaking news, feature news, documentary, commercial ads, public service announcements, action/adventure shows, sitcoms, game shows, talk shows, cartoons, and reality shows).

When we encounter a new message, we must categorize it by using either a leveling or a sharpening strategy. With the leveling strategy, we look for similarities between the new message and previous messages we have stored away as examples in our categories. We look for the best fit between the new message and one of remembered messages. We will never find a perfect fit; that is, the new message always has slightly different characteristics than our category calls for, but we tend to ignore those differences. In contrast, the sharpening strategy focuses on differences and tries to maintain a high degree of separation between the new message and older messages (Pritchard, 1975). To illustrate this, let's say two people are comparing this year's Super Bowl with last year's Super Bowl. A leveler would argue that the two games were similar and point out all the things the two had in common. The sharpener would disagree and point out all the differences between the two Super Bowls. Levelers tend to have fewer categories so that many things can fit into the same category, whereas sharpeners have many, many categories. In our example, the first person would likely have only one category for Super Bowls, feeling that all the Super Bowls are the same. A sharpener might have a different category for every Super Bowl, treating each one as unique.

## Emotional Intelligence

Our ability to understand and control our emotions is called emotional intelligence. Emotional intelligence is thought to be composed of several related abilities, such as the ability to read the emotions of other people (empathy), the ability to be aware of one's own emotions, the ability to harness and manage one's own emotions productively, and the ability to handle the emotional demands of relationships.

Those of us with stronger emotional intelligence have a well-developed sense of empathy; we are able to see the world from another person's perspective. The more perspectives we can access, the more emotional intelligence we have. When we are highly developed emotionally, we are more aware of our own emotions. We also better understand the factors that cause those emotions, so we are able to seek the kinds of messages to get us the emotional reactions we want. In addition, we are less impulsive and are able to exercise more self-control. We can concentrate on the task at hand rather than become distracted by peripheral emotions.

## Tolerance for Ambiguity

Everyday, we encounter people and situations that are unfamiliar to us. To prepare ourselves for such situations, we have developed sets of expectations. What do we do when our expectations are not met and we are surprised? That depends on our tolerance level for ambiguity. If we have a low tolerance for ambiguity, we will likely choose to ignore those messages that do not meet our expectations; we feel too confused or frustrated to work out the discrepancies.

In contrast, if we are willing to follow situations into unfamiliar territory that go beyond our preconceptions, then we have a high tolerance for ambiguity. Initial confusion does not stop us. Instead, this confusion motivates us to search harder for clarity. We do not feel an emotional barrier that prevents us from examining messages more closely. We are willing to break any message down into components and make comparisons and evaluations in a quest to understand the nature of the message and to examine why our initial expectations were wrong.

During media exposures, people with a low tolerance encounter messages on the surface. If the surface meaning fits their preconceptions, then it is filed away and becomes a confirmation (or reinforcement) of those preconceptions. If the surface meaning does not meet a person's preconceptions, the message is ignored. In short, there is no analysis.

People with a high tolerance for ambiguity do not have a barrier to analysis. They are willing to break any message down into components and make comparisons and evaluations in a quest to understand the nature of the message and why their own expectations were wrong. People who consistently attempt to verify their observations and judgments are called scanners because they are perpetually looking for more information (Gardner, 1968).

## Nonimpulsiveness

This refers to how quickly people make decisions about messages (Kagan, Rosman, Day, Albert, & Phillips, 1964). People who rush to a decision are impulsive. In contrast, people who take a long time and consider things from many perspectives are reflective or nonimpulsive.

Typically, there is a trade-off between speed and accuracy. Impulsive people are most concerned with speed; they feel overwhelmed by decisions, so they want to have things resolved as soon as possible. For them, it is worth the risk to make a bad decision as long as they can quickly end the worry that comes with being faced with a decision-making task. Reflective people are most concerned with accuracy; they dread being wrong, so they think about all the options of a decision, even if it takes a long time.

How much time we take to make decisions is governed by our emotions. If we feel comfortable encountering new information and like to work through problems carefully, we are likely to act reflectively and take our time. However, if we feel a negative emotion (such as frustration), we tend to make decisions as quickly as possible to eliminate the negative emotional state.

# Experience

Substantial gains in media literacy can come about from experience both in the media world and the real world. In this section, I explain what I mean by experience and why it is so important to increasing media literacy.

By experience, I do not simply mean time spent with the media. Two people can spend 100 hours with the media, and one of those people may have encountered 100 different experiences, whereas the other has encountered only one experience 100 times. The first person may have spent the 100 hours with many different media, many different vehicles, and many different kinds of messages. At the end of the 100 hours, the person has a greater appreciation for the range of messages, and this comprehension of range provides him or her with a much better context to understand any one message. This person can compare and contrast across many more kinds of messages to perceive patterns. This person also understands that there are many more options out there in the media channels and therefore makes a better selection of which of those options can best achieve his or her personal goals. The person who has used the 100 hours to have one experience 100 times has lost all these opportunities.

By experience, I mean that certain media exposures have altered the way you think or feel about something in the real world or that a real work occurrence has altered the way you think or feel about media messages. For example, can you remember back to when you were in early elementary school and you saw an ad for some fantastic toy that you "just had to have"? If you are male, the toy was probably a GI Joe or some sort of action toy such as a truck or helicopter. In the ad, the thing moved and made action noises and did really cool things. But when you got the toy, it just sat there like the inert piece of plastic that it was. You felt betrayed. This taught you to be skeptical about advertising. If you did not have this real-world experience to match against the similar media world experience, you would have lost the opportunity to learn something valuable.

Higher levels of media literacy are keyed to a wider range of experiences, both with real-world encounters as well as with media messages. Ask yourself about how broad your real-world experiences are. Do you have lots of friends, but they are all pretty much the same as far as background, values, political attitudes, personality, and so on? Do you spend your time pretty much the same every week—that is, stuck in habits? Do you shop at the same stores? Do you commute to school or work the same way every time? When you take trips, do you go to the same places?

Think about your habits in life and with the media. The more you are governed by habits, the less you think about options and the narrower your experience base becomes. Increasing media literacy requires you to expand your base of experiences so that you perceive more options about people, about how to spend time, and about emotional reactions. With more options, you can make better decisions. And when you make your decisions consciously—rather than being continually governed by automatic routines and habits—you are exercising more control over your life.

# Active Application of Skills

Although exposing yourself to a wider range of experiences contributes to the potential of attaining higher levels of media literacy, you also need to pay careful attention to those experiences and really think about them. This requires the active application of skills. Cognitively, this means using analysis and evaluation more when encountering messages. It also means that we need to use the skills of grouping, induction, deduction, synthesis, and abstracting more when taking information from those messages and incorporating it into our knowledge structures.

We also need to be more active in using emotional skills. Salovey and Mayer (1990) say that we can develop emotional literacy by working in five areas: reading emotions (empathy), having emotional self-awareness, harnessing emotions productively, managing emotions, and handling relationships. The first three of these have relevance to media interactions and how we deal with those messages. First, we need to develop greater empathy, which refers to our ability to see the world from another person's perspective. Second, we also need to be aware of our own emotions as well as understand what causes and alters them. Third, we need to be less impulsive and exercise more self-control on concentrating on the task at hand rather than becoming distracted by peripheral emotions.

Being emotionally literate requires an understanding of how emotions are evoked by the media and how we can control those effects when we are confronted with different types of messages. We can use the media to achieve the emotional effects we want if we are conscious of what we are doing and aware of how the effects processes work.

When we are unaware of emotional effects, the media can exercise unwanted influences, such as reducing our sensitivity to things about which we should care. For example, people who watch a great deal of violence on television become desensitized to the suffering of victims not only on television but also in the real world.

Unfortunately, few people continue to work at expanding their experiences and developing their skills consciously. This can be seen in figures that indicate that most people do not even begin to process most of the information to which they are exposed—rather, they screen it out and do not remember it even a short time after exposure. Most people remember only about 40% of what they see and only 10% of what they hear (Adams & Hamm, 1989).

The moral skills are linked closely to the cognitive and emotional skills. When we encounter a message, we need to analyze and evaluate it from a moral perspective. Our emotions play a part in the drive to dig deeper in our analyses and to set standards in our evaluation. That is, our emotions will guide us in determining what is right or just.

We need to apply our skills consciously to filter out some messages that we evaluate as inaccurate, misleading, or not useful. We need to analyze messages to get below their surface and perceive deeper meanings. We need to compare what we see in media messages with what we know from our knowledge structures. In short, we need to be active in interacting with the media.

If we are passive during our media exposures, we can still pick up a good deal of information in our media-saturated culture, but that information will not be balanced or complete. To illustrate this point, let's say a person needs 100 facts to have a commanding knowledge base in a particular area. Passive exposure to the media might result in the person being exposed to maybe a dozen facts. The mainstream flow of messages from the media will never provide you with the full range of information you might need. The media have a narrow agenda for information and a narrow repertoire for entertainment stories. Passive exposure will not get you outside these limits. If we stay fixed in this passive state, the continual flow of messages will only serve to reinforce a narrow, unbalanced set of information. Unless you actively seek a wider variety of sources of information, your knowledge structure will not become stronger, and you will fall into the trap of believing that you are well informed—because of all your exposure—but really becoming less informed as the world changes without you seeing it.

Unless we stay active in processing messages, our position on the media literacy continuum can degrade to lower levels. Without continually practicing skills, those skills will deteriorate. Without continually updating and adjusting our knowledge structures, they quickly become out of date and cluttered with unprocessed information. For example, the ownership, control, economic, and organizational patterns of the media industries change each year; each week brings a flood of new messages; and social scientists conduct hundreds of important studies each year that require us to expand as well as alter the way we think about effects. If we don't keep up, we will slide behind.

# Conclusion

Media literacy can be developed through maturation, improving one's natural abilities, gaining meaningful experience, and actively applying one's skills. During childhood, maturation can hold up development, but by about age 12, the gaining of experience and the active processing of that experience are the dominant ways of continuing our development. This is why children's exposure cannot be compared to adults. Children are not people who differ from adults simply because they have less experience. The essential difference is not experience; the key difference is that children have less capacity to make sense of their experiences. With maturation, children have more capabilities open to them. As they reach adolescence, they have passed through the last cognitive maturation gates. From this point onward in life, people cannot depend on maturation to help them continue to develop higher levels of media literacy. If they want to continue to develop, they need to actively apply their skills and expose themselves to a wider variety of media experiences.

The four factors of development work together. For example, a 7-year-old girl will be able to read because she has passed through the gate of cognitive maturity where her mind has developed to a point where she can learn to read. If she reads a simple book on gardening, she will be able to recognize most words and be able to recognize how the words are assembled into sentences to convey an idea. She has a basic competency in reading. If she also has a good deal of experience in gardening, this experience, along with her reading skill, will combine to allow her to read the book more quickly and acquire a good deal more meaning from it than a child who has not had any experience in gardening. As her experience with gardening increases, her need for more information will also increase. She might subscribe to gardening magazines, listen to tapes on gardening, and seek out television programs on the subject. As her knowledge base grows, she will seek information from related areas—perhaps botany and landscape architecture. If she carefully analyzes the messages as she is exposed to them, she will be developing a better "eye" for the artistry of gardening, and thus her ability to appreciate will be increased. Thus, the combining of experiences from the media along with real-life experiences and the conscious application of advanced skills along the way moves her further down both the gardening path as well as the media literacy path.

Media literacy can be developed. That development is easier among people who keep improving on their natural abilities, who keep searching for a wide range of experiences in both the media as well as the real world, and who keep applying their skills actively to build more elaborate and useful knowledge structures.

# Further Reading

Goleman, D. (1995). *Emotional intelligence.* New York: Bantam. (352 pages with index)

In this very readable best seller, Goleman argues that there is an emotional IQ, not just an intellectual one. He challenges the long-held belief that a person's intelligence, as measured by a narrow IQ test, is an inadequate predictor of success or ability. First, he broadens the conception of intelligence, and then he shows how a person's emotional development interacts with a broad range of cognitive abilities. He cites physiological data to show that emotions are part of the brain and are triggered by the capacity of the body.

Kohlberg, L. (1981). *The philosophy of moral development: Moral stages and the idea of justice.* New York: Harper & Row. (428 pages, including references and index)

Kohlberg lays out his moral development scheme of three stages, each with two substages. There are many examples relating this structure to how people come to understand the concept of justice.

Pulaski, M. A. S. (1980). *Understanding Piaget: An introduction to children's cognitive development* (Revised and expanded edition). New York: Harper & Row. (248 pages with index)

This is a very clear, well-organized description of most of Piaget's thinking and research. Many drawings illustrate key concepts.

# KNOWLEDGE STRUCTURES OF MEDIA CONTENT

# CHAPTER 5

# Reality and Media Messages

**Key Idea:** The media spin reality to make it appear more exciting and thus attract people away from their real lives.

**What Is Reality?**
    Magic Window
    Multidimensions of Reality
**Organizing Principle: Next-Step Reality**
    Audience's Perspective
    Programmers' Perspective
**The Importance of Media Literacy**
**Conclusion**

We all live in two worlds: the real world and the media world. Most of us feel that the real world is too limited; that is, we cannot get all the experiences and information we want in the real world. To get those experiences and information, we journey into the media world. For example, you might feel that your life is too boring and you want to experience some exciting romance. You could read a novel, go to a movie, or watch a television program to get this kind of experience. Or you might be curious about what happened in your city today, so you watch the evening news, where reporters take you to all the places of the day's actions—crime scenes, fire locations, courthouses, sporting arenas. Although these are all real-world locations, you are not visiting them in the real world. Instead, you enter the media world to visit them.

We are continually entering the media world to get experiences and information we cannot get very well in our real lives. We enter the media world to expand our real-world experience and to help us understand the real world better. But those experiences we have in the media world are different than if we had experienced them directly in the real world. We often forget this as we bring media-world experiences back into our real world. As we constantly cross the border between the real world and the media world, the border sometimes gets blurred, and over time we tend to forget which memories are from experiences in the real world and which were originally experienced in the media world.

This blurring of the line and the interlacing of memories makes it important that we spend some mental energy considering the nature of reality and how the reality of the two worlds is different.

# What Is Reality?

Reality is one of the most difficult concepts to define in any context. Philosophers have been trying to define it for millennia, and ever since the field of psychology was founded more than a dozen decades ago, psychologists have been almost exclusively dealing with the fundamental problem of how the human mind encounters the world and seeks to make sense of what is real.

With media studies, it would seem as if the task of delineating reality would be easier by simply drawing the line of reality between the media world and the real world. The real world is real, and the media world is fantasy. But this is far too easy a distinction, and drawing the line in this way will be highly inaccurate and misleading. Still, we do have to make a distinction because developing a sophisticated understanding of the nature of reality is very important when trying to gain control over media effects. Let's begin by examining how scholars have examined how people make this distinction.

## Magic Window

Media scholars have encountered the issue of determining reality primarily as a concern in dealing with children. The assumption has been that children see the media, especially television, as a magic window on the world. Psychologists believe that young children perceive television as the simple, unvarnished truth of what is happening in the real world. Media researchers have found that very young children (younger than 3 years of age) do regard television as a magic window, but as children's minds mature cognitively (especially from ages 3 to 5), they develop a skepticism about the literal reality of media messages, and they are better able to distinguish reality from fantasy (Taylor & Howell, 1973). By age 5, children can distinguish between fictional programs and news or documentary. At this point, children clearly know what fiction is, but they continue to develop a better understanding about nonfiction as they grow older and as their experience with news shows messages (Wright, Huston, Reitz, & Piemyat, 1994).

Researchers have labeled this shift away from a magic window belief in the literal reality of media messages as "adult discount," where children begin thinking like adults and are more skeptical of the reality of the messages (Hawkins, 1977). Most researchers seem to believe that children have fully incorporated an adult discount into their thinking by age 12.

There is evidence, however, that not all people apply an adult discount by the time they reach age 12. For example, Van der Voort (1986) found that although children's perceptions of reality decreased from ages 9 to 12 for fantasy programs, there was no change in their perceptions of the reality of so-called reality programs. It appears that children base their perceptions of reality not on the accuracy of portrayals or information but on the probability that something could occur in their lives. By age 12, they have not developed an understanding that, in many ways, news is a construction by journalists, just as fiction programming is a creation of writers.

It appears that many adults may not have reached this stage (see Box 5.1). The people who wrote to the Coast Guard, begging them to rescue Gilligan and his friends from the island, appear silly. You might be thinking that such a problem with reality is rare in adults. But is it? How many adults believe the matches in the World Wrestling Federation television programs are real? How many adults who watch docudramas have difficulty perceiving the line between what actually happened and what was fictionalized? How many adults have trouble distinguishing between the reality and fantasy in facts presented by political candidates in mediated debates? How many adults realize that news programs, with their filtering processes and story construction formula, substantially change the picture of what actually happens and instead present a distorted version of what the world is like?

---

**Box 5.1**

In 1964, Sherwood Schwartz produced a show called *Gilligan's Island*. This was a farcical comedy where seven characters who had been on a pleasure cruise encountered a storm that left them shipwrecked on an island somewhere in the Pacific Ocean. After about six episodes had aired, Schwartz was contacted by the Coast Guard and told that it had received several dozen telegrams from people who were complaining that the military should send a ship to rescue these seven people. Those telegrams were serious. Schwartz was dumfounded, calling this the "most extreme case of suspension of belief I every heard of." He wondered, "Who did these viewers think was filming the castaways on that island? There was even a laugh track on the show. Who was laughing at the survivors of the wreck of the *S. S. Minnow*? It boggled the mind" (Schwartz, 1984, p. 2).

Now in the first years of the new millennium, one of the most popular shows on television is *Survivor,* which bills itself as reality television. This show purportedly takes 16 real people and puts them in a wilderness setting where the individuals depend on each other for survival (food, shelter, fire). At the same time, they are competing against one another for $1 million. In what sense is this show real? The players were selected from thousands of applicants not because they were ordinary people but on the basis of their potential attractiveness to audiences and their ability to generate conflict. The situation is artificial in the sense that none of these people lives their typical life in the wilderness, and none (with the exception of the all-star season) has played this game before—or any game for $1 million. Although the setting looks like a deserted wilderness, the players are not really alone. There are dozens of production people, including camera crews, sound engineers, crews to design and build sets for the challenges and tribal councils, and the host Jeff Probst. Where do these production people live? How do they get to the survivors' camps to tape them? Are there helicopter and boat crews? How do all these production people eat—are there cooks? How does their food get to the island? The show is not scripted in the sense that dialog has been written by a member of the Writers Guild of America. But each contestant carefully writes his or her own lines, in the sense that the contestant's interactions are highly calculated to put himself or herself in the best position to win the game. Also, the show is carefully edited to present to the viewing public the most dramatic version of what takes place. The 960 hours over the course of the 40 days of the game are edited down to about 10 hours that are shown to the public. That is only 1% of what happened. This example makes us confront the issue of where we draw the line between reality and fantasy when something appears in the media. Also, do most adults make this distinction better than most children?

As we age, we do not automatically acquire the ability to make accurate differentiations between reality and fantasy. Believing that we do may be the strongest evidence that our belief in what we think is the reality of the situation is actually a fantasy. Misperceptions of reality are not limited to children. *If we are to understand how people make decisions about what is real in the media, we need to look at more dimensions than the magic window one.*

## Multidimensions of Reality

Frequently, the judgment of reality is multidimensional; that is, we consider multiple characteristics in making judgments of reality. For example, it is possible to judge some science fiction movies (such as *Aliens* or *Star Wars*) as being more realistic than many situation comedies on television. A science fiction movie may take place in a fantasy world where no human has ever gone, contain characters that exist only in the imagination, and have laws of physics that are unlike anything on earth; however, the plots, dialog, and themes could be judged as very realistic. In contrast, although a situation comedy may take place in a house very much like the viewers' own and have characters that dress like everyday people and engage in everyday problems, many viewers may roll their eyes and feel that those comedies have nothing to do with real life. Real people do not act like situation comedy characters act, and problems in the real world never get neatly resolved in 30 minutes like they do in situation comedies.

The beginning point of judging reality is usually with an assessment of whether a portrayal actually happened. But viewers rarely stop at this judgment. There is more to judging reality. Viewers—especially with fictional content—make assessments about whether something *could* happen as portrayed. That which could never happen is fantasy. So the judgment must move beyond the *actualities* of occurrence and consider the *possibilities* that different characters could be people encountered in real life and that particular situations could actually occur.

Researchers have found that people will go beyond magic-window considerations and also judge the reality of media messages along the dimensions of social utility and identity (Dorr, 1981; Hawkins, 1977; Potter, 1986). The social utility judgment is based on whether viewers believe they can use the information in the portrayal in their own lives. The more fantastic the characters and actions, the less viewers believe they can translate that information into something they can use in their day-to-day interactions with people. The identity judgment is based on a feeling of parasocial involvement with particular characters. The closer a viewer feels to a character, the more real that character is to that viewer.

Viewers make judgments on these three dimensions in an independent manner; that is, if a program is perceived as highly realistic on one dimension, the person may or may not perceive the show as being realistic on the other two dimensions. For example, *Star Trek* is likely to be regarded as fantasy when considering it along the magic-window dimension, but it could be regarded as highly realistic by many on the identity and social utility dimensions.

More recent research also supports the notion of reality having multiple dimensions. For example, Albada (2000) provides evidence that people talk about the families on television in terms of their realism and structure. Furthermore, people feel that the way families are portrayed on television influences their own expectations of family life, valued features of family, and communication with family members. Also, Hall (2003) conducted a series of focus groups in which she asked participants to conceptualize media realism. She found complex definitions that varied by genre and were based on six ideas: factuality, plausibility, typicality, emotional involvement, narrative consistency, and perceptual persuasiveness. *Factuality* is what actually happened. *Plausibility* is what could happen. *Typicality* is what usually happens. *Emotional involvement* is the degree to which a person's feelings and sense of identity are pulled into a message. *Narrative consistency* refers to the plot of a story and how well it makes people feel that sequence actions are believable. *Perceptual persuasiveness* refers to how real the images look. Of all these six dimensions, it appears that plausibility is the most often used conceptualization employed by people to determine the degree of reality in a media message (Hall, 2003).

Another important point to consider is that differences in judgments of reality in media portrayals are likely to be larger across people of the same age compared to the differences in judgments across different age groups. Not every child of the same age is making the same judgments about reality. For example, Van der Voort (1986) reports that perceptions of reality and the degree of identification with characters vary substantially at any given age. In his research, he found that some children became absorbed in watching the violent videos and judged the violence to be realistic, which led to a stronger emotional reaction, which led to a belief that the violence was terrible, which did *not* lead to aggressive behavior in real life. In contrast, other children who were also absorbed in viewing violence and believed it to be realistic had an uncritical attitude toward program violence, which led to them being more jaded and less emotionally involved, which led to more aggressive behavior in real life.

Up to this point in the chapter, I have shown you how complex the idea of reality can be. We must consider multiple dimensions that are independent from one another. We must consider that children are less capable than adults in making certain kinds of judgments about reality but become more sophisticated on certain dimensions as they age. We must consider that there is wide range of sophistication in making reality judgments across adults. And we must consider that many adults overestimate the degree of reality on so-called reality programs as well as news.

How can we simplify this complex array of ideas so that we can focus attention on why all this should matter to media literacy? What do people really need to know about the nature of the reality of media messages to be literate and protect themselves from harmful effects?

# Organizing Principle: Next-Step Reality

Much of the complexity in the research about perceptions of reality can be explained simply by the idea of what I call "next-step reality." When we think about what audiences really want from media messages, we can see that many of their exposure decisions are guided by a desire for "next-step reality." Also, when we look at decisions from a programmer's perspective, we can again see the emergence of "next-step reality." This idea is embedded in how media messages get produced and why certain messages attract large audiences whereas other messages do not. In this section, I bring this idea to the surface and show you how it serves as a useful organizing principle for thinking about all kinds of media content.

## Audience's Perspective

Why do people expose themselves to media messages? At the most fundamental level, they expose themselves to the media to find messages that they cannot get in real life. If people were getting all the messages they needed in real life, they would have no motivation to go to the expense (money and time) to search through the media for these messages.

There are two reasons why people are motivated to get certain messages but go to the media rather than get those messages in real life. One reason is that it is impossible for them to get those messages in real life. For example, for most people, it is impossible to know what the Earth looks like from outer space or what the surface of other planets look like. It is impossible to know what it was like to live on a farm during the American Civil War, to be a knight of the Round Table in medieval England, or to watch Jesus Christ preach. To get access to these images, sounds, and emotions, people must access messages from the media.

A second reason that motivates people to get messages from the media instead of real life is because the costs of getting those messages in the media are far lower than the costs required in real life. For example, it is easier to watch a 1-hour travelogue on France than to pay the money to travel there for a week. It is far easier to watch a presidential news conference on television than it is to go to journalism school, get a job on a major newspaper or television service, get credentialed as a White House reporter, and attend the press conference in person. And it is less costly emotionally to watch characters in a movie try to meet each other, establish relationships, break up, and learn from their mistakes than it is to go through all of that in real life to learn the same thing.

Audiences therefore have a strong, continuing motivation to seek out messages in the media. They search for messages that have two general characteristics. First, those messages must appear real. They must have many elements that signal viewers that they are real; that is, they are close enough to resonate strongly with a viewer's experience of everyday reality, and thus those messages are accurate representations or at least plausible and probable. If they do not appear real, then audiences will not trust that the information is useful enough to bring it back into their everyday lives. Second, those messages must present a little more than everyday reality. Without this something extra, there is no reason to search out the media message because the person is already getting the message in his or her real life. This is what I mean by next-step reality—the message is presented as reality to resonate with the audience's experience and make it have the potential to be useful in everyday situations, but the message is "sweetened" by an extra added ingredient that takes it one step outside of the audience's everyday existence.

Therefore, people want media messages that are not so real that they are the same as their everyday lives. But neither do they want media messages that are so far removed from their experiences and needs that the messages have no immediate relevance. So people want messages that are one step removed from real life; they want messages that show what is easily possible and make it seem probable and even actual.

## Programmers' Perspective

Programmers intuitively know that to attract audiences, they must take their audience's sense of reality and tweak it a bit to make it seem more interesting. Thus, the producers of media messages typically keep the elements of their messages anchored in the real world as much as possible so that they can accurately resonate with the audience's experiences in real life. But producers of media messages also know they cannot simply reproduce those messages; there would be no point to this because it would be easier for people to stay with the real-world messages.

Producers of fiction know that their art is in telling stories that are "bigger" than life in some way. Producers can take an ordinary setting and a typical plot (boy meets girl) but change the characters so that they are a little more attractive or a little more interesting than people in real life. Or producers can take ordinary characters and put them in a plot that is a bit more dramatic in events and consequences than what happens to most people in real life. Skilled producers can take the audience on a journey by removing the audience one step at a time until they have taken them willingly to an absurd place. This is the formula with farce. The story begins with what looks like an ordinary everyday situation; then, step-by-step, the producer takes the audience far away from that reality but does it in a way that the audience is not lost but willingly awaits each new step. Thus, producers depend on viewers' willing suspension of disbelief. To make people willing, producers must take it one step at a time.

The next-step reality is also easy to understand with persuasive messages. For example, the typical problem-solution advertising message shows ordinary people with an ordinary problem, such as bad breath, a headache, dirty laundry, hunger for a good lunch, and so on. The advertiser invites the audience to take the step of faith into a solution, that is, to buy and use the advertised product on the promise that it will solve the problem better than any other solution—that is, more quickly, more completely, more cheaply, or more satisfying emotionally.

The next-step reality is a bit more difficult to understand with information-type messages. For example, if the purpose of news organizations is to report the events of the day, how can the next-step reality apply to journalists? The answer is that when journalists select what gets reported, they are not as interested in the typical events as they are the anomalous events. Recall the old saying that if a dog bites a man, it is not news, but if a man bites a dog, that is news. The twist in the event makes it news. Crimes are news because they are aberrant behaviors. Violent crimes are more newsworthy than are property crimes because they are more aberrant and more rare.

All kinds of messages—entertainment, persuasion, and information—are all crafted to retain the appearance of a high degree of reality, but all are really one step removed from reality. The more skillful this one-step remove transforms the reality, the more interesting the message will be and the more likely it will attract and hold people's attention.

Because we spend so much time with the media world in addition to the real world, and because the boundary between the two is often obscured, we can often get confused.

This is especially the case after thousands of hours of automatic processing of both the mundane real-world messages and the massive flow of media-world messages. In all of that continuous flow, there is a constant intermingling of perceptions.

# The Importance of Media Literacy

Increasingly, the border between our real world and the media world is becoming harder to discern. More and more often, the media do not wait for us to cross over into their world; they bring their messages into our world. Because much of our exposure to media messages is not planned by us, we don't realize how much we are exposed to the media. Consider the exposure you have to media messages everyday in your real world without you being aware of them. For example, there are radio messages coming out of other people's cars as you walk down the street in your real world; you pass messages on kiosks, billboards, cars, clothing, and so forth. As the media pump messages into our world at an ever increasing rate, the borderline becomes blurred. We take almost all of this for granted.

There are many places where the border between the real world and the media world is not so clear. To illustrate this, consider the following question: Is the news real? Some of you may reply, "Of course it is real. It is what happened. Journalists do not make up news stories." But when you expose yourself to the news, aren't you in the media world? Reading a newspaper or watching the evening news on television means that you have left your world of direct experience and crossed over into the media world. If you were present when an event happened, then that happening took place in your real world. However, if your exposure to the event is on television, you are experiencing the event in the media world—not the real world—and this makes a difference. Often, news coverage is very different from the real-world occurrence; if we were at the newsworthy event and then later saw the news story, we could clearly see those differences, and the line between the real world and the media world would be very clear to us. But what if we did not attend the event and have only the news coverage to tell us what happened? In this case, all we have is the media-world account of the real-world event, and we blur the lines between the two worlds when we believe that we are being exposed to real-world events when we are not. We are being exposed to the media-world interpretation of real-world events. This might at first seem to be a very subtle, insignificant difference. But this is actually a profoundly important difference.

Also contributing to the blurring of the line is the media presenting many of their messages as "reality" programming. Think about what makes the following programs real, as the media claim: *Cops, The Bachelor, Extreme Makeover, Blind Date, Fifth Wheel, Cheaters,* and *Monday Night Football.* To what extent do these shows fit into your real world and resonate with your real experiences?

As genres change and the line between reality and fantasy programming becomes even more blurred, we must avoid falling into the trap of debating which types of shows are more real. This is why the next-step reality is so fundamental to media literacy because it shifts the question and hence the focus of our attention. The question should *not* be, How real are media messages? The next-step reality organizing principle shows us that every media message is a mix of reality and fantasy. Instead, the question should be, Which elements in this message reflect reality and which elements are removed from reality in some way? When you are guided by the organizing principle of next-step reality, you need to analyze media messages to answer these more appropriate questions. This analysis will help you develop a sensitivity to how big of a step you usually tolerate in the one-step remove messages. Some people will tolerate a very small step and limit themselves to messages that very closely match their own experiences and knowledge. On the other end of that spectrum are people who insist on radical departures from what their everyday lives provide them. These are the people who wrote to the Coast Guard about rescuing Gilligan, and these are the people who take on the personae of fantasy characters.

The key to becoming media literate is not in how close we move to the reality end of the spectrum; that would only limit our range of information and emotional reactions. Instead, the key to media literacy is to be flexible and aware. Being flexible means being willing to traverse the entire spectrum of messages and being willing to enjoy the full range of messages. Being aware means thinking about where you are in the spectrum and knowing the different standards of appreciation to apply to different places on the spectrum of reality. By being both flexible and aware, you can much better enjoy the enormous variety of messages in the media and, at the same time, control the effects of those messages so that you avoid the negative ones that usually come from automatic exposure and instead more intensely enjoy the positive effects that can result from any media message.

All of us must continually decide how closely media messages reflect real life and what the implications of those differences are on our beliefs about reality. Sometimes, these decisions about what is real are relatively easy; it is simple for most of us to understand that there is nothing in real life anything like *Gilligan's Island*. But some of the decisions are harder to make accurately—especially when they are subtly shaped over a long period of time by the accumulation of thousands of journeys into the media world. Over time, we have come to accept much of the media world as the real world. For example, who is the president of the United States? Are you sure? Have you ever met him? If you have not met him, how do you know he really exists? If you have met him, how do you know he is who he says he is? I am not trying to make you paranoid. I am only asking you to consider the degree to which you trust the information and experiences you bring back from the media world into your real world. When encountering some of that information, you should have a high degree of skepticism, but other information should be accepted by you with a feeling of trust. Do you know which is which?

This is why being media literate is so important. Media messages are not always the way they seem. There are often many layers of meanings. Some of those layers are highly unrealistic (never happened in actuality, never will happen, and never could happen), but they are interlaced among layers of realistic elements that could transform the overall message in your perception from "fantasy" to "it might happen" to "it is likely to happen" to "I need to try this." The more you are aware of the layers of meaning in messages, the more you can control the selection of which meanings you want. Being more analytical is the first step toward controlling how the media affect you. If you are unaware of the meanings, then the media stay in control of how you perceive the world.

When you understand this organizing principle of next-step reality, you can better appreciate media content. You can focus your analysis on how different media, different vehicles, and different artists achieve the resonance of reality and then take that one step to remove their message from that reality. This is where the artistic talent comes into play. So a good understanding of this concept can help you develop a keener aesthetic sense as you experience individual messages. Also important, this concept should motivate you to ask questions about patterns in the one-step remove. There are patterns of life in the real world, and there are patterns of stories in the media world. The two patterns are not the same. The more you recognize the story patterns and how they are different from real-world life patterns, the less trouble you will have in recognizing the border between reality and fantasy. The next three chapters focus on those media-world patterns and the ways they deviate from real-world patterns.

# Conclusion

Clearly, the issue of reality entails more than making a simple decision about whether something actually happened. People are able to think in terms of degrees of reality, and when they are assessing the degree of reality, they consider more than one dimension.

It is also important to understand that there is not a huge gap between children's ability to perceive reality accurately and adults' ability. This is a trap that adults frequently fall into. Being in this trap gives those adults a false sense of security that they do not need to think carefully about the reality of media messages because they are no longer children and therefore are protected by the adult discount. Because the degree of belief in reality is associated with higher negative effects, adults are vulnerable, as are children (Potter, 1986; Rubin, Perse, & Taylor, 1988).

The most useful way to think about reality is with the "next-step reality" organizing principle. This focuses your attention on the degree to which media messages are both real and fantasy. This then sets up more important questions: Which elements in the message do I regard as real, and how did I arrive at that perception? Which elements in the message do I regard as fantasy? To what extent am I attracted to the fantasy and willing to try to make it my reality? Keep these questions in mind as you read through the next three chapters on different types of media content.

**Exercise 5.1**     Delineating the Elusive Line Between Reality and Fantasy

1. *Analyze Television Programs:* For each of the genres of programs listed below, pick one particular program and analyze it.

   - Situation comedy
   - Drama (police drama or family drama)
   - "Reality" program (such as *Survivor, The Bachelor, Extreme Makeover, The Apprentice,* and *Cops*)
   - News program

     For each program, take a sheet of paper and write the name of the program at the top. Then draw a vertical line down the middle of the page. Label the left column as "Reality Indicators" and list in the column all the things about the program that you think would lead someone to believe that the program content is real, that is, depicts reality. Then label the right column "Nonreal World" and list in that column all the things about the program that you think would lead someone to believe that the program was not real.

2. *Tabulate Lists:* Count all the items you have listed in the Reality Indicators column and write that number at the bottom of that column. Then count all the items you have listed in the Nonreal World column and write that number at the bottom of that column. Do the same for all sheets, so that you have two totals at the bottom of the page for each program you have analyzed for reality.

   Turn totals into percentages. For example, if on one sheet you listed five things in the left column (reality items) and five things in the right column (nonreality items), then this would compute to 50% reality and 50% nonreality. If instead you had one item in the reality column and four items in the unreality column, this would compute to 20% and 80%.

3. *Check for Patterns:* If you were a perceptive television viewer, you are likely to have at least a handful of items in each column. No program is purely reality—there are all kinds of production decisions (about characters, plot, settings, customs, makeup, dialog, camera placement, editing, etc.) that take messages out of the pure reality realm. Also, no program is purely fantasy—there are character types, situations, language, settings, and so forth that are very much like the real world.

   Look at the pairs of percentages at the bottom of each page. Are the splits in percentages favoring the first types of shows, which are the more fantasy shows? Or are they favoring the more reality types of shows, which are the second two genres? Or is there no difference?

Now try this exercise again

- With movies
- With stories in magazines
- With newspaper stories
- With Internet sites
- With video games

Do reality proportions vary across the medium?

# CHAPTER 6

# Entertainment Content

**Key Idea:** Media entertainment content follows clear formulas that are designed to attract and hold our attention.

M ost of us feel that we have a good understanding of media content because we recognize the names and faces of movie stars. We know the words and melodies of popular songs. We can tell our friends about what happened in detail on our favorite television shows.

But how much do we know about the patterns of characters, actions, and themes across the media entertainment landscape? For example, what *types* of characters are most prevalent in entertainment? What are the typical plot formulas? Do you know what themes underlie most of media entertainment?

These questions are addressed in this chapter, where the focus is on television entertainment. Why television? Because television is the most pervasive medium for entertainment. Almost all of us get more of our entertainment from television compared to any other medium. And we take much of this exposure for granted. We are not conscious of the broad patterns of characterization and plot that we constantly see. But those patterns— even though they are fictional—can influence what we think about the real world.

# Entertainment Formula

On the surface, it appears that the media present a wide variety of entertainment messages. But when we analyze those messages, we can see that they follow standard patterns. For example, a wide variety of songs have been presented as popular music in recordings, cassettes, CDs, and on the radio over many decades. Each of those songs follows certain formulas. None of those songs is a purely random sequence of notes. Musical formulas tell musicians which notes are played in sequence (melody progressions) and which notes are to be played together (chords). There are a small number of standard rhythms. All of the songs are creative variations off the standard formula. The same can be said for any media message.

## General Story Formula

There are formulas for telling stories. All stories begin with a conflict or a problem. The conflict is heightened throughout the story, and the main characters try to solve the problem. Finally, during the climactic scene, the problem is solved, and the conflict is eliminated.

This general formula is used not only by the creators of media messages; the formula is also used by us—the audience—to help us easily recognize the good and bad characters and to quickly find where we are in the story. Stories that follow the formulas the closest usually have the largest audiences, because they are the easiest to follow. The more experience we have with entertainment messages, the more we learn the story formula. We are conditioned to expect certain plot points, certain pacing, certain types of characters, and certain themes.

## Genres

The overall entertainment story formula is elaborated in different ways across different genres of entertainment. Let's examine the story formula in the genres of drama, comedy, romance, and reality programming.

### *Drama*

The drama genre has three basic subgenres that illuminate three types of drama entertainment: tragedy, mystery, and action/horror (Sayre & King, 2003). Tragedy must have characters that are perceived by the audience as noble and good. However, bad things happen to these characters either because they have a fatal flaw they cannot get around (as is the case in Shakespearean tragedies) or because fate has conspired to do them in (*Titanic*). What audiences enjoy about tragedies is the opportunity to compare themselves with the tragic characters and feel better off than those poor characters.

With the mystery formula, an important element of the plot is missing. For example, in a "whodunit" mystery, the *who* is missing. The crime triggers the story, and someone must use the information available to figure out who committed the crime. The suspense is in solving the puzzle. Audiences are drawn into the story as they try to solve the mystery for themselves.

The action/horror formula is primarily plot driven as good and evil fight it out in ever deepening conflict. Characters are stereotypes or comic book types. Within several seconds after being introduced to a character, we know whether that character is a hero or a villain.

Characters are static and don't change. The plot relies on fast-paced action that maximizes arousal in the audience. The primary emotions evoked are fear, suspense, and vengeance. Violence is a staple in almost all of these stories. The formula of violence tells us that it is okay for criminals to behave violently throughout a program as long as they are caught at the end of the show. This restores a sense of peace—at least until the commercials are over and the next show begins. Also, we feel that it is permissible for police officers, private eyes, and good guy vigilantes to break the law and use violence as long as it is used successfully against the bad guys.

## Comedy

With the comedy formula, minor conflict situations flare up and set the action in motion. The conflict is heightened verbally, through deceit or insults. Characters are developed through their unusual foibles and quick wit. The action is neatly resolved at the end of the show, and all the main characters are happy.

One subgenre of comedy is the character comedy or comedy of manners. Here the humor arises out of character quirks that illuminate the craziness of everyday situations. Characters find themselves in difficult situations that we all encounter everyday. As characters try to work their way through these situations, the absurdity of certain social conventions is illustrated, and this makes us laugh. Examples include *Seinfeld* and *Frasier*. Another subgenre of comedy is the put-down comedy, where certain characters have power over other characters and exercise that power in humorous ways. Examples include *MASH* and *Fresh Prince of Bel Air*.

The situation comedy formula is so well known by viewers that Nickelodeon has created some 60-second sitcoms. This cable network inserts these mini-sitcoms between the old 30-minute sitcoms it programs on Nick at Nite. These include *The Gaveltons*, which is about the adventures of America's most litigious family; *Spin & Cutter*, a buddy show about the stupid schemes of two lovable goofballs; and *All's Well*, a father-knows-best-style family comedy (Maurstad, 1998). We have no trouble recognizing the character types of these highly truncated plots.

## Romance

A romance story begins with a young person experiencing either loneliness from a lack of a relationship or a relationship that is bad due to betrayal, jealousy, or fear. We identify with the main character and feel her pain. But she is full of hope for what seems like an unattainable goal. Through hard work and virtue, she gets closer and closer to her goal—even though she experiences frequent heart-rendering setbacks—until the story climaxes with the fulfillment of the goal, which transmits intense emotions to the audience.

Writers who have mastered this formula are very successful. For example, among all paperbacks sold in the United States, about half are in the genre of the romance novel. One romance novelist who has really understood the formula is Nora Roberts. She has published 127 romance novels, all following the same basic romance formula. In 1998 alone, she had 11 titles on the *New York Times* best-seller list. In total, she has 85 million books in print, and her work has been translated into 25 languages (Riggs, 1999). Has she produced a body of great literature that will be read for centuries? No, of course not. Has she recognized a market for a particular kind of story and manufactured many products to meet that need? There is no doubt of this.

## Reality Series

A new genre of the reality series began appearing in 2000. This type of show was popular with programmers because they are less expensive to produce (Einstein, 2004). The public also liked these new series, and audiences quickly grew.

The most popular of the reality series has been *Survivor*. Even before airing the first episode, CBS received 6,000 applicants who wanted to be marooned on a small island in the South China Sea and compete for $1 million (Bauder, 2000b).

The popularity of *Survivor* quickly generated a slew of other entries into this genre of reality programming. What these shows have in common is that each takes a handful of real people and puts them in a competitive situation. As the participants compete and reveal their personalities, audience members begin to identify with (or at least root for) certain players. For example, on *The Bachelor,* a young man who is looking for a wife is introduced to 25 beautiful women. Each week, he eliminates some of the women until he gets it down to 1 woman and proposes marriage to her. Another example is *The Apprentice,* where 16 men and women compete in the business world to get hired as an apprentice to entrepreneur Donald Trump. The reality series is a new genre, so it will take some time to see whether it becomes an enduring staple of television programming or whether its popularity fades away.

The most dominant two genres in prime-time television from the 1970s to the 1990s were dramas and situation comedies. The type of drama shifted from action/adventure and westerns in the 1960s to crime/detective dramas in the 1970s. The comedy genre accounts for half of the top 100 television shows and top 100 movies of all time (Sayre & King, 2003).

After years of watching stories on television and in the movies, we have become adept at following the formulas about characters, plots, and themes. We know these formulas so well that many of us think we can write and produce our own shows. Perhaps some of us can, but producing a successful show is a very difficult undertaking. The formulas are deceptively simple.

## Constraints

Although these formulas are relatively simple for audiences to understand, they are exceedingly difficult for producers to follow well when creating television series. The reasons for this are that producers must work around so many constraints. Some of these constraints are introduced by the media, and other constraints are introduced by society's norms.

### *Constraints by Medium*

Telling an entertaining story presents a different challenge as you move from one medium to another. If you plan to tell a story in print, you have only one perceptual channel (eyes), and you need to use words to trigger vivid images in the minds of the readers. If you plan to tell a story in song, you again need to trigger vivid images and strong emotions, but you must do this through the audience's ears, not their eyes. With a song, you also need to use words that sound good; that is, they must have a certain cadence that goes along with the rhythm of the music, and often there is a rhyming pattern. Also, the words must tell their story in 2 or 3 minutes.

Television is by far the most challenging medium for telling stories. At first, it might seem the least challenging because it appears to have few constraints; that is, you can use audio as well as video elements. Also, you are not dependent on the reading abilities of audience members. But there are two significant challenges with the television medium. First, stories must be enormously compelling. When people watch a show on television, it is extremely easy to use the remote control and switch to another channel and keep switching, never to come back to the story. Also, television stories are frequently interrupted by breaks for commercials, and some of these breaks have a dozen or more ads and last for 4 or more minutes. Viewers can forget about the story or lose their motivation to stay tuned unless that story has really intrigued them. Therefore, storytellers on television must do things to catch the audience's interest right from the beginning; they must build the action to a high point before each commercial break so that the audience will want to stay tuned throughout the commercial pod and find out what happens when the show returns, and they must keep the action interesting every minute so that people who are flipping through channels will want to stop and watch the show.

Second, stories must be very simple. This is why formulas are so standard. People might tune into a story in the middle. If the story is formulaic, people can easily understand where the story is when they start watching. Audiences must instantly be able to know who the characters are. Also, unlike print, people can't control the pacing of the story or turn back a few chapters and reread an earlier part. (Of course, with VCRs, people can now do this, but they rarely do.) As a result of this constraint, television stories must be simple and very easy to follow; people must get the gist of the story, even if they are not paying much attention to it.

With television programs, not only must producers use the well-known formulas so well that any potential audience member can tune in at any point of the story and easily pick up the action; producers must also be creative enough to break with the story formula to keep their stories fresh to viewers who have seen the same plot hundreds of times. These two tasks seem impossible to attain at the same time, and this is why the percentage of television series that have lasted more than several dozen episodes is small.

## Societal Constraints

The public has certain expectations about what it will and will not tolerate in entertainment. We can see where this line of acceptability is when the public gets offended and complains—particularly in the areas of bad language, sexual portrayals, and violence. Television programmers are essentially conservative and fearful of offending viewers, so they present content that they believe reflect mainstream American values.

This line of acceptability, however, changes over time as people get over their shock at a new kind of portrayal, then eventually get used to it. For example, writing more than a decade ago, George Comstock (1989) pointed out that

> much of what is on television today [the late 1980s] would not have been considered acceptable by broadcasters or the public 20 or even 10 years ago. Public tastes and social standards have changed, and television has made some contribution to these changes by probing the borders of convention accompanying each season. . . . These conventions of popular entertainment provide television, as they do other media, with rules that minimize the possibility of public offense. (p. 182)

The public tastes and social standards have continued to change since that time, and they will continue to change.

The same evolution of a formula has been occurring with popular music. The basic formula of popular songs is a story about love or sex. For example, in one content analysis of themes in popular music over the past 60 years, it was found that 70% of all songs have dealt with the topics of sex and love (Christianson & Roberts, 1998). What has changed in the formula is the way this theme is treated. Love used to be treated as an emotion, and the lyrics were symbolic; that is, the words suggested actions but left it up to the listeners to imagine the sex. Now love is treated as a physical act, and the lyrics are much more explicit in describing those acts, so listeners do not need their imaginations.

Storytelling formulas evolve as public tastes change over time. People get bored with too much repetition and look for something slightly different. Producers need to know how far they can push the line of acceptability at any given time without offending people and hence losing audience members. The media have become much more sensitive to these changes in taste because they know if they can push the line and not offend audiences, they will be the first to present a new twist in the old familiar formula, and this will attract large audiences.

The Fox television network is especially known for pushing the line of television programming. It aired shows such as *When Good Pets Go Bad* and *World's Scariest Police Shootouts.* When these shows came under harsh criticism, Sandy Grushow, director of programming for Fox, made public apologies. In the late 1990s, Grushow spent a lot of time apologizing. Then, in February 2000, Grushow made the decision to air *Who Wants to Marry a Multimillionaire?* The show was a sensation, drawing 23 million view-ers, but it again was an embarrassment when it was revealed that the selected bride, Darva Conger, had not really intended to get married on the program but went through with it only to get an annulment several weeks later. Grushow apologized again but this time offered an explanation for continuing to program these types of shows: "It's like someone who goes to their boss and says, 'We can make something at half the cost that will make twice as much money.' The boss would say, 'Go do it, but don't embarrass us.' This has turned into an embarrassing situation and now they have to fix it" (Bauder, 2000a, p. 3E).

# Character Patterns

The population of characters on television is very different from the population of people in the real world. This is not to say that there are not types of people in real life like almost every character on television. Instead, in the aggregate, the pattern in the population of TV characters is different from the pattern of people in the real world. These differences can be seen most clearly in two ways. First, when we look at patterns in the aggregate, we see that the demographic balance is very different in the television world compared to the real world. Second, we see that the characters are presented as stereotypes.

## Demographic Patterns

When we look past the individual characters and focus instead on patterns across the entire population of television characters, we can see that the television world is very dif-ferent from the real world (see Table 6.1). The patterns of gender, ethnicity, age, marital status, socioeconomic status (SES), and occupations are very different in the television world compared to the real world. If we notice these demographic patterns in the televi-sion world and assume that they are the same in the real world, we will be creating faulty information for ourselves.

**Table 6.1**        Demographic Patterns

| | |
|---|---|
| Gender: | Males outnumber females three to one in the television world. The gender difference has been moving more toward a balance over the years but very gradually. Even today, male main characters are more prominent. For example, one study found that among main characters, males spoke for 1.7 minutes for every minute a female character spoke. |
| | This gender imbalance varies by type of program. In soap operas, there is a balance among the genders. Also, in situation comedies and family dramas, there is almost a balance, but in police/detective shows, males outnumber females 5 to 1. |
| Ethnicity: | 80% of all characters are White Americans. |
| | African Americans comprised only 2% of television characters until the late 1960s, when they jumped to about 10% of all characters. Now, African Americans account for about 16% of the main and minor roles, which is larger than their percentage (12%) in the real-world population of the United States. |
| | Hispanics, however, have not fared as well. Although Hispanics make up about 9% of the U.S. population, only about 2% of all television characters are Hispanic. |
| | Asian Americans and Native Americans combined account for about 1% of all television characters. |
| Age: | Three quarters of all television characters are between the ages of 20 and 50, but in the real world, only one third of the population is between these ages. Young children and the elderly are underrepresented on television. Fictional characters younger than age 19 make up only 10% of the total television population, even though they make up one third of the U.S. population. Also, characters older than age 50 account for about 15% of all television characters. |
| | The most dramatic imbalance is in the over-65 age group. Barely more than 2% of television characters are at least 65 years old, but 11% of the real-life population is in this age bracket. |
| Marital status: | Marital status is obvious with about 80% of the women and 45% of the men. Of those for whom you can tell their marital status, more than 50% of the women are married, whereas less than one third of the men are married. |
| Socioeconomic status (SES): | Almost half the characters on television are wealthy or ultra-wealthy, and very few (less than 10%) are lower class. |
| Occupations: | The higher prestige occupations are overrepresented on fictional television. Nearly one third of the television labor force is professional and managerial, whereas in real life, the figure is only 11%. |
| | Working-class people are greatly underrepresented, except for a few television world professions. For example, prostitutes outnumber machinists by 12 to 1; there are twice as many doctors as welfare workers, 8 times more butlers than miners, and 12 times more private detectives than production line workers. But the world of work may be changing a bit. Vande Berg and Streckfuss (1992) analyzed occupations in prime-time television and found that there was a slight increase in the representation of women and in the variety of their occupational portrayals. Still, women remain underrepresented and limited in their depictions in organizational settings. Males outnumbered females 2 to 1 in the workplace. |

SOURCES: Comstock, Chaffee, Katzman, McCombs, and Roberts (1978); Davis (1990); Glascock (2001); Greenberg, Edison, Korzenny, Fernandez-Collado, and Atkin (1980); Mastro and Greenberg (2000).

The entertainment stories in the mass media also have a fairly standard set of characters, and this set of character types does not change much across media or vehicles. For example, one study of characters appearing in shows across 32 channels on a typical cable system found the same patterns of gender, race, and age across all channels (Kubey, Shifflet, Weerakkody, & Ukeiley, 1996).

On almost all of the demographic indicators, the television world has very different patterns than the real world. However, it is interesting to note that one minority—African Americans—has fought for better representation on television programs and is now proportionally more likely to be represented in the television world (16%) than in the real world (12%). This group continues to fight successfully for representation. For example, during the fall 1999 television season, African American leaders severely criticized the big four television networks that premiered 26 new series; in all of those series, the lead characters and nearly all the cast regulars were White, even those on shows where the action takes place in urban high schools and New York City nightspots (Lowry, Jensen, & Braxton, 1999).

What can account for this dominance of males, Whites, and youthful adults? Perhaps it is due to the demographics of the people who are television writers. Turow (1992) pointed out that according to the Writers Guild of America, White males account for more than three quarters of the writers employed in film and TV. Minorities accounted for 2% of all writers. And it appears that the demographics of the writers are not getting more diverse. In a survey of the age, gender, and ethnicity of writers working in Hollywood's television and film industries in 1985, it was reported that it was dominated by White males. In 2002, the same pattern was found as far as gender and ethnicity (Bielby & Bielby, 2002), and Glascock (2001) reported that males outnumber females 3.6 to 1 among creative personnel, which includes producers, directors, and writers.

## Stereotypical Portrayals

There is a positive as well as negative side to stereotypes. Stereotypes are positive from the point of view that they are easy for viewers to recognize. But stereotypes can also have a negative effect because they are often inadequate as well as biased; they often serve as obstacles to rational assessment; and they are resistant to social change.

We use stereotypes in dealing with real-world information, not just media portrayals. For example, when we meet a new person, we try to "type" that person based on the characteristics we can immediately see, such as age, gender, appearance, how they talk, and so on. Once we have typed someone, we have a set of expectations for that person. For example, if we see a 5-year-old girl in a fancy dress playing with a doll on the steps of a church, we would immediately call up a specific set of expectations. In contrast, if we see a middle-aged man with a beer belly straining through his dirty tee shirt, chewing tobacco, and cleaning a rifle, we would call up a very different set of expectations. Stereotypes provide us with a set of expectations that we can access quickly as we encounter people and

**Table 6.2**     Examples of Prevalent Stereotypes

- The strong, self-reliant police detective who uses unconventional methods to deal with the scum on the street
  He is irritated by his authoritarian bosses but always gets the job done using his own unorthodox methods.
- The nurturing mother who has kooky kids and an idiot husband
- The sexy young female actress/model/nurse/secretary who becomes a romantic interest of a male hero
- The dumb blonde who is superficial, cares only about physical appearance and dress styles, and has no common sense
- The young street punk who commits petty and violent crimes, usually for drugs
  He is tough and sassy until police intimidate him into making a plea bargain.
- The nerdy male adolescent who displays hilariously dysfunctional social skills
  Although he is very sensitive, he never learns from his social mistakes.

events. They are a necessary mode of processing characters, especially when there are thousands of messages coming at us quickly everyday and we need to create order out of "the great blooming, buzzing confusion of reality" (Lippmann, 1922, p. 96).

Characters in the television world are developed as stereotypes according to certain formulas, which make the characters easily and quickly recognizable to viewers. Look at the examples of stereotypes in Table 6.2. For each of these stereotypes, a clear image likely comes into your mind. You have seen each of these characters many times. When one of them appears in a story, it only takes a few seconds for you to recognize who that character is.

Stereotypes, however, can be harmful when they lead audiences to believe that all people of a given type share certain negative characteristics. This is why two groups—African Americans and women—are vocal in their complaints about how their demographic groups are stereotypically portrayed in television stories. Stereotypes in some other areas, such as occupations, families, the elderly, and body images, can also be harmful.

## *African Americans*

It appears that the stereotype of African Americans on television has changed. In a review of the literature on ethnicity on television, Busselle and Crandall (2002) drew three conclusions. First, the world of situation comedy is one in which African Americans are approximately as prevalent as they are in the real world. But unlike the real world, discrimination, poverty, and crime do not exist. Second, drama programs about Black families are rare. And as argued by several researchers, when Black families are portrayed, their lives are consistent with the beliefs that opportunities abound and that hard work begets economic comfort. Third, we know relatively little about the roles of African American characters in programs with predominantly White casts. From the extant evidence, it appears that Black and White characters most often interact in the workplace, and Blacks most often occupy positions of superiority over Whites rather than positions of subservience or equality (Entman & Rojecki, 2001). Finally, when African American characters are not members of the middle or upper class, they are portrayed as social undesirables rather than as the working poor.

## Gender

There is a good deal of gender stereotyping. Females are more likely to complain about these gender stereotypes because there are more negative female stereotypes compared to male stereotypes. Males are usually portrayed with positive personality characteristics such as competency, leadership, and bravery. As for females, there are two primary stereotypes. If a woman is single, she is often portrayed as a sex object. There is a strong emphasis on the female body being attractive, desirable, and youthful. If a woman is a mother, she is usually portrayed as wise and nurturing. The profile of women on prime-time television has not changed much in 50 years (Elasmar, Hasegawa, & Brain, 1999).

Gender stereotyping is also in educational programming. Barner (1999) examined sex role stereotyping within children's educational programming mandated by the Federal Communications Commission (FCC). A content analysis revealed that males had a greater representation than females, and both male and female characters exhibited sex role stereotypical behavior. Also, males were more likely to evoke some consequence for their actions, whereas female actions tended to be ignored altogether.

## Occupations

Research has consistently found that the world of work is dominated by male characters and that more women than men cannot be categorized by occupation (Signorielli, 1990; Signorielli & Bacue, 1999; Vande Berg & Streckfuss, 1992). In the 1990s, for example, Signorielli and Bacue (1999) found that 4 out of 10 female characters did not work (20.3%) or their occupation was unknown (19.2%). By comparison, fewer than 1 of 4 male characters could not be classified in an occupation (12.4%) or were seen as not working (12.3%). These images may ultimately suggest that working outside of the home is not as important for women as for men.

In the world of work, female characters usually have less status than do males, but this does reflect the real world. As Farley (1998) notes, on average, males still make more than females, and male participation (or lack thereof) in household tasks is often related to the discrepancy in earnings between spouses.

Interestingly, marital status is an important predictor of employment for women. Content analyses of programming in the 1970s and 1980s indicated that married women were less likely to be employed outside the home, whereas single women and women who were divorced or widowed were more likely to be portrayed as working outside the home. By comparison, the marital status of male characters did not restrict their employment. Most male characters were portrayed as working, with single men the smallest group of male characters who did not work (Signorielli, 1982, 1990; Signorielli & Kahlenberg, 2001).

Ethnicity also plays a pivotal role in the depiction of occupations on television. Fewer non-Whites than Whites are professionals, but proportionally, more non-Whites have law enforcement jobs. Compared to the U.S. labor force, professionals and law enforcement agents are overrepresented, whereas managerial jobs, laborers, and service workers are underrepresented (Signorielli & Kahlenberg, 2001).

Governmental employees do not fare well in television stereotyping. An analysis of 1,234 prime-time series episodes from 1955 to 1998 reveals that governmental employees are often portrayed in negative roles. With politicians, 51% were in negative roles—either as corrupt (such as Boss Hogg on the *Dukes of Hazzard*) or scatterbrained (such as New York Mayor Randall Winston on *Spin City*) (Aversa, 1999).

## Families

There have been some changes in the way families are portrayed on television. In a study comparing families in TV situation comedies from the 1950s through the 1980s, Scharrer (2001) found that fathers in the more recent seasons were portrayed as fools compared to fathers in earlier seasons. On domestic comedies, the adult members of families are now more likely to interact more openly, and there is more expression of feelings in spousal relationships (Douglas & Olson, 1995). But the adults are also shown as having more conflicts with children. As a result, the relational environment has become more conflictual and less cohesive in modern TV families than in families from earlier decades. Also, modern families are less able to manage day-to-day life and less able to socialize children effectively (Douglas & Olson, 1996).

## Elderly Characters

Older characters are typically not revered or treated with respect in television entertainment. They are typically portrayed as being eccentric, infirm, stubborn, and foolish.

## Body Image

A content analysis of three magazines from 1967 to 1997 found that male bodies were portrayed as more lean, muscular, and V-shaped. This fits with the male body image ideal of thin and athletic. "Sociocultural standards of beauty for males emphasize strength and muscularity" (Law & Labre, 2002, p. 697).

# Controversial Content Elements

In the world of media entertainment, everything can be forgiven except dullness. When TV was being criticized for having so much violence, then–CBS president Howard Stringer was arguing against standards to clean up television by saying, "We don't want to turn the vast wasteland into a dull wasteland" (*USA Today,* July 1, 1993, p. 2A). And that is the key—TV and all the entertainment media must avoid being dull.

Recall from an earlier section in this chapter that it is very difficult for producers to apply the story formula in a way to attract and hold audiences. It takes a very talented writer to create a story that is not dull. Less talented writers can rely on three staples to avoid dullness. These are sex, violence, and "bad" language. Each of these three is controversial because if writers and producers go too far, there will be many complaints from viewers. Still, producers frequently use these elements to arouse their audiences and keep otherwise uncreative plots and uninteresting characters from appearing dull.

## Sex

### Frequency

Sexual activity on television has been prevalent since the 1970s (Buerkel-Rothfuss, 1993; Cassata & Skill, 1983). If we limit our definition of sex to visual depictions of intercourse, the rate fluctuates around one (Greenberg et al., 1993) or two (Fernandez-Collado, Greenberg, Korzenny, & Atkin, 1978) acts per hour of prime time. In soap operas, the rate is even higher.

If we expand the definition to include all visual depictions of sexual activity, such as kissing, petting, homosexuality, prostitution, and rape, the hourly rates go up to about 3 acts on prime time and 3.7 acts per hour on soap operas (Greenberg et al., 1993). And when the definition is further expanded to include talk about sex as well as sexual imagery, the rate climbs to 16 instances per hour on prime time (Sapolsky & Tabarlet, 1990). Most of this talk about sex is on situation comedies in the early evening, when it is presented in a humorous context.

The most recent major set of studies was conducted from 1997 to 2002, which analyzed thousands of programs across 10 channels and found that about two thirds of all shows (64%) contain some sexual content and 14% have sexual intercourse. Among the 20 top-rated shows among teens, 83% contained sexual portrayals. The overall rate was about three scenes per hour. Two thirds (67%) of all network prime-time shows contain either talk about sex or sexual behavior, averaging more than five scenes per hour (Kaiser Family Foundation, 2003).

## Consequences

Most depictions of sexual behavior are not presented responsibly from a health point of view. Schrag (1990) reports that American children and teens view an average of more than 14,000 sexual references and innuendos on television each year. Of these, less than 150 refer to the use of birth control, so the rate of unprotected sex is very high, yet there is a very low incidence of sexually transmitted diseases (STDs) or pregnancies depicted in these stories. This situation may be changing for the better. For example, by the 1997–1998 television season, about 9% of shows dealing with sex presented safe-sex messages, and this had increased to 15% of shows in the 2001–2002 television season (Kaiser Family Foundation, 2003). Although sexual portrayals are improving in their depiction of safe practices, fewer than one in every six shows that present sexual content will have any mention of the possible risks or responsibilities of sexual activity or any reference to contraception, protection, or safer sex.

## Homosexuality

The U.S. television industry has a long history of ignoring, stereotyping, and marginalizing homosexuality (Harrington, 2003). Gay and lesbian issues or characters were virtually invisible on television in the 1950s and early 1960s. Then, in the 1970s, gay characters began to appear, but they were limited to two treatments. One treatment was the coming-out story, and the other was the "queer monster" script. Furthermore, although the 1970s ushered in prime-time shows about gay characters, they were typically played by straight actors and marketed to a straight audience, a trend that continues today.

In the 1980s, depictions of homosexuality declined dramatically due to the conservatism of the Reagan years and the growing concern about HIV/AIDS (and its association with gay male sexuality) (L. Gross, 2001). Gay characters began to appear in greater frequency throughout the 1990s in part due to a growing stigma attached to antigay prejudice and a growing recognition of a gay consumer market (L. Gross, 2001). By the late 1990s, about 50 network series had lesbian, gay, or bisexual recurring characters, more than twice the total of all previous decades of television. In 1997, prime-time viewers witnessed the first lesbian lead actress/character on network television, which was the comedienne Ellen DeGeneres, who played Ellen Morgan on ABC's *Ellen.* The following year, NBC featured the first network gay male lead in its hit show *Will & Grace.* During the fall 1999 television season, the big four television networks premiered 26 new series. There were 17 gay characters on the four major networks and about the same number of black, Asian, and Latino characters combined. A big reason for this is that there are many gays in Hollywood and not many minorities (Brownfield, 1999).

In many respects, the 1990s seemed to transcend the longstanding "rules" for representing homosexuality on television: (a) Gay or lesbian characters must be restricted to one-time appearances in television series or one-shot television movies; (b) gay and lesbian characters can never be "incidentally" gay—instead, their sexuality must be the "problem" to be "solved"; (c) their problem should be explored in terms of its effects on heterosexuals; and (d) gay and lesbian erotic desire must be completely absent (Dow, 2001, pp. 129–130; see also L. Gross, 2001).

Although there are more representations of homosexuality than ever before, scholars caution against the presumption that these are necessarily more progressive representations. As throughout television history, gays and lesbians are still more likely to appear in comedies than dramas, where the line between "laughing with" and "laughing at" remains strategically ambiguous. Also, gay and lesbian characters are still typically portrayed by straight (or not "out") actors and marketed to straight audiences (Battles & Hilton-Morrow, 2002; Dow, 2001; L. Gross, 2001).

Although the representation of homosexuality on prime-time TV since the 1990s has certainly been different from that of the 1970s, it remains constrained by a complex set of competing organizational norms, priorities, and practices. In this "fiercely imitative" cultural arena, networks are most open to approving gay or lesbian content when gay issues are high profile in the national news or when an existing show with gay characters is generating high Nielsen ratings.

## Violence

Violence is the most studied form of content in all of the mass media. Scholars have been monitoring the amount of violence on television ever since the early 1950s, and there have been at least 60 major content analyses over the past half century (see Potter, 1999).

Depending on the definition used, violence has been found in 57% to 80% of all entertainment programs (Columbia Broadcasting System, 1980; Greenberg, Edison, Korzenny, Fernandez-Collado, & Atkin, 1980; Lichter & Lichter, 1983; "NCTV Says," 1983; Potter & Ware, 1987; Schramm, Lyle, & Parker, 1961; Signorielli, 1990; Smythe, 1954; Williams, Zabrack, & Joy, 1982).

The most consistent examination of television violence has been conducted by Gerbner and his associates (e.g., see Gerbner, Gross, Morgan, & Signorielli, 1980). Since the late 1960s, they have documented the frequency of violent acts that fit the definition: the overt expression of physical force (with or without a weapon) against self or other, compelling action against one's will on pain of being hurt or killed, or actually hurting or killing. Signorielli (1990) reports that from 1967 to 1985, the hourly rate has fluctuated from about four to seven violent acts, with peaks occurring about every 4 years.

The most comprehensive analysis of violence on television has been conducted with the National Television Violence Study (NTVS, 1996), which analyzed the content of a total of 3,185 programs across 23 television channels for all day parts from 6 A.M. until 11 P.M., 7 days a week, over the course of a television season. NTVS researchers report that 57% of all programs analyzed had some violence and that one third of programs presented nine or more violent interactions.

The numbers in the above paragraphs are limited to physical forms of violence, and they do not include verbal violence. Verbal violence is even more prevalent on television than is physical violence. For example, Williams et al. (1982) reported finding a rate of 9.5 acts of verbal violence as well as 9 acts of physical violence per hour on North American (United States and Canada) television. Potter and Ware (1987) found about 8 acts per hour of physical violence and an additional 12 acts of verbal violence on American television. Also, Greenberg and his colleagues (1980) reported that an average prime-time hour of television contains 22 acts of verbal aggression and 12 acts of physical aggression. In a comparison of rates of violence on television from the mid-1970s to the mid-1990s, Potter and Vaughan (1997) found that the rates of physical violence remained stable but that the rates of verbal violence had increased dramatically. They reasoned that programmers were wary of increasing physical violence because such an increase would trigger a public outcry, but the substantial increase in verbal violence was tolerated by the public, so the increase continued.

There have also been some scientific studies of the amount of violence in films. For example, the top-grossing 50 films of 1998 contained a total of 2,300 acts of violence, according to the Center for Media and Public Affairs, based in Washington, D.C. "Violence was not only a staple of popular entertainment, it was often portrayed as laudable, necessary or relatively harmless activity," said S. Robert Lichter, the center's president (Goldstein, 1999, p. B1). In another analysis of violent films, Sapolsky, Molitor, and Luque (2003) content analyzed popular slasher films in the 1990s and found more acts of violence in them than similar films from the 1980s. One change was that recent slasher films rarely mixed scenes of sex and violence. The researchers also posed the question about whether females were more victimized than males, and they concluded that in all slasher films, there were more male victims than there were female victims. But they did not stop with this conclusion; they also found that the ratio of female victims is higher in slasher films than in commercially successful action/adventure films of the 1990s. This means than when a female is shown in a slasher film, she has a greater chance of being victimized. Also, females are shown in fear longer than males.

Movie previews also a present a high degree of violence. In one study of video rentals, it was found that the majority of previews on rental tapes contained violence, and these portrayals were common across MPAA ratings (G/PG, PG-13, and R) (Oliver & Kalyanaraman, 2002). Rates of aggression in previews were positively associated with increased marketing and distribution costs for the previewed films.

Violence on television has been examined not only for its frequency but also for its context—that is, the way it is presented. For example, Potter and Ware (1987) found that with much of the violence, the perpetrator is rewarded and the victims are rarely shown with much pain and suffering. This was also the case in the NTVS studies, where violent acts were rarely punished, and rarely were victims shown as suffering any harmful consequences.

Also, 37% of the perpetrators of violence were portrayed as being attractive, and 44% of the acts were shown as being justified. These patterns led the researchers to conclude that violence not only was prevalent throughout the entire television landscape but was also typically shown as sanitized and glamorized (see Potter & Smith, 2000).

This level of violence in the media is far higher than the real-world levels of violence and crime. This was demonstrated by Oliver (1994), who analyzed pseudo-reality-based police shows, such as *Cops*. She found that the Federal Bureau of Investigation (FBI) figures for murder, rape, robbery, and aggregated assault were 13.2% of all crimes, but in the television world, these four violent crimes accounted for 87% of all crimes. Also, the FBI reports that 18.0% of crimes are cleared, but on television, 61.5% are cleared—that is, the perpetrator is arrested, is killed, or committed suicide. Again, television focuses on the most arousing crimes rather than the dull ones. Also, there is a more satisfying resolution to crimes than there is in the real world.

## Language

It appears as if "bad" language has broken the barrier on television and is here to stay. For example, Kaye and Sapolsky (2001) examined 1 week of prime-time programs aired on the ABC, CBS, NBC, and Fox networks in 1990, 1994, and 1997 to ascertain whether usage of offensive language increased throughout the 1990s when a content-based rating system was implemented. The per-hour rate of objectionable words increased between 1990 and 1994 but decreased in 1997 to a level slightly below that found in 1990. Although the FCC deems the "seven dirty words" as too offensive for television, five of these words have made their way onto the prime-time airwaves.

# Health

The television world is a generally healthy one when we look at patterns across all kinds of shows. Some of this pattern is deceptive; that is, it presents a very misleading message. But part of the pattern is very responsible in presenting healthy messages to viewers.

## Deceptive Health Patterns

Although there are many indicators of deceptive health, I'll present only five in this section. First, although most characters are not shown having particularly healthy habits (eating responsibly, regularly exercising, and getting medical checkups to prevent illnesses), most characters appear healthy, fit, and thin. It has been estimated that 64.5% of the American population is overweight or obese (American Obesity Association, 2004), but on television, only 6% of the males and 2% of the females are. Furthermore, characters do not gain weight from their high-caloric diets. Eating and drinking are frequent activities on entertainment programs. About 75% of all shows display this activity. But eating is usually unhealthy. The traditional meals of breakfast, lunch, and dinner combined account for only about half of the eating; snacking accounts for the rest. Fruit is the snack in only 4% to 5% of the episodes.

Second, although there is a high degree of violence on many shows, few characters are portrayed as suffering any harm. In fact, most characters are portrayed as being healthy and active. Only 6% to 7% of major characters are portrayed as having had injuries or illnesses that require treatment. Pain, suffering, or medical help rarely follows violent activity. In children's programs, despite greater mayhem, only 3% of characters are shown receiving medical treatment. Prime-time characters are not only healthy but also relatively safe from accidents, even though they rarely wear seat belts when they drive. And they are rarely portrayed as suffering from impairments of any kinds as a result of an accident.

A third indicator of deceptive health is that the everyday normal health maladies are rarely shown. Most health problems that are portrayed are serious and life threatening. When help for medical problems is portrayed, it is not in a preventative or therapeutic manner but in a dramatic and social way. Hardly anyone dies a natural death on television.

Prime-time characters are not shown with any kind of physical impairments. Rarely does a character even wear glasses; even in old age, only one out of four characters wears them. Only 2% of characters on prime-time shows are physically handicapped. When they do appear, they tend to be older, less positively presented, and more likely to be victimized. Almost none appear on children's shows.

Fourth, mental health is portrayed in a dangerously stereotypical manner. Mentally ill people are usually depicted as the bad guys, that is, the crazed criminals who are very dangerous. They are typically shown to be active, confused, aggressive, dangerous, and unpredictable. In real life, mentally ill people are usually passive and withdrawn, frightened, and avoidant.

Fifth, doctors are greatly overrepresented on television compared to their numbers in real life. Health care professionals dominate the ranks of professionals, despite the paucity of sick characters on television. They are five times their numbers in real life proportionally. Only criminals or law enforcers are more numerous. However, it is interesting to note that health care professionals are largely absent from children's programs. Also, many of these doctors are shown making house calls and devoting far more time to individual patients than real-life doctors are able to do.

## Responsible Health Patterns

The use of alcohol, tobacco, and illegal drugs has dramatically declined over the years on television. Smoking was a frequent activity until the mid-1980s, until it almost completely disappeared except for reruns of old movies.

Alcohol use has also substantially declined. When it is presented now, it is frequently shown with negative consequences. Until the mid-1980s, alcohol consumption was common on television. The drinking of alcohol was shown twice as often as the drinking of coffee and tea, 14 times that of soft drinks, and 15 times that of water. It was shown as sociable, happy, and problem free. Also, alcohol use was rarely portrayed with any negative consequences. When negative consequences were shown, they were usually very slight, such as a temporary hangover. Despite high rates of consumption across many characters, only 1% of television drinkers are portrayed as having a drinking problem.

Although television is showing more responsible portrayals of drug and alcohol use, the movies do not fare so well. An analysis of the 200 most popular movies of 1996 and 1997 reveals that characters frequently abuse drugs and alcohol. Moreover, these characters are not portrayed as worrying about the consequences (Hartman, 1999).

# Values

Examining the arts within a culture is a way to determine the values of that culture. For example, the ancient Greek and Roman cultures exhibited the values of perfection, harmony, and beauty in their art. During the European Middle Ages, the art reflected the dominance of the Catholic Church, with its focus on the life of Christ, especially his birth, miracles, crucifixion, and resurrection. Earthly existence was mundane and painful, whereas the afterlife was glorious. During the Renaissance, the art reflected the values of a scientific approach to understanding the world. During the European Romantic era, the focus shifted from the logical and intellectual concerns that were dominant during the Renaissance to the emotions of humans. During the Modern era, the arts were decoupled from the church and political institutions. Art glorified the individual and his or her unique way of looking at the world and constructing meaning (Metallinos, 1996).

Today, we can examine the broad span of messages from the mass media and ask, What do our stories tell us about our current culture? Some researchers and social critics have attempted to answer this question. Table 6.3 shows what two media scholars have observed to be the themes in television entertainment. Notice that the first of Comstock's (1989) themes deals with material consumption. Comstock is not referring to the ads in the stories but to the values in the stories themselves. He says, "It is not solely that so many stories revolve around the rich, but that in so many instances dwellings and their furnishings are beyond the means of those portrayed as occupying them" (p. 172). For example, the popular situation comedy *Friends* features Monica, a part-time cook, and Rachel, a waitress in a coffeehouse, who are shown supporting themselves in a well-furnished two-bedroom apartment in downtown Manhattan.

Notice also how the lists of Comstock (1989) and Walsh (1994) overlap. For example, Walsh is also concerned with the value of materialism, which he argues is at odds with a

**Table 6.3**     Values Underlying Entertainment Messages

**Comstock's (1989) List**

1. Material consumption is very satisfying.

2. The world is a mean and risky place. There is a great deal of crime and violence throughout the television world.

3. The TV world has turned the social pyramid upside down by showing most characters as wealthy and powerful and very few of them as working class.

4. Males are more powerful than females in terms of income, job status, and decision making. This is slowly changing, but we are still far from a balance of power.

5. Occupational status is highly valued. Professional occupations are depicted as worthwhile, whereas manual work is uninteresting. People attain the status of a worthwhile profession through upward mobility from the middle class. This upward mobility is accomplished through self-confidence and toughness; goodness of character alone is not enough. The movement upward is usually quick and painless.

6. There are a few privileged professions in which the people are almost always shown as doing good and helping others. However, most businesspeople are shady. Businesses are frequently portrayed as taking advantage of the gullible public and abusing their power.

7. Law enforcers are overrepresented as being successful, strong, and justified. Private eyes are almost always shown as better than the police.

8. There is a belief in the occult, life on other planets, life after death, and hidden, malevolent purposes behind the inexplicable.

9. A person's self-interest is very important. People are motivated to get what they want regardless of the feelings of others. Examples include extramarital affairs, crime, hard-driving businesspeople, and police who disregard the rights of others to achieve their goals.

10. There are often truly heroic acts portrayed where there are daring rescues, selflessness, loyalty to others, and the struggle against difficult odds to do the right thing.

**Walsh's (1994) List**

1. Happiness is found in having things.

2. Get all you can for yourself.

3. Get it all as quickly as you can.

4. Win at all costs.

5. Violence is entertaining.

6. Always seek pleasure and avoid boredom.

healthy society. Walsh also argues that the values of the marketplace are as follows: happiness equals wealth, instant gratification, and me first. In contrast, the values of a healthy society are the following: self-esteem comes from within, moderation, tolerance, understanding, and social responsibility.

In complaining about the direction of programming on TV aimed at young people, *U.S. News & World Report* columnist John Leo (1999) said,

> These shows are also carriers of heavy cultural messages, the most obvious being that parents are fools. In the teen soap operas, parents are absent, stupid, irrelevant, zanily adulterous, on the lam, or in jail. The unmistakable message is that kids are on their own, with no need to listen to parents, who know little or nothing anyway. This helps the TV industry certify teenagers as an autonomous culture with its own set of ethics and consumption patterns. (p. 15)

Young people are a very important target for many Hollywood films, and a particular kind of film is believed to be the best draw for them. For example, in a profile of a literary manager, Warren Zide, *L.A. Times* reporter Claudia Eller (1999) examines the values operating in Hollywood. She said,

> When it came to getting the script for *American Pie* in shape to be sold, Zide said he and his colleagues advised [the writer] "to write the raunchiest script possible without worrying about the rating." Apparently it was good advice. The R-rated comedy about four high-school buddies who make a pact to lose their virginity before graduation piqued the interest of several studios before it was sold to Universal Pictures for $650,000. (p. C5)

Eller also quotes Zide on his reaction to a script about teenagers on a spring break:

> "I hated when I was growing up and you go to see some R-rated movie and there's no nudity in it, and you're like, 'Oh, man, I was gypped.'" So, now as a literary agent, Zide asks, "Do we have enough T&A in it?" (p. C5)

# Becoming Media Literate With Entertainment Messages

Recall from the previous chapter that media messages contain many elements to make them appear like the real world, but those messages must also contain elements that remove them from the mundane real world. In this chapter, you have seen how the entertainment messages depart from the real world when it comes to character portrayals, controversial content, health, and values. The more you know about these discrepancies, the more you can separate your media-world knowledge from your real-world knowledge and thus prevent the media-world distortions to influence your expectations for the real world.

Television and film ignore things that are not visually interesting, such as thinking by ourselves, reading, walking, and other quiet activities that make up much of our lives. Activities such as housework, running errands, and small talk with neighbors are vastly underrepresented. Instead of ennobling our ordinary experiences, television suggests that they are not of sufficient interest to document.

However, producers are under no obligation to present an accurate account of the mundane world. Their task is to build as large an audience as possible. To do this, they must rely on all their creative powers to achieve a dramatic effect, so they deliberately distort the world to surprise and startle us. Some creative people produce fantasy that, by definition, is totally unlike real life—they do this to allow us to escape our lives and to see imaginative occurrences. Other producers who try to capture real life must do so in an intriguing manner. That is, they avoid presenting the mundane mainstream of real life and instead highlight the occurrences at the margins where there are particularly interesting people or events. This is real life in the sense that it could happen or even did happen. For example, family dramas appear to be very realistic in their settings, characters, and types of problems encountered. But they are unrealistic in their pacing, with most problems solved in 60 minutes.

The purpose of storytellers who use the mass media is simply to tell a good story so as to attract people and keep them coming back. The writers are not psychologists or sociologists; they are not usually trying to tell us much about how the human mind works or about how society works, but they still do present us with elements that we use to generalize our own conclusions about how the human mind works and how society works.

The danger to us as viewers of these stories is that we gradually absorb the individual fantasy elements. Over time, we start to confuse the "one-step remove" elements from the more realistic elements. Eventually, we come to believe that the patterns of fantasy that we continually see in media stories should be how we live our real lives.

The way to deal with the unrealistic picture presented by television entertainment is *not* to pressure producers to make their world of fiction more realistic. That would be silly. Instead, the best way to deal with this situation is to educate yourself about the content patterns in the media world and to become more sensitive, recognizing where those patterns diverge from real-world patterns. Learn to appreciate the divergences as fantasy and limit yourself to being entertained by their unreality. And avoid being guided by unrealistic expectations based on what media characters look like and how they act.

Now that you have more information about patterns of characters, plots, and values of entertainment stories in the media, you have a stronger knowledge structure about media content. When you use this knowledge structure to guide yourself through your exposures to media stories in the future, you will be able to see much more in those messages. Table 6.4 shows the cognitive, emotional, aesthetic, and moral skills you will need to do this in a conscious, active manner. But do not restrict yourself to the specifics in Table 6.4; instead, use the information presented there to stimulate your thinking about other skills

**Table 6.4**     Types of Skills and Knowledge Needed to Deal With Entertainment Messages in a Media-Literate Manner

|  | *SKILLS* | *KNOWLEDGE* |
|---|---|---|
| COGNITIVE | Ability to analyze entertainment content to identify key plot points, types of characters, and themes | |
| | Ability to see entertainment formulas | |
| | Ability to compare/contrast plot points, characters, and themes across vehicles and media | Knowledge of elements in entertainment formula |
| EMOTIONAL | Ability to analyze the portrayed feelings of characters | |
| | Ability to put one's self into the position of different characters in the story | Recall from personal experiences how it would feel to be in the situation depicted in the story |
| | Ability to control emotions elicited by the plot and themes | |
| AESTHETIC | Ability to analyze the craft and artistic elements in the story | Knowledge of writing, directing, acting, editing, sound mixing, and so on |
| | Ability to compare and contrast the artistry used to tell this story with that used to tell other stories | Knowledge of good and bad stories and the elements that contributed to those qualities |
| MORAL | Ability to analyze the moral elements as evidenced by decisions made by characters, implications of those decisions revealed by the plot, and underlying theme | Knowledge of what moral systems say about different decisions as well as knowledge of the moral implications of your decisions |
| | Ability to compare and contrast ethical decisions presented in this story with other stories | Knowledge of other stories that have portrayed this topic, both good and bad |
| | Ability to evaluate the ethical responsibilities of the producers and programmers | Knowledge of values of people in the media industries |

and knowledge. Then, during your exposures to media entertainment, recall the knowledge you will need and consciously apply the skills in all four domains.

During exposure to the media, remember that entertainment messages follow a formula. The people who create this world must be creative within a rigid formula. Viewers want formulaic characters and plots so the entertainment is easy to follow. Look at how closely those stories follow the formula. Also, notice how stories deviate from the formula and try to assess the magnitude of those deviations. How much can a story deviate before you become confused and lose sense of what is happening? Look at the stories that are most popular, that is, highest-rated television programs and movies with the largest box office. How closely do they follow the formula? Examine the actors and actresses in those popular stories. What do they do that would make them so popular?

Keep asking questions about these stories. Be skeptical. Take nothing for granted. If you stay active during your exposures, you will be increasing your media literacy and thus gain more control over setting expectations for life that are both realistic and special to you.

# Further Reading

Cantor, M. G. (1980). *Prime-time television.* Beverly Hills, CA: Sage. (143 pages, including index)

Written by a sociologist who spent 10 years interviewing actors, writers, and producers, this book explains how decisions about content are made in the television industry. She develops a model to show that many forces shape the development of any television program. The examples in the book are dated, but the principles still apply.

Greenberg, B. S. (1980). *Life on television.* Norwood, NJ: Ablex. (204 pages, including index)

This is a classic content analysis of American television drama in the mid-1970s. Each of the 13 chapters addresses a different content topic, such as the demography of fictional characters, sex role portrayals, antisocial and prosocial behaviors, family interaction patterns, sexual intimacy, and drug use.

Lichter, S. R., Lichter, L. S., & Rothman, S. (1994). *Prime time: How TV portrays American culture.* Washington, DC: Regnery. (478 pages)

This is a look at what is on television, written from a critical humanistic perspective. There are few statistics but lots of examples from programs to illustrate their main point that the world of television is very different from the real world of families, work, sex, crime, and so on.

Medved, M. (1992). *Hollywood vs. America: Popular culture and the war on traditional values.* New York: HarperCollins.

This film critic argues that Hollywood has a value system that is very different from that of mainstream America. Hollywood glorifies the perverse, ridicules all forms of mainstream religion, tears down the image of the family, and glorifies ugliness with violence, bad language, and America bashing. Then the industry is puzzled why attendance is dropping and criticism is increasing.

Metallinos, N. (1996). *Television aesthetics: Perceptual, cognitive, and compositional bases.* Mahwah, NJ: Lawrence Erlbaum. (305 pages with index)

This book lays out many principles of aesthetics from both a social science as well as an artistic perspective. He demonstrates that humans are bound by their perceptual capabilities and the functioning processes of their brains. However, people also create culture through their art. A person who is visually literate needs to have information in the areas of perception, cognition, and artistic composition.

Postman, N. (1984). *Amusing ourselves to death: Public discourse in the age of show business.* New York: Penguin. (184 pages with index)

This is a strong, well-written argument about how the media, especially television, have conditioned us to expect entertainment. Because our perceptions of ideas are shaped by the form of their expression, we are now image oriented. We respond to pleasure, not thought and reflection.

Sayre, S., & King, C. (2003). *Entertainment & society: Audiences, trends, and impacts.* Thousand Oaks, CA: Sage. (422 pages, including end notes and index)

This book spans the entire gamut of media-provided entertainment in 16 chapters. It provides some history of thinking about entertainment, a theory of entertainment content and effects, conceptions of audiences, medium comparisons, and even predictions for the future of entertainment.

**Exercise 6.1**  Practicing Media Literacy Skills on Entertainment Programming

Watch a television program, then think about the following tasks:

1. *Analysis:* Break down the program by
   a. Listing the main characters
   b. Listing the main plot points
   c. Were there violent elements? If so, list them.
   d. Were there sexual elements? Is so, list them.
   e. Were their health-related elements? If so, list them.

2. *Grouping:* Select the two main characters.
   a. How are they the same/different demographically?
   b. How are they the same/different by personality characteristics?
   c. How are they the same/different in the way they move the plot forward?

3. *Evaluation:* Think about all the characters and make the following judgments.
   a. In your judgment, which character was the most humorous? Why?
   b. In your judgment, which character was the most ethical in his or her behavior? Why?
   c. In your judgment, which actor or actress displayed the best acting skills? Why?
   d. In your judgment, which of the plot points were the strongest? Which were the weakest?
   e. In your judgment, what is the theme of this show?

4. *Abstracting:* Describe your show (characters and plot) in 50 words or less.

5. *Generalizing:* Start with particular characters and particular happenings in your show, then infer general patterns of people and events in general.
   a. Think about the demographics of the characters in your show. Do those demographics in your show match the patterns of demographics in the real world?
   b. Think about the plot elements (sex, violence, health) in your show. Do these elements in your show match the patterns of these elements in the real world?

6. *Appreciating*
   a. Emotional: Was the show able to evoke emotions in you? If so, list those emotions and explain how the show triggered those particular emotions.
   b. Aesthetic: Is there something about the writing, directing, editing, lighting, set design, costuming, or music/sound effects that you found of particular high quality? If so, explain what led you to appreciate that element so much.
   c. Moral: Did the show raise ethical considerations (either explicitly or implicitly)? If so, did you appreciate how the show dealt with those ethical considerations?

**Exercise 6.2**   Analyzing the Content of Television Entertainment

1. Write a definition for sexual behavior. This is not as easy as it might seem. You must consider issues such as the following: What must the characters do, what are their intentions (a kiss or a hug is not always sexual), and what do they talk about (if a character talks about what he or she wants to do, does that count)?

2. Watch two different situation comedies and count how many acts occur that meet your definition. Note the gender, age, and ethnic background of the characters.

3. Discuss your results with others in class who did their own content analyses of sex.
   a. What is the range in the numbers of acts found? Can this range be attributed to differences in definitions or differences in shows?
   b. Profile the types of characters who were most often involved in sexual activity.
   c. Are there any noticeable differences in character profiles across types of situation comedies?

4. Now try using your definition to analyze the content on soap operas, music videos, and action/adventure dramas.
   a. Do you see any big differences in the number of sexual acts across different types of shows?
   b. Do you see any big differences in the profiles of characters involved in sexual activity across shows?

5. Now think about how sex is portrayed in the television world.
   a. What types of activity are the most prevalent?
   b. How responsibly is sex portrayed in the television world—that is, are the physical and emotional risks often discussed or considered? Is sex portrayed as a normal part of a loving, stable relationship, or is it portrayed more as a game of conquest or a source of silliness?
   c. Did you find anything in the patterns that surprised you?

6. What do you need to know about how sex is portrayed in the media and the role of sex in the real world for you to construct a strong knowledge structure on this subject?

# CHAPTER 7

# What Is News?

---

**Key Idea:** News is not a reflection of actual events; it is a construction by news workers who are subjected to many influences and constraints.

---

I n America, we appear to revere the press. For example, we often quote Thomas Jefferson, who said in 1787, "Were it left to me to decide whether we should have a government without newspapers or newspapers without a government, I should not hesitate a moment to prefer the latter" (quoted in Jensen, 1997, p. 11).

However, we also like to criticize the press. Even Thomas Jefferson himself delivered one of the most strident criticisms of the press after he became president and had to deal with it on a daily basis. In 1807, he said, "The man who never looks into a newspaper is better informed than he who reads them." Jefferson took the position that "he who knows nothing is nearer to truth than he whose mind is filled with falsehoods and errors" (quoted in Jensen, 1997, p. 11). Thus, Jefferson was arguing that nothing printed in a newspaper could be believed.

What Thomas Jefferson experienced more than two centuries ago is the same thing that people since him have experienced when they take part in a real-world event and then expose themselves to the news story in the media. People expect the news story to be a simple, accurate reflection of the real-world event. But this has never been the case, and it never will be.

# Is News a Reflection or a Construction?

If you were to ask someone how the news differs from entertainment programming, most people would say that entertainment is fiction and therefore made up by writers, whereas news presents actual events that happened. We think of news as a reflection of the events of the day; that is, the media are merely holding a mirror up to reality.

But when we take a closer look at the news, it becomes clear that news does not *reflect* reality. Instead, it is a construction by journalists. News coverage is triggered, of course, by actual occurrences. But what we see presented as news by the media are not the events themselves. Instead, the media present us with stories *about* the events, and those stories are constructed by journalists who are influenced by constraints that are largely outside of their control. Journalists are also profoundly influenced by other factors that frame what gets presented as news.

## Constraints

Three basic constraints limit what is presented in news stories. These constraints are usually regarded as being outside the ability of journalists to control them, although this is changing. Those three constraints are deadlines, resource limitations, and geographical focus.

### *Deadlines*

Sometimes an event will begin before a deadline but continue beyond the deadline, so the journalist cannot get all the information on the ongoing event. In this case, the journalist must file a partial story. What is left out of the story may eventually prove to be more important than what is put into the partial story.

Deadlines often prevent journalists from gathering all the facts and presenting a complete and accurate story about the event. For example, daily newspapers have a deadline every single day. Morning newspapers usually have a deadline about 11 P.M. the night before. Let's say a fire breaks out in a well-known building 2 A.M. on a Wednesday morning and firefighters battle the blaze until 4 A.M., when the fire is out and the building is gone. People reading their Wednesday morning newspaper over breakfast would want to learn about the fire, but no report of it will be in the Wednesday morning paper. The editor of the newspaper must then decide whether to print a story of the fire in the Thursday morning edition, which would make the story old news. The deadline constraint has prevented the newspaper from reporting the fire as "news." Deadlines are even more troublesome for weekly newspapers and news magazines; by the time their readers get their stories, the stories seem less like news because much time has elapsed between the event occurring and the "news" story being made available to the audience.

Some media channels, such as radio, television, and the Internet, are not constrained much by deadlines because journalists working in these media can continue to file updates of stories as new information becomes available. However, these journalists are still subject to other constraints and influences.

## Resource Limitations

Although the news-gathering departments of the major media organizations—especially broadcast networks and the major daily newspapers—are very large and have considerable resources, there are still limits to those resources. There are never enough resources to be able to cover all the events that happen in a given day, and assignment editors must decide which stories will get covered and which will not.

This used to be an especially difficult problem for local television stations. To cover a story, a local TV station would have to send more than just a reporter; it would also have to send a crew of camera and sound people in a relatively large van to hold the people and equipment. But with new technological developments, this constraint is not as limiting as it once was. For example, E. Slater (2004) points out that "reporters from every television network and cable outlet now carry miniature broadcast-quality digital video cameras. In addition to at least one cell-phone, many journalists carry a digital voice recorder, at least one hand-held e-mail device and a wireless modem" (p. A11). This allows many more stories to be covered. Of course, other resource constraints, such as a limit on the column inches a newspaper devotes to news, is not changing to allow for more stories to be printed, so these technological enhancements are putting more pressure on other constraints to hold the status quo.

The argument that resource constraints are responsible for limiting what we see as news is often faulty. This is revealed in the way a lot of the resources duplicate their efforts, thus making for inefficient use of limited resources. For example, the Associated Press news service has more than 100 reporters in Washington, DC, alone, and many of them are trying to develop the same contacts at the White House. Every 4 years, the two major political parties hold nominating conventions to select their party's candidate for president. News organizations send a total of about 16,000 journalists to these nonevents; I call this a nonevent because the person who is nominated is usually known months in advance of the "nominating" conventions, so the news value of the convention is very small. If those journalistic resources that were assigned to the convention were instead directed to other locations, the news audiences would likely receive a much wider and richer span of news from those same limited resources. This same principle applies every day on smaller scales in every town of the United States, with several newspapers, magazines, radio stations, and TV stations all sending reporters to the same police stations, city halls, and athletic contests.

The major news organizations all had budgets greatly expand over decades without providing an expansion in the amount of news. For example, the annual budget of the ABC network news department grew from about $1 million in the early 1960s to more than $300 million in the late 1980s, but with that enormous growth in resources, the amount and/or quality of news did not increase 300 times during that period.

Also, CNN and all-news radio shows have significant budgets and a very large news hole. But the number of stories they cover is very small compared to the space they have.

Their news perspective has not allowed them to provide a greatly expanded breath of stories. Instead, CNN maintains a narrow vision of what is important and continually presents a small set of stories over and over all day.

## Geographical Focus

Each news organization is focused on covering the events in its own locale so it can report those stories to its local audiences. With few exceptions in the United States, newspapers each have their own geographical territory and focus their coverage within the bounds of that territory.

There is another form of geographical constraint, and this refers to the condition that, even outside of a news organization's local area, there appears to be a belief that certain parts of the world are more important (more newsworthy) than others. For example, Larson (1983) examined international news coverage on television and found that events in the Third World (the poorer, less industrialized countries) were covered less than events in industrialized countries and that what coverage there was about the Third World was crisis oriented. The same pattern was found by Potter (1987b) in newspapers. Kim and Barnett (1996) show clearly that the news flow of information around the world is dominated by the Western industrialized countries at the center. This power is associated with the degree of economic development. So, for example, if a dozen people are killed by a bomb in a London department store, this is likely to get far more coverage in the United States than if 100 people are killed in an earthquake in Guatemala.

Even within this country, the news coverage is not balanced geographically. In the United States, events occurring in the Northeast and on the Pacific Coast are covered the most, whereas events happening in the rest of the country are undercovered in the national news services (Graber, 1988).

## News-Framing Influences

News-framing influences are like constraints in the sense that they can be seen as forces that shape what gets selected and presented as news. However, these news-framing influences are different from constraints because they are purely constructions of journalists to help them do their jobs more easily and to fulfill the goals of the businesses that employ them.

## Commercialism

Arguably, the strongest influence on the construction of news is its commercial nature (Altheide, 1976). News organizations are in the business of constructing large audiences so they can rent those audiences to advertisers. The larger the audience, the higher the rent and the more money the news organization generates. Therefore, the ultimate goal of news is a commercial one, and journalists are driven to construct stories that will appeal to large audiences. Therefore, news organizations must be careful not to run hard-hitting stories that would offend their advertisers (Lee & Solomon, 1990). For example, the harmfulness of tobacco has been greatly underreported because tobacco advertising is so important to the survival of many magazines and newspapers. Television has also been affected, even though no tobacco products have been advertised on television for three decades. The tobacco companies are large conglomerates with many products. A television news show that offends a tobacco company is in danger of losing advertising of other brands controlled by the large tobacco conglomerates.

Also, journalists will write stories that are not strictly news but that instead have the value of promoting other commercial products being marketed by the organization that owns the news organization. For example, Kaniss (1996) criticized news shows in the Philadelphia area by pointing out that during the November 1996 sweeps month, the local CBS affiliate on its evening news show ran nine stories on the *Titanic,* a ship that sank 84 years prior but was the subject of a CBS mini-series. The local ABC affiliate frequently runs news stories about Mickey Mouse because the ABC network is owned by Disney. Local affiliates also frequently run news stories about stars on their network series, and they often run soft news stories on topics of made-for-TV movies appearing that night on the network.

## Marketing Perspective

The pressures of commercialism set up a conflict between two perspectives on news. One of these is the professional responsibility perspective. This is where journalists regard themselves as having a responsibility to inform the public about the most important and significant events of the day so that people can use the information to make better decisions as citizens of that society. For example, journalists operating within this perspective would strive to provide in-depth information on candidates and issues during a campaign so that voters can make a more informed decision. These journalists would also try to present clear explanations about economic conditions, implications of government policies, the patterns of changes in society, and other broad-scale issues so the public is exposed to the context behind individual issues. But there is a danger of providing such in-depth coverage of complicated issues; that is, such coverage is likely to bore most audience members.

In contrast, there is the marketing perspective. This is where news workers pay careful attention to what kinds of stories and presentation formats generate the largest audience. For example, journalists operating under the marketing perspective are more likely to present stories that grab the attention of large audiences by highlighting the unusual so as to shock people.

The influence of commercialism has moved the news away from the professional responsibility perspective and placed it squarely under the marketing perspective. As a result, the news has attempted to be more entertaining. The stories are shorter. There is more focus on personalities than genuine leaders. There is more focus on celebrities than on people of substance. And there is more focus on gossip than news.

This ambivalence between social responsibility and entertainment is evident in public opinion polls. For example, when Americans were asked whether television stations should broadcast live coverage of a hostage being held at gunpoint, only 22% said yes. But when those same people were asked whether they would watch such coverage, 59% said yes (Luntz, 2000). Most of us know that it is not responsible for certain events to be broadcasted. However, we are attracted to such events and would watch if we could.

This marketing perspective has led news workers to believe that the public wants more soft news items than stories about the government, the economy, and political matters. In a content analysis of 13,000 items in 12 daily newspapers, it was found that newspapers with a strong market orientation publish fewer items about government and public affairs and more items about lifestyle and sports than do newspapers with a weak market orientation:

> Today, the newsrooms of hundreds of U.S. newspapers, magazines, and television stations have embraced, to greater or lesser extents, this approach to making news. Typically a market-driven organization selects target markets for its product, identifies the wants and needs of potential customers in its target markets, and seeks to satisfy those wants and needs as efficiently as possible. (Beam, 2003, p. 368)

Also, Schudson (2003) reports that soft news increased from 35% in 1980 to 50% in 1998 in television networks, major news magazines, and leading national newspapers.

People like deviance, so the news media are interested in presenting things that deviate from the normal (Shoemaker, 1987; Shoemaker, Danielian, & Brendlinger, 1991). Deviance covers those things that are out of the ordinary, and the more they differ from reality, the more they are considered newsworthy.

With news coverage, there are two types of deviance (Shoemaker & Reese, 1996). There is statistical deviance, which "causes things that are unusual (either good or bad) to be considered more newsworthy than commonplace events" (p. 47). For example, if a woman gives birth to four children over a decade, that is not news. But it a woman gives birth to quadruplets, that is unusual and therefore is newsworthy. The statistical probability of giving birth to four children at once is very low, so this gets covered.

The other type of deviance is normative, which refers to ideas or events that break norms or laws. For example, if a person goes to a bank and puts money in his account, that is normal and will not get covered. But if a person goes to a bank and withdraws money from other people's accounts at gunpoint, that breaks the law and gets covered. Thus, the media like to focus on crime because it occurs outside the norm. Within crime news, there is a preference for violent action (Antunes & Hurley, 1977; Windhauser, Seiter, & Winfree, 1990) and crimes against people (Ammons, Dimmick, & Pilotta, 1982; Fedler & Jordan,

1982), which are rarer and more deviant than property crimes. Also, deaths due to violence are more likely to be reported that deaths due to disease (Combs & Slovic, 1979). This over-reporting of crime is also found in other countries, such as England (Roshier, 1981).

The irony is that we depend on the news to tell us what the norm is. To be well informed, we need to know how things typically work, what is likely to happen tomorrow, and what the relative risks of harm are. But the news media focus our attention on the deviant. Because we see so many portrayals of the deviant, we come to believe that the deviant is the norm.

## Organizational Structures

Organizational structures vary. Small companies are more flexible and entrepreneurial. They search out new needs and quickly adapt. In contrast, large companies are compartmentalized, with each division having a special function and its own staff of technical people. Large bureaucracies are more resistant to change.

## Ownership

Ownership patterns can also influence the content. For example, the *New York Times* has remained in the hands of one family for more than 100 years. There is very high potential for the members of that family to have a strong influence on that newspaper. In contrast, other newspapers might be owned by a large media conglomerate with thousands of shareholders, each with a very low potential for influence.

Although there are some examples of newspapers changing their editorial stance because of pressure from an owner, these are rare. What is more typical is strong pressure from owners that the newspaper make a larger profit. This reinforces the marketing perspective.

## Use of Sources

News is shaped by the sources that journalists use to gather information. The dominant sources of news are public information officers in businesses and governmental units. Most companies and institutions have public relations departments whose sole job is to establish themselves as experts and feed information to journalists. Once a person is established as an expert source, he or she is called by journalists when they want an expert opinion on that particular issue.

How do journalists know who is an expert? Most journalists don't. They lack the experience or education to evaluate the credentials of many people who could serve as experts in news stories, so they chose people not on the basis of knowledge but on their *appearance* of expertise and their willingness to tell a good story. This point is illustrated by Steele (1995), who examined how television news organizations selected and used expert sources to interpret the news. She found that news organizations chose expert sources that reflected journalists' understanding of expertise. Experts were selected according to how well their specialized knowledge conformed to television's "operational bias," which places its emphasis on players, policies, and predictions of what will happen next. Steele concluded that these processes undermine the ideals of balance and objectivity as well as severely limit how news is framed.

The major news organizations all use the same sources, many of whom are unnamed, so the same type of stories always get covered. This is a clear conclusion of two journalists—Lee and Solomon (1990)—who wrote a book titled *Unreliable Sources: A Guide to Detecting Bias in News Media,* in which they expressed strong criticism of American journalistic practices. These journalists observed that over time, reporters become close friends with their sources and stop looking for other points of view. This makes their jobs easier because these reporters do not have to continually develop new and better sources of information. But the problem with this practice is that the sources have their own agendas. Frequently, the sources are public relations people for various governmental agencies, businesses, or political action groups. Thus, these sources are not trying to provide unbiased expertise to help journalists understand the issue better; instead, these people are paid to present only their one side of the issue and to make their side appear as the only valid position on the issue. For example, the military establishment has always had a sophisticated public relations operation that works to maintain strong public support for its goals and its need for increasing funding. In the 1960s, when the Soviet Union had 100 long-range missiles and the United States had 2,000, the Pentagon convinced the American people that the United States lagged far behind Russia in weapons, and the public ended up supporting greater defense budgets. During the Reagan administration, the Pentagon had an annual public relations budget of $100 million and employed 3,000 staff people.

Sources often have an incestuous relationship with journalists. Many journalists go into government and serve as press secretaries or public information officers. Also, press secretaries go into journalism. Over time, the two professions converge, and this revolving door homogenizes the coverage. Schudson (2003) observes, "Political institutions and media institutions are so deeply intertwined, so thoroughly engaged in a complex dance with each other, that is not easy to distinguish where one begins and the other leaves off" (p. 154). Bennett (2003) argues that this close relationship leads to what he calls indexing. By this, he means that journalists take their direction from the government when deciding the range of public opinion. What the government recognizes as the range of public opinion, journalists accept and limit their reporting to that range.

## Branding

News shows brand their reporters. Notice that at the beginning and end of news reports, the reporters will often mention their names, and sometimes their names will be in graphics superimposed over the visuals. Local TV stations do this so that audience members will follow the reporters in addition to the stories. If the stories are not particularly good one evening, audience members will still tune in to see their favorite reporters. This has the effect of turning news reporters into celebrities. When these news celebrities become really well known, they begin commanding very large fees for speaking at private functions. For example, Cokie Roberts of ABC commands a fee of $35,000 per appearance, and Ted Koppel gets $50,000 (Schudson, 2003).

Some journalists get involved in making the news events themselves. For example, *Newsweek* columnist George Will helped Ronald Reagan prepare for the televised debates during the 1980 presidential election. Also, former CBS news anchor Dan Rather made a speech at a Democratic fund-raiser in 2001 (Schudson, 2003).

## Values

Journalists believe that Americans hold certain core values, so they try to tell stories that resonate with these values. This becomes one of the important characteristics in telling a good story and holding the audience's attention. What are these values? Shoemaker and Reese (1996) say there are eight of them (see Table 7.1).

## Story Formula

Journalists are very busy people. Their days are filled with an incredible amount of detail that must be processed on short deadlines. A reporter at a daily newspaper may have to write several dozen stories every day. Do reporters spend hours thinking about the best way to communicate the essence of each story, then several more hours polishing draft

**Table 7.1**     Core American Values

- Individualism—Audiences like to hear about people who do things their own way, even against powerful odds.
- Moderatism—Fanaticism of any kind arouses skepticism.
- Social order—Peace and order are valued; people who deviate from this are labeled as wrongdoers.
- Leadership—There are high expectations for leaders; those who are found to be weak, dishonest, or immoral are investigated.
- Ethnocentrism—Other countries are judged against American standards.
- Altruistic democracy—There is a democratic ideal of efficient government and participation by all citizens; deviations from this are news.
- Responsible capitalism—There should be fair competition without unreasonable profits or exploiting workers.
- Small-town pastoralism—Small towns and rural areas are the font of virtue.

after draft? No. Rarely do they have this kind of time. Instead, they must assemble the facts of a story in a matter of minutes, then move on to the next story. How do they do this? They use story formulas (Fishman, 1980).

Formulas are the procedures that journalists learn as shortcuts to help them quickly select and write stories. The most popular information-gathering formula is the series of questions: Who? What? Where? Where? Why? and How? Journalists confronted with a new story begin by asking these questions.

One popular news-writing formula is the inverted pyramid. This formula tells the journalist to put the most important information at the beginning of the story, then add the next most important set of information. Journalists move down their list of information, ranked according to importance until all the information is in the story. This formula was developed in the early days of the telegraph, when journalists in the field would send their stories to their newspapers over telegraph lines. If the line went dead halfway through the story, the journalist would know that at least the most important information got through. We are way past the days of dependence on unreliable telegraph lines, but the formula still has value because editors will cut stories if they run too long. For example, a newspaper editor might want to use a reporter's 12-inch story but only has room for 8 inches, so the editor will typically cut off the last 4 inches.

Another popular formula is to use a narrative to tell a story in an entertainment format. Journalists who use this formula will begin the story with a heated conflict, a gruesome description, or an unusual quote—all designed to grab the reader's attention in an emotional manner. Then the writer moves through the plot, much like a fictional story-teller would.

Perhaps the most popular formula for telling stories in the news is what I call simplified extended conflict (SEC). When covering a story, journalists look for some angle of conflict that appears very simple. They believe that a story that has no conflict will not *grab* the audience's attention, but if the conflict is complex, the story will not *hold* the audience's attention. Furthermore, if the story can be played out over several days—or longer—so much the better. Political elections offer lots of good examples of the SEC. Campaigns always involve conflict between the candidates, and this can usually be reduced to two people. Also, the campaign, which goes on for weeks or months, can be portrayed as a race, with one candidate ahead and the other candidate running hard to catch up. If the conflict is focused on the finer points of complex issues, the story will not appeal to a large audience. Therefore, journalists look for a simple form of conflict, and that is best seen in the "horse race" metaphor. Political coverage is much more about who is winning and whether the challenger can come from behind and close the gap than it is about issues. Other examples of SEC are O. J. Simpson against the court system, the United States against Iraq, various crusaders against Congress, the little guy against city hall, and the forces of pro-life against the forces of pro-choice. The press can present the conflict in these situations in a very simple manner and keep the conflict going for a long time. It does this by polarizing the people or issues in the conflict, inviting the audience to identify with one side, then playing out the fight with lots of drama.

When the press has a big story that will consume news space for several weeks or months, it has an opportunity to more fully develop the nuances of the parties in the conflict. With political issues, the press could choose to tell the story of how competing interests have some common ground and how compromise is crafted. With criminal trials, the press could choose to tell the story of how humans can go astray and what justice means in each situation. Instead, the press rarely digs deep into a story—illuminating its complexity and educating the public about the underlying nature of the problem. The press stays with the surface information—polishing it to a more glitzy finish to make it more attractive to passive viewers.

## News Perspective

All of the constraints and news-framing influences shape how journalists select which events to cover and how they construct their stories. When we take all these influences and constraints together, we call this the "news perspective." This news perspective is not something that is consciously imposed by the owners of the media. Instead, it grows naturally out of the practices of the status quo and leads us to ask, How could the news be any other way?

People who are hired as journalists become socialized by this news perspective as they learn their jobs. The news perspective is so pervasive and common among journalists that it is taken for granted. It is also generally shared by journalists in all kinds of vehicles and all media, as evidenced in several research studies. One of these studies found that there is a considerable overlap in news stories at local television stations in the same market. Davie and Lee (1993) found that 56% of stories were the same, with network sources having more similarity. The nonoverlapping stories were more likely to be from local sources. Also, Davie and Lee (1995) analyzed local television newscasts and found that there is a distinct preference for sensational stories that feature acts of sex and violence and are easy to explain. There was little differentiation among the stations, leading to the conclusion that the news sense of all local producers is almost the same.

Hudson (1992) also arrived at the same conclusion as a result of an experiment on more than 100 news directors and executive producers from all size markets all over the country. He showed them a violent incident and asked them how much of the incident they would show in a newscast. Editors exhibited the same news judgment in all size markets and across all kinds of stations.

### Advantage

The advantage of the news perspective is that it helps journalists simplify and organize the overwhelming amount of material they must sift through on a daily basis. The use of this perspective can be seen in "the routines of news detection, interpretation, investigation, and assembly" (Fishman, 1980, p. 18). Because this news perspective is shared among news workers of all levels (reporters and editors) as well as across different media, it serves as a kind of code of professionalism that legitimates the "intertwining of political and corporate activity" (Tuchman, 1978, p. 14).

### Disadvantage

The disadvantage of the news perspective is that its limited vision results in a very narrow view of what is news. It also leads journalists to treat those selected stories superficially, thus distorting reality. Altheide (1976) argues that "the organizational, practical, and other mundane features of news work promote a way of looking at events which fundamentally distorts them. . . . In order to make events news, news reporting decontextualizes and thereby changes them" (pp. 24–25).

### Changes

The news perspective has changed over time from social responsibility to marketing because of the business constraints as mentioned above. The news perspective used to be guided by the criteria of significance, proximity, and timeliness. The more an occurrence had these characteristics, the more likely it would be covered. But now the criteria are different because of the desire to build large audiences. The news perspective criteria now are conflict, appeal to emotions, and visualization. For an event to be covered today, it must meet these newer criteria.

To illustrate this change, Slattery and Hakanen (1994) compared local television newscasts from 1976 and 1992. They found that hard news coverage of the government declined dramatically from 64% to 19%, whereas coverage of human interest stories and sensationalism climbed from 10% to 41%. During the same time, there was shrinkage in the news hole of the late-evening newscasts from 13 minutes to 11.8 minutes, thus allowing more time for advertising. This is the classic pattern of the marketing perspective.

## Can Journalists Be Objective?

There is a strong ethic of objectivity in journalism (Parenti, 1986). But what does this mean? Editors may be objective in the sense that they don't want to publish a "slanted" story. However, they have no choice but to use their personal judgment in deciding which stories get assigned, which stories get written by the best reporters, which stories get edited down, and which stories get printed on the front page.

The idea of objectivity has many layers of meaning. Let's work our way through some of these layers to develop an appreciation for this most important of all journalistic standards.

## Fabrication

Everyone would agree that it is a serious violation of objectivity if journalists make up facts and sources. Fabrication is always a threat because sometimes journalists do not have enough time or are too lazy to get all the facts they need, so they make some up or accept some facts without checking them out fully. Also, Jamieson and Waldman (2003) point out that sometimes journalists are tempted to tell a good story and ignore facts that get in the way of telling that story.

Fortunately, there are not many examples of fabrication, but a few major instances have emerged lately. Lori Robertson (2001), in a recent *American Journalism Review* article, talks about almost two dozen such acts of ethical violations that resulted in the firing of journalists. The problem seems to be in all kinds of print vehicles, including high-profile magazines (*Time, New Republic, Business Week*), large newspapers (*Wall Street Journal, New York Times, Boston Globe*), and small newspapers (*Myrtle Beach SC Sun News, Bloomsburg, PA Press Enterprise, Owensboro, KY Messenger-Inquirer*), and cuts across all kinds of reporters, including sports, business, general news, columnists, and arts critics.

Perhaps the most publicized ethical problems were perpetrated by *New York Times* reporter Jayson Blair, who was found to have frequently fabricated facts in his stories. His motivation was to write interesting stories that would be selected for publication in prominent places in the newspaper and thus make him more famous and further his career as a journalist. When *Times* editors finally began checking his stories, they found many fabrications and quickly fired Blair. But the damage to the credibility of the *Times* was done, and the editors felt compelled to publish a 14,000-word apologia on its front page (Wolff, 2003).

## Bias

When we dig a little deeper beyond fabrication, we find the idea of bias. Uncovering bias requires interpretation, and this makes it a more difficult violation of objectivity to spot. Assessing whether a fact was fabricated requires relatively little interpretation, but with bias, we must infer whether the story has essential elements that the journalist failed to report because those elements supported a side of the issue that the journalist did not want supported. Therefore, bias is a willful distortion on the part of a journalist, but it is difficult for audiences to recognize when this is occurring. If you agree with the journalist, you conclude that there has been no bias; in contrast, if you are a critic of the journalist, you argue that bias exists. Let's examine two ways bias can influence journalists' decisions: bias in ignoring stories and bias in the writing of a story, particularly political stories.

### Bias in Ignoring Important Stories

News organizations cover only a tiny fraction of the occurrences on any given day. Does bias influence how they decide what to cover? Some people make a strong case that bias is a major influence. For example, let's look at the findings of Project Censored, which is a yearly analysis that compares happenings in the real world with events covered by the news organizations (Jensen, 1997). This project began in 1976 to monitor news coverage in the mass media and determine if there were major events or issues that were not being covered. Jensen says,

> The essential issue raised by the Project is the failure of the mass media to provide people with all the information they need to make informed decisions concerning their own lives. Only an informed electorate can achieve a fair and just society. The public has a right to know about issues that affect it and the press has a responsibility to keep the public well-informed about those issues. (p. 10)

Jensen (1997) argues that the media are biased in the way they select which events they choose to cover. He says,

> The media are more concerned with their next quarterly profit than with the unique opportunity given them by the First Amendment. And most journalists are more concerned with keeping their jobs and increasing their income than with fighting for the public's right to know. . . . America's mainstream mass media basically serve three segments of society today—the wealthy, politicians, and the sports-minded. The news media have done an exceptional job providing full and, on the whole, reliable information to those who are involved in or follow the stock market and to those who are involved in or follow politics and to those who are involved in or follow sports. (p. 12)

Jensen says that there is no conscious conspiracy among journalists to censor the news.

> News is too diverse, fast-breaking, and unpredictable to be controlled by some sinister conservative eastern establishment media cabal. However, there is a congruence of attitudes and interests on the part of the owners and managers of mass media organizations. That non-conspiracy conspiracy, when combined with a variety of other factors, leads to the systematic failure of the news media to inform the public. While it is not an overt form of censorship, such as the kind we observe in some other societies, it is nonetheless real and often equally as dangerous to the public's well being. (pp. 14–15)

In his book *Censored: The News That Didn't Make the News—And Why,* Jensen (1995) describes many seemingly important stories that did not receive much, if any, coverage by the news media. For example, in 1985, the National Institute for Occupational Safety and Health (NIOSH) found that more than 240,000 people were in danger in 258 work sites around the United States. It is the purpose of NOISH to monitor safety in the workplace and to inform workers when they are in serious danger of contracting life-threatening diseases from exposure to chemicals and other hazardous materials in the workplace. By 1995, NIOSH had informed less than 30% of the people who it had found to be in daily danger a decade earlier. Thus, NOISH knew that 170,000 people were working in highly risky environments every day and let 10 years go by without telling them. The news media ignored this governmental negligence for more than a decade.

## Bias Toward Particular Political Views

Those who follow the media closely often complain about a liberal or a conservative news bias, or they say that there is too much negativism. In an analysis of Gallup public opinion data, it was found that more than half of Americans felt that the media were influenced by advertisers, business corporations, Democrats, the federal government, liberals, the military, and Republicans (Becker, Kosicki, & Jones, 1992). The newspaper industry itself finds the same thing in its own surveys. For example, a survey by the American Society of Newspaper Editors found that most people believe the media have political leanings (Jeffres, 1994).

What is interesting is that conservatives feel that the media have a generally liberal leaning, whereas liberals feel that the media are conservative. Conservatives complain that most news reporters are liberal in their own views, and these liberal journalists show their bias when they present their stories. In contrast, liberals feel that conservative commentators have too much power and have redefined the American agenda to stigmatize liberals.

In the early days of the United States, most newspapers were founded by men who had a clear political viewpoint that they wanted to promote. Towns had multiple newspapers, each one appealing to a different niche of political thinking. Newspapers were biased politically, and the bias was clearly labeled. But by the late 1800s, newspapers had shifted from a political focus to a business focus, with the goal of building the largest circulation. To do this, newspapers lost their political edge so as to avoid offending any potential readers. This business focus still underlies the mass media. Decisions are made to build audiences, not to espouse a political point of view. Sometimes, arguing for a particular political point of view can be used as a tool to build an audience, but these instances are usually found within those media with a niche orientation. Instead, the large national news organizations such as the television networks and the large newspapers try to present both sides of any political issue so as to appear objective and balanced because they want to appeal to all kinds of people across the political spectrum. This conclusion has been supported by D'Alessio and Allen (2000), who conducted a meta-analysis of 59 quantitative studies of news bias in presidential campaigns since 1948. They found no evidence of bias with newspapers or magazines and only an "insubstantial" bias in network television news.

It is important to be sensitive to whether particular news vehicles present either a liberal or conservative bias. But it is far more important to be sensitive to the broader bias underlying all news vehicles—that is, the bias of commercialism, entertainment, and superficiality. If all we do is debate the liberal-conservative issue when it comes to news bias, we are in danger of missing the larger picture that the news media are providing us with a worldview that determines not only what we think about (as in agenda setting) but also what we think, how we think, and who we are.

## Partial Story

At an even deeper level of analysis is the idea that journalists are not objective because they are telling us only part of the story. This type of distortion is not usually regarded as bias because there does not seem to be an intention by the journalist to mislead the audience. Instead, the journalist has run out of time or does not have enough sources or ability to tell the entire story. Even though the journalist is not trying to mislead the audience, people exposed to a partial story are still shown a distorted picture of the occurrence, and therefore the story cannot be regarded as being objective.

One form of partial story is when a major story stops getting covered, even though important events continue to occur. An example of this is the $21 billion settlement by the tobacco industry that was covered during negotiations. But then the press stopped covering the story as the tobacco companies began paying billions of dollars to state governments between 2000 and 2002. Why would it be important to cover how the money was used? The settlement specified that states should spend the money for health care and to educate people, especially children, about the health risks of smoking. But only 5% of this total payout went toward antismoking efforts as it was intended. Instead, it got funneled to all sorts of pork barrel projects across the 50 states, and in North Carolina, much of it went to subsidize tobacco farmers. These subsidies did not go to help tobacco farmers transition to other crops; instead, much of it went to modernize their tobacco farms (Mnookin, 2002). Also, the press did a poor job of educating the public about where the money for the payout was coming from. Most people know that it is from the major tobacco companies, but most people do not know where the tobacco companies get much of their revenue that they use to make their payments to states in the tobacco settlement. Each of the major tobacco companies now controls hundreds of brands of all kinds of food products in supermarkets. So the payout was likely financed by a rise in prices of crackers, cereals, peanut butter, dog food, soups, and so on.

Another type of partial story is when a journalist will tell a story from a single point of view. American journalists typically will tell their stories from the point of view that America is always justified in its military actions, and those we aggress against are not justified. For example, Fishman and Marvin (2003) analyzed 21 years of photographs appearing on the front pages of the *New York Times*. They focused on violence and found that non-U.S. agents were represented as more explicitly violent than U.S. agents and that the latter are associated with disguised modes of violence more often than the former. The recurring image of non-U.S. violence is that of order brutally ruptured or enforced. By contrast, images of U.S. violence are less alarming and suggest order without cruelty. Thus, violence is associated more with out-group status than with in-group status.

## Context

Perhaps the deepest level of analysis of the idea of objectivity arrives when we consider the nature of context. This is the concern over how much background-type information to present to help readers make sense of the event. Without context, the story has ambiguous meaning. For example, a story could report that Mr. Jones was arrested for murder this morning. That fact can convey very different meanings if we vary the context. Let's say that the journalist put in some historical context that Mr. Jones had murdered several people a decade ago, was caught and convicted, served time in prison, but was recently let go because of a ruling of an inexperienced and liberal judge. In contrast, let's say that Mr. Jones, one of the candidates running for mayor, was arrested despite the fact that police had in custody another man who possessed the probable murder weapon and who had confessed. The fact of the arrest takes on a very different meaning within different contexts.

Let's consider another example of context. In the summer of 1995, Allan Little, a veteran foreign correspondent for the British Broadcasting Corp., was covering the war in Bosnia. One day, as the Serbian soldiers were approaching a Muslim town, he wanted to tell the story of an impending massacre, but his editor told him that such reporting would not be objective. Little was told to report just the facts of the day, with no background and no interpretation, which he did. Although he knew that it was the practice of the Serb forces to slaughter all the Muslims they could and that the town was unprotected and would soon fall into Serb hands, he could not put that context into his news story. On July 11, the Serb soldiers captured the town, rounded up the thousands of men and boys in the village, and killed them all. Little says, "I still to this day feel sullied and tainted that I pulled my punches on that one" (Randolph, 1997, p. A5). The accurate or complete coverage would have been to report the event in the context of Serbian goals and past behaviors during the war. In that way, viewers could see the true horror of the aggression and get a much better understanding of what was taking place. Instead, to preserve an editor's sense of "objectivity," Little was limited to reporting only the details of how far the Serb army advanced each day. Which way of reporting would have been more meaningful to readers? In situations such as this one, a journalist and his editor are both trying to be what they think of as "objective," but they mean very different things when they talk about "objectivity."

Although contextual material is very important, many stories present very little context (Parenti, 1986). For example, the many stories about crimes that we see reported everyday are each limited to the facts of that one crime. Rarely is there any context about crime rates or how the particular crime reported in the story matches some kind of a pattern—historical, social, economic, and so forth. Crime stories are like popcorn for the mind. Each story is small, simple, and relatively the same. They give our mind the sense that it is consuming information, but those stories have little nutritional value. After years of munching on this information, we have come to believe that most crime is violent street crime and that it is increasing all around us. But the real-world figures indicate that most crime is white collar (embezzlement, fraud, forgery, etc.) and property crimes (larceny, shoplifting, etc.) rather than violent crime (murder, rape, armed robbery, etc.). But it is the more rare violent crime that gets reported because it is more deviant and thus more likely to capture the attention of the news audience.

Asking journalists to build more context into their stories presents two problems. First, journalists vary widely in talent, and it takes a very talented and experienced journalist to be able to dig out a great deal of relevant contextual information on deadline and then to present that context without being slanted to favor only one side of the story. Second, when journalists have the responsibility of constructing the context, they may be manifesting a lot of power to define the meaning of the event for the readers. Journalists can substantially change the meaning if they leave out (whether intentionally or through an oversight) an important contextual element.

Bagdikian (1992) argues that the most significant form of bias in journalism appears when a story is reported with a lack of context. The fear is that context is only the journalist's opinion, and opinion must be avoided in "objective reporting." Bagdikian continues, "But there is a difference between partisanship and placing facts in a reasonably informed context of history and social circumstance. American journalism has not made a workable distinction between them" (p. 214). He says that "there are powerful commercial pressures to remove social significance from standard American news. Informed social-economic context has unavoidable political implications which may disturb some in the audience whose world view differs" (p. 214). So the media report undisputed facts about things but ignore the meaning behind the facts and, in so doing, severely limit our ability to see that underlying meaning.

The news media are often criticized for providing only superficial information. Thus, the news media are not providing the public with enough guidance to make sound opinions about the important issues of the day. We can see evidence of this in public opinion polls that reveal that the public is missing key information. For example, in public opinion polls, only 17% of people think that crime is a big problem in their own community, whereas 83% of Americans think that crime is a big problem in society (Whitman & Loftus, 1996). That is, most people do not experience crime in their own lives and therefore do not think it is a big problem where they live. But they hold the opinion that the country is in bad shape.

Let's examine an example of a story reporting facts that are accurate but that leads readers to a wrong conclusion because the reporter does not provide an adequate context for those facts. In 2004, *Los Angeles Times* reporter Larry Stewart wrote a story from a report by a group calling itself the Institute for Diversity and Ethics in Sport. In his newspaper story, Stewart (2004) reported that the report said that it found six of the schools in the 2004 National Collegiate Athletic Association (NCAA) basketball tournament sweet 16 had graduation rates no higher than 50%. This leaves the reader with the impression that universities (at least six) were exploiting their athletes. But what the reporter did not put in the story is that, nationwide, only about 50% of students who enter a 4-year program as a freshman end up graduating with a bachelor's degree. Therefore, the problem is not with basketball teams having unusually low graduation rates, which is what the story implied. The real issue is the relatively large dropout rate of all college students. Also, the reporter said that the report complained that only 3 of the 16 teams had an African American head coach. Why is this number bad? What should the number be? If the number should be proportional to the number of African Americans in the United States, then we should expect 12% of coaches to be African American, and that would make it two coaches. Or instead, should the number of African American coaches be proportional to the number of African American players on NCAA basketball teams? This would be a much larger percentage, but then this begs the question that perhaps African Americans are overrepresented on these basketball teams and that the problem is that there needs to be better representation from non–African Americans on NCAA basketball teams—why are there not many more Hispanic or Asian American players? The determination of adequate representation is a complex issue. If newspapers see themselves as having the function of informing their readers so those readers can make good decisions, then journalists must provide more detailed contexts. If, instead, a journalist writes a superficial story that features only a controversy, then this serves to stir up negative emotions instead of educating readers.

In summary, you can see that objectivity is a complex concept, with many layers of meaning. This makes it difficult to understand what people really mean when they use the term. Thus, it is useful to move past objectivity and focus on something else, such as balance, as a reasonable criterion for quality news coverage.

# Balance

As we have seen from earlier sections of this chapter, all journalists must make many decisions about news coverage, and although they use a news perspective to make these decisions, this perspective does not contain a formal list of steps to follow. Each journalist interprets the news perspective through his or her personal perspective. So the idea of objectivity is an unattainable goal. If we hold the work of journalists up to the criterion of objectivity, we will always be finding serious fault. Therefore, we need to shift to a more reasonable and useful criterion—such as balance.

Many journalists prefer the criterion of balance, which is the recognition that when an event has more than one side to it, journalists should present those viewpoints. With some stories, there are many sides. In stories of simple conflicts, there are usually two sharply differing sides. To be fair, journalists present both sides and try to do so with equal weight.

Are news stories balanced? Fico and Soffin (1995) looked at balance in newspaper coverage of controversial issues such as abortion, condoms in schools, and various governmental bills. Balance was assessed by examining whether both sides of an issue were illuminated in terms of sources interviewed for both sides and whether assertions for both sides were in the headline, first paragraph, and graphics. They found that 48% of stories analyzed were one-sided; that is, a second side was not covered at all. They counted the number of story elements that illuminated the different sides of each issue and found that, on average, one side received three more elements compared to the other side—therefore, the average story was imbalanced. Only 7% of stories were completely balanced. The authors concluded that professional capability and/or ethical self-consciousness are lacking in many journalists.

Although balance is a simpler criterion than is objectivity, it still has a problem. To test for balance, we check to see that all sides to an issue are presented in an equal manner so that the audience can make up its own mind on the issue. But the problem is, how many sides does each issue have? Simple issues have two sides. Unfortunately, journalists cover most issues as if they were simple, so journalists will recognize only two sides. In their analyses of national news programs, Croteau and Hoynes (1994) found a relatively narrow range of opinion projected there and that most of the sources are either highly visible government officials or elites. They found that elites were from two sides of any political argument, but rarely were there more than two sides portrayed. Also, news shows neglect the broader public beyond the visible elites. Croteau and Hoynes say this has negative consequences:

> One of the significant consequences of this presentation is a view of the United States without any deep-seated or lasting conflict. On the contrary, domestic conflicts are presented as technical problems that can be solved by competent managers. Political disagreements are depicted as tactical differences, rather than differences in values, goals, or power. And if they are included at all, those who do not play by the rules of political civility are depicted as extremists who do not understand that Americans are all part of the same team. Ultimately, the depiction of the political world as a game carries with it a clear message about the rules of the game: insiders are the players and only players can win. (pp. 57–58)

If journalists are unable to provide us with balance, then we must construct it for ourselves if we are to be media literate. This means we must seek out information from all sides of an issue. But how do we know how many sides there are? We can't. So instead, we must develop skepticism about all issues so as to never be confident that we have all the information from all sides.

# Becoming Literate With News Content

How can we protect ourselves from the illusion that we are being informed about the important events of the day when we faithfully expose ourselves to news messages in the media? The key is to develop higher media literacy with more elaborated knowledge structures and stronger higher order skills.

Now that you have more information about news as a construction, the news perspective, the myth of objectivity, and the importance of balance, you have a stronger knowledge structure about media content. When you use this knowledge structure with advanced skills, you will be able to see much more in messages of news and information. Table 7.2 shows the cognitive, emotional, aesthetic, and moral skills you will need. It also provides some examples of knowledge across these four domains. These lists are not exhaustive. There are other examples of skills and knowledge that you could use to increase your media literacy during exposures to media messages.

Keep this template in mind as you watch the news. Think about how useful your knowledge structures are. Seek to elaborate your existing knowledge structures by using five strategies: (a) analyze the news perspective, (b) search for context, (c) develop alternative sources of information, (d) be skeptical of public opinion, and (e) expose yourself to more news, not less.

## Analyze the News Perspective

Remember, news is a construction by news workers. Journalists make their selections and decisions based on their news perspective. So when we watch a news program on TV or read a newspaper, we are seeing as much (or more) about those news organizations as we are seeing the events in the story—if we know what to look for. By keeping this in mind, we will be learning a great deal about news values while at the same time protecting ourselves from accepting the false belief that news is a complete, accurate, and balanced picture of our world. Getting a more accurate picture should be our goal. But to achieve that goal, we must seek out many sources and be actively critical of their information.

## Search for Context

Often, we hear the term *news and information* and read this as a single concept rather than two. But it is important to make a distinction between news and information. News is that which is "new" in some sense. If it is something we already know, it is not news. Therefore, it must be out of the ordinary—that is, deviant. It must make us think, "Gee whiz, I never knew that! Isn't that strange." It must entertain or excite us in some way. In contrast, information tells us something of value about our world. It makes us think, "That is something I should know; that is something I can use."

**Table 7.2**  Types of Skills and Knowledge Needed to Deal With News and Information Messages in a Media-Literate Manner

|  | *SKILLS* | *KNOWLEDGE* |
|---|---|---|
| COGNITIVE | Ability to analyze a news study to identify key points of information | |
| | Ability to compare and contrast key points of information in the news story with facts in your knowledge structure | Knowledge on topic from many sources (media and real world) |
| | Ability to evaluate veracity of information in story | |
| | Ability to evaluate if story presents a balanced presentation of the news event/issue | |
| EMOTIONAL | Ability to analyze the feelings of people in the news story | |
| | Ability to put one's self into the position of different people in the story | Recall from personal experiences how it would feel to be in the situation in the story |
| | Ability to extend empathy to other people contiguous to the news story | |
| AESTHETIC | Ability to analyze the craft and artistic elements in the story | Knowledge of writing, graphics, photography, and so on |
| | Ability to compare and contrast the artistry used to tell this story with that used to tell other stories | Knowledge of good and bad stories and the elements that contributed to those qualities |
| MORAL | Ability to analyze the moral elements in a story | Knowledge of criticism of news and knowledge of the meaning of bias, objectivity, balance, and fairness |
| | Ability to compare and contrast this story with other stories | Knowledge of other stories on this topic and how those journalists achieved balance and fairness |
| | Ability to evaluate the ethical responsibilities of the journalists on this story | Highly developed moral code for journalism |

Of course, this is not a neat, categorical distinction; something can be both news and information. For example, a news story might begin with the announcement that J. J. Jones was arrested for jumping out of a tree and mugging an old woman as she walked through the city park. This is highly unusual and deviant, so it would get covered as news. People watching this story would say, "Gee whiz. What is the world coming to?" If the story ends at this point, it is merely news. But if the story continues by putting the arrest in context, then it most likely would contain information, such as changes in the rate of crime in the park, reasons for the changes, the police department's success rate of solving those crimes, and the like. This context provides readers with something they can use—not just a fleeting emotional reaction. At higher levels of media literacy, people can more clearly see this distinction between news and information—and demand more information.

## Develop Alternative Sources of Information

In their book *How to Watch TV News,* Postman and Powers (1992) say that for people to prepare themselves to watch television news, they need to prepare their minds through extensive reading about the world. In short, if individual messages in the media do not provide much context, then you need to search that context out for yourself. With important social, political, and economic issues, this usually means reading books and magazines. But when you do this, make sure you read a variety of viewpoints. Context is more than getting exposure to one perspective on a problem—no matter how in-depth. A fully developed knowledge structure requires in-depth exposure to the issue from as many different points of view as possible. So if you find a detailed article on a topic in a conservative magazine, try to find the same topic treated in liberal, middle-of-the-road, and nonpolitical magazines. Following this strategy will result in your knowledge structure on this topic being much more elaborate, and your resulting opinion will be much sounder.

## Be Skeptical About Public Opinion

The problem with public opinion is not with measuring it accurately. Good technology can do this well when opinions exist. The problem is that often people don't have an opinion about something, or they are not sure what their opinion is—they are ambivalent. To illustrate this, take your own informal opinion poll. Ask several of your friends for their opinions on the deficit, health care reform, campaign finance reform, capital punishment, and some local issues of concern to you. Notice that most respondents will feel that they should have an opinion, and they will give you one. Then ask them why they hold those opinions. Do they quote many facts in a logical, well-reasoned argument that provides a strong foundation for their opinions? Or do they act kind of embarrassed and defensive? Are those opinions deeply held and of strong value to them? Or are those opinions superficial and based on a few random facts? How do you feel about national policy being formulated on the basis of these opinions?

When we do these things, we will attain a higher level of media literacy with the news. This requires an interplay between our knowledge structures and our skills (see Table 7.2). Stronger skills translate into stronger knowledge structures.

## Expose Yourself to More News, Not Less

When Americans were asked in a recent survey about their opinion of the press, 46% said they had a favorable opinion, and 45% said they held an unfavorable opinion (Luntz, 2000). This opinion split is also in evidence in exposure patterns. Only about 45% of American adults read newspapers regularly, and only 61% watch television news ("Fewer Adults Reading Papers," 1995). Furthermore, there is reason to believe that news exposure will continue to decline. A 1998 survey reports that only 38% of young people had read the newspaper the day before, whereas 69% of seniors had (Pew Research Center, 1998). If this trend continues, with the younger generation of news avoiders replacing the older generation of news seekers, the rates of news exposure in the general population will continue to drop.

Why are younger people more likely to avoid seeking out news? The answer seems to lie in the larger trend of people feeling overwhelmed by information. We cannot process it all. We feel fatigued and look for ways to reduce the exposure. With news, people do not want to seek out information unless it is relevant to them. For example, Chew and Palmer (1994) conducted a survey and found that people's need for information varies according to how relevant the issue is to them. With low relevant issues, people are primarily concerned about information about how that issue would affect them. With high relevance issues, people are more interested in gathering information that will help them form a good opinion, so they want information covering different viewpoints and want to hear from experts.

Also, many people feel fatigued with bad news. In surveys, most people will complain about the amount of bad or negative news and ask for more good news, saying that is what they prefer (Galician, 1986). They say that bad news is not necessarily more interesting. But the news organizations continue to predominantly feature bad news (such as crime, scandal, and controversy).

The reasons cited above—too much news is irrelevant and bad—are understandable explanations for why people are increasing their avoidance of news. But avoiding news limits one's experience, and this is a mistake. Instead, people need to expose themselves to a wider range of news from a wider range of news organizations. In this way, people can find the positive as well as the negative and find the coverage that is relevant to their needs. With more information, people can make better decisions about which facts are more accurate. And with more information, people have more options in filtering in certain facts and constructing their knowledge structures that are more useful to them.

# Conclusion

News is not a reflection of actual events; it is a construction by news workers who are subjected to many influences and constraints. Each day, journalists must select from all of human activity those things that they feel should be reported. For each event selected, journalists must then decide what the focus of the story should be so that it will hook an audience. Finally, journalists must assemble the news elements into some structure to tell the story. In performing these tasks, news workers cannot be objective, so they try for the goal of being balanced. However, careful analyses of the news indicate that most stories are not balanced.

Formulas guide the construction process. The purpose of these formulas is to help news workers do their jobs efficiently. The formulas are part of the news perspective, which is shaped by many influences and constraints. This news perspective shifts the goal of news workers from informing the public to entertaining as many people as possible, thereby generating the maximum revenue for the news organization. This has led to a focus on the sensational and the superficial. News now asks only for our eyeballs, not our gray matter.

Many of us feel we have a good understanding of current events because we read newspapers and magazines and keep up with news on radio and television. But without a complete knowledge of the day's events themselves, we cannot tell if the news coverage is complete, balanced, or accurate. Instead, we must trust the media to give us the full picture. However, the media are highly selective in what they choose to show us each day.

Being media literate requires us to search out a wide range of sources and build stronger knowledge structures that provide us with the context that mainstream news programs do not provide. We need to be careful about analyzing the news perspective, search for context, develop alternative sources of information, and be skeptical. In short, we need to be more active and conscious in using higher order skills to process news messages.

# Further Reading

Altheide, D. L. (1976). *Creating reality: How TV news distorts events.* Beverly Hills, CA: Sage. (221 pages)

This is an ethnography about how people in the newsroom create a community to get their news work done. Altheide's central thesis is that "events become news when transformed by the news perspective, and not because of their objective characteristics" (p. 173). He develops a construct called a "news perspective" to explain how the staff select and treat the news. News perspective is a sort of bias that helps journalists simplify and organize the overwhelming amount of material they must sift through. This news bias is influenced by the constraints of commercialism, scheduling, technology, and competition. He argues that "the organizational, practical, and other mundane features of news work promote a way of looking at events which fundamentally distorts them" (p. 24). "In order to make events news, news reporting decontextualizes and thereby changes them" (p. 25). The biggest influences on the news scene are commercialism (ratings and the drive for profit), competition (from other media), and the community context (especially political ties).

Jensen, C. (1995). *Censored: The news that didn't make the news—and why.* New York: Four Walls Eight Windows. (332 pages with index)

Begun by the author in 1976, Project Censored invites journalists, scholars, librarians, and the general public to nominate stories that they feel were not reported adequately during that year. From the hundreds of submissions, the list is reduced to 25 based on "the amount of coverage the story received, the national or international importance of the issue, the reliability of the source, and the potential impact the story may have" (p. 15). A blue-ribbon panel of judges then selects the top 10 censored stories for the year.

Lee, M. A., & Solomon, N. (1990). *Unreliable sources: A guide to detecting bias in news media.* New York: Carol. (420 pages with index)

Written by two journalists, this book is a strong criticism of American journalistic practices. The central thesis is that economic norms govern the news much more than the quest to fulfill the public's right to know.

Postman, N., & Powers, S. (1992). *How to watch TV news.* New York: Penguin. (178 pages with index)

These authors argue that what television news says it is presenting and what it actually presents are two different things. The authors say that TV presents the important happenings of the day that all citizens should know. But what it really presents is superficial constructions designed to create large audiences for advertisers. The authors say that for people to prepare themselves to watch television news, they need to prepare their minds through extensive reading about the world.

Schudson, M. (2003). *The sociology of news.* New York: Norton. (261 pages including end notes and index)

Schudson sharpens and clarifies many points in the argument that journalists "not only report reality but create it" (p. 2). He digs deep into the issue and offers explanations about how the news construction occurs and the effect those constructions have on the public. After providing a brief history of journalism, he identifies two criticisms as being especially salient today. The first is that news coverage of politics is critical and this promotes cynicism in the public. Second, news itself has gone soft; that is, it is a mix of information with entertainment rather than a legitimate effort to explain complex situations.

Shoemaker, P. J., & Reese, S. D. (1996). *Mediating the message: Theories of influences on mass media content* (2nd ed.). White Plains, NY: Longman. (313 pages)

In this book, the authors review research on media content and build toward a theory with assumptions, propositions, and hypotheses. The strength of this book is its broad look at research on news. It includes much empirical social science work, many industry examples and anecdotes, and an entire chapter on a cultural approach to ideology. It has two shortcomings. First, its span purports to be all media content, but it focuses almost exclusively on news. Once we get to Chapter 5, there is almost nothing on entertainment content. And nowhere is there anything on ad content. Also, the focus is limited to the media of television and newspapers. A second limitation is that there is really nothing new here. Their "theory" is really several lists.

Tuchman, G. (1978). *Making news: A study in the construction of reality.* New York: Free Press. (244 pages)

The author hung out in newsrooms over a 10-year period to find out how news workers constructed reality. She found that news workers developed a code of professionalism that was based on the interests of the organizations they worked for and that the central concept of this professionalism is the "news frame." The news frame is what news workers use to put up to events to determine whether those events "fit" as news.

**Exercise 7.1** Practicing Analyzing the News

1. Take a blank sheet of paper and draw the structure of Table 7.2 on it. That is, create two columns: label one column "Skills" and the other column "Knowledge." Now create four rows, labeling them "Cognitive," "Emotion," "Aesthetic," and "Moral." Your table should have eight blocks. Make a copy of this table so that you have two of them.

2. Watch a news story on television. Videotape the story so that you can watch it more than once.

3. After a single viewing, write down the skills and knowledge you needed to achieve a basic minimal understanding of what the story says. Think in terms of your everyday viewing of news, where you just want to monitor the surface facts to keep up with the day's major events.

4. Think about the skills and knowledge you would need to achieve a much more complete understanding about the meaning of the event in the news story. Think in terms of what it would take for you to be an expert on the event. This may require you to view the tape several times.

5. Look at what you have written in response to Question 4. Does it differ much from what you have written in response to Question 3? How much detail do you have in each of the eight blocks? With which blocks did you struggle the most? Why do you think you struggled there?

6. Compare the results of your tables with those of a friend. Did your friend have more details in certain blocks compared to yours? If so, did that additional detail extend your thinking? The more people's work you compare, the more you can see a range of differences.

**Exercise 7.2**   Inferring News Workers' Decisions

Gather together three or four newspapers for the same day—the more the better.

1. Look at the composition of the first page across those newspapers, and think about the differences and similarities of news perspective.
   a. What are the major stories in terms of placement and size?
   b. What pictures and graphics are used? Are they used to present substance, or are they used merely to make the page more appealing to the eye?
   c. How much of the front pages is composed of non-news matter?

2. Read the major news stories.
   a. What criteria must have been used to select them?
   b. What types of elements are emphasized in the stories? What are the facts that make this story news? What facts provide background context?
   c. Is the story balanced, or are obvious viewpoints ignored?

3. Look at the sections of the newspapers.
   a. Which sections are there? (such as sports, women, business, etc.)
   b. Look at how the space is allocated. How much space is given to ads? How much to hard news? How much to soft, entertainment-type news?

4. What happened within the last 24 hours that did not get covered?

5. In summary, which of these newspapers do you think is the best and why?

6. Later today, listen to some news on the radio and watch some on television. How is the news different in these media compared to newspapers?

**Exercise 7.3**    Exercising Your Skills

1. Think of some current event of interest to you. Now pretend you are an editor of a newspaper. What elements would you want to have in the story?
   a. What sources would you want to interview?
   b. What facts and figures would you want to gather?
   c. What historical contextual factors would you want?
   d. Would you want visuals—graphics or photographs?

# CHAPTER 8

# Advertising

**Key Idea:** We live in a culture saturated with advertising messages. Some popular criticisms of advertising form the public discourse, but the issues of more important concerns lie at a deeper level.

Let's begin with the question: What are the products of advertising? Some of you might interpret this to mean what the clients of the ad agencies want to sell—laundry soaps, cars, soft drinks, hamburgers, and so on. Others might think that the products are the ads we see—after all, that is what the people in the industry create and show to us constantly. Both of these interpretations have some truth to them on the surface, but both miss the point of the real nature of advertising. The most important product of advertising is you.

Advertisers have trained you and all members of the public to give them your time, attention, and money. Advertisers have spent hundreds of billions of dollars over your lifetime to craft special messages that have put hundreds of thousands of images, jingles, ideas, and desires into your memory banks. They have done this with your permission and even your blessing. And they have even convinced you to pay them for conditioning you.

## Advertising Is Pervasive

Our country is saturated with advertising. With about 6% of the world's population, the United States absorbs almost half of the world's advertising expenditure. We are literally surrounded by ads constantly (see Table 8.1). Estimates range from 300 to 1,500 for the number of ads that each of us is exposed to per day (Jones, 2004). Even if we take the low end of this range, that is about 110,000 messages each year or almost 20 ads for every waking hour.

Each year, the amount of money spent on advertising grows dramatically. In 1900, about $500 million was spent on all forms of advertising in the United States. By 1940, it was $2 billion, so it took 40 years to multiply four times. In 1980, it was $60 billion, or a growth of 30 times in those 40 years. By 2000, it had grown to more than $220 billion per year. These numbers are so large that they are difficult to comprehend. Let's break down the expenditures

*(Text continued on page 136)*

---

**Table 8.1**     Pervasiveness of Advertising in America

---

**Newspapers**

- Sixty percent of the typical newspaper is advertising. Newspapers are now primarily vehicles for ads more so than for news. For example, the *New York Times* Sunday edition contains 350 pages of ads.
- Despite the growth in the size of most newspapers, the space given to the news (the news hole) has remained the same. Newspapers have given about the same amount of space to news content since 1910, but because the overall size of newspapers doubled during that time, the percentage of the newspaper that contains news has shrunk by half.

---

*(Continued)*

**Table 8.1** (Continued)

**Film**

- Movie theaters bombard viewers with ads. A series of ads is projected on their screens while the audience waits for the show to begin. When the film begins, there are usually ads for the theater's concession stand. The ticket a person buys usually has an ad on it.
- Films themselves are full of ads in the form of paid product placements. Product placement in Hollywood movies took off in 1982, when Reese's Pieces were shown in the movie *ET* and their sales increased by 300%. Huggies paid $100,000 to be the diaper shown in *Baby Boom* (1987). *Menace II Society* (1993) was one of the biggest advertising features, with 10 brands of drinks (340 images), 8 car brands (20 images), 3 types of tobacco/drugs (15 images), and many other products, including clothing, candy, magazines, and condom brands clearly shown (Sayre & King, 2003). Other prominent examples of product placement are Lays potato chips in *Poltergeist*, Wheaties in *Rocky III*, Budweiser in *Tootsie*, and Milk Duds and Zagnut in *48 Hours*. In *Santa Claus—The Movie*, McDonald's paid $1 million to the filmmakers to have a scene set in a specially constructed McDonald's restaurant; McDonald's also spent $18 million on promotion and network advertising. Some films have up to 46 different products prominently displayed and paid for by their sponsors (Fuller, 1997). There are more than 30 companies operating in Hollywood to place products within movies and TV shows.

**Radio**

- Some radio stations present 40 minutes of ads per hour.

**Television**

- On television, there are now more than 17 minutes of ads and promotions each hour on broadcast television (Croteau & Hoynes, 2001). Most television stations present at least 40 ads per hour. In primetime, the big 4 networks (ABC, CBS, Fox, and NBC) air 14 minutes and 15 seconds of ads and promos on average during every hour, and in daytime, the time is even higher, with the average across all channels being almost 19 minutes per hour. From 1965 to 1995, ads on network TV got shorter and more frequent—the average length shrunk from 53.1 seconds to 25.4 seconds, and the number of ads per minute increased from 1.1 to 2.4 (Koenenn, 1997).
- The average American household has the TV on more than 47 hours per week. Out of this time, about 12 hours are ads. By the time a person leaves high school, the typical American has seen more than a quarter of a million TV commercials.
- Ads are embedded in some TV shows. CBS's *The Price Is Right* gets $1 million in payments from product producers each year—this is in addition to the prizes the manufacturers give away on the show.
- TV advertising is now in airports, in elevators in high-end hotels, and in doctors' waiting rooms—all beaming messages to captive audiences (Croteau & Hoynes, 2001).

**Computers**

- The Internet Advertising Bureau says that in 1998, advertising on the Internet neared $2 billion. Almost half of this money came from computers and software advertisers (Maddox, 1999). This figure continues to grow dramatically each year.

## Nonmedia

- Ads are on the sides of buildings, on taxis and buses, and even on the clothing of people walking the streets.
- Third-class mail (junk mail) in the 1980s grew 13 times faster than the population (Koenenn, 1997).
- There are now talking billboards that are fitted with a low-power radio transmitter that tells motorists where to tune for more information on the product advertised on the billboard (Horowitz, 1996).
- Ads have even moved into public toilets. Chicago's United Center sports arena charges advertisers $1,000 a year for an 8-by-11-inch space on its bathroom walls (Horowitz, 1996).
- Ads appear on police cars in Oxnard, California, where the city council approved a money-raising plan to sell advertising space on police cruisers ("Police Cars," 1995).
- Pepsi-Cola has produced the first TV commercial in space by paying Russia to have its cosmonauts aboard its space station, *Mir*, deploying a can of Pepsi into space (Horowitz, 1996). PepsiCo, owners of Pizza Hut, have also sponsored the Russian space program in another way. In November 1999, the Russians launched a Proton rocket that had a 30-foot logo of Pizza Hut painted on it ("Pizza Pie in the Sky," 1999).
- Sporting events are themselves vehicles for ads. Even the Olympics are advertising events. In 1984, the Olympic games in Los Angeles became the first to be supported entirely by commercial sponsorship, and it made a big profit. VISA alone spent $25 million on the rights and on promotions. One by one, all major sporting events are turning to sponsorships for funding.
- Ads are in public schools. Whittle Communications gives to all participating public schools the equipment needed to receive satellite programming and provides them with a 12-minute news program daily. Inserted in those programs are 2 minutes of ads paid for by companies interested in getting their ad messages in front of youngsters. About 65% of the public in national polls objected to this, but Whittle went ahead in the schools that did not object (Turow, 1992). Also, by the late 1990s, Channel One was in more than 12,000 schools in the United States and commanded a daily audience of more than 8 million children. The schools get television sets for each classroom, VCRs, and a satellite link along with the programming. Channel One rents this captive audience out to advertisers (Croteau & Hoynes, 2001).
- Even the pope has been commercialized. The Vatican acknowledges that the pope's visits are costly, so they have agreed to sponsorship. The pope's 4-day visit to Mexico in the winter of 1999 was sponsored by Frito-Lay and PepsiCo. Some Catholics criticized this practice. But the church defends it.
- In Sweden, advertisers have tried interrupting personal phone calls with ads.
- Ads are everywhere: stickers on fresh fruit, walls of toilet stalls, gas pumps, backs of store receipts, tickets to theaters and sporting events, and church bulletins (Croteau & Hoynes, 2001).

(Continued from page 133)

by number of people in the population. In 1940, the industry spent $16 on each person in this country; by 1980, it was $260, and now it is more than $900 per person per year.

An advertiser who wants to introduce a new product and break through the existing clutter to get consumers to realize that there is a new product on the market must spend about a $50-million minimum to introduce a new product in grocery or drug stores nationally. Of course, the new advertisements add to the clutter, making it even more expensive for the next product introduction. All of this behavior serves to increase the clutter exponentially. And we are still in a growth cycle.

Why can we expect continued growth? Because we—the public—do not mind all this advertising. Of course, we sometimes criticize certain ads we don't like, and sometimes we get upset when we watch television and have our shows repeatedly interrupted by commercial breaks. Americans have positive beliefs and attitudes about advertising. About 45% say they have a generally favorable attitude toward advertising, whereas only 15% have an unfavorable attitude. The rest are neutral. Thus, advertisers have done a good job conditioning us to accept the flood of advertising messages with few complaints.

Our criticisms are minor compared to our unthinking support of advertising. By "unthinking" support, I mean that most of us do not realize how much advertising exposure we experience everyday and how it has shaped our attitudes and behaviors. We accept the saturation, and we allow our behavior to be shaped by it. I'll present two examples of this point to help you understand how much you have been influenced by advertising.

The first example deals with how much money we spend on advertised products when we have a choice of buying brands that are unadvertised and sell for much less money. For example, Jones (2004) points out that Cheerios, which is the leading brand in cold cereals, has a unit price of $5.10 per pound, but most stores sell a very similar cereal as a house brand for about $2.66 per pound.

> The taste of the store brand is quite satisfactory, although most people would slightly prefer the taste of Cheerios. But Cheerios is 92 percent more expensive. Consumers are perfectly aware of the prices of the two brands because the cereals are displayed alongside one another, yet Cheerios outsells the store brand by about four to one. (p. 25)

The minor difference in taste alone does not account for the fact that 80% of consumers spend the extra money to buy the advertised brand. It appears that Cheerios advertising has made most consumers believe that something special about Cheerios warrants the very high price relative to the same cereal in the house brand box.

A second example is how much you voluntarily participate as an advertiser. Look at the clothing you have on now. How many clothing logos are you displaying on your shirt, pants, shoes, hat, book bag, and so on? You are advertising those products everywhere you go. How much are those companies paying you to advertise for them? Had you bought the same piece of clothing without the prized logo, it would have cost you less money. Therefore, you have chosen to pay more for the privilege of wearing a particular brand. This is a good deal for those manufacturers who have you working for them *and* having *you* pay *them!*

# Popular Surface Criticisms

Over the years, there has been public criticism of advertising for all sorts of reasons. Six of these types are analyzed in this chapter. With each of these issues, we will start with the surface criticism on which the public generally fixates. Then we will analyze each in more depth. Through this analysis, you should learn two types of things. First, you should learn more about the nature of advertising and its potential power over you. Second, you will learn more about your own opinions and behaviors concerning advertising.

## Advertising Manipulates Us Into Buying Things We Don't Need

This is a popular surface criticism. Parents say this to their children who pester them for the toys, candy, and cereals the children see advertised on television.

How do we define a need? If we stick to basic survival needs, then, yes, advertisers ask us to buy many things beyond our absolute basic needs for survival. At base, we really only need a set of clothes, a shelter, and some daily food.

The psychologist Abraham Maslow has pointed out that there are levels of needs beyond survival. Once humans have met the basic survival needs, they become concerned with other needs such as safety needs, social needs, and self-actualization needs. We need to feel accepted by friends and colleagues. Dressing right helps with this. For social needs, we need many different outfits of clothes. We need a certain type of car. We need to live in a certain kind of home. We need certain kinds of foods and beverages to go along with our lifestyles. We use all these products to define ourselves in social situations. Are these products luxuries or necessities? Each person must define what is a necessity for himself or herself.

## Advertising Makes Us Too Materialistic

Some critics claim that advertising makes us too materialistic. How much is *too* much? Some people believe we should conserve natural resources and live at a lower level of consumption. Other people believe that we should always strive for more of everything; if it looks like we might run short of resources, we will be able to figure out a way to solve the problem.

With less than 6% of the world's population, the United States consumes nearly 30% of the planet's resources. Americans can choose from more than 30,000 supermarket items, including 200 kinds of cereal. Do we really need all these material products?

Americans say they are dissatisfied with materialism despite all the abundance. In surveys, more than 80% of Americans typically agree that most of us buy and consume far more than we need. And about two thirds agree that Americans cause many of the world's environmental problems because we consume more resources and produce more waste than anyone else in the world (Koenenn, 1997). Yet we continue to consume at a greater rate each year.

Thus, the public is schizophrenic about consumption. We believe we are too materialistic but keep asking for more products.

## Advertising Is Deceptive

Perhaps the most damaging criticism of advertising is that it is generally deceptive. In everyday language, we think of deception as lying. Do ads lie? The answer is no in the sense that lying is presenting a blatant falsehood. Advertisers know that if they present a claim they cannot support, they can be fined, so they avoid making explicit claims that can be checked for truth. Also, major advertisers know that their products differ from their competitors' products in very minor ways, so there is no point in making claims that their product is clearly superior in some way. Instead, advertisers are fond of using what is called "puffery," which is the making of implicit claims that cannot be tested for truth. For example, advertisers will claim that their product is the best in their class without specifying what that class is. Advertisers puff up their products with exaggerations that are expressions of opinion rather than claims of some objective quality or characteristic of the product. Puffery gives the illusion to viewers that they are being given important information about the product, but this illusion evaporates when we look more closely at the ad. For example, have you ever seen an ad where any of the following claims were made: "the best of its kind," "the most beautiful," or "the finest"? These slogans at first seem to be telling us something, but upon closer examination, they are empty claims because they cannot be tested.

Also, some ads present implied superiority claims, such as "Nothing beats a great pair of L'eggs" (pantyhose), "The ones to beat" (Chrysler K cars), and "Nobody does it better" (Winston Lights cigarettes). On the surface, these slogans imply that their products are superior, but when we examine them more closely, we realize that they are not really making a clear comparison with another product.

Another element of puffery is when an ad tells the truth—but not the whole truth. For example, many brands that are labeled as a fruit juice drink contain only 10% fruit juice; the ad contains an element of truth, but it is misleading. Also, ads for many cereals show a brand as "part of this complete breakfast," which features several nutritious foods such as fruit, bread, and milk. This statement is literally truthful, but almost none of the nutrition in the claim comes from the cereal.

How do advertisers use puffery to suppress the truth? Jamieson and Campbell (1988) list the following tactics:

- Pseudo-claims: An example of this is "X fights cavities," but we are not told how. Is it a chemical in the toothpaste, the movement of the brush on the teeth, or the habit of brushing?

- Comparison with an unidentified other: "X has better cleaning action." Better than what? Better than another brand? Better than not cleaning? There is an implied comparison that makes the product sound superior, but it really is a meaningless claim.

- Comparison of the product to its earlier form: "X is new and improved!" Again, on the surface, this seems like a good thing—until we start thinking about it. What was wrong with the old version? And what is wrong with this current version that will end up being new and improved again next year?

- Irrelevant comparisons: "X is the best-selling product of its kind." What kind? Maybe *kind* is defined so narrowly that there is only one brand of its kind. Also, maybe it is the best-seller because it is the cheapest or because it wears out so fast.

- Pseudo-survey: "Four out of five dentists surveyed said they recommend X." Who are these five? Maybe they were paid to recommend it.

- Juxtaposition: A smiling person holds a product so that viewers associate happiness with the product.

Thus, advertising messages are designed to use puffery to trick us into believing there is more to the product than there really is. They give us the illusion of making a strong claim when in fact the claims are weak or nonexistent.

This leaves us stuck in the place between truth and a lie. Although most advertising is not technically false, it cannot be considered true (Preston, 1994). The ads cannot be regulated because they are not technically false. But neither are they true. Apparently, Americans regard this puffery as a form of deception because in public opinion polls, 80% of people feel that television advertising offers primarily deceptive persuasion. Also, only 17% regard TV advertising as a source of good information (Norris, 1983; Soley & Reid, 1983).

## Companies Manipulate Us Through Subliminal Advertising

Is there such a thing as subliminal persuasion; that is, are there subliminal messages that have a powerful effect on us? To answer this question, we first need to be clear about what *subliminal* means. The popularized version of subliminal persuasion reflects a conscious effort on the part of the sender to deceive viewers by adding something to a message that is not consciously perceivable by the audience—but the person's unconscious mind sees that "extra message." For example, in the 1950s, James Vickery inserted messages of "Eat Popcorn" and "Drink Coke" into a theatrical film and claimed that the theater audience bought much more popcorn and Coke, even though no one reported seeing the ads because they were projected too quickly. Later, it was found that Vickery's results were a hoax. But this story has entered our folklore, and many people believe that unscrupulous advertisers are exposing us to subliminal messages all the time.

The idea of subliminal advertising having an effect on us is a hoax. The word *subliminal* means below our threshold to perceive. For example, the human eye cannot see an image if it is shown for less than about one sixteenth of a second—that is below our line of ability to perceive an image. This is why we perceive movies as a smooth flow of moving images when, in actuality, what is being projected on the screen is a series of still shots. If those shots are projected at about 12 per second, we see flicker in between shots, but we still perceive motion. Once those individual images are projected at 16 per second, the flicker disappears; that is, it happens too fast to register an impression on us. The flicker between the individual images is still there, but we can no longer perceive it. Hollywood films are projected at 24 or more frames per second. At this speed, there is no chance for any individual frame to register a unique impression on us. So even if an advertiser placed an ad in 1 frame every second, each of those exposures would be too brief to cross the line of our ability to perceive them. If our sense organs cannot perceive an image, then it can have no effect on us. I'll further clarify this point with an audio example. You can train a dog to come to you when you blow a dog whistle, which emits a very high-pitched sound that the dog can hear but you cannot. The pitch of the sound is outside of the hearing range of humans; that is, the sound does not cross the line into our perceptual ability to hear it. Can you train a person to come to you every time you blow a dog whistle? If people cannot hear the whistle, they cannot know when you are blowing it, and therefore, they cannot respond to a stimulus that they cannot perceive. Thus, subliminal stimuli—because they are outside a human's ability to perceive them—can have no effect on humans.

When some people use the term *subliminal advertising effects*, what they really mean is "unconscious effects of advertising." This unconscious influence *is* a powerful effect with which we should be concerned. There is a difference between subliminal and unconscious. With subliminal, we do not perceive the message, but with unconscious, we do perceive the message but do not think about it; thus, the message gets put into our subconscious without us knowing it.

Advertising alters reality by creating worlds that do not exist and makes us want to be a part of those worlds. Advertising does this by showing us that we can change our attractiveness, body image, smell, whiteness of smile, relationships, self-image, and degree of happiness by using certain products.

Also, by using technology, advertisers can make the world look different. They can electronically morph people's appearance. They can insert their products into old movies. They can insert their products into real locations; for example, at sporting events, they can electronically paint the field with their product's logo so the television viewing audience can see it even though the logo does not exist at the stadium.

Advertisers can alter our perceptions of what is real. For example, until about the 1970s, advertisers used White actors almost exclusively, thus making audiences believe that minorities did not exist or, if they did, that they were unimportant. Then in the 1970s, African Americans began appearing on TV and eventually grew to about 10% of the actors in ads and in television shows; however, other ethnic minorities are still almost invisible in ads (Mastro & Stern, 2003). Because television commercials not only promote consumption but also shape images and "sustain group boundaries that come to be taken for granted" (Coltrane & Messineo, 2000), it is important to consider how such representations might influence racial/ethnic minority viewers.

Because advertisers continually present the same kinds of messages, over the years, we also learn many general lessons about consumption and how to solve problems. Although each ad is trying to get you to buy a particular product, at a deeper level, all ads are teaching you lessons about who you should be and how you can get there. To illustrate, let's consider an example of an ad for toothpaste, which on the surface is only an ad for a particular toothpaste. But it comes with several layers of deeper meaning embedded in the message. At a deeper level, the ad is a message about the importance of health. At an even deeper level, it conveys a message about consumerism—that is, the ad tells you that you need to buy something to clean your teeth; you cannot simply use water to brush your teeth. Also at a deeper level is implied permission to eat foods that might contribute to decay because as long as you use the product to brush your teeth, you need not feel guilty about eating things that promote tooth decay. You can see that a "simple" ad for a toothpaste carries with it several layers of meaning, some of which may be consciously processed (the surface claims made in the particular ad) and some of which are unconsciously processed (how to solve problems, the nature of health, etc.).

## Advertising Is Excessive

As you saw earlier in this chapter, our culture is saturated with advertising. Whether this is excessive requires an evaluative judgment. This means you must have an awareness of what is an acceptable amount. This amount then becomes your standard for excessiveness. If you have a high standard for excessiveness, then you will likely conclude that the amount of advertising has not yet reached that level, and therefore advertising is not excessive.

In public opinion polls, when people are asked, "Do you think there is too much advertising on television?" about 70% of people say yes. But if they are asked, "Do you think that your being shown all this advertising is a fair price for you to pay to be able to see 'free' television?" again 70% will say yes (Miller, 1989).

But television is hardly free; it just seems free. Now a large part of the cost of many products is advertising. For example, when you buy soap or toothpaste, about 35% of the cost goes for advertising. Also, most households now have cable television; these house-holds pay for television, and they also pay more when they buy advertised products.

Is advertising excessive? You must decide whether you are getting value for what you are paying for in terms of better entertainment, news, and products. For most people in their everyday lives, they act as if the amount of advertising is not excessive. Then, when they are presented with figures about how much advertising saturation there is in our cul-ture, they are shocked. But then they return to their everyday lives and continue to act as if the huge amount of advertising is not excessive.

### Advertising Perpetuates Stereotypes

Almost all advertisers must use stereotypes. A 15-second television commercial can-not develop a character in all the rich detail needed to make us feel that the character is not a two-dimensional stereotype. Advertisers must present their messages very quickly. This requires simplifying everything, including characters.

When we analyze this criticism, we can see that the problem has less to do with stereotyping than it has to do with whether portrayals are negative or positive. If an entire class of people (such as all women or all African Americans) is portrayed with negative characteristics, then it is reasonable to argue that this is bad. If all young blonde women are portrayed as dumb, this is a negative stereotype and is offensive to many people. However, if an entire class of people is portrayed as being attractive, smart, and successful, it is not likely that people would be offended by this, although this too is a stereotype.

# Social Responsibility Versus Economic Responsibility

Sometimes, advertisers are criticized for not being responsible. What this criticism really means is that they are not *socially* responsible. And advertisers often do things to warrant such criticism. For example, for 50 years, liquor manufacturers had not used television to advertise their products because of a sense of social responsibility, in a voluntary attempt to protect children and teenagers from seeing liquor ads. This was an admirable display of social responsibility. But during the fall of 1996, Joseph E. Seagram & Sons began airing spots for two whisky brands on independent TV stations around the country. The com-pany was motivated by the single desire to increase sales and felt it was bad business to continue avoiding the use of the powerful advertising medium of television. In defense of his company's move, Tod Rodriguez, general sales manager, said, "There are a lot worse things than alcohol ads on TV" (Gellene, 1996, p. D2). Many people found this incident very upsetting and the Seagram Company's reasoning very self-serving. Incidents such as this illustrate the shift away from social responsibility toward marketing.

Anheuser-Busch—the number-one brewer—found beer sales flat in 1998. Its typical target audience was young men, who are typically reached in sporting shows. To increase sales, Anheuser-Busch decided to increase beer drinking among women, who accounted for only about 17% of its sales. So Anheuser-Busch decided to break its self-imposed barrier of not targeting women in the television audience and began advertising in daytime TV. A consultant to the company said, "It should be done. For the beer people not to be selling full-bore ahead on one gender is absurd" (Arndorfer, 1998, p. 8).

Until the 1980s, pharmaceutical companies marketed their drugs only to physicians. Then in the 1980s, they began marketing to the general population to get people to request certain drugs from their doctors. What this does is extend the belief that people should live a perfect life, free of all physical and psychological barriers. This is especially the case with ads for antidepressants, in which people are told they never need to feel depressed (Critser, 2004). Pharmaceutical companies knew they could increase sales of prescription drugs if they went directly to people and bypassed physicians. In this way, people would imagine symptoms and put pressure on their doctors to prescribe the advertised drugs.

Psychologists, parents, and social critics are concerned about protecting children from a barrage of advertising. Recall from Chapter 4 that young children have not developed to a point where they can understand certain elements about ads and therefore cannot protect themselves. Also, children have had less experience with products than have adults, and therefore children are not as sophisticated in making decisions about how to spend their money. However, from an advertiser's point of view, children are regarded as an important market. American kids (ages 4–18) have a combined annual allowance of $70 billion, which is the total of Finland's gross domestic product ("Material Kids," 1994). The younger children are targeted with ads on Saturday mornings, when almost all the ads are for toys or food. Among the food ads, 90% are for junk food, such as sugary cereals, candy bars, potato chips, and fast food (Wharton, 1991). By 1998, more than $2 billion was spent on advertising to children. This was 20 times more than in 1988. The average American child now sees more than 30,000 TV commercials per year (*Time*, 1999, August 16).

Children are regarded as a highly desirable target market for many advertisers who are spending more money each year to convince children to consume their products. For example, tobacco companies have been targeting young people (ages 14–24) for decades as a prime market. In 1991, the Joe Camel campaign was launched to appeal to teens by focusing a lot of ads around high schools and colleges. In 5 years, the sale of Camels to teens went from $6 million to $476 million (Holland, 1998). Teenagers are three times as likely as adults to respond to cigarette ads; 79% smoke brands depicted as fun, sexy, and popular ("Study Links Teen Smoking," 1996).

The problem of a lack of social responsibility is not limited to how some advertisers aggressively target women or children. The problem is much broader and extends to the very nature of all advertising. For example, Harvard economist and social critic John Kenneth Galbraith (Arens, 1999) argues that advertising is fundamentally a negative force on society because it serves to shift a society's resources from benefiting the public to benefiting only individuals, and this leads to a great deal of waste. When we sell large cars and SUVs to individuals who rarely travel with many passengers, there is a waste of fuel, and we need to build more and more expensive highways and parking lots. But if that money were put into public transportation, the resources would be used much more efficiently, and everyone in the public would benefit more. Advertising is what drives private demand. If it weren't for advertising, consumers would buy much less, and some of the resources that currently go into satisfying private demand could be reallocated for the common good, such as public education, public parks, and public transportation.

In contrast to Galbraith, historian David Potter (Arens, 1999) regards advertising as a positive force on society. He sees advertising as a social institution comparable to the school and the church in its power to convey information and to teach values. An important value in America is the transforming of natural resources into abundance. Advertising supports this value and reinforces our inherent need to consume and enjoy it.

Potter, however, does express some concern that advertising has no overriding responsibility to society. Other institutions (such as the family, education, religion, etc.) are altruistic; they try to improve the individual and society. Advertising is very different. Advertising is selfish; its only responsibility is to serve the marketing objectives of the company that pays for it.

# Becoming More Literate

With entertainment and news-type messages, we are typically more active in searching for exposures and processing the information in those messages compared to advertising messages. In contrast, we encounter almost all advertising messages in a state of automaticity, where we are unaware of how much exposure we are experiencing. For example, we plan our exposures to the morning newspaper, our favorite TV shows, films, books, and magazine stories. We rarely plan to expose ourselves to an ad; however, exposures to ads still occur at a rapid pace as we are searching for entertainment and news messages.

To protect ourselves from all this unplanned advertising exposure, we remain in a state of automatic processing so we don't have to pay attention to all of the ads. However, exposure to the ads continues even though we are not paying attention to them, and this makes our exposure unconscious, which is what most advertisers want. During unconscious exposure, advertisers can plant their messages into our subconscious, where they gradually shape our definitions for attractiveness, sex appeal, relationships, cleanliness, health, success, hunger, body shape, problems, and happiness. For example, we might have the radio on in the car as we concentrate on driving, and when ads come on, we do not pay much attention. Then later, we find ourselves humming a jingle, or a word phrase occurs to us, or we pass by a store and "remember" that there is a sale going on there. These flashes of sounds, words, and ideas emerge from our subconscious, where they had been put by ads that we did not pay attention to. Over time, all those images, sounds, and ideas build patterns in our subconscious and profoundly shape the way we think about ourselves and the world.

Almost all exposure to advertising is unconscious, yet it still works. Advertising works because it gets into the audience's unconscious without the audience attending to those messages and analyzing them. A very sophisticated marketing research industry spends more than $7 billion each year to find out how to shape people's needs and behaviors; this is more money than the federal government spends each year on all of education.

To increase your media literacy about advertising, you need to have elaborate knowledge structures about advertising and about your own needs. To build a stronger knowledge structures about ads, do the exercises at the end of this chapter. Exercise 8.1 will help you notice more of the advertising in your environment. Exercise 8.2 will help strengthen your skills and thereby make you more in control of how advertising influences you. Exercise 8.2 will also help you become more aware of your needs. As you work through the exercises, think about what ads are really selling, what the intended effect of the ad is, and what your needs really are.

## What Are Ads Really Selling?

Ads are designed to present a single product claim. This claim is presented as the reason you should buy the advertised product, that is, the product will do something of value for you. That something of value can be in the form of a physical feature, a functional feature, or a characterizational feature. Physical features focus attention on the product itself and its ingredients (e.g., Buy our toothpaste because it contains XW7, which is the strongest decay-fighting chemical ever!). Functional features focus attention on how the product is used (e.g., Buy our toothpaste because it comes in an easy-to-use pump!). Characterizational features focus attention on the psychological consequences of the consumption (e.g., Buy our toothpaste because it will make you feel safe from tooth decay—no matter what you eat!).

Ads usually present one simple claim and emphasize that over and over. If the claim focuses on a physical or functional feature, it is very easy to spot. Characterizational ads are more ambiguous. They are usually designed to make you feel something, then link that feeling with the product.

## What Is the Intended Effect of the Ad?

Most people think that ads are designed to convince people to buy the product. Very little of the advertising we see has this intention. Many ads, especially those for new products, are intending only to establish our awareness that the product exists. Some ads are designed to create an emotion in us and link that emotion with the product. Some ads are designed to inoculate us against the claims of competitors so that when we see an ad for one of their competitors, we will not come under its influence. But the most prevalent intention of ads is reinforcement. Most ads are aimed at target groups of people who already use the product. Thus, the advertisement is designed to remind those customers that the product still exists and that it is a good one. People usually remember ads for products they already buy, so most of the effect of advertising is one of reinforcement of existing attitudes and behaviors. Thus, reinforcement is the powerful effect of advertising. Most ads are designed to make people feel good about the products they already have bought so that they will buy them again.

## What Are Your Needs?

The more you are aware of your needs, the more you can use advertising to control your life. If you are not aware of your needs, the constant flood of advertising messages will create and shape your needs—often without you knowing it. Stop reading this chapter now and go to Exercise 8.3.

How did you do on Part I? Were you able to come up with a long list of needs, or could you think only of one or two? Was it easy or hard to rank order your needs? Then in Part II, were you surprised by how many products you have brought into your home? Were you surprised about how many were well-advertised brands?

Now ask yourself, How aware am I of my needs? Make a comparison of your rank-ordered list from Part I with how you spend your money and time as indicated in the inventories in Part II. Is your primary need (from Part I) reflected in the inventories of your possessions and time (from Part II)? For example, let's say your number one–ranked need was health. Did the inventory of your closet reveal more clothes for workouts than any other type of clothes? Did your inventory of your kitchen reveal an absence of highly advertised, high-caloric, high-fat, high-sugar, high-salt snacks? Did your inventory of your bathroom reveal more products for sore muscles or more for beauty? Is your toothpaste a decay preventer or a tooth whitener? Did the inventory of your time reveal that you are very active or mostly passive?

If your self-reported needs (from Part I) matched closely your inventories (from Part II), then congratulations! You are aware of your needs and know how to spend your resources to satisfy them. But if there are discrepancies between your self-reported needs and where you spend your money and time, then you have a faulty sense of your needs. You might be telling yourself that your needs are A, B, and C, but your real needs are X, Y, and Z. You are satisfying your real needs even though you are not aware of what they really are. More typically, discrepancies exist because you are not able to satisfy your needs; that is, you are very aware of what your needs are. But when you go to the store, you end up buying lots of things that really do not address those needs, but you hope they will because you want to believe the puffery in the ads. But the will to believe is not enough. As time goes by, you become frustrated that you cannot fulfill your major needs, although it seems like you are doing what society (as channeled by advertisements) is telling you to do.

**Table 8.2**     Types of Skills and Knowledge Needed to Deal With Advertising Messages in a
Media-Literate Manner

|  | *SKILLS* | *KNOWLEDGE* |
|---|---|---|
| COGNITIVE | Ability to analyze an advertisement to identify key elements of persuasion | |
| | Ability to compare and contrast key elements of persuasion in the ad with facts in your real-world knowledge structure | Knowledge on topic from many sources (media and real world) |
| | Ability to evaluate veracity of claims in the ad | |
| EMOTIONAL | Ability to analyze the feelings of people in the ad | |
| | Ability to put one's self into the position of different people in the ad | Recall from personal experiences how it feels to have a need for the advertised product |
| AESTHETIC | Ability to analyze the craft and artistic elements of the ad | Knowledge of writing, graphics, photography, and so on |
| | Ability to compare and contrast the artistry used to craft this ad with that used to craft other types of ads | Knowledge of successful and unsuccessful ads and the elements that contributed to those qualities |
| MORAL | Ability to analyze the moral elements of an ad | Knowledge of criticism of advertising and knowledge of how ads can manipulate our attitudes and behaviors |
| | Ability to evaluate the ethical responsibilities of advertisers | Highly developed moral code |

# Conclusion

Some people regard advertisers as unscrupulous manipulators who will do or say anything to get you to give them your money. They think advertising has changed the culture for the worse by making us too materialistic—creating a throwaway society of products, ideas, and people.

Other people regard advertisers as American heroes who are responsible for keeping the economy fired up by creatively encouraging more and more consumption. This has produced the richest society ever—one with the highest standard of living and the most variety in everything. They see advertising as a glamorous profession for creative people—a fast track to a rewarding career.

Who is right? Is advertising good or bad? What is the myth, and what is the truth? You must decide for yourself. In making such a decision, it is risky to base your decision on a few intuitive impressions. Instead, it is much better to base your decision on a strong knowledge structure. Building such a knowledge structure requires you to be sensitive to the issues of how advertising influences businesses, the economy, critics, the public, and individual consumers—especially children. On almost all of these issues, there is a range of opinion. When you understand that range and the philosophies underlying different positions, you are better able to construct a well-reasoned opinion for yourself.

# Further Reading

Jones, J. P. (2004). *Fables, fashions, and facts about advertising: A study of 28 enduring myths.* Thousand Oaks, CA: Sage. (305 pages, including glossary and index)

This author is a college professor with 25 years' experience working in a major advertising agency. In this book, Jones confronts more than two-dozen beliefs that the public holds about advertising and shows how each of these is faulty.

**Exercise 8.1**     Becoming Sensitized to Advertising

1. How much advertising are you exposed to on a daily basis?

   For one day, carry around a sheet of paper in your pocket and write down every time you are exposed to an advertising message. Record the time, the product advertised, and the channel. Remember channels can be media (newspapers, television, radio, etc.) or other types such as posters (on walls, cars, kiosks, sidewalks, etc.) and ads on clothing (sweatshirts, hats, footwear, etc.).

   How many ads were you exposed to in one day? How many different channels were used? How many of these exposures did you seek out?

2. Watch 1 hour of television and write down each ad. Remember that a promo for a station or a television show counts as an advertisement.

   How many did you record? Were you surprised at the number?

3. Go through your local newspaper page by page and count the ads.

   Are you surprised about how many ads there are? Does this amount bother you—if so, would you be willing to pay more for the newspaper if all ads were eliminated? About 80% of a newspaper's revenue comes from advertising. So if your newspaper currently costs 50 cents, that cost would increase to about $4.00 per issue if subscribers like you had to contribute all the revenue to your newspaper.

4. Get a piece of paper and make two lists. For one, list all the breakfast cereals you can remember. Then turn the paper over and list all the shampoos you can remember.

   Go to a supermarket and count how many different cereals and shampoos are on those shelves. Were you able to name them all? What percentage were you able to name? Of those you did not have on your list, can you recall anything about their advertising campaigns? If so, why do you think you could not remember them when you made your list?

5. Next time you go to the drug store or the supermarket to shop, try buying as many nonadvertised products in place of the advertised brands you usually buy.

   How much money did you save? Are the savings worth it, or do you feel that you have made a big mistake?

6. Run a taste test for your friends. Buy several brands of advertised cola and some obscure brands. Pour different brands into their own cups. Ask your friends to taste each and tell you which cola is in which cup. Could your friends guess the right brands? Were they sure of their choices, or were they making wild guesses?

**Exercise 8.2**    Practicing Media Literacy Skills With Advertising Messages

Look at several print ads from magazines and newspapers. Also, watch several ads on television. Use this set of ads in the following tasks.

1. *Analysis:*
   a. What is the main product claim (reason for buying the product) of the ad?
   b. Is the claim presented explicitly or implicitly (you have to infer it)?
   c. Do any of the ads use puffery?
   d. What is the intention of the ad (awareness, positive emotion, change attitude, inoculation, reinforcement, buying product)?
   e. Look beyond the surface of the ad and the particular product, and then list some values that these ads are teaching.

2. *Compare/Contrast:*
   a. How are product claims the same and different across the ads?
   b. Which product claims show up most often?
   c. How are intentions the same or different across ads?
   d. Which intention do you find most often?

3. *Evaluation:*
   a. In your judgment, which of the claims works best? Why?
   b. In your judgment, which of the claims does not work? Why?

4. *Deduction:* Can you see any patterns in these ads that exemplify any of the criticisms of advertising?

5. *Appreciation:*
   a. Emotional: Were any of the ads able to evoke strong emotions in you? If so, list those emotions and explain how the ad triggered those particular emotions.
   b. Aesthetic: Is there something about the writing, directing, editing, lighting, set design, costuming, or music/sound effects that you found of particular high quality? If so, explain what led you to appreciate that element so much.
   c. Moral: Did any of the ads raise ethical considerations (either explicitly or implicitly)?

**Exercise 8.3**     Needs Inventory

**Part I**

Take out a sheet of paper and write down your needs.

1. Begin by simply listing all your needs as they pop into your head.

2. Once you have a list, organize the elements into categories. Group all like needs together. For example, you might have several social needs (e.g., make more friends, become more popular), health needs (lose weight, exercise more, etc.), career needs, family needs, school needs, and so forth.

3. After you have your categories, rank order your groups. Which set of needs is most important to you? What set is second, and so on?

Now put this paper aside and go on to Part II.

**Part II**

1. Go through your clothes closet. How many changes of clothes (outfits) do you have? How many pairs of shoes?

   If you have one or two changes of clothes, you are operating at a functional level; that is, you are satisfied to protect your body from the elements and for the sake of being modest. If you have many sets of clothes, group them according to your needs; that is, which are your social clothes, your business clothes, your exercise clothes, and so on? Which set of clothes contains the greatest number of outfits? Why? Do you have the most clothes in an area that is the same as what you designated as your highest ranked need area in Part I?

2. Go through your kitchen cabinets and pantry.

   How many prepared foods (in boxes, cans, and bags) do you have compared to natural foods (milk, fresh fruit, fresh vegetables, etc.)? What proportion of those products are advertised brands, and what proportion are unadvertised or generic?

3. Check your bathroom. How many "health and beauty" aids do you have?

   How many of those products are for basic health needs, and how many are image enhancers? What proportion of those products are advertised brands, and what proportion are unadvertised or generic?

4. Think about how you spend your time.

   How much time do you take getting washed, groomed, and dressed each day? How much time do you spend eating and snacking (how many times)? What do you do with your leisure time—are you active in satisfying your needs, or are you passively sitting in front of the TV or listening to music, where you are being told by others what your needs should be?

# KNOWLEDGE STRUCTURES OF MEDIA INDUSTRIES

# CHAPTER 9

# Development of the Mass Media Industries

*Key Idea:* The development of the media industries generally moves from the innovation stage to growth, peak, decline, and then adaptation.

E ach of the mass media industries has a unique history shaped by particular innova-
tors, special needs for consumers, and distinct content. However, the media industries
also follow some consistent patterns. When we focus our attention on those patterns that
are common to all the media industries, we can develop a better appreciation for the nature
of the mass media that have developed over time and why they are so powerful today.

In this chapter, I'm asking you to think like a historian. This does not mean that I want
you to memorize lots of names, facts, and dates. Instead, I want you to focus your attention
on the big picture—that is, the broad patterns about how the media have developed over
time and the factors that have shaped that development. It is the big picture that is important; the details are only important insofar as they help you understand what has happened over time to explain why we have the mass media we do today.

# Patterns of Development

To illustrate the patterns common to all media as they have developed and grown over
time, I use a life cycle metaphor as a template. The life cycle metaphor provides a useful
framework for examining the media industries because it focuses your attention on how
the industries have gone through changes and why. The life cycle metaphor contains
five stages: innovation (or birth), penetration (or growth), peak (maturity), decline, and
adaptation.

## Innovation Stage

Each of the mass media industries began as an innovation. The innovation stage of a
medium's development is characterized by a technological innovation that makes a channel of transmission possible. For example, there would be no film industry if someone had
not invented the motion picture camera and projector. However, technology by itself is not
enough to create a mass medium. A mass medium is more than an invention; there have
been many technological innovations that have failed or that are still sitting on a shelf
somewhere. So the innovation stage is also characterized by *marketing* innovations in
addition to *technological* innovations. This means that someone had to create a business
that would use a new channel of transmission and thus begin building an audience for the
messages flowing through that channel. A successful marketing innovation begins with an
entrepreneur recognizing a need in the population, then using a new technology to satisfy
that need in a way that people begin recognizing the value of the new medium and how
it can help them. To do this, the entrepreneur must have a mass-like orientation; that is,
he or she must exploit the channel's potential to reach very large and broad audiences.
Furthermore, the entrepreneur must use the channel in a way that develops a habit of

exposure among audience members. For example, in the early 1900s, after the motion picture camera and projector were invented, some entrepreneurs turned their living rooms into theaters and began charging people to watch movies. These entrepreneurs found that there was a market for this kind of entertainment, so they took steps to grow that market by renting out storefronts to accommodate larger audiences; then they began renting concert theaters, and then built their own theaters that were primarily for the showing of films. This demand from the theaters led other entrepreneurs to create film production companies to make and distribute films to the theaters. Without all these marketing entrepreneurs who recognized a public need and marketed their services to grow that need into a habit, the invention of the motion picture camera and projector would never have grown into more than a curious invention.

## Penetration Stage

Once an innovation has created a new mass media channel, that channel needs to appeal to a very large, heterogeneous population if it is to be effective as a mass medium. This is called penetration. The penetration stage of a medium's development is characterized by the public's growing acceptance of that medium. The public's reaction to a new medium is based on the medium's ability to satisfy existing needs or to create new needs.

Sometimes, the public has a need that is already being satisfied by existing media, but a new medium comes along that can satisfy those needs better in some way. For example, in the 1940s, people were satisfying their need for entertainment with radio and with films. But then broadcast television came along and was better than radio because it offered pictures in addition to sound; people received more in return for their attention. Also, television was better at satisfying many people's need for entertainment compared to film because television brought many hours of entertainment into a person's home each and every day, so there was no need to leave the house, get a babysitter, find a parking place, or buy a ticket. Television was much more convenient.

A new medium can be successful in the penetration stage by generating a new need or increase an existing need. Television is credited with increasing the American public's appetite for entertainment. The amount of viewing has steadily increased since television was first introduced; now, the average household has the set on for more than 47 hours per week, most of which is entertainment programming.

As each medium grows, it is influenced by factors that shape its growth. These factors include the public's need and desire for the medium, additional innovations that change the appeal of other competing media, political and regulatory constraints, and the economic demands of the private enterprises that own and operate the mass media.

## Peak Stage

The peak stage is reached when the medium commands the most attention from the public and generates the most revenue compared to other media. This usually happens when the medium has achieved maximum penetration; that is, a very high percentage of households has accepted a medium, and the medium cannot grow in penetration any more. Of course, it can continue to absorb a greater proportion of an audience member's time and money. For example, broadcast television reached a peak in the 1960s after taking audiences away from radio and film. Broadcast television also had taken national advertisers away from magazines and radio. Until the mid- to late 1990s, broadcast television remained at a peak as the most dominant mass medium because people were spending more time with broadcast television everyday compared to any other medium. Also, most people regarded broadcast television as their primary (and often only) source of entertainment and news.

## Decline Stage

Eventually, a peak medium will be challenged by a newer one and go into a decline. In the decline stage, the medium is characterized by loss of audience acceptance and therefore by a loss in revenues. A decline in audience support results not from an atrophied need but by the needs being satisfied better by a competing medium that is growing in penetration and moving toward its own peak.

## Adaptation Stage

A medium enters the adaptation stage of development when it accepts the challenge of redefining its position in the media marketplace. Repositioning is achieved by identifying a new set of needs that the medium can meet because the old needs it used to fulfill are now met better by another medium. For example, after radio lost its audience to television, it adapted by doing three things. First, it stopped competing directly with television by eliminating its general entertainment programs such as soap operas, situation comedies, and mystery dramas. Instead, radio shifted to music formats where disk jockeys would play popular songs one after another. Second, it abandoned its strategy of trying to appeal to a general audience and instead segmented the market according to musical tastes, and each station aimed its programming at the people in one of those niches. So in a given market, there is likely to be a top 40 station, a rhythm and blues station, a jazz station, an album-oriented rock station, a golden oldies station, a country and western station, a classical music station, and so forth—each appealing to a different set of listeners. Third, it realized that with the invention of the transistor radio, it could be portable whereas television could not. So radio developed playlists that formed a kind of background mood-shaping experience as people drove in their cars, laid out on beaches, and talked on the phone.

# Comparisons Across Mass Media

In this section, we'll look at the big picture across the media industries. For more detail about each of the mass media, see Appendix A.

## Life Cycle Pattern

Take a minute to look at the life cycle patterns displayed in Figure 9.1. Notice that the print media of books, newspapers, and magazines are the oldest, with each of them moving out of their innovation stage more than a century ago. Computers are the newest mass medium, with its innovation stage finishing about the time you were born. Notice also that all of the mass media, with the exception of cable TV and computers, are currently in the adaptation stage. This means they are all trying to figure out how to coexist with the other up-and-coming media.

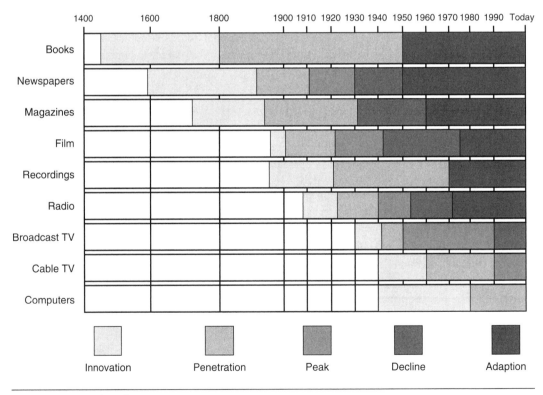

**Figure 9.1**    Life Cycle Patterns

Although the life cycle metaphor is a good template for showing patterns, it is not perfect. For example, notice that several of the media (books, magazines, and recordings) never reached a peak. This does not mean that those media are not important or successful; it only means that those media never achieved dominance as the most important mass medium at a given time.

## Indicators of Peak

We are at an interesting time in the development of the media industries. Broadcast television has left the peak stage, which lasted for almost 40 years, during which time it accounted for almost all of the television audience. But cable channels have been eroding broadcast television's hold on the audience, and now broadcast television has slipped below 50% of the television-viewing audience, and its revenues are now lagging behind that of cable television.

When a medium is at its peak, it is usually the dominant medium; that is, it is the most important medium to the greatest number of people. This can be seen in terms of how much money the industry generates and how much time people spend with that medium. Given these criteria, it appears that cable television (along with its satellite delivery services) is the most dominant medium. Table 9.1 shows that this medium accounted for more revenue in 1998 and that, since then, it has grown even stronger as a dominant medium. Broadcast television is still growing, but it is lagging further and further behind the revenue-generating capability of cable. Also, notice the recent revenue growth of the Internet. If it keeps growing at the rate that it did in the 3-year period between 1998 and 2001, it will soon overtake newspapers and eventually compete with cable as the dominant medium.

**Table 9.1**     Revenue Change From 1998 to 2001 (U.S. Dollar Figures in Millions)

| *Medium* | *1998* | *2001* | *Change (%)* |
|---|---|---|---|
| Cable/satellite TV | 29,033 | 51,984 | + 79.1 |
| Film (theater and video) | 27,106 | 27,208 | + 0.4 |
| Broadcast TV | 24,026 | 29,820 | + 24.1 |
| Newspapers | 22,135 | 23,728 | + 7.2 |
| Recorded music | 9,544 | 9,208 | − 3.5 |
| Consumer magazines | 7,311 | 7,460 | + 2.0 |
| Consumer Internet | 4,527 | 12,326 | + 172.3 |
| Consumer books | 3,952 | 4,552 | + 15.2 |
| Radio | 3,500 | 6,766 | + 93.3 |

SOURCE: U.S. Bureau of the Census (2004, Table 1124, p. 720).

NOTE: The change column reflects percentage change from 1998 to 2001.

**Table 9.2**    Comparison Across Media Industries by Hours and U.S. Dollars Spent Per Person Annually

| Medium | Hours Per Year | | | | Dollars Per Year | | | |
|---|---|---|---|---|---|---|---|---|
| | *1998* | *2001* | *2005* | *Change (%)* | *1998* | *2001* | *2005* | *Change (%)* |
| Radio | 936 | 983 | 1,062 | + 13.5 | | | | |
| Broadcast TV | 884 | 815 | 790 | − 10.6 | | | | |
| Cable/satellite TV | 667 | 846 | 881 | + 32.1 | 167.38 | 210.58 | 269.18 | + 60.8 |
| Recorded music | 283 | 238 | 203 | − 28.3 | 61.67 | 60.57 | 54.30 | − 11.9 |
| Daily newspapers | 185 | 177 | 170 | − 8.1 | 53.37 | 54.12 | 56.57 | + 6.0 |
| Consumer magazines | 125 | 119 | 113 | − 9.6 | 46.45 | 43.57 | 46.26 | − 0.4 |
| Consumer books | 120 | 109 | 104 | − 13.3 | 84.16 | 86.13 | 92.37 | + 9.8 |
| Consumer Internet | 54 | 134 | 199 | + 268.5 | 27.63 | 62.08 | 111.76 | + 304.5 |
| Video games | 43 | 78 | 101 | + 134.9 | 18.49 | 27.96 | 38.38 | + 107.6 |
| Home video | 36 | 56 | 120 | + 233.3 | 92.58 | 109.60 | 141.35 | + 52.7 |
| Movies in theaters | 13 | 13 | 14 | + 7.7 | 31.23 | 36.57 | 45.82 | + 46.7 |

SOURCE: U.S. Bureau of the Census (2004, Table 1125, p. 720).

NOTE: The columns labeled "2005" are projected figures. The change column reflects percentage change from 1998 to 2005.

Let's now take a look at how much time and money each individual spends with the different mass media on average (see Table 9.2). Notice that radio is in first place with the number of hours people spend with it per year; broadcast television is second, cable TV/satellite is third, and then there is a big drop to the next medium (recorded music) in terms of hours spent per year. Does this mean that radio should be the dominant medium? The answer is no—for several reasons. First, although people spend a lot of time with their radios on, they are using the medium for background noise; that is, they are not really paying much attention to those messages. When radio was at its peak in the 1920s and 1930s, its programming commanded listeners' full attention. That programming included a wide range of genres that are now seen on television. People would listen to soap operas, detective shows, game shows, and comedies. But now, most of radio listening is background music. While listening to this music, people are typically exposing themselves to other media (such as reading books, magazines, and newspapers), or they are doing something else (such as talking on the phone, jogging, or working) that requires more attention. Even though the radio is on for so many hours in the lives of so many people, it does not hold people's full attention.

Second, radio does not generate as much revenue as other media. Notice that in Table 9.2, both radio and broadcast TV have no figures listed in the dollars spent per year columns. Does this mean people do not spend money on these media? Of course not. It means that these media do not get any income *directly* from the consumer. People must buy receivers, but that money goes to Circuit City, Best Buy, or wherever people buy their sets. Broadcast radio and television get almost all of their revenue from advertising, which comes from consumers but only indirectly. Table 9.2 includes only direct revenues from consumers to the media businesses themselves.

Look at the contrast between broadcast television and cable television. As recently as 1998, people on average spent a good deal more time with broadcast than with cable TV, but this is now reversed. Also, cable's revenues from consumers will have grown by more than $100 per person in the 7-year period from 1998 to 2005. This makes cable television and satellite clearly the most dominant medium. For more evidence of this dominance, see the advertising revenue growth displayed in the next chapter.

The newest and fastest growing medium is the Internet. It has already surpassed theatrical movie attendance, books, and magazines in terms of time spent and money spent. It will soon surpass newspapers and recorded music. The Internet is well into the penetration stage and, within a decade or so, may be in a position to challenge cable television for the peak.

Keep an eye on computers and the Internet; as of today, this is a new industry still in the penetration stage, but it is growing rapidly and may reach a peak within the next decade. As I type this chapter on my computer, I have a cable wire screwed into a jack on my computer that allows me to access the Internet and brings me 500 digital channels of broadcast stations, cable stations, and music. The line between cable television and the medium of computer/Internet is blurring, with computer/Internet taking over many of the functions of cable alone and adding to it many new features. For example, on my computer, I can download Hollywood movies and edit them together with my own home movies so that I can star in a feature film. I can also download music and edit it into my own film and slap on an introduction from a television show to begin my film. I can then e-mail my creation to several friends, who can each insert themselves into the film and e-mail it back to me. Try doing that without a computer!

Several other media—video games and home video—are growing fast in terms of hours per year and dollars per year. It will be interesting to follow what will happen to these newer media. Perhaps they will be folded into another medium, such as computers, or perhaps they will figure out a way to remain distinct and use a separate technology to market a distinct kind of service to consumers and thus grow in their own right.

# General Employment Trends

Related to the growth and development of the media industries are the following questions: How large are the various mass media industries in terms of employees, and what are the characteristics of the people who work in the mass media?

## Overall Size of Workforce

The media are healthy and expanding in terms of employment. The total workforce across the media industries generally grows about 3% each year. But it might surprise you to see that the number of people who work in these industries is rather small, given the high visibility and powerful influence of these industries.

Newspapers are by far the largest employer (see Table 9.3), although there are fewer newspaper establishments than there are software publishers or film/video companies. Although there are many (19,269) film/video production companies, they tend to be small, averaging only about 13 employees per establishment (see Table 9.4). Even smaller are the sound-recording companies, which average about 7 employees per establishment. The larger establishments are with broadcast television stations and newspapers. For example, the average broadcast station employs about 65 people, including on-air talent (anchorpeople and news, weather, and sports reporters), camera operators, sound technicians, directors, engineers, salespeople, promotion people, traffic people, managers, secretaries, receptionists, and so on. Newspapers average about 46 people per establishment—including editors, reporters, photographers, graphic artists, salespeople, managers, secretaries, receptionists, and so forth.

## Salaries

Average salaries are generally highest in software firms (see Table 9.5), and they are growing faster in that industry than any other mass media industry. One caution about

**Table 9.3**    Changes in Number of Employees and Number of Establishments

| | Number of Employees | | | Number of Establishments | | |
|---|---|---|---|---|---|---|
| *Medium* | *1998* | *2001* | *Change (%)* | *1998* | *2001* | *Change (%)* |
| Newspapers | 403,400 | 414,000 | + 2.6 | 8,758 | 8,540 | 2.5 |
| Software publishers | 266,400 | 353,300 | + 32.6 | 12,090 | 10,353 | − 14.4 |
| Film/video production | 254,500 | 270,100 | + 6.1 | 19,269 | 19,532 | + 1.4 |
| Cable TV | 174,400 | 245,400 | + 40.7 | 4,679 | 6,692 | + 43.0 |
| Magazines | 137,600 | 133,200 | − 3.2 | 6,298 | 6,248 | − 0.8 |
| Radio | 126,700 | 142,700 | + 12.6 | 6,894 | 7,297 | + 5.8 |
| Broadcast TV | 123,000 | 126,700 | + 3.0 | 1,895 | 1,937 | + 2.2 |
| Books | 89,000 | 89,700 | + 0.8 | 2,684 | 2,698 | + 0.5 |
| Sound recording | 21,500 | 27,000 | + 25.6 | 2,935 | 3,250 | + 10.7 |

SOURCE: U.S. Bureau of the Census (2004, Tables 1121 and 1124, pp. 718, 720).

NOTE: The change column reflects percentage change from 1998 to 2001.

**Table 9.4**     Employment Patterns in 1998

| Medium | Employees | Establishments | Average Number of Employees/Company |
|---|---|---|---|
| Newspapers | 403,400 | 8,758 | 46.1 |
| Software publishers | 266,400 | 12,090 | 22.0 |
| Film and video production | 254,500 | 19,269 | 13.2 |
| Cable television | 174,400 | 4,679 | 37.3 |
| Magazines | 137,600 | 6,298 | 21.8 |
| Radio | 126,700 | 6,894 | 18.4 |
| Broadcast television | 123,000 | 1,895 | 64.9 |
| Books | 89,000 | 2,684 | 33.2 |
| Sound recording | 21,500 | 2,935 | 7.3 |

SOURCE: U.S. Bureau of the Census (2004, Table 1119, p. 717).

interpreting the average salary figures in Table 9.5: remember that these are averages. These averages were computed by taking the total payroll in an industry and dividing it by the number of paid workers in that industry. In some media industries, such as film, there are many, many people working for almost minimum wages, whereas a few earn tens of millions of dollars per year. Although averages can be misleading if you use them to estimate what your entry-level salary should be in an industry, they are still useful as a relative indicator of how much money is paid out to employees.

**Table 9.5**     Comparison of Average Annual Pay Per Employee From 1997 to 2001 (in U.S. Dollars)

| Medium | 1997 | 2001 | Change (%) |
|---|---|---|---|
| Software publishers | 69,025 | 104,600 | 51.5 |
| Sound recording | 51,671 | 67,778 | 31.2 |
| Broadcast television | 50,913 | 58,082 | 14.1 |
| Magazines | 43,571 | 56,637 | 30.0 |
| Books | 40,522 | 53,545 | 32.1 |
| Cable television | 35,280 | 47,800 | 35.5 |
| Film and video production | 32,540 | 37,600 | 15.6 |
| Newspapers | 29,228 | 35,621 | 21.9 |
| Radio | 28,455 | 37,708 | 32.5 |

SOURCE: U.S. Bureau of the Census (2004, Tables 1119 and 1121, pp. 717, 718).

NOTE: The change column reflects percentage change from 1997 to 2001.

## Demographic Patterns

When looking at the total labor force in this country, we can see a trend toward more and more women becoming employed outside the home. Now, about 45% of the labor force is female. With the mass media industries, there has been a growth in the number of women employed, but there are still many more men working in the mass media than there are women.

The media industries that have the highest percentage of women employed are magazines and books, where women make up more than 50% of the labor force. The most growth in terms of the percentage of women has been in the newspaper industry. In 1960, only 20% of all people working on newspapers were women, but this percentage has been growing slightly each year. A major reason for this increase has been because newspapers have been moving away from the traditionally male-oriented press jobs and into more clerical and technologically oriented jobs. In broadcasting, 23% of all employees were women in 1960. This remained fairly static until 1972, when the federal government began monitoring hiring practices in businesses. Since that time, there has been a gradual increase to the current figure of about 30%.

In motion pictures, about 40% of all employees are women, but this varies depending on the sector of the industry. In the large exhibition sector (ticket takers, concession clerks, projectionists, etc.), about 45% of all employees are women. But with the production sector (actors, directors, producers, and writers), 95% are men.

### Journalism

A popular profession within the media industries is journalism. In this journalistic community, there are about 67,000 reporters and correspondents, 23,000 writers and editors, and 67,000 radio and television announcers and newscasters. Most are male, White, and young. About one third of working journalists are women, which is an unusually low percentage given that about two thirds of students in journalism schools over the past decade have been women. Only about 8% are minorities (3.7% are African American, 2.2% Hispanic, 1% Asian American, and 0.6% Native American). More than half of U.S. journalists are younger than 35, and only 10% are 55 or older. Almost all have a college degree, either with a major in the skill of journalism or another content-based area, such as English, American studies, and political science. In the United States, there are more than 300 universities with journalism/mass communication programs, and each year, about 20,000 bachelor degrees are granted by those journalism programs.

### Writers

In the television and film industries, most writers are men, and most of these men are young. Bielby and Bielby (2001) collected data on the careers of 8,990 television and film writers and found that writers are getting younger. The researchers explained this trend by saying that marketing strategies in television and film have been shifting to target younger audiences more, so these industries are hiring younger writers to tell stories that would attract that target market.

## Advertising

According to the American Association of Advertising Agencies, there are about 100,000 people currently employed in advertising agencies in the United States: about 24% in creative, 15% in account management, 10% in media, 10% in financial, 8% in special support services, and the rest in secretarial and clerical areas (i.e., about 33%). Employment in ad agencies grows at about 3% each year. Women account for 34% of people in advertising and only 17% of top executives ("Ad Agency Women," 1996).

The gap in salaries between men and women is closing. In the 2003, an *Advertising Age* salary survey (Endicott, 2003) indicated that there were still differences between salaries for men and women working the same jobs; however, those differences had typically shrunk to less than 10%, and in some jobs (such as creative director and account planner), the pay was about equal.

## Status

Women who are employed in the media industries are usually in positions of lower status, earn less money, and have less education. For example, in newspapers, women hold about 120 managing editorships at 1,700 newspapers in the United States. As far as policymaking positions on newspapers, women hold about 361 (11%), whereas men hold 3,057 (89%). With book publishing, about 64% of editors, vice presidents, and professionals are men; however, there is better representation in the smaller publishing houses.

# Conclusion

The development of the media industries generally moves from the innovation stage to growth, peak, decline, and then adaptation. Remembering this will help you understand how the media industries start, how they grow, and where they are today.

There are nine major mass media industries: book, newspaper, magazine, film, recording, radio, broadcast television, cable television, and computer. Each of these industries was born out of a combination of technological and marketing innovations. Technological developments created the new channel of communication, but it took marketing entrepreneurs to figure out how to use the new channels to deliver messages to the largest audiences possible.

After an innovation stage, each industry entered a stage of penetration, where it increased its appeal to more and more people. Acceptance of a medium is based on its ability to satisfy an existing need or to create a widespread need that it can then satisfy.

A peak stage is reached when the medium commands the most attention from the public and generates the most revenue compared to other media. This usually happens when the medium has achieved maximum penetration.

Eventually, a peak medium will be challenged by a newer one and go into a decline. In the decline stage, the medium is characterized by a loss of audience acceptance and therefore by a loss in revenues. A decline in audience support results not from an atrophied need but by the needs being satisfied better by a competing medium.

A medium enters the adaptation stage of development when it accepts the challenge of redefining its position in the media marketplace. Repositioning is achieved by identifying a new set of needs that the medium can meet because the old set of needs it used to fulfill is now met better by another medium.

Most of the mass media are currently in the adaptation stage, where they share audiences and advertisers by serving a different function from the other competing media. There is reason to believe that they will continue refining their messages and thereby continue to survive in a healthy manner.

The media industries employ fewer workers than most people would guess. And those workers do not reflect the demographics of the population of the country. Although the media have been trying to hire a larger proportion of women and minorities, those groups are still very much underrepresented in the media workforce.

This chapter has focused your attention on the big picture of how the media develop and change as industries. Now that you have a basic knowledge structure about the development of the media industries, you can pick up more information to elaborate that knowledge structure by reading the detailed profiles of the media industries in Appendix A. Also, this growing knowledge structure will help orient you when you read the next two chapters. While reading those chapters, think about continuing to elaborate this knowledge structure by adding in information about the economics and control of the media industries.

# Further Reading

Croteau, D., & Hoynes, W. (2001). *The business of media: Corporate media and the public interest.* Thousand Oaks, CA: Pine Forge Press. (302 pages, including appendix, endnotes, references, and index)

This book takes a critical perspective on how the media industries developed in the United States. The authors say, "We are concerned with the tension between the media industry's insatiable quest for profits and a democratic society's need for a media system that serves the public interest"

(p. xiii). The book presents seven chapters organized into three sections: (1) Profits and the Public Interest: Theoretical and Historical Context, (2) Industry Structure and Corporate Strategy: Explaining the Rise of Media Conglomerates, and (3) Neglecting the Public Interest: Media Conglomerates and the Public Sphere.

Greco, A. N. (Ed.). (2000). *The media and entertainment industries.* Needham Heights, MA: Allyn & Bacon. (279 pages, including index)

Each of the 10 chapters in this edited book illuminates one of the mass media industries. Authors describe how their industry is structured to gather all the resources they need to produce messages and get those messages out to all the target segments in their audiences. Most chapters present numerous tables of quantitative data to show how the numbers and names of the business in the industry have changed over time, as well as the amount of time and money people spend with the products produced by those businesses. Most of the chapter authors have expanded on their topic in a book published as part of the Allyn & Bacon Mass Communication Series.

# CHAPTER 10

# Economic Perspective

*Key Idea:* The businesses in the media industries are in strong competition with each other to acquire limited resources, play the high-risk game of appealing to audiences, and achieve a maximum profit.

The mass media industries are a huge economic force that generates total revenues of about $700 billion a year (U.S. Bureau of the Census, 2004). Clearly, there is a great deal of money being exchanged for services in the mass media industries. To understand how the industry acquires and uses its resources, we need to understand the mass media from an economic perspective.

How much of your money do you personally contribute to the media? Before you read on in this chapter, take a few minutes to complete Exercise 10.1.

# The Media Game of Economics

Economics is a huge game, with many players and lots of resources at stake. Each player brings particular resources to the game. Players trade away their resources to get other resources they want more. The overall strategy of good game players is to negotiate the exchanges well so that they give up relatively few of their personal resources to get relatively large resources from other players.

## The Players

There are four types of players who vary in terms of their goals, resources, and abilities to play the game. The players are (a) you the consumer, (b) the advertisers, (c) the media companies, and (d) the media employees.

As a consumer, you are in the largest group. This includes all 285 million of us in the United States (actually, the game is going global, so there are 6 billion people, but in this chapter, I will focus attention on the United States). Consumers' resources include their time and money. They seek to exchange that time and money for entertainment and information.

Consumers as an aggregate form the group that has the greatest amount of power in the game because this is the largest group, and its size represents a huge amount of time and money. If this group pulled out of the game entirely, the game would collapse. However, this power is dispersed over so many people that no one consumer has much power by himself or herself. This is why individuals often feel powerless in this game. When this happens, they continue to play the game (because they cannot avoid it) in a resigned state, hoping to avoid feeling much frustration in making poor economic exchanges.

The advertisers are a second group of players. Advertisers bring money to the game. They negotiate an exchange of their money for time and space in the media to present their ads to their target audiences. Advertisers want to get access to their target audiences for the lowest cost possible. So they look for media vehicles that have constructed the largest assemblages of the audience members they want without also including other kinds of audience members they do not want. For example, sellers of tennis rackets want to get their ad messages in front of as many people who play tennis as possible, but they do not want to buy a large audience if that audience also contains toddlers, invalids, and people who hate tennis. So they look for media vehicles that have constructed an audience of only tennis players and negotiate a good ad price to rent that audience.

The media companies are the third group of players. These businesses bring money, messages, and audiences to the game to compete in three different markets simultaneously. First, each media business competes in the talent market to try to get the best actors, directors, writers, journalists, and so on under contract to them. They try to keep these costs low, but because talent is in short supply, their expenses escalate each year. Second, media businesses compete in the audience market; that is, they present the messages produced by their talented employees in such a way to attract the greatest number of people within certain types of audiences. With messages offered in the media of magazines, newspapers, cable, and Internet, those companies sell subscriptions, so they want to maximize their revenue by attracting as many subscribers as possible. Media companies also sell messages in the form of books, recordings (music and movies), and theater tickets. Third, media companies compete in the advertising market. When media companies have constructed quality niche audiences, they have something valuable to offer advertisers who want to get their messages in front of certain types of consumers.

The media employees comprise the fourth group of players. Employees bring talent and time to the game. Their goal is to increase their income and benefits for each hour worked. In the media, we make a distinction between below-the-line employees and above-the-line employees. Below-the-line employees are typically the crafts and clerical people. Talent has much less an influence in determining how well they do their job than does training and effort. That is, with the proper training and motivation, most people could do a good job as a lighting technician, sound boom operator, ticket taker, secretary, or receptionist. There is a very large number of people who potentially could do these jobs, so the supply (people wanting these jobs) is much larger than the demand (number of these jobs available). Therefore, the pay for people in these positions is relatively low.

The above-the-line employees are the creative types, and this requires talent much more than training or effort, although training and effort are also important. These above-the-line people are the actors, writers, producers, and directors. For the mass media industries, talent is not viewed in terms of artistic ability as much as it is regarded in terms of ability to attract large audiences. Sometimes, the two are the same, but more often than not, they are very different. For example, the best singers or musicians are hardly ever the most popular. Celine Dion has an exceptionally gifted singing voice and is also popular. However, the singing ability of Madonna or Britney Spears, although good, cannot alone account for their huge popularity. Also, there are many television stars who are not particularly good actors (they have never won an acting award), yet they are in high demand by television producers because these people can attract large audiences. This kind of talent is in short supply, so these people are paid extremely well for their services. According to *Forbes* magazine ("The Celebrity 100," 2004), Mel Gibson and Oprah Winfrey were the highest paid media celebrities in 2003, each with an income of $210 million (see Table 10.1).

**Table 10.1**    Income of Media Celebrities, 2003

| *Millions (U.S. Dollars)* | *Person* | *Profession* |
| --- | --- | --- |
| 210 | Mel Gibson | Director/producer |
| 210 | Oprah Winfrey | Talk show host |
| 147 | J. K. Rowling | Author |
| 75 | Steven Spielberg | Director/producer |
| 66 | Jim Carrey | Actor |
| 64 | Bruce Springsteen | Musician |
| 60 | Nora Roberts | Author |
| 57 | David Copperfield | Magician |
| 40 | Ray Romano | Actor |
| 40 | David Letterman | Talk show host |
| 40 | Jerry Bruckheimer | Director/producer |
| 39 | Kelsey Grammar | Actor |
| 35 | Peter Jackson | Director/producer |
| 35 | Robert De Niro | Actor |
| 32 | Cameron Diaz | Actress |
| 31 | Howard Stern | Talk show host |
| 30 | Rush Limbaugh | Talk show host |
| 30 | Sandra Bullock | Actress |
| 28 | Celine Dion | Musician |
| 28 | Olsen Twins | Actresses |
| 27 | Tom Hanks | Actor |
| 27 | Cher | Musician |
| 25 | Judge Judy | Talk show host |
| 20 | Regis Philbin | Talk show host |
| 17 | John Madden | TV announcer |

**Table 10.2**    Wealth of Media Owners, 2003

| Billions (U.S. Dollars) | Person | Media Company |
|---|---|---|
| 46.0 | Bill Gates | Microsoft Computers |
| 22.0 | Paul Allen | Microsoft Computers |
| 13.0 | Michael Dell | Dell Computers |
| 12.2 | Steven Ballmer | Microsoft Computers |
| 9.7 | Sumner Redstone | Viacom |
| 5.1 | Jeff Bezos | Amazon.com |
| 5.0 | Gordon Moore | Intel |
| 4.0 | David Geffen | Music |
| 3.0 | George Lucas | Filmmaker |
| 1.6 | David Filo | Yahoo Inc. |
| 1.4 | Jerry Yang | Yahoo Inc. |

SOURCE: "The Super Rich" (2003).

Another elite set of employees are the media company managers, who are often also partial owners of the companies. The talent of these managers is to oversee the construction of messages and their distribution so that those messages are experienced by the greatest number of targeted consumers. In essence, the talent of managers is to construct these audiences by attracting consumers with above-the-line talent and try to maintain those audiences by making the exposures continually rewarding and at low cognitive costs to the audience members. These media managers also have a talent in short supply and are therefore paid very well year after year and have amassed great wealth (see Table 10.2). With few exceptions, these people are not nearly as well known as the media "stars," but they are far more powerful than any of the stars and have been able to generate personal wealth well beyond what any of their employees have.

## The Goal

For all four types of players, the general goal is to maximize the value of the exchange for themselves. But value is computed in very different ways for different players. For the media businesses, employees, and advertisers, value can be computed quantitatively—numbers of dollars. But for individuals, value is not a quantitative concept—it is satisfaction. Individuals rarely engage in the media economic game to increase their financial resources. Instead, they desire satisfaction from their exposure to media messages. As long as they feel satisfaction, they will continue feeling a net winner. People continually assess their satisfaction by comparing the benefits gained from the media messages to their personal costs for those exposures. Audiences want to increase the value of their exposure by searching for more useful information and entertainment while reducing their costs.

One form of costs is financial. For example, people can reduce their financial costs by finding information on the Internet rather than paying magazine and newspaper subscriptions. Another form of cost is time. People can go to sources of information with which they are familiar, and this saves time over seeking out new sources. And another form of cost is cognitive energy. Making decisions and thinking through their implications requires cognitive effort; it is easier for people to stick with habits and not have to think about everything they do.

Another important thing to realize when understanding the goals of this economic game is that the game is ongoing. Because it does not end, there is no ultimate winner or loser. Instead, the goal is a process; this means that at any given time, the players can assess if they are winning or losing. Of the four players, the media businesses are the best at making this assessment. They can do this by performing the simple calculation of adding up all their revenue and then subtracting out their expenses, thereby determining their profit. If the profit continues to grow each year, the business is doing well. For advertisers, it is a bit more difficult to tell how well they are doing because they must compare the money they spend on advertising with the amount of sales they have. For employees, it is yet more difficult; they know what they are being paid, but assessing their true value for talent, effort, and ability is difficult. Many people think they are being underpaid, but how can they be sure they are assessing their talent accurately?

Consumers have the most difficult task of assessing how well they are playing the economic game. This difficulty stems from their lack of ability to specify what they get in return for their time and money. Without a clear articulation of their goals, they default to an intuitive feeling of satisfaction. If they feel satisfied by media messages, they continue to spend their time and money with those messages. Much of this continued exposure to the same media messages is conditioned and not consciously reasoned. Therefore, consumers, with their mindless exposure, become pawns in the game. Although consumers have the greatest potential power of any single group in the game, they are typically the weakest group. This is why it is so important to be media literate. It makes you a better game player, and when you play the game better, you get much more in return from the exchange of your resources.

Notice that the goals of the four groups are very different from one another. Also, there are times when the goals are in direct conflict. For example, a film company will prefer to pay an actor little money to reduce its business expenses on the film and thus maximize its profit. In contrast, the actor in the negotiation wants to be paid a huge amount of money and be handsomely rewarded for his talent to attract a huge audience for the film company. Thus, the negotiations are more often competitive than cooperative. This means that often there is one player who benefits more than other players, given the outcome of a particular negotiation. This competitive stance leads certain players to approach the game with the attitude that they have to increase their wealth in the negotiations, even if it means that other players must reduce theirs.

## The Rules

The most central rule of this economic game is that to play, you must bring resources and a willingness to exchange them for other resources. If you lack either the resources or the willingness to exchange, you cannot play. All the other rules are made up by players as they negotiate. When rules are made up, it is done to maintain a sense of fairness in the exchange. Players who begin to perceive the game as unfair will cease to trust the other players and will stop playing, and this diminishes the game. For the game to remain exciting, it must have many players exchanging many resources.

Although there are few rules, many characteristics guide the play of the game. These characteristics are illuminated in the next section.

# Characteristics of the Game

To understand more about how the economic game is played with the mass media, you need to understand six characteristics of that game. These characteristics are as follows: the importance of valuing resources well, indirect as well as direct support, the complex interdependency among players, the nature of competition, the principle of relative constancy, and advertising as the engine. An understanding of this set of principles will help you comprehend how the negotiation for resources takes place.

## Importance of Valuing Resources Well

The key to negotiations is to value the resources accurately. If one player can do this and the second player cannot, the second player is at a real disadvantage. There are two considerations that go into resource valuation, and both of these require considerable skill to do well. One factor in valuing a resource is making an assessment about how well the resource will achieve a particular goal. A second factor that is important in valuing resources is to consider supply and demand.

The more skill people have in these areas, the better they will be able to make accurate assessments of the value of resources, and the more valuable those people will be in a negotiation. For example, let's say you find something in your parents' attic that you think may be valuable. You take it to an antique dealer to sell it. The dealer gives you a price of $60 for it. Should you accept the $60 and sell it to the dealer? If you have no knowledge of antiques and no idea about how rare the piece is, you are operating in the dark. You might think you are savvy and ask for $100, then settle for $80, feeling good that you "got the dealer to raise her price" $20. But maybe the piece is worth $1,000. If you don't have a good operating knowledge about what your resources are worth, you will continually fall into one of two traps. One trap is to overvalue your resources, and no one will want to enter into exchanges with you. The other trap is to undervalue your resources, in which case you make lots of exchanges, but you continually are shortchanged. When you have little knowledge of the value of your resources, you can only play the game to lose.

## Indirect as Well as Direct Support

Recall that this chapter began with the statement that the media industries generate about $700 billion revenue a year. This figure breaks down to about $2,400 for every man, woman, child, and infant in the United States. If you are an average person in your media spending habits, you contribute about $800 annually *directly* to these media companies—buying books, recordings, and movie admissions; subscriptions to magazines and newspapers; and purchasing hardware, such as TVs, VCRs and DVD players, tape players, and other media products. But there is a big difference between this $800 and the $2,400 that the average person contributes to the total revenues of the media companies. What accounts for this difference? The answer is that the remaining $1,600 is what the average person in the United States contributes *indirectly* to the media by buying advertised products. For example, if you buy a tube of toothpaste for $3, about one of those dollars goes into the toothpaste company's advertising budget and eventually finds its way into a newspaper, magazine, or television station. If you added up all these hidden contributions to advertising for each product you buy, it would sum to about $1,600 each year.

The media of books, films, recordings, and computers are supported almost entirely by direct costs to the consumer. There are a few examples of ads being stuck in books and recordings and displayed before films or in computer programs, but this revenue from these ads is minor compared to direct costs. With magazines, newspapers, and now cable TV, the costs are split between direct (subscription or newsstand selling price) and indirect (advertising). With broadcast television and radio, there is no direct cost for exposure to a program, but there is a high cost for purchasing the means to receive a program (radios and television sets), in addition to indirect costs in the guise of advertising.

The balance between direct and indirect support is shifting from direct to indirect payment. The reason for this is that the costs of some hardware such as TVs, radios, CD players, VCRs and DVD players, and computers is coming down each year while the revenues generated through advertising increase each year.

To put this $700 billion in perspective, look at Table 10.3, which shows the per capita spending on personal items. Direct spending on the media ranks behind only food, clothing, and physicians. When we add in the indirect spending, media expenditures per person would be in first place on this list. Also look at Table 10.4, which shows that the federal

**Table 10.3**    Per Capita Expenditures for Various Items in 2003

| Per Person (U.S. Dollars) | |
|---|---|
| 2,067 | Food from grocery stores |
| 1,380 | Food at restaurants and fast-food establishments |
| 937 | Clothing |
| 936 | Physicians |
| 778 | Household utilities (electricity, gas, water, etc.) |
| 584 | Motor vehicles (new and used) and parts |
| 307 | Higher education |
| 225 | Furniture |
| 114 | Air travel |

SOURCE: U.S. Bureau of the Census (2004, Table 667, p. 444).

**Table 10.4**    Expenditures of the Federal Government in 2003

| Billions (U.S. Dollars) | |
|---|---|
| 86.3 | Education, job training, and social services |
| 64.2 | Transportation (highways, airports, trains) |
| 30.6 | Natural resources and environment |
| 20.8 | Agriculture |
| 20.7 | International affairs |
| 376.3 | National defense |

SOURCE: U.S. Bureau of the Census (2004, Table 476).

government spent a total of $222.6 billion on education, transportation, agriculture, natural resources, and international affairs combined. This is about the amount we as consumers spent on the media directly. Add to those federal figures the $376.3 billion that the federal government spent on national defense, and the sum grows to about $600 billion—still far short of the $700 billion in total revenues to the media industries. This should give you some idea of how big the media economic game is.

## Complex Interdependency Among Players

Some exchanges are relatively simple—that is, where two people make an exchange and no one else is affected or concerned with that individual exchange. For example, a newspaper wants to minimize its costs. Let's say you are an employee of the newspaper, and you want a raise in pay and benefits. If you are a receptionist or a secretary, the negotiating power is with the newspaper because there is a very large supply of people with these skills relative to the demand. The newspaper will offer you a wage not much above the minimum wage. Either you take this offer or you look for work elsewhere.

There are, however, many times when the negotiations are more involved, and this illustrates the complex interdependence among the different players in the media economic game. For example, let's say a radio station wants to attract more advertisers, so it cuts the price of its ads by 20% in its highest rated show. Advertisers fight to buy those ad times (called avails), so demand for the avails at this station increases. The station, which used to air 9 minutes of ads during an hour, decides to air 20 minutes of ads, thus increasing its supply of avails to meet the increasing demand. The station likes this because even though it has cut its income per ad by 20%, it is now selling more than twice as many avails; the station has almost doubled its total revenue. But the audience notices this change and becomes upset that there are so many ads and not nearly as much music. Most of the audience switches channels during the ads and never comes back. The station's ratings drop dramatically. Then advertisers become unhappy because it is no bargain to get a 20% discount on ads if the audience they expected is almost gone. Advertisers begin feeling they are wasting their money, so they stop buying those ads.

Three other characteristics make this interrelationship even more complex. First, the situation is highly dynamic and interrelated. When a person at one media company makes a decision, it can often have an impact on other companies in the same industry and perhaps other media industries. Returning to the radio station example above, when advertisers flocked to the station to get the discounted price for the avail, other radio stations (as well as television stations, newspapers, and local magazines) most likely lost advertising revenue. So when the revenues of one vehicle dramatically increase in the short term, the revenues of other competing vehicles are affected and usually go down. The same ripple effect can be seen with expenses of the media companies. For example, if several media companies started paying writers more money, then the better writers would be attracted to those companies, and the other companies would either have to pay more or else make do with lesser talented writers, which would lower the quality of their shows and result in losing audience size and hence lower revenue. When something changes in a tightly linked industry, that change ripples outward and affects other players.

A second characteristic that contributes to the complexity is that sometimes decision makers are conflicted because they are experiencing cross-purposes; that is, a decision maker might be a member of more than one group—each with a different economic goal. Let's say you work at a small newspaper and also own half of the newspaper company. As an employee, you might want a raise in salary, but this would increase expenses and therefore reduce profits, making your investment less valuable. On a different scale, let's say you work for a large newspaper and own stock in the company that owns the newspaper. A raise in your wages will benefit you a great deal more than would a nonraise benefit shareholders. So your needs as an employee greatly outweigh your needs as an owner.

Third, media vehicles compete in different markets. A market is a segment of the audience to which you offer your product or service. Markets differ in size, with the largest market in the United States being the national one. Only a few vehicles, such as television network prime-time broadcast programs, *USA Today* newspaper, *TV Guide* magazine, and major Hollywood movies, see themselves competing in a national market. More typically, vehicles carve out a special niche. One way of identifying a niche is geographically, such as the case with newspapers, radio stations, and broadcast television stations. Media vehicles in these industries have their own geographical locale, such as a city or a limited region. Another way of identifying a niche is by audience interest, which is common with magazines, books, and radio. For example, *Surfer* magazine appeals to a very different audience niche than does *Ladies' Home Journal.* College texts are marketed very differently than religious books. Country and western–formatted radio stations appeal to a very different audience than does a rap station.

Clearly, the economics of the mass media industries are complex. The complexity can be traced to the fact that there are many different components, each with its own needs that are most often in conflict with the needs of other components. This requires a constant negotiation process, and as decisions are made, effects ripple out and influence the decisions of others. All parties are profoundly interlinked.

## Nature of Competition

Although this economic game involves many people and businesses, there are a limited number of resources. Competition for those resources is strong—especially for the most valuable of those resources. However, because the game is ongoing, we must consider that certain companies and people get stronger and stronger at the game and, as a result, become more powerful. Some of these companies are attaining near-monopoly status within segments of the market. Thus, we have evolved into a situation referred to as monopolistic competition—*monopolistic* because each firm is large relative to the size of the market for its products (also, there are very high barriers to entry in most media industries) and *competition* because firms in an industry compete.

Unusually high profits in an industry typically attract new firms, which results in greater competition. With greater competition, there are more firms and hence expanded output, lower prices, reduced profits, and greater benefits for consumers. But this trend is not apparent in most mass media industries. In most media industries, there are a few companies that make very high profits. Although these companies compete with each other, the industry does not attract other companies because the cost of entry into those industries has become so high.

Another characteristic of the competition is that within a market, all products are relatively indistinguishable; that is, the messages are not identical but very similar. For example, the stories in *Newsweek, Time,* and *U.S. News & World Report* are very similar in terms of content, depth, and perspective. A situation comedy on ABC is very similar to one on CBS; the characters have different names, but the stereotypes, settings, and plot points are very similar. With computer software, all spreadsheet application programs are pretty much the same; also, Web browsers are almost identical in features. The key to competition is making consumers believe that your product is different from the others. Media businesses do not really compete on product features as much as they compete on product images. This is why advertising is so important. Advertising gets people to look beyond the product features to consider product images as well as psychological advantages of using the product.

## Principle of Relative Constancy

The consumer's proportion of economic support for the mass media is approximately constant to the general economy. This is the principle of relative constancy.

Mass media products have become staples of consumption in our society much like food, clothing, and shelter. As staples, they receive a fixed constant share of the economic pie, a relatively fixed proportion of all expenditures. This was true in 1929 and still is more than seven decades later.

Although the percentage of consumer spending on the mass media has remained constant at around 3% of gross national product (GNP) since 1929, that money breaks down differently year by year depending on the media available and the relative attractiveness of their messages. When one medium increases its share of revenues, other media experience a decrease in revenues.

The percentage of media expenditure spent on newspapers and magazines peaked in 1933; movie admission peaked in 1945; books peaked in 1970. Expenditures for radio, television receivers, recordings, and computers are still growing.

## Advertising as the Engine

Advertising is the engine that drives the growth of the media industries. The cost of doing business in the United States has greatly increased as advertising continually becomes a stronger economic force. In 1900, about $500 million was spent on all forms of advertising. By 1940, it was $2 billion, so it took 40 years to multiply four times. In 1980, it was $60 billion or a growth of 30 times in those 40 years. Now it is more than $200 billion. Television (broadcast and cable) and newspapers account for well over half of all the revenue that goes to the media industries. With cable television becoming more aggressive in the advertising market, it is likely that their revenues will grow the fastest, thus keeping it in first place at least for the foreseeable future.

Why is advertising so important to our economy? There have been some dramatic changes of the economy of this and other Western countries over the past 100 years and especially over the past 50 years that have worked in combination with advertising to increase both the sale of goods and services as well as the importance of advertising. First, there has been a decline in the proportion of farmers and blue-collar workers and an increase in the proportion of white-collar professional workers. This means that people are not as self-sufficient and must buy their food and clothing. Second, there has been a high level of employment, which gives people the resources to buy goods and services. We have more discretionary income, which makes it possible for us to purchase things at a point well beyond the mere subsistence level. Over time, the standard of living has steadily increased as people's earning power increases and their expenditures for food, clothing, automobiles, housing, media, and luxuries have all increased.

Advertising has been the engine for this growth. Advertising makes it possible for new goods to enter markets and let us know immediately that they are available. With more product successes, more and more companies are willing to introduce an even wider range of new products. These companies fuel advertising agencies with money, which is passed through to the media. As the media grow, they offer more information and entertainment to us. More of us spend more time with the media, thus generating many more audiences, which the media rent out to advertisers. The money cycles from us to products, to the manufacturers of those products, to those companies' advertising agencies, to the media. Advertising drives this cycle faster and faster each year. If we stopped buying advertised products, the cycle would slow down and eventually stop.

# Media Industries' Strategies

The media industries have developed some general economic strategies over the years that make them successful at playing the economic game and achieving their goals. Three major strategies are illuminated in this section.

## Maximizing Profits

Almost all mass media are profit-oriented enterprises. As businesses, they are run to make as large a profit as possible. Remember that profit is the payoff or reward for doing business. This reward can be conceptualized in several different ways. First, it can be regarded as the difference between a company's revenue (total income) and expenses (total costs)—usually expressed as a percentage of revenues. For example, let's say you run a small magazine and at the end of the year, you total up everything and find that your revenues (all income through subscriptions and advertiser's fees) came to $100,000. Your expenses (paying writers, editors, photographers, printers, distribution, taxes, office supplies, utilities, etc.) sum up to $90,000. That means you have $10,000 left over after having paid all your expenses for the year. This is your reward. You get to keep 10% of all your revenues; that is, your return on revenues (ROR) is $10,000 divided by $100,000.

A second way of computing your reward is to compare your profit to your assets, which is the money you have invested in the business. Let's extend the same example above where you had a $10,000 profit at the end of the year. If you had $50,000 invested in the business (office furniture, computers, printers, fax, and other equipment), then your return on assets (ROA) would be 20%, which is very good.

Both ROR and ROA are very important indicators of the reward of doing business, but they look at reward in different ways. For example, let's say you bought a radio station for $1 million and at the end of the year you had generated a profit of $10,000 on revenues of $100,000. That 10% ROR is pretty good, but the ROA is only 1%, which is terrible! You could have invested the $1 million in a passbook savings account at the bank and done much better. In another example, let's say you start a small weekly newspaper and your only assets are a computer and a few pieces of furniture totaling $4,000. Your newspaper generates revenue of $50,000, but your expenses are $49,000 so your profit is only $1,000. Your ROA is a very high at 25% ($1,000 profit divided by assets of $4,000), but your ROR is only 2% ($1,000 profit divided by revenues of $50,000).

Let's look at the ROR and ROA of the mass media industries (see Table 10.5). Newspapers appear to be the best of the mass media industries because they have very high percentages on both ROR and ROA. Remember these are industry-wide averages; some newspapers do much better than these figures, and others have been losing money.

On the weaker end is the audio recording industry, with the lowest ROR. However, 7% is still better than the average for all industries in the United States. As for ROA, the cable television and film industries are the lowest, but both of these industries have huge asset bases, and this is what tends to make their ROA percentages appear smaller.

**Table 10.5**     Comparison of Profits Across Media Industries

| Industry | ROR (%) | ROA (%) |
| --- | --- | --- |
| Television broadcasting | 22 | 18 |
| Radio | 20 | N/A |
| Newspapers | 17 | 26 |
| Cable and pay television | 15 | 9 |
| Magazines | 11 | 24 |
| Films | 11 | 9 |
| Books | 10 | 14 |
| Audio recordings | 7 | 14 |

SOURCES: Format adapted from Picard (1989, p. 89); data from Standard & Poor's (1996) *Index to Surveys* and U.S. Bureau of the Census (2000).

NOTE: ROR = return on revenues; ROA = return on assets.

In the simplest situation, profit is what a company has at the end of the year after paying all its expenses. So profit is the difference between revenue, which is the total amount of income for the business, and expenses. This strategy to maximize profits is best achieved when media businesses maximize revenues while minimizing expenses.

## Increasing Revenue Streams

Because revenue is linked to audience size, media businesses have a strong incentive to increase the appeal of their messages so they can attract larger audiences. With a larger audience, the businesses receive more revenue from consumers directly (through sales and subscriptions) as well as indirectly (through advertisers).

In the highly competitive media environment, there is a limit to how attractive you can make your messages and how much you can grow any one audience. So media businesses try to create multiple audiences and thus benefit from multiple streams of revenue. For example, movie studios know they can grow the box office audience for films only so much. Although they typically spend $50 million advertising a film, they know that spending much more than this will not necessarily increase box office sales. So they put the movie on videocassettes and DVDs so that people can rent or buy the movie. This increases revenue streams. They also lease the movie to foreign distributors, and this adds another revenue stream. They market the film to the airlines for showing during flights. They also market the music from the film on CDs. Often, they try to produce toys, clothing, or other artifacts from the film and sell those to the public. They sometimes hire someone to write a book about the making of the movie. Or they could hire someone to translate the movie into a comic book format. And they also sell product placements in the films. All these revenue streams increase the total revenue and thus make the film more profitable.

Once the media company has created a message, it wants to develop multiple revenue streams to benefit from that message. This tactic has been very successful. This is a big reason why movie companies want to buy other media companies. When a media company becomes a conglomerate, controlling the distribution of messages in many media channels, it can easily market a single message across all channels and thus quickly create multiple revenue streams for that one message.

Even the older media of newspapers and magazines have been aggressive at developing additional revenue streams. For example, Table 10.6 shows that although these media still depend on print advertising and subscriptions for the majority of their incomes, they now also derive a significant income from many other sources.

## Minimizing Expenses

One of the largest expenses across all the media industries is personnel, which can be subdivided into two broad categories: talent and clerical. Talent is not so much artistic mastery as it is the ability to generate revenue. Some people have sales talent and can sell

**Table 10.6**    Examples of Multiple Revenue Streams

| *Newspapers* | *Magazines* | |
|---|---|---|
| $32,973 | $17,898 | Advertising revenues from print |
| 9,394 | 13,816 | Subscriptions and newsstand sales from print |
| 109 | 856 | Subscription revenue from Internet |
| 324 | 293 | Advertising revenue from Internet |
| 1,788 | 934 | Contract printing |
| 75 | 231 | Licensing rights of content |
| 977 | 110 | Distribution of flyers, inserts, etc. |
| 42 | 44 | Graphic design services |
| 14 | 161 | Sales of mailing lists |

SOURCE: U.S. Bureau of the Census (2004, Table 1129, p. 722).

NOTE: Figures are in millions of U.S. dollars for the year 2001.

advertising space and time. Some people have writing talent and have large followings of readers who buy their books, magazines, and newspapers. Some have musical talent and continually produce records that go platinum. Some have acting talent and generate huge sales at the theater box offices or high ratings for television programs. There is never enough talent to meet the demand, so media companies bid up the prices for the services of people who have this talent. The few talented people at the top of their industries make large sums of money.

However, most of the positions in the media industries are fairly low-level jobs that entail routine assignments that can be done by many different people with little training. These are the secretaries, receptionists, ticket takers, and low-level craftspeople. A bit higher than this are the assistant producers, camera operators, disk jockeys, and the like. Some of these people have special talent and quickly move up to the top of their industry, but most of them do not.

The media pay the people with a lot of talent a lot of money because these people are required for a company to generate large revenues. To counterbalance the large payments to talent, companies reduce expenses by paying clerical people as little as possible. Because the supply of potential workers for entry-level positions is so much larger than the demand, media companies can pay near minimum wage and get good workers.

The media reduce expenses through economies of scale and economies of scope. Economies of scale exist when marginal costs are lower than average costs, that is, when producing an extra unit of a good falls as the scale of output expands. Large production runs are good because they spread out the start-up expenses over many units; thus, with each additional unit manufactured, the per-unit cost continues to go down (Doyle, 2002). To illustrate, let's say you are a newspaper publisher and your daily cost of operation (cost of paying all your reporters, editors, salespeople, office staff, rent on building, depreciation of all your equipment, supplies, phones, other utilities, etc.) is $6,000. This is your fixed cost. If you print only one copy of the newspaper, you will have to sell it for $6,000 just to cover your fixed costs. If you print two copies, you would have to sell each for $3,000 to cover all your costs; your average fixed cost per copy is cut in half. If you print 60,000 copies, your average fixed cost per copy is only 10 cents. Thus, your average fixed costs keep going down as these costs are spread over more and more copies.

However, when you print more copies, the cost of paper, ink, and distribution increases; these are your variable costs because they vary according to how many copies you print. The more copies you print, the more paper and ink you will need, and the price you pay for a roll of paper or a gallon of ink will go down because you can buy these materials in bulk and get big discounts. Although your total cost for ink and paper will go up when printing more copies, your *average* variable cost for these will go down. This is known as economies of scale. The bigger the scale of your business, the more likely your costs will go down either through the ability to demand greater discounts or because you are able to operate more efficiently beyond a certain point.

The more copies you print, the more your distribution costs will go up—both in total and on average. To illustrate this point, imagine that you publish only 1,000 copies of your newspaper. You could hire 10 youngsters each to deliver 100 papers after school and pay them a nickel for each paper delivered. Thus, your average distribution cost is 5 cents per newspaper. But let's say you wanted to publish 50,000 newspapers. You would need to hire 500 youngsters, and this would require you to develop a whole new layer of administration to recruit, train, and keep track of all these paper carriers. You would have to buy some trucks and hire drivers to get the newspapers out to these 500 carriers quickly every day. You would also have to hire some bookkeepers to keep track of all the subscriptions and billing. So the average variable cost might increase from 5 cents to 15 cents *per newspaper* delivered as you go from 1,000 to 50,000 in circulation.

The media companies, like any business, want to keep their expenses down, so they will find the point at which the combination of both their average fixed costs and their average variable costs are lowest. Beyond this point, distributing more copies only serves to increase unit costs and thus reduce profit. So newspapers, magazines, books, and recordings each seek the point where their average total costs (the sum of average fixed costs and average variable costs) are lowest.

With economies of scale, broadcast television and radio are different from the other media. They have no variable costs, only fixed costs. For example, with broadcast television, there is no cost to the station of adding an additional viewer to the audience. Viewers pay for their own television receivers, and they pay for the electricity to run them. The station has no distribution costs other than the electricity of the broadcast signal, and the power used to broadcast a station's signal is the same whether 100 or 100,000 sets are tuned in.

It is fixed. With no variable costs and with a very high first-copy fixed cost, broadcast television stations keep dropping their average total costs with each additional audience member added. For this reason, the broadcast media (both radio and television) are strongly motivated, more than any other medium, to increase the size of their audiences.

Economies of scope also serve to reduce a firm's expenses per unit. Economies of scope are achieved through multiproduct production; that is, there are variations on the product produced. Recall the example above about a movie company generating many revenue streams for a single movie. As the revenues increase for each new revenue stream, the expenses remain relatively low; that is, once you have produced the movie, it is relatively inexpensive to record it on videocassettes and DVDs. By increasing the scope of distributing the same product, very little additional costs are incurred, and yet the potential for revenues increasing is great.

Digitization has made economies of scope even more attractive because it creates little cost to retransmit a message in many different channels. Also, digitization allows for compression of greater amounts of data or more layers of content to be packed into a product. Now you can buy a DVD disk with an entire movie; it also can have interviews with the writer, director, and stars; outtakes; director's cut; alternative endings; and so on. Yet the DVD disk is much smaller than the videocassette, which holds much less information.

## Constructing Audiences

Because advertising is the principal source of revenue for most of the commercial media throughout the world, media companies are in the business of constructing desirable audiences and renting them out to advertisers. A medium builds an audience by recognizing where there is a need for entertainment or information, then providing those products and services to satisfy those needs. This can be done generally in one of two ways. A media business can either (a) orient toward a quantity goal (i.e., attract as large an audience as possible) or (b) orient toward a niche (i.e., attract a special kind of audience).

The dominant mass media in the past have always followed a quantity goal. They tried to present whatever content they felt would attract the greatest number of consumers. This is what the commercial television networks have done in the past, especially for their prime-time period (8 to 11 P.M. each night). A prime-time show that gets a rating of 11 will be regarded as a failure. This means that only 11% of all households—"only" 19 million people—watched it. Even though this is more than all the people who saw the Broadway smash hit *Chorus Line* in its extraordinarily long 10-year run, the television networks are not satisfied by such a small audience. A difference of 1 rating point for a show over the course of a single season could mean almost $100 million in advertising revenue to the network, so networks are strongly motivated to increase the size of their audiences as much as possible. But this quantitative goal is now unrealistic for broadcast television, and there are indications that this industry is going to a niche-oriented approach, as have all the other mass media industries.

## Attracting People to Niches

The radio and magazine industries have been very successful for years in attracting people to their niches. For example, a radio station will develop a certain sound to appeal to one kind of listener, then try to attract as many of those kinds of listeners as possible. So one station will use rap music to attract urban youth, whereas another station will use golden oldies to attract the aging baby boomers. The audience for each of these stations is relatively small compared to an audience for broadcast television. But small, highly targeted audiences have great value to many advertisers. Special groups of people have special needs. Businesses that are marketing products for a special audience will pay a premium to the media vehicles that attract that special audience. For example, joggers as a group have a special need for information on running practices, equipment, and training techniques. They support several magazines that publish nothing but this type of information. Manufacturers of jogging equipment pay a premium to place ads in these magazines, knowing that the buying of advertising space in these magazines is a very efficient purchase because the ads placed there will be reaching their most likely customers.

## Conditioning Audiences

Once a mass media business has constructed an audience, it needs to keep that audience, so it can continue to rent it out to advertisers. Recall from the definition of mass media that the business is not interested in providing a message for a single exposure, like a rock concert promoter might. The mass media want to stay in business over the long term, and this requires that they maintain their audiences. Therefore, they must condition their audience members so that they develop a habit of exposure.

## Reducing Risk

Constructing messages that will appeal to the tastes of the public is a very risky endeavor. Many messages fail to attract their hoped-for targets. To reduce this risk, media businesses have shifted to the "marketing concept." With the marketing concept, managers conduct research to identify particular niche audiences, then find out what their unmet needs are. Then the media develop messages to meet those previously unmet needs. Beginning with research first and product development second reduces risk of product failure once the products are put into the market.

This procedure is used frequently by the media industries. Researchers look at what works, then develop shows that are sequels or spin-offs of successful shows. Also, in the magazine industry, a large conglomerate will do market testing for unmet needs for magazines; once a need is found, the company will develop a magazine to reach that niche audience, then rent those consumers to a particular set of advertisers who need to expose that particular audience to their ad messages.

# Consumers' Strategies

We as consumers follow strategies just like the media industries do. However, our strategies are quite different from the profit-maximizing strategies of the mass media. We have two options for strategies. We can follow a default strategy, or we can follow a media literacy strategy.

## Default Strategy

The default strategy follows a goal of maintaining a minimal level of uninterrupted satisfaction. We continually expose ourselves to media messages in a habitual pattern. If we did not read any novels last year, we avoid reading novels this year. If we usually watch the evening news during dinner, we continue to watch the evening news during dinner. If we like a half-dozen music groups, we follow their new releases and typically ignore the music of other groups and are completely unaware of the music in other genres. We watch a few favorite shows on television and go to a few movies—usually the same kinds of movies with the same stars. We follow these habits because it is easy. These habits were developed in the past when we tried something new and felt it was a pleasant experience, so we continue with it without thinking much. We rarely search out the experience for a very different type of message, either because we are not sure what other messages are out there or feel that searching out those messages will entail much more effort than it is worth; that is, we will not feel more rewarded by them. Although the messages we currently experience are not providing huge rewards, they have almost no costs to us because they are routine habits.

## Media Literacy Strategy

People who follow a media literacy strategy understand the economic game and how to be a better player. This means they have higher expectations for a return on the resources they expend. They want more than minimal satisfaction from exposures. They think much more about the value of their own resources, and they want to negotiate a better exchange for those resources.

What separates the use of the default strategy and the media literacy strategy? The answer is the strength of one's personal locus. People with a weak personal locus will settle for little in the exchanges because it requires too much effort to become a better player in the economic game. In contrast, people with a strong personal locus find it essential that they become more of a winner at this game. Expending the greater effort of using skills better and building more elaborate knowledge structures (see Table 10.7) is fun because it pays them back with much more interesting experiences.

**Table 10.7**    Types of Skills and Knowledge Needed to Deal With Media Industries in a
Media-Literate Manner

|  | *SKILLS* | *KNOWLEDGE* |
|---|---|---|
| COGNITIVE | Ability to analyze reports on media industries and companies to determine revenue, expenses, and profits | Knowledge of revenue, expenses, and profits of media industries and specific companies |
|  | Ability to compare and contrast across industries and companies on economic indicators |  |
|  | Ability to evaluate the economic health of media industries and companies |  |
|  | Ability to generalize from particular companies to industry trends |  |
|  | Ability to synthesize a prediction for future trends in the media industries and companies |  |
|  | Ability to analyze media industries and companies to recognize the operation of the six economic characteristics |  |
| EMOTIONAL | Ability to analyze your feelings in reaction to the economic practices of media | Knowledge of your experiences in buying and using media products |
| MORAL | Ability to analyze the moral implications of economic decisions | Knowledge of values in the media and knowledge of your own ethical system |
|  | Ability to compare and contrast the moral implications across different companies |  |
|  | Ability to evaluate the ethical responsibilities of the mass media to society |  |

# Conclusion

When you add the economic information from this chapter to your knowledge structure about the media, you develop a deeper understanding about how decisions are made. Remember that the media industries are composed of businesses that are run to make as large a profit as they can. They do this by attempting to maximize revenues and minimize expenses. Each of the media industries does this well, and each earns a profit much higher than the average of all industries in the United States.

The media businesses play the economic game very well because they follow three strategies. First, media have a strong drive to maximize profits, and they achieve this by increasing revenue and decreasing expenses. Second, they construct niche audiences, then condition audience members into habits of continual exposures. Third, they reduce their risks by following the marketing concept.

We as consumers have two strategies available to us. One strategy is the default strategy, where we follow habits conditioned by the media. By following this strategy, we exchange our resources of time and money for a continual state of satisfaction with our habitual exposures. The alternative is to follow a media literacy strategy, where we expend more effort to develop our skills and knowledge structures *so that we profit by using the media better to fulfill our own needs for entertainment and information.*

# Further Reading

Albarran, A. B. (2002). *Media economics: Understanding markets, industries and concepts* (2nd ed.). Ames: Iowa State University Press. (229 pages, including index, glossary, and appendices)

This is a very readable introduction to economic principles and how they govern the behavior of media companies, primarily in the United States. Each of the 14 chapters begins with a list of learning objectives and ends with a clear summary, a set of discussion questions, and some exercises so readers can test their understanding of the chapter's topic. Appendix A offers a valuable list of reference sources for those who want to research particular companies or segments of the media industries.

Alexander, A., Owers, J., & Carveth, R. (Eds.). (1993). *Media economics: Theory and practice.* Hillsdale, NJ: Lawrence Erlbaum. (391 pages with glossary, indexes, and appendices)

There are 15 chapters in this edited volume, which contains a good deal of technical economic information but is presented in a readable manner. Also, a 13-page glossary defines the key terms presented throughout the book.

Picard, R. G. (1989). *Media economics: Concepts and issues.* Newbury Park, CA: Sage. (136 pages)

This is a short, straightforward introduction to the major economic principles that underlie the media industries.

**Exercise 10.1**    Estimating Your Personal Expenditures on the Media

1. Before you go any further, stop and make a general estimate about how much money you spent on all forms of the media over the past year.
   Write your estimate here: $ _____

2. Now, let's itemize those expenditures. Think back 1 year from today and try to remember how much money you spent on each of the following over the past 12 months. If you want to do this accurately, get out your checkbook register and credit card receipts.

   $_____ Cable subscription (take monthly bill and multiply by 12)
   $_____ Magazine subscriptions
   $_____ Buying individual issues of magazines
   $_____ Newspaper subscriptions
   $_____ Buying individual newspapers
   $_____ Textbooks
   $_____ Other books (pleasure reading, gifts, reference books, etc.)
   $_____ Movie theater admissions
   $_____ Rental of movies from video store
   $_____ Buying videotapes (blank and prerecorded)
   $_____ Buying CDs, tapes, and other recordings
   $_____ Buying blank audio tapes and CDs
   $_____ Buying video (Nintendo, etc.) or computer games
   $_____ Playing video games at arcades
   $_____ Buying computer software and/or manuals
   $_____ Subscription to computer services (America Online, Prodigy, etc.)
   $_____ Buying hardware (radios, televisions, VCRs and DVD players, Walkman, computers, etc.)
   $_____ Repairs on media equipment

   $_____ TOTAL (sum of all the figures down the column)

3. How close are your figures in #1 and #2?

4. Does the amount of money you spent surprise you? Why?

**Exercise 10.2**    Financial Analysis

1. Go to the library and get a list of media companies. Try the *Hoover's Guide to Media Companies* or get your reference librarian to help you. Find two media companies that look interesting to you.

2. For each company, do a brief financial analysis by answering the following questions:

   a. How much revenue did the company have last year?

   b. What were the major sources of that income?

   c. Given the sources of income, would you say that the company is primarily concerned with media businesses, or are media businesses really a sideline to other more important businesses?

   d. What were the company's expenses for the year?

   e. What was the company's profit margin? (Can you get both ROR and ROA?)

   f. What did the company do with its profits? Did it disperse all or part to the shareholders who invested in the company? Or did the company keep all or most of the profits for investing in additional media properties or other businesses?

3. Given your two analyses of the companies, in which would you rather invest your money? Why?

# Who Owns and Controls the Mass Media?

Ownership and control are not always the same thing. If you own a computer, you can decide who you will allow to use it and when. You control it as well as own it. But let's say you own 10 shares of stock in a large media company. Although you are part owner of the company, your control over that company is negligible. The ownership of almost all of the powerful media corporations is spread out across thousands of shareholders, but the control of each of those companies is in the hands of one person, the chief executive officer (CEO). Although the CEO is accountable to the shareholders, the amount of power he or she has in comparison to any one of the shareholders is enormous. Even if you were able to round up 100 of your closest millionaire friends and invest a total of $100 million in one of these powerful companies, your group as a whole would still own only a small percentage of the company.

When we think about the control of the media companies, we should not think of the owners. Instead, we need to focus our attention on the decision makers or the CEOs. Recall from the previous chapter that media companies are one of the primary players in the media economic game. The CEO then is the person who makes the major decisions for his or her company in that game. Also, recall that the primary goal of the media companies is to maximize their profits. This goal is accomplished most efficiently when a company is powerful enough to control all phases of the production and distribution of messages. Therefore, media companies have a strong drive to buy up other media companies to acquire additional revenue streams. Also, when a company owns many other companies that supply it with materials to produce their messages, that company does not have to compete with other buyers for those materials; the company has its subsidiaries supply it with the materials at cost, and this keeps expenses low. When expenses are low and there are many lucrative revenue streams, the company can generate large profits. This is why there is such a strong drive among the powerful media firms to buy up other media firms. The media businesses get more efficient and wealthy through the concentration of ownership.

As you can see, there is a strong drive among companies to merge and consolidate. But is this a good thing for the public? The American public is often skeptical about too much power being given to any one company or any one individual. American society has had a history of venerating another value that is in direct opposition to the concentration of power in the hands of a few CEOs. This competing value is called localism. Localism is the belief that power should be dispersed among as many people as possible. In fact, the United States was founded on a value of localism, and the value of localism has been in competition with the value of concentration throughout the country's history.

## Competing Forces

These key forces of localism and concentration operate in opposite directions. The localism force drives toward the goal of empowering all people and keeping them involved in as many important decisions as possible. The concentration force drives toward the goal of efficiency by consolidating resources and putting the power into the hands of a few people. This essential tension between dispersion of power and concentration of power can be seen clearly in the development of the media industries. Consumers favor localism; they want a marketplace with as many voices as possible so they have lots of choices about how to satisfy their various needs for information and entertainment. CEOs favor concentration; they focus on the capitalistic business environment where the goal is maximizing profits. In the section below, let's examine how these two forces have been competing.

## Localism in American Culture

Localism is a populist perspective. It is based on the belief that control of important institutions should be in the hands of all of the people and that the best way to do this is to keep control decentralized, that is, at the local level, where it is closest to individuals.

The founding fathers created a democratic form of government rather than a more efficient totalitarian one at the national level; they also allowed for state governments and all sorts of local governments. Political power was structured so that it was spread out over many layers. There are 18,000 municipalities and 17,000 townships. Within these, there are 500,000 local governmental units directly elected by local residents, and 170,000 of them have the power to impose taxes.

Localism is a part of the American tradition. This country was founded on the belief that the individual is more important than are institutions or governments. When government is necessary, it should be decentralized so as to be closer to the people's needs and more accountable to them. Over time, the American public has retained its value for dispersion of power and has continued to support the overlapping, multilayered structure of government, even if it often seems inefficient. The American public has also held the general belief that in the economic realm, monopolies are bad and that it is better to preserve competition among companies.

Concerning the mass media, there is also a strong feeling by many that the media voices should be kept local if they are to serve best the needs of individuals and society. The media started as innovations at the local level. When a government was called upon to regulate them, the governmental agencies have usually favored this localism ethic in their policymaking. A good example of this is how the federal government handled the development of the broadcasting industries. If you want to broadcast a radio or television signal, you must send your signal out on a frequency. If you and I want to use the same frequency to broadcast our different signals, then we will interfere with each other, and consumers will receive a garbled signal. A very limited number of frequencies are set aside for broadcasting on what is called the electromagnetic spectrum. Someone has to decide who gets to use which frequencies, then enforce these decisions so that others don't come along and interfere. The federal government decided that it was the one to make the decisions, reasoning that the electromagnetic spectrum belonged to all Americans much like a national park or any other resource that should be shared by all citizens.

In the early days of radio broadcasting, the federal government decided to require individuals to apply for a broadcast frequency with the Federal Communications Commission (FCC). The FCC was immediately flooded with applications for AM radio frequencies. But the AM band on the electromagnetic spectrum allowed for only about 117 frequencies. The FCC could have chosen 117 applicants and awarded each of them their own frequency. This would have led to 117 AM radio stations, with each using their frequency to broadcast their signal to the entire country. But that is not what the FCC did. Instead, the FCC divided the country into many local market areas and awarded some frequencies to each market. Also, each radio station was limited in the amount of power it could use to broadcast its signal so that the signals would not go beyond their local markets. This allowed the FCC to assign the same frequency to many different markets without having to worry about signals interfering with one another. The FCC chose this alternative because it wanted to spread the limited resource of broadcast frequencies around to as many different people as possible.

By keeping ownership of radio licenses at the local level, the FCC believed it was setting up a system whereby the stations would be operated in the best interests of their local communities. Private businesses were allowed to broadcast on these frequencies, provided they operate "in the public interest, convenience, and necessity." Therefore, the rationale for regulation in broadcasting is based on the following points: spectrum scarcity, localism, public interest, promoting diversity of content, and the prevention of monopolies.

Now the country has grown to about 215 broadcasting markets with 6,894 radio stations. When television came along in the 1940s, the FCC used the same procedure of allocating broadcasting licenses to local stations in the local markets. Now we have 1,895 broadcast television stations (U.S. Bureau of the Census, 2004).

For decades, the FCC prevented broadcasting monopolies from developing by limiting the number of stations any one company could own to 7 AM, 7 FM, and 7 TV stations in total, with no two being in the same market. In the 1980s, the rules were relaxed to 12 AM, 12 FM, and 12 TV stations. Then the Telecommunications Act of 1996 further relaxed the limits to a significant extent in the guise of opening up competition. Now companies can control TV stations serving up to 45% of the country; they can also own as many radio stations as they want as long as those stations do not cover more than 50% of the country's population (FCC, 2003). Also, the ban was lifted prohibiting a company from owning a TV and radio station in the same market. This deregulation triggered many mergers among media companies. During the 1990s, there was more than a total of $300 billion worth of major media deals in which companies bought multiple television and radio stations (Croteau & Hoynes, 2001).

Why would the FCC deregulate the broadcasting industry? The answer is that broadcasters put a great deal of pressure on the federal government to deregulate. Broadcasters argued that they were being unfairly limited in their rights to own multiple businesses. They pointed out that there were no ownership limits for magazines, book publishers, newspapers, cable operators, and Internet sites; also, the previous limits on film studios had been relaxed. Consumer groups could present no convincing evidence that multiple ownership of broadcasting businesses caused harm to the public. Broadcasters showed that when businesses are consolidated, they are more efficient.

## Concentration as a Goal of American Business

Straining against this ethic of localism is a very strong trend toward concentration, consolidation, and centralization. Although almost every media company began as a small, local operation, they take on the characteristics of big business as they grow. Big businesses are complex organizations that market many different products and services but do so under a strong centralized system to achieve a more efficient operation. Big businesses grow by claiming a larger share of the markets in which they compete. They accomplish this by acquiring control of more resources, and this often leads to buying—or at least investing in—other companies.

General industry-wide trends show that fewer and fewer people control more and more of the media. And this trend will probably continue as the cost of buying and operating a media voice keeps going up and as entry into the industry becomes more difficult. Today, a person needs a great deal of money and expertise to attempt to buy a mass media voice. Because of this, only companies that already own media voices are successful in acquiring new voices. This is no longer a place for the amateurs who were so instrumental in the innovation stage.

As media companies grow larger and more centralized, there is a danger that they will narrow the range of voices that will get heard. For example, if you send a letter to the editor of a newspaper with a circulation of 1,000, there is a good chance that your letter will get published. But if you send the same letter to a newspaper with a circulation of 1 million, your chance of being published is much smaller. Thus, the larger and more powerful the media company is, the less access you have for making a contribution to its messages or influencing the way it makes decisions. Larger companies must filter out more requests, and in this filtering-out process, there is a danger that some types of voices will not get heard at all.

With all the recent mergers and acquisitions in the media industries, ownership patterns have changed rapidly, but the one constant is the trend toward even greater concentration. For example, Bagdikian conducted an analysis of media ownership patterns in 1983 and found that the control of the media was essentially in the hands of 50 people— these were the CEOs of the largest media companies that, in combination, controlled more than half of the revenues and audiences in their media markets. Less than a decade later, Bagdikian (1992) found that the number had shrunk to 23 CEOs of corporations that control most of the business in the country's 25,000 media businesses. Eleven companies controlled most of the daily newspaper circulation. In magazine publishing, a majority of the total annual industry revenues went to two firms. Five firms controlled more than half of all book sales. Five media conglomerates shared 95% of the recordings market, with Warner and CBS alone controlling 65% of that market. Eight Hollywood studios accounted for 89% of U.S. feature film rentals. Three television networks earned more than two thirds of the total U.S. television revenues (Bagdikian, 1992). Then in 2000, Bagdikian published an updated version of his analysis and concluded that "six firms dominate all American mass media" (Bagdikian, 2000, p. x). Each of these six companies (Bertelsmann, Disney, General Electric, News Corp., Time Warner, and Viacom) owned media vehicles in almost all of the mass media. Bertelsmann is based in Germany; News Corp. is owned largely by Rupert Murdock, an Australian; and the other four are American corporations. However, all six own subsidiaries in many countries and market their messages all over the world.

# Cross–Ownership and Control

## Types of Concentration

There are three different trends toward concentration. First, there is the horizontal merger. This is when one media company buys another media of the same type. An example is a newspaper chain buying another newspaper. This pattern was very popular during the 1980s, when newspapers were being gobbled up by chains at the rate of 50 to 60 per year.

Second, there is the vertical merger. This is when one media company buys suppliers and/or distributors to create integration in the production and distribution of messages. An example is a book publisher buying a printing plant and some bookstores. Another example is Viacom, which owned television stations in Philadelphia, Boston, Dallas, Detroit, Pittsburgh, and Miami. It added significant vertical integration through its ownership of Paramount Pictures, thus allowing Viacom to control the production and distribution of television programs to the television networks (CBS or UPN) and through the Blockbuster stores that it owned. In addition, it could promote those shows' soundtracks on MTV and VH1 and do book tie-ins through Simon & Schuster—all of which are also owned by Viacom.

Third, there is the conglomerate merger. This is when a media company buys a combination of other media companies and/or companies in a nonmedia business. An example is a film studio that buys a newspaper, several radio stations, a talent agency, and a string of restaurants. Paramount Communications owns Paramount Studios, which is one of the leading producers of motion pictures, television shows, and cable programming. It also owns Simon & Schuster—the world's largest book publishing company. It is a major maker of entertainment videocassettes, and it controls 1,100 movie screens in the United States and 11 foreign countries (Bagdikian, 1992). Then in 1994, Viacom, which owns cable television services such as MTV, VH1, and Nickelodeon, took over Paramount Communications for $9.6 billion.

From the business point of view, cross-media ownership is very attractive. Not only is it very profitable, but the arrangement also allows for cross-promotion of products. For example, when Paramount released its movie *The Brady Bunch,* Viacom put on several weeks of Brady TV reruns on its Nickelodeon cable channel as a way of promoting the movie.

## Megamergers

During the 1980s, there were 2,308 mergers and acquisitions involving media companies for a total of $214 billion (Ozanich & Wirth, 1993). This activity served to consolidate resources in fewer companies. Thus, the CEOs of these newer, larger companies hold a greater concentration of power as they manage those resources. During the 1990s, mergers became more and more popular as media companies bought other media companies (see Table 11.1), and nonmedia companies were also buying media properties (see Table 11.2) because they are so profitable. For example, Westinghouse Electric Corporation, which began as a manufacturer of railroad air brakes in Pittsburgh in 1886, decided to change its line of business. By 1995, it had bought one of the major television networks—CBS—for $5.4 billion, then spent another $9 billion buying cable channels and radio stations over the next 2 years. In 1997, it moved its headquarters to New York City and took the name CBS ("CBS Headquarters," 1997).

Phone companies keep looking for entertainment companies to buy. For example, GTE has 17 million phone lines and $20 billion revenue annually. BellSouth is the biggest regional phone company with 19 million phone lines, which bring in a total of $16 billion per year. With all their cash, the phone companies are looking to invest in profitable businesses, especially those that would give them access to customers who want to buy information and entertainment.

## International Perspective

It is not uncommon for foreign companies to buy or invest in American media companies. In 1 year, companies from the United Kingdom made 188 deals totaling $23.6 billion to buy U.S. media companies, Japanese companies made 45 transactions for $11.9 billion, Canadian companies made 46 deals for $9.7 billion, French companies made 26 deals for $3.0 billion, and German companies made 27 transactions for $1.2 billion. Also, through the decade of the 1990s, foreign companies were buying American media properties, especially film studios. For example, Pathe, a French-Italian firm, bought MGM and United Artists. Sony, a Japanese electronics manufacturer, bought Columbia Pictures from Coca-Cola. Also, about 13% of all American newspapers are owned by non-American companies (Albarran & Chan-Olmsted, 1998).

**Table 11.1**     Media Megamergers

---

- January 1986: Capital Cities Communications, Inc. purchases American Broadcasting Company for $3.5 billion to create Capital Cities/ABC, Inc.
- November 1989: Sony Corp. buys film and television producer Columbia Pictures Entertainment, Inc. for $3.4 billion.
- January 1990: Warner Communications, Inc. and Time, Inc. complete $14.1 billion merger, creating world's biggest media conglomerate at the time.
- January 1991: Matsushita Electric Industrial Co. of Japan buys MCA, Inc. for $6.9 billion.
- September 1993: The New York Times Co. buys Affiliated Publications, Inc., parent company of *The Boston Globe,* for $1.1 billion, the biggest takeover in U.S. newspaper history.
- July 1994: Viacom, Inc. buys Paramount Communications, Inc. for $10 billion after winning a bidding war against QVC, Inc. to buy the movie, publishing, and sports company.
- August 1994: Viacom, Inc. buys video rental chain Blockbuster Entertainment Corp. for $8 billion.
- August 1995: Walt Disney Co. acquires Capital Cities/ABC, Inc. for $19 billion, making it the largest media company at the time. ABC had been concerned about the fragmentation of the television audiences due to cable, so it diversified and bought ESPN and Lifetime cable channels as well as the Disney channel. This made Disney the first media company with four distribution systems: filmed entertainment, cable television, broadcasting, and telephone wires.
- October 1996: Time Warner and Turner Broadcasting System complete $7.6 billion merger. This becomes the world's biggest media company, with annual revenues of more than $20 billion.
- November 1996: Penguin Group, the international publisher, buys Putnam Berkley Group, a U.S. subsidiary of MCA (owned by Seagram Co.) for $336 million. Penguin is strong with backlist books (Arthur Miller, Gabriel García Márquez, Toni Morrison, E. L. Doctorow, Joyce Carol Oates), and Putnam has a strong front list (Stephen King, Terry McMillan, Tom Clancy, Patricia Cornwell).
- February 1997: A merger of two radio companies created Chancellor Media Corp., which took control over 103 radio stations that generate more than $700 million annually in revenue. The top-ranked radio group is Infinity Broadcasting ($1.1 billion in revenue annually), which is owned by Westinghouse Electric Corp.
- January 1998: Compaq Computer Corp. buys Digital Equipment Corp. for $9.6 billion. This made Compaq one of the three largest computer companies in the world in terms of sales. This was the biggest buyout in the history of the computer industry to that point.
- May 1998: Condé Nast Publications, Inc. buys *Wired*—the San Francisco–based cutting-edge bible of the cyberspace revolution. The deal was in excess of $75 million. The magazine was cofounded by a husband-and-wife team in 1993. At the time of the sale, *Wired*'s circulation was 400,000 and had $31.5 million in ad revenue. Condé Nast is a unit of Advance Publications (publishers of the *New Yorker, Vanity Fair,* and *Vogue*), which in turn is a division of the Newhouse newspaper publishing chain.
- December 1998: CBS Corp. raises $2.9 billion by selling a 17% stake in Infinity Broadcasting Corp., its radio and outdoor advertising business. The initial public offering of stock is the largest ever in the media industry.

---

*(Continued)*

**Table 11.1** (Continued)

- April 1999: CBS Corp. announces an agreement to buy King World Productions, Inc., the leading syndicator of television programs, for $2.5 billion.
- September 1999: Viacom announces a merger with CBS Television Network for $38 billion, making it the biggest deal between any two media companies. The merger combines film, television, radio, Internet sites, book publishing, and many other businesses.
- October 1999: Clear Channel Communications, Inc. agrees to buy AMFM, Inc. for $16.6 billion in stock, creating the nation's largest radio company.
- November 1999: Spelling Entertainment Group, Inc. sells Virgin Interactive Entertainment to concentrate it resources on its television and film operations (*Melrose Place* and *Beverly Hills, 90210*). Virgin produces video games (Nintendo) and computer games. Spelling is owned by Viacom, Inc.
- November 1999: American Media, Inc., publisher of the *National Enquirer* and the *Star,* among other newspapers, acquired Globe Communications, Inc., publisher of the *Globe* and the *Sun*, for $105 million. David Pecker, chairman of American Media, said that the merger would create "one of the largest publishers of celebrity-driven content in the world." The new company is projected to generate about $400 million in annual revenue.
- January 2000: America Online, Inc. agrees to buy Time Warner, Inc. in a $135 billion merger agreement, the largest ever combination in the media industry.
- January 2000: Time Warner, Inc. (record labels of Atlantic, Elektra, and Warner Brothers) and Britain's EMI Group (record labels of Virgin, Priority, and Capitol) agreed to merge their music businesses, thus creating the world's biggest music company, with combined annual revenues of $8 billion. The new firm would represent 2,500 musicians.
- February 2000: Germany's Mannesmann AG merged with Britain's Vodafone AirTouch PLC for $180 billion, making it the largest merger in the history of the world. The combined company would have 42 million customers and be the leader in mobile phone service in 11 European countries.
- March 2000: The Chicago Tribune Company took over the Times Mirror Co., which publishes the *Los Angeles Times.* The $6.3 billion deal made the Tribune Company the country's third largest newspaper group, with control of 3.6 million in daily circulation across 11 daily newspapers. The company also owns 22 TV stations (in Chicago, Los Angeles, and New York) and Internet sites. The new company reaches 75% of the country's households through its broadcast and cable TV services.

SOURCES: Compiled from AP Online (2000); Fabrikant (1995); Greimel (2000); Hofmeister (1997a, 1997b); Holstein (1999); Lorimer (1994); Lyall (1996); McDonald (2000).

An example of how American companies attract foreign investors is Rupert Murdoch, an Australian who owns newspapers in most of the major cities in Australia along with the country's only national daily, television stations, publishing houses, record companies, and a major airline. He went to Great Britain and bought the *London Times,* two sex and scandal sheets with a combined circulation of more than 8 million, a string

**Table 11.2**    Nonmedia Companies Buy Media Companies

---

- June 1986: General Electric Co. buys RCA Corp., parent company of National Broadcasting Co. and the NBC television network, for $6.4 billion. At the time, the deal was the largest nonoil acquisition in U.S. history. In the same year Capital Cities bought ABC.
- May 1993: US West, a telephone company, pays $2.5 billion for 25.5% of Time Warner. The new company plans to integrate the technologies that would provide a service where people could instantly order whatever programming they want (movies on demand), shop for products, do their banking, listen to CDs, watch live sports and concerts, make travel plans, play video games, and so on.
- June 1995: Seagram Co. buys MCA, Inc. from Matsushita for $5.7 billion and renames it Universal Studios.
- November 1995: Westinghouse Electric Corp. buys CBS, Inc. for $5.4 billion, giving the new company 15 TV stations and 39 radio stations that, combined, give it direct access to one third of the nation's households.
- November 1996: Seagram Co. now owns about 80% of MCA, which owns Putnam publishing, films, records, and theme parks.
- December 1996: Westinghouse Electric Corp.'s CBS unit buys Infinity Broadcasting Co. for $4.7 billion, combining the nation's two biggest radio station operators.
- September 1997: Seagram Co. buys half of the USA Networks (reaches 70 million homes and includes USA and Sci Fi channels) from Viacom for $1.7 billion in September 1997. Seagram also owns Universal Studios, so it can now produce and distribute programming.
- December 1997: Westinghouse Electric Corp. changes its name to CBS, Inc. shortly after deciding to sell its traditional businesses such as power generation equipment and light bulbs.
- December 1998: Seagram Co. buys the PolyGram music company for $10.4 billion.
- February 1999: AT&T joins with Time Warner, Inc. in a deal to offer local and long-distance telephone service, cable TV, and high-speed Internet access over Time Warner's cable systems in 33 states. Because AT&T has already acquired Tele-Communications, Inc., AT&T raises its access to 40% of U.S. households. This deal also lets AT&T back into providing local phone service, which it had been prevented from doing since its breakup in 1984.

---

SOURCES: Compiled from AP Online (2000); "CBS Headquarters" (1997); Hofmeister (1997a, 1997b); Lyall (1996); Maney (1995).

of magazines, a string of provincial newspapers, and companies for manufacturing paper, printing, and distributing newsprint. He came to the United States and bought the *New York Post, New York Magazine, Village Voice, Chicago-Sun Times,* two other daily newspapers, and 17 suburban weeklies. He has also bought Metromedia's seven television stations in New York, Boston, and other major cities, giving him access to 21% of the total television audience. His empire earns more than $1 billion a year. Recently, Murdoch's Australian firm, News Corp., bought the remaining 18% of its U.S. Fox Entertainment Group, Inc. unit, giving it full ownership of 20th Century Fox film studios and the Fox network and channels.

Globalization works both ways. American companies market their entertainment services worldwide. For example, by 1993, MTV was in cable systems in more than 71 countries, reaching more than 500 million people (Barber, 1995). By 1995, ESPN was offering programming to 150 countries in 18 languages.

Media economist Alan Albarran (2002) regards globalization as one of the most important economic trends in recent years. He explains that markets for media messages have been saturated in the United States, so for American media companies to open up even more revenue streams and to increase the flow of income even more, they need to market their messages in other countries.

# Concentration in Advertising

As the media become more concentrated, so too does the advertising industry. The large, national agencies are becoming larger so that they can deal better with the larger media companies. As ad agencies grow bigger, they become much less interested in local retailers and local markets, instead favoring the much larger national market where they can make bigger deals and more money. Thus, most of the advertising today is for national brands. For example, when most people think of hamburgers, they think of McDonald's, Burger King, and Wendy's—not the local restaurant run as a family business. So the trend toward concentration is not just within the media industries; it is also with retail stores and with advertising agencies.

The world of advertising has also been exhibiting a strong drive toward concentration, especially over the past two decades. This can be seen with advertisers as well as with advertising agencies.

## Concentration Among Advertisers

Manufacturers are buying each other up in an effort to get bigger and bigger. This gives them more power in the marketplace, helps them increase profits by diversifying into several businesses, and gives them more power as advertisers. For example, Proctor & Gamble has usually been the number one advertiser in the world since 1913. It sells its products in 140 countries and advertises heavily in all. It will spend more than $3 billion on advertising this year. On TV alone, it will buy more than 28,000 ads, which would take you 10 days of solid viewing (24 hours per day continuously) to watch them all. Therefore, Proctor & Gamble exerts an enormous amount of power. Other examples include McDonald's, which has 17,000 franchise restaurants in 90 different countries, including 760 in Japan; their largest restaurant is in Beijing (Barber, 1995). Coca-Cola is in 160 countries (Barnet & Cavanagh, 1994), and two thirds of Coke's revenue comes from outside the United States (Barber, 1995).

Some very large companies have so many products that we as consumers do not realize that many of the products that appear very different are marketed by the same company. For example, PepsiCo, Inc. markets beverages (Pepsi, Slice, Mountain Dew, and root beer), but it also owns and controls the largest restaurant system in the world, which includes Kentucky Fried Chicken, Pizza Hut, and Taco Bell. In fall of 1998, Coca-Cola bought Cadbury Schweppes beverage brands (Schweppes, Dr. Pepper, Crush, Canada Dry) outside the United States for $1.85 billion. Also, Quaker Oats is only a cereal, right? Not exactly. It markets its oatmeal and also other cereals (Cap'n Crunch), Gatorade, Van Camp's Pork & Beans, Rice-A-Roni, Gaines dog food, Ken-L Ration dog food, granola bars, rice cakes, Aunt Jemima breakfast foods, and Fisher-Price toys. Quaker Oats is typically one of the top 30 companies in the world in terms of advertising budgets.

How about cigarettes? Are you trying to be socially responsible and not buy products that would support companies that market harmful products? You recognize the name of Phillip Morris as a cigarette company—it manufactures and sells Marlboro, Merit, Virginia Slims, and Benson & Hedges. Did you know that Phillip Morris Co. owns General Foods and Miller Brewing? General Foods includes Maxwell House coffee (Maxwell House, Sanka, International Coffees, Brim, and Yuban), Birds Eye frozen foods, Post cereals (Raisin Bran, Grape-Nuts, Honeycombs, Fruit & Fibre, 40% Bran Flakes, Crispy Critters, Pebbles, Super Golden Crisp, Alpha Bits), Tang, Country Time, Kool-Aid, Minute Rice, Stove Top Stuffing, Dream Whip, Jell-O, Crystal Light, Ronzoni, Shake 'n Bake, Log Cabin syrup, Oscar Meyer meats, Louis Rich, and many, many others. Miller of course makes Miller High-Life, Miller Lite, and Miller Genuine Draft, but it also makes Henry Weinhard's, Hamm's, and Milwaukee's Best.

RJ Reynolds is another tobacco company. It manufactures and markets Salem, Vantage, Ritz, Doral, Magna, Camel, Now, More, and Winston. But it also owns Life Savers, Carefree gum, Del Monte Foods, and Nabisco. Notice that what we think are just two tobacco companies actually are responsible for many more products than cigarettes.

## Concentration Among Advertising Agencies

Just as businesses that manufacture the products are getting bigger and bigger, so are ad agencies. Half of all the advertising placed in the United States each year is handled by one of the world's top 20 advertising agencies. This means there is an enormous amount of concentration, with many instances of an agency handling the accounts of direct competitors.

In 1986, three agencies—BBDO, Doyle Dane, Bernback and Needham Harper—joined together to become the world's biggest. A month later, Britain's Saatchi & Saatchi took over the Ted Bates agency, creating a new number-one agency ($7.5 billion worth of business). Agencies keep buying each other and consolidating so that every few months, there is a new "largest advertising agency in the world." In May 2000, the London-based WPP Group PLC (which previously had bought the U.S. ad agencies of J. Walter Thompson and Ogilvy & Mather) bought the American agency Young & Rubicam. This consolidated firm now handles the business of the following huge advertisers: AT&T, Cadbury Schweppes, Colgate-Palmolive, Ford Motor Co., Kraft Foods, and Sears.

# Issues of Concern

All this merger activity has raised many issues of concern. I will present four of them in this section: the fallout from deregulation, the reduced level of competition, the lack of access by the public to media voices, and how to deal with the Internet.

## Deregulation

As you saw earlier in this chapter, the merging of media companies has been taking place for decades, although governmental regulations imposed some limits. Also, the Federal Communications Commission and the Federal Trade Commission watched the media industries closely for problems with certain firms getting too powerful. But then in 1996, Congress passed the Telecommunications Act and largely removed the last remaining limitations to consolidation. In that year alone, there were $25 billion in merger activity in the broadcasting industry and another $23 billion in the cable industry (Jensen, 1997). Since 1996, the FCC has been less concerned with preventing monopolies within the United States and more concerned with allowing American companies to grow significantly stronger to compete and dominate in the world market (Albarran & Chan-Olmsted, 1998). FCC Chairman William Kennard said that he is merely recognizing the realities of globalization and new technologies.

One feature of the 1996 deregulation eliminated the longstanding restriction of allowing one company to own two television stations in the same market. It had long been believed that broadcast television stations were far too precious a local resource to allow one company to own more than one in a given television market. Almost all local markets had very few broadcast stations (typically three to five broadcast television stations), so it was important to have as many owners as possible to ensure a diversity of voices. However, over time, as greater numbers of people subscribed to cable television services, regulators came to believe that people in all local communities had access to many different voices, and therefore the limits on broadcast station ownership were no longer important.

The media industries have been moving steadily toward greater concentration both within each industry and especially across media industries. Critics fear that this trend has already put too much power into the hands of a very few people. For example, Table 11.3 shows that the top eight firms in the recording and motion picture industries account for virtually all the revenue in those industries. Even in the book industry, which is fairly unconcentrated relative to the other media industries, the top eight companies account for half of all book revenue. Furthermore, the figures in Table 11.3, which reveal a high degree of concentration, are likely to underestimate the degree of concentration in the media industries because they do not take into consideration cross-ownership patterns; that is, they do not account for a firm owning and controlling revenue in several mass media industries at once. To see how much cross-ownership there is, look at what the top seven media conglomerates each control (see Table 11.4).

**Table 11.3**   Indicators of Concentration in Segments of the Mass Media

| CR4 | CR8 | Mass Medium |
|-----|-----|-------------|
| 98 | 99 | Recording industry |
| 78 | 99 | Motion pictures |
| 77 | 91 | Magazine |
| 77 | 88 | Radio |
| 53 | 80 | Cable and satellite television |
| 48 | 69 | Daily newspapers |
| 30 | 50 | Book |
| NA | NA | Broadcast television |
| NA | NA | Internet |

SOURCE: Compiled from Albarran (2001).

NOTE: CR4 = concentration ratio of top four firms (percentage of total revenues of the major four players in the industry); CR8 = concentration ratio of top eight firms: percentage of total revenues of the major eight players in the industry; NA = not applicable.

**Table 11.4**   Most Powerful Media Companies in the United States, as of 2003

**AOL Time Warner** ($41 billion)

- Broadcast television—WB network; Kids' WB!
- Cable—Time Warner Cable (11 million subscribers); pay cable channels (HBO and Cinemax); 9 local news cable channels; Turner Broadcasting (CNN, Headline News, TBS, TNT, Turner Classic Movies, The Cartoon Network)
- Film—TV production and film production (Warner Brothers Pictures, New Line Cinema, Fine Line Features, New Line International, New Line Television, Castle Rock Entertainment, and Telepictures Productions [produced *Friends, Lord of the Rings*]); library of more than 6,000 films, 25,000 TV programs, and thousands of animated shows (such as Looney Tunes and Hanna-Barbera); Warner Brothers International Cinemas (123 screens in the United States and 650 screens in other countries)

*(Continued)*

**Table 11.4** (Continued)

- Recordings—Warner Brothers Music Group, Atlantic, Elektra, and numerous smaller labels
- Magazines—largest publisher of magazines in the United States, with 130 magazines reaching more than 300 million people worldwide, including *Time, Life, People, Fortune, Money, Sports Illustrated, Entertainment Weekly, In Style, Sunset, Parenting, Southern Living,* and *Teen People*
- Internet—America Online (30 million subscribers); Compuserve; McAfee Virus Scan, Mapquest, Netscape, Winamp
- Newspapers—7 dailies
- Books—Little, Brown; Book of the Month Club; DC Comics (Superman, Batman, *Mad* magazine, and 60 other titles)
- New media—AOL, with its 20 million Internet subscribers
- Sports—Atlanta Braves (baseball), Atlanta Hawks (basketball), Atlanta Thrashers (hockey); World Championship Wrestling
- Other—Warner Brothers Studio Stores (more than 150 worldwide); MovieFone

**Walt Disney** ($25.3 billion)

- Broadcast television—10 TV stations; ABC Television Network
- Cable—ESPN, Fox Family, Toon Disney, and Disney Channel; also holdings in Lifetime, A&E, History Channel, and E!
- Radio—59 radio stations; ABC Radio Network
- Film—Walt Disney Studios; Touchstone Films, Miramax Films, Hollywood Films, Buena Vista Filmed Entertainment, Walt Disney Feature Animation, Buena Vista International, and a partnership with Pixar
- Magazines—*Discover, Los Angeles Magazine*
- Books—Hyperion books
- Recordings—Hollywood Records, Mammoth Records, Walt Disney Records
- Sports—Anaheim Angels (baseball), Mighty Ducks of Anaheim (hockey)
- Other—theme parks; consumer products; The Disney Store; petroleum and natural gas production interests

**Viacom** ($24.6 billion)

- Broadcast television—CBS and UPN television networks; Paramount Television Studio (*JAG, Entertainment Tonight*), Spelling Television, and King World Productions (*Jeopardy, Wheel of Fortune*); Viacom Stations Group (39 TV stations)
- Cable—Comedy Central, Nickelodeon, MTV, VH1, TV Land, TNN (now Spike TV), CMT (Country Music Television), Showtime, BET (Black Entertainment Television)
- Radio—Infinity Broadcasting chain of 183 radio stations; CBS radio network; Westwood One; Metro Networks
- Books—Simon & Schuster, Scribner, Pocket Books, Anne Schwartz Books, Archway Paperbacks, Lisa Drew Books, Fireside, Free Press, MTV Books, Nickelodeon Books, Pocket Books, Star Trek Books, Washington Square Press

- Film production—Paramount Pictures (including a library of more than 2,500 titles), Nickelodeon Movies, MTV Films, Nickelodeon Studios, United International Pictures (33%), Spelling Films, Republic Entertainment, Worldvisions Enterprises
- Film theaters—Paramount Theaters, Famous Players Theaters (1,700 screens in 13 countries), United Cinemas International
- Recordings—Famous Music (copyright holders of more than 100,000 songs)
- New media—MTV Networks On Line and Marketwatch.com, CBS.com, CBSSportsLine.com, CBSMarketWatch.com, and Country.com
- Other—Blockbuster Video; five amusement parks; TDI Worldwide and Outdoor Systems, which sell ad space on 210,000 billboards nationwide; Star Trek franchise

**Comcast** ($21.1 billion)
- Cable—nation's leading cable television operator
- New media—high-speed Internet access

**Sony** ($17.2 billion)
- Television—Columbia TriStar Television (*Dawson's Creek, The Young & the Restless*); Game Show Network
- Film—Sony Pictures Entertainment, Columbia TriStar Motion Picture Group, Columbia TriStar Home Video, Columbia TriStar Television Group (*Spiderman, Men in Black*)
- Recordings—Sony Music Entertainment, CBS Records, Columbia Records, Epic, Legacy, Tri-Star Music
- New media—Sony PlayStation video games

**News Corp.** ($15.2 billion)
- Broadcast television—Fox network; 35 stations in the United States
- Radio—Fox Sports Radio Network
- Cable—FX, Fox Sports Net, Fox News Channel, Golf Channel, National Geographic
- Magazine—*TV Guide*
- Newspapers—*New York Post* and 175 newspapers internationally
- Books—HarperCollins, William Morris Books, Avon Books, Regan Books
- Film—20th Century Fox, Fox 2000, Fox Studios, Fox Searchlight, Fox Animation Studios Studio
- New media—DirectTV
- Sports—Los Angeles Dodgers (baseball); part owner of Staples Center

**General Eletric** ($13 billion)
- Television—NBC television network and 14 stations
- Cable—MSNBC, CNBC, Bravo
- Film—Universal Studios
- Other—theme parks

SOURCES: Compiled from Albarran (2001); Baker, Falk, and Manners (2000); Bettig and Hall (2003); Croteau and Hoynes (2001); Flanigan (2003); Polman (2003); Verrier and James (2003).

## Lack of Competition

Critics argue that as competition among media companies decreases, the quality of media products declines. But has the quality of the media products declined? There is no evidence that it has. For example, research has not found that when a radio station is bought by a conglomerate the content degrades. Lacy and Riffe (1994) looked at the news content of radio stations and compared group ownership effects. They found that group ownership had no impact on the financial commitment or the local and staff emphasis of news coverage.

Also, a study done on newspaper content could find no change in content after a newspaper was bought by a chain (e.g., see Picard, Winter, McCombs, & Lacy, 1988). No evidence of change was found with the stories, the range of opinions on the editorial page, or the proportion of the newspaper displaying news.

This criticism that concentration of ownership reduces competition in a market seems valid on the surface, but it breaks down when analyzed. To illustrate, let's say a city has two newspapers. A chain buys one of those newspapers. The chain-owned newspaper cuts subscription costs and ad rates. Readers and advertisers switch to the chain newspaper because it is less expensive. Eventually, the other newspaper goes out of business. The degree of concentration in that market goes up. But this does not mean that the newspaper has no competition simply because it is the only newspaper in the market. The newspaper must compete for audiences and advertisers along with the radio, television, and cable stations in the market. Thus, if the newspaper degrades its news product, people will drop their subscriptions and turn to other sources of news. With lower circulation rates, the newspaper will need to drop the rate it charges advertisers, and this will produce less revenue. With less revenue, the newspaper will need to lay off reporters, and the news product further degrades. This downward cycle continues until the newspaper is out of business. But this almost never happens because chain-owned newspapers are driven by making large profits, and to do that, they must do everything they can to expand their circulations and hence their appeal to advertisers.

Newspapers, as well as all the other media, expand their revenues only by providing more and better services to consumers. How do they know what consumers want? They are constantly doing market research to test out new ideas. Also, they carefully monitor the public reactions, verbal as well as monetary, to their messages. When the public's tastes or wants change, the media know this, and they offer new types of products and messages.

Many critics argue that the media industries lose diversity when the industries become more concentrated. Fewer voices should mean fewer opinions getting aired. However, Einstein (2004) points out that "in study after study, scholars have determined that there is no proven causality between media ownership and programming content" (p. vii). Einstein argues that the reduction in the number of program choices is not due to consolidation but to television's reliance on advertising as its primary source of revenue. Because of this reliance, there are severe limits on content, which include time limes for length of program, the "lowest common denominator" mentality, and an avoidance of controversy. In an analysis of the TV industry over the past four decades, Einstein reveals that as the industry became more concentrated, programming became more diverse. She said that diversity was at its peak in the late 1960s and then declined when the FCC imposed regulations about sharing programs through syndication. Then, when those syndication rules were relaxed and broadcasters could keep the programs they produced to themselves, diversity increased sharply in prime time.

Although the businesspeople in media organizations generally leave the creative people alone to do what they do best and attract large audiences, the business side can spill over onto the editorial side at newspapers in some cases. This was clearly illustrated in the fall of 1999, when the *Los Angeles Times Magazine* devoted coverage of the Staples Center, a new sports arena. The publisher, Kathryn M. Downing, had entered into a partnership agreement on the issue with the Staples Center, agreeing to have the Staples Center promote the magazine in return for sharing profits. Downing did not tell her reporters or editors about the business partnership. When the journalists found out, they complained about not knowing the magazine had been turned into a public relations device for the Staples Center. Downing, whose background was as a business manager and not as a journalist, apologized, saying that she did not realize that her actions would damage the journalistic integrity of the newspaper ("*L.A. Times* Publisher Errs, Apologizes," 1999).

The danger presented by so much consolidation is not in lost quality in the production of messages. The media companies have a huge stake in attracting and holding audiences, whether they have competition or not. The danger instead is that the messages are too slick and too commercial; this would greatly limit the scope of possible messages available to the public.

## Lack of Access

Critics argue that as concentration increases, the individual's access to the media is reduced. *Access* here can mean two different things. One meaning is ownership; that is, how much access does an individual have to own a media property? Because most media companies are public corporations, any individual can buy a share of any company. But can a person own a media property fully? The answer still is yes. There are comparatively low barriers to entry in the magazine, book publishing, weekly newspaper, and computer industries. With several thousand dollars, a desktop computer, and a strong initiative, most people could begin a company in one of these media industries. Of course, he or she should be prepared to face very stiff competition to gain the attention of an audience and the confidence of advertisers. But it is possible to create one's own media voice in those industries. In contrast, barriers to entry are much higher in the radio, television, cable, and film industries, and the conglomerate mergers over the past several decades have raised those barriers much higher, almost to the point of being prohibitive for anyone except the wealthiest individuals and the biggest companies.

Access can also mean the ability to get your particular point of view heard through someone else's media property. This is still relatively easy to do at the local level, such as with newspapers and small-circulation magazines. Most still print letters to the editors, and most buy articles from people with little journalistic experience. Also, most markets have call-in radio programs where you can get your voice heard. In contrast, national media properties, such as *Newsweek* magazine or a TV or cable network, require a great deal of skill and good connections to get your voice heard because the competition to use those channels is so strong.

## Internet

Because the Internet is new and was created as such a diversified means of communication, researchers are still working on the problem of how to keep track of all the activity of hundreds of millions of people visiting billions of Web sites and pages. Until companies can deliver accurate exposure figures, it is difficult to convince advertisers how much value they are getting for their advertising dollar. Also, until the major media conglomerates can figure out how to harness all the Web surfing to channel people to certain sites only and condition their habits on those sites, those major companies will not be willing to invest large sums in owning those sites.

Although the Internet is still very new, there are signs that some of the challenges laid out in the previous paragraph are being met. For example, estimates indicate that the top 100 visited Web sites account for half of all Web sites visited. Also, between March 1999 and March 2001 the total number of companies controlling half of U.S. user minutes online shrank from 11 to 4 (Bettig & Hall, 2003). This is indeed powerful evidence that the Internet is also becoming highly concentrated despite its newness and the wide variety of Web sites available.

One tool that has helped this concentration occur so quickly is the search engine. People use search engines—such as Google and Yahoo—to tell them which sites they should visit to get information on various topics. Users type in a keyword describing the topic, and the search engine provides the user with a list of sites. For example, as I write this, I get on Google and do a search for the keyword *news.* Google searches for 0.14 seconds, then tells me that there are 407 million hits—that is, this search engine found 407 million Web sites concerned with the topic of "news." Google then shows me the addresses of the first 10 of those 407 million Web sites, so that I can click on one of those addresses and go to that Web site. Those 10 sites in order are as follows: CNN.com, BBC News, ABC News, FoxNews.com, Google News, usnews.com, wired.com, news.cnet.com, CBS News, and Yahoo News. These 10 are presumably the most popular. But let's think about how they got to be the most popular. They show up at the top of Google's list because they are the most popular, and because they are the most popular, they are presented first by Google. Kind of a circular process, isn't it? Then how does a Web site break into this cycle? The answer is to pay for placement on Google. This is why Google makes so much money as a company—it sells placement on its searches. You can buy popularity. If you buy a high enough placement in a Google search, then the most people will see your address and likely visit your Web site. When you get the most visits among all your competitors, you are the most popular and will continue to place high on the Google searches. The companies with the most money can buy the highest placements. Thus, the Internet becomes more and more concentrated in terms of a few Web sites on each topic area consuming the most visits.

# Conclusion

Media critics are wary of the degree of concentration in the media industries. Their concern is focused on the central issue of which is more important: efficiency (brought about by industry integration and economics of scale) *or* independence (diversity of content and easier entry into the market, thus allowing alternative voices).

This is an issue about which you likely have an opinion. But to synthesize a good opinion, you need to build it up from an analysis of the situation. This chapter provides such an analysis to begin your thinking. You should continue your thinking on this topic by considering which ethic you think should be dominant in the formulation of the media industries. Do you favor localism, with its focus on the power of society—through citizen activism and government regulations—to make the media be responsive to the different needs of the broad spectrum of people in the society? Or do you find more favor with concentration as a goal of businesses driven to operate more effectively and efficiently and thus generate as large a profit as possible for the owners?

Once you get interested in this issue and begin formulating your opinion, you need to monitor changes in this dynamic situation and continually update your knowledge structures. Over time, the government has been relaxing regulations, and as a result, businesses have been moving strongly toward concentration. But there is still a great deal of competition among the media industries as they try to claim more of our attention and more of a share of the advertiser's dollar.

# Further Reading

Bagdikian, B. H. (2000). *The media monopoly* (6th ed.). Boston: Beacon. (288 pages with endnotes and index)

Since 1983, Bagdikian has been conducting an economic analysis of the media industries to track the degree of concentration. With each new edition, the number of powerful companies shrinks as their media (as well as nonmedia) holdings dramatically grow. This book is a must-read for anyone concerned about how much power is being concentrated in the hands of a few CEOs of media holding companies.

Bettig, R. V., & Hall, J. L. (2003). *Big media, big money: Cultural texts and political economies.* Lanham, MD: Rowman & Littlefield. (181 pages with bibliography and references)

In this book, two professors at Penn State University argue that the media have been unfettered in their drive for greater profits and control over constructing meaning in our culture. They present a great deal of detail in support of this thesis in their six chapters. The authors demonstrate that the result of this media consolidation is that a few very powerful companies are becoming even more invasive in our lives and are successfully supplanting family, friend, religion, and education as the controlling source of constructing meaning.

Doyle, G. (2002). *Understanding media economics.* London: Sage. (184 pages, including references and index)

This book was written for people who do not have a background in economics but who want to learn about how the media industries operate along economic principles. Although the examples are primarily from Great Britain and Europe, they illustrate economic trends and principles that also operate in the United States.

Einstein, M. (2004). *Media diversity: Economics, ownership, and the FCC.* Mahwah, NJ: Lawrence Erlbaum. (249 pages, including references, appendices, and indexes)

The author examines the issue of whether the consolidation in the media industries has led to a lessening of diversity. This book offers strong historical and economic perspectives on the issue. She concludes that despite a clear consolidation of ownership of media properties and the narrowing in the number of people making decisions about media content, there is even more diversity in messages now than there was four decades ago.

Maney, K. (1995). *Megamedia shakeout: The inside story of the leaders and the losers in the exploding communications industry.* New York: John Wiley. (358 pages, including index)

This is a well-written description of the major players in the technologies landscape in the mid-1990s. There are lots of anecdotes and stories about what has been happening in the telephone, cable, computer, wireless, and entertainment industries. The book is full of facts and personal descriptions of the personalities involved. However, things are happening so fast in these industries with new rollouts and buyouts that the book is likely out of date.

**Exercise 11.1**     What Is the Concentration of Media Ownership in Your Local Market?

This exercise asks you to be a detective to search out information in your local media market. See how creative you can be in coming up with strategies to get the answers to the following questions.

1. How many movie screens are there in your market?
   a. How many theaters control those screens?
   b. Are the theaters owned by chains? If so, how many chains control the total set of screens?

2. How many radio stations are there in your market?
   a. How many are group owned?
   b. How many of the stations are owned by companies that also own other media businesses in your market?

3. How many broadcast television stations are there in your market?
   a. How many are group owned?
   b. How many of the stations are owned by companies that also own other media businesses in your market?

4. Is your local newspaper owned by a chain? If so, does it own other media businesses in your market?

5. Are there any magazines published in your market and distributed only in your market? If so, does the controlling company also own other media businesses?

6. What is the name of the company that provides your market with cable TV service? Is that cable company a multiple system operator?

7. In total, how many different media outlets (voices) are there in your market? How many individuals or companies control these voices?

8. If you wanted to express yourself through the media in your market, how hard do you think it would be to gain access to one of these outlets?
   a. For example, assume that you wanted to criticize some new governmental regulation or tax policy in your local area. Which outlet would be most likely to give you space or time to speak out?
   b. Which outlet(s) do you think would be the hardest or impossible?

9. Given your answers to the questions above, how concentrated do you think your market is—that is, do you think the outlets are in the control of too few individuals?

# CHAPTER 12

# What Is an Audience?

*Key Idea:* We are members of many different niche audiences that are constructed by the mass media, then maintained by conditioning our habits.

Each of us spends a great deal of time with the mass media. Recall from Table 9.3 that the *United States Statistical Abstract* indicates that the average American is spending about 10 hours per day with the media. Some researchers put this figure at almost 12 hours per day (Consoli, 1998), and others claim that this amount will continue to increase due to steady increases in time spent on the Internet (Merli, 1998) and video games (Kaiser Family Foundation, 2002). Because we spend so much time with the media, it is tempting to think that people are actively seeking out exposures and are therefore responsible for constructing the audiences to which they belong. This is inaccurate because it makes it seem that people are the active agents and that the media are responding to our demands for messages. It is more accurate to regard the media as the active agents—that is, they are actively constructing audiences, and we respond by allowing them to do this.

The media actively construct audiences by crafting certain kinds of messages to lure certain kinds of people. Once they have attracted those people, they do everything they can to reinforce that exposure behavior by conditioning those audience members into exposure habits. A key to becoming media literate is to understand how this process works. This understanding will sensitize you to examine what audiences you currently inhabit, and once you realize this, you can gain more control over the decision about which audiences you want to continue to be a part of and which other audiences you would like to join.

This chapter will provide you with the background information about audiences to help strengthen your locus. Then the exercises at the end of this chapter will help you examine your audience memberships.

# The Nature of Audience

What is an audience? At first, this question may seem very simple with an obvious answer. But the way media programmers have been thinking about audiences has changed from perceiving the audience as a large mass of undifferentiated people to regarding audiences as many niches of people as defined by their special interests.

## What Is a Mass Audience?

Until fairly recently, many media programmers and researchers believed there was something called a "mass" audience for the mass media. The term *mass communication* came into use about a century ago, when early social philosophers posited that newspapers, magazines, and books communicated their ideas to all audience members in roughly the same way. If a message affected one member a certain way, it would affect all audience members the same way.

The term *mass* did not refer to a *large* audience as much as it referred to a certain *type* of audience. Early sociologists focused on the way people felt about themselves and others in social networks in industrialized societies. They felt that people in the modern mass society were becoming both isolated and alienated from other members of society because increasing technology was making people into machines.

To be a "mass," an audience needs four characteristics. First, the audience composition is heterogeneous. This means that the audience is composed of people of all kinds, and no one is excluded. Second, the audience members are anonymous. The message designers don't know the names of anyone in the audience—nor do they care to—because the designers regard everyone to be the same and interchangeable. Third, there is no interaction among the members in the audience. People don't talk to each other about the media messages, so the messages do not get modified in conversations. Instead, those messages have a direct effect on each person in a uniform manner. And fourth, there is no leadership. The mass is very loosely organized and is not able to act with the unity that marks a crowd (Blumer, 1946). Blumer (1946) also pointed out that a mass has no social organization, no body of custom and tradition, no established set of rules or rituals, no organized group of sentiments, and no structure or status roles.

Starting with the industrial revolution in the mid-1800s, the United States and Western European countries were regarded as having mass societies. Because the countries were heavily industrialized, it was believed that this technological progress had shaped the lives of people. Less industrialized countries did not have mass societies because people there were tightly integrated into social networks in which they interacted continually with others on a daily basis. So the United States was regarded as having a mass society and India was not, even though the population of India was much larger than that of the United States.

Because it was believed that communication did take place in a mass-like fashion, it was assumed that a message reached everyone in the same way and was processed by everyone in the same manner. It was also believed that the processing itself was very simple; that is, people were vulnerable and had no psychological defenses against messages because they did not discuss messages with other people.

As evidence for this position, social critics pointed to the way that Adolph Hitler used the mass medium of radio in the 1930s to mobilize the German population to support him. Kate Smith's radio telethons for war bonds, in which she raised millions of dollars, were also offered as evidence that people were highly susceptible to media messages. Another often-cited example of the public's seeming lack of defense against media messages is provided by the widespread reaction to Orson Welles's 1939 Mercury Theater presentation of *War of the Worlds*. Some listeners to the radio play believed what seemed to be news bulletins interrupting the show were real reports of Martians landing in New Jersey. These people panicked, and this reaction was frequently cited as evidence that the media exert a powerful effect.

Sociologists of the 1930s and 1940s were very vocal in their warnings about the dangers of mass communication. A more careful analysis of the three examples mentioned, however, reveals that most people were not affected by those messages (Cantril, 1947). Furthermore, it was later shown that the people who were affected were not all affected in the same manner, nor did they all react in the same way. Thus, the idea of mass audience and its supporting belief that all audience members reacted to the messages in the same way was breaking down.

## Rejection of the Idea of Mass Audience

By the 1950s, it became apparent to many scholars that the assumption of the audience as a "mass" was incorrect. Friedson (1953) was the first to criticize this view of the audience. He felt that people attend movies, listen to the radio, and watch television within an interpersonal context. Discussions of media material frequently take place before, during, and after exposure. There is a well-developed web of organized social relationships that exists among audience members. This social environment influences what audience members will expose themselves to and how messages will affect them. Media behavior is merely a part of their more general social behavior. Friedson warned that "the concept of mass is not accurately applicable to the audience" (p. 316). Since Friedson made this point, many other researchers have supported this position (Bauer & Bauer, 1960).

Today, the term *mass communication* is still used. But rarely is there a time when everyone is exposed to the same message. Even with events such as the Super Bowl, only about 60% of people watch. And more important, those people who do watch the Super Bowl do not all experience the same thing. Some viewers are elated as their team is winning, others are depressed as their team is losing, some are happy that there is a reason to party and have no idea who is playing, and many are bored as the game becomes one-sided. There is no common experience. Also, during the viewing, people talk to each other and help each other interpret events.

There is no "mass" communication because there is no "mass" audience. Instead, there are many audiences, some with structures and leadership and others without these characteristics. Some audiences last for only a few hours (Super Bowl viewers), whereas others last for a whole season (diehard football fans). Some audiences are based on a need for immediate information (viewers of CNN) or in-depth information (readers of news magazines); a need for a religious experience; or a need for political stimulation, musical entertainment, romantic fantasy, and on and on.

## The Idea of Niche Audience

Mass media programmers and product marketers know that there is no mass audience. Therefore, they almost never attempt to sell a product, service, or media message to everyone. Instead, media programmers select particular kinds of messages to appeal to particular kinds of people. They send those messages out in their media channels, hoping to attract as many of those targeted people as possible. Once they have attracted them, they rent that audience's attention out to advertisers, who want to get their messages in front of those targets and persuade them to buy their products and services. Thus, media programmers are in the business of constructing niche audiences. For example, if a radio station wants to attract an upscale, highly educated, older audience, the station programmer is likely to select a classical music format and play only a certain type of music as well as present interviews and news about certain artists. Once the station has attracted this upscale, highly educated, older audience, the sales staff will rent this audience out to advertisers such as luxury cars dealers, jewelers, and travel agencies.

Each person is a member of multiple-niche audiences. You are a member of a local community that the local newspaper and cable TV franchise targets. You are a member of virtual communities when you get on the Internet—communities that quickly form and may last for only one evening. You are a member of certain hobby groups that are targeted by certain magazines, although other members of your audience are spread out all over the world and will never meet you in person.

# Conceptions of Segmented Audiences

One of the key challenges for mass media programmers is to determine how the total population can be divided into meaningful segments. Over the years, audience segmentation schemes have become more complex in an effort to generate more precise groupings. This is illustrated by showing the development of thinking over five types of segmentation methods: geographic, demographic, social class, geodemographic, and psychographic.

## Geographic Segmentation

This type of segmentation scheme is most important to newspapers, radio, and local television where there are geographical boundaries to their coverage areas. But it has also been useful to other media in thinking about getting their messages out to certain regions of the country.

This is the oldest form of segmentation, and it worked well when regions of the country were culturally diverse. A company would begin a business in a certain locale and produce products that the people in that locale wanted. Because of limits on distribution, that company would only do business and only advertise in that one area. If that company wanted to expand, it would move out from its home locale to other places in the region where the product met a need. If there was a nationwide need, then the company could expand into national distribution and advertising—but then there would be no need to do geographic segmentation. As many businesses took their products into the national market, regional differences eroded.

Geographic segmentation is becoming less useful as the country becomes more geographically homogenized. We are a mobile society. Each year, about 20% of the population moves to a new home. Therefore, regions are not as insulated as they once were. Also, regions are not as different from one another as they once were. Over time, there has been much more of a sharing of foods, music, clothing styles, and other cultural elements across regions.

## Demographic Segmentation

Demographics focus on the relatively enduring characteristics about each person—such as gender, ethnic background, age, income, and education. These are fairly stable characteristics and have been quite useful in classifying us into meaningful audience segments. Although people can change their status on some of these (such as education and income), such change requires a great deal of effort.

The usefulness of demographics as an audience segmentation device has been diminishing. Decades ago, when adult women stayed home and raised children, it made sense to market household and child care products to women only. Also, radio and television presented female-type programs during the daytime hours when women were home. But now that the percentage of women in the labor force is the same as that for men, gender is less useful as a segmenter.

Ethnicity also used to be a stronger demographic segmenter than it is today as the range of income, education, political views, and cultural needs is much greater within any ethnic group than it is across ethnic groups. With the tremendous growth of credit, household income has not been as useful a segmenter. Educational level is also less useful. Fifty years ago, having a college degree put you in an elite—the top 5% of the population. But now, 20% of American adults have at least one college degree, and another 20% have earned some college credit.

## Social Class Segmentation

We could think of social class solely in terms of household income level, but then social class would mean the same thing as the demographic of income. Why would we need both types of segmentation schemes if they put the same people into the same groups? Instead, social class is a mix of characteristics. One of those characteristics is income, but psychological characteristics are also part of the mix. For example, being in the lower class, of course, means a low income. But you as a college student have a very low income. Do you consider yourself lower class? No, obviously there is more to the definition. Being in the lower class means taking the psychological perspective that what happens in life is not under your control. Lower class people feel that they were born into a situation with not much opportunity and that they must struggle to maintain their existence. Because fate has put them in this situation, all they can do is to try to make the best of it when they can. Therefore, when they get a windfall of money, they want to have as much fun as they can before someone takes it away from them. There is no point in saving for a tomorrow that will never come.

Being middle class means holding the value that it is good to put off immediate pleasures for more important longer term goals. Thus, middle-class people have a strong work ethic, believing that work is good for them and for society in general. The fact that you are in college is a good indication that you hold a middle-class perspective. You believe that it is a good idea to make economic, time, and lifestyle sacrifices for 4 years now so that later you will receive much larger rewards for your efforts. You believe that your current actions influence your future. You believe that you control your fate—not the other way around.

Being upper class does not mean simply having more money; it means being able to control more resources—yours and those of others. It means the ability to raise large sums and wield a high degree of power.

## Geodemographic Segmentation

A relatively recent innovation in consumer segmentation is geodemographic, which is a blend of geographic and demographic segmentation. It is based on the assumption that we choose to live in neighborhoods where other people are like us. So neighborhoods tend to be homogeneous on important characteristics, and these characteristics are very different across neighborhoods.

One example of geodemographic segmentation is the PRIZM scheme, which was developed by the Claritas Corporation in 1974. PRIZM is based on a complex analysis of the U.S. census data. It began with the 35,000 ZIP code neighborhoods and concluded that there were 40 different kinds of neighborhoods in the United States. It gave the clusters memorable (and trademarked) nicknames such as "sun belt singles" (which are southern suburban areas populated by young professionals), "Norma Rae-ville" (named after the movie of a working-class woman who unionized factory employees), "Marlboro country" (evoking a western rural area with rugged men on horses), "furs and station wagons" (typified by new money living in expensive new neighborhoods), and "hardscrabble" (which represents areas in the Ozark mountains, Dakota badlands, and south Texas border).

## Psychographic Segmentation

Psychographics is the current cutting edge of segmentation schemes. It is not limited to one or two characteristics of people but uses a wide variety of variables to create its segments. Typically, a psychographic segmentation scheme will use demographics, lifestyle, and product usage variables in segmenting consumers. There are many examples of psychographic segmentation. Two stand out as being very influential.

## Twelve American Lifestyles

William Wells, director of advertising research at Needham, Harper & Steers in Chicago, developed the 12 American lifestyles that include Joe the factory worker and his wife Judy, Phyllis the career woman and her liberated husband Dale, Thelma the contented homemaker, and Harry the cigar-chomping middle-aged salesman. Each of these creations represents a different lifestyle. For example, Joe is a lower-middle-class male in his 30s who makes an hourly wage doing semiskilled work. He watches a lot of television, especially sports and action/adventure programs; he rarely reads. He drives a pickup truck and knows a lot about automotive parts and accessories. In contrast, Phyllis is a career woman in her 30s with a graduate degree. She reads a lot, and when she watches television, it is usually news or a good movie. She likes fine food, dining out, and travel.

## VALS Typology

VALS was developed at SRI (Stanford Research Institute) by Arnold Mitchell. After monitoring social, economic, and political trends during the 1960s and 1970s, Mitchell constructed an 85-page measurement instrument that asked questions ranging from people's sexual habits to what brands of margarine they ate. He had 1,635 people fill out the questionnaire, and the answers became the database for his book *Nine American Lifestyles,* published in 1980. In the book, Mitchell argued that people's values strongly influence their spending patterns and media behaviors. So if we know which value group a person identifies with, we can predict a great deal about the products and services he or she will want. For example, one of the groups is called Experientials. The people in this value grouping like to try new and different things to see what they are like. They like to travel. They are early users of new types of products. And they are constantly looking for something different.

The VALS typology has made SRI very successful, with income more than $200 million per year. By the mid-1980s, SRI had 130 VALS clients, including the major TV networks, major ad agencies, major publishers such as Time, and major corporations such as AT&T, Avon, Coke, General Motors, P&G, RJ Reynolds, and Tupperware. For example, Timex, a giant corporation best known for its watches, wanted to move into the home health care market with a selection of new products, including digital thermometers and blood pressure monitors. It decided to focus on two VALS segments: Societally Conscious and the Achievers. Everything about the packaging and the advertisements was chosen with these two groups in mind. Models were upscale, mature in comfortable surroundings with plants and books. The tagline was "Technology where it does the most good." Within months, all of Timex products were the leaders in this new and fast-growing industry.

Over the years, as the American culture has changed, VALS has changed its segments to keep up. Today, the VALS typology of segments looks very different than it did in the early 1980s. By keeping up with changes in people's lifestyles over the years, VALS has remained a valuable tool to mass media programmers and marketers.

# Media Conditioning

Before we begin this section, look at Exercise 12.1 and estimate how much you are exposed to the media in an average week. Make a quick estimate about how many hours you are exposed during a typical week. Then return to this point in the chapter.

The mass media have conditioned us to certain behavioral patterns of exposure. These are continually reinforced and become habits. The mass media employ three tactics to do this. First, they try to appeal to your existing needs and interests. Second, they reinforce exposure inertia. And third, they break down barriers between media.

## Appeal to Existing Needs and Interests

Recall from the previous chapters that the media typically follow the marketing concept, where they begin their message design with research that seeks to identify what the existing needs and interests are in the population. Not everyone has the same needs and interest, so the media can identify a range of different types of people as defined by those different needs. For example, some people are very interested in sports, but other people are more interested in news and public affairs. These are two important niches for the media. Each of these has subniches. Some sports fanatics might like baseball, whereas others cannot stand baseball but love football.

How do media companies know what the existing needs are? The easiest way to answer this question is to look at what messages are already being consumed. The messages that already are attracting the most attention within a niche audience demonstrate that there is a particular existing need. The new competitors then try to create their own messages to attract that same audience by appealing to that same need. This is why many new shows typically look like already existing shows.

Programmers know that we have a relatively narrow exposure repertoire—that is, a set of message types we attend to—so if the new competitors can make their messages very similar to what we are already attending to, we will likely pay attention to those new messages also. Messages that are too different than what we are already exposing ourselves to will not break through the automaticity. We typically stay in this state of automaticity until something triggers our attention, and then we pay attention to it. Therefore, media programmers look for what has triggered our attention in the past, and they construct their messages in a similar manner so their messages will also trigger our attention.

Although we have a wide variety of media and messages available to us, we usually select a small subset of them that tend to serve our needs best. We each have our preferred media and our preferred vehicles, and we use these preferences to develop our habits of media exposure. For example, most of us watch television, but we do not watch all of television. Only when the number of channel choices is low (around three or four) will we expose ourselves to a high proportion of those available channels. But when there are a large number of channels available (such as 100 or more on most cable services), we will tend to select only one or two types of programming (from the genres of news, drama, comedy, education/information, talk, soap operas, music, game shows, etc.) and limit our viewing to the channels with this type of programming. Thus, each of us has our own channel repertoire of about 3 to 6 channels; rarely do we check out the options outside our repertoire. Having a VCR or remote control does not increase our channel repertoire. In cable households, the repertoire is a bit larger (about 5 to 8 channels), although the number of channels available to viewers is much higher (Ferguson, 1992).

## Reinforce Exposure Inertia

Media exposures are inertial. This means that when we are paying attention to a particular message, we tend to keep paying attention to that message, and when we are in an automatic state, we tend to stay in that state and filter out all the messages around us. For example, let's say we turn on our television set at 8 P.M. to watch a show we like—one that is in our viewing repertoire, so we have developed the habit of watching it each time it is on television. Let's say the show is a 30-minute situation comedy. At 8:30, the show will be over. Television programmers know that if they present another situation comedy of the same type at 8:30, there is a high probability that you will continue to watch that station. This is called audience flow-through. Television programmers try to attract you early in the evening and then present similar types of shows to keep you and your fellow audience members viewing that station and flowing through all the way to the end of the evening. The best predictor for a program's rating is the rating of the lead-in program and the lead-out program (Cooper, 1993). For this reason, television programmers will put similar-type programs together (like four situation comedies back-to-back) to hold onto its audience. If they interrupted the block of situation comedies with a game show, they would lose all the viewers who did not have that type of program in their viewing repertoire.

## Break Down Barriers Between Media

Several decades ago, media programmers were most concerned about branding their particular vehicles and trying to build loyalty to those vehicles. For example, local television stations wanted you to watch only them. A newspaper wanted you to be loyal to that newspaper and get your news only there—not from magazines, television, or the radio.

But with the rise of media consolidation, media programmers have shifted their focus to the message and away from the vehicle as primary. So, for example, a conservative commentator on the radio might also be asked to do a TV show on that television station that is also owned by the company that owns the radio station. That company might also own a magazine and book publishing firm, in which case the commentator would be encouraged to write a column for the magazine and publish a book. When this media conglomerate company brands its message—the commentator—the company then tries to market that message through as many media and vehicles that it owns so as to increase the number of revenue streams without adding much to the already existing expenses. Therefore, media companies think of audiences more in terms of messages that would attract them rather than as groups of people limited to one medium or one vehicle.

Differences across media are also blurring over time. Newspapers are becoming more like magazines in their editorial outlook, featuring more soft news and human interest pieces that are not time sensitive and that appeal more as entertainment than as information. Trade books are becoming shorter and less literary. And computers with their games, encyclopedias, and Web pages are becoming more like films, books, magazines, and newspapers. Given the focus on messages and the convergence of channels, the content is becoming much more of a focus than is the delivery system.

Some futurists argue that we are moving toward convergence where all the media will be one—"a single, high capacity, digital network of networks that will bridge what we now know as the separate domains of computing, telephony, broadcasting, motion pictures, and publishing" (Neuman, 1991, p. x). Just as the cotton gin and assembly line symbolized the onset of industrialization and mass society, the personal computer may come to symbolize the onset of deindustrialization and the decentralization of information processing.

# Conclusion

This is an exciting time to be in our culture. The media are aggressively looking for the needs and interests we have, and then they construct messages to attract our attention in satisfying those needs.

If you are media literate and carefully monitor your exposures to make sure that they are truly guided by your needs, and if you carefully search for those messages that best satisfy your needs, then you will be using the media well as a tool. If you do not do these things, then the media will be using you as their tool to achieve their goals. They will be altering your tastes and needs to conform to the messages they want you to pay attention to, and then they will condition you into the habit of seeking out those messages. And ultimately, they will condition you to believe that your needs came from you and that you are simply using the media to satisfy those needs. However, it was the media that guided you into certain audience memberships, then reinforced those habits until you have gradually come to believe that the origin of the needs was you and not the media.

After reading through this chapter, you should be more sensitized to your media exposures, and you should be more aware of those exposures. Now do Exercise 12.2, which asks you to keep a diary of your media exposures. If you are like most people, your diary will reveal that you are exposed much more than you thought when you made your initial estimate. The reason for this is that the media have conditioned many exposure patterns so well that we don't think about them during the actual exposures, and we cannot remember them later when we try to recall them. Much of our exposure is automatic.

# Further Reading

Neuman, W. R. (1991). *The future of the mass audience.* New York: Cambridge University Press. (218 pages)

Neuman begins with a good, balanced discussion of the difficult idea of postindustrialism and with the conflict between fragmentation and homogenization. He argues that education contributes to fragmentation, with people now able to peruse their specialized interests. Family is changing as women enter the workforce in large percentage. He also shows that media use is fragmenting.

He says the central question is whether the proliferation of new communications channels will lead to fragmentation of the mass audience. He says that this is not a new issue but is a continuing and central problem of political communications. The key issue is that of balance: balance between the center and the periphery, between different interest factions, between competing elites, and between an efficient and effective central authority and the conflicting demands of the broader electorate (p. 167). This is the conflict between community and pluralism.

**Exercise 12.1**    Estimate Your Media Exposure

Try to estimate how many minutes and hours you spend with each of the following media during a typical week.

_____ Watching television (cable, broadcast, movies played on a VCR or DVD player, etc.)

_____ Watching films at a theater

_____ Listening to radio (at home, in your car, etc.)

_____ Listening to recordings (CDs and tapes)

_____ Reading newspapers

_____ Reading magazines of all kinds

_____ Reading books (texts for class, novels for pleasure, etc.)

_____ Computer usage (games, word processing, surfing the Internet, etc.)

_____ TOTAL

**Exercise 12.2**    Track Your Media Exposures

Keep a Media Exposure Diary for 1 week. Get a small notebook—one you can carry with you wherever you go for 7 days. Every time you are exposed to a message from the media either directly or indirectly, make an entry of the time and what the message was.

Direct exposures are those where you come in contact with a medium and experience a message during that contact. For example, if you watch *The Simpsons,* then write, "Message: *The Simpsons;* Time: Monday 8–8:30." Listening to KXXX for 30 minutes in the car is also a direct exposure.

Indirect exposures are those where you see a reminder of a media message, such as seeing a title of a movie on the marquee or at a bus stop. You don't see the film itself (which would be a direct exposure), but you see something that reminds you of it. Also, listen to conversations. If people talk about something they heard from the media, then you have been exposed to that media message indirectly. For example, if you heard your friends talk about *The Simpsons,* then write, "Message: Talked with friends about *The Simpsons;* Time: Tuesday morning 10–11:30." If you happened to hear your roommate humming a popular song that is played often on the radio, then write, "Message: Roommate hummed X song; Time: Wednesday all day!"

At the end of the week, analyze the entries in your diary to answer the following questions:

1. How much total time were you exposed to media messages?

2. How many exposures did you experience in that 1 week?

3. What proportion of the exposures was direct and what proportion was indirect?

4. What proportion of media exposures were initiated by you (active) and what proportion just happened (passive)?

5. How do your diary data compare to your estimates from Exercise 12.1?

6. What kinds of messages were most prevalent?

**Exercise 12.3**    What Segments Are You In?

1. Pick three of your favorite television shows. Write the name of each on the column heading line below. Then watch each of these shows and list the products being advertised in each commercial on the lines in the column for that show.

Show 1: _____    Show 2: _____    Show 3: _____

2. Now look at the lists of products and try to imagine who the advertisers had in mind as a target audience when they decided to advertise in these shows.

   - Are those products oriented more toward males or females, or doesn't it matter?
   - What age group are the products aimed at?
   - What economic level are the products aimed at?
   - What educational level are the products aimed at?
   - What geographical location are the products aimed at, or doesn't it matter?
   - What values do the advertisers think you have?

3. Did you notice any ads for other TV shows? If so, what other shows where those ads trying to get you to watch? Do you watch those other shows? Why or why not?

4. Now try the same exercise using three magazines that you like.

5. Monitor the junk mail you receive for a month as a result of being added to marketing mailing lists.

# PART IV

# KNOWLEDGE STRUCTURES OF MEDIA EFFECTS

# CHAPTER 13

# Broadening Our Perspective on Media Effects

**Key Idea:** When we take a four-dimensional perspective—timing, type, valence, and intentionality—of effects, we can appreciate the broad range of effects the media are constantly exerting on us.

**Four-Dimensional Perspective on Media Effects**
>> Timing of Effects
>> Type of Effects
>>> *Cognitive-Type Effect*
>>> *Attitudinal-Type Effect*
>>> *Emotional-Type Effect*
>>> *Physiological-Type Effect*
>>> *Behavioral-Type Effect*
>> Valence of Effects
>> Intentionality of Effects
> **Conclusion**

S uzanne is babysitting her two younger brothers, ages 7 and 10. She is reading a magazine while they are watching the *Power Rangers* on television. She sees an ad for a new shampoo and tears out the coupon in the magazine ad, making a mental note to buy some of this brand when she is out shopping later today.

Her brothers are starting to shout at the television screen. Suzanne yells at her brothers to be quiet, then puts on her headphones to listen to some music to calm her down. A song starts playing on her radio, and she starts to pay more attention to the lyrics and puts down her magazine. She begins to really like the song and wonders, "Who is singing this? I've never heard it before."

She begins to daydream about her date tonight. "I hope Tim takes me to another horror flick. It's so much fun to scream my lungs out and to attack him during the bad parts."

When the song on the radio is over, the DJ goes right into an ad, not telling her the title or artist. She is frustrated, so she tries to remember the melody by humming it so later she can ask one of her friends.

Suddenly, her thoughts are interrupted as her brothers begin screaming at each other and then wrestle around on the floor. Suzanne runs into the TV room and breaks up the fight. "You guys better behave yourselves or I won't let you watch *Power Rangers* anymore! Get back in your own chairs now."

Peace restored, Suzanne picks up a newspaper and notices a story about a drive-by shooting where a gang of youths imitated some action in a recent movie. She thinks, "The media have such a bad effect on young kids. My brothers are going to end up in jail if they keep watching those shows. Thank goodness the media don't have any effect on me!"

Many of us have a narrow view of media effects. We look for high-profile tragedies as evidence of a media effect and use those isolated incidents to conclude that there are media effects. Although these high-profile tragedies are indications of media effects, they are rare in number, and this leads many people to think that media effects do not happen often. This is faulty thinking. Media effects are happening all around us every day. And those effects are not just happening to other people; they are happening to *all* people, including Suzanne and us. For example, in the scenario above, Suzanne was persuaded to buy a new shampoo; she changed her mood by listening to the radio to try to calm herself down, and then the radio changed her mood to frustration when the DJ neglected to provide her with the information she wanted; she looked forward to a movie later that day; and she learned about a crime by reading the newspaper, then generalized from that one story to an unreasonable fear about her brothers ending up as convicts.

If we have a narrow perspective on what media effects are, then we will not be able to perceive the many effects that are constantly occurring all around us. Such a narrow perspective does not eliminate the effects; those effects still happen, but they influence you without your awareness and, more important, occur outside your control. A key to media literacy is an

---

**Box 13.1**    The Weather as an Analogy for Media Effects

Media effects are like the weather in many ways.

Weather is always there, but it can take many forms. Sometimes it makes you shiver, sometimes it makes you wet, and sometimes it gives you a painful sunburn—but it is all weather. Also, it is very difficult to predict the weather with any precision because the factors that explain the weather are large in number, and their interaction is very complex. Supercomputers are used to try to handle all those factors in highly complex models. They help increase the predictive accuracy on the broad level; that is, they can tell us how much rainfall and how many sunny days a particular locale will have this year. But they cannot tell us with accuracy who will get wet on which days. Although the Weather Bureau cannot control the weather, we as individuals can control the weather's effect on us. We can carry an umbrella, use sunscreen, or close ourselves off from elements we don't like. And we can run out to embrace a beautiful day.

Like the weather, the media are pervasive and always around us. Also, like the weather, media influences are difficult to predict because the factors that explain such effects are large in number, and their interaction is very complex. We use powerful computers to examine large sets of variables in trying to make such predictions, and we have learned much about media effects. We know in general that certain types of messages will lead to certain kinds of opinions and behaviors, but we cannot predict with precision whose opinion or behavior will be changed. And as individuals, we do not have much power to control the media, but we have a great deal of power (if we will use it) to control the media's effects on us. To know how to use this power, we must be sufficiently literate about media effects.

There is an important difference between the weather and the influence of the media on us. With the weather, we all recognize its different forms and know when they are happening. It is fairly easy to tell the difference between rain, fog, and snow because there is much tangible evidence whenever these occur. But with media influence, the effects are often difficult to perceive until someone points them out. Then they become easier to spot.

---

awareness of the variety of media effects. When you have this knowledge, you can decide which effects you want to experience and which you want to avoid. You can gain control.

# Four-Dimensional Perspective on Media Effects

The purpose of this chapter is to make you more aware of the variety of media effects by expanding your perspective. Many, many effects can occur from media exposures. For a list of some of these, see Appendix B. But before you look for a list of individual effects, focus on the big picture; that is, read through this chapter and build a better knowledge structure by learning to think of media effects in four dimensions. These dimensions are time, type, valence, and intentionality.

## Timing of Effects

Media effects can either be immediate or long term. This distinction focuses on *when the effect occurs,* not on *how long it lasts.*

An immediate effect is one that happens during exposure to the media message. If it does not happen during the exposure, the opportunity is lost. If the effect does happen, it might last only for a short period of time (such as becoming afraid during a movie) or it might last forever (such as learning the outcome of a presidential election), but it is still an immediate effect because it changed something in you during the exposure. For example, when you watch a news program, you learn about the events of the day. Or while reading a newspaper, you immediately feel happy when you learn that your favorite sports team won an important game. And when you watch an action/adventure film, you might begin jumping around in your seat and wrestling with your friends. These are all immediate effects because something happened to you during the exposure.

Long-term effects show up only after many exposures. No single exposure or no single message is responsible for the effect. Instead, it is the pattern of repeated exposures that sets up the conditions for a long-term effect. For example, after watching years of crime programs and news reports, you might come to believe that your neighborhood is a high-crime environment. No single exposure or event "caused" this belief; the belief is slowly and gradually constructed over years of exposures until one day it occurs to you that you better buy another set of locks for your doors.

Immediate effects are much easier to notice than are long-term effects. There are two reasons for this. First, immediate effects usually exhibit themselves as some kind of change. You notice that a change in your behavior or a particular emotion—such as anger or lust—flares up all of a sudden. Long-term effects also take the form of changes, but those changes happen so gradually and take so long to build up that it is very difficult to notice any one of those slivers of changes.

A second reason immediate effects are easier to notice is because they occur during an exposure to a particular message, and this makes it easy to link the effect to the media message as a cause and conclude there was a media effect. By the time people notice a long-term effect, it is well after many media exposures and many other things happening in their lives, so it is more difficult to link the effect to media exposures.

## Type of Effects

Most of the concern about the media focuses on behavioral effects. For example, there is a belief that watching violence will lead people to behave aggressively, that watching portrayals of sexual activity will make people engage in illicit sexual acts, and that watching crime will make people go out and commit the crimes they witness in media messages.

However, there are five types (four types in addition to behavior) of media effects. They are cognitive, attitudinal, emotional, physiological, and of course behavioral.

## Cognitive-Type Effect

Media can affect what we know by planting ideas and information into our minds. This happens all the time and may be the most prevalent media effect. We are constantly acquiring information during every exposure to the media. But rarely do people credit the media with this type of effect when they are thinking about media effects. Think about all the information you now possess that got into your mind from your exposures to books, magazines, and newspapers.

This cognitive learning is not limited to factual information; we also learn a great deal of social information from the media. As children, we learn a great deal about our world by observing role models—parents, older siblings, friends, and so on. Observation of social models accounts for almost all of the information communicated to children up until the time they begin school. And media provide an enormous number of models and actions from which children might learn. Given the large amount of time children spend with the media, pictorially mediated models (especially TV) exert a strong influence on children's learning about social situations.

Even as adults, we continue to pay careful attention to social models. When we do not have the social models we need in our real lives, we can usually find them in the media. Some of us want to learn most from social models who are powerful, extremely witty, physically attractive, or very successful in a particular career. We develop a vicarious relationship with a professional athlete, famous actor, powerful politician, or wealthy role model. By observing these role models in the media, we gather lots of social information about what it takes to be successful and happy. Think of all the information you have in your memory about characters in television shows and movies you have seen; think about all those names, faces, behaviors, witty lines, and emotions they portrayed.

## Attitudinal-Type Effect

The media can create and shape our opinions, beliefs, and values. Attitudes can also be learned immediately. We could hear a new song on the radio and immediately like it, that is, create a positive attitude about the song. Or we could watch a new television show and immediately hate it.

The media also exert long-term attitudinal effects. One long-term attitudinal effect is cultivation. Over years of watching criminals hurt people and steal their wealth, we come to form the attitude that the world is a mean and violent place. We come to believe that the crime rate is rising dramatically each year, when in fact it is going down. Another long-term attitudinal effect is reinforcement. Most advertising messages are aimed at existing customers of particular products; the advertisers want to give their current customers additional reasons to keep buying those products and to continue feeling good doing so. Advertisers want to reinforce our brand-loyal habits and prevent us from trying competitors' products. As long as those advertisers can keep reinforcing our positive attitudes about their brands, those attitudes will become stronger and stronger over time and thus less likely to change.

## Emotional-Type Effect

The media can make us feel things. They can trigger strong emotions such as fear, rage, and lust. They can also evoke weaker emotions such as sadness, peevishness, and boredom. Emotional reactions are related to physiological changes. In fact, some psychological theoreticians posit that emotions are nothing more than physiological arousal (Zillmann, 1991). If we feel a very high level of arousal and don't like it, we might label it hate. But if we like it, we might label it love.

We have all experienced emotional changes while exposing ourselves to media messages. Horror movies trigger extreme fear, newspaper editorials can make us feel outrage, magazine pictures can make us feel lust, and calm music can help us feel more peaceful.

The media also exert long-term emotional effects. One long-term emotional effect is desensitization. Over years of watching violence in the media, which rarely show victims suffering and instead focus on the perpetrators of the violence and how attractive they are, we gradually come to lose the ability to feel strong sympathy for victims both in media portrayals and in real life. We might regard the homeless as people who are victims of their own bad judgment and don't deserve much sympathy from us.

## Physiological-Type Effect

Media can influence our automatic bodily systems. These are usually beyond our conscious control, such as the contraction of the pupil of the eye when we look at a bright object. We cannot control the degree to which the pupil dilates, but we can look away from the object and thus prevent the iris from contracting.

With the media, there are many physiological effects that usually serve to arouse us. A suspenseful mystery serves to elevate our blood pressure and heart rate. A horror film triggers rapid breathing and sweaty palms. Hearing a patriotic song might raise goose bumps on our skin. Viewing erotic pictures can lead to vaginal lubrication, penile tumescence, and increased heart rate (Malamuth & Check, 1980). A farce might make us laugh so hard that we are unable to stop, even when laughing becomes painful. Or listening to music can calm and relax us by reducing our heartbeat and bringing our rate of breathing down to a regular, slow rate.

Over time, our physiological responses to particular media messages can change. For example, when we see our first horror movie, our heart rate might go through the roof, and we are so scared that we need to run out of the theater. But if we keep watching horror movies, we might find that it takes more and more gore to trigger any rise in heart rate. Gradually, over many exposures to horror films, our physiological responses wear down.

### Behavioral-Type Effect

Media can trigger actions. For example, after seeing an ad for a product, we might leave our house and go buy the product. Or we read about something in a magazine and call a friend to talk about it.

There are also long-term effects to our behavior. For example, we might buy a computer and get on the Internet. For the first several weeks, our Internet sessions are relatively brief, perhaps 15 minutes or so. But over several years, the time we spend per day on the Internet has grown to several hours. The Internet behavioral habit is displacing other activities, such as watching television, exercising, or even talking to other people.

## Valence of Effects

The effect can be in a positive or negative direction. These terms are value laden. Who is to decide what is positive and negative? The answer can be approached in two ways: the individual and society.

From the individual perspective, a positive direction is one where the effects help you achieve your personal goals. In this situation, you are usually aware of your goals and you use the media strategically to achieve those goals. For example, if your goal is to get some information to satisfy your curiosity, then finding facts in a book, in a newspaper, or on television can be very satisfying. This can move you toward a goal of having more information and achieving a higher level of knowledge. In contrast, a negative effect is when the media use you as their tool to achieve their goals, if their goals are in conflict with your goals. For example, advertisers want you to spend more and more of your money on their products. If you do this, you may be going bankrupt trying to solve problems you really don't have.

We can also look at the valence of effects from a broad societal point of view. If the media teach people how to commit crimes and trigger that behavior, then the media are exerting a negative influence. However, the media also make a great deal of information available, which can serve to make the public more informed and therefore choose better leaders and support the best solutions for social problems. When this happens, society is stronger, and therefore this is a positive effect.

## Intentionality of Effects

Oftentimes, we intend for an effect to happen, so we consciously seek out particular messages in the media to get that effect. For example, we may be bored and want to feel high excitement. To satisfy this conscious need, we go to a movie that presents a great deal of action and/or horror. During the movie, our blood pressure and heart rate go way up, and we are on the edge of our seat with fear. We have satisfied our need.

Also, when we seek out factual knowledge in the media, we are consciously trying to achieve a positive cognitive effect. For example, you read the morning paper to learn about which sports teams won their games yesterday, you watch a cooking show to copy down a new recipe, or you listen to your car radio driving to work to learn how to get tickets for a concert. The information does not need to be extremely important, and it need not be remembered for more than a few minutes for an effect to have occurred. Every day, there are dozens of examples where you intentionally use the media to pick up a fact that you can use.

Many times, we expose ourselves to the media for one reason, but other effects that we were not seeking also occur. To illustrate, most of our viewing of prime-time television is purely for purposes of entertainment. We are looking for funny portrayals so we can laugh, or we watch our usual dramatic programs to see what happens to our favorite characters. During these exposures, we will usually have our intended effects occur; that is, we will laugh and get some information on the travails of our favorite characters. But other effects are also occurring—effects we did not seek out and perhaps effects that we are not even aware of until someone later points them out. For example, our program may be interrupted by a series of advertisements, and some of those jingles or sayings stay with us. Or perhaps we begin snacking after seeing so many food products advertised. Our body did not tell us we were hungry—the media did. Also, we listen to CDs primarily to be entertained, but we also unconsciously pick up the attitudes of the rappers. Thus, we frequently experience effects different from our intentions.

Unintentional effects are not limited to immediate learning. They can be long term as well, and they can be attitudinal, emotional, physiological, and behavioral. For example, after years of watching exciting movies, you develop a belief that the real world should be much more exciting. Also, your emotional and physiological reactions may have become desensitized; that is, it takes more excitement to make you happy. You did not intend for this to happen, but it happened anyway.

Even when you are receiving an intentional effect, you may be experiencing unintended effects at the same time. For example, you watch a violent movie solely for the excitement, and the movie does deliver the excitement you wanted. However, the movie may also be delivering other effects with the excitement. You may be experiencing an emotional desensitization effect. Also, you have the elements forming to generalize to a belief that the world is a mean and dangerous place, which is a long-term cognitive effect.

Unintentional effects frequently occur when you are in the state of automaticity because your defenses are not engaged. You are not aware that any learning is taking place, and hence you are not actively evaluating and processing the information. However, even when you are trying to be an active viewer, unintended effects can occur. For example, let's say you watch a news program such as *Crossfire* or *Meet the Press*. You understand that the people on that program are spinning the story in a way to reach their own particular goals. They are not there to inform you about the complexity of the situation; they do not want to reach a compromise or a synthesis of a higher realization on the issue. Instead, they dumb down the issue and present their polarized position so the general public does not get lost, and they make their position look as attractive as possible so that most of the public will agree with them. Now, if you are actively watching this and processing this information, you can protect yourself from the influence of either message by acting media literate and trying to synthesize the two positions and construct a more common ground on the issue. This is much better than simply accepting one of the polarized positions. You feel good. You feel that you have avoided being swept away with superficial argument. However, there is a residue left behind. There is a distrust of political figures. There is a belief that politics is argumentation rather than compromise and resolution. There is a feeling that government is about process and not resolution of problems.

The highest form of media literacy is the ability to move beyond the active controlling of an exposure and to conduct a self-reflexive examination of the residue. This is impossible to do until you recognize all the effects that are possible from the exposure. Because the residue really is more than what it seems—it's the transparent dust that gradually builds up into an effect much later. It is hard to see in the present, and it is hard to understand how something so insubstantial as some residue of a particular exposure could amount to an important effect.

# Conclusion

A key step in increasing your media literacy is to expand your perspective about what is a media effect. Don't get trapped into thinking of the media only as kind of a candy store (see Box 13.2). Don't think that the media only affect others, such as young children who don't know any better or the criminal types who claim they copy what they see in the media.

We live in a media-saturated environment, and the effects are constantly happening to us as they shape our knowledge patterns, attitudes, emotions, and behaviors. They even trigger physiological reactions, such as our heart rate, blood pressure, and other bodily functions. And we don't even need to experience a change in order to see that the media have had an effect on us because a prevalent effect is reinforcement—that is, solidifying our existing beliefs and behaviors.

In our everyday lives, the immediate and long-term processes work together. The immediate process gives us a new fact that either extends our learning or adds weight to our already existing structure. In the long term, we look for patterns across these facts and infer conclusions about how the world operates. These generalized conclusions then become part of our knowledge structures. If we are not aware that we are making generalizations, then we cannot control that process and ensure that they are reasonable and accurate. Thus, faulty principles will get into our knowledge structures and lead us to make more defective conclusions and guide our search for facts in a faulty manner.

---

**Box 13.2**   Candy as an Analogy for Media Effects

Many people think of media effects as if they were candy.

As we walk down the street, there are people passing out all kinds of candy for free. They want us to taste their sweets, then come into the store and buy something. We are tempted. When we take a piece, it tastes good and makes us want another piece. Often we sneak another piece or two, thinking it can't hurt. But then a few minutes later, we experience a sugar rush followed by a crash of energy. Also, there is this lingering sweet taste in our mouths that becomes unpleasant as time goes by. We envision the sugar eating holes in our teeth. If we have kids with us, we find they are rambunctious and whine for more candy. And now we have to act like the bad guy and tell them no; it will spoil their dinner.

A lot of people think of the media as a candy store. Their messages are tempting, and we let ourselves sample and often like the experience. But afterwards, we feel guilty. We feel we should have been doing something more substantial or productive with our time. We feel that those messages are now eating holes in our brains as we can't get a jingle, a song, or stupid joke out of our minds. If we have kids with us, we fear that they are soon going to imitate the bad language, bad attitudes, or bad behavior they have seen in the messages.

Yes, the media do offer lots of "candy" messages. If we indulge ourselves with a steady diet of candy over the years, we will clog up our arteries with fat and experience all sorts of negative health effects. But the media offer many other kinds of messages. If we can resist the initial temptation of candy at the door and instead find the more nutritious messages in other parts of the media cafeteria, we can consume a more balanced and full range of vitamins and minerals. To live a more healthy life, we need to know what to consume and exercise some self-discipline.

---

Being media literate requires that we understand the full range of media effects. We need to recognize when those effects are having a negative influence on us so we can protect ourselves. And we need to recognize when the effects are having a positive influence on us so we can appreciate and enhance their power.

Now that you have a broader appreciation for media effects, take a look at the list of effects in Appendix B. This list is not exhaustive. Instead, the list provides illustrations of all kinds of effects. Look for these media effects in your own lives, and let this selection of effects sensitize you to look for many other media effects.

**Exercise 13.1**    Thinking About Media Effects

1. Pick some child with whom you have spent a fair amount of time. Can you think of any effects that child exhibited that could be regarded as a media effect? (List them below.)

_____

_____

_____

2. Pick some adult with whom you have spent a fair amount of time—perhaps a parent or a neighbor. Can you think of any effects that adult exhibited that could be regarded as a media effect? (List them below.)

_____

_____

_____

3. Pick a friend about your own age. Can you think of any effects that friend exhibited that could be regarded as a media effect? (List them below.)

_____

_____

_____

4. Now think about yourself. Can you think of any effects that you exhibited that could be regarded as a media effect? (List them below.)

_____

_____

_____

**Exercise 13.2**     Recognizing Immediate Effects

Think about the differences among cognitive, attitudinal, emotional, behavioral, and physiological effects. Then think about what has happened to you in your life after particular media exposures.

On a blank sheet of paper, divide the page into five rows, labeling them cognitive, attitudinal, emotional, behavioral, and physiological effects.

For each row, see if you can list at least two effects that have happened to you immediately after being exposed to the media. Name the immediate effect, and then describe a specific example of how the media have affected you or someone you know.

Use the list below to guide your thinking.

a. Cognitive: Media can immediately plant ideas and information.

b. Attitudinal: Media can influence attitudes and feelings about things.

c. Emotional: Media can trigger an immediate emotional reaction, such as fear, attraction, sadness, and laughter.

d. Behavioral: Media can trigger behavior.

e. Physiological: Media can arouse or calm you.

**Exercise 13.3**    Recognizing Long-Term Effects

Think about how the media may have exercised a subtle effect on you over the long term. On a blank sheet of paper, divide the page into five rows, labeling them cognitive, attitudinal, emotional, behavioral, and physiological effects.

For each row, see if you can list two long-term effects. Next to each effect, describe specifically how long-term exposure to media has led to that effect on you.

Use the list below to guide your thinking.

*Long-term effects:* Slow accumulation of information, attitudes, and images leads to beliefs about the real world.

a. Cognitive: Oftentimes, people will not expose themselves to the media with the purpose of learning anything. Rather, they will be interested in seeking escape or entertainment. This is especially true with television, radio, and film. However, acquisition of information and attitude change does take place. This type of learning is called *incidental learning*.

b. Attitudes: Erosion or building up of certain attitudes.

c. Emotional: People can build up a tolerance against emotional reactions over time and thus become desensitized.

d. Behavioral: New behaviors can be learned in the short term but not performed until much later.

e. Physiological: Increased tolerance for certain content; physiological dependency on a medium or certain content.

**Exercise 13.4**     What Have You Internalized From the Media Culture?

1.  When you are driving and listening to your car radio, do you switch the channel, looking for something else, even when you are satisfied with the song you are currently hearing—thinking maybe a better song is on another station now? Do you flip through the channels on the television set looking for something better?

2.  In romantic relationships, which is more important to you: commitment or perfection?

    When you are in a romantic relationship, are you happy when you make a lasting, strong commitment to the other person? Or do you worry that this person may not be the absolute best one for you and perhaps there is someone a little better out there?

3.  In college, do you value learning or efficiency more?

    Do you make a commitment to each course, attend every session, and try to get all you can from them? Do you take a wide range of courses (some you know nothing about) to expand your experience?

    Or do you look for ways to spend your time better during class, such as going on a job interview, finishing a term paper for another course, or catching up on sleep? Do you look for courses on the basis of which ones require the least amount of work for the highest grades?

4.  In your career, which will be more important to you: loyalty or success?

    Will you find a job and build your entire career there to pay back your employer for your first big opportunity? Or will you take the first job as a stepping stone to something better and leave as soon as you have learned all you can in that job?

5.  When you have a major problem, are you upset when you cannot solve it in a short period of time?

# CHAPTER 14

# How Does the Effects Process Work?

> *Key Idea:* People need to be proactive—rather than reactive—in understanding how the media affect us. We also need to realize that there are many factors interacting in the effects process. When we understand these two ideas, we can gain control over that process of effects.

Two boys go to the movies and watch *The Deer Hunter,* a film in which American prisoners during the Vietnam War are forced by their captors to play the game of Russian roulette. Russian roulette is a game where one chamber in a revolver contains a bullet while the other chambers are empty. Each player in the game takes a turn pointing the gun at his head and pulling the trigger. If he is lucky and the chamber is empty, the gun does not fire and the player is saved. If he is unlucky, the chamber contains the bullet, which is then fired into his brain, killing him instantly.

Several days after watching this movie, the boys are playing in their parents' bedroom and find a revolver under the bed. They decide to play Russian roulette. Eventually, the gun fires, killing one of the boys.

Should the media portrayal be blamed for this death? This is a very important question. Some people would argue that the boy caused his own death. Some would argue it is the fault of the parents for having a loaded gun available. Some would blame the producers of *The Deer Hunter.* And still others would generalize this example into an argument about how irresponsible all media are.

This chapter will deal with this issue by emphasizing two important ideas. The first idea is that it is better to be proactive than it is to be reactive. By this, I mean that if we wait until a negative effect occurs, the most we can do is try to assess blame; it is too late to prevent the negative effect. Instead, it is better to learn how to take a proactive stance so you can continually assess how close you—as well as others—are to manifesting a negative effect. Learning how to be proactive will give you greater control over the process leading up to a negative effect. Also, it will allow you to position yourself better to achieve positive effects while you are avoiding negative ones.

The second important idea that is foundational to this chapter is that usually many factors work together to bring about any media effect. These many factors interact in a complex process of influence that is constantly changing the probability that you will experience a particular media effect.

This chapter is organized to illuminate each of these ideas more fully. When you finish reading this chapter, you should have a basic knowledge structure about how the effects process works. This will give you a much better perspective on controlling the process and thereby achieving the effects you want. However, this chapter cannot give you much detail about all the different factors that change the probabilities of all the media effects that could occur. I can alert you to the different types of factors that have been found to influence many effects. But for you to elaborate this basic knowledge structure, you will need to take additional media effects courses and do additional reading of the relatively large literatures of media effects research studies.

# The Proactive Approach

A lot of people think of media effects categorically—that is, either an effect occurs or it does not. The problem with this type of thinking is that it is reactive. If an effect occurs and it is negative, then all we can do is feel bad about it and try to assess blame. Or if an effect occurs and it is positive, then all we can do is be thankful that it occurred and hope it occurs again. This stance does not give you much control over the effects. Even more of a problem is when an effect does not seem to occur; in this case, we think the media have not had any influence, but this is rarely the case. The media are constantly influencing how we think, feel, and act. Just because we do not see an outward manifestation of these things does not mean that the media are without influence.

It is much better to be proactive rather than reactive when dealing with media effects. Being proactive means having the knowledge to predict the risk we are experiencing with our media exposures. With media literacy, effects are important, but even more important is understanding what leads up to these effects because the more we understand the process leading up to the effects, the more we can control that process. We can do more than complain about negative effects; we can prevent them. Furthermore, we will know how to control the effects process so that we experience more positive effects more often.

The proactive approach requires that you understand the difference between a manifestation of an effect and a process effect. Also, you need to understand that we are constantly being subjected to factors that alter the degree of risk of manifesting an effect; that is, our risk levels are constantly changing. And you need to understand that each of us has a risk set point that indicates where we typically are located on what I call the risk continuum.

## Process and Manifest Effects

When we talk about media effects, we typically mean only manifest effects, that is, those changes in behavior or knowledge that we can observe. For example, while watching television, we notice that our siblings begin wrestling or insulting each other. Or we notice that we are going to the kitchen to get that bag of potato chips to eat after watching a commercial for that product. Or we watch a news program covering a campaign and notice that our attitude toward one of the candidates has changed. These examples are of effects we can observe; they have manifested themselves to outside observers.

----------------------------------------------------------------------------> EFFECT MANIFESTED

0                              Influence Line                              100

**Figure 14.1**     Risk Continuum

If we look only for manifest effects, we are missing a great deal of the process of influence. Far more numerous and interesting than the manifest effects are the process effects. The process effects are the changes in our risk level along the risk continuum (see Figure 14.1). Notice that the left end of the risk continuum is labeled 0 (which means that there is no risk of a manifest effect), and the right end of the risk continuum is labeled 100 (which means that the probability of the effect occurring is 100%). When the probability of risk is 100%, it manifests itself; that is, we all notice it and conclude that the effect has occurred. Therefore, at one end of the continuum, there is virtually no chance that an effect will be manifested. At the other end of the continuum, there is a certainty that the effect will occur. If we can shift our thinking away from reactions to effects after they have occurred and think more about where we are in the process of influence, we can be proactive and monitor our risk levels much better.

## Constant Alteration of Risk Levels

Every day, our level of risk is moving back and forth along the risk continuum as we experience factors from the media and factors in our own lives. Some of those factors increase risk—that is, move us toward a manifestation—whereas other factors decrease risk by moving us away from the manifestation point. All of these movements are process effects. Thus, effects are constantly occurring as a result of our unfolding experiences with the media. The arrows labeled with numbers in Figure 14.2 represent factors that push our risk level higher, and the arrows labeled with letters represent factors that push our risk level lower. These factors are in constant interaction. Some of these factors are stronger than others, but none is strong enough by itself to move you all the way from 0 to 100 along the risk continuum.

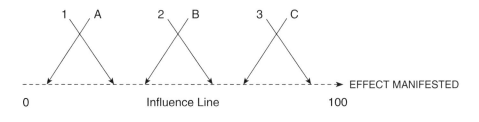

**Figure 14.2**     Factors Influencing Risk Continuum

The more we know about where we are along the continuum and those factors that move us in the direction we want to go, the more we can control the effects process and how media literate we are. Such control will allow us to reduce the probability of a negative effect occurring well before it has a chance to manifest itself. Also, such control will allow us to accelerate the manifestation of a positive effect and, if it is a long-term effect, allow us to take comfort in the fact that we are moving toward such an effect even though we have not yet manifested it. Because the purpose of media literacy is to empower people to control effects, it is far better for people to regard effects as movements along a continuum rather than the either-or manifestation of an effect.

## Risk Set Point

Typically, our movement back and forth along the risk continuum is not a wild one, taking us from one end to the other in a given media exposure. The factors from the media and the factors in our own lives, although influential in moving us along the continuum, typically exert a more modest movement. The reason for this is that we each have a "home neighborhood" along this continuum that anchors us to a particular level of risk. This is our "risk set point."

This idea of a "set point" comes from how physicians sometimes talk about dieting and weight loss. Each of us has a certain set point for our body weight. This set point is determined by genetics as well as long-term habits of eating and exercise. If you eat a lot of extra food around a holiday time, chances are that you may experience a temporary weight gain, but your body will return to its set point weight within a week or so as your eating habits return to normal. On the other hand, if you go on a crash diet for a month, you might lose a significant amount of weight, but when you stop dieting, your body will return to its set point weight. The way to lose weight and keep it off is to change your set point; this requires a gradual increase in exercise along with a gradual decrease in caloric intake over a period of years. Set points take a long time to alter.

With media effects, it is helpful to think in terms of risk set points. These are determined by long-term conditioning. Some people are conditioned in a way that their set point is very close to the manifestation of an effect, so with these people, it does not take much in a media exposure to result in an effect being manifested. In contrast, other people have been conditioned in a way that their set point is very far away from a manifestation, so it is unlikely that any one media exposure will result in a manifestation (see Figure 14.3).

Typically, people's risk set points are fairly far away from behavioral manifestations; that is, it would take a media message with many (or unusually strong) characteristics to push a person all the way up to the manifestation of a behavioral act. In contrast, on cognitive effects, people's risk set points are fairly close to a manifestation. Thus, with some effects, there is a long distance between a person's risk set point and the manifestation point; it would require many factors to move a person all the way to the manifestation. In contrast, some people have a risk set point very close to the manifestation point; it would

Let's consider an example of a disinhibition effect, that is, the manifestation of aggressive behavior after watching a violent movie.

```
   Person A                              Person B            MANIFESTATION

------- X ------------------------------------------------ X -------->         OF

0                                        100             DISINHIBITION
```

   Person A has a risk set point far away from the manifestation level of 100. She is likely to have been raised by loving parents who taught the golden rule, has high trait empathy, and is rarely frustrated. She is likely to have avoided exposure to the typical violent portrayals found in movies and television series. When she has been exposed to media portrayals of violence, she has learned that violence is ugly, harmful to victims, and unsuccessful for perpetrators.

   Person B has a risk set point fairly close to the manifestation level of 100. She is likely to have been raised by parents who have either abused their children (physically and emotionally) and/or taught their children to fight back when provoked. This person also has high trait aggressiveness and low empathy. She is likely to have been exposed to many violent portrayals in which the perpetrators were glamorized and the victims were not shown suffering much.

   Thus, people's risk set points are determined by a combination of their traits, typical lifestyle situations, and patterns of media exposure.

---

**Figure 14.3**     Risk Continuum for Disinhibition Effect

---

not take much to move the person to the manifestation point. When people are aware of the factors that go into the determination of a risk set point, they can better assess the impact of different types of messages on bringing about a manifested effect.

# Factors Influencing Media Effects

As I pointed out earlier in this chapter, many factors interact in the media effects process. In this section, I point out many of the more influential types of factors that are responsible for positioning a person's set point and then are active in moving a person off that set point back and forth across the risk continuum. Remember that there are many different kinds of media effects, and the factors that are influential in the processes leading up to those effects vary by effect.

## Set Point Factors

   What are the general factors that are responsible for fixing a person's set points? I discuss seven of them in this section. Each of these seven types of factors exerts a subtle but continuing influence on a person, and this serves to make a person's risk set point relatively fixed and enduring.

## Developmental Maturities

We mature cognitively, emotionally, and morally as we age. When we are very young, our minds, emotions, and moral reasoning are beginning to develop and thus have a lower ceiling of capacity than when these are more fully developed. As we mature in these areas, we are able to process more information and to apply more sophisticated skills well. This gives us the capacity to move our set point closer to the manifestation for the effects we want to experience and away from the manifestation point for effects we want to avoid.

Cognitively, as children mature, they are not so limited to perceptual elements in media messages and can process the information at a more conceptual level; they are less influenced by a central, salient feature of a message and can process many elements in a message; they are not limited to concrete thinking but get better at making inferences accurately; they are more sophisticated in making distinctions between fantasy and reality; and perhaps most important, they can think about thinking itself—that is, engage in meta-thinking—which helps them monitor their media exposures and the potential effects of those exposures on them (Strasburger & Wilson, 2002).

Recall from Chapter 4 that Piaget has shown that infants operate at a very low level of cognitive functioning. But as infants grow older, their minds mature, and they move up one level at a time until, by age 12, their minds have developed to a point where they can function like an adult. For example, preschoolers have difficulty in comprehending and making use of the order of isolated events in a plot. They lose track of the order in which things happen and relationships among events separated in a plot. They have difficulty in making inferences about the causes and meanings of actions, and they have difficulty in understanding characters' motives and the consequences of their actions. When they watch television, they focus their attention on the microelements of particular sound effects, voices, bits of music, and small segments of motion or color. As they age, they are able to organize these individual elements into meaningful chunks. This conceptual chunking allows them to begin to understand plot and character development.

Because of differences in cognitive development, children learn different things from the media at different ages. Younger children are not able to follow the narratives in news stories or dramatic plots, so they construct less meaning from them. Thus, they cannot engage in much generalization, and this protects them from constructing false images of the world or internalizing many of the themes in the culture. But they are more susceptible to the claims of advertisers because they are not skeptical of that information. Also, young children are more likely to be frightened by monsters and scary sound effects. As they age, children develop the ability to protect themselves from certain kinds of messages, but they become vulnerable to the negative effects of other kinds of messages.

As for emotional reactions, Smith and Wilson (2002) found that fear reactions from news are affected by age. Older children are more likely to comprehend news stories, and this leads them to be more frightened by the happenings reported. Also, emotional reactions to violent action/adventure films are influenced by humor, but there is a gender difference. For example, females find that wisecracking heroes add to their emotional distress, whereas male viewers find that wisecracking heroes reduce their distress a bit (King, 2000).

People at lower levels of maturity are limited in how much information they can understand and work with, and they are also limited in their capacity to control their emotions and behavior. These limitations make their set point less fixed—that is, more susceptible to movement—and they are less able to control that movement.

We must be careful not to fall into the trap of believing that everyone of the same age has reached the same level of development cognitively, emotionally, and morally. For example, Piaget's theory says that children are fully developed cognitively and therefore are capable of adult thinking (formal operations) at age 12. However, King (1986) conducted a review of the published literature that tested the formal reasoning abilities of adults and concluded that "a rather large proportion of adults do not evidence formal thinking, even among those who have been enrolled in college" (p. 6). This conclusion holds up over the 25 studies she analyzed, including a variety of tests of formal reasoning ability and a variety of samples of adults 18 to 79 years old. In one third of the samples, less than 30% of the respondents exhibited reasoning at the fully formal level, and in almost all samples, no more than 70% of the adults were found to be fully functioning at the formal level.

Ability to reason morally is not always shown to be more advanced with age. For example, Van der Voort (1986) found no evidence that children judge violent behavior more critically in a moral sense as they age. He found no reduction in the approval of the good guys' behavior. And as children aged, they were even more likely to approve of the violent actions of the bad guys. So although children acquire additional cognitive abilities with age, they do not necessarily acquire additional moral insights. There is a range of moral development among people of any given age. Also, older children are not automatically more highly developed morally than are younger children.

## Cognitive Abilities

The developmental maturities suggest potentialities; that is, at a given age, there are limits to what people can understand and how they go about reasoning. But developmental potentialities are not the same as actual abilities; that is, not everyone who has the same potential exhibits the same level of cognitive abilities.

Recall from Chapter 4 that there are four cognitive abilities—field dependency, type of intelligence, type of thinking, and conceptual differentiation—that are most relevant to media literacy. Each of these has an influence on establishing a person's risk set point for media effects. For example, people who are more field independent, higher on both fluid and crystalline intelligence, and more likely to conceptually differentiate information into categories will be more likely to control their set points.

## Knowledge Structures

People with the largest amount of knowledge learn most from media (Comstock, Chaffee, Katzman, McCombs, & Roberts, 1978). When people have a great deal of knowledge on a particular topic, they have a strong, well-developed knowledge framework. They are usually motivated to acquire more information on various topics and thus seek out media that will provide them with this information. When they see a new message on the topic, they are able to integrate that new information quickly and efficiently into their existing knowledge structure.

If a person's knowledge structure is composed primarily of information only from the media, then this structure may be dominated by media-stimulated generalizations and internalizations from the media world. With many topics, we have no choice but to rely primarily on media information. This is what makes the media so powerful a socializing influence—we cannot check out the media information by comparing it to information from other sources such as real life. For example, almost no one knows what it feels like to be a professional athlete. We are given some insights about what the life of a professional athlete might be like, but almost no one has an opportunity to check those insights out for themselves. This is true for almost all content of news. The same is true for much fictional programming. Viewers do not know what it feels like to be a professional comedian, a multimillionaire, a detective, or many other portrayals on TV. Because viewers do not have an opportunity to check it out in real life, it is impossible to prove the messages false or inaccurate. When people are asked if TV entertainment is credible and a reasonable representation of the way people live, most people say yes. As you increase your amount of viewing, your perceptions of the reality of TV entertainment programs increase. This is especially true among children and those who have the least amount of variety of real-world experiences.

## Sociological Factors

The degree of socialization is related to the amount of influence the media will have. People who have been socialized with consistent norms for a long period of time will have a relatively weighty risk set point. That set point is then hard to move. If those norms are far away from the manifestation point, then it is unlikely that the media will ever be able to exert a strong enough influence to cause a manifestation. For example, if a person is a senior citizen and has been exposed consistently to anti-aggression norms all her life from parents, friends, educational institutions, church, and so on, she has a risk set point far away from a behavioral manifestation of aggression. She could watch an entire evening of *The Matrix, Kill Bill,* and other highly aggressive media messages and not move anywhere near the point of manifesting aggressive behavior herself. If, on the other hand, another person has been taught to fight back by his father, been taught that only the strong survive in a tough school, and been shown by his friends that the only way to get respect is to fight, he has a risk set point fairly close to a behavioral manifestation of aggression, and it would take very little media influence to push him into a manifestation state.

We learn norms by observing other people in real life and through the media. The media provide many characters that communicate a great deal of social information to viewers. These messages are especially influential on the socialization of children because young people have less experience in real life to counterbalance the media portrayals. The media stories and character portrayals also convey a lot of information to adults. The media messages are especially influential on adults who have limited social contacts in the real world. For example, people who have never served in government, never become active in a political party, and never attended a political rally or meeting depend on the media to provide them with all their information about how the political system works and the qualities of the people serving. These people with highly limited political experience have no way to check the media portrayals against the real world, so they must accept the stories the media present.

We are all influenced by institutions, parents, friends, and other social forces. For example, with children, parental involvement in media exposure serves to influence learning. Children increase their understanding and recall of both central and incidental program content when adults provide comments to guide their children's attention and understanding during viewing. However, most parents do not usually provide critical insights during TV viewing with their children (McLeod, Fitzpatrick, Glynn, & Fallis, 1982). Also, people with strong interpersonal ties will use them to filter media messages (Comstock, 1980). The more a person identifies with a peer group and the more cohesive is the group, the more the person will be influenced by the group and the less effect the media will have by themselves. Parental support for aggression as a means of problem solving has been found to have a greater influence on attitudes favorable to the use of aggression than the viewing of TV violence (Comstock, 1980; Hawkins & Pingree, 1982; McLeod et al., 1982). Potter, Pashupati, Pekurny, Hoffman, and Davis (2002) report that people have a shared schema they have learned about violence from years of viewing violent narratives in the media.

## Lifestyle

People who have active lifestyles where they interact with many people and institutions are generally less affected by the media. But those people who have fewer real-life experiences because of lack of money, education, or vitality are more likely to have much higher exposure to media that is not counterbalanced by other experiences. This is why the poor, low socioeconomic status (SES) individuals, ethnic minorities, and the elderly are particularly susceptible to the influence of the media, especially television, because they expose themselves to a great deal of TV due to their sociological and psychological isolation. TV becomes their window on the world and their primary source of information.

## Personal Locus

This may be the most important factor so far because it reflects the five factors above and, more important, activates the power of those five factors. Furthermore, it determines the seventh factor, which is a person's media exposure habits. When a personal locus is strong, the person has the drive energy to make the most of his or her maturities, skills, knowledge structures, sociological factors, and lifestyle.

People who have a strong personal locus have more awareness of the effects process, so they have constructed their risk set points to conform to their personal goals. This means that there are some effects they want to achieve with the help of the media; for these effects, they have constructed a risk set point fairly close to the manifestation point so that a single exposure to the proper media message can achieve the effect. People with a strong personal locus are also aware that there are some effects that they do not want to manifest themselves, so they construct risk set points for those effects far from the manifestation point.

## Media Exposure Habits

Each of us has a set of media exposure habits that focuses our attention on certain media and certain types of messages presented by those media. For example, some people like television and watch all kinds of TV shows indiscriminately. Given this pattern, these people will likely have a relatively high set point for a cultivation effect; that is, they are at high risk to manifest a belief that the world is a mean and violent place because there is so much crime and violence across the television landscape (Gerbner, Gross, Signorielli, Morgan, & Jackson-Beeck, 1979). The risk set point will be especially high when a person's media habits focus on exposures to crime shows and action/adventure programs (Potter, 1991). In contrast, people who habitually expose themselves to a great deal of television such as *Mister Rogers' Neighborhood, Sesame Street,* and similar programs will likely have a very low risk set point for such a cultivation effect.

When the media present a relatively constant picture of a social world, their effect is more powerful because all the content is pointing to the same type of effect. When the media present messages that are the same as those presented by other institutions such as family, education, religion, and the legal system, then all those messages reinforce one another. But when there are differences across messages, the media messages are often regarded as the most important. This is especially true for people who spend more time with the media than other institutions and for people who like, trust, or are aroused more by the media messages than messages from other sources.

## Factors Special to a Type of Effect

While understanding where your risk set points are in the processes of influence, it is also important to monitor the factors that will move you away from your set points. In this section, I present three types of factors about the media as well as three types of factors about you that are important in assessing such movement.

### Content of the Messages

It matters what you expose yourself to in a particular exposure session. Let's say you have a habitual exposure pattern of horror and action/adventure shows, and your risk set point is very high for a disinhibition effect. If you watch another hour of television, will that be enough to push you into the manifestation category? It depends on what content you watch. If you watch a comedy program in which the characters help each other and the themes are prosocial, then you are likely to move away from the manifestation point. But if you watch a highly violent program, then you will be more likely to move toward the manifestation point.

### Context of Portrayals

The meaning of the messages is in the way they are portrayed, especially social lessons. When the characters in a story are portrayed as being highly attractive, when their actions are portrayed as being justified, when they are rewarded for those actions, and when the consequences to other characters are minor, then audiences will likely identify with those attractive characters, experience the action from their point of view, and learn from this vicarious experience. Audiences will accept the meaning of the experience that was portrayed by those characters.

This is why the portrayal of violence in the media is so dangerous. The "good guys" are as likely as the "bad guys" to commit acts of violence. The good guys' violent acts are always portrayed as being justified, and they are rarely punished. The meaning of violence, then, is that if you are a good guy, violence is an essential and successful means of resolving conflict. Because each viewer regards himself or herself as a good guy, viewers learn that it is okay for them to use violence.

### Cognitive Complexity of Content

When the message makes few cognitive demands on people, they can process its meaning easier. For example, verbal recognition decreases when content pacing increases and arousal increases. The reason is because these content changes increase the resources that a viewer must use to process the messages. It appears that visual recognition does not also decrease. Therefore, visual recognition may be a more automatic task not requiring as many resources (Lang, Potter, & Bolls, 1999). Children's comprehension of educational content from media messages is dependent on the degree to which the information is central to the narrative. If facts are tangential, they will be learned less well.

The more demands the narrative makes on the working memory, the less well will facts be comprehended and remembered (Fisch, 2000). For example, children remember news better from TV than from print, regardless of their reading proficiency. This is because TV news can provide information in several channels at once, and when the information is semantically redundant—that is, it complements and reinforces each other—learning is achieved better. TV can present pictures, words, and sound (Gunter, Furnham, & Griffiths, 2000). Adults were also found to remember more of political news when the emotional elements in the story were redundant. People read the emotional eliciting cues in political news messages (Bucy & Newhagen, 1999).

## Motivations

When people have a conscious need for a particular kind of information, they will actively seek out this type of information in the media, and the chance of them learning from this experience is high. When people are passive, learning can still occur, but it is not as likely.

People who have a higher education and higher intelligence are more motivated to seek out information from the media. These people select the information that has the greatest utility to them. Also, sensation seeking was found to be a predictor of exposure to television violence (Krcmar & Greene, 1999).

## States

A state is a drive or emotional reaction that occurs in response to some temporary stimuli. It is relatively short lived. Oftentimes, something will happen in our lives that will cause us to feel angry or frustrated. This state can interact with media content and lead to certain effects. For example, someone who is frustrated and then views violence will be much more likely to behave aggressively than if only one of these conditions is present.

The media frequently generate states. Perhaps the most important state is arousal. When viewers are aroused, their attention is more concentrated, and the experience is more vivid for them. They will remember the portrayals more and will be more likely to act while aroused (Comstock et al., 1978; Zillmann, 1991). When viewers are aroused, their attention is more concentrated, and the experience is more vivid for them. They will remember the portrayals more and will be more likely to act while aroused (Comstock et al., 1978; Zillmann, 1991).

Certain production techniques tend to arouse viewers. These techniques include fast cuts, quick motion within a frame, loud music, and sound effects. Also, certain narrative conventions (such as suspense, fear, life-threatening violence, and erotica) can lead to arousal.

Although most states are regarded as physiological or emotional ones, there are cognitive states also, and these are especially important with media literacy. If you find yourself confronting information about a topic where you have no context or background information, you will likely find yourself in a state of ignorance. This cognitive state of ignorance is usually associated with emotional states of frustration or despair. But the cognitive part of this state is keyed to a lack of informational context. Like all states, cognitive states are short lived because people will typically avoid the message or search out more information on the topic. Either response is sufficient to end the experience of ignorance on that topic.

## Degree of Identification

Identification with particular characters is also a key factor in the effects process because people will pay more attention to those characters with whom they identify. We become involved in media-depicted events through a psychological relationship with the characters in a two-step process. First, we make a judgment about how much we are attracted to the character and how much the character is like us—or how we would like to be. Second, we engage in an "as if" experience in which we imagine ourselves in the role of the character. Viewers form strong attachments to certain characters, depending on what those characters do and say (Hoffner & Cantor, 1991). The stronger the attachment, the stronger the probability of an effect (Bandura, 1986, 1994).

People identify with characters who have similarities to them but who also have qualities that they would like to possess but do not. Generally, there is a greater liking (positive affect and emotion) for characters who are more similar in age, gender, ethnicity, or interests (Himmelweit, 1966). Although most people tend to select the same-gender character, girls often choose male characters as role models; boys rarely choose female characters. Girls look for physical attractiveness in their selections for role models; boys look for physical aggressiveness. Usually, identification is with a positive object, but it can also be induced through negative sentiment.

# Media Literacy and Blame

Let's return once again to the Russian roulette situation from the beginning of this chapter and readdress the question: Should the media be blamed for the death of the boy who shot himself? This question is continually asked when we hear about a killing that is modeled after a portrayal in a movie or a video game. Although a death resulting from someone imitating something he or she saw in the media is cause for public attention, the public discourse about this problem is very weak. People will typically blame the media, the gun, or the parents of the killed boy. There is little understanding that these three and many other factors are all contributing influences. If we are to blame one, we should blame them all.

We need to understand that in our complex society, seldom does a single element cause an effect. Influences work in combination to move us away from our risk set point. This is not hard for us to understand when it comes to knowing what causes a fire, for example. A fire requires fuel, oxygen, and heat. All three must be present to have a fire. With media effects, there are many factors about the media portrayal, factors in the life of the people involved, and factors about the real-world situation that all contribute to a probability that an effect will occur. No one of these factors will increase the probability from 0 to 100%.

Who is to blame? It depends on how you ask the question. If the question is, "Should the gun manufacturers be held solely responsible for crimes committed using their guns?" the answer is no, of course not, because there are other influences involved. If the question instead is, "Are the gun manufacturers blameless?" the answer again is no because their guns have been essential ingredients in certain violent crimes. The key here is to recognize multiple influences and not allow any one of the influences to be absolved simply because it was not the only influence.

The effects process is a complex one. That is why it requires a person of relatively high media literacy to appreciate the situation. People who are at low levels of literacy will believe there is no effect because they do not know what to look for, or they will focus on artifacts that might not be attributable to the media. Either way, low-level media literacy misleads people into a false sense of awareness.

Despite the complexity in determining what is a media effect, we do know there is a wide range of them from minor to serious, from rare to widespread. Taking a proactive perspective on media effects helps you plan for what you want to have happen to you. This proactive perspective also helps you control the process of influence by positioning your own risk set points and managing your media exposures to reduce the risk of experiencing negative effects while increasing the probability of achieving positive effects.

# Further Reading

Bianculli, D. (1992). *Teleliteracy: Taking television seriously.* New York: Continuum. (315 pages)

David Bianculli was a TV critic/columnist for 15 years before writing this book, which is a defense of television. Although admitting that 90% of TV content is "crap," he feels that it has a great deal of value. He presents a manifesto of 10 points, all intended to get TV more respect. The most interesting part of the book is in the first section, where he presents a 150-question literacy quiz (75 questions about TV and 75 about classic literature and music). The TV questions are very easy to answer, but the other questions are very difficult. His point here is that the population is very TV literate. He also presents a fascinating history of criticism of various forms of literature and music dating back to Plato; this clearly shows that there are people who think every new piece of art is bad and that every new medium is dangerous.

Mander, J. (1978). *Four arguments for the elimination of television.* New York: Morrow. (371 pages)

Mander has written a strong criticism of television. His arguments are more anecdotal and casual than scientific or compelling. His arguments are as follows: (a) TV mediates experience, and this removes viewers from experiencing real life; (b) TV colonizes experience, that is, a few people control the content, and this perspective is imposed on all viewers; (c) TV makes us sick physically (ingesting artificial light) and mentally (dims the mind, hypnotizes, suppresses imagination); and (d) TV has inherent biases against subtlety, away from the sensory, and toward the extraordinary.

Neuman, S. B. (1991). *Literacy in the television age: The myth of the TV effect* (2nd ed.). Norwood, NJ: Ablex. (233 pages with indexes)

Neuman argues that television viewing has not reduced literacy, which she defines in terms of reading ability. She says the arguments that TV has reduced literacy fall under four theories: displacement, information processing, short-term gratification, and interest stimulation. She shows that the empirical evidence does not support any of these theories; that is, the criticism that the media have hindered literacy is unwarranted.

Strasburger, V. C., & Wilson, B. J. (2002). *Children, adolescents, & the media.* Thousand Oaks, CA: Sage. (539 pages, including appendices, references, and indexes)

This is a very readable book with lots of cartoons, pictures, and graphics. The content deals with how both children and adolescents are influenced by the media, particularly the content of advertising, violence, sexuality, drug use, music, and portrayals of food. It also has special chapters on the media of electronic games and the Internet. The authors take a public health perspective in showing the risks of different kinds of media content on individuals and society. The book concludes with chapters on recommendations to help individuals protect themselves as well as recommendations to others, such as programmers, advertisers, policymakers, educators, parents, and researchers.

**Exercise 14.1**    Profiling the Probability of an Effect

1. Analyze a particular media effect along with its pattern of factors that would influence the probability of the effect actually occurring. For example, choose the viewing of a violent movie and its potential effect on you behaving aggressively immediately after the viewing the film.

   a. Look at the list of 13 factors (7 set point factors and 6 factors special to a type of effect) in this chapter and use them to write a profile of the characteristics that would need to be present in the film and that would increase the probability of you behaving aggressively. For example, with context of portrayals, what contextual characteristics would need to be in the film to increase the probability of an aggressive effect?

   b. Now using the same 13 factors as a guide, write a profile that would keep the probability of an aggressive effect as low as possible.

   c. Look at the two profiles. Which one is closer to what you experience in your life? Are there factors about you personally that put you at risk for this type of effect? Are there characteristics about the films you typically see that increase your risk?

2. Do the same exercise above with another effect. Refer to Appendix B for choices.

3. Think about the possible effects of the media in your life and try to apply the following ideas:

   a. *Thresholds:* Have you noticed no effect in some area until you passed a certain level of exposure? What was the effect and level of threshold exposure?

   b. *Direct and indirect:* Can you think of any effects the media have had on you indirectly? For example, have your friends formed an opinion from media messages and then persuaded you to adopt that opinion without you ever being exposed to the original media messages?

## Exercise 14.2    Diagnosing Risk

Each of the five following scenarios features a person interacting with some media message(s). For each of the five scenarios, think about the following five things:

    a.  Pick an effect that the person is at risk of manifesting.

    b.  Think about where the person's risk set point is for that effect. What factors went into positioning that risk set point where it is?

    c.  What factors about a media exposure are likely to push the person toward the manifestation point?

    d.  What factors about the person's exposure experience or the person himself or herself are likely to push the person toward the manifestation point?

    e.  What could this person do to avoid being pushed toward the manifestation point?

*Scenario 1: Bobby*

Bobby is a 5-year-old who loves to watch action/adventure cartoons on Saturday morning television. His mother is happy that the television serves as a babysitter for Bobby, freeing time up for her to work in another part of the house.

*Scenario 2: Jennifer*

Jennifer is disgusted by watching political ads on television. She thinks all ads are negative and will not watch them. Also, she thinks all politicians are crooks and refuses to vote or pay attention to any news coverage of campaigns.

*Scenario 3: Cool Dude*

Cool Dude is a sophomore in college. For the past 4 years, he has been closely following heavy metal and rap music. He also watches a good deal of MTV. He stays up partying all night every night and sees himself as the center of social life at the school because of his dress, his talk, and his style.

*Scenario 4: Alison*

Four-year-old Alison has just watched Bambi's mother die in the movie. She is so grief stricken that she cannot take her nap.

*Scenario 5: Percy*

Percy is a teenager who has seen every horror film made. But now the thrill is gone. Recently, he has lost the ability to be scared while at the movies. Still, he continues to go to every new horror film—hoping that there will be some awesome special effect or super gruesome scene that can excite him.

# CHAPTER 15

# Effects on Institutions

**Key Idea:** The media, especially television, have fundamentally changed many of our institutions.

The effect of the media is not limited to individuals. The media also profoundly influence our institutions. Some institutions, such as politics, have fundamentally changed due to the direct influence of the media, especially television. Other institutions—such as the family, society, and religion—have changed because of many different social pressures, and the media have served to heighten these pressures.

In this chapter, we examine how the media have influenced these four institutions. The changes that have taken place in these institutions over the years have been caused by many factors, not by the media alone. However, the media's role cannot be ignored. Also, notice that many of those changes are positive.

The more you know about the present character of these institutions, the more you can appreciate the power of the media. Also, this chapter illustrates how the media can have an indirect effect on you through these institutions. The more you understand about these dynamics, the more media literate you will be.

# Family

## Decline in the Traditional Family

In the span of just one generation, the makeup of the American family has changed radically. The number of traditional two-parent families has shrunk, eclipsed by childless couples, single parents, and people living alone (Perkins, 1996). From the early 1970s to 1998, the percentage of American households made up of married couples with children dropped from 45% to 26%. Marriage has also dropped from 75% of all adults in 1972 as being married to 59% in 2002 ("U.S. Divorce Statistics," 2002). Also, the percentage of children living with single parents went from 4.7% in 1972 to 18.2% in 1998 (Irvine, 1999).

One argument for the cause in the decline of the traditional family is that the rates of divorce are very high in the United States, and they have been climbing since television first penetrated our culture. In 1960, 16% of first marriages ended in divorce, and by 1996, the figure had climbed to 40% (Whitman, 1996). Critics claim that the rise of the divorce rate and the portrayals of broken families on television are not a mere coincidence; they claim that the television portrayals have socialized people to believe that divorce and having children out of wedlock are acceptable. Critics point out that television too frequently portrays divorce, single-parent households, and alternative lifestyles. These portrayals, presented over many different kinds of shows and over many years, tend to be internalized by viewers. Over time, people become dissatisfied with their own marriages and seek adventure with other partners. Also, there are popular television series, such as *Married with Children,* that portray married life in a negative manner, thus giving young people the idea that marriage is an unattractive lifestyle.

## Family Unity

Television, as well as other media, has the potential to bring the family together to share a common experience. Families can build a bonding ritual around television by agreeing to watch a particular movie or series and then spend time talking about it after the exposure. In the 1970s, many households had only one television, and viewing was a common family activity (Medrich, Roizen, Rubin, & Buckley, 1982). However, few families now use television or other media in this way. In contrast, patterns of media use within a family usually indicate that media exposure is an individual rather than a group activity. For example, more than two thirds of all American households have more than one television set, so individual viewing is possible in most homes. Also, with 65% of households having cable and the average cable service providing more than 100 channels, individual viewing is desirable, so family members do not have to compete for the television. Each family member can watch what he or she wants by viewing a separate TV in a separate room.

Even when family members view television together, there is less interaction than if the televisions were off and the family members had to entertain one another. For example, more than one third of families have TV on during meals, and this reduces the conversation among family members.

When it comes to the media, parents have changed their roles over the years. For example, Pipher (1996) points out,

> Good parents used to introduce their children into the broader culture; now they try to protect their children from the broader culture. Good parents used to instill the values of the broader culture; now they try to teach their children values very different from the ones the world at large teaches. (p. 11)

Also, parents have reduced the time they spend with their children—40% less time from the 1950s to the 1990s (Pipher, 1996). Pipher argues, "Rapidly our technology is creating a new kind of human being, one who is plugged into machines instead of relationships, one who lives in a virtual reality rather than a family" (p. 92). "When people communicate by e-mail and fax, the nature of human interaction changes" (p. 88). The conveniences of technology serve to cut us off from others. We depend less and less on others (at least face-to-face). People are things or services, not human beings. Pipher says that 72% of Americans don't know their neighbors, and the number of people who say they have never spent time with the people next door has doubled in the past 20 years.

## Other Contributing Factors

Even if we accept the argument that television has influenced the trend toward the breakdown of the traditional family, we must realize that there are also other influences, such as economic ones. For example, it takes more money to support a family. The median household income is now just more than $30,000. So both adults are likely to work, and this makes it harder for them to have children and raise them at home. The percentage of women in the labor force has been steadily climbing—now, about 60% of all women 16 years old and older work (U.S. Bureau of the Census, 2000).

Another reason that family structure and family interaction have changed is that careers have become more important to many people than their families. Wage earners work longer hours, and this takes them away from the home for a higher proportion of their waking hours. There are strong stressors of time, money, and lifestyle, which make people regard the home as a place to recover from the workplace, not a place where they have high energy. No longer is family of paramount importance in most people's lives (Pipher, 1996).

Clearly, family structures and interaction patterns have been changing over the past four decades. There are many reasons for this. Television is a key element, but not the only one, in this change. The additional elements of economic demands, the rise in the importance of careers, and changes in lifestyle preferences have all contributed to the probability of change in the institution of family.

# Politics

The mass media have always had an influence in shaping the way politics have been conducted. Since the founding of the United States, candidates for political office have always relied on coverage of their campaigns in newspapers and magazines, and they have bought ads in these media to get their messages out to the electorate and to create an image for themselves. When William Henry Harrison ran for president in 1840, he wanted to change his image so he would appeal more to the voters who were mostly common people who distrusted the rich. He was afraid of being perceived as an aristocrat because he was the wealthy son of a governor and the owner of a palatial Georgian mansion on a 2,000-acre estate worked by tenant farmers. Instead, he wanted to be perceived as a farmer and backwoodsman to increase his appeal to the electorate. In his newspaper ads, he was shown wearing a coonskin cap and drinking cider by a log cabin. This image was everywhere during the campaign.

About the same time, Daniel Webster created the first political pseudo-event for the press. He camped out with Green Mountain boys in the woods and challenged to a fistfight anyone who called him an aristocrat.

Harrison won his election, but Webster lost his. Using the media does not guarantee victory. But not using the media can guarantee defeat. Candidates for public office, from city council member to president of the United States, must establish name recognition among the electorate, and along with a recognized name, they must instill a positive image. The media are the channels that make it possible for candidates to achieve these goals quickly and across many people.

As radio came along, politicians used it to reach more of the electorate. In the 1930s, Thomas Dewey, a crusading New York City district attorney, ran for governor. On the final day of the campaign, he was on radio from 6 A.M. until midnight, inviting people to phone in and ask him questions. Most of the calls were from one of his assistants who spent the day in a phone booth with a pile of coins.

When television came along in the 1950s, politics began to change dramatically. Since that time, people who want to run for office have been developing much more direct access to the public; thus, there has been a gradual and continual erosion of the amount of influence the political parties are able to exert. This shift in power away from political parties to the public is seen in the areas of primary elections, nominating conventions, campaign spending, campaign staffs, content of advertising, and news coverage.

## Primaries

Television has increased the importance of primary elections for presidential candidates. The nomination of presidential candidates used to be decided in party caucuses and conventions. In 1940, primary elections were held in only 13 states. By 1976, 30 states had primaries. Now almost every state has either a primary election or a caucus. This change has been stimulated by television coverage, which sets the agenda for the public early in an election year and gets people thinking about the candidates.

Now, someone who wants to run for president must do well in the early primaries to get press coverage. Those candidates who do not do well are not put on the press's agenda, and the public rarely hears about them. Those candidates who do well get a great deal of coverage, and this is free publicity for those campaigns.

## Nominating Conventions

The media have changed the presidential nominating conventions of political parties by focusing so much of the public's attention on them. The historical purpose of these conventions was for the loyal party members to gather at a national meeting to exercise their power and to cut deals about party platforms and candidates. The result of all this negotiation was to select a candidate to represent the party in the presidential election. Now, the candidates are known well in advance of the "nominating" conventions, so those meetings have been transformed into advertising platforms for the parties. Thus, the delegates are instructed to portray a favorable impression of the party to the public. This means showing harmony and togetherness rather than debating important issues. From the rise of television in the 1950s, the major television networks used to cover both the Democratic and Republican nominating conventions from "gavel to gavel" until the 1990s, when they began cutting back coverage. In 2004, they covered only the major speeches.

## Campaign Spending

Television's increasing importance in political campaigns has resulted in great increases in campaign spending. In the early days of television, expenditures on the media for political advertising increased 600% (adjusted for inflation) between 1952 and 1974 (Comstock, 1980). By 1972, spending was greatly increased in the presidential election, with McGovern spending $30 million and Nixon $60 million. The reason for the increase was a major shift in the way the campaigns allocated their money. For example, in 1956, 85% of presidential campaign expenditures was spent on setting up rallies for in-person speeches by the candidates. Three elections later, with total expenditures four times greater, more than half the money was spent on television ads (Comstock, 1989). And the television budget continued to increase dramatically, resulting in smaller budgets for field operations, such as setting up rallies, local campaign offices, buttons, and bumper stickers.

Shortly after the 1972 presidential election, in which the candidates spent $90 million, Congress passed some campaign reform legislation that placed strict limits and regulations on spending. In the 1976 election, both candidates spent about $9 million.

However, despite the limits imposed by Congress, the money required to run for president is increasing dramatically again, and a good deal of it is being spent very early in the campaigns. Candidates must spend huge amounts of money early to get name recognition. For example, in 1984, Democratic front-runner Walter Mondale spent more than $30 million to win a single primary. His two challengers (Jackson and Hart) spent a total of more than $21 million in a losing effort—that is, more than $55 million spent by Democratic candidates in a single state! Ronald Reagan, who was an incumbent president at the time, ran unopposed in the Republican primaries and spent $18 million. When the primary campaigns were over, Mondale was nominated as the Democratic candidate and Reagan as the Republican candidate. During the general election that fall, the two presidential candidates were each allowed to spent $40 million, which was the limit imposed by Congress. But political action committees (PACs), which were not regulated, could raise as much as they could and spend it any way they wanted. The wealthy right-wing National Conservative Political Action Committee spent $14 million to campaign for Reagan.

Politics has become a very big money game. In the 1996 presidential election, more than $152 million of federally approved funds were spent—this is the money raised and spent by the presidential candidates according to limits and procedures imposed by the Federal Election Commission. Also, more than $477 million of federally approved funds were spent on congressional races. In addition to federally approved spending, political action groups can raise their own money and spend it on their own public relations campaigns to support a candidate or to run negative ads against his or her opponents. In 1996,

PACs spent $430 million for these campaigns. Thus, more than $1 billion was spent in 1 year's election campaigns for president and Congress (U.S. Bureau of the Census, 2000). It is interesting to note that in the 2000 elections for federal offices, media companies donated more than $75 million to candidates (Lewis, 2000).

When people say that "too much" is spent on political advertising, it is not clear what they mean by the "correct" amount. This is the point made by the columnist George Will (1996), who says that the annual sum spent on political campaigning is less than that spent on yogurt. Also, when you take a 2-year period and include all the money spent by all candidates campaigning for state and federal offices, it equals the same amount as that spent by the nation's two largest commercial advertisers—Proctor & Gamble and Philip Morris. This $700 million works out to be a combined total across all elections of $1.75 per eligible voter per year.

The 2004 presidential election set records for both spending and for getting around campaign financing laws. During this campaign, about $1 billion was contributed from a total of about 1.23 million contributors, which was more than double the 500,000 people who contributed money to political parties during the 2000 presidential campaigns. Also, campaign regulations increased the allowable donation from $1,000 to $2,000 per person. The $1 billion does not include money spent on the 2004 presidential campaign by PACs and state political parties (Getter, 2004).

## Campaign Staffs

The increase in television involvement in political campaigns has altered the makeup of campaign staffs. The most important person in a campaign used to be the campaign manager, who had extensive contacts among party workers so he or she could pull in favors and get lots of members active in setting up rallies, passing out bumper stickers, and going door-to-door to hand out party literature. Now the most valued people in the campaign are the public opinion polling expert and the media consultant.

The polling expert finds out what the public wants in a "leader"—that is, how the person should look, how the person should act, and what stand the candidate should take on important issues. The media consultant then crafts ads and pseudo-events for the media to make the candidate appear like that ideal image.

Some U.S. media experts are so successful that they are being hired to influence elections in other countries. For example, both major political parties in Israel hired expensive American consultants to win their 1999 election of prime minister (Makovsky, 1999).

## Content of Advertising

Critics also complain that much political advertising is either negative or fluff (non-informational). Roger Ailes, the media consultant who produced the new Nixon in 1968, agrees, saying that television is only good to cover three things: visuals, attacks, and mistakes. As a result of this reasoning, there have been high proportions of negative ads in presidential campaigns. For example in the 1988 presidential election, 70% of ads were negative. In the 1996 campaign, about half of all the money spent by PACs was on ads against a particular candidate (U.S. Bureau of the Census, 2000).

## News Coverage

Campaigns that are played out in the media are typically dominated by sound bytes—the short quote with a catchy phrase. Sound bytes are so short that they do not give the candidate an opportunity to convey his or her positions with any sophistication or depth. The sound byte has gotten so short that it appears that it cannot shrink any more. Lowry and Shidler (1995) report that in the 1992 presidential campaign, the size of the sound bytes stopped shrinking. In 1968, the average sound byte was 43.1 seconds, and it decreased to about 9 to 10 seconds in 1988. In this study, the average sound byte for candidates was 9.4 seconds, and the average for noncandidates was 7.3 seconds. Thus, a 20-year trend seems to have bottomed out.

Schudson (2003) reports that negative coverage in the 1980 presidential campaign was about 25%, and this figure had climbed to 60% in the 2000 presidential election. This negative news coverage has also made its way to the Internet. Wicks and Souley (2003) examined the news releases that were posted on the official campaign Web sites of George W. Bush and Al Gore during the 2000 presidential campaign. Three quarters of those releases were negative—a similar percentage to television political advertising. This is support for the political competition model, which says that close races produce significant negativity. This model explains that candidates who hold comfortable leads will present more positive information about themselves (called acclaims), whereas trailing candidates will try to contrast their positions with those of the front-runner. When the race is close and there is no clear front-runner, each candidate will frequently attack the opponents because each perceives that attacking an opponent through the media can be an effective way of attracting voters (Ansolabehere & Iyengar, 1995).

The press usually presents campaigns as horse races. In an analysis of more than 1,300 election stories carried by ABC, CBS, and NBC during the 1988 primaries, more than 500 dealt with who appeared to be winning, and another 300 dealt with campaign strategies, for a total of more than 60% of the coverage clearly exhibiting the horse race mentality. In contrast, only about 1 in 6 stories covered the issues.

The front-runner is the candidate who wins the very first primary. The press then creates expectations for candidates and the campaign outcome. Throughout the campaign, the press reports polls to set up these expectations about who is winning and by how much. When something different than the expected occurs, it is deemed newsworthy.

Media coverage fluctuates with the performance of the candidate in the preceding contest. The most attention generally goes to the candidate who was the winner or who has emerged surprisingly as the challenger. Candidates who falter become progressively less able to compete because they begin slipping off the agenda (Patterson, 1980).

There is a trend toward using new sources of information on politics—such as on MTV and talk shows (*Larry King*). Hollander (1995) found that attention to MTV and late-night shows is not related to gains in political knowledge, but attention to talk shows is.

Media can directly affect how people process information about political events, and this priming effect influences behavior (Iyengar & Kinder, 1987). By focusing on certain issues and ignoring others, the media set the agenda for the campaign. The agenda alters the public's priorities. The high-priority issues then are what the public focuses on when examining the stance of candidates. Thus, if a candidate is strong on many issues and weak on one, and the press makes that one issue a priority, then the public will think that issue to be very important and therefore rate that candidate low.

In summary, television has made it possible for candidates to quickly build name recognition and plant a favorable image in the minds of the voters. But this comes with a high price. Television advertising is very expensive and thus requires candidates to continually raise large sums of money. There is also a price to the institution of politics, which has been forever changed.

There are some key benefits to this change. As voters, we are given a lot more information about candidates, and significant coverage of campaigns begins earlier. Also, with this additional information and the opportunities to vote in primaries, we are given more power to select the candidates who will run in the general elections. But there is also a downside— the information we are given about the candidates is usually very superficial and often negative. And the mainstream media also set the agenda, thus channeling our interest to a few selected topics and away from all others. We can counteract this downside by being careful to analyze the information we do get and to seek out more extensive and intensive information and build stronger knowledge structures about the political process and its players.

Although the addition of primaries and caucuses to choose presidential candidates was at first seen as a populist move—that is, to give the individual voters more say in picking their party's standard bearers—the effect has been to concentrate power into the hands of only a few of those voters. For example, before the 2004 primary races, Howard Dean had worked for more than a year to put together a grassroots political organization through the Internet. When the first voter test rolled around—the Iowa caucuses— Massachusetts Senator John F. Kerry unexpectedly came in first in a crowded seven-person field of Democratic candidates. Kerry won with about 125,000 votes or about 22% of Iowa's Democratic voters (Dallek, 2004). This first caucus was seen as so important that candidates who did not finish well began dropping out, and Howard Dean's "loss" (he still came in second in a field of seven candidates) was something he could not shake. He went on the next week to finish second to Kerry in the New Hampshire primary and again was perceived as a loser. Although he continued to get votes and amass delegates over the course of the next month of primaries, he could not shake his loser image, and he eventually had to withdraw from the race, leaving Kerry virtually unopposed.

The way political campaigns are conducted has certainly changed over the past 50 years, with the rise of the importance of television as a mass medium. And it appears that more changes are in store for politics as newer media become more important. Internet Web sites are being used extensively by candidates for all kinds of political offices. Candidates can post information and interact with voters in chat rooms. Also, some of the "older" media are being used in new ways. For example, talk radio is an important outlet for candidates as well as television newsmagazines, electronic town meetings, and MTV (Davis & Owen, 1998). Even entertainment programs such as late-night talk shows (*David Letterman* and *The Tonight Show*) and Comedy Central are being used by candidates to get more exposure.

# Religion

About 80% of Americans consider themselves religious and believe in life after death. But only 57% attend a church or synagogue on a regular basis. One of the reasons for this difference in percentages is because commitment to religious institutions has been dropping in the United States, especially among younger people, such as the 76.5 million people in the generation known as the baby boomers, who were born between 1946 and 1964. About two thirds of these baby boomers dropped out of organized religion during the 1980s, although some of them were starting to return by the end of that decade (Woodward, 1990). Another reason is perhaps because people are able to use the media much more for worship and are less likely to attend religious services in person.

The media have always provided people with religious information. For example, the Bible is still the all-time best-selling book. Sales continue to grow—up 50% over the past few years. And 91% of all Americans own an average of three versions. However, fewer people are spending time reading it, and there is Bible illiteracy. More than half of Americans can't name even five of the Ten Commandments, and two thirds don't know the names of the four gospels. Religious organizations are trying to jazz up the old book, and now there are more than 3,000 different editions designed to appeal to different readers. It is being promoted by celebrities such as M. C. Hammer, the rap artist, and Sinbad, the comedian. Newer versions of the bible include the *TouchPoint Bible,* which is organized by topics such as anger and self-control; the *Positive Thinking Bible,* by Norman Vincent Peale; the *Devotional Bible for Dads,* which is folksy and chatty; and the *Complete Idiot's Guide to the Bible.*

Some newer versions of the Bible display a high degree of political correctness. For example, some versions have changed "Son of Man" to "Human One," and the Lord's Prayer reads, "Our Father-Mother who art in heaven" (Watanabe, 1999). Sales of all religious books continue to climb. For example, sales in 2003 were up about 33% from the previous year (Association of American Publishers, 2003).

## Religion on Television

Religious programs have been on television ever since its earliest days in the 1950s, but it was not until the 1970s that this type of programming became very visible. There is a controversy about how large the viewing audience is for religious television. The televangelists claim that the audience is very large. In contrast, Fore (1987) says that the audience for the electronic church is far smaller than claimed. In surveys, about 71 million people say they have watched one of these programs each week. But Nielsen diaries put the figure at about 24.7 million a week, and this is a duplicated audience; the unduplicated figure is about 13.3 million who watch at least 15 minutes a week. The number of people who watch for an hour or more is less than 4 million. Only the top religious programs draw an audience of more than 2 million viewers (Horsfield, 1984). The demographics of the audience are more female, older, lower education, lower income, and more blue-collar occupations (Hoover, 1988; Horsfield, 1984).

The best predictor of religious program viewership is whether a person is affiliated with a church. It is the churchgoers who watch religious TV. Thus, religious programs are preaching to the converted and do not serve to convert those who are not churchgoers (Horsfield, 1984). Fore (1987) says that about 77% of the heavy viewers are church members who attend services fairly regularly. About 14% said they watch religious television instead of going to church. The viewing of religious television is to be associated with church attendance, giving, and private religious behaviors such as prayer and Bible reading (Hoover, 1988). Therefore, the effect of these shows is possible reactivation of inactive members or channeling members from one church to another.

Religious programming on television is shaped by the same forces that shape television content in general (Horsfield, 1984). The three major forces are as follows:

1. Sensationalism: There is a strong emphasis on producing material that will quickly capture and hold viewers' attention.

2. Instant gratification: Programmers strive to provide immediate answers to easily defined problems.

3. Oversimplification: Programming avoids in-depth demanding analyses of issues, events, and human relationships and instead relies heavily on stereotyped characters, plots, and relationships.

Religious themes are not common in television entertainment. However, there are examples of successful series (*Touched by an Angel* and *Seventh Heaven*) that make religious themes a central part of their programs.

# Money

A big theme on all religious programs is the appeal for money. In 1983, Abelman (cited in Fore, 1987) conducted a content analysis of the 40 leading religious shows and found that in an average hour, the viewer was asked to donate $328; a person who watches 2 hours a week is subject to direct appeals of about $31,500 a year. Most of these appeals are to allow the televangelist to stay on the air, not to fund missions of helping clothe or feed people.

Figures for yearly contributions in the late 1970s are as follows: $60 million to Oral Roberts, $46 million to the Christian Broadcasting Network, and $20 million to Jimmy Swaggart (Horsfield, 1984). By 1983, Pat Robertson's CBN brought in $101 million, of which $89 million came in as donations. In 1985, Jim Bakker's PTL Club had an income of $72.1 million, with 42 million in direct contributions and the rest earned from a new $30 million Victorian-style hotel and biblical theme park, the 2,500-acre Heritage USA. PTL's expenses that year were $89.7 million. Jimmy Swaggert generated about $45 million a year; 80% was spent to keep his show on the air (Fore, 1987).

# Television's Influence on Individuals' Religious Experiences

What do viewers get from watching religious television programs? Hoover (1988) argues that the electronic church has had a revitalizing effect by recognizing individuals' experiences of dissonance, frustration, and cultural crises. By depicting the culture as out of control, these programs present themselves as offering stability and a clear purpose. They have done this by developing a total, universal explanation of life that proposes to resolve the dissonances felt in contemporary life.

What is the appeal of the electronic church? Fore (1987) explains that the electronic church appears authoritative at a time when authority appears to be in disarray. It highlights competition between God and the devil. It places emphasis on individuals as the foundational societal unit and charges them to act. And it is generally affirming of the social values most people hold and reinforces this belief system with attractive personalities.

# Television's Influence on the Institution of Religion

Some social critics, such as Hoover (1988), argue that the main effect of the electronic church has not been the changing of people's beliefs. Instead, the main effect of the electronic church has been the changing of the institution of religion in America. How has religious television done this? It has broken down denominational boundaries, thus bringing evangelicals and fundamentalists into the mainstream. And it has changed the way we see politics and religion—the electronic church has taken on a political prominence.

## Television as Religion

Some scholars think of television as becoming a dominant institution that has taken over some of the functions of religion (Gerbner & Gross, 1976). They say that television implicitly communicates values and interpretations of the world by presenting lessons about success, power, and dominance. By conveying status to certain people, television identifies those people much like priests who guide our thinking.

Television is seen by some as the new American religion.

Television is the new "cultural storyteller," an agent of norms and values as much as of news and information. Television fulfills this function very much in the way traditional storytellers did—by a process of dialectic, not didactic—where the stories evolve with the culture, retaining most, but not all, of their formal integrity by changing to suit its audiences and new contexts of expression. (Hoover, 1988, p. 241)

Fore (1987) says that television is

beginning to replace the institution that historically has performed the functions we have understood as religion. Television, rather than churches, is becoming the place where people find a worldview which reflects what to them is the ultimate value, and which justified their behavior and way of life. Television today, whether the viewer knows it or not, and whether the television industry itself knows it or not, is competing not merely for attention and dollars, but for our very souls....

Television is itself becoming a kind of religion, expressing the assumptions, values, and belief patterns of many people in our nation, and providing an alternative worldview to the old reality, and to the old religious view based on that reality. (pp. 24, 25)

These writers are very critical of the idea that television is becoming the dominant religion in this society. "The values, assumptions, and worldview of television's 'religion' are in almost every way diametrically opposed to the values, assumptions, and worldview of Christianity and the historic Judeo-Christian tradition in which the vast majority of American profess to believe" (Fore, 1987, p. 25). Also, Hoover (1988) cautions that contemporary religion is at odds with many of the messages of television—the messages of materialism rather than sharing and asceticism; force and violence dominate the value systems instead of love and cooperation; classes of people are objectified and manipulated, not encouraged and cared for. Many evangelists see TV as secular humanism that is competing with the values they espouse; therefore, TV is the enemy.

Critics fear that the technological worldview poses three threats to religion (Fore, 1987). First, it is diverting a major portion of the world's interests, motivations, satisfactions, and energies away from a religious center. Second, it is robbing genuine religious vocabularies of their power as people know more about TV characters than religious symbols and figures. Third, the new technological environment encourages the growth of religious concern that rejects or ignores organized religion. People spend more time with electronic devices than they do with people. With increasing channels and content options, people can pick only those things that reinforce already held beliefs. This puts the development of beliefs into the hands of individuals rather than the institution of religion. Thus, communication is treated more as a commodity to serve an individual's immediate needs, rather than as a broad cultural phenomenon that brings us together into a large community where the needs of the community are more important than the needs of any individual.

Fore (1987) contrasts the central myths of television with the central values of religion. He says television presents five myths:

1. The fittest survive (social Darwinism).

2. Power and decision making start at the center and move out (Washington, DC, is the center of political power; New York the center of financial power; Hollywood the center of entertainment power).

3. Happiness consists of limitless material acquisition (corollaries include that consumption is inherently good and that people are less important than are property, wealth, and power).

4. Progress is an inherent good (it is good to keep moving, but it is less important to have a goal).

5. There exists a free flow of information (this is a myth because there is almost no chance for nonestablishment information from getting a wide hearing).

Television is forcing churches to adapt. Comstock (1989) says that "in the case of cultures in which traditional religious observances have a visible and important place, television is one of the central components of modernization that channels public energies toward secular pursuits" (p. 246). As people become more secular, religion has to adapt by fighting against the trend of secularization, thus becoming less relevant to people's everyday lives, or it must change its values. For example, in Israel, television took time away from participation in celebrations and activities associated with Jewish religious practice, so television broadcasting was outlawed on the Sabbath. But the public demanded that the prohibition be lifted, and it was (Katz & Gurevitch, 1976).

In summary, the key benefit of religious messages in the media is that it provides more experiences to worship for those people who are already religious. But critics are concerned that television itself has become a religion, as evidenced by the ritualized viewing by many people. This has critics worried because the values presented on television are very different from the values presented by organized religion.

# Society

The same forces that are fragmenting politics, religion, and the family are also fragmenting society. But there is an irony to this situation because on the surface, the media appear to be a unifying force. The mass media give us the illusion that we all are experiencing the same messages. When we see a show on TV or hear a song, we often assume that everyone else has also seen it. Or when we read about a national figure in the newspaper or magazine, we assume that everyone else in our society also knows who that person is. People get the feeling that everyone else is tied into the same things that they are. But this is an illusion.

Instead, the media are serving to fragment us; that is, we are becoming more and more different from one another as we share a smaller and smaller set of shared experiences over time. How? Although we all have *access* to the same messages, we cannot possibly *expose* ourselves to them all. For example, you probably have access to at least 100 different television stations, but you can watch only one at a time. You must make choices. It's our choices that fragment us. Because each of us has a different set of interests, we are all screening out a different set of messages. Although our *access* to the media may be the same, everyone is paying attention to a different set of messages. Over time, our knowledge structures develop very differently; we have very few shared experiences.

These knowledge structures are what we use for context when we interpret new messages. Because our contexts are so different from one another, our interpretations then differ. These differences remind us of how little we have in common. This trend toward differences continues as more messages are made available and as we screen in only a very small subset of them.

When we look at this fragmentation phenomenon from the media point of view, we see an irony. The mass media are driven to appeal to as many of us as possible. For example, programmers at ABC, CBS, Fox, and NBC, as well as Hollywood producers and publishers of general magazines and best-selling books, want to construct messages that will appeal to as wide an audience as possible. So they strip away as much context as possible so that they don't require much in the way of interpretation from their audiences. When you watch a situation comedy on prime-time television, you don't need much contextual information. You are not required to know anything about the history of situation comedies, their economic nature, or the political environment of getting one on the air. You don't even have to know what the characters did on the last episode to follow this episode. Very little is asked of you as a viewer, compared to what is asked of you if you were to watch a documentary on Egyptian hieroglyphics or a Shakespearean play, for example. With situation comedies, you don't need to bring much context to the viewing. And the viewing of situation comedies does not contribute much to the contexts you already have, so this common viewing along with millions of other people does not really build a common context.

Donnelly (1986) describes this fragmentation of society when he says that we are currently living in an Autonomy Generation that will soon change to a Confetti Generation. The Autonomy Generation people believe that each individual is the center of all relevant values.

> We are responsible only to ourselves, and we alone can decide which activities and ways of behaving have meaning for us and which do not. We live subjectively according to our own feelings with little need for outside reference.... We interpret life in terms of what's in it for us, seek authenticity by transcending society and external value systems, and insist on being ruled only by the laws of our character.... We live in the present, responding to momentary perceptions, relationships, and encounters. To us, what is most important is how outside events are perceived and understood by the individual. (p. 178)

He says we experience what Durkheim called *anomie,* the peculiar pain derived from individuals' inability to identify and experience their community.

Donnelly (1986) says that the new electronic media have five characteristics that will affect society: quantity (in terms of availability and use), speed (delivery and satisfaction), weightlessness of images (no context), remoteness (bring faraway information close), and choice (explosion of alternatives). Because the present generation does not possess the cultural tools to absorb such an explosion of information, we will become the Confetti Generation. The Confetti person is inundated by experience but ungrounded in any cultural discipline for arriving at any reality but the self.

> We will witness an aggregated version of today when all ideas are equal, when all religions, life-styles, and perceptions are equally valid, and equally indifferent, and equally undifferentiated in every way until given a value by the choice of a specific individual. (pp. 181–182)

Whether Donnelly (1986) is overstating the problem remains to be seen. He may be right if the literacy of the people in society does not keep up with the changes in our world.

# Conclusion

The media have changed institutions, especially television and especially over the past four decades. These institutions affect us, so the media exert an indirect effect on us through these institutions.

The family has changed from the traditional two parents, with one working outside the home and the other staying home taking care of the children. Television has been blamed for making people more materialistic, so more people have to work longer hours to get the means to buy all the new products that have become necessities: multiple cars, multiple TV sets, stereos, computers, cellular phones, and on and on. Thus, people spend more time in the workplace and less time with family members. When the family is together, the individuals are likely to watch TV in separate rooms. Parents are less likely to watch with their children and talk about the shows with them. With little adult supervision on television viewing, video game playing, and computer usage, children experience worlds apart from the family. The shared experience is disappearing.

Politics has changed from a process of interpersonal persuasion, speech making, and backroom power deals to one of opinion polling, broad-scale negative television ads, and images that look good on television. The power of the primaries (especially the first few) has greatly increased, whereas the purpose of nominating conventions has evaporated. Now, more than ever, the campaigning process is driven by big money so that candidates can produce slick ads and saturate television audiences with them. Spending lots of money will not guarantee a victory, but having little money will guarantee a loss.

Religion has moved onto television to provide messages to the already religious. Without advertising, these religious programs depend on the donations of viewers. And they are able to raise a great deal of money each year. For many people in this society, television is becoming a religion, as they structure their time around television viewing in a ritualistic manner, seek to learn the fundamental lessons about life from television, and take great comfort in hearing the news and watching the entertainment.

Society is fragmenting. Television has the ability to bring everyone in society together by giving us all common, shared experiences everyday. In the early days of television broadcasting, this was perhaps the case. But now, with most households able to access 100 or more channels, no two people's viewing habits are the same. We each have an incredible variety of messages at our fingertips. In the pursuit of this variety, we lose the sense of shared community.

The media, especially television, have influenced these changes. But we must be careful not to think that they are the only influence. We live in a complex society where family, politics, religion, society, and many other forces are constantly working, often at cross-purposes. The media are an important player in all this because they transmit information about change so quickly and broadly. The pace of life is accelerating. Those who are media literate can have an influence on the direction of that pace—at least for themselves.

# Further Reading

Croteau, D., & Hoynes, W. (1994). *By invitation only: How the media limit political debate.* Monroe, ME: Common Courage. (218 pages, including index)

The authors have conducted a careful analysis of news programs to determine who are portrayed as sources of national news. They found that there is a relatively narrow range of opinion projected there and that most of the sources are either highly visible government officials or elites.

Davis, R., & Owen, D. (1998). *New media and American politics.* New York: Oxford University Press. (304 pages with index)

After presenting chapters that define the new media and explain the environment in which they operate, the authors offer eight more chapters in three areas: the role and content of new media, the audiences and effects of new media, and the effects of new media on traditional media, campaigns, and public policy. This book is now dated because so many elections, including two presidential elections, have taken place since this book was written. But it serves as a good historical piece about the initial use of the so-called new media. Also, the book does a good job at sensitizing readers to what are the important issues in using alternative media in American politics.

Donnelly, W. J. (1986). *The confetti generation: How the new communications technology is fragmenting America.* New York: Holt. (239 pages with index)

Donnelly is a former adman and professor who retired from Young & Rubicam (Y&R) to write this book. His main point is that people (especially Toffler and other futurists) who make predictions about new media focus on the technologies and ignore the audience. Because of this, their projections of media use in the future are way off (e.g., 200 channel cables by 1990).

Jamieson, K. H., & Waldman, P. (2003). *The press effect: Politicians, journalists, and the stories that shape the political world.* New York: Oxford University Press. (220 pages with index)

This book is one of the latest and best books dealing with the topic of how journalists manufacture news. This book focuses on how journalists use their lenses (the shifting perspectives that color what reporters see of the world) to select what gets covered. The journalists use frames, which are the structures they use to tell stories; the book also provide an in-depth analysis of two topics.

McChesney, R. W. (1999). *Rich media, poor democracy: Communication politics in dubious times.* Urbana: University of Illinois Press. (427 pages with index)

The author makes a strong argument that the trend toward consolidation of media businesses has been seriously undermining democracy in the United States. McChesney defines democracy as the practice of the majority of citizens making the core political decisions. As fewer and fewer people have greater control over the information industries, the average person has less chance to participate in legitimate debates about issues.

**Exercise 15.1**    Becoming Sensitive to Changes in Institutions

1. Interview your parents by asking them the following questions. Ask them to think back to when they were your age or younger for their answers.

   A. Family
     1. What was the most important medium in the household?

     2. How many televisions were in the house, and who controlled them?

     3. Were there viewing rules? Restrictions on kids?

     4. Did family members ever read books or magazines to one another?

     5. Did family members listen to radio or music together?

   B. Politics
     1. Where did people get most of their information about political campaigns? Conversations or media? If media, which ones?

     2. Did they go to political events, such as rallies, speeches, or meetings?

     3. Can they remember any political ads? If so, what sticks out in their minds about those ads? Images? Negativity?

     4. Do they have any strong memories about news coverage of nominating conventions, the campaign, or election returns?

   C. Religion
     1. Did they used to listen to religious programs on the radio or watch them on television?

     2. What was their opinion of religious leaders at the time?

     3. Do they feel that religion has changed in the past several decades? If so, do they think the media had any influence?

2. Next interview your grandparents and ask them the same questions.

3. Ask yourself the same questions.

4. Compare the pattern of answers across three generations. Do you see any changes in attitudes, perceptions, or the way people live their lives? If so, can you attribute any of these changes to the media?

**PART V**

# INCREASING MEDIA LITERACY

# CHAPTER 16

# The Importance of Real-World Knowledge

> ***Key Idea:*** The more primary knowledge we have about our world, the stronger the context we have for evaluating the accuracy and the usefulness of information from the media.

**Importance of Information**
    Orienting Function
    Confirming Function
**Types of Information**
    Need for Factual Information
    Need for Social Information
**Examples of Faulty Beliefs**
    Crime
    Government
    American Products
    Causes of Death and Risks
**Conclusion**

Children recite jingles instead of poetry and they know brand names instead of the names of presidents. More students can identify Mr. Peanut and Joe Camel than can identify Abe Lincoln or Eleanor Roosevelt. They can identify twenty kinds of cold cereal but not the trees and birds in their neighborhoods. (Pipher, 1996, p. 94)

B ack in 1922, before the mass media became so dominant in our culture, journalist Walter Lippmann wrote a book called *Public Opinion,* in which he said,

Each of us lives and works on a small part of the earth's surface, moves in a small circle, and of these acquaintances knows only a few intimately. Of any public event that has wide effects, we see at best only a phase and an aspect. (p. 79)

Our world is far more complex today, which makes his comments even more significant. Are our opinions and beliefs keeping pace with our world? Are we willing to search out more information from a wider variety of sources so that we can use the complexity to arrive at more reasoned opinions? Or do we uncritically accept partial sets of facts and infer simple conclusions? There is a far greater challenge to be media literate today than there was 80 years ago.

## Importance of Information

We are immersed in a flood of information. We cannot avoid being bombarded by information every day. But all this information does not necessarily make us more knowledgeable. Recall that there is a difference between information and knowledge. Information is facts, data, and impressions. Knowledge is the construction of information into meaningful structures. To construct useful knowledge structures, we must scan for useful information, screen out the faulty facts, and knit together the elements of the good information into a useful pattern. Unless we have good knowledge structures to guide us in our constant encounters with media messages, we will have little context to help us make good decisions about what is useful.

To be media literate, you need to develop strong knowledge structures on a wide range of topics—about the media and about the real world. This requires that you have a plan that identifies important topics. Then you must actively seek out information on these topics so you can build knowledge structures. This book cannot provide a plan for you; you must construct your own plan that builds on your abilities and moves you toward your goals for life. What this book can do is give you some things to think about, and it can stimulate you to think about developing a plan for yourself.

This chapter is not a catalog of all knowledge that a media-literate person should have. Such a list would be impossible to provide in the space of one chapter. Several authors have made strong arguments for the importance of such a list (Bloom, 1987; D'Souza, 1991). Also, a few scholars have attempted to build such a list (Hirsch, 1987; Hirsch, Kett, & Trefil, 1993).

There is a core of information that arguably everyone should have. This is why public education for everyone through Grade 12 is so important. Without a sharing of basic definitions, concepts, and procedures among the members of each new generation, the possibility for efficient communication withers away. However, we should not expect public schools to provide each of us with all the information and skills we will need to function well and achieve our individual goals in life. There are substantial differences across people in what information they will need to become media literate. People operate in different cultures and have different interests and different sets of experiences, so their needs for information differ.

Good knowledge structures are essential in protecting media-literate individuals from unwanted effects from the media. The broader and more accurate your knowledge structures are, the more you will be able to orient yourselves toward positive effects and avoid the influence of negative effects. Knowledge structures serve two functions in this process: the orienting function and the confirmation function. When we are not very media literate, the media control these functions. Being highly media literate means that we have shifted control of these functions over to ourselves.

## Orienting Function

Seldom are messages complete enough for us to understand them without having to draw from some contextual information outside the message. For example, if we see a story that the United Nations has sent troops into Fallujah, at minimum we need to know what the United Nations and Fallujah are. It would also help to know what the intention of the United Nations is and why it would want to send troops into Fallujah.

It is helpful to think about any media message as a core cluster of facts that sits at the center of a set of progressively larger concentric circles. Each successive circle contains a wider array of facts that help us to make meaning of the media story that sits in the middle. The more developed our knowledge structure, the wider is our context of understanding. Therefore, we must be able to access a good deal of general information to be able to make meaning from any media story that we might encounter.

Where do people get this orienting knowledge? They need a liberal education. *Liberal* in this sense means broad. People who have a very narrow education—no matter how much in depth it has been—will have difficulty making meaning out of the many media messages that fall outside of their areas of experience.

# Confirming Function

When we are exposed to a fact, we have a choice to either accept it or to try to judge it for accuracy. If we accept the fact and it is inaccurate, we then distort our knowledge structure and have a faulty foundation for our beliefs. Of course, it is better to try to confirm the accuracy of a fact, especially if that fact will be used to justify an important decision or belief.

When we evaluate the accuracy of a fact, we must compare it to a standard. If the new fact meets the standard of accuracy, we confirm it as true. The problem then becomes in choosing the standard of accuracy. We could use our existing knowledge structure as the standard, but if our knowledge structure has inaccurate or out-of-date information in it, the standard will be faulty, and we will make a bad judgment on the new fact. Instead, it is better to confirm the new fact by looking for more information. This is why it is so important to be continually aware of what information you need and to constantly look for it in the real world as well as the media world. In looking for that new information, it is helpful to think of two strategies. First, we could go to credible sources of information. Typically, primary sources are more credible than secondary sources. For example, if we read an article about a candidate's position, that article is a secondary source—the primary source is the candidate. The secondary source may have presented a complete and accurate account of the candidate's position, but maybe the reporter misstated something or left something out. Thus, the possibility of distortion is part of the risk of using secondary sources.

Second, we could search out multiple sources and compare the resulting accounts. Following through on the example of the candidate above, we could search out other magazine, newspaper, and broadcast reports of the candidate's position. We could also ask the candidate's opponent and other people active in politics. From this set of resulting information, we can get a much more accurate fix on what the candidate believes. None of these sources by itself presents the full picture. Even the most primary source of the candidate herself might be flawed because she might not point out inconsistencies with her voting record or how her position has changed over time.

These strategies are especially important when dealing with facts illustrated through numbers and percentages. Percentages are the comparison of two numbers; that is, you take a figure and compare it to some base number. Sources might faithfully report a percentage using accurate numbers, but had they made a comparison to a different base number, the entire meaning of the situation would change. For example, after the U.S. Department of Health and Human Services released the results of a 16-year tracking study of drug use among the nation's adolescents (12–17 years old), the lead sentence in a story by the Associated Press was the following: "A 105 percent jump in teen-agers' drug use since 1992 instantly became a campaign issue" ("Teen Drug Use," 1996). In the ninth paragraph, the story explains that in 1992, 5.3% of adolescents said they had used an illegal drug in the last 30 days, and in 1995, the figure was 10.9%. Thus, if we compare 5.3% to 10.9%, we get an increase of 105%. But if we compare the increase of 5.6% to the 1992 base of 5.3%, the increase is 5.6%. Which percentage is accurate? They both are—but the two convey a really different picture about drug use.

Another example is the reporting of a survey about women and abortions (Leo, 1996). The Guttmacher Institute, which is strongly in favor of abortion rights, released a report that said that Catholic women have an abortion rate 29% higher than Protestant women. This makes it sound like Catholic women are the heaviest users of abortion. But this is not the case. A closer look at the data indicates that Catholic women have an abortion rate right at the national average. Protestant women have an abortion rate much lower than the national average. So when you compare Catholic women to Protestant women, the rate of abortion is higher with Catholics. But if you compare Catholic women with nonreligious women, we find that the rate of abortion among Catholics is only one quarter the rate among nonreligious women. Again, which set of facts is accurate? They both are. But the interpretations are very different.

Even if we are highly media literate, we will, of course, still rely on media messages as sources of information. But we will also seek out information from other secondary sources as well as primary sources. By assessing the relative credibility of the sources, we can then weight the relative value of information from each source. And by looking for patterns of consistency in the information across the sources, we can arrive at a more solid understanding of the topic.

# Types of Information

There are two types of information: factual and social. We use the media as well as real-world institutions as sources for these types of information.

Recall that factual knowledge refers to parameters about the world that are usually not in dispute (not open to individual interpretation). Examples include the size of the population of the United States, names of political leaders, final scores of sporting contests, and the distance between cities.

Social knowledge relates to shared understandings about human interactions. Examples include the way people should behave in certain roles (such as parent, professor, partier, stranger, colleague) and the moral themes within a culture or institution.

## Need for Factual Information

Social critics have a lot of ammunition when they target the educational system in the country. For example, the National Assessment of Educational Progress monitors the learning of our nation's youth in public schools. The results of its recent testing were that the majority of America's high school seniors did not know basic facts about U.S. history, and they could not use what they did know to back up their opinions. Among 12th graders, only 43% attained at least the basic level, 11% were proficient, and 1% was advanced. Scores on math and science have been improving, but scores on reading and writing have been going down (Buzbee, 1995).

However, children don't seem to have trouble identifying those celebrities who get the most media coverage. When children ages 9 to 12 were asked to identify names of people, Michael Jordan and Michael Jackson topped the recognition list at 96% of respondents. Hillary Rodham Clinton was recognized by 82%. Boris Yeltsin got 21%, and Nelson Mandela was low at 20% ("Names & Faces," 1995).

Thus, it seems that the media, especially television, are the dominant teachers of the nation's youth. But television is largely focused on entertainment and popular culture. Television does not teach useful skills (such as writing, critical reading, analysis, and problem solving) that are the essential tools of an educated person. Television does present a wide range of content, much of it highly educational, but viewers prefer to focus on the mainstream entertainment products typically found on the major broadcast networks—the situation comedies, action dramas, soap operas, and game shows. On this point, the media cannot be faulted; they are businesses responding to markets, and the largest markets are for entertainment, not in-depth information.

The institution of public education is entrusted with teaching basic skills, imparting a wide range of knowledge structures, and instilling an appetite for learning. If this institution fulfilled these goals, then we would have a highly informed populace creating a strong market for all kinds of information. However, critics point out that the institution of education is failing to achieve these goals in any substantial way. For example, E. D. Hirsch (1987), who wrote a book titled *Cultural Literacy,* argues that the public's base of knowledge is very narrow. He believes that there is a set of core information that the educational system needs to instill in every individual. Without this broad base of general information, individuals cannot be regarded as being educated; that is, they are not literate about the culture within which they live.

The public's level of higher order skills is also not very strong. For example, in a poll of 400 chief executives conducted by *Fortune* magazine, 77% rated the American public education system as fair or poor—the lowest ratings possible. These business leaders said that they needed an educated workforce that could think, write, analyze, and solve problems to function in the information age. They felt that the American educational system was failing in this task.

Social critics present a bleak picture. But what they fail to acknowledge is the enormous amount of learning that does take place everyday. All of us have some very good knowledge structures. All of us have mastered the basic competencies of literacy, and many of us operate at high levels of proficiency on the advanced skills. Of course, the population could be better, and the social critics perform a useful function in reminding us of this. But bringing this issue down to the personal level, it is important for you to realize that there is a range of knowledge and abilities in society. You must decide for yourself where you want to be in that range. To help you think through this issue, look at Exercise 16.1.

## Need for Social Information

Social information is perhaps even more important than factual information. The media, especially in the entertainment messages, show how people behave, how they achieve success, how they form relationships, what they do when they are unhappy, and so forth.

Real life offers a wide latitude on these social lessons. This latitude includes many if not almost all of the media portrayals. However, those media portrayals do not cover the gamut of human experience; those portrayals tend to emphasize the unusual and the dramatic. When people's knowledge comes overwhelmingly from media messages, they will construct beliefs on information that often does not translate into the real world very well. They will have faulty explanations and faulty beliefs. To correct for this problem, people need to have real-life experiences to see more of a range of social lessons.

# Examples of Faulty Beliefs

A *Newsweek* poll (June 8, 1996) found that 48% of Americans believe UFOs are real, and 29% think we have made contact with aliens. Another 48% think there's a government plot to cover up the whole thing. What makes the results of this poll especially interesting is that almost none of these people claimed to have had direct contact with UFOs or aliens. However, almost half the population believes that there are UFOs and that there is a government plot to cover it up. Where do people get these beliefs? Apparently, they have seen something in the media that has led to this belief. Instead of checking it out with real-world information and finding that none exists, they have decided on pure faith to believe that real-life evidence does exist, even if they have not seen it—thus the need for the companion belief that the government is covering it up. Almost half the American population—at least on this one issue—is satisfied to hold a rather strange belief and base it on absolutely no real-world evidence.

There are many examples of people holding faulty beliefs. Examples on four topics are presented below. On each of these, you can see that public opinion may have been different if people had been provided with a more complete set of information by the media or, in the absence of that, if people had searched out a wider range of information in real life.

## Crime

Most people overestimate the rate of crime, especially violent crime. A Gallup poll commissioned for the White House Office of National Drug Control Policy found crime and violence to be the top national concern among adults (Ostrow, 1996). Most people have not been involved in a crime. Where do they get this idea that crime should be the most important problem facing our country? The media continually show us criminal portrayals both in the news and in entertainment programming. With all this vicarious exposure to crime, most of us generalize to a pattern that there is a great deal of crime in this country and that it continues to increase.

But is this opinion an accurate generalization? Despite the public thinking that crime is a top concern, it has been decreasing steadily since the early 1990s. From 1986 to 1996, the total number of crimes committed per year dropped 7.3%; murder was down 14.0%, rape down 4.7%, robbery down 10.1%, and burglary down 29.9% (U.S. Bureau of the Census, 2000). In 2003, fewer than 24,000 people were murdered—this is only about 40% of those killed in traffic accidents. Yet people are more likely to want more police than to want safer cars or safer highways.

In his book *Crime and Punishment in America*, Elliott Currie (1998) argues that most Americans believe that our legal system is soft on crime; that is, the criminal justice system is much too lenient with criminals. But most people have no idea what the arrest, conviction, and incarceration rates are.

Critics say that there are 10 million violent crimes a year, but only about 100,000 people go to prison each year. Let's analyze this claim. The first problem is that most violent crimes (60%) do not get reported to police. Many of these are schoolyard fights or barroom altercations; however, many serious violent crimes are not reported to police. Only two thirds of robberies, one half of aggregated assaults, and one third of rapes are reported, according to victim surveys (Currie, 1998).

The next problem is that only a small percentage of crimes is cleared by an arrest. Out of the 10 million violent crimes, only about 640,000 (6%) involve an arrest and thus have a perpetrator enter the criminal justice system.

Once in the system, only 165,000 cases end in a conviction. The rest are dropped for lack of evidence, or the defendant is acquitted. Once a person is convicted, about 90% go to prison, and prison sentences are tough. For murder, the average time served is more than 10 years (and this does not include those with life sentences or condemned to death); sentences for rape average more than 7 years; and robbery averages more than 4 years. Prison sentences for convicted criminals are much stiffer in America than in other industrialized countries. Clearly, America is not soft on crime *once a person is convicted.*

Currie (1998) points out that from 1971 to 1996, the number of people in state and federal prisons in the United States went up six times, from 200,000 to 1.2 million inmates. There are also another 500,000 inmates in local jails. This 1.7 million is the size of the city of Houston and twice the population of San Francisco. From World War II to the early 1970s, there were about 100 inmates for every 100,000 people in the U.S. population. By the mid-1990s, that number had climbed to 427 per 100,000.

## Government

Politicians have been running for president on a platform of reducing the size of the federal government ever since 1980. They promise to cut inefficiency and waste and to lower taxes. Have they done so? The answer is no. The overall size of the federal government has remained at about 22% of the gross domestic product, which is the total of all goods and services. The growth has been in the areas of debt servicing, Medicare, and Social Security. In contrast, state and local governments are growing—up 23% since 1980. Most Americans are paying less in federal income tax, but this is more than offset by increases in state and local taxes.

Another myth about the federal government is that it spends huge amounts of money on foreign aid. In 1998, the federal government spent about $13.8 billion in foreign aid—that is three quarters of 1% of the federal budget (U.S. Bureau of the Census, 2000). Most people think that this number is much higher. Also, most people think that this money is simply sent to other countries. Not so. The Business Alliance for International Economic Development said that 80% of the foreign aid budget is spent in the United States, explaining that "the livelihoods of hundreds of thousands of Americans—farmers, truckers, assembly line workers, software developers—depend on U.S. foreign assistance" (Rothberg, 1996, p. F2).

## American Products

Some people argue that allowing foreign-made products into our market will take away jobs from Americans. This argument sounds reasonable on the surface, but let's look at it in more depth using the automobile market as an example.

What is an American-made automobile? Did you know that Jaguar cars are made by a wholly owned subsidiary of Ford Motor Company? Lamborghini, the Italian sports car maker, is wholly owned by Chrysler Corp. The Lotus is a General Motors (GM) product. The Mazda Navajo four-wheel drive vehicle is made in the Ford Explorer plant in Kentucky, and 50% of Saab is owned by GM. Ford now markets Jaguar, Volvo, Aston Martin, and Land Rover in its line of luxury cars (Holstein, 2000).

Also, some purportedly American-made cars are not made by Americans. For example, the Ford Festiva is made by Kia of Korea. The Plymouth Laser is a Mitsubishi Eclipse and vice versa. The Ford Probe is really a Mazda MX-6 made by Mazda in Flat Rock, Michigan. And the Geo Prizm, which seems to be a model of Chevrolet, is really a Toyota Corolla made in Fremont, California ("It's Pretty Hard to Tell," 1993).

In addition, many American companies are part owners of foreign car companies and vice versa. In 1998, the European carmaker Daimler-Benz bought Chrysler, and the next year, DaimlerChrysler AG purchased a controlling interest in Japan's Mitsubishi Motors Corp. General Motors has paired with Fiat. Ford Motor Company has paired with both

Mazda and Volvo. This merging and buying is motivated by a desire for car companies to achieve efficiencies in sharing parts (Hyde, 2000).

The global economy is very interdependent, with overlapping ownerships. The idea of a purely made American car is passé. If the automobiles were assembled in an American plant, many of the parts would come from all over the world. For example, in the June 21, 1999, issue of *USA Today,* General Motors had a full-page ad (p. 5A) in which it said in bold headlines, "The men and women of GM proudly salute the General Motors 'Suppliers of the Year.'" Underneath this headline, GM listed 185 companies "whose efforts have helped raise the quality standards of GM products." Of these companies, 114 were in foreign countries—spread across 26 foreign nations. This raises the following question: What does it mean to buy an American car?

A foreign-made automobile sold in the United States benefits the U.S. economy because the dealership that sells and services the vehicles supports American salespeople, managers, mechanics, and so on. Also, gasoline and oil are purchased from local stations, and the taxes paid (sales, gasoline, licensing, and tolls) all benefit local governments.

The idea that buying a seemingly foreign-made product does not benefit workers in this country is very superficial reasoning. Economists tell us that foreign trade does not lessen or add to jobs; instead, it shifts them from lower unskilled positions to higher paid skilled jobs (Quinn, 1996).

## Causes of Death and Risks

The reporting of high-profile crimes makes us believe that most of us will eventually meet a violent death. But we are 10 times as likely to die a natural death (such as from heart disease, cancer, or even pneumonia) than a violent one. With the violent death category, we are more likely to die in an accident than to be murdered. We are even more likely to commit suicide than to be murdered. The suicide rate is 32,000 per year, compared to 24,000 murders per year (U.S. Bureau of the Census, 2000).

When we rely on the media exclusively for information, we come to believe that we are at risk of being injured by the high-profile catastrophes that are frequently covered in the news. Those things that are not covered make us believe that there is much less risk than there really is. For example, when we compare causes of death per 100,000 people, smoking accounts for 21,900; motor vehicle accidents, 1,600; diagnostic X-rays, 75; lightning, 3; and asbestos in school buildings, 2. However, among the things on this list, the public is most concerned about asbestos in school buildings, and when the media focused on this story in the late 1980s, the asbestos removal industry grew from almost nothing to a $4.2 billion enterprise (Matthews, 1992). And there are people who will feel uncomfortable about a dentist X-raying their teeth but who will feel much less uncomfortable smoking, which is 293 times riskier.

Another way to compare risk is to look at how many days, on average, a behavior will cut from your otherwise normal life span. On average, smoking cigarettes cuts 2,500 days from a man's life and 800 days from a woman's life; being overweight by 30% cuts 1,300 days; working as a coal miner, 1,100 days; being poor, 700 days; and nuclear reactor accidents, .02 days (Allman, 1985).

Some people are terrified of flying but feel no risk when riding in a car. Wurman (1989) says the number of passenger deaths per billion miles is 2,154 in an automobile compared to 214 in an airplane. Also, most people travel much more in automobiles, so their risk is far higher in an auto than in an airplane.

We all feel an uncomfortable sense of risk at times. Perhaps it is when we drive through a "bad" neighborhood, walk alone at night, or fly in an airplane. Where do we get these feelings of risk? For most of us, it is the memory of a story we saw in the media of a mugging or a plane crash. Those gruesome images, although very small in number, stay with us and lead us to unrealistic assessments of risk. With many risky behaviors, the media are silent. If we depend exclusively on the mainstream media messages for our information, we will generalize to a very unrealistic world in which our sense of danger will be very much misplaced.

# Conclusion

The media can greatly expand our knowledge by giving us information on topics that we cannot experience for ourselves. They can take us deep under the sea, into outer space, back in history, and into the Oval Office. But the picture they give us of these places, events, and people is partial and often without much context. If we accept this information as is and do not check it, analyze it, or expand it, we only get a limited picture and may be inferring patterns and themes that are faulty.

How do we know how our government works and who has the real power? How do we know about historical figures? Most of our information comes to us through the media. We depend on this media information because it is impossible for us to have firsthand exposure to historical events or even to current events. So we are dependent on the media for information. Some of this information is good, and some of it is not so good. We must develop the skills to know the difference. It is not always clear what is accurate and what is faulty.

Being media literate means consciously processing the information in all messages as well as being able to recognize useless information and screening it out, then keeping the useful information and building a strong knowledge structure. This requires searching out multiple sources of information, determining the relative credibility of the different sources, and evaluating the variety of claims. It requires analyses of the relevant positions, then synthesizing the worthwhile elements into a reasoned opinion that has been consciously derived and able to be defended. The media provide you with the resources, but you must do your part in developing a strong personal locus that drives you to seek a wider array of information to satisfy all your personal needs rather than to be content to accept what the mainstream media make easily available to you.

# Further Reading

Bloom, A. (1987). *The closing of the American mind.* New York: Simon & Schuster. (392 pages with index)

This is a critique of the state of higher education by a professor of social thought at the University of Chicago. His primary criticism is that universities no longer have a vision for what students should learn to be educated human beings. When the decisions of curriculum are left up to students, they decide to take easy, unchallenging courses so they graduate without having an understanding of the past or a vision for the future.

D'Souza, D. (1991). *Illiberal education: The politics of race and sex on campus.* New York: Free Press. (319 pages with index)

In this criticism of higher education, D'Souza argues that the movement toward political correctness has led to an "anything goes" curriculum at most universities. As a result of this, students are not getting rigorous educations.

Hirsch, E. D., Jr. (1987). *Cultural literacy: What every American needs to know.* Boston: Houghton Mifflin. (251 pages with index)

Hirsch points out that reading is more than recognizing words; it also requires the person to decipher the meaning in the words and stories. To do this, he argues, we need to educate students to have a core knowledge about our world and our culture. He lays out a plan for doing this along with 63 pages of key terms and concepts that he feels every educated person should know.

Hirsch, E. D., Jr., Kett, J. F., & Trefil, J. (1993). *The dictionary of cultural literacy* (2nd ed.). Boston: Houghton Mifflin. (619 pages with index)

This is a dictionary of the "core concepts" of our culture. It is organized into 23 sections, such as life sciences, business and economics, world politics, technology, and fine arts.

**Exercise 16.1**    *Assess Your Learning Experiences*

1. *The Template*

   To do this exercise, you will need to start with a template of knowledge. There are several templates of knowledge you could use. Pick one of the following, then fit your learning experiences into that template.

   - One kind of template of knowledge is reflected in how your college or university is organized into areas or schools, such as arts, humanities, social sciences, and physical sciences. Within each of these areas are departments. For example, social sciences usually has departments of anthropology, sociology, psychology, political science, and economics.
   - Or you could go to the library and look at how knowledge is organized there either by the Dewey decimal system or the Library of Congress system.

   Draw your template graphically on a piece of paper. Sketch a set of blocks to represent the different areas and subareas. The big blocks (such as physical science) should be composed of smaller blocks (such as physics, chemistry, and biology). Some of these smaller blocks (such as biology) may also be composed of subsets (such as botany and zoology). Don't spend more than an hour sketching this out. The goal is not to be inclusive of every detail; instead, try to come up with a reasonable picture of how human knowledge is generally organized.

2. *Graph Your Experiences on the Template*

   Think back over the past 2 years and try to remember *significant learning experiences* you have had during that time. A significant learning experience is something you remember as valuable to your learning, such as the following:

   - A course that really challenged you and made you think
   - An interest in something that made you read a series of books (or search out information in other media) and want to discuss the issues

   Write these *significant learning experiences* in the appropriate content blocks in your template in red ink.

   Now think back over the past 2 years and remember the *"just okay" learning experiences.* These are courses where you learned something but not a whole lot. Or these were minor interests you had in searching out information from the media.

   Write these *"just okay" learning experiences* in the appropriate content blocks in your template in blue ink.

3. *Look for Patterns*

   Look for blank areas:

   Where are the blank areas where there is no red or blue ink? Have you been broadening yourself as a student in college, or have you been playing it very safe so you don't experience new areas? What does this tell you about what you value in a college education and the kind of person you want to become as a graduate?

Look for clusters:

Where are the red areas? Are they all in one small part of the template, or are they sprinkled all over? What does this pattern say about you as a learner and what it takes to make something a significant learning experience?

Where are the blue areas? What do these have in common? How do these blue areas differ from the red areas? What does this pattern tell you about yourself as a learner; that is, to what extent were these experiences less than optimal because of outside forces (such as the teacher, the course materials) or because of something within you (such as motivation, previous knowledge structures)?

4. *Your Personal Goals*

   Think about your goals for life in the following areas:

   - Career
     What industry do you want to get into upon graduation?
     Do you plan to move around to different industries or stay in one?
     How do you plan to advance in your chosen industry?
     What do you see as your last job—highest achievement?

   - Relationships/Family
     What kind of a person do you see as your life partner?
     Where do you plan to meet this kind of person?
     Why would this kind of person be attracted to you?

   - Hobbies
     How do you plan to spend your leisure time?
     Do you plan to travel?

5. *Are You Off to a Good Start?*

   Compare your personal goals to your pattern of significant learning experiences. For example:

   - If you plan a high-powered career, do you have the significant knowledge structures and skills that would make you attractive to people in that industry?
   - If you plan to attract an interesting life partner, have you developed a wide range of interests that would help you attract such a person?
   - If you plan to travel the world, have you studied languages, art, history, political systems, and so on that would give you the basis to appreciate those different cultures?

# CHAPTER 17

# Personal Strategy for Increasing Media Literacy

**Key Idea:** Only you have the power to increase your own level of media literacy.

**Ten Techniques**
1. Strengthen Your Personal Locus
2. Focus on Usefulness as a Goal
3. Develop an Accurate Awareness of Your Exposure
4. Continually Practice Literacy Skills in Mindful Exposure Sessions
5. Acquire a Broad Base of Useful Knowledge
6. Think About the Reality-Fantasy Continuum
7. Make Cross-Channel Comparisons
8. Examine Your Opinions
9. Change Behaviors
10. Take Personal Responsibility

**Illustrations**
  Learning Ladders
  *Cognitive Ladder*
  *Emotional Ladder*
  *Moral Ladder*
  *Aesthetic Appreciation Ladder*

Examples of Levels of Literacy
    *Beavis and Butthead*
    *Soap Operas*
    *Nightly News*
**Conclusion**

C ongratulations for having worked on your knowledge structures in the previous chapters. By now you should have a fairly good awareness about what it means to be media literate. You should now be asking yourself: How can I preserve the skills and knowledge structures I already have? How can I improve?

The answers to these questions require you to think about developing a consistent strategy. In this chapter, I can help direct your thinking, but I cannot give you *The* Strategy. You must develop that for yourself in response to your particular needs. Think about what I say in this chapter as a platform—a jumping-off point for you to take greater control of the trajectory of your thinking as you glide through the rich atmosphere of media messages throughout the course of your life.

The purpose of developing a personal media literacy strategy is to gain control over the process of influence that the media currently dominate. This is not to say that you forsake all automatic processing of information. That is an unrealistic goal. Instead, the strategy should be one where you gradually improve your awareness of the process of influence and gradually exercise more and more control over it. In the next section, I present 10 suggestions to guide your thinking in developing your personal media literacy strategy.

# Ten Techniques

## 1. Strengthen Your Personal Locus

Remember that your locus is a combination of an awareness of your goals and the drive and energy to search out information and experiences to attain those goals. Therefore, you need to analyze your goals. What really makes you happy? What do you really want to achieve in life? Are the answers to these questions things that have been programmed by the media? Think about where those answers came from and how comfortable you are with those answers.

Also, you need to increase your willingness to expend mental effort. We all have expectations about the appropriate amount of mental effort that is necessary to read a book, listen to a lecture, or watch television. Compared to print, TV elicits lower expectations about mental effort. The amount of invested mental effort (AIME) while viewing is a voluntary matter (Salomon, 1981). Because we can control our mental effort, we can also control the degree of our learning. The greater the mental effort expended, the higher the comprehension, learning, and eventual recall.

## 2. Focus on Usefulness as a Goal

There are different reasons for media exposure. All can be valid and highly useful. But uses vary. We need to be clear about what our goals really are during each exposure session. We should remember that we are placing ourselves at risk for unwanted effects if we expose ourselves mindlessly. With a little effort, we could increase our control over the content—and perhaps even increase our enjoyment of the content by experiencing a stronger emotional reaction or a greater appreciation of some aesthetic characteristic in a message.

Continually ask yourself what you want to get from this media exposure. If it is facts and information, then process the material actively to select those facts and categorize them well. If instead you want to be entertained by establishing a parasocial interaction with a particular character who is attractive to you, then be aware of attraction and how it might be affecting you. Remember that this character lives in a world very unlike your own and is a product of a production system with particular goals that are likely to be very different from your personal goals.

## 3. Develop an Accurate Awareness of Your Exposure

Periodically (maybe once a year), keep a diary of media usage for a week. By repeating this exercise, you can monitor your changing interests in media, vehicles, and messages. As you monitor changes, ask yourself the following types of questions:

Am I broadening my exposure to different media, or am I staying primarily with only one or two?

Am I broadening my exposure to different vehicles? (If you used to watch mainly sports and action/adventure on television, are you now spreading your viewing around to a wider range of genres?)

Am I planning my media exposures to serve specific goals of which I am aware, or am I just exposing myself to whatever comes along?

Try to increase the variety in your media exposures. Variety will broaden your interests and perhaps lead you to ask for different kinds of content from the media. But even if you find you don't like any of the new messages you are trying, you can always cut back. However, the cutting back in this situation is your idea, based on your own reactions, and not something programmed by the media.

# 4. Continually Practice Literacy Skills in Mindful Exposure Sessions

Try to reduce the amount of mindless exposure. But remember, mindless exposure is not necessarily associated with a particular type of content—any content can turn your mind off, and any content can potentially have value and engage the mind. For example, a bland situation comedy can turn our minds off, but so too can a great work of literature—but for different reasons. If we watch a Shakespearean tragedy, we might find our mind wandering because it requires so much mental effort to follow the Elizabethan language, the poetic expression, the historical settings, and the many characters involved in multiple plots.

It is important to develop active media use habits and not to practice bad habits. When you are passive, the media effects occur outside your awareness and therefore outside your control. Remember that active processing and high involvement with media reduce unwanted effects. People who are conscious of what they are exposed to and actively interact with the content will retain control over the learning process. Such people will consciously discount certain messages and carefully encode other information for memory storage. People who are not active processors of information will let the media, especially television, happen to them.

The context of the exposure can also influence the activity of information processing. When watching a message, analyze the contextual elements. For example, with ads, ask the following: Who is the spokesperson, and is he or she credible and trustworthy? What are the product claims? With entertainment messages, look closely at the action. Is it rewarded? What are the character's motivations? What appear to be the producer's motivations? What values underlie this portrayal?

Beware of factors that increase mindlessness in exposure. Factors that distract your attention during exposure serve to move you into a low-involvement state. In this state, you use peripheral modes of information processing; that is, your mind goes on automatic pilot. Advertisers rely on this to get their message into your subconscious without your defense mechanisms being activated.

# 5. Acquire a Broad Base of Useful Knowledge

The key to knowledge is that it is useful; acquiring knowledge that is not useful does not help. This means we must be consciously aware of our needs for knowledge.

There is always a gap between the knowledge we already have and the knowledge we need to understand the world better. We can close the knowledge gap for ourselves. But we must do this on a topic-by-topic basis. The means for closing the knowledge gap on a topic is under our control because the knowledge gap is influenced more by our interest in a topic than by our general level of education (Chew & Palmer, 1994). If we have high interest on a topic, we will search out information from many different media and many different sources. But when we have low interest on a topic, we allow the media to determine for us how much information we get.

## 6. Think About the Reality-Fantasy Continuum

Continually ask yourself the degree to which something is real or fantasy; this is a continuum. Some programs will be easy to spot as fantasy, such as *Looney Toons*. But other programs may not be so obvious. Some have a realistic setting and some realistic situations but are still fantasy, such as *Married With Children*. Others may have a fantasy setting but deal with situations in a realistic manner, such as *Star Trek*. Distinguishing reality from fantasy in the media is often a difficult task that requires you to think about the many different characteristics of a message. So you must think analytically and break a message down into its component parts, then assess which parts are realistic. Do not swallow the message whole as being either real or fantasy; media messages always have elements of both.

Do not go on a quest to avoid fantasy merely because fantasy elements are dangerous to use in real-world expectations. There is a place for fantasy in the enjoyment of the media. Fantasy messages can be very entertaining because of their imaginative or humorous appeal. They can stimulate our thinking creatively; however, we must realize that it is a stimulating tool, not a model to imitate. The important thing is to know when you are being exposed to fantasy so that you can process those messages differently. If you aren't sufficiently analytical, many messages with embedded fantasy might appear realistic.

Being aware of the fantasy-reality continuum is especially important now, when there are so many so-called reality programs on television. Although all of these programs have reality elements, they also contain many fantasy elements. And some of these "reality" shows may have a mix of elements that make them less real than some fictional programs. The distinction between shows labeled reality and those labeled fiction is not a sharp, clear line. Be careful of accepting these labels.

## 7. Make Cross-Channel Comparisons

Although media literacy is a generic concept that spans across all media, there are some special challenges presented by different channels. For example, reading a magazine article requires some skills not required when watching a situation comedy on television. This point, of course, is obvious. But the nature of the differences themselves is not so obvious. To illustrate this, watch a news story on CNN, and then look for that story in your local newspaper. Analyze those similarities and differences—are they important?

These differences will become even clearer if you attempt to create a message for different channels. Try writing a news story for a radio station and a magazine that comes out once a month. Try constructing a message that will make people laugh when they hear it in a song on a CD. Now translate that humor onto the computer screen for Internet browsers. Designing good media messages, especially humorous ones, is very difficult. Exercises such as these will help increase your aesthetic appreciation.

## 8. Examine Your Opinions

Ask yourself the following: Are my opinions well reasoned? For example, Americans say they are dissatisfied with materialism despite all the abundance. In a recent survey, 82% of Americans agreed that most of us buy and consume far more than we need. And 67% agreed that Americans cause many of the world's environmental problems because we consume more resources and produce more waste than anyone else in the world (Koenenn, 1997). And yet we in the United States continue to consume nearly 30% of the planet's resources and services each year, although we account for less than 5% of the world's population. We can choose from more than 30,000 supermarket items, including 200 kinds of cereal. Do we really need all these material products?

Although people criticize television in general, their opinions are inconsistent. For example, The Roper Organization, under the sponsorship of NBC in the early 1980s, had respondents in a national survey express their reactions to 17 particular TV shows—16 of which had been the targets of complaints about sex and violence from religious organizations. Only 13% of respondents said there was too much violence on the *Dukes of Hazard,* and 10% said there was too much sex on *Dallas*—these were the most negatively rated shows! But when asked about television in general, 50% of the respondents said that there was too much sex and violence on TV (The Roper Organization, 1981).

As can be seen in the above examples, we are not very systematic in gathering information and carefully assessing it in constructing our opinions. Instead, we operate fairly intuitively. As a result, we have a lot of superficial opinions that may conflict with one another.

## 9. Change Behaviors

To what extent do your behaviors correspond with your beliefs? For example, if you think society is too materialistic, do you avoid buying many material goods? If you do keep your consumption of material goods at a minimum, then there is a match between your behaviors and your beliefs. But there are people who continually complain about waste in our materialistic society, then go out and buy lots of new things they don't need. The first step in behavioral change is a realistic assessment of the match between your beliefs and existing behaviors.

Changing your behavior to correspond with your beliefs demonstrates commitment to a moral responsibility of following through on your beliefs rather than simply blaming someone else and doing nothing, which has become a popular strategy for many of society's problems. For example, let's examine what has been happening in the area of the environment and pollution. The media have put the issue of pollution on the public agenda as the prominence and length of these stories have increased dramatically since the 1970s (Ader, 1995). During that same period, air pollution went down about a third, but solid waste went up about 25%. This shows us that as Americans become more concerned about pollution, they have put pressure on the government to clean up the air by regulating manufacturing plants and requiring emission controls on cars. But solid waste, which is under the control of individual citizens through voluntary recycling programs, has not been so successful. This means that individuals are not cutting back on their waste through lower consumption or recycling. Again, people are looking to the government or someone else to solve problems.

You could boycott advertisers, cancel subscriptions, and write letters when you see something you don't like in the media. This action, of course, will have almost no effect on the media themselves, unless large numbers of other people feel as you and do the same things. However, that is not a reason to stop yourself from doing these things. By taking action, you give yourself a sense of gaining control over the media.

## 10. Take Personal Responsibility

This may be the hardest to do. We as Americans are fond of placing blame on others. This allows us to feel that the problem lies elsewhere and therefore it is someone else's problem to fix. For example, let's consider the problem of overeating. The American Medical Association tells us that one third of Americans are obese and another one third are overweight. This would seem to be a personal problem, but most people continue to eat too much and exercise too little. They wait for a government to impose some solution. In spring of 2002, the California legislature was considering the California Childhood Obesity Prevention Act. This act would have essentially banned the sale of carbonated beverages in public schools (Bartholomew, 2002). By summer of 2002, there were already eight states restricting junk food sales in some form, and another dozen states were considering their own legislation. Furthermore, people were filing lawsuits against fast-food chains (Tyre, 2002). Are people really that weak willed that they need the government to ban something before they will stop consuming it?

# Illustrations

To help make you aware of differences in media literacy development, let's look at some examples of how people can react to different types of media content. Those reactions are best understood when compared to positions on the learning ladders of cognitive, emotional, moral, and aesthetic appreciation.

# Learning Ladders

The learning ladders remind us that we can improve our degree of media literacy in four areas: cognitions, emotions, morality, and aesthetics. Progress up each of these ladders is accomplished by mastering the key skills of analysis, evaluation, grouping, induction, deduction, synthesis, and abstracting.

## Cognitive Ladder

The first step is awareness, which is the ability to perceive information elements in media messages. This requires the use of analysis. The next step is understanding. This is the ability to perceive the relevant components in any messages and then group them to see how those elements are related to each other. The next step is evaluation, which requires a good deal of contextual information to have templates with which to compare current messages. To do this well, a person needs a great deal of context in the form of elaborate knowledge structures. At the highest step, people are able to appreciate a message by comparing it to their understanding of the constraints and resources of the people who produced the message. The more elaborated a person's knowledge structure is about the media industries, the more the person will be able to appreciate the valuable elements in those messages and discount the other elements.

## Emotional Ladder

At low levels of emotional development, people's emotions control them. They get aroused and angry without being able to control those reactions. They experience fear so strong they cannot shake it. Or they cry at a movie and cannot stop even though they are very embarrassed. Or they are unable to feel any emotions even though they long to do so.

At higher levels of emotional development, people can use the media to shape and control their emotions. For example, stressed women watch more game and variety shows as well as more television in total, whereas stressed men watch more action and violent programming (Anderson, Collins, Schmitt, & Jacobvitz, 1996). Depressed people especially use television to escape unpleasant feelings and real-world stimuli that could exacerbate those feelings (Potts & Sanchez, 1994).

If people are aware of what they are doing, then the use of media to manage moods is a sign of high levels of media literacy; that is, people are consciously using the media as a tool to satisfy a particular need. If, in contrast, people are depressed and don't know what to do, they may watch television by default until they are tired enough to fall asleep. This is not an example of people controlling their exposure, so this is evidence of a low level of media literacy.

## Moral Ladder

This requires the development of opinions about the ethical nature of media messages. Typically, we infer themes from shows by comparing elements in the portrayals against our personal values.

At the lowest level on this ladder, you construct your moral judgment of a message based purely on intuition or because someone else, whom you respect, gives you the judgment. You see the elements in the show as an undifferentiated mass or blur. You make quick intuitive reactions about whether the show feels right or not, according to your values. If there is a fit, you are happy; if there is no fit, you have a negative reaction. You really can't articulate your reaction very well because it is primarily emotional. For example, if a respected friend tells you that *NYPD Blue* is a morally reprehensible program, you will likely accept this opinion without watching the show. If you accidentally find yourself exposed to it, you immediately have a negative reaction and turn it off.

At the middle levels of this ladder, you make a distinction among characters on their values and find yourself identifying with those characters who have the same values as you do. If those characters are portrayed positively (rewarded, successful, attractive, etc.), then you are happy.

At the higher levels, you think past individual characters to focus your meaning making at the overall narrative level. You separate characters from their actions so that you might not like a particular character, but still you like his or her actions in terms of fitting in with (or reinforcing) your values. You do not tie your viewing into one character's point of view but try to empathize with many characters so you can vicariously experience the various consequences of actions through the course of the narrative. During a narrative, you are able to assume different moral perspectives as to more fully appreciate the action from all participants' points of view.

## Aesthetic Appreciation Ladder

This development is oriented toward the cultivation of an enhanced enjoyment, understanding, and appreciation of media content. At lower levels on this aesthetic ladder, people have a very simple categorical opinion that the show is either good or bad. Not much reasoning goes into the intuitive decision, so viewers are not able to explain why they like something.

At the middle levels, people are able to distinguish acting from writing and directing. Viewers have the ability to perceive that one of these might be good while another is bad. Also, people are able to compare an artist's performance within this message with past performances and infer a trend in the work.

At higher levels, there is an awareness of media content as a "text" that provides insight into our contemporary culture and ourselves. An awareness of artistry and visual manipulation is also needed. This is an awareness about the processes by which meaning is created through the visual media. What is expected of sophisticated viewers is some degree of self-consciousness about their role as interpreters. This includes the ability to detect artifice (in staged behavior and editing) and to spot authorial presence (style of the producer/director).

Learning about visual conventions is not a prerequisite for interpreting visual messages. However, learning these conventions can help heighten our appreciation of artistry; it also provides viewers with the ability to see through the manipulative uses and ideological implications of visual images. This helps enhance critical viewing.

Can you make a quick assessment of your position on each of these four ladders? If you can, then your awareness is fairly high. But if you are unclear how to position yourself, then think about these ladders as you watch television or read a newspaper. As you reflect on your media exposures as they are happening, you will develop more insights about the levels at which you normally operate. Remember, you will move your positions on the ladders depending on the type of message and your mood. If you are simply looking for fantasy to help you relax, you are likely operating at lower levels. But you may be capable of operating at higher levels at other times. As you are exposed to media messages over a long period of time, develop a sense of where your "home position" is, that is, at what level you usually operate.

Now let's use these learning ladders as templates to examine some examples. This analysis will highlight the important differences across levels of media literacy.

## Examples of Levels of Literacy

There are many different reasons why people expose themselves to different kinds of content, and there are many different benefits people can get out of any particular message. Because of this, it is not possible to analyze a message and assume that all those who are exposed will extract the same meaning or have the same experience from it. Below, we explore several examples to illustrate this point.

### *Beavis and Butthead*

There has been a great deal of criticism of the television show *Beavis and Butthead.* Many people find it offensive. However, it can be viewed in different ways depending on how literate you are.

At one level, you might really like the characters and identify with them. You feel that those characters see the things the same as you do—something is either cool or it sucks. You think that finally there are characters who are not afraid to tell it like it is. You might watch it and realize that they ARE you. You use them as role models and feel confirmed that there are other people like you, so it is okay to be the way you are. This reaction to *Beavis and Butthead* illustrates a low level of media literacy. The viewer demonstrates no real analysis of the show, so the cognitive level is low. There is no evidence of moral or aesthetic development. But there is a moderate emotional reaction of liking for the characters. However, overall, the pattern on the learning ladders is at or near the lowest level.

At a higher overall level of literacy, people would be aware enough to regard the characters as simple stereotypes. By comparing and contrasting Beavis and Butthead with other characters on television, it is clear that these characters are less developed. This might lead to an emotional reaction of frustration that the characters never change or learn from their mistakes. Also, it might lead to a moral reaction that the characters are reprehensible.

At an even higher level of literacy, the show could be regarded as a satire on the insipid values of Generation X. This would require more cognitive effort of analysis, comparing/contrasting, and evaluation to construct this conclusion. It would also require a broader knowledge structure about what Generation X is supposed to be. This might lead to a strong humorous emotional reaction; however, the laughter is *at* the characters, not *with* them. This stance on laughter is evidence of an awareness of a moral position that abhors the values of the characters and, in so doing, finds them funny in their fool's paradise. An aesthetic analysis of the program would reveal the characters to be very flat from an artistic point of view. This could lead to an admiration of the producer's ability to keep things so consistently flat. The artistic perspective is flat. The character development is flat; that is, the characters do not change or mature. The dialog is flat; it does not develop into deeper levels of insight. This consistent flatness is not easy to sustain over many episodes. At this level, there is a strong aesthetic appreciation, along with strong cognitive, emotional, and moral reactions.

## Soap Operas

Soap operas as a genre can appeal to viewers of all levels of media literacy. At a low level of literacy, people feel some kind of unarticulated attachment to the program. They cannot explain why they like the characters or the show. Because they don't analyze it, they just let it be.

At a bit higher level of development, people will watch soap operas because they feel a personal identity with the characters and have substituted the soap world for their barren existence. This leads to a strong emotional reaction. Other people will watch soaps because they want to learn how attractive characters dress and act; this leads to some cognitive processing and evaluation of how characters look and act.

At a higher level, some people view soaps in groups so they can discuss the action as it unfolds. Or they will call their friends later and use the action as an important topic of conversation. These people use the viewing to maintain a community of friends that they would not have without the soap opera. This requires a considerable amount of cognitive processing and emotional attachment.

At a higher level still, the viewing takes on an in-depth analysis of the aesthetic and moral elements displayed there. Viewers marvel at the writing, directing, and acting challenges of mounting a multiplotted program 5 days a week for an open-ended time period, often stretching over decades. Also, the complexity of the changing moral sensibilities can be intriguing. It is a truly remarkable achievement that the creative people on these shows can sustain a sense of drama and suspense under such severe pressures in a genre with so many constraints.

## Nightly News

At a low level of media literacy, looking at the news each night (whether in the newspaper, in a magazine, on radio, or on television) can be nothing more than a mindless habit that provides people with a sense that they have been exposed to what is important each day. As a ritual, it provides structure to one's life, even if it does not provide any information of value.

At a higher level, people consciously monitor certain stories for new developments. They add new information to their existing knowledge structure on the story and feel some emotion as they derive a sense of satisfaction about learning more.

At the highest levels of media literacy, people use this regular exposure as a starting place for learning about the events of the day. They notice what is on the agenda and immediately use that information to elaborate their existing knowledge structures. But then they seek out alternative messages in other vehicles and other media to augment this information and serve as a confirmation as to its completeness. They have a constant skepticism that there may be more to the story. They have developed a keen aesthetic awareness of the strengths and weaknesses of various reporters and news organizations. They use these insights to evaluate the worth of each new story. Finally, they are very aware of the visual framing, the use of camera movement, the use (or lack of use) of graphics, and other production techniques that subtly construct the tone of the stories.

Remember that it is not the type of shows you watch that make you media literate or illiterate. Instead, literacy is keyed to what you think and how you feel while you are being exposed.

# Conclusion

Media literacy is a perspective. To achieve this perspective, you need to increase your awareness and control. The exercises in this chapter are designed to help you make an assessment (and continue this practice over time) of your awareness about your own knowledge structures, about how your mind works, and about your ability to apply knowledge of the key elements in the effects process.

Media literacy is most clearly diagnosed when we compare people's patterns of thoughts and feelings to the positions on the learning ladders. Keep these ladders in mind during your exposures.

**Exercise 17.1**    Awareness of Your Knowledge Structures

Below is a list of chapters in this book. Each one presents a knowledge structure on its topic.

1. For each chapter in the book, try to recall the structure of the content.
   a. Can you remember the key idea of that chapter? Can you remember major ideas or sections of the chapter?
   b. Then go back to the first page of that chapter and check your recall. If you remembered the key idea, give yourself 1 point, and give yourself another point for your recall of *each* major idea (the major points in the outline). Thus, your score should be somewhere between 0 and 5 for that chapter.
   c. Enter your score in the left column, which is labeled "Book."
   d. Do the same procedure for each of the chapters listed below.

| Book | AdExp | | |
|------|-------|---|---|
| | | | FOUNDATIONS |
| _____ | _____ | Chapter 1 | Why Increase Media Literacy? |
| _____ | _____ | Chapter 2 | Defining Media Literacy |
| _____ | _____ | Chapter 3 | The Media Literacy Model |
| _____ | _____ | Chapter 4 | Developing Media Literacy |
| | | | KNOWLEDGE STRUCTURES OF MEDIA CONTENT |
| _____ | _____ | Chapter 5 | Reality and Media Messages |
| _____ | _____ | Chapter 6 | Entertainment Content |
| _____ | _____ | Chapter 7 | What Is News? |
| _____ | _____ | Chapter 8 | Advertising |
| | | | KNOWLEDGE STRUCTURES OF MEDIA INDUSTRIES |
| _____ | _____ | Chapter 9 | Development of the Mass Media Industries |
| _____ | _____ | Chapter 10 | Economic Perspective |
| _____ | _____ | Chapter 11 | Who Owns and Controls the Mass Media? |
| _____ | _____ | Chapter 12 | What Is an Audience? |
| | | | KNOWLEDGE STRUCTURES OF MEDIA EFFECTS |
| _____ | _____ | Chapter 13 | Broadening Our Perspective on Media Effects |
| _____ | _____ | Chapter 14 | How Does the Effects Process Work? |
| _____ | _____ | Chapter 15 | Effects on Institutions |
| | | | INCREASING MEDIA LITERACY |
| _____ | _____ | Chapter 16 | The Importance of Real-World Knowledge |
| _____ | _____ | Chapter 17 | Personal Strategy for Increasing Media Literacy |

2. Next, think about additional reading you undertook after studying each chapter.

   a. For each book or article you read from the "Further Reading" list or from the reference list, give yourself 2 points.

   b. For each additional book you have read relevant to the topic since studying the chapter, give yourself 1 point.

   c. For each significant experience you have had concerning that topic since studying the chapter, give yourself 1 point. (A significant experience is an extended conversation you had with someone on the topic of the chapter, consciously trying to apply the principles in that chapter, etc.)

   d. Record your point totals for each chapter in the column labeled "AdExp" for Additional Experiences.

3. Look at the pattern of numbers across the chapters. What does this tell you about the state of your current knowledge structures?

   a. Look down the "Book" column. If you have mostly 4s and 5s, you have a very strong set of knowledge structures. If you have mostly 3s, you have a good beginning set of knowledge structures. If you have some zeros, you need to go back and reorient yourself to the structure of information in those chapters.

   Remember that having strong knowledge structures does not necessarily mean you have a great deal of knowledge on that topic, but it does mean that you are aware of the main ideas, and this will help you acquire additional knowledge much more efficiently.

   b. Look down the "AdExp" column. If you have 3s or above, you are showing a strong commitment to extending your knowledge and elaborating your knowledge structures. Look where you have zeros and ask yourself why you were not willing or able to extend your knowledge.

   c. Look at the total pattern of numbers. Were you stronger on certain chapters than others?

   It is understandable that you may have more interest in particular topics than others. But remember that balance is important. Be proud of your accomplishments—now build on them to overcome your weaknesses.

# CHAPTER 18

# Helping Others Increase Media Literacy

*Key Idea:* You have the power to develop media literacy strategies to influence society and other individuals.

I n the previous chapter, the focus was on helping yourself increase your level of media literacy. This chapter shifts the focus to helping others increase their levels. The first section of this chapter helps you think about interpersonal settings—small-scale opportunities to help others. Then the second section helps you think about institutional settings—the larger social structures of the educational system and the media industries. Whether you undertake the challenge of working with people one-on-one or on a large scale, it is essential that you first have developed your own media literacy to a relatively high level so that you have something worthwhile to offer other people.

# Interpersonal Techniques

Interpersonal techniques orient you toward helping other individuals with their media literacy. You begin by identifying individuals who might be at risk for negative effects from the media and work with them. Many people target children. Children are a special group because children are still at a low level of development and require more care to shape their media habits and their awareness of potential effects.

## Current Situation

We are all exposed to thousands of media messages each day, especially children who are seeking information about their world. Jordan (2001) reports the result of a nationwide random sample that found that 87% of American households with children have at least two working TV sets in the household. Children are reported spending about 2.5 hours per day watching television and almost another hour a day in front of a screen playing video games or on the computer. This is far more time than time spent on homework at about 1.1 hours per day. This degree of exposure has many parents concerned, and they want to do something to protect their children from potentially harmful effects.

A wide variety of techniques are being used with children. These can be usefully grouped into three categories as follows: rules (or restrictive mediation), coviewing, and active mediation (Nathanson, 2001a; Valkenburg, Krcmar, Peeters, & Marseille, 1999).

### Restrictive Mediation

Restrictive mediation involves setting rules about how much, when, and which types of television can be viewed. It appears that many households do not have any rules for TV viewing in general. For example, about half (49%) of all children have no rules for TV viewing in their households, and 42% of children say that TV is on most of the time in their house (Rideout, Foehr, Roberts, & Brodie, 1999). However, Jordan (2001) reports that about 61% of parents say they have rules for TV viewing.

What are the rules? Of those families who say they have rules, 92% say they prohibit certain programs, 76% say they require their children to finish homework or chores before viewing, and 69% say they limit the amount of hours their children are allowed to watch (Stanger, 1997).

Who uses the rules? The parents who have rules for TV use tend to be mothers who are educated and highly concerned about the negative effects of television (Brown, Childers, Bauman, & Koch, 1990; Bybee, Robinson, & Turow, 1982; Valkenburg et al., 1999; Van der Voort, Nikken, & van Lil, 1992). The children who receive restrictive mediation tend to be younger, but there are no gender differences (Abelman, 1999; Brown et al., 1990). Among children age 8 and older, 61% say they have no rules for television viewing (Rideout et al., 1999).

Parents who have rules appear to be motivated not by a general concern about exposure but more by a fear that certain content will trigger negative effects. For example, Valkenburg et al. (1999) found in a Dutch survey that parents who have viewing rules are motivated by the concern that their children will watch something that will either scare them or teach them to behave aggressively. This concern was also found by Krcmar and Cantor (1996), who reported that 90% of parents in an American sample said they limit their children's viewing of violent content. Also, Jordan (2001) reports that more parents are concerned about what their children watch on TV (70%) than they are about the amount of TV they watch (19%).

## Coviewing

Coviewing involves parents and children watching TV together. No conversation is required.

There is a discrepancy in the research about how often coviewing occurs. For example, Jordan (2001) reports that 93% of parents say they watch TV with their children at least once in a while. Also, Sang, Schmitz, and Tasche (1992) found that although coviewing decreases with age, even with adolescents at 14 years of age, about half were still coviewing with at least one parent. Valkenburg et al. (1999) found coviewing to be more common than active mediation.

Other researchers have found that coviewing occurs rarely. For example, Lawrence and Wozniak (1989) found that most viewing is solitary and that when children do view with a family member, it is usually a sibling. Dorr et al. (1989) say that coviewing is more common with older children who are likely to watch shows the adults also like. More recently, Rideout et al. (1999) report that among children age 7 and older, 95% never watch TV with their parents; also, even among children ages 2 to 7, 81% say they never watch with their parents.

Notice that the discrepancy in findings may be due to who the researchers ask. When researchers ask parents if they watch with their children, coviewing appears to be common. But when researchers ask children if parents view with them, coviewing appears to be rare.

## Active Mediation

Active mediation consists of conversations that parents or other adults have with children about television. This talk need not be evaluative. An analysis of the literature on active mediation studies over the years has revealed four types of mediation approaches that parents use when viewing with the children (Austin, Bolls, Fujioka, & Engelbertson, 1999). These are nonmediators (parents who talk about television with their children infrequently), optimists (those whose discussion primarily reinforces television content), cynics (those whose discussion primarily counters television content), and selectives (those who use both positive and negative discussion techniques, depending on the situation). There is a difference between positive mediation, which is pointing out the good things in television messages as well as encouraging children to emulate those good things, and negative mediation, which is pointing out the bad behaviors of characters and being critical of what is portrayed.

Active mediation is rare. Several studies have found that there is generally no dialogue when a parent and child are viewing together (Austin, 1993; Himmelweit, Oppenheim, & Vince, 1958; Mohr, 1979). And a Gallup poll indicates that when parents and a child are viewing television and some offensive material comes on the screen, parents are seven times more likely to ignore it by quickly changing the channel than to discuss the offending content with their child (Austin, 1993). There is evidence that active mediation comes at the request of children (Reid & Frazer, 1980; Stoneman & Brody, 1982); that is, sometimes this is initiated by children who ask their parents questions while viewing.

Active mediation has also been found from caregivers at day care centers. Nathanson, Eveland, Park, and Paul (2002) conducted a survey of 265 nonparent caregivers of second through eighth graders. They found the caregivers provided more active mediation and censorship for violence than for sex on television. They found that when caregivers thought they had effective techniques of active mediation, they were more likely to use mediation when there were high-threat situations. But when the caregivers did not feel they could mediate effectively, they were more likely to use restrictive mediation.

## Use of Program Ratings

There are some tools available to parents to help children monitor their exposure. One of these tools is the ratings of films provided by the MPAA (Motion Picture Association of American) for the past three decades. However, in repeated studies, about one third or fewer parents use the MPAA age-based ratings system (Abelman, 1999; Bash, 1997; Mifflin, 1997).

Then, in the mid-1990s, Congress mandated program ratings for television programs so that this information could be fed into the V-chip, which was required on all television sets sold in the United States after 1999. However, parents were slow to learn about the ratings. Six months after the introduction of the ratings, a survey found that children and adolescents seldom used the ratings (Greenberg, Rampoldi-Hnilo, & Hofschire, 2000). The survey was repeated a year later, and the findings were the same; it was found that about 30% of mothers were not aware of the ratings at all, and those who were aware of the ratings gave them below-average grades for clarity (Rampoldi-Hnilo & Greenberg, 2000). Similar results were found in a pair of studies funded by the Kaiser Family Foundation. In a Kaiser study, 82% said they were aware of the ratings, but among those who were aware, only half said they used the ratings (Foehr, Rideout, & Miller, 2000), and these figures remained largely unchanged a year later when the survey was repeated (Kaiser Family Foundation, 1999). It appears that parents who are most in need of the ratings are least likely to use them; the ratings are used most by parents who already carefully monitor their children's viewing (Abelman, 1999; Greenberg & Rampoldi-Hnilo, 2001). The development of the TV ratings has done little to stimulate other parents to become more involved in the monitoring of their children's viewing.

In a nationwide random sample, 72% say that they are aware of the TV ratings systems and that their children are also aware of the ratings system. However, only 39% say that they use the ratings on a regular basis (Jordan, 2001). Also, in a Kaiser Family Foundation (1998) report, it was reported that only 7% of parents could correctly interpret the symbol (FV) for violence in children's programming.

## Criticisms

This is a dreadful situation. Parents think they are doing much more than they are, if children's take on things can be believed. If parents are coviewing with children, laying down rules, and actively mediating their television exposures, this is not making an impression on many of those children.

For years, media advocates for children have been pressuring the industry to provide program ratings for parents to help them monitor their children's exposures. With the mandating of the V-chip, advocates secured a victory, but the television ratings system that the television networks developed has been widely criticized as not being accurate or useful. For example, there is evidence that the V-chip is not as helpful as hoped (Kunkel et al., 2002). They found that although the age-based ratings (TV-G, TV-PG, TV-14, and TV-MA) were reasonably accurate, the content descriptors (V, S, D, and L) were not being used on the vast majority of programs that contained violence, sexual behavior or dialogue, and adult language. Furthermore, there is evidence that only a small minority of parents is even aware of the meanings of the labels (Kaiser Family Foundation, 1999; Schmitt, 2000). For a more detailed discussion of this topic, see Potter (2003).

The problem with parents and other adults providing so little help to children seems to be traceable to two characteristics. First, it appears that parents have little real motivation to help in this area. Of course, parents say they are concerned, and of course they care about the well-being of their children. But parents do not behave in a way that follows through on that concern. Most television viewing and other media exposures go unmonitored, which leads to my second criticism: Many parents do not know what to say to their children to help them become more media literate, nor do they have an educated rationale for viewing rules. Unless parents themselves are media literate, their help is likely to lead to negative effects rather than truly helping their children.

## What Techniques Work

Many techniques have been tried. In reviewing this literature, Nathanson (2001a) concludes that some of these techniques work, whereas others do not; some work with certain kinds of parents or certain kinds of children; and the effects are varied, ranging from cognitions (learning about television messages), attitudes (developing skepticism for ads and news), perceptions (of television reality), and behaviors (including aggression, viewing habits, and response to advertising). For example, Nathanson (2001b) found that parental attitudes were a strong predictor of what techniques parents used and the effect those techniques would have on their children. Parents with negative attitudes concerning violence on television used active and restrictive mediation, whereas parents with positive attitudes used coviewing. From the child's perspective, restrictive mediation signaled parental disapproval of the content, and coviewing signaled approval of the content; interestingly, children interpreted active mediation as parental approval of the content (Nathanson, 2001b).

### Rules

There is a difference of opinion about the effectiveness of restrictive mediation. Desmond, Singer, Singer, Calam, and Colimore (1985) argue that it has been found to be a useful technique. In contrast, Nathanson (2002) found that restrictive mediation was related to less positive attitudes toward parents, more positive attitude toward the content, and more viewing of the content with friends. This appears to be the opposite of what parents intend as an outcome of using this technique. Nathanson says, "Unfortunately, parents' good intentions in using restrictive mediation may actually contribute to the harmful outcomes parents wished to prevent in the first place" (p. 221).

### Coviewing

Coviewing, like restrictive mediation, has had mixed results in the research literature. Coviewing has also been associated with negative outcomes such as coming to believe that television characters are like real-world people (Messaris & Kerr, 1984) and learning aggression from violent television (Nathanson, 1999). Also, Nathanson (2002) found that coviewing was related to more positive attitudes toward viewing of television violence and sex. These were interpreted as unintended effects. Nathanson concludes that "parents' consistent pattern of coviewing objectionable television with their adolescents encourages the youngsters to develop similar media habits" (p. 223).

Coviewing has been shown to have positive outcomes, such as increasing the learning of educational content (Salomon, 1977). Children who coview with their parents say they enjoy the programs more (Nathanson, 2001b). However, even when positive effects are found, they are usually fairly weak. For example, Austin and Pinkleton (2001) found that although coviewing had a positive effect on political socialization, other factors, such as skepticism and negative mediation, had more impact.

Peers are also influential during the adolescent years. Nathanson (2001c) found that peer mediation is more influential than parental mediation during adolescence. Specifically, she found that peer mediation promotes more of an orientation toward antisocial behavior, which then leads to aggression. Thus, the positive influence of parental mediation serves to reduce aggressive behavior, but the negative influence of peer mediation serves to increase it.

## Active Mediation

Active mediation techniques have been found useful in helping children reduce unwanted effects from viewing television (Austin, 1993; Nathanson & Cantor, 2000; Nathanson & Yang, 2003). Active mediation seems to work better than more punitive techniques. Parents who try to reason with their children while disciplining them are more effective in reducing the harmful effects of exposure to violence than those parents who use physical punishment (Singer, Singer, & Rapaczynski, 1984).

Children who experience active mediation in general are less vulnerable to negative effects of all kinds—cognitive, attitudinal, emotional, and behavioral. As for cognitive effects, active mediation has been found to be successful in teaching children to be more skeptical toward television news (Austin, 1993) and creating better understanding of television plots (Desmond et al., 1985). With children, parental involvement in media exposure serves to influence learning. Children increase their understanding and recall of both central and incidental program content when adults provide comments to guide their children's attention and understanding during viewing. When parents actively mediate during television viewing, they can influence their children's interpretations (Austin, 1993). Parents can make viewing active for their children by continually asking questions about meaning and structure, such as, "Who did what to whom?" and "Why?" This gets them practicing making connections.

As for attitudes, active mediation has been found to reduce perceptions of the reality of television messages (Messaris & Kerr, 1984), even with television news (Austin, 1993), and reduce negative cultivation effects (Rothschild & Morgan, 1987). Nathanson and Botta (2003) reported the results of a survey of adolescents and their parents, which found that when parents commented on body images of characters on television, adolescents were more likely to process the images more and experience negative emotions more. These negative emotions had an impact on behaviors in the form of unhealthy eating or eating disorders.

Active mediation has been helpful in shaping emotional responses to media. Cantor and Wilson (1984) found that negative emotional responses to frightening films could be allayed with active mediation, at least with older children (older than 9 years old). Cantor (2001) provides some good advice for parents of children who are experiencing negative emotional effects from the media, especially horror content. Also, Hoffner (1997) says that prior knowledge of a happy outcome can reduce fear for some children.

These techniques can move beyond cognitive aspects and can also include emotional and behavioral aspects. Children who experience emotional media messages when they are among peers or adults will exhibit a reduced likelihood and intensity of immediate emotional effects, especially fear effects from scary movies. Also, the probability of a child behaving aggressively when watching violence can be reduced if adults verbalize comments and interpretations while observing with the child—such as pointing out unrealistic and inappropriate behavior in programs.

Children are likely to model their behavior after attractive characters they see in the media. This modeling can be shaped by interpersonal techniques. For example, Austin and Meili (1995) found that children use their emotion and logic to develop expectations about alcohol use in the real world when they see alcohol used by characters on television. When children rely on both real life and televised sources of information, children are more likely to develop skepticism about television portrayals of alcohol use when they rely on parents as primary sources of information and behavioral modeling.

As for behavior, active mediation has been found to lower levels of aggression (Corder-Bolz, 1980; Grusec, 1973; Hicks, 1968; Nathanson, 1999; Nathanson & Cantor, 2000; Singer et al., 1984) and reduce the influence of advertising (Reid, 1979).

Nathanson (2001c) found that peer mediation was more effective than parental mediation. She found that peer mediation led to more positive orientations toward antisocial television, which in turn led to greater aggression. Of course, the intention of parental mediation is to inhibit negative media effects, but peer mediation facilitates harmful outcomes.

The success of mediation techniques is also tied to the type of person who is the target. For example, Nathanson and Yang (2003) demonstrated that certain techniques worked well with younger children (ages 5–8). These techniques focused on emphasizing the factually inaccurate nature of a show as well as emphasizing how socially unrealistic the portrayals were. But these techniques were not found to work well with older children (ages 9–12). The authors speculated that perhaps the older children already understood those lessons and did not want to hear a lecture, feeling that such advice was pedantic or condescending.

Also, some techniques work better with one gender. For example, Nathanson and Cantor (2000) tested a mediation technique of getting children to become involved with victims of violence in cartoons rather than the aggressors. This worked with boys but not girls, that is, it was successful in preventing boys from increasing their aggressive behavior subsequent to viewing the violence in the cartoon.

Mediation works better when parents are more active during television viewing (Austin, 1993). Parents need to ask questions continually and engage their children in discussions about the meaning of actions. Parents need to explain the meaning of words, pictures, narratives, and so on.

Emotional reactions of children can be controlled through the use of both cognitive as well as noncognitive techniques. For example, Cantor (2001), who is an expert on children's fright reactions to horror shows in the media, explains that, in general, preschool children benefit more from noncognitive than cognitive techniques. Among elementary school children, both types of techniques work well, but children prefer the cognitive techniques. Cognitive techniques rely on a person verbally casting the threat in a different light. "When dealing with fantasy depictions, the most typical cognitive strategy seems to be to provide an explanation focusing on the unreality of the situation" (p. 215). In contrast, noncognitive techniques "do not involve the processing of verbal information and appear to be relatively automatic" (p. 214). One noncognitive technique is visual desensitization, which involves showing a person repeated images that are sequenced to build from nonthreatening to very threatening depictions so the person is gradually desensitized. Also, Desmond (1997) provides some detailed suggestions about how parents can do things in their homes to increase the media literacy of their children, particularly to help them with their perceptions of reality, and to increase their knowledge about production techniques and the commercial nature of the media.

Role modeling has been found to be a successful technique. Oftentimes, children will select their own role models, but parents in active mediation can influence the models children choose and sensitize them to certain characteristics of those characters that make them good role models. Children are likely to model their behavior after attractive characters they see in the media. This modeling can be shaped by interpersonal techniques, especially from parents themselves as good role models (Austin & Meili, 1995; Hogan, 2001; Slater & Rouner, 2002). For example, Austin and Meili (1995) found that children use their emotion and logic to develop expectations about alcohol use in the real world when they see alcohol used by characters on television.

Slater and Rouner (2002) observe that social cognitive theory has been a useful explanation for the effectiveness of educational messages in entertainment programs because of the role modeling. However, they argue that the elaboration likelihood model is an additional explanation, especially for those people who do not have role models on shows; these people are likely to have low involvement, which makes them even more susceptible to the influence of such messages. Thus, if these people were highly involved and were likely to argue against the messages, their low involvement would defuse the counterarguments.

When you become a parent, you will need to be careful in monitoring your children's experience with the newest of the media—the Internet. People can (and do) put out lots of questionable information and entertainment services. There are primarily three types of risk for children or teens who use the Internet. One is exposure to inappropriate material such as sexual matter and hate speech. A second is developing inappropriate relationships with strangers. The third is harassment. ("Is Your Child," 1995).

Therefore, parents need to be careful in monitoring what sites their children visit. Parents need to tell their children never to give out any identifying information, such as an address, phone number, school name, and so forth, and never allow a child to arrange a face-to-face meeting with someone online. Parents who find information that may be illegal (such as child pornography or hate speech) should report it to authorities. Parents should build skepticism in their children because people on the Internet may not be who they claim to be; people can make up a persona in terms of gender, age, background, and so on. Parents should set time rules of access; too much contact can lead to addiction. And finally, surfing the Internet can be a fun activity for all family members to do together.

# Public Education

This section shifts our attention to a more macro level. First, I briefly show the fragmentary nature of media literacy curricula in this country, then examine the barriers that prevent a more unified approach to media education. This section then concludes with a critique of curriculum concerns and recommendations.

## Current Situation

Critics have observed that the United States lags behind many other countries in developing media literacy courses and curricula in public schools (Brown, 1991, 1998, 2001; Considine, 1997; Davies, 1997; Kubey, 1997; Piette & Giroux, 1997; Sizer, 1995). They point to a long list of countries that are far ahead of the United States with media literacy curricula. These countries include Australia, Canada, Great Britain, South Africa, Scandinavia, Russia, and Israel, as well as many other countries in Europe, South America, and Asia (Brown, 1991; Piette & Giroux, 1997). For example, Australia has had mandated media education from kindergarten to 12th grade since mid-1990s. This curriculum stresses aesthetics and semiotics, with a liberal humanist approach to the popular arts (Brown, 1998).

In the U.K. and some Latin American counties, empowerment of media consumers is paramount often focusing on industry control through corporate and governmental hegemony. Media education there stresses "representational" and oppositional ideologies, power, and politics and ways to participate in mainstream media or construct alternative media outlets. (Brown, 1998 p. 45)

Critics point out that the relative lack of attention to media education in the United States is a serious problem because the United States is the most media-saturated country in the world. More time and money are spent on media consumption in this country than any other country in the world, yet our educational system virtually ignores media education (Sizer, 1995). This is not to say that there are no media literacy efforts in America's schools; however, their existence is rare and largely unsupported by the institution of education. For example, Brown (2001) characterizes the teaching of media literacy in this country as "isolated teachers introduced mass media topics into their classrooms, usually within the context of traditional content such as English or history social studies" (p. 683). He continued, "Schedules already crowded with curricular mandates had no time for yet another addition, so whatever media study could be introduced was typically integrated into already existing courses" (p. 683).

Some states have been discussing media literacy and trying to get initiatives going. Kubey (1998) reports that there have been "significant statewide initiatives" in New Mexico and North Carolina, with "noteworthy developments" in Wisconsin and Minnesota. A few years ago, Hobbs (1998) reported that media literacy concepts were included in the curriculum frameworks in more than 15 states. And this is growing as "ongoing efforts are in place in many U.S. school districts. Interest in media education is even growing among mainstream education organizations and health professionals, including the National Association of Secondary School Principals and the American Academy of Pediatrics" (Hobbs, 1998, p. 24). Initiatives are growing, but we need to monitor whether this talk about the importance of media literacy and its inclusion in mission statements translates into meaningful implementation.

## Barriers

Why is there so little sustained effort at developing and implementing media literacy curricula in the United States while there are many good efforts in other countries? There appear to be many obstacles for further development of media literacy (for a more complete treatment, see Brown, 2001; Considine, 1997; Davies, 1997; Kubey, 1997).

Arguably, the most critical obstacle is the lack of centralized decision making concerning education in the United States. Brown (1998) points out that curriculum decisions are spread out over 15,000 school districts, each with its own school board and administrators. Kubey (1990) elaborates on this argument by pointing out that the United States is a huge country with a highly diversified population and no central governmental policy on media literacy to pull things together. Also, only 4% of educational expenditures in the United States come from the federal government (Kubey, 1998). Thus, in this country, the power for curriculum decisions lies at the state and especially local levels. Each of these decision-making bodies has its mix of personalities, needs, and political agendas.

Not paying attention to the special circumstances in each school's culture has been credited in large part for the failure of media literacy efforts that were tried in the 1970s (Anderson, 1983). Hobbs (1998) extends this point by saying, "Media literacy initiatives have been most successful in school communities where teachers, parents and students have a shared, common vision about their love-hate relationship with media culture" (p. 23). Brown (1998) says, "If media literacy studies are to survive and grow, administrators in school systems and at individual schools must endorse and support them. They should not be left wholly dependent on the initiative and energy of isolated teachers" (p. 52). Brown calls for a more holistic and continuing approach.

> To succeed, a curricular program of media literacy must be developed through collaboration among teachers, administrators, specialists, and parents, who together must build it into the systematic education process. Media study should not be a mere appendage of a random elective course, nor should media technology be used merely as a tool or aid to teach other subjects. That means developing studies geared to the participants' successive levels of cognitive development based on educational and behavioral research findings. It also means continuing and integrating studies into successive grade levels through the school years. (p. 52)

But all this comes with a high cost. Other curricula must be replaced with the media literacy one. Teachers need significant training, and this will require reduced teaching loads. Parents will need to become much more involved.

It also requires a sustained commitment that includes substantial training of media literacy teachers. Hobbs (1998) says,

> The most successful efforts to include media literacy in schools have taken 2 or more years of staff development to build a clearly defined understanding of the concept as it relates to classroom practice among a substantial number of teachers and school leaders within a school district. (pp. 23–24)

Then once trained, the teachers need to be supported continually by the institution rather than left on their own. Hobbs (1998) explains that a study of teacher performance in Great Britain yielded depressing results. Among the teachers who completed training in media literacy education, about 40% ended up doing nothing, 25% did something moderately well, 10% did something creatively exceptional, and the remaining 25% did something embarrassing, dangerous, or just a waste of time.

Unless resources are provided, there are significant barriers to implementation. For example, one recent study reports that although most high school teachers believe the study of media is important, 40% did not teach it at all because of constraints on time and curriculum space (cited in Brown, 2001). The same pattern was found in Maryland with language arts teachers; once again, the teachers regarded media literacy as important to teach, but the lack of training, materials, and time prevented many from teaching it (Koziol, 1989). Brown (2001) observed that few teachers receive training to deal with the challenge of teaching media literacy either in their college degree programs or in workshops for teacher certification. Most teachers, however, do feel that they are qualified to teach media literacy, even though only about one third had any training.

Curriculum designers often look to media literacy scholars for guidance. However, there is the lack of agreement among scholars about what media literacy is and what its goals should be (see Chapter 2). Two of the more pressing definitional issues when it comes to curriculum design are tone and texts. Regarding tone, Brown (1991) complains that "many media workshops and curricula are protectionist and defensive. They seek to inoculate consumers against blandishments of images and messages of media entertainment, news, and advertising" (p. 45). As for texts, Hobbs (1998) observes that although media texts have always been essential in education, rarely are those texts "considered beyond their function as conveyers of information" (p. 25). They need to be the objects of inquiry (Kress, 1992). Students need to analyze the people and corporations who produce and disseminate those texts and understand their motives. Also, the texts themselves need to be analyzed for what they leave out, how they are structured, and their basis for claims both from an aesthetic and moral perspective.

This diversity of opinion gets magnified as we move out to consumer activists, teachers, and school administrators. There is also a wide variety of opinion concerning the composition of a media literacy curriculum, what should be taught, how it should be taught, and how the effect of the teaching should be assessed. The good thing about this diversity is that it provides a wide range of ideas for instruction and a variety of curriculum models to the many different school systems in the United States. If most of the school systems were entrepreneurial and willing to search out the techniques that would fit the special culture in their district, then this variety would pay big dividends. But most school districts are very conservative about change. The teachers and administrators already feel they are asked to cover too many topics, so they cannot add another one without a great deal of debate.

The diversity of ideas among scholars appears more as an academic debate than as a convincing argument to shift resources. For scholars to present a convincing argument, they must present a perspective that integrates the best thinking into a clear set of principles that can guide their decision making in three key issues: curriculum design, teaching, and assessment.

## What You Can Do

When you become a parent, you can insist that your school district provide some sort of media education. You might have to begin small by volunteering in your child's classroom. Develop some mini-instructional units based on your own knowledge about media literacy. Typically, children will really like these sessions because it involves them in something they use every day. If your mini-units work well, students will talk about them, and other students will create a demand for similar instruction. By beginning small, you can grow a demand locally in your child's school.

# Societal Techniques

With societal techniques, the focus is on exerting pressure on a particular part of the industry, the government, or some institution to increase public awareness about a problem or to bring about some particular change. To do this successfully, you will first need a strategy supported by a great deal of commitment. Your strategy will require many years of effort to effect a change. Also, it requires money. Often, people will start a PAC (political action committee) or a consulting firm that will then apply for grants to support its work.

Contacts are also extremely important. By linking up with other powerful people and groups, you could become part of something that could potentially have enough power to get the attention of the large media companies. Look at the list of citizen action groups in Appendix C. Contact those that are of most interest to you and ask them to send you information.

Changing media industry practices or content is very difficult. Remember that the industries have grown and developed in response to demands from the public. If an industry or a vehicle does not respond well to the demand, it loses money. Successful CEOs have confidence that their decisions will result in greater profits. So don't expect change when you ask them to ignore their experience and to change their practices when they might risk losing millions of dollars by making those changes you suggest. This is why the public concern about television violence has resulted in so little change over the past 50 years. In explaining this nonaction, Stuart Fishoff (1988), a psychologist who writes for television and movies, said,

> Let's suppose the results, the conclusions were incontrovertible—TV and film modeling of aggression and other anti-social values has significant effects on the viewing audience. Would it really make any difference to the gate keepers of media fare in Hollywood and New York? I submit the answer is not on your life! (p. 3)

He cites an important principle in psychology for his conclusion:

> The more far-reaching and costly the consequences of accepting a message, the more facts needed before an audience will be persuaded as to the accuracy of the message—and the more energy will be expended in denigrating both the message and the messenger in order to maintain existing belief. (p. 3)

Therefore, the media industries have been very slow in acknowledging the value of any of the research on negative media effects while using the research on positive effects to show that they are acting responsibly. This attitude has outraged many media critics and stimulated many average citizens to want to do something to remedy the problem.

Another example of a societal technique is the concern over protecting very young children from the effects of television advertising. In the early 1970s, some consumer groups were formed to protect children from what was being seen as abuses by broadcasters. Prominent among these groups was Action for Children's Television, which found examples of children's programs that contained as many as 16 minutes of ads per hour—far above the industry's self-imposed limit of 9.5 minutes. And the products advertised were largely nonnutritious snacks and deceptively presented toys. Many products were being pitched by characters from the programs, thus making the distinction between the show and the ad indecipherable, especially for young children.

This pressure influenced the Federal Trade Commission (FTC) to hold hearings throughout the 1970s. The FTC considered banning certain types of ads. But in the end, the FTC concluded that although there was evidence that television advertising created risks for children, no practical effective remedies were open to federal policymaking. The primary problems were determining who is a child; that is, at what age is a person no longer a child? Also, there was the fear that regulating advertising on children's television might cause broadcasters to stop programming for children.

Another example of a societal strategy took place in the fall of 1995, when some well-known political figures began a campaign to clean up talk shows on television. Headed by former Education Secretary William Bennett, Senator Joseph Lieberman (D-Conn.), and Senator Sam Nunn (D-Ga.), the campaign did not seek regulation of television content. Instead, it sought to influence public opinion and to shame certain television producers by characterizing the content of daytime talk shows as "lethal." These critics acknowledged that some of the 20 nationally syndicated talk shows dealt with serious issues of domestic abuse, drug abuse, and racism in a constructive way that enlightens viewers. But they pointed out that some shows had a circus atmosphere that included shouting matches, fistfights, foul language, and audience members yelling out unqualified advice. As an example of sleaze, they cited examples from the *Sally Jesse Raphael* show, which featured girls who were sexually active at the age of 10, and Jerry Springer, who hosted a show about a 17-year-old who had four children with her 71-year-old husband, whom she called "Dad" (Hancock, 1995).

There are many other examples of people and groups who have tried to influence public awareness of problems with media content and to bring about change in the media industries. These efforts have been more successful in raising public consciousness about these problems than they have been in bringing about changes in programming. This leaves us with the following question: Should we continue to try? The answer, of course, is yes.

With societal techniques, we should have modest expectations for what it means to have a successful societal strategy. And we need to have a long time frame. Societal change of this type moves at glacial speed—it takes decades to see change. But remember that a glacier is exerting constant pressure, and change is happening constantly—but we can't see it happening because it is happening very slowly. The same is true with societal campaigns. If we exert constant pressure, we will eventually be able to perceive changes. If you are impatient and want to see change happen more quickly, then try some interpersonal and personal techniques.

**Exercise 18.1**    Fantasizing About Your Societal Strategy

Let's say that next year, you win $10 million in the lottery. After you pay your taxes, pay off all of your current debts, and splurge on all sorts of luxuries, you still have $3 million left over. So you decide to do something more worthwhile with your money and your life—you decide to set up a citizen action group that will help people become more media literate and change some of the things in society. Think about techniques as you address the following issues.

1. Goals: What would the goals be for your organization?
   a. List some interpersonal goals you would want to achieve.
   b. List some societal goals you would like to achieve.

2. Targets
   a. To reach those goals set above, which groups would you target for change (see Appendix C)? List those targets.
   b. For each target, what specifically would you want them to change?

3. Techniques: How would you stimulate that change?
   a. What things would you do to get the people in your targets to understand your point of view?
   b. What things would you do to get the people in your targets to change their behaviors?

4. Barriers: What do you think would be the key barriers that might prevent you from achieving your goals?

# PART VI

# ISSUES IN
# MEDIA LITERACY

# CHAPTER 19

# Media Influence on Sports

Professional sports have changed dramatically over the past four decades. The reason is money—big money. Not only have the revenues been increasing each year, but those revenues also have been increasing at an increasing rate. The key to making sense of these increases as well as the nature of sports today is to understand the money cycle.

The mass media have been an integral part of making the money cycle possible. The media provide the means for advertisers to inject mammoth amounts of money into the cycle. Also, the media provide so much continual exposure for professional as well as college sporting events that millions of people have made sports an essential ritual in their lives. And the media have transformed hundreds of athletes into celebrities who can themselves command huge payments—both for playing their games and for endorsing the products of commercial advertisers.

# The Money Cycle

Professional sports are driven by a money cycle. This cycle has the following five components:

1. *Athletic talent* demands higher salaries plus bonuses each year. Because athletic talent is in short supply, talented athletes will find a team willing to pay a high salary and bonuses.

2. *Owners of teams* are in the business of attracting fans to their games as well as fans to telecasts of their games, so they must field a competitive team to make the games exciting. Also, the fan base grows in size and is more loyal when teams are winning, so the owners must buy players who are better than the players on the teams they compete with; this requires them to bid high for the limited amount of athletic talent.

3. *Television networks* are in the business of creating audiences for their telecasts and renting out those audiences to advertisers. Network programmers know that sporting events can attract large numbers of fans, so they bid high for the rights to telecast sporting contests. Network programmers know that when they own the rights to telecast sports, their network generates higher revenues and the network gets stronger; in contrast, a network gets weaker when it lets a competing network outbid it for the telecasting rights.

4. *Advertisers* of certain products find sports fans an especially desirable audience. They pay sports telecasting networks a premium to get their persuasive messages in front of their highly desirable target audiences.

5. *We, the public,* receive a lot of satisfaction in following our favorite sports teams, so we follow the games on television, tolerate the commercial interruptions, and buy the advertised products. Also, we find certain sport events to be highly entertaining (*Monday Night Football,* Super Bowl, playoffs), so we watch them even when we do not have a favorite team in the contests.

When the five segments of the cycle cooperate and work well together, the cycle attracts more money. The public watches more games and buys more advertised products, especially those products endorsed by athletes. With higher viewership for sports shows, television networks charge advertisers more for access to the viewers. The television networks make more money and can afford to pay the sporting leagues higher fees for the rights to televise the games. The leagues and owners make more money and can afford to pay more to attract the best players and thereby win more games, which attracts more fans.

The cycle keeps going around and around, each time at a higher level of salaries for players, which requires more income for owners and leagues, which demand bigger contracts from television networks, which must charge more for commercial time to advertisers, who want larger audiences, who want more exciting games, which requires better players, who want more money . . . and the cycle continues.

Let's take a closer look at each of these segments of the money cycle. I make a distinction between the more active agents and the more responding agents in the cycle. The more active agents—the owners and players—have the most power in negotiating for money. The remaining agents—television networks, advertisers, and the public—are still essential to the money cycle, but their actions are largely in response to another agent; rarely do they initiate change.

## Players

Salaries for players in all professional sports have been escalating in the past few decades. To illustrate this trend, let's begin by turning the clock back to 1959, when Ted Williams, a future hall of fame player for the Boston Red Sox baseball team, was offered a contract for $125,000. Williams returned his contract unsigned to management; he was rejecting their offer. His reason for rejecting the contract was that it was for *too much money*. Williams argued that he was not worth that much money because he was coming off a year in which he hit "only" .259, which was a bad year for Williams, although it would be a better than average year for almost everyone who ever played professional baseball. Williams asked for a pay cut of 25%, which was the maximum pay cut possible.

As an example of how high professional sports salaries are getting, consider the case of Orlando Pace, a 6-foot, 7-inch, 320-pound offensive lineman who, as a rookie in 2003, signed a 1-year contract with the St. Louis Rams for $5.73 million. If he did not get hurt and played all offensive plays for the entire season as well as four playoff games, his salary would break down to $5,000 per play ("Pace Signs," 2003). Thus, Orlando Pace was earning more money in one half of one football game than Ted Williams earned in an entire 6-month season of baseball.

Over the past 30 years, salaries for major league baseball (MLB) players have been increasing rapidly. In 2004, the median salary for major league baseball players was $775,000 per year, but this average figure masks how much money some players are paid. To be ranked in the top 25 highest paid players in the 2004 season, a player would have to make at least $12.5 million for the year, which is almost $80,000 per game. The highest paid player was Manny Ramirez at $22.5 million, which is about $140,000 per game. The highest paid pitcher was Pedro Martinez, who was paid $17.5 million or about $175,000 per inning if he has a good year and pitches 100 innings. With the highest annual payroll in all of sports, the New York Yankees spent $184 million for players in 2004 alone. The team has two of the five highest paid players, with Alex Rodriquez at $22 million and Derek Jeter at $18.6 million—both shortstops. At the other end of the spectrum is the Milwaukee Brewers, with a total player salary expense of $27 million. With the Yankees's payroll almost seven times as large as the Brewers's payroll, the talent level is not evenly distributed across teams ("Baseball Salaries," n.d.).

As for the National Basketball Association (NBA), Michael Jordan was earning $4 million during the 1995–1996 season, when he led the Chicago Bulls to their fourth championship in professional basketball in 6 years. He was named the most valuable player of the year, and many basketball fans regard Jordan as the best basketball player of all time. A year later, he was a free agent and signed a new contract for $18 million, making him the highest paid player in the league—temporarily (Rhodes & Reibstein, 1996). Less than 10 years later, the highest paid player (Kevin Garnett) was being paid $29 million for the season, and 29 players were being paid more than $12 million each for the year ("Hoops Hype," n.d.).

Salaries for players in the National Football League (NFL) have also escalated dramatically. For example, the median earnings of the 2,000 NFL players in the 1999 season were $430,000. Five players (Troy Aikman, Drew Bledsoe, Brett Favre, Deion Sanders, and Warren Sapp) were each paid more than $6.2 million that year. Another 50 players were paid more than $3 million, and an additional 400 made more than $1 million ("National Football League 1999 Salaries," 2000). A short 3 years later, the median average player salary was $540,000, and a salary of $6.2 million per year would not even rank you in the top 30 highest paid NFL players. The highest paid football player in 2002 was Michael Strahan, a defensive end for the New York Giants who was paid $20.6 million, which is more than a million dollars per game, counting all games including preseason games ("Football Salaries," n.d.).

Athletes can also command large fees for endorsing products. Companies are willing to spend huge fees to athletes who endorse their products because such endorsements work to increase sales. For example, in 1985, when Boris Becker signed a multi-million-dollar deal to promote Puma tennis shoes and rackets, the company's sales increased 25%. John McEnroe's endorsement of Bic disposable razors increased the company's market share from 12% to 23% of total razor sales.

Sports marketing has really grown by focusing on product endorsements by athletes. By 1983, $25 million was spent on endorsements; by 1988, it had doubled to $50 million. By the time he retired as a basketball player in 1999, Michael Jordan was making more than $40 million per year in product endorsements.

## Owners and Leagues

Until several decades ago, the owners and leagues were much more in control of players' contracts and salaries. Whitson (1998) explains that sport was commercialized early in the 20th century in the United States, where sports developed

> labor markets of athletic talent, in which wealthy teams offered "traveling players" financial inducements to come and play for them. It was this, of course, that

created the phenomenon of the professional athlete, even though labor market mobility (and hence salaries) would quickly be contained by the emergence of cartels in all the major sports. (p. 60)

These cartels controlled player salaries and player movement, but this arrangement broke down as a result of labor challenges in the 1970s, and now there is a great deal of player movement and escalation of salaries.

To help control the rise of salaries and to try to create parity among teams, several professional sports have established salary caps for teams in their leagues. However, many owners routinely ignore the caps. For example, in the 1995 NFL season, the salary cap was $37.1 million per NFL team, and 26 of the 30 teams in the league went over that maximum. The Dallas Cowboys spent the most at $62.2 million; owner Jerry Jones spent almost $40.5 million in signing bonuses, including $13 million to Deion Sanders ("NFL Teams," 1996). Four years later in the 1999 season, salaries were even higher. Dallas paid its players $55 million in salaries and bonuses, but the Cowboys's spending was matched by the Arizona Cardinals and was outspent by the Tennessee Titans ($56 million), the New England Patriots ($57 million), and the Tampa Bay Buccaneers ($58 million). Even the most frugal team (Oakland Raiders) spent $40 million on players' salaries.

Also, in the 1990s, the NBA instituted a salary cap per team. The 1996–1997 salary cap for the Chicago Bulls was $24.3 million, but the Bulls were able to pay Jordan $18 million that was not counted against the salary cap because the salary cap did not apply to the resigning of a team's existing players (Rhodes & Reibstein, 1996). All salary caps have loopholes. Owners and players' agents who are determined to make a deal can find away around any limits on salaries and bonuses.

Why do owners continue to escalate salaries? The answer is that a star player at any price is a great investment. Not only can star players help their teams to win, but, more important, they also bring fans out to the stadiums and, even more important, attract television viewers for their games. This greatly increases the value of the franchise. For example, the Chicago Bulls franchise was valued at $17.5 million in 1985—Jordan's rookie year. In 1996, after the Bulls won their fourth NBA title, the franchise was valued at $178 million. The owner had a huge yearly income from broadcast rights, merchandising, and ticket sales. The Bulls play at the United Center, where there are 216 suites each selling for $175,000. In 1996, all games were sold out, and there was a waiting list of more than 17,000 fans for season tickets (Rhodes & Reibstein, 1996).

In most professional sports, the leagues negotiate television contracts, then share the money with team owners. This serves to preserve parity among all teams, regardless of the size of their local television market. For example, the NFL used this model and, in so doing, was able to keep the Green Bay Packers as a viable franchise. Green Bay, Wisconsin, is a town of well under 100,000 in population and is an outlying part of the Milwaukee television market, which is a relatively small media market. If the Green Bay Packers relied primarily on local television revenue, there is no way it could generate income anywhere near the revenue of teams in New York City or San Francisco, each with about 10 million viewers in their local markets.

MLB, however, has allowed owners to negotiate their own local television contracts and keep that money. This has resulted in a very wide disparity of television revenue across local markets. This is the major reason why the New York Yankees is the most valuable professional sports franchise, even though baseball is a much weaker sport financially than football or basketball. The New York Yankees is valued at $832 million and has an annual revenue of $238 million. Thus, it can afford to spend more than $180 million on player salaries. The least valuable baseball team is the Montreal Expos (now the Washington Nationals) at $145 million, with an annual revenue of $81 million ("Most Valuable Franchise," 2004). It is rare for a low-revenue team to have a successful year, but it does happen. In 2003, the Florida Marlins, which was the 25th ranked team in value at $172 million and an annual revenue of $101 million, won the World Series. But the next year, when it could not renegotiate all its players' contracts, many of the players moved on.

When the NBA shifted to the NFL model in the 1970s, it began attracting many more fans. By the 1990s, basketball revenues had risen dramatically and surpassed those of baseball and hockey (Whitson, 1998).

But even with TV money, owners have been aggressive in cultivating additional revenue streams, such as luxury skyboxes at stadiums and apparel merchandising. The owners frequently raise the prices of tickets, concessions, parking, apparel, and other souvenirs. The NFL also has other revenue streams, such as more than $4 billion per year in gross licensed merchandise sales (Bellamy, 1998).

With television and advertisers putting so much money into these sports, they demand that the leagues make their sports even more exciting and more amenable to advertising. The leagues have complied. For example, the coverage of a football game is more than 3 hours long, although the game itself takes 60 minutes, and there is less than 10 minutes of action on the field during those 60 minutes that the clock is running. So the announcers must provide lots of anecdotes, statistics, and color commentary. The director must provide lots of replays, slow motions, shots of the crowd and cheerleaders, and so on. The NFL changed the extra point rule so that teams could go for 2 extra points, thus helping the team behind to catch up faster and make the game more interesting. Rules were changed to provide more protection for the most valuable offensive player—the quarterback—who needed more time to engage in the game's most exciting play, which is the long pass. Basketball now has a shot clock that requires players to shoot the ball at least every 24 seconds. Basketball also instituted the 3-point play, which is much riskier and hence more exciting.

To accommodate advertisers, the NFL instituted the 2-minute warning in the mid-1960s to guarantee a break for commercial messages at a time when viewership is usually high. Also, the NFL and the NBA have frequent television time-outs. Uniforms are more colorful. All of these changes to the games were instituted to increase viewer interest and thereby provide advertisers with the largest possible audiences.

## Television Networks

The biggest increase in sports revenue is from television. Without a television contract, no sports league could survive. The American Football League got started in the early 1960s with a TV deal of $1.7 million. Although this does not seem like much money today, it made the difference in whether the league survived in the early 1960s. In 1965, CBS paid $14.1 million to broadcast NFL games. By the mid-1990s, the NFL was charging $500 million per year for broadcasting rights, and this sum was so large that it had to be shared by five networks: ABC, NBC, ESPN, Fox, and TNT. The most recent contract pays the NFL $2.2 billion per year in TV revenue, and this is likely to increase dramatically in 2005, when this current multiyear contract expires. In addition, the National Football League signed a 5-year contract with DIRECTV for $2 billion to sell its subscription package and deliver it by satellite ("NFL Notes," 2002).

The big three television networks felt that they had reached a limit to what they could spend for the rights to telecast sporting events in the early 1990s and vowed not to increase their bids because they were losing money (Bellamy, 1998). For example in 1990–1993, CBS lost $500 million broadcasting major league baseball games, so CBS was conservative in submitting its bid to continue its longstanding tradition of broadcasting NFL games. CBS bid $300 million, whereas Fox bid $400 million per year, so the NFL dumped CBS and went to Fox. CBS immediately realized that it made a mistake in losing all that NFL programming, so when the NFL contract came up for renewal again, CBS became competitive again, bidding $500 million a year for 8 years.

The television networks know they cannot depend on teams winning to keep increasing their viewership. With the four major professional sports (football, basketball, baseball, and hockey), each contest has only two teams, which means the number of losers is always the same as the number of winners. There is no way to increase the number of wins relative to the number of losses. Therefore, winning competition is not enough to market sports successfully. The television networks have had to develop other means to increase the size of the sports audience. The way they have done this is to shift the focus from sports to an entertainment formula. This means that the announcers must be good storytellers. The announcers must fill in the history of the teams and tell compelling stories about "there is a tradition of bad blood between the teams" or some other subplot to keep people watching the games, especially when the score is lopsided. Announcers must tell human interest stories about the struggles of individual players both on and off the field. And they must turn certain players into larger-than-life heroes, who can take over a game at any instant with their courage or superhuman abilities.

Certain players are pushed into the spotlight each season, and those who performed well there became legends—players such as Babe Ruth, Wayne Gretsky, Magic Johnson,

O. J. Simpson, and Michael Jordan. Even nonsports fans knew who these people were, and those reputations attracted a lot of new fans to the games.

The television networks have branded their sports shows, such as the *NBA on NBC* and *ABC's Monday Night Football* (Bellamy, 1998). They have done this to generate viewers loyal to shows and not just teams. If the game is bad, which it often is, the networks have to hold on to their audiences so that they can guarantee to advertisers that the audiences will be large.

## Advertisers

Advertisers pay huge fees to television networks to get their messages to their target audiences. The biggest—and most costly—showcase for advertising in sports is the annual Super Bowl. For example, ABC generated revenues of $130 million in its 2000 broadcast of the Super Bowl. The network's three dozen advertisers paid an average of $2.2 million per 30-second spot.

Advertisers have also turned stadiums into advertising vehicles with the naming of the stadiums, and by putting ads on scoreboards, walls, ticket stubs, concession stand product packaging, and so on. Some basketball courts have ads painted on them; hockey has ads in the ice and around the rink's walls. Some football teams have ads on their jerseys (Nike swoosh), and in car racing, the drivers' uniforms as well as the cars are covered with ads.

In the spring of 2004, major league baseball even tried putting ads on the bases, but criticism flared up, and it has backed off, for now. One critic said that this "undermines the character of America's pastime at every level." This criticism makes one wonder whether the critic has seen a baseball game in the past two decades, with all the advertising that is already at the stadium. It is interesting to consider what another critic said as a way of thinking about what might be coming in the future: "How low will baseball sink? Next year, will they replace the bats with long Coke bottles, and the bases with big hamburger buns?" (Penner, 2004, pp. D1, D8).

Businesses are happy to contribute large sums of money to sports—as long as those businesses get high visibility for themselves in return. For example, Frito-Lay gave $15 million to the Fiesta Bowl and in return received 3 years of sponsorship rights to that college football game. This means that the name of the game was changed to the Tostitos Fiesta Bowl, and this name had to appear on all the signage and be mentioned by all announcers referring to the game.

As early as 1986, there were already more than 2,100 companies sponsoring sporting events and spending a total of more than $1 billion a year on all kinds of sports. This money bought some companies the leverage to change the names of some sporting events. The Boston Marathon was renamed the John Hancock Boston Marathon, and the Sugar Bowl football game was renamed the USF&G Sugar Bowl. This advertising money gives sponsors a stronger presence at particular sporting events, and sometimes their ads can overwhelm the sporting event itself. For example, Budweiser sponsored the Marvin Hagler–Sugar Ray Leonard middleweight fight in 1987. For $750,000, it got the right to cover the ring mat and the ring posts with its logo.

## Public

The public has always been interested in sports. But for the money cycle to grow, the number of fans has to grow each year. Also, the commitment of those fans needs to grow each year so that those fans spend even more time watching the games, going to the stadiums, buying the team merchandise, and supporting all the advertisers. And most important, the general public in each locale must identify and support its local teams. All of these things have happened and continue to happen.

People spend a great deal of time watching sports on television. A few years ago, two researchers counted more than 8,000 sporting events televised that year, and there are times when there are 10 events televised at the same time (Kinkema & Harris, 1998). The most popular televised sport is the NFL, with an average rating of 16; major league baseball is second, with a rating of 11.1. The cost of a 30-second ad is about $130,000 and $80,000 for football and baseball, respectively. Golf and tennis are the least popular sports, but they still have a loyal following and generate average ratings of about 4.5 and 3.8, respectively. Also, these sports deliver a high-quality audience, that is, one that is very affluent and hence very attractive to companies that advertise luxury products.

Not only does the money cycle depend on continued support from fans, but it requires support from nonfans also. This is most clearly seen in the building of new sports stadiums across the country. The major sports leagues have been successful in getting local municipalities to finance a large part of these stadiums through public financing and taxes. For example, the NFL has been a very successful negotiator in getting cities to build new stadiums, parking facilities, and so forth to hold onto or to attract new football franchises. In the 5-year period from the summer of 1998 to the summer of 2003, 12 new NFL football stadiums were opened—many in cities with existing football stadiums. Each of these new stadiums had between 82 (Seattle) and 208 (Washington, D.C.) premium skyboxes that the owners of the NFL teams could rent out to wealthy clients and businesses. But the sweetest part of most of these deals is that the NFL got the cities to pay for most of the construction costs. Only one owner (Daniel Snyder, owner of the Washington Redskins) paid for at least half of the construction costs, and with three of the stadiums (Raymond James stadium in Tampa, Florida; Reliant Stadium in Houston, Texas; and the Coliseum in Nashville, Tennessee), the NFL saw to it that the cities paid the entire cost of the stadiums. Therefore, if you rent a car or rent a hotel room in a city with an NFL team (or a major league baseball team or NBA team), you are likely paying a tax that helps that city finance its stadiums (Metropolitan Sports Facilities Commission, n.d.).

Most cities feel that it is important to have major sports teams. Cities with such teams are willing to spend a great deal of public money to keep them, and those cities without such a team are willing to spend a great deal of public money to attract such a team away from another city. In the mid-1990s, four teams left their home NFL city to get a better deal. For example, the Los Angeles Rams went to St. Louis when St. Louis offered a brand-new stadium, plus guaranteed $16 million per year in gross ticket sales along with other financial considerations (Bellamy, 1998). After Los Angeles went several years without a football team, the NFL was getting pressure from advertisers that there was no team in the nation's second largest media market. In 1999, the NFL put pressure on Los Angeles to build a stadium and other facilities (parking lots, training areas, etc.) so the NFL could put a team back in that city. A Los Angeles billionaire put together an ownership group, and the city put in $150 million in state revenue bonds to build parking structures around an existing facility—the Los Angeles Coliseum. But the NFL commissioner, Paul Tagliabue, objected to the deal, saying that the municipality was not putting in enough taxpayer money, and because of this, the team would not be profitable for its owners—projecting an annual profit of only $25 to $28 million per year. The city of Houston offered $200 million in public money for a new stadium plus private investment in an adjacent football museum. When the city of Los Angeles would not put more taxpayer money into its offer, the NFL awarded the franchise to Houston, which is also a very important media market (Flanigan, 1999). In 2004, Los Angeles again received pressure from the NFL to invest hundreds of millions of dollars of taxpayers' money to build a suitable facility to satisfy the NFL.

The costs of building professional sports stadiums are going up dramatically, and it is costing taxpayers a lot of money to have a team. For example, let's look at what happened in Houston, Texas. The city built the Astrodome at a cost of $35 million and opened it in 1965. It was the home of both football and baseball teams. Then, in 2000, Houston opened Minute Maid Park, which cost $250 million to build and was designed for baseball only. Then 2 years later, Houston opened the brand-new Reliant Stadium for football only, at a cost of $449 million. The Houstons Rockets, the NBA team, began playing in the Compaq Center, which cost $27 million and opened in 1975. This was replaced by the Toyota Center in 2003, which was built at a cost of $175 million (Reinken, 2003).

# Olympics

The ancient Olympics were a venue for amateur athletes to compete every 4 years. Of course, at the time, there were no professional sports. The ancient Olympics continued for more than 1,200 years, died out, and then were revived in 1896 as the "modern" Olympics. For a long time, the modern Olympics preserved its focus on amateur athletes and banned any professional athlete of any kind from participating.

Cities competed to host the Olympic games every 4 years. By 1932, the cost of hosting the games had increased to a point where cities could not make back all the money they spent, so it was a sacrifice to host the games. Still, many cities competed because it was prestigious to be the host city. It also provided a great public relations opportunity to show off the host city to the world.

Eventually, with the rise of television, networks were willing to pay the International Olympic Committee fees for the rights to broadcast the games, and this helped host cities defray the costs of building all the venues and the cost of running the Olympics. In 1964, NBC paid $1.5 million to the International Olympic Committee for the rights to broadcast the Tokyo Summer Olympics. By 1980, the cost had skyrocketed to $85 million when NBC acquired rights to the Moscow Summer Olympics, despite the fact that the Soviets wanted $210 million plus $50 million in production equipment to be left behind. The broadcast was never made, though, due to the boycott of the 1980 games by the American government. ABC paid $225 million for the Los Angeles summer games in 1984 and $91 million for the winter games in Sarajevo. Despite losing money on the winter games, ABC came back with an even higher bid of $309 million for the 1988 winter games in Calgary. NBC got the 1988 summer games in Seoul, Korea, for $300 million. NBC paid $456 million for the 1996 Atlanta games, and CBS bid $375 million to broadcast the 1998 Nagano games in the Winter Olympics. NBC broke its record by bidding $705 million for exclusive U.S. rights to broadcast the 2000 summer games in Sydney, Australia, and another $545 million for the 2002 winter games in Salt Lake City. The total NBC package is worth about $1.3 billion—none of the other U.S. networks entered a bid (Nelson, 1995). NBC also bid $2.3 billion for the rights to the summer games in 2004 and 2008 and the winter games in 2006, even before the sites were decided ("NBC Gambles," 1996).

Where does this money go? It is paid to the International Olympic Committee (IOC), which also sells rights to broadcast the games to media in other countries. When ABC paid $309 million for the 1988 winter games, the European Broadcast Union (EBU, which represents 32 countries and a population of several hundred million) paid $5.7 million, and the Soviet Union (along with it Eastern European allies), North Korea, and Cuba paid a combined total of $1.2 million. Thus, it is clear that the United States (or, rather, advertisers on U.S. television) really supports the games—without U.S. support the Olympics would be very different.

The IOC also sells to advertisers the rights to sponsor the games or show their products during the games. Real (1998) explains that American TV has increasingly borne the cost of hosting the Olympic games. In 1960, American TV money contributed about 0.3% of the cost of the games; in 1980, American money supported 6% of the cost; and in 1984, it contributed 50%. Now American TV totally supports the cost and allows the host city to make a big profit.

The Olympics have become a major venue for advertising. The modern Olympics have always accepted advertising. In 1896, there were ads for Kodak. Coke began its association with the games in 1928. But as the games got more expensive, planners needed more advertising revenue. The 1976 games in Montreal experienced a $1 billion deficit.

**Table 19.1**     Television Broadcast Contracts for Olympics

|  | *Summer Olympic Games* | *Fee in Millions (U.S. Dollars)* |
| --- | --- | --- |
| 1960 | Rome | 0.6 |
| 1964 | Tokyo | 1.6 |
| 1968 | Mexico City | 4.5 |
| 1972 | Munich | 12.5 |
| 1976 | Montreal | 25.0 |
| 1980 | Moscow | 95.5 |
| 1984 | Los Angeles | 225.0 |
| 1988 | Seoul | 305.0 |
| 1992 | Barcelona | 401.0 |
| 1996 | Atlanta | 456.0 |
| 2000 | Sydney | 705.0 |
| 2004 | Athens | 793.0 |
| 2008 | Beijing | 894.0 |

SOURCE: Adapted from Real (1998, p. 19).

In 1984, when the Olympics were held in Los Angeles, the games not only covered their enormous costs but also made a huge profit of $215 million (Manning, 1987). They did this by selling corporate sponsorships of various events and locales. VISA alone spent $25 million on the rights and on promotions, and 146 corporations were official sponsors of various events. By the 1996 games in Atlanta, the IOC had signed up 180 companies and brands that used the Olympics for promotions (Grimm, 1996). The top 10 of these official sponsors (such as Coke and IBM) paid a total of $2.1 billion (Jensen & Ross, 1996). This more than offset the total cost of $1.7 billion for holding the 1996 Atlanta games (Boswell, 1996). Now, almost all athletes have corporate logos on their clothing. Sponsorships are sold for each event and for the games in general. Companies use the event as an opportunity for global marketing.

Ever since the Los Angeles games in 1984, the Olympics have been highly commercial and highly profitable for the host city. Now, competition among cities to host the event is very strong.

The Olympics are less profitable for the television network that outbids its competitors and is awarded the rights to broadcast the games. This huge expense for the broadcast rights is only the beginning. Production is another big expense. In the 1984 Los Angeles Summer Olympics, the United States sent 500 athletes to compete; ABC sent 3,500 people (1,400 engineers, 1,800 support personnel, and 300 network production and management people). To produce 188 hours of coverage, they used 205 cameras, 660 miles of camera cables, 4 helicopters, 3 houseboats, 26 mobile units, 35 office trailers, and 404 hardwired commentary positions. There were microphones on basketball backboards, underwater in the diving pool, in boxing ring posts, and on equestrian saddles. The cost of covering the games was $100 million. This is why the television networks must sell a great deal of advertising. For the 1996 games in Atlanta, NBC sold a total of $675 million of ad time to 50 advertisers. More airtime was devoted to commercials than to the actual sports action (Farhi & Shapiro, 1996).

Even though television networks often lose money televising the Olympic games, they continue to bid up the price for future telecasting rights. They reason that the Olympic telecasts attract large audiences that they can target their promotions for new entertainment shows. Thus, if those promotions can generate larger audiences for the shows premiering after the Olympics, the networks will more than earn enough to cancel out the loss of telecasting the Olympics and generate a larger overall yearly profit for the network.

Because of the highly commercial nature of the Olympic games, the IOC was unable to maintain the prohibition against professional athletes. Now the Olympics are very different than they were even 25 years ago. They are a showcase for the best athletes—professional as well as amateur—in the world. But even more important, they are a showcase for international companies that want to develop markets worldwide for their products and services.

# Conclusion

Professional sports have become more exciting and entertaining to the general viewer over the past several decades. The public is showing increased interest in sporting events and personalities of all kinds. But the price for this continues to climb. As a fan, you support your teams by buying tickets, parking, refreshments, and souvenirs at the games. If you do not go to the stadium, you can still support your teams by watching them on television and buying products advertised on those telecasts. And even if you do not go to the games or watch the local teams on television, you are still supporting those teams financially through local taxes and paying the interest on revenue bonds your city council has sold to build the fancy new stadiums that will keep owners from moving their teams elsewhere.

There are three key concerns you should ponder with the issue of media and sports. First, how far can the money cycle go in changing professional sports? Is there a limit to what players can earn? Is there a limit to what we are willing to pay for tickets, concessions, parking, and clothing with the logos of our favorite teams? Is there a limit to what municipalities will add to the local tax burden to hold onto a local team? Is there a limit to how many commercial breaks we will tolerate when watching professional sports on television?

A second thing for you to ponder is a larger concern with all sports. How far have the changes in professional sports filtered down to college sports, high school sports, and recreational sports? Do the changes in professional sports change the expectations of those who play little league baseball; that is, is the pressure too high to win? Does it take the fun away from watching intramural sports or a community league game?

Third, the ultimate concern is with the value of these changes to us. How can we avoid experiencing potentially negative impacts on our own lives? How can we benefit more from the advantages offered to us by the positive changes?

# Further Reading

Wenner, L. A. (Ed.). (1998). *MediaSport*. New York: Routledge. (336 pages with index)

This edited book contains 17 chapters in four parts: playing field, institutions, texts, and audiences. Although this book is now a bit dated, with most of its research coming from the early to mid-1990s, it still presents valuable insights into how sports have developed primarily in the United States to become such a powerful economic and social force.

**Exercise 19.1**     Extending Knowledge

In this chapter, I have presented you with some facts to illustrate the money cycle with sports. Use this information as a jumping-off point and see what research you can do to update and expand on the points in this chapter by considering the following questions.

1. *Extend your knowledge:* Pick one of the main points in this chapter, and do your own research to expand your knowledge and update the information. Some topics are the following:

   - Product endorsements by professional athletes
   - Cost of sports stadiums and how they are financed
   - Comparison of player salaries across sports
   - Track advertising expenditures by sport
   - Find the demographic profiles of fans in different sports
   - How have the games changed to make them more attractive to viewers?
   - Who are the owners of the sports teams, and how did they make enough money to be able to buy a sports franchise?

2. *Analyze advertising content:* Watch several broadcasts of a particular sport. But instead of paying most attention to the game, pay attention to the advertisements. Keep track of all ads. Then answer the following questions:

   - Which companies advertise the most on particular sports?
   - Which product categories are most often advertised by sports?
   - Given your answers to the above two questions, who do you think the target audiences are for those big advertisers?
   - What kinds of appeals are used in those ads; that is, what are the advertisers telling you about their products and why you should use them?

3. *Project trends:* Pick one sport and see if you can find salary information for what the average salary was and what the highest paid players made in each decade.

   - Project that information into the future for one, two, and three decades. How much will the average player be making when you are 30, 40, and 50?
   - Break those salary figures down by game; that is, what will the average player and the highest paid player make per game in the future?
   - What do you think your salary will be when you are 30, 40, and 50? How long will it take a pro player to earn what you make in a year?

4. *Get a historical perspective on these issues.* Talk to your father (or mother) and grandfather (or grandmother) about sports behaviors 40–50 years ago. Ask them the following questions:

- Did they used to attend sporting events in person?
- Did they follow sports through the media? Is so, which sports and which media?
- Are they aware of any changes in their favorite sports over the past few decades? If so what is their reaction to those changes?
- What is their reaction to the salaries paid to athletes today?
- What is their reaction to the amount of advertising at the games and during media coverage?

5. *Develop an informed opinion* about the amount of money spent on professional athletes.

- Think about the pros and cons. Try to list all the positive reasons for the accelerating salary increases, and then list all the negative reasons.
- Think of the ramifications on things beyond sports, such as the following:
     Local taxes
     Traffic patterns and congestion
     Teaching your kids to play sports
     Taking your family to sporting events
     The cost of advertised products
     The overall economy
     Our sports as perceived by the rest of the world

- On balance, what is your informed opinion?
- What, if anything, should people do?
     Elected leaders
     Television networks
     Future athletes
     Advertisers

**Exercise 19.2**     *Personal Inventory*

This exercise is designed to guide you through a cost-benefit analysis of sports. Some of the questions in this cost-benefit analysis will require you to do some research on the Internet.

Begin by thinking about how many sports you follow. The big four are football, basketball, hockey, and baseball. But also think about golf, tennis, track, horse racing, car racing, volleyball, and so on. Think beyond professional sports and include college level and high school level. Also, think about city leagues, YMCA leagues, children's leagues, and so forth.

*Estimate your direct costs:* Think about how much time and money you spend following sports and estimate your answers to the following questions:

1. For each sport, estimate how much time you spend going to games.

   What is the cost of tickets?
   What is the cost of transportation to the games?
   What is the cost of parking at the games?
   How much do you spend on food and drink at the games?
   How much do you spend on souvenirs—programs, pennants, and so forth?

2. How much do you spend on items with team logos?

   Clothing (hats, shirts, jackets, etc.)
   Items for your car (flags, license plates, bumper stickers, etc.)
   Items for your desk (cups, pens, calendars, etc.)
   Sports gifts for others

3. How much money do you spend watching games on television?

   Cost for special cable or pay TV sports services?
   Cost of parties for friends who watch the games with you?
   Cost of food and drink at sports bars while watching games?

4. How much time do you spend in all the above activities?

5. How much time do you spend doing the following:

   Talking about sports teams, players, and scores of games?
   Reminiscing about past good times?
   Complaining about bad games, plays, and players?
   Projecting into the future of your team, players' careers, or games?

*Estimate your indirect costs:*

1. How much money do you spend buying products advertised on sporting events? (To answer this completely, you need to analyze all the products advertising on all sports programs you watch and then find out what percentage of the purchase price of each of those products was spent on advertising of sports. To estimate your answer, think of the major sponsors of the teams you follow and add up all the money you spend each year on those products.)

2. How much money has your city spent to support the local sports teams? Think of the cost of building the stadiums, parking lots, and access roads to the professional, college, and high school sports. Try to estimate how much of your taxes goes into supporting all these sports.

*Estimate your direct benefits:*

1. How much satisfaction did you derive last season from the performance of the sports teams you followed?

   If you are a rabid fan and your teams all won championships, your satisfaction level should be extremely high. But think about the satisfaction you obtained from experiencing individual games and the performances of individual players.

2. How much satisfaction did you derive from displaying your teams' logos on your clothing, car, desk, and so on?

   Is it important to you that other people know which teams you support? If so, why? Do you identify so closely with a team that you, as a fan, feel partially responsible when they lose and that you have earned a celebration when they win?

*Estimate your indirect benefits:*

1. How important are your teams to their home cities?

   What economic benefits do the cities get by having those teams?
   What public relations benefits do the home cities get from supporting their teams?
   Do the teams need to win for the city to achieve these benefits?

2. Now considering what the cities experience as benefits, how much of that passes down to individuals such as yourself?

*Compare costs to benefits:*

   Now that you have thought about the questions raised in the above four areas, make a comparison of the costs to the benefits. Do you feel that the benefits you derive (of all kinds) are more than enough to pay you back for all the time and money you put into your fan-ship?

- If yes, what is your most valuable benefit? Why do you value that so highly?
- If no, how can you bring this cost-benefit comparison more in line with the value you expect? Is there some way to reduce your costs while still getting the same benefits? Is there some way to increase the benefits without increasing your costs?

Finally, think about where you might be 5 years from now given the money cycle. The monetary costs to you are likely to be much higher than they are today. Do you think the media will be able to grow the benefits proportionally so that you still feel that your money and time spent with sports are worthwhile?

# Media Violence

People seem to have been complaining about violence in the media ever since storytellers have used the media. Criticism has spiked in the past few decades as television has become so pervasive in American households and since violence has become so pervasive in television programs (see Table 20.1).

In this chapter, we will address the issue of media violence by focusing on the two fundamental topics underlying this issue. First, we will analyze the topic of effects, and then we will analyze the topic of the nature of violence in the media. The public has a very narrow conception of both of these topics. When people are limited by a narrow perspective on a problem, they are prevented from seeing many of the problem's key facets, and this limitation will distort their perceptions and prevent their criticism from being useful. The purpose of this chapter is to get you to expand your perspective on media violence and help you see the problem in a more complete and realistic manner. Thus, you will be able to craft a better informed opinion about media violence.

**Table 20.1**     Public Opinion About the Amount of Violence in the Media

- A 1975 Gallup poll found that two thirds of Americans found the present level of violent programming unacceptable (Cooper, 1996).
- In a 1993 poll, 70% of Americans feel that entertainment TV has too much violence, and 57% think that TV news gives too much attention to stories about violent crime (Galloway, 1993).
- A 1994 *Parents* magazine poll found that an overwhelming majority of Americans—87% of those questioned—said that the media "contains too much violence" (Diamant, 1994).
- In a 1995 Time/CNN survey, 52% of adult Americans said they are very concerned about the amount of violence depicted in movies, television shows, and popular music; another 25% said they were fairly concerned; only 9% said they were not concerned at all (Lacayo, 1995).
- A 1997 nationwide poll by the *Los Angeles Times* found that two thirds of people think that television programming has gotten worse over the past decade, with 90% believing that television now has more violence and sex than it did 10 years ago (Lowry, 1997).
- A 1997 *USA Weekend* write-in poll generated 21,600 responses, with 92% of those respondents saying they regarded television content more offensive than ever, especially with violence, sexual content, and vulgarity.

# Effects

If you ask the typical person, "Does violence on television and the movies have any effect?" most people will say yes—recalling a horrible instance when someone copied a violent criminal act that was in a movie or in the news. However, if you were to ask those same people if violence on television and movies has had an effect on them, most would say no. Thus, most people believe that other people are at risk but think they are free from risk. This difference in perception between one's self and others has been labeled the "third-person effect."

The reason for this third-person effect with media violence is because few people believe they behave aggressively after watching violence, but they have ample evidence that others are influenced to behave aggressively. There are frequent examples of copycat crimes and of kids going on shooting sprees at school in imitation of movie and video game violence. Also, many adults notice their children imitating violent television characters they see on action/adventure shows or on the *World Wrestling Federation.* We all remember children (or even ourselves as children) racing around the house, chasing siblings and pets while imitating sounds and movements from violent portrayals. But we recognize we do not behave that way now, so there is no effect on us. What makes this opinion possible is a narrow conception of what effects are possible from exposure to media violence. Recall from Chapter 13 that I showed you how to broaden your perspective on media effects. Let's work on broadening your perspective again, this time in the specific area of media violence.

## Narrow Perspective

The public largely limits its view of effects of exposure to media violence as aggressive behavior. The public rarely considers that there may be effects that are physiological, emotional, attitudinal, and cognitive. Furthermore, they are limiting their concern to three groups as being susceptible to these aggressive behaviors; those groups are children, criminals, and young boys who play video games. Are these three groups at risk for negative effects? Yes, of course. To illustrate, let's examine video games more closely. Video games are very popular, with marketing surveys revealing that 92% of all children and adolescents ages 2 to 17 play video games. The average child spends 20 to 33 minutes a day playing these games. The most popular types of games are combat (42%), sports (41%), and adventure (36%). About 89% of the top-selling games contained violence, and 17% featured violence as the primary focus of the game (Kaiser Family Foundation, 2002). A recent study reports that games rated for mature users are more likely to feature violence than are those rated for general audiences. Differences also emerged in the context of violence. When compared to general-audience games, mature games are not only more likely to feature child perpetrators but also justified acts of repeated gun violence that are graphic in nature (Smith, Lachlan, & Tamborini, 2003). Also, Slater (2003) reports that adolescents seek out more violent media content (and violent Web sites) when they are high on traits of sensation seeking and aggressiveness. Also, boys and those who are alienated are more likely to seek out violent content.

Clearly, young boys who play video games are at risk for aggressive behavioral effects. But there is also a wide range of effects to which we are all susceptible, even if we do not play video games and even if we are not a child or a criminal. Look at the list of effects displayed in Table 20.2. Each of these has been well documented by research. Notice that some are immediate effects (meaning that they occur during exposure to the media violence), whereas others are long-term effects (which take many exposures over a long period of time to build up to a manifestation). Notice also that although there are behavioral effects, there are also effects that are more physiological, attitudinal, emotional, and cognitive. When we don't understand the range of effects, it is easy to overlook what may be the most widespread effect of exposure to media violence.

## The Overlooked Effect

Perhaps the most prevalent effect of constant exposure to violence is an effect that is so subtle that most people overlook it. This is the effect of a cultivated belief that the world is violent and a related fear of being victimized. Of course, real-world violence and

**Table 20.2**    Immediate and Long-Term Effects From Exposure to Media Violence

**The Immediate Effects**

*Behavioral Effect*

1. Imitation/Copying Behavior: This is the effect that the public focuses on most when thinking about protecting people from the influence of media violence. This is understandable because copying behavior is very easy to spot and very easy to see the link back to the media content. This type of effect is much more prevalent with children than adults.

2. Triggering Novel Behavior: Triggering refers to a behavior that is neither imitated (mimicking a just-seen behavior in the media) nor activated (putting in motion a previously learned behavior). Triggering refers to the media stimulating a person to act in a violent manner but that person acts out in a novel way.

3. Disinhibition: Exposure to media violence can reduce viewers' normal inhibitions that prevent them from behaving in a violent manner. This effect has the largest research base.

4. Attraction: Many people are attracted to violence, maybe not all the time, but there come times when people want to see a violent show. If it were not for this effect, violent CDs would not sell, and horror movies would have no audiences. When you add up all the time and money spent by millions of people each year in seeking out this kind of content, this must be regarded as a major effect.

*Physiological Effect*

5. Fight/Flight: Exposure to violence can temporarily arouse people physiologically. During exposure, a person's heart rate and blood pressure increase. These physiological changes are the body's way of getting ready to respond to the violence as if it were a real threat to the viewer. This type of arousal dissipates usually within an hour after exposure.

6. Excitation Transfer: Violence presented in the media tends to arouse viewers and hence is an energizer. People do not necessarily need to use that energy in an aggressive manner—they can transfer that energy to other outlets. For example, people who are exposed to a strongly violent portrayal can become highly aroused (heightened heart rate) and are ready for action. If there are sexual reminders in their environment, they will be likely stay highly aroused but shift into a sexual mode. The arousal needs direction because arousal by itself is not guided. If the viewer guides the energy into positive directions, then the exposure to violence will have a prosocial value. Whatever the direction, the energy from the arousal is short-lived and usually dissipates within several minutes after exposure.

*Emotional Effect*

7. Temporary Fear: Violence in films and on television can produce intense fright reactions. Fright as an immediate emotional response is typically of relatively short duration, but it may endure on occasion for several hours, days, or even longer. It is composed of the components of anxiety, distress, and increased physiological arousal that are frequently engendered in viewers as a result of exposure to specific types of media productions.

*Attitudinal Effect*

8. Immediate Creation/Change of Attitudes: A person's attitude can be created or changed with as little as a single exposure. For example, researchers have shown that when people are exposed to a violent television program, they will show an immediate drop in sympathetic attitude.

*Cognitive Effect*

9. Learning Specific Acts and Lessons: People can learn behavior patterns by watching characters perform in the media. For example, children might watch a cartoon where characters beat each other over the head with rubber hammers and show no harm. The children do not imitate the behavior patterns they see because there are no rubber hammers available to them. But this does not mean they have not learned how to perform a certain aggressive behavioral sequence. Also, they have learned that such behavior is funny and not really harmful to the person who is hit in the head.

## Long-Term Effects

*Behavioral Effect*

10. Training Behavior: Violent video games train players to kill. When children watch graphic violence in movies and on TV shows and also play realistic, violent video games, it breaks down their natural resistance to killing. This training follows the same principles used by the U.S. military to transform peaceful young men into soldiers who must kill their enemies. The game playing has a physical component of training; that is, players are trained in eye-hand coordination, thus practicing the ability to fire at and kill moving targets. It also has an emotional component, whereby players overcome their natural resistance to killing, are rewarded for such behavior, and can experience intense pleasant emotions when they are highly successful at killing.

*Physiological Effect*

11. Physiological Habituation: This is building up or increasing physiological tolerance over the long term. With repeated fight-or-flight responses, the human body gradually builds up a resistance to the exposure to media violence. For example, the first time people see a horror film, their bodies respond with a fight-or-flight reaction that substantially increases heart rate and blood pressure. As they continue to view horror films over the years, the body's reaction is not as substantial to this stimulus; the heart rate and blood pressure still increase but not as much. With repeated exposures, people build up a higher tolerance to this type of message physiologically. In the extreme case, with massive exposure to this type of message, people might even extinguish all physiological reactions to horror.

12. Narcoticizing: Not only does habitual viewing of violence over time dull our reactions, but some people also continue to crave the strong "arousal jag" they used to get from violent exposures. But to experience the same degree of arousal, they search out more graphic and stronger forms of violence. Thus, violence acts like a drug in the sense that people grow a stronger dependence on it over time while the drug loses its strength. In its extreme case, this narcotic of violence can lead to addiction.

*(Continued)*

**Table 20.2** (Continued)

*Emotional Effect*

13. Desensitization: Some portrayals are presented so often that we can no longer treat them with wonder or awe. Our tolerance has been increased so that those things that used to horrify or even upset us no longer do. This is especially important with the issue of violence. Viewing TV violence leads to lowered sensitivity to aggression and violence. And when people are exposed to violence continuously for a long period of time, this lowering of sensitivity is reinforced.

14. Cultivation of Fear: There is a good deal of research support for the hypothesis that heavy exposure to the world of television, which is saturated with violent portrayals, leads people to construct unrealistically high estimates of risk of victimization and a corresponding belief that the world is a mean and violent place.

*Attitudinal Effect*

15. Long-Term Reinforcement of Attitudes/Beliefs: Because the media provide so many messages of violence and because those messages are usually presented with the same cluster of contextual factors, viewers' existing attitudes about violence are reinforced over time. This makes the attitudes stronger and therefore harder to change as time goes by.

*Cognitive Effect*

16. Learning Social Norms: The learning of social norms is a special case of generalizing patterns. People can generalize patterns from individual media exposures without that pattern being a social norm. For example, through repeated exposure to media violence, a person overestimates the rate of crime and the percentage of crimes that are cleared by an arrest. Although these are generalizations, they are not social norms. Social norms are generalized patterns from social information rather than factual information. Social norms deal more with the rules of behavior in social situations rather than society's factual parameters, such as the numbers of lawyers, crimes, trials, and executions—all of which have a real factual indicator. But social norms have no factual basis.

*Effects on Society*

17. Changing Institutions: When violence permeates the media year after year in all kinds of programming, it puts pressure on institutions to change. For example:

The criminal justice system—when the public believes crime is one of the most important social problems, candidates for elective office run on a platform of getting tough on crime. Municipalities hire more police officers, arrests for certain crimes escalate, people are asked to give up certain rights, courts are under pressure to give stiffer sentences to criminals, the prison population increases, and states must build more prisons so they raise taxes.

The educational system—because of some high-profile shootings in public schools, many schools now have metal detectors at their doors; there are searches of lockers and restrictions on who can walk into a school building. Teachers are wary of aggressive students, making it harder to concentrate on the higher goals of education, and focus instead on survival in many school districts.

Religion may be changing as people turn to that institution more out of a generalized fear or out of a rejection of the changing norms of society. Also, religions may be more aggressive at drawing the line of acceptable behaviors to stop the shift of society in an antisocial direction. Thus, religion becomes more concerned with moral issues than spiritual ones. The focus may be shifting more toward prescribing everyday behaviors and away from focusing on the awe and mystery of creation and human's place in the universe and eternity.

The institution of family may also be changing as a result of these forces brought about by media violence. Perhaps the generalized fear makes parents less trusting of their children. Perhaps couples are less willing to deal with their arguments by looking for peaceful solutions and being willing to compromise. Instead, couples may be looking for more fights to act on their aggressive impulses, feel more justified in those confrontations, and thus want to dominate the other in their resolutions. Such adversarial behaviors are likely to lead to more breakups and more people choosing to live alone.

---

crime do exist, but they do not exist to the levels that the general public has been conditioned to believe. For example, Lowry, Nio, and Leitner (2003) report that from March 1992 to August 1994, public perceptions of crime as the most important problem in the United States jumped from 5% to 52%. Although crime rates did not increase and even decreased slightly during that period, public perception went way up. The researchers report that the jump was due to network TV news and its focus on crime, particularly violent crime.

What is the reality about crime? The crime rate has been falling, both in terms of crimes reported to the police as well as actual victimization rates. Also, home burglary rates have dropped 50% over the past two decades. Yet in a recent poll, only 7% of Americans believed that violent crime had declined in the past 5 years (Whitman & Loftus, 1996). The news does not give us an accurate picture of crime in society; instead, it continually tries to shock us with coverage of untypical events.

# Conception of Violence

When the public criticizes media violence, what is the public really criticizing? And when the public calls for less violence, what is the public really asking to be reduced? These are extremely important questions, and they are often overlooked. But if we are to get to the heart of the topic of media violence, we must find answers for them.

## Public's Definition

The research evidence on this point indicates that the public is focused only on a particular kind of violence—that which is graphic. For example, Potter et al. (2002) reported that graphicness and explicitness were two of the important predictors of their participants' judgments of the degree of violence. Thus, audiences' judgments about the degree of violence are related much less to the number of violent acts than to the degree of graphicness. For example, people might not think an action/adventure movie with wall-to-wall car chases and gunfire is more violent than a drama in which one character is unexpectedly shot and we see the bullet tearing through flesh and bone. One highly graphic scene can earn a movie a perception of being more violent than another movie with repeated acts of sanitized violence.

Closely related to graphicness is the characteristic of offensiveness. If portrayals are not offensive—that is, evoking a negative reaction—then viewers do not pay much attention to violence compared to other program features (British Broadcasting Corporation, 1972), or when they do pay attention, it is not an important element that takes away from their enjoyment of programs (Diener & De Four, 1978; Diener & Woody, 1981). But when a violent portrayal is unusually graphic, it interrupts viewers' flow of enjoyment, and viewers experience strong negative emotions.

Another key element in the public's definition of violence is that humor is a camouflage. It appears that when humor blankets violence, the public does not see the violence. This is taken for granted by all kinds of people. An anecdote will illustrate this. In the winter of 1996, I was meeting with the staff of the Viacom Standards and Practices Department in New York City. These seven women are charged with previewing the content to be aired on Viacom's cable channels of MTV, VH1, and Nickelodeon. I was watching a music video while the seven women in the room explained how they screened music videos to determine if those videos met their standards or, if in their judgment, there were things in the portrayals that would offend viewers. For an hour, the women showed parts of music videos and explained how they asked the various music groups to remove or tone down certain images that they felt were demeaning to women. Finally, when I was given a chance to ask a question, I said, "What about violence in the videos?" Several women were eager to answer that they were sensitive to that issue and that the videos did not have any direct scenes of violence, although violence was implied in certain lyrics. Then I asked about violence on Nickelodeon. There was a rather long pause as the women looked at me as if I were a third grader who had just claimed that two plus two equals seven. One of the women looked very puzzled and said, "But there is no violence on Nickelodeon." I returned the puzzled look and replied, "What about your Saturday morning shows such as *Bugs Bunny* and *Ninja Turtles*?" Her puzzled looked turned into a big smile as she said, "But those are not violent. Those are cartoons!" Were these women naive? No, they had a highly sophisticated understanding of violence—as defined by the general viewing public. These women knew that the public was not concerned by the actions—even the most brutal—portrayed in cartoons.

What is the reason for humor camouflaging the violence? It appears that humor tends to remove the threat of violence. For viewers to consider something violent, they need to feel a degree of personal threat. This insight can be found in the work of Barrie Gunter in Great Britain. He reported that viewers' ratings of the seriousness of violent acts were higher as the fictional settings were closer to everyday reality in terms of time and location. In contrast, "Violence depicted in clearly fantastic settings such as cartoons or science-fiction were perceived as essentially non-violent, non-frightening and non-disturbing" (Gunter, 1985, p. 245). Other researchers also report that people were much more concerned with acts that had a higher probability of occurrence, meaning the likelihood of the act happening to them in everyday life (Forgas, Brown, & Menyhart, 1980).

In summary, the public uses a conception of violence that is keyed to three factors. First there is graphicness. The more blood and gore shown in a portrayal, the more the portrayal risks offending viewers, and the more viewers will object to the act as being violent. Second, the seriousness of the action itself and the way the act is portrayed are more influential in the decision of violence than is the portrayed of harm to the victim. Third, people allow humor to camouflage violence. Humor reduces the feeling of personal threat to viewers and thereby eliminates the sense of violence.

## Ironies

The way the public defines violence creates an irony. The kind of violence that upsets people the most is precisely the type of violence that they need to be exposed to more. In contrast, it is the violence that most people do not complain about—or even perceive—that is doing them the most harm.

If a show presents a highly graphic act of violence without humor, people will be offended and complain that this type of portrayal is too violent and has no place in media messages. Their intention is to pressure the programmers to eliminate this type of content. The implication is that if the graphicness were reduced or if it were shown in a humorous context, the action would not be offensive to them.

The irony is that when people are shown violence, they *should* be offended, and they *should* complain. Such a reaction is the appropriate one to violent actions; it shows that they are sensitive to the violence. When they do not complain, there is evidence that they have been desensitized to the violence. There is a great deal of violence portrayed in the media, and the overwhelming majority of it is not met with complaints; thus, most people are desensitized to almost all of the violence they continually witness on TV.

When television programmers hear complaints about too much violence, the inclination of many creative types is not to reduce the amount of violent acts; instead, their typical response is to sanitize those acts. This means making them less graphic by showing less harm to the victims or to mask the harm with humor. Sanitized violence leads viewers to believe that violent acts are not such a big deal. So the less harm shown to the victims in television stories, the more harm to viewers in the form of the negative effect of desensitization. Conversely, the more harm shown to victims of violence in television stories, the more positive the message is that violence is really damaging and should therefore be regarded with disgust.

Another irony is that when people complain about the amount of violence, they are basing their complaints on only the graphic instances. This means that they are missing more than 90% of the violence presented—that is, violence that is formulaic and therefore coming into their subconscious, underneath their radar, which is only attuned to that which is highly graphic and therefore offensive.

## Developing a Broader Sensitivity

Being media literate requires a broader sensitivity to media violence. This means getting beyond the defining of violence purely in terms of high graphicness. To begin this task, stop reading this chapter at this point and get a pencil and a piece of paper. Attempt to write your definition of violence in one sentence. When you finish, think about the violent portrayals you have seen in movies and on TV. Does your definition work well? Does it identify what would be violent in news shows? In an episode of the *Three Stooges*? In Saturday morning cartoons? With video or computer games?

The task of defining violence appears to be an easy one at first. But it turns out to be very difficult to write a definition that would provide adequate guidance to judge whether something is violent across all the nuances of portrayals across all media. Most people become frustrated with this task as they realize how complex it is to articulate precisely what they had previously believed they understood clearly. The reason for this is that *violence* is a primitive concept; that is, we all know it when we see it, but it is nearly impossible to write down a good definition. Another example of a primitive term is *red*. You cannot

**Table 20.3**      Key Elements in Definitions of Violence

1. Does the act have to be directed toward a person? Gang members swing baseball bats at a car and totally destroy it. Is this violence?

2. Does the act have to be committed by a person? A mudslide levels a town and kills 20 people. Do acts of nature count? Remember that nature does not write the scripts or produce the programming.

3. Does the act have to be intentional? A bank robber drives a fast car in a getaway chase. As he speeds around a corner, he hits a pedestrian (or destroys a mailbox). Do accidents count?

4. Does the act result in harm? Tom shoots a gun at Jerry, but the bullet misses. Is this violence? Or what if Tom and Jerry are cartoon characters and Tom drops an anvil on Jerry, who is momentarily flattened like a pancake. A second later, Jerry pops back to his original shape and appears fine.

5. What about violence we don't see? If a bad guy fires a gun at a character off-screen and we hear a scream and a body fall, is this violence, even though we do not see it?

6. Does the act have to be physical (such as assaults), or can it be verbal (such as insults)? What if Tom viciously insults Jerry, who is shown through the rest of the program experiencing deep psychological and emotional pain as a result? What if Tom embarrasses Jerry, who then runs from the room, trips, and breaks his arm?

7. What about fantasy? If 100 fighting men "morph" into a giant creature the size of a 10-story building, which then stomps out their enemies, does this count as violence?

8. What about humorous portrayals? When the Three Stooges hit each other with hammers, is this violence?

---

write a definitional rule for what is red and what is not, but you have high confidence that you know what it is and can spot it when it occurs.

We deal with many primitive concepts in our everyday life—love, chair, freedom, sex. We all "know" what these mean, even though it is very difficult to specify an adequate definition for any of them. But examining our definitions is an important task. For us to understand our world better and how we assess the meaning of it, we need to analyze the definitions we have for things. This helps us understand those things better; it also helps us understand ourselves better. So let's continue on this definitional task by looking at the questions in Table 20.3. Answer each of the eight questions. Then, when you are finished, compare your definition to your answers to each of the eight questions. Do you want to make any changes to your definition? After you have completed these tasks, try doing Exercise 20.1.

# Conclusion

The public continually complains that there is too much violence in the media, especially television. The public, however, underperceives the degree of violence because its perceptions are limited to violent acts that are graphic and therefore offensive to them. The implication of the public criticism is that the violence should be sanitized by making it less graphic. Sanitizing media violence, however, would increase the probability that viewers would become desensitized to the violence, and this is a negative effect.

The public also has a narrow perspective on the harm of exposure to media violence. Most people believe that continued exposure to media violence primarily harms unstable people who will behave aggressively or commit crimes. There are many, many negative effects, however, that result from exposure to media violence. These effects are not limited to behaviors but also include cognitive effects, attitudinal effects, emotional effects, and physiological effects.

Becoming more media literate with the issue of media violence requires that people think more broadly about the effects and understand the full range of risk to themselves and other people. Also, people need to change their criticism either to push for the reduction of violent acts or to increase (not decrease) the graphicness of the portrayals. If media programmers keep increasing the number of violent acts and keep sanitizing those portrayals to avoid public criticism, this exacerbates the situation where the public is increasing its risk of many negative effects of which people are largely unaware.

# Further Reading

National Television Violence Study. (1996). *Scientific report.* Thousand Oaks, CA: Sage. (568 pages with index)

The National Cable Television Association funded this $3.3 million project to examine the prevalence and context of violence on American television, the effects of warnings and advisories placed before violence programs, and the effect of public service announcements advocating the avoidance of violence. Some of the chapters are very technical and contain many statistics. But the overall report is the most comprehensive analysis of the issue of violence on television to date.

Potter, W. J. (1999). *On media violence.* Thousand Oaks, CA: Sage. (304 pages with index)

In this book, I take a narrow focus by looking at only one form of media content—violence. But I try to provide an in-depth analysis of the effects of exposure to this one type of content.

Potter, W. J. (2003). *The 11 myths of media violence.* Thousand Oaks, CA: Sage. (259 pages with index)

This book begins with a chapter illuminating the current state of public debate over media violence and ends with a chapter reflecting on the prognosis for change. In between are 11 chapters, each dealing with a faulty belief about media violence. Taken together, these myths lock people (the general public, people in the media industries, media regulators, and media researchers) into a maze of unproductive thinking. These myths include the following faulty beliefs: There is too much violence on television, the media are only responding to market desires, and reducing the amount of violence in the media will solve the problem.

**Exercise 20.1**   Analyze Media Content for Violence

1. Watch a television show that has a reputation for presenting a lot of violence. Use your definition and see how many actions fit your definition. Count them.

   How many acts would you have counted using a definition that was based on a "no" answer to all eight questions in Table 20.3?
   How many acts would you have counted using a definition that was based on a "yes" answer to all eight questions in Table 20.3?

2. Watch another program with violence; this time, pay attention to how the violence is portrayed.

   How much of the violence is committed by bad characters and how much by the "good guys?"
   How many of the violent acts are punished in the scene, that is, where the perpetrator is stopped in his or her actions or sanctioned in some way?
   How many of the violent acts show realistic harm to the victims?
   How many of the violent acts are portrayed as being justified?
   What does this pattern of context tell you about whether committing violence is good or bad? That is, what are the producers of this program teaching you about whether using violence is good or bad?

3. Watch a situation comedy and count the number of acts of verbal violence—that is, verbal put-downs, slurs, insults, and comments designed to embarrass another character.

   What kinds of characters commit the most verbal violence? Are they the main characters? Are they attractive?
   What happens to characters who commit acts of verbal violence? Are they punished or rewarded (by laughter) or neither?
   Are the victims of the verbal violence shown as being harmed? If so, what kind of harm, and how long does the harm last?
   What does this pattern of verbal violence and its context tell you about whether committing verbal violence is good or bad?

**Exercise 20.2**     Can You Identify the Negative Effects?

1. Do you or your children feel like wrestling after watching several hours of cartoons or the *World Wrestling Federation?*

2. After watching a horror movie late at night by yourself, do you have a difficult time relaxing and falling asleep? Or do you lie awake in bed thinking that you should get up and check the locks once again or perhaps leave a light on in the hall?

3. You have seen a violent movie that took place in an inner-city ghetto. African American teenagers were dealing drugs and killing rivals with guns. You shake your head and think, "Inner cities are such war zones. I'm glad I don't have to travel through one of them!"

4. You're thumbing through the newspaper and notice that a new Steven Seagal action/adventure film has just been released. You feel excitement and can't wait until you get to see it.

5. You are watching the evening news and you hear about two brutal murders that took place last night in your town. You think back and remember previous newscasts about murders in your town over the past year. You conclude that the murder rate is sharply increasing.

6. You see a teenage boy slip on a puddle in a supermarket and fall down. You do not go over to help him thinking, "Silly boy. It's his own fault for not looking where he was going. Besides, he is not really hurt." You walk away and not give it another thought.

**Interpreting Your Answers to Exercise 20.2**

I have titled this section "Interpreting Your Answers to Exercise 20.2" because these are possible interpretations, not definitive psychoanalysis. There may be a lot of reasons for each of your answers. What I am doing in this exercise is suggesting a media violence explanation so as to increase your awareness of possible influences.

1. This is the standard imitation effect. In this situation, it is harmless, unless you get really carried away! But what is happening is that the viewing is getting you involved in the mayhem. Your heart rate and blood pressure increase. You are moving into a fight-or-flight mode. When you see your partner in a similar condition, you agree that wrestling would be a fun thing to do.

2. This is a temporary fear reaction. The movie has planted strong images in your mind and a strong feeling of fear in your heart. Although your bedroom and surroundings are familiar, on this particular night, there is "something else in the

room." That something else is not really a monster in the flesh but an apparition in your mind. This apparition can make your palms sweat and your heart pound—not very conducive to sleep!

3. This is likely a reinforcement of attitude effect. Most of the images the movie presented are probably not new to you. Although you have never seen a gang war in an inner city, you have these images through previous media exposures. And you have already held the attitude that inner cities and African American teenage males are highly dangerous. These are both stereotypes, of course. And the stronger the stereotypes, the less likely you will seek out real-world information to see if your attitude is distorted.

4. This is an attraction effect. You have a history of arousing and pleasurable experiences with past action/adventure films, especially those starring Steven Seagal.

5. This is a cognitive effect of generalizing patterns. Your recollection of several stories about local murders has led you to see a pattern. You can't recall many murders 5 years ago or when you were a child, so you see a trend to the pattern—there is an increase in the murder rate in your town.

   What may be happening is that the actual murder rate in your town is down (the murder rate in the United States as a whole has been declining the past decade), but the local news is getting better at presenting gruesome images that stay in your mind longer.

6. This may be a desensitization effect. From watching so many acts of violence in the media, a simple fall is nothing. Also, because the victims of the serious acts of violence in the media rarely show any pain or harm, you think, "How can a silly slip hurt a young boy?"

# CHAPTER 21

# Privacy and Piracy With the Media

The topics about privacy and piracy are treated together as one large issue in this chapter because they are so closely related. Whether something is privacy or piracy depends on your perspective. For example, let's say you join a record club and buy a CD. When you buy a CD, you feel you own it and can share it with whomever you want; it is your private business. If the record company tracks your sharing, you feel the company is invading your privacy, but the record company thinks you are pirating its music—even though you bought the music from the company. Also, if you bought the CD off the Internet or through mail order, the record company collected information about you when you joined; you willingly gave the company your address (so the CDs could be mailed to you) and your musical interests (so the company could send you catalogs of music you would like to buy). But the company likely shared (or sold) this information to other companies. When you find out the record company sold your personal information to other companies, you feel that it invaded your privacy and acted like pirates by taking something from you and selling it for its own benefit without compensating you or even asking for your permission.

The concerns about privacy and piracy are all about drawing lines—lines between what is private and what is public, as well as lines between what rights come with ownership and what rights do not.

With the new technology of computers and the Internet, it is easier than ever for individuals and companies to invade your privacy. Because computers and the Internet are so new, most people are relatively inexperienced with the medium and do not understand how open to abuse this channel of communication is. In the early 1980s, fewer than 5% of all American households had a computer, but within 20 years, that number had climbed to almost two thirds (http://www.commerce.gov). Government regulators are just beginning to grapple with the complexity of these problems as information is digitized and put out in all media channels, especially the Internet. Digitization and computers make it possible and easy for people to invade your privacy and for you to make copies and distribute any form of information, regardless of who is protected by copyright. These problems raise fundamental questions about what rights to privacy you really have and what rights other people have of using information about you. Also, the concept of a creative message and who owns it is getting more complex. Legislators, regulators, and the courts are struggling with these questions.

Until these thorny questions are resolved by policymakers and the legal system, we will not have meaningful guidelines and enforcement. However, in the meantime, we need to answer these questions for ourselves and take steps to protect our private information and our creative rights while at the same time availing us of rich sources of information and creative messages circulating on the Internet and through all the other media.

# Privacy

We all have a set of things that we want to be kept private and another set that we want to share. For example, many people do not want to share information with strangers about their income, where they live, or their age. Many people want their friends and business associates to know their phone number and e-mail address, but they want to keep this contact information away from telemarketers and other advertisers who might inundate them with unwanted messages. Also, when we give information about ourselves to our close friends, we expect them to follow a fundamental principle of fairness that they not share that information with a third party unless they first ask our permission or, at least, that they tell us that they have passed that information along to a third party.

## Invasions of Your Privacy

This section outlines six ways that people and companies are already invading your privacy, primarily through the Internet. These six are dumping, monitoring, selling information, identity theft, hijacking, and infecting. The more you know about possible invasions, the better you can proactively take steps to protect your privacy.

## *Dumping*

People with e-mail service know that their e-mail address is quasi-public. That is, it is posted in various places so that old friends, potential business associates, and the like can contact them even if we have not given them our e-mail address. Many universities give their students free access to the Internet and a personal e-mail account. The universities usually have a directory where anyone can type in your name and get your e-mail address. There are many positive reasons to be listed in such a directory. But there are also risks of unwanted attention. For example, advertisers might get into your university's directory and download all the addresses so they can e-mail everyone with their ads for books and other products. There are times, of course, that we might like getting such announcements for good products we need at good prices. But often we are bombarded with messages for all kinds of products in which we have no interest or ability to buy. These unwanted messages clutter our mailboxes and can make huge demands on our time to sort through all the junk mail to get to the e-mails we value. This unwanted e-mail has been given the name of "spam."

Many of us regard our e-mail account as being only for person-to-person communication, where we know the people we are sending our specially written e-mails to and that those who send us e-mails know us. We do not regard our e-mail address as an invitation to advertisers to inundate us with their messages that are often sent out impersonally to hundreds of thousands of people at the same time. We are offended when our e-mail box becomes cluttered with dozens of messages from spammers offering special deals on products for which we have no use.

Marketers who use e-mail to get their messages out to a wide variety of people see the Internet as a great tool to inform people of their products and services. They are not concerned with the additional costs to recipients of their messages. Instead, they are driven purely by e-mailing as many people as possible. Skilled spammers can each send out 30 million e-mails a day and thus put them on equal footing of a major advertiser such as a *Fortune* 500 company, which spends millions of dollars in television advertising a week to get their messages in front of that many people. Spammers are concerned with only one thing—maximizing their coverage of people with e-mail addresses. Because spammers operate on a hit rate of 25 sales per 1 million e-mails, they must send out extremely large numbers of e-mail offers to generate any sales. Projections are that by 2006, there will be 200 billion e-mails sent each day (Stone & Lin, 2002).

In their quest for reaching large numbers of people, spammers will buy long lists of e-mails addresses either legally or illegally. Spammers can buy CDs with 100 million e-mail addresses on them for as little as $2,000. Or they might hack into a company's private e-mail directory and steal those e-mail addresses. Sometimes, an employee of an Internet Service Provider (ISP) will sell the company's addresses. For example, in the summer of 2004, AOL, after fighting a daily battle with spammers who were clogging their service with unwanted e-mails, found out that one of its employees had sold AOL's list of 92 million e-mail addresses to a spammer for $100,000. The spammer used the addresses to promote his online gambling business, then sold those addresses to other spammers for tens of thousands of dollars himself (Gaither, 2004c).

ISPs are especially wary of spammers because a sudden inundation of hundreds of thousands of messages can slow their systems down, and a flood of a million messages can crash their systems. Slow service and crashed systems anger customers and cause ISPs with many of these problems to lose customers, so ISPs must hire technical people to filter out the spammers. A war between spammers and Internet companies has developed. The Internet companies have technicians set up spam traps—called honey pots—to collect spam e-mail and analyze it to figure out what spammers are doing; then they devise antispam software to screen it out. In response, spammers buy the antispam software to figure out how to get around it. Each week, the sophistication increases as the ISPs war with the spammers. As of now, it appears that the spammers are winning the war. By 2003, spam accounted for half of all e-mail traffic, and the volume continues to rise.

One example of a huge spammer group calls itself the Alabama Spammers. This group dialed into Earthlink's high-powered servers and established several dozen connections simultaneously. Earthlink's spam abuse team spotted the attack within minutes, but it usually takes a hour to identify the accounts and manually terminate all the connections; meanwhile, the Alabama Spammers were able to send out thousands of messages. Earthlink filed civil lawsuits against 100 companies accusing them of hijacking Earthlink customer accounts to send spam under the RICO Act (Racketeer Influenced and Corrupt Organizations Act), which has been used to attack Mafia operations (Gaither, 2004b). The suit contends that in 2003, spam cost U.S. businesses $10 billion. One of the companies named in the suit is OptInRealBig.com and its owner, Scott Richter. This company uses contests and promotions to gather information on Internet users, then sells those addresses to other spammers. Richter's promotions include selling a diet pill named Inferno, a copy of Jennifer Lopez's engagement ring, Iraq's most-wanted playing cards, and an herbal supplement for "penile fitness." He sends out several hundred million e-mails each day, making his company one of the largest spammers. Richter does not like the term *spammer* and says, "We're a powerhouse in the e-mail marketing world. I stand up for what I do" (Jerome & Bane, 2004, pp. 125–126).

Some antispam services have been targeted by spammers. For example, for a year and half, Ron Guilmette published blacklists of spammers on his Monkeys.com Web site until September 2003, when he was inundated by a mass e-mail assault for 10 days until he had to shut down his Web site. Guilmette said, "I underestimated both the enemy's level of sophistication, and also the enemy's level of brute malevolence" (Gaither, 2004b, p. C1).

In the spring of 2004, the New York State Attorney General and Microsoft Corporation filed a suit against a handful of spammers that had sent billions of illegal and deceptive e-mail messages. The e-mails were illegal because the spammers used forged sender names, false subject lines, and fake sender addresses (Jerome & Bane, 2004).

Public opinion is very much against spam, with 77% of public saying that spam had made their online experiences unpleasant and annoying. Also, 29% said spam had caused them to use e-mail less. The public is taking steps to protect itself, but at great cost. It has been estimated that the public spent almost $1 billion in antispam software and services in 2004, which is an increase of 50% in 1 year (Gaither, 2004b).

## Monitoring

ISPs, marketers, and other companies have a technology to monitor activities on your computer by planting a small file called a "cookie" on your hard drive. ISPs and advertisers either avoid telling customers about this practice or, when customers find out about cookies, companies say that cookies are designed to help Internet users achieve a more efficient experience.

Netscape created cookies in 1994 as a special browser feature to make life easier for people browsing the Web. The concept is similar to that of a computer's preferences file. It keeps track of how the user wants a site to look or function. Once the preferences are set, the user does not have to input routine information upon each visit.

Netscape thought cookies would be especially useful in enabling "shopping cart" services on Web sites, such as Amazon.com. The idea was to allow consumers to click from page to page, choosing items to buy, while a virtual clerk kept track of the items by listing them in a small file called a cookie. Then the customer checks out of the virtual store by typing in credit card and address information so the company receives payment and knows where to send the purchases. But this information about the customer does not evaporate when he or she turns off the computer; instead, the information is preserved in a cookie that can be accessed during the customer's next shopping session. The advantage to the customers is that they will not have to reenter their addresses and credit card numbers, thus making subsequent trips to the online store more convenient for the customer. However, these cookies are accessed by the online store, which uses the information about past purchases to guide the customer to future purchases. For example, if you buy a book about dinosaurs from Amazon.com in one visit to its online store, in subsequent visits, you will miraculously be presented with ads about other dinosaur books, toys, and games. Virtual stores access the information stored in the cookies on people's hard drives to tailor how they present their products on the screen.

Online stores access the information stored in cookies for their own purposes. They use this information to track which sites in their virtual stores attract the consumers' attention the most. They can also use this information to e-mail customers about sales and new products, and thus they can try to generate sales even when customers do not visit their online stores. They can also pull the information from cookies and create mailing lists along with customer profiles to sell to other stores.

Cookies are now used by other companies in addition to ISPs and online stores. There are now "third-party advertising networks," which use cookie files to track a user's activities all across the Web and trigger advertisements according to each user's apparent interests and needs. One of these third-party advertising networks is Doubleclick, which sprang up to oversee banner ads on Web sites.

Cookies themselves are not inherently bad or necessarily invasive to one's privacy. But they open the door for widespread abuse. In the most comprehensive and extreme cases, a Web company could build a profile of an Internet user that combines information about her purchases, her taste in music, the investment information she seeks, the health issues that concern her most, and the kind of news stories that seize her interest (Pew Internet & American Life Project, 2000).

When Netscape first developed cookies, it did not tell consumers how they worked. As the use of cookies grew in frequency, there were few complaints from consumers. But eventually, some consumers figured out that there was this clandestine activity taking place on their hard drives. A firestorm of criticism erupted. There seemed to be no anticipation at the time that the use of cookies would create a problem. In 1996, Alex Edelstein, Netscape's product manager for Navigator 2.0, declared that cookie technology was an insignificant issue and would "blow over" (Pew Internet & American Life Project, 2000).

After the media reported on the technology in January 1996, people began realizing how their privacy was being invaded without their knowledge and got upset. More than half (54%) of Internet users believe that Web sites' tracking of users is harmful because it invades their privacy. Just 27% say tracking is helpful because it allows the sites to provide information tailored to specific consumers, and 54% of Internet users have chosen to provide personal information to use a Web site. An additional 10% say they would be willing to provide it under the right circumstances, and 27% are hard-core privacy protectionists and would never provide personal information (Pew Internet & American Life Project, 2000).

Under pressure, Netscape added a tool to disable cookies for the next version of their Web-browsing software. But it was not very easy to do the disabling. Web site users had cookies implanted on their machines unless they took affirmative steps to reject cookies—a classic "opt-out" scheme. A user had to dig two menu screens down in the browser to find the place to opt out of cookies.

Microsoft built in cookie controls in its more recent versions of Internet Explorer. Internet users are now alerted when a site tries to place a third-party cookie—that is, one that could help track their activities all across the Web. But even with these new tools provided by Internet browsers, only about 10% of people set their browsers to block cookies (Pew Internet & American Life Project, 2000).

Some shocking uses of cookies have come to light. These examples show how powerful cookies are in monitoring activity on one's computer. The federal Office of National Drug Control Policy (the so-called drug czar's office) was found to be using cookies to track Web surfers' drug-related information requests. After a storm of criticism that this might allow the drug czar's office to clandestinely record citizens' online activities, the federal Office of Management and Budget banned the use of cookies on federal government Web sites. Also, the Federal Bureau of Investigation (FBI) came under fire from Congress and civil liberties groups for developing "Carnivore," a wiretapping device that silently intercepts all traffic to and from a suspect's e-mail account.

In the private sector, Pharmatrak, Inc., a Boston technology firm, acknowledged tracking consumers' activities on health-related sites without informing the public. Also, Dow Chemical Company fired 50 employees after a search of their e-mail revealed pornography or violent images (Pew Internet & American Life Project, 2000).

## Selling Information

Once a company accesses the information in cookies, there is a temptation to aggregate it into long lists of customers (along with addresses and buying habits), then sell it to other companies. For example, Toysrus.com was accused of feeding shoppers' personal information to a data analysis firm without revealing this transaction to consumers. In response to complaints, Toysrus.com added information to its privacy policy about how customer data were treated.

Many companies regard the selling of customer data as just another lucrative revenue stream. In early 2000, Internet advertiser Doubleclick decided it would combine two databases and sell the information. One database was the anonymous Web-surfing habits of millions of people that were gathered through cookies. The other was an offline database that included people's geographical addresses and other private information.

Some companies that collect information from their customers promise not to sell it but then are later forced to do so. For example, in 2000, Toysmart.com filed for bankruptcy, and the Federal Trade Commission forced the company sell off customer data to the highest bidder. The firm had promised site users that it would not divulge information gleaned from tracking users' activities on the site, but a court-appointed overseer believed the customer list was a valuable asset that could be sold to help pay off the firm's creditors. In this case, the court ruled that it was more important for a bankrupt company to partially pay back some of its creditors than it was to protect the privacy of its customers.

## Identity Theft

With the rise of the Internet comes the risk of identify theft. This crime feeds on the inability of consumers to control who has access to sensitive information and how it is safeguarded. The Federal Trade Commission (FTC) reported that in 2003, about 7 million people became victims of identity theft. That breaks down to 19,178 people per day, 799 per hour, and 13.3 per minute ("U.S. Tallies," 2004).

Identity theft remains the number one concern among consumers contacting the FTC. A recent study found that 91% of respondents do not see an "end to the tunnel" and expect a heavy increase in victimization. Almost half (49%) also stated that they do not feel they know how to adequately protect themselves from this crime (Pletcher, 2003).

Approximately 85% of victims found out about the crime due to an adverse situation—denied credit or employment, notification by police or collection agencies, receipt of credit cards or bills never ordered, and so on. Only 15% found out through a positive action taken by a business group that verified a submitted application or a reported change of address.

Victims now spend an average of 600 hours recovering from this crime, often over a period of years. Based on 600 hours times the indicated victim's hourly wages, this equals nearly $16,000 in lost potential or realized income. Also, victims spend an average of $1,400 in out-of-pocket expenses. Although victims are finding out about the crime more quickly, it is taking far longer than ever before to clear their records and recover from the situation.

Even after the thief stops using the information, victims struggle with the impact of identity theft, which often includes increased insurance or credit card fees, inability to find a job, higher interest rates and battling collection agencies, and issuers who refuse to clear records despite substantiating evidence of the crime. This negative fallout may continue for more than 10 years after the crime was first discovered. The emotional impact on victims is likened to that felt by victims of more violent crime, including rape, violent assault, and repeated battering. Some victims feel dirty, defiled, ashamed and embarrassed, and undeserving of assistance. Others report a split with a significant other or spouse and of being unsupported by family members.

Identify theft creates significant costs to law enforcement agencies. The Government Auditing Office (GAO) conducted a study (GAO-02–363, issued March 2002) of the impact of the crime of identity theft on various federal agencies. The executive office for U.S. Attorneys estimates that the cost of prosecuting a white-collar crime case is $11,443. The Secret Service estimates that the average cost per financial crime investigation is $15,000. The FBI estimates that the average cost per financial crime investigation is $20,000. And the average arrest rate (according to law enforcement) is under 5% of all reported cases by victims.

A common scam of identity thieves is to set up an electronic auction site where people bid on items (Lee & Light, 2003). The person who wins is told to send his or her name and address so the merchandise can be mailed. The recipient is told to wait until the merchandise arrives and check it out before paying for it, so it sounds like a good deal from a reputable company to the recipient. But what the recipient does not know is that the thief uses the information to obtain a credit card in the recipient's name and charges the purchase on it.

## Hijacking

Another invasion of privacy is when your computer is hijacked. This can take several forms. One form is when someone accesses your hard drive and uses it as a server to send out messages under your IP address, thus hiding his or her own IP address. Another form of hijacking, which is done by advertisers, is to take over your homepage with a browser or to implant a search engine in your computer. This appears innocent enough, but this browser or search engine is designed to direct you only to certain advertised Web sites. One is SearchCoolWeb, which provides a page of all kinds of interesting topics that you can click on to play games or go shopping. Although this page looks like a service helping you in your Internet surfing, what really is taking place is that your browser has been hijacked and your Internet browsing is being controlled by the hijacker.

Even the traditionally used search engines are not what they seem. For example, Google is a highly successful Internet search engine. Many observers thought it was making its money by leasing its search technology to other search engines. But when it released its financial records in May 2004 in preparation for taking the company public, it was revealed that out of its nearly $1 billion sales in 2003, 95% came from selling advertising. Google is now regarded as the major advertising agency for the Internet, with about 19% of all Internet advertising now going through Google. The way advertising on Google works is that advertisers pay Google to have their Web address linked with key terms that people use when they do a Google search (Gaither, 2004a). Thus, when you type in a key word to activate the search engine, Google does not necessarily respond with a list of most relevant or most visited Web sites on that topic; instead, Google is likely to give you relevant sites for which advertisers have paid them the most money.

## Infecting

There are hackers who create computer viruses for the sole purpose of corrupting computer files. Unlike the people who invade your privacy using any of the methods above, these virus disseminators are not motivated by stealing information from you or by directing your attention to certain sites so they can benefit financially. Instead, these people are motivated by purely destructive goals.

A virus is a hidden element of computer code that lurks unobserved in the computer until it is activated. The most common computer virus acts as a string of code that attaches itself to a normal software program, often affixing itself to file extensions that end in .COM or .EXE. All computer programs are made up of thousands of lines of software code, the actual language that creates the program. The string of viral code hides itself among the normal code. Once infected, software programs frequently change in size as the virus adds code to the beginning or end of the program. The most common computer viruses range in size between 2,000 and 4,000 bytes of code.

Computer viruses are highly contagious. Every time a user saves an infected program to a floppy disk, the virus gets saved too. Whenever that disk is loaded onto a new computer, the virus gets loaded too. When that computer connects to a network server, the virus connects too. Because most viruses remain hidden, most users have no idea they are passing around the virus until it is too late. The viral code replicates itself and spreads quickly, infecting more and more computers as it grows.

With a single user, a virus can make dozens of perfect, identical copies of itself within minutes of infection. Once a computer is hooked up to a computer network system, that same virus can infect every other computer in an office environment in a very short period of time. Networks themselves do not necessarily become infected; instead, they may act as carriers of the virus, infecting all computers currently hooked up to the network system, as well as those that eventually log on. All computer systems can be exposed to viruses. Computer viruses can infect any form of writeable storage medium—including hard disks, floppy disks, tapes, CD-ROMs, optical media, and all forms of memory.

When a virus attack occurs, the most common setbacks to your system are that data files are lost or corrupted, program files are corrupted, floppy disks are destroyed, hard drives are reformatted, and file addresses can be lost, making it impossible to retrieve files that still exist.

Computer viruses can be extremely damaging both to businesses and individual users. A survey showed that in North American corporations with more than 400 PCs, more than 50% of companies had experienced a virus attack. The study also found that the rate of corporate PCs infected with a virus is increasing at an alarming rate, with 26% of all sites discovering an infection in a single month. In another study, more than 9% of companies interviewed said they had experienced "disastrous" data losses due to a computer virus. In 2003, computer viruses cost at least $82 billion worldwide, and this does not include the emotional distress of crashing computers and lost files (Winik, 2004). Computer viruses have been reported in well over 100 countries around the world, reaching every continent on the globe.

The number of viruses has grown dramatically in less than two decades. In 1986, the National Computer Security Association estimated that there were only 4 known computer viruses. Today, there are more than 5,000 known computer viruses, with an average of 110 new viruses discovered each month ("What Is a Computer Virus?" n.d.).

## Protecting One's Privacy

Public opinion is strongly in favor of personal privacy. However, it is difficult for regulators to establish laws that draw a clear line distinguishing what is private and what is public. Although there are a few laws in existence, it is exceedingly difficult to prosecute and punish offenders. Until regulators can catch up with the technology, the burden falls largely on us as individuals to protect ourselves.

## *Public Opinion*

Privacy has become a much more important issue to the American public in the past few decades. A Lou Harris poll found that the percentage of Americans concerned about their privacy rights grew from 34% in 1970 to 90% in 1998 (Identify Theft Center, 2002).

A lot of this concern is directed at the Internet. The Pew Internet & American Life Project (2000) reports two strong conclusions from its survey of Americans and their Internet habits. The first conclusion is that American Internet users overwhelmingly want the presumption of privacy when they go online. The second conclusion is that a great many Internet users do not know the basics of how their online activities are observed, and they do not use available tools to protect themselves.

The Pew Internet & American Life Project (2000) reported that 84% of Americans were "very concerned" or "somewhat concerned" about their personal information being accessed by people they did not want to have it. Internet privacy has emerged as a central policy concern about the Internet as more Americans go online every day and as the news media continually report on new allegations about privacy violations by Internet companies.

A majority of Internet users (54%) are against online tracking because it invades their privacy. Advocates of cookies make the case that consumers will eventually come to appreciate cookies because cookies allow sites to provide information that is important and relevant to an individual Web user. In the case of advertising and marketing, cookie advocates argue that there is a great deal of waste that everyone hates in mass marketing through the mails (junk mail) and the media. These advocates argue that the ideal world created by cookies and tracking is one where the clutter of information and advertisements is cut to a minimum, and only useful material is put in users' and consumers' hands. However, what these cookie advocates fail to understand is that many Internet users want to make their own decisions about which messages show up on their computer screens; that is, they do not want any advertisers aggressively invading their screens. Only 27% of Internet users feel that advertisers' use of cookies is helpful in tailoring information exposure to their particular needs. Almost three quarters of Internet users would prefer to make their own decisions about which messages to access (Pew Internet & American Life Project, 2000).

Internet users overwhelmingly call for strict enforcement of their privacy; 94% of Internet users want privacy violators to be disciplined. If an Internet company violated its stated privacy policy and used personal information in ways that it said it wouldn't, 11% of Internet users say the company's owners should be sent to prison, 27% say the owners should be fined, 26% say the site should be shut down, and 30% say the site should be placed on a list of fraudulent Web sites (Pew Internet & American Life Project, 2000).

## Opt-In Versus Opt-Out

One of the biggest concerns facing regulators dealing with privacy is to determine the degree to which consumers control their level of privacy. Legislation can be written either to favor consumers (opt-in) or businesses (opt-out). With opt-in, the default is privacy, and consumers have to do something to grant advertisers permission to send them a message or to record information in a cookie; that is, advertisers cannot send e-mail to consumers or record information in cookies on consumers' computers unless they first ask those consumers and are explicitly granted permission. With opt-out, the default is that businesses have the right to send any information and to create cookies until consumers tell them to stop. Businesses overwhelmingly prefer the opt-out option because they can do whatever they want until a person tells them to stop, and few people tell businesses to stop because most people are not aware of how those businesses are invading their privacy. When this is explained to people, 86% of Internet users say they prefer "opt-in" privacy policies.

Most regulations, however, are being crafted to favor businesses. For example, the policy negotiated by the Clinton administration, the FTC, and a consortium of Web advertisers gave Web sites the right to track Internet users unless the users take steps to "opt out" of being monitored. These privacy standards were regarded as being so favorable for online advertisers that shares in Doubleclick rose 13% in 1 day (Pew Internet & American Life Project, 2000). So far, this law has not been viewed as a success for consumers because fewer than 3% of consumers opt out (Stern, 2002). A primary reason why this figure is so low is that so few consumers know (a) that they have this option, (b) the consequences of not opting out, and (c) how to opt out.

To protect their privacy, a relatively small number of savvy users are devising their own "opt-in" policies and deciding that some Web sites are not worthy of getting their personal information. Also, 24% of Internet users said that they have provided a fake name or personal information to avoid giving a Web site real information, 9% of Internet users have used encryption to scramble their e-mail, and 5% of Internet users have used "anonymizing" software that hides their computer identity from Web sites they visit. But most people do not know how to protect themselves, and 56% of Internet users did not know what cookies were, much less know how to avoid them. Only 10% of Internet users have set their browsers to reject cookies (Pew Internet & American Life Project, 2000).

## Regulations

There are laws preventing the use of a person's name and address in a postal mailing list without his or her consent. "Although courts have yet to apply such statutes to list of e-mail addresses, given the rise of unsolicited e-mail advertisements, the time is ripe" (Lee & Light, 2003, p. 307). Part of the reason why such laws have such lax enforcement is that it is costly to track down violators, and when those lawbreakers are identified, they simply move out of the country and thus avoid punishment. For example, the first financial penalties to a spammer were handed down in California in October 2003. PW Marketing and its owners, Paul Willis and Claudia Griffin, were fined $2 million for sending unsolicited or misleading e-mails. The spammers have fled the country to avoid the judgment (Healey, 2003). Also, on January 1, 2004, a new law took effect outlawing many of the tricks spammers use. In response, many spammers have moved their operations outside the United States to avoid prosecution. Therefore, it appears useless for U.S. legislators to pass laws against spammers, identity thieves, and virus disseminators when those people can easily continue their practices in other countries where these actions are not illegal. The virtual geography of the Internet does not lend itself to the traditional ways of thinking about laws and enforcement.

# Piracy

Piracy is the unauthorized use of copyrighted material. Protecting the rights of creators to benefit from their work has been a serious issue ever since the earliest mass media were made possible by the printing press. The mass media are both an essential tool to help authors disseminate their work and thus receive an income and grow their reputation; at the same time, the mass media are a danger to authors by allowing pirates to make unauthorized copies of their work. Recently, with the digitization of information and with the easy access to the Internet that interlinks hundreds of millions of computers worldwide, this issue has reached a critical stage.

To make the treatment of this issue manageable in the few pages of this chapter, I will focus on piracy of musical recordings, which is at the forefront of this issue. However, piracy of print, still pictures, and video are also important facets of piracy.

Making sense of this issue requires the consideration of two factors. First, we must decide what a creative unit is; second, we need to determine what a person owns when one buys a message. Before reading any further in this chapter, work through the questions in Exercise 21.1 and Exercise 21.2.

As with privacy, the issue of piracy is about drawing lines. As you worked through the exercises, you in essence were drawing lines between what you thought were your rights as an owner of a CD and the rights of the artists who created the messages on that CD.

## Some History

Piracy has been a problem for the music industry for decades. As early as the 1950s, people could use tape recorders to pirate music by recording it off the radio, but the quality was poor. Or people could make a copy of a record or tape on a tape cassette using home-recording equipment, but to do so, they had to already have a copy of the recording and could make only one copy at a time.

In 1992, Congress passed the Audio Home Recording Act (AHRA), an amendment to the federal copyright law. Under the AHRA, all digital recording devices were required to incorporate a Serial Copy Management System (SCMS), which allowed digital recorders to make a first-generation copy of a digitally recorded work. However, the technology prevented people from making a second-generation copy to be made from the first copy, but users could still make as many first-generation copies as they wanted. The AHRA also provided for a royalty tax of up to $8 per new digital recording machine and 3% of the price of all digital audiotapes or disks. This tax is paid by the manufacturers of digital media devices and distributed to the copyright owners whose music is presumably being copied. In consideration of this tax, copyright owners agree to forever waive the right to claim copyright infringement against consumers using audio-recording devices in their homes. This is commensurate with the fair use exception to copyright law, which allows consumers to make copies of copyrighted music for noncommercial purposes. The SCMS and its royalty requirements, however, only apply to digital audio-recording devices. Because computers are not digital audio-recording devices, they were not required to comply with SCMS ("Music Piracy and the Audio Home Recording Act," 2002).

The recording industry experienced steady growth in sales throughout the 1990s, reaching a high of almost 1 billion units (CDs, cassette tapes, and records of all kinds) sold per year. But then in 2000, there was a drop in sales. The recording industry immediately concluded that this drop in sales was due to the widespread sharing of music on the Internet, which had been growing in popularity throughout the 1990s. There was some truth to this conclusion. Public opinion polls showed that this practice of using the

Internet to share music was indeed growing. In 1999, about 2% of Internet users said they shared music; 2 years later, more than 30% said they downloaded music (Moody, 2002). Also, in a *USA Weekend* poll of teenagers conducted in May 2002, 54% responded that they saw nothing wrong with downloading music off the Internet; only 10% thought it should not be done. About 48% said they burned their own CDs, but only 45% said they frequently or occasionally downloaded music from the Internet ("Tunes & 'tudes," 2000).

## How Big Is the Problem?

About 5 years ago, a debate flared up concerning how big the problem of music piracy really was. The recording industry claimed the problem was huge and growing. The industry was releasing figures such as that an estimated 3.6 billion songs were illegally downloaded each month in the United States. In 1999, the music industry estimated that one in four compact disks of new music was actually an unauthorized copy. By the end of 2001, the industry estimated that as many CDs were burned and copied as were bought ("Music Piracy and the Audio Home Recording Act," 2002). The music industry used these figures to claim that illegal file trading was responsible for reducing legitimate music sales (Newscientist.com, 2004).

The Recording Industry Association of America (RIAA), which represents the world's largest record companies, points to several studies suggesting a link between declining record sales and the growth of illegal file trading. For example, a series of surveys conducted by a Houston-based company, Voter Consumer Research, has indicated that those who download more songs illegally are less likely to buy music from legitimate retailers. "Countless well respected groups and analysts have all determined that illegal file sharing has adversely impacted the sales of CDs," says RIAA spokeswoman Amy Weiss.

People outside the recording industry claimed that recording companies were greatly exaggerating the problem. For example, Felix Oberholzer-Gee at the Harvard Business School and Koleman Strumpf at the University of North Carolina tracked millions of music files downloaded through the OpenNap file-trading network and compared them with CD sales of the same music and concluded that, "at most, file sharing can explain a tiny fraction of this decline." Oberholzer-Gee and Strumpf monitored 680 albums, chosen from a range of musical genres, downloaded over 17 weeks in the second half of 2002. They used computer programs to automatically monitor downloads and compared these data to changes in album sales over the same period to see if a link could be established. The most heavily downloaded songs showed no decrease in CD sales as a result of increasing downloads. In fact, albums that sold more than 600,000 copies during this period appeared to sell better when downloaded more heavily. For these albums, each increase of 150 downloads corresponded to another legitimate album sale. The study showed only a slight decline in sales as a result of online trading for the least popular music. "From a statistical point of view, what this means is that there is no effect between downloading and sales," say Oberholzer-Gee and Strumpf (Newscientist.com, 2004).

Although the debate over the extent of music piracy within the United States rages on, there is little debate that music piracy is a serious problem internationally. For example, the International Federation of the Phonographic Industry (IFPI, which is an organization representing the international recording industry and has a membership of 1,500 record producers and distributors in 76 countries) says that music piracy is an international problem, with worldwide sales of pressed pirate CDs of 500 million units in 2001, up from 475 million in 2000, with pirate CD-R discs estimated at around 450 million units, up from 165 million in 2000. The value of the global pirate market is estimated to have risen slightly, from U.S.$4.2 billion in 2000 to U.S.$4.3 billion in 2001. This increase was contained by falling pirate disk prices. This value figure does not equate to the actual losses suffered by record companies, which are far greater. For example, in territories with high piracy levels, such as China or Russia, it is exceptionally difficult to develop a legitimate market for recorded music.

## Antipiracy Technology

The largest record companies are developing antipiracy technology to protect their copyrighted music against the information technology industry's movement toward increasingly user-friendly digital hardware and software. A few of the "big five" major music labels are currently experimenting with antipiracy technologies designed to combat the online file sharing of their products through peer-to-peer networks, such as Napster. These copy protection programs encode electronic impediments onto commercial CDs, which prevent the disks from being played on any device that is not a simple CD player.

Sony has developed its own antipiracy technology, called "key2audio." The music label announced in January 2002 that it had produced a total of 10 million disks for 500 different albums that could not be played on personal computers by using its key2audio program, which prevents consumers from listening to CDs on any type of CD-ROM or DVD player. A second version of the software, key2audio4PC, is a bit more lenient than key2audio in that it does permit listeners to play copy-protected CDs on their personal computer. However, the disks are encrypted to limit usage to a single PC. For example, once the CD is played on the consumer's home computer, that person would not be able to play the same CD on his or her DVD player in the next room or on his or her computer at the office. Downloaded music files may be copied from the PC hard drive to a blank CD, but that CD would likewise be playable only in the specific PC on which the copy was made from an authorized download.

Another music label is licensing antipiracy technology from outside developers. BMG Entertainment began using the Cactus Data Shield antipiracy program, developed by Midbar Technology. Cactus is designed to prevent consumers from reformatting songs into MP3 files and burning copies or making them available on file-sharing systems. The software prevents listeners from playing the disks on CD-ROM drives, which means that the music will not play on the Sony Playstation 2, a number of car stereos and DVD players, or on PCs. The Cactus patent application states that the resulting playback distortion on an unauthorized copy would not only distort the sound but would also be "potentially damaging" to amplifiers and speakers. The Cactus system also disables stand-alone CD burners.

Digital rights management companies are also developing and marketing solutions for entertainment companies. Macrovision, in collaboration with TTR Technologies, developed multiple versions of an antipiracy technology called SafeAudio, a 100% software-based, audio copy protection technology for music CDs. SafeAudio Version 2 allows CDs to operate in CD players and PC-based CD-ROMs but spoils any copy made to the hard drive or a CD burner by adding background noise to the playback sound. SafeAudio Version 3 allows CDs to be played in simple CD players but not in a CD-ROM or copied onto a hard disk drive. Products such as SafeAudio are proving to be a difficult sell to record labels in the United States, which are concerned about negative consumer backlash. Perhaps in response to this concern, Macrovision recently released its SafeAuthenticate product, which permits CDs that are authenticated by the product's software to be a genuine pressing to be played from the computer's CD-ROM drive or copied onto the hard drive for playback through Microsoft's Windows Media Player.

## New Legislation

It is clear from the language of the AHRA, as well as subsequent judicial interpretations of the statute, that Congress did not anticipate 10 years ago that the SCMS would be inadequate to contain the impending home digital recording explosion that was galvanized by the Internet. Although music copyright owners are taking technological action to protect their content, the U.S. Senate is considering legislation that would require manufacturers of information technologies to implement safeguards against unauthorized copying of music. In March 2002, Senator Ernest Hollings (D-S.C.), chairman of the Senate Commerce Committee, introduced the Consumer Broadband and Digital Television Promotion Act (CBDTPA). This proposed legislation, which is heavily supported by music industry lobbies such as the Recording Industry Association of America, would require all new digital media devices to be encoded with security technology to prevent unauthorized copying of copyrighted works.

Critics of this legislation think that it goes too far. For example, members of the information technologies industry believe that the charge to make them responsible for inhibiting unauthorized copying is an impossible task because it is not technologically feasible to protect a digital work once it is in the public domain. Consumer groups such as DigitalConsumer.org feel that the bill violates individuals' rights to postpurchase flexible use of copyrighted materials. Media critics declare that as a cure, the CBDTPA would be far worse than the disease of digital content piracy. They say that making it more difficult to play a copy-protected CD on more than one digital media device would be only a speed bump for pirates who might easily circumvent antipiracy technology, but it could turn out to be a roadblock for the average music buyer.

Also, critics of the legislation point out the absurd argument used by the recording companies that they are not releasing high-quality digital content to the general public because of fears that it will be pirated. They argue that once the legislation passes, they will release that content, and the public will then benefit. Interestingly, they do not specify what this withheld content is.

Using the old antipiracy legislation, some law enforcement agencies have been going ahead with crackdowns on pirates. In April 2004, the U.S. Justice Department completed its largest investigation of the piracy of intellectual property over the Internet. This included an investigation of more than 100 people in 27 states and abroad who were involved in the theft of more than $50 million in music, movies, games, and computer software ("100 People Identified in Piracy Raid," 2004).

# Summary

Industry groups are working hard right now to shape up practices to protect their business interests. If they get their way, they will have the right to send advertising to your e-mail address, plant cookies on your hard drive, sell your e-mail unrestricted, and sell information they collect about you to other advertisers. They will also prevent you from making copies of the recordings, videos, and software you buy. Furthermore, these businesses would like to impose restrictions on your use of their messages without suffering any restrictions on their use of your information. And when these businesses offer you options to restrict their use of your information, they place the burden on you to tell them no, rather than accept the burden themselves to ask for your consent.

Legislators are considering these issues and formulating laws and regulations. If you have interests that are different from those of the businesses providing you with media messages, you need to clarify what those interests are and make them known to the legislators now before they pass laws to prevent you from doing what you think is fair and allowing businesses to do what you feel is unfair.

With these issues of privacy and piracy, it is essential that you become an informed consumer. If you remain ignorant of what is happening, you could lose your privacy, your identity, and perhaps be arrested.

# Conclusion

This book is now ending. What kind of an effect have you let it have on you?

Did you read it critically by analyzing the information and arguments? Did you compare and contrast the points made here with your existing knowledge structures? Did you evaluate my arguments and positions, agreeing with some and disagreeing with others? Did you synthesize the information you found most useful into your own perspective on media literacy and your own set of techniques to achieve that perspective? If you answered yes to these questions, then you have reacted well cognitively to the book. The key to a high-quality cognitive reaction is not whether you agree with me and accept all this information. Instead, the key is that your mind was continually active as you read the book.

Did you have some strong emotional reactions while reading the book? For example, did you get upset with some of the information or arguments? Do you feel challenged and motivated to become more media literate? If you answered yes to these questions, then you have reacted well emotionally to the book. The key to a high-quality emotional reaction is not whether you have positive feelings about me or about the book. Instead, the key is that you were able to let your emotions become engaged by hating parts of the book and loving others.

Did you take moral positions throughout the book? For example, did you develop a sense of what is right with our culture (and what is wrong) because of the media? Did you make a strong commitment to yourself to do certain things to help yourself and others? If you answered yes to these questions, then you have reacted well morally to the book. The key to a high-quality moral reaction is not whether you agree with my positions. Instead, the key is that you are able to perceive a sense of right and wrong about certain conditions and to take a stand for yourself.

Finally, were you aware of aesthetic reactions to the book? Were there times when you appreciated the way I structured a chapter or the way I illuminated an important point? Did you find certain examples useful and creative? Did you feel that certain sections could have been written better? If you were able to answer these questions, then you were sensitive to the aesthetic features of the book. I, of course, hope that your aesthetic reactions were favorable. But whether favorable or not, the more aesthetic reactions you had and the more aesthetic awareness you exercised, the better for your media literacy development.

Most important, I hope you can see that you have achieved a significant degree of media literacy. You have many useful knowledge structures and many useful skills. As you continue developing these knowledge structures and skills, remember to be aware of what you are doing and stay in control of your progress. And make it fun!

**Exercise 21.1**    Where Do You Draw the Line?

1. Let's say you buy a CD. What do you really own? How much control do you have over using that music? Read each item in the list below and consider your rights of ownership. Put a check mark next to each item you feel comfortable doing. For each item you think is wrong or illegal, do not put a check mark.

_____Listen to the CD alone in the privacy of your room

_____Listen to the CD in your room with friends

_____Take your CD to your friends' room and listen to it there

_____Play your CD in your car with all the windows down so everyone on the street can hear it

_____Make a backup copy of your CD

_____Make a copy of your CD and rearrange the songs in the order you prefer

_____Make a compilation CD with songs from several CDs you own

_____Lend a CD that you own to one of your friends so he or she can make a copy for his or her own personal use

_____Lend a CD that you own to a dozen of your friends so they can make a copy for their own personal use

_____Copy the songs on a CD you own onto your computer so you can listen to them while you are on your computer

_____Copy the songs on a CD you own onto your computer and then send an e-mail to a friend and arrange for one of those songs to play in the background as your friend reads your e-mail

_____Copy the songs on a CD you own onto your computer and then send a song to your friend to let him or her check it out

_____Copy the songs on a CD you own onto your computer and then send all those songs to your friend

_____Copy the songs on a CD you own onto your computer and then make those songs available to anyone in cyberspace to make a copy

_____Take your CD to a secondhand store and sell it to the store

_____Sell your CD to another person on e-Bay

_____Make copies of your CD and sell those copies to other people

2. Now go back over the list above, and every time you see something such as "a CD you own" or a "CD you bought," substitute it with "a CD you borrowed from the public library." Read each item in the list above and consider your rights of usage of borrowed material. Put a plus sign (+) next to each item you feel comfortable doing. For each item you think is wrong or illegal, do not put a plus sign.

3. Now compare the pattern of checked statements to the pattern of statements with plus signs. Look at the statements that have check marks but no plus signs; these are the special rights you feel you have as an owner of a CD compared to a user of someone else's CD.

**Exercise 21.2**     How Big Is a Creative Unit?

1. Now think about the size of the unit that is copyrighted. Where would you draw the line between what is protected by copyright and what is too small to be protected by copyright? Check those elements in the list below that you think should be protected by copyright.

   _____ An artist's entire body of work
   _____ An album
   _____ A song
   _____ A chorus in a song
   _____ A chord progression or a lyrical phrase
   _____ One note or word

2. Now think about how big a unit of information you would feel comfortable copying. At what point does the resulting CD stop being the work of other artists and become your artistic product? From the list below, check those products that you believe would be primarily your own creation.

   _____ Make a compilation CD of songs of one artist from several different CDs
   _____ Make a compilation CD of songs of different artists from different CDs
   _____ Make a compilation CD of songs of different artists along with recordings of your own original music
   _____ Make a compilation of CDs of songs of another artist—some performed by that artist and some performed by you
   _____ Record a song from a CD that you own as a soundtrack on a home movie that you made and will give to your parents on their anniversary
   _____ Record a song from a CD that you own as a soundtrack on a movie that you make for a grade in a film production course
   _____ Record a song from a CD that you own as a soundtrack on a movie you that make and enter into a contest to win a scholarship to college
   _____ Record a song from a CD that you own as a soundtrack on a movie that you make to show on a public-access cable TV program

3. Now that you have considered the options in #1 and #2 above, what is the key criterion that defines a creative unit?

# Appendix A

## *Profiles of the Mass Media Industries*

Appendix A presents a profile of each of the nine mass media industries illuminated in Part III of the book. Each profile begins with key indicators showing how that mass media industry has developed according to the life cycle metaphor. Notice that some of those industries have not gone through all five stages. Each profile contains information about its economic nature and indicators of concentration and then concludes with key indicators revealing the current nature of that industry.

The industries are treated in the following order, which roughly corresponds to their ages:

1. Book

2. Newspaper

3. Magazine

4. Film

5. Recording

6. Radio

7. Broadcast television

8. Cable television

9. Computers/Internet

Before we get started on these profiles, I need to clarify the distinction between a vehicle and a company. For example, *Time* magazine is one such vehicle. *Time* publishes 52 weekly issues each year, but the issues are not the same as the vehicle. Also, we need to make a distinction between the company that publishes the vehicle and the vehicle itself. Time Warner is the company that publishes *Time* magazine, but Time Warner also publishes many other magazine vehicles such as *Money, Discover,* and *Fortune.* So when we talk about magazines, we must be clear about whether we are referring to the media channel (of all magazines), a vehicle (which is a title of a single magazine), an issue (which is the set of stapled pages laying on your coffee table), or the company (which usually owns and publishes several vehicles).

Unless otherwise indicated, the information in the profiles below is from the 2004 *Statistical Abstract of the United States* and July 1996 Standard & Poor's *Index to Surveys.*

# 1. Book Industry

## Innovation Stage

- The key technological innovation for book publishing—as well as all of the print media—was the invention of moveable type by Gutenberg in the mid-1400s.

- Book publishing was already well developed when the United States was first colonized. However, until the 19th century, books were not a mass medium because they were purchased and read by only the educated and the affluent.

- During the late 1800s, some entrepreneurs recognized that the reading literacy rate was relatively high, given the effects of compulsory education. They began selling paperback books that were affordable to the masses.

## Penetration Stage

- By 1900, public schools were widespread, and reading literacy was commonplace.

- Large publishing houses were being established, so many more books were being published and marketed, thus bringing the unit price down so that books were affordable to more of the general population.

## Peak Stage

- The book publishing industry has never reached a peak; that is, it has yet to achieve dominance among the mass media.

## Adaptation Stage

- The book industry has adapted to competition from other mass media by becoming niche oriented. Many publishers sell books to only one niche, such as college-level science texts, library reference books, religious books, children's mystery novels, and so on.

- This is a healthy industry economically, and it continues to grow each year both in terms of revenues and titles produced. Annual revenues did not break the $1 billion mark until about 1960, and as recently as 1980, the revenue was only $4 billion.

- There has been a strong trend toward concentration in the bookstore segment of the industry. In 1958, companies that owned more than one bookstore (chains) accounted for only 28% of all sales, and there were no chains with more than 50 stores. Now there are chains such as Barnes & Noble and Borders, which own more than 1,000 bookstores. Chain-owned bookstores now generate more than two thirds of all the revenue in the book industry.

- Consolidation has been taking place in book publishing, although the deals are not as big as with mergers of film and television companies. For example, in the mid-1990s, The Penguin Group acquired a U.S. subsidiary of MCA for $336 million. The Penguin Group publishes primarily classics and reference-type books (Lyall, 1996). The Putnam Berkley Group is known for its successful best sellers from authors such as Tom Clancy, Dick Francis, Patricia Cornwell, and Amy Tan. The merged company accounted for about 12% of all book sales in the United States.

## Current Nature

- There are about 2,700 book publishers.

- The industry produces about 68,000 new titles and sells about 2 billion books each year. The largest segment is the adult trade book, which includes general interest fiction and nonfiction, advice, and how-to books. These are the books typically found in the bookstores in malls.
Each year, about one third of published titles are mass-market-type publications; 24% are trade books, 20% are textbooks, 10% are book clubs, and the rest are religious, professional, and specialty books.

- Most of the books are sold through retail bookstores. Most of the sales in this segment are in the very large chains such as Waldenbooks or Barnes & Noble.

- Revenue: The book industry now has an annual revenue of about $26.4 billion for consumer books, another $5.1 billion for professional books, and another $7.4 billion for educational books (Albarran, 2002).

- Expenses: There are many elements that go into the expense of book publishing. Let's take a typical example of a hardbound trade book that lists for $19.95 in a retail bookstore. When this sells, the store keeps about 48% for its own expenses and profit and sends the remaining $10.37 to the publisher. It costs the publisher about $2.00 to manufacture the physical copy of the book (composition, typesetting, jacket design, paper, ink, printing, binding, etc.). Another $3.00 is for overhead, which includes the expense of editors, office staff, marketing, and so on. The author gets about $2.00 in royalties. The remaining $3.37 is profit unless the stores return the unsold copies—a common practice—and wipes out the potential profit.

- Risk: Only one book in five is successful, meaning it makes money for the publisher after all the expenses and returns are subtracted from sales. The small number of successful books, in essence, subsidizes the industry and makes it possible for publishers to take chances on all sorts of "risky" books and new authors.

Out of the 68,000 new book titles published each year, well under 1% make it onto any best-seller list. For example, in 1997, only 88 fiction titles made the lists; 85% of these books were written by authors who had been on the list before (Gulbransen, 1998a).

Because of the high risk, publishers aggressively use the marketing concept; that is, they search for books they think the public wants instead of books they think are the best from a writing or education point of view. Publishers believe the public likes books on scandal, celebrities, cooking, self-help, and dieting; this is why there are so many books published on these topics each year.

- Bookstores are going online on the Web. Amazon.com began in July 1995 and reached $15 million in sales the next year; however, its costs were $20 million that year. In May 1997, Barnes & Noble went online to add another revenue stream to its successful "brick-and-mortar" stores.

- Now, when a publisher comes out with a new book, it is frequently offered in both paper and electronic form. Called E-books, these electronic books are handheld, battery-powered devices where the words appear on a screen rather than a paper page. Introduced in 1998, fewer than 10,000 books were sold that first year. By the following year, there were more than 1,500 fiction and nonfiction titles available (Stroh, 1999).

- Concentration: Out of the 2,700 book publishers, 1,200 do not publish as many as five books a year. The top 8 companies typically generate half the revenues (Albarran, 2002). Book publishing is a segmented field, with different sets of publishers specializing in certain submarkets. But even within these submarkets, there is a trend toward concentration. For example, in mass-market paperback publishing, the top 7 firms account for more than 80% of all sales.

As for the best-seller list, six major publishers (Random, Simon & Schuster, Penguin Putnam, Bantam Doubleday and Dell, HarperCollins, Time Warner) typically account for about 85% of the hardcover slots and 83% of the paperback slots. If you add in the titles of six other smaller houses, you account for 98% of all best sellers (Gulbransen, 1998a, 1998b).

# 2. Newspaper Industry

## Innovation Stage

- The innovation stage of newspapers dates back to before United States was formed. Some key technological developments took place in Europe beginning in the 1400s. Also, in the 1600s, entrepreneurs set up newspaper publishing businesses and home delivery distribution systems.

- In the American colonies, publishers typically started newspapers not to make money but to shape political opinion. These early newspapers were more like propaganda leaflets, and each had very small circulation. By 1776, there were already 30 weekly newspapers in the colonies, and these newspapers went into a total of 40,000 homes. These newspapers were run by political parties, which dictated their content. The parties used their own newspapers to present their version of the news.

## Penetration Stage

- By the 1830s, a big shift in the purpose of newspapers was taking place. Publishers became much more interested in making money with their newspaper businesses, and newspapers evolved into a mass medium. To increase revenues, publishers needed to build large circulations. They were no longer interested in appealing to a small, select group of political partisans. Instead, they needed to broaden their base. So publishers began hiring professional editors who could produce a product that responded to broader social needs and human interests rather than narrow political ideologies. By the 1870s, newspapers had truly become a mass medium and the only one at the time.

- Technological developments made it possible for newspapers to create a better product and to distribute that product more widely and faster. For example, newer printing presses were invented, and these newer presses made the printing of the papers faster and cheaper. The telegraph allowed reporters in locations away from the newspaper office to wire their stories to the newspaper. By 1900, improved transportation allowed distribution to a larger territory.

- Newspapers were being run in a more business-like fashion. They used economies of scale to lower their unit costs. And even though they were selling copies for a penny apiece, their profits were increasing dramatically because their volume was growing so fast.

- With the decline of political partisanship, more and more readers found a broad range of newspapers interesting and useful. Advertisers also found the medium very useful.

- Between 1880 and 1900, the number of newspaper businesses in America more than doubled from 850 to 1,967. In 1870, about 2.6 million copies were circulated daily to the 7.6 million households in America (1 out of every 3). By 1900, 93% of all households were subscribing.

## Peak Stage

- In 1919, newspapers reached a peak of penetration as the average household was receiving an average of 1.4 newspapers per day.

- The number of daily newspaper organizations was at a peak at almost 2,500 firms.

## Decline Stage

- Newspapers began to decline as the most important mass medium in the 1930s and 1940s as radio, then television, took away newspapers' functions of providing information and entertainment.

- Even more devastating was that the newer media eroded the base of advertising, especially among the national advertisers.

- The number of daily newspapers declined to about 1,750 in 1945.

## Adaptation Stage

- Since the 1950s, newspapers have redefined their role as a local medium for audiences and advertisers.

- Although the newspaper industry has experienced overall growth, most of that growth has not been in big cities; the circulation of city newspapers has remained static. Most of the growth in circulation has been in the daily and weekly newspapers of smaller communities.

## Current Nature

- There are 8,540 newspaper establishments; about 1,480 are daily newspapers, and the other 7,060 are weeklies. Also, there are an additional 1,000 online newspapers in the United States (Albarran, 2002).

- Revenue is now about $47.5 billion a year.

- Newspapers now have many major streams of revenue that include advertising, home delivery subscriptions, newsstand sales, Internet subscriptions, contract printing, licensing rights of content, distributions of inserts, graphic design services, and sales of mailing lists.

- Expenses: The biggest expense of newspapers is personnel costs, which account for about 60% of all expenditures. Although this cost goes up each year, it has been doing so at a slow rate of about 3% to 4% a year.

- Profit: The average profit margin for a newspaper company is about 17%, which is more than triple the median profit margin for companies in *Fortune* 500. Lacy and Blanchard (2003) analyzed 77 daily newspapers and found that publicly held daily newspapers produced higher profit margins than did privately held dailies. Public ownership and higher profits were associated with smaller newsroom staffs. The public dailies also had higher starting salaries.

- Chain-owned newspapers are even more profitable. The primary purpose of a chain-owned newspaper is to maximize the profits of the parent company. Therefore, chain-owned newspapers have a strong incentive to increase revenues (eliminating competition) and reduce expenses (by using economies of scale). Of course, non-chain-owned newspapers also have a similar profit motive, but chains have more economic power. They use the following: (a) first-copy expenses are amortized over larger circulations, thus resulting in a lower per unit cost (first-copy costs are fixed, and these are very large in small-circulation newspapers—that is, as high as 40% of total revenue—so the more papers sold, the lower the per unit cost); (b) reproduction costs decline as circulation goes up (additional pages do not cost as much as the first few pages); and (c) the distribution process is more efficient with a denser circulation pattern, and this works against multiple deliverers of multiple papers.

- Localism: Almost all of the 1,500 daily newspapers printed in the United States have a local orientation; that is, they circulate to readers in their home city and the immediate surrounding suburbs. Only a small number of newspapers (such as *USA Today, Wall Street Journal, Christian Science Monitor*) truly have a national circulation and national editorial focus. In this way, America is unique in newspaper localism compared to other industrialized countries of the world. In most foreign countries, newspaper circulation emanates from a few large cities and spreads out across the entire country. For example, Tokyo has 11% of Japan's population, but daily newspapers from there account for 70% of the total newspaper circulation in that country. London, with 14% of England's population, accounts for 70% of circulation. In America, New York City and Washington, D.C., combined have 7% of population but account for only 10% of the country's daily newspaper circulation. Clearly, in this country, newspaper publishing is done at the local level.

- Concentrated ownership: Although publication takes place at the local level, ownership of the newspapers is becoming more and more concentrated; that is, there are fewer people controlling more and more newspapers. The trend toward greater concentration is evidenced in two ways: reduction in competition among newspapers and an increase in ownership by chains.

- Competition among newspapers has been greatly reduced. For example, the number of cities with competing daily newspapers is decreasing. In 1900, more than 65% of all U.S. cities had competing newspapers, but now less than 1% do. Two reasons have been cited for the decline of newspaper competition. First, political parties do not support newspapers anymore as they once did, and there has been a decline in the partisanship in the U.S. press. Second, advertisers are demanding large circulations without duplicate readership. As a result, the larger newspaper in a two-newspaper town gets the advertising and continues to grow. The smaller circulation newspaper loses advertising and eventually goes out of business.

- Chains have increased in size and number. In 1909, there were only 13 chains, and they owned only 2% of all newspapers. Chains grew slowly until 1970, when the majority of newspapers were owned or controlled by small private groups—often a single family. By the 1990s, three quarters of all newspapers were chain owned (Picard, 1993).

- As for control of circulation, the eight largest newspaper chains accounted for only 10% of daily circulation in 1900, but by the 1990s, chains controlled a total of 85% of the nation's newspaper circulation. However, no single newspaper or chain dominates the nation's news dissemination. For example, the two largest chains are Gannett Co., whose 82 newspapers have a combined circulation of about 6 million, and Thomson, whose 125 newspapers have a combined circulation of about 4 million. Together, these two chains control more than 200 newspapers but less than 16% of the nation's circulation (Picard, 1993). In contrast, the three television networks have far greater control of the news flow than any combination of newspaper chains.

- With concentration of newspaper control, access by individuals becomes harder. In 1900, there was one newspaper for every 36,000 people in the United States, but now there is only one newspaper for about every 170,000 people. Access to get one's voice heard is much more difficult.

- The largest circulation newspaper is the *Wall Street Journal* at 1.75 million daily circulation, followed by *USA Today, New York Times,* and the *Los Angeles Times,* each with daily circulations of more than 1 million (Albarran, 2002).

# 3. Magazine Industry

## Innovation Stage

- The same technological innovations that made the book and newspaper industries possible were essential to the beginning of the magazine industry.

- The magazine industry began in the United States in 1741, but until 1800, no American magazine lasted more than 14 months. Advertising support was hard to find, so magazines struggled to stay in business.

- Circulations were very small, with the average circulation for a magazine being about 500 copies and large-circulation magazines selling between 2,000 and 3,000 copies.

- New magazines kept springing up, and by the time of the Civil War, there were about 700 magazines published in the United States.

## Penetration Stage

- Throughout the late 1800s, the magazine industry continued to grow because of several factors that benefited all of the print media: Literacy rates increased, household incomes grew so people had more money for discretionary spending, and people had more leisure time. Also, another factor that was especially helpful to the growth of the magazine industry was that in 1879, the U.S. Postal Service made low-cost mailing available.

- The magazine industry began a boom. By 1885, there were about 3,300 magazines, and by 1990, about 50 of those magazines had become well-known national magazines, each with a circulation of more than 100,000.

- In the 1890s, magazines cut their prices to below production costs to increase circulation. Thus, advertising revenue became essential to the survival of magazine companies.

- By the end of the 19th century, magazines became a mass medium.

## Peak Stage

- Magazines have never reached a "peak" in the sense that they became the dominant mass medium.

- Magazines, however, exhibited some peak-like characteristics in the first few decades of the 1900s. They were the only national mass medium. Unlike newspapers, which had their circulations limited to small geographical areas in and around their home cities, magazines were mailed to subscribers all across the country. Advertisers who wanted to reach a national audience flocked to magazines.

## Decline Stage

- From 1930 to 1960, the magazine industry declined primarily because of heavy competition from radio, then television, for advertising revenue.

- National magazines had the hardest time surviving not only because of the loss of advertising revenue but also because of steep rises in postal rates. In 1950, there were 40 magazines with a circulation of more than 1 million; within 25 years, all but 10 had gone out of business.

## Adaptation Stage

- To survive, magazines became more specialized. They changed from trying to construct very large audiences with content that had mass appeal and instead targeted narrow, specialized audiences. Some magazines focused on news only, some focused on young women, some focused on particular hobbies, and so forth.

- As an industry, magazines have adapted very well. Both the number of magazines and circulation are up. The number of magazines and other periodicals has increased steadily from 5,500 in 1900 to 6,900 in 1950 to more than 10,000 today. Now, more than 50 magazines have circulations of over 1 million. Monthly circulation of magazines is 350 million copies, whereas newspapers have a total circulation of 2 billion copies per month.

- There has been a generally steady growth in sales for more than 50 years. During that time, the price of subscriptions and newsstand sales have increased. Subscriptions, which average $30.50 a year, are increasing in popularity because they are more convenient and more economical for consumers than buying individual issues at the store.

## Current Nature

- There are currently 6,248 periodical establishments.

- There are about 18,000 magazine vehicles published in the United States. Only about 750 of these are commercial publications, as designated by the Audit Bureau of Circulations (ABC), which provides the official certification of magazine circulation and exposure (Albarran, 2002).

- Revenue: The magazine industry now generates about $21.5 billion in revenue per year. Sales revenue is about $10 billion per year, of which one third is newsstand sales and the remaining two thirds from subscriptions. Ad revenue is another $11.5 billion annually. Magazines attract about 7% of all ad dollars spent each year (Albarran, 2002).

- Expenses: As with newspapers, the biggest expense of a magazine is personnel, but this has not been climbing very fast. In contrast, expenses for paper and mailing have been increasing rapidly over the past few decades.

- The magazines that exist today do not really compete with each other for readers or advertisers. For example, *Boy's Life* does not compete with *Forbes,* and *Newsweek* does not compete with *Cosmopolitan.* Instead, each magazine tries to create a distinct audience base that it can rent to its own special set of advertisers. Magazines are niche oriented as they aim less at *quantity* of circulation and more for a *quality* audience. Within a niche, there are usually a small number of magazines that do compete against one another. For example, *Newsweek* competes against *Time* and *U.S. News & World Report* for essentially the same readers and same national advertisers.

- The magazine industry is subdivided into niches. The big niches are consumer magazines (such as *Reader's Digest, TV Guide*), news (*Time, Newsweek*), sports (*Sports Illustrated, Runner's World*), opinion (*National Review, New Republic*), intellectual (*Commentary, American Scholar*), men's interest (*Esquire, Gentleman's Quarterly*), women's interest (*Cosmopolitan, Better Homes and Gardens*), humor (*National Lampoon, Mad*), sex (*Playboy, Playgirl*), and business (*Forbes, Money*). Within each of these niche markets the magazine vehicles compete with one another for readers and for advertisers, but typically, a small handful of magazines account for most of the circulation and ad dollars within a niche.

  The large media conglomerates publish magazine vehicles in several of these niches. For example, Time Warner publishes *Time, Sports Illustrated,* and *Money.*

- The magazine industry is very concentrated. Of all firms that publish magazines, the top four account for 77% of all magazine revenue each year (Albarran, 2002), and the top 160 firms account for 85% of the industry's total revenues (Daly, Henry, & Ryder, 2000).

# 4. Film Industry

## Innovation Stage

- The film camera and projector were invented in the 1880s by Thomas Edison, who owned the early patents and therefore had a monopoly.

- By 1900, there were three companies marketing film equipment. These three companies also provided films and sold them outright to users as a way to encourage the sale of equipment.

- Theaters began to be an alternative to live entertainment during vaudeville shows.

# Penetration Stage

- In 1902, film exchanges were established so theaters could share films. Small producers consolidated their resources and formed studios for production and distribution. By 1905, there were more than 100 film exchanges, and the producer-wholesaler-retailer chain in the film industry became institutionalized. Five years later, there were 10,000 small theaters, each run by entrepreneurs who parlayed small investments into quick profits.

- By 1912, producers were making full-length feature films. During this time, audiences began to regard movies less as a novelty and more as a habit.

- The Hollywood star system was devised as a way to lure people to the movies by attaching identifiable names to an otherwise unknown film and by merchandising the star as an important part of the distribution process. The stars of those early films were chosen not on their acting skill but on their ability to attract audiences.

# Peak Stage

- The peak of the film industry was reached in the 1920s and lasted into the late 1940s. In 1927, an average of 60 million people attended motion pictures *every week.* By 1929, this figure was more than 110 million people.

- Sound movies were introduced in 1927, and color was introduced in the late 1930s.

- The number of commercial films released to theaters grew to a peak of 497 films in 1941.

- The number of theaters in the 1940s was about 20,000. The number of movie seats, including car spaces at drive-ins, reached a peak of 11.1 million in 1935.

# Decline Stage

- Starting in the late 1940s, the industry went into a decline because of competition from television. The number of commercial films released to theaters decreased steadily from a peak in 1941 to a low of 203 films released in 1963. Costs skyrocketed. Massive advertising and marketing campaigns were necessary to build audience interest for each picture.

- The federal government regarded some of the very large film companies as monopolies and forced them to sell parts of their operations. For example, it became illegal for a single film company to produce, distribute, and exhibit films. So the large film studios sold off their theaters. After divestiture, film production companies lost some of their incentive because they no longer owned their own theaters. Production of films dropped.

## Adaptation Stage

- Film studios adapted first by reducing their workforces and selling off their property.

- In 1965, film studios began making films primarily for television showing and have experienced steady growth since then.

- Not until 1970 did the production-distribution sector turn around financially. For example, the exhibition sector adapted by creating multiscreen theater complexes.

- Production costs skyrocketed through the 1980s but stabilized by the mid-1990s at about $50 million per Hollywood picture; at the same time, box office receipts went from about $1.2 billion in 1980 to $7.5 billion in 1999 (Albarran, 2002).

## Current Nature

- The motion picture industry is now considered the motion picture and video industry because so much of its production is done for television, and much of its distribution is on video.

- The film industry is divided into three distinct sectors: production, distribution, and exhibition. It has 19,532 establishments as follows: production, 10,595; distribution, 537; and exhibition, 5,353. The central sector of the film industry is distribution, which is controlled by the Hollywood studios.
The exhibition sector is composed of the theaters, with their total of about 26,000 screens (DeFleur & Dennis, 1996).

- Revenue: Annual revenues are now about $57.2 billion. The studios have several major revenue streams: domestic movie rentals to theaters, foreign rentals, sales of videos, and the licensing of films to television outlets.
This year, theaters will sell about 1 to 1.3 billion tickets for total revenues of about $5 billion. The revenues increase from year to year but not due to more people attending the movies; instead, the increases come from higher ticket prices. About 70% of this revenue is sent to the film distributor. Movie theaters generate revenues of about $7.8 billion through their two revenue streams: (a) the portion of the ticket sales they get to keep and (b) high-margin concessions, such as popcorn, soda, and candy, which account for about 30% of their revenue.
The United States is the world's largest film market and, for more than 50 years, has been the world's largest exporter of filmed entertainment to other countries.
Home video revenues were projected to be $26 billion by 2004; international distribution to the world's 6 million people is very profitable, but loss of revenues due to piracy is estimated to be $2 billion annually (Albarran, 2002).

A new and growing revenue stream for Hollywood studios is selling product placements in their films. Commercial advertisers now spend about $360 million annually to get their products used in Hollywood movies (James, 2003b).

Another revenue stream is sponsorship of movie premiers. For example, Coors is now the sponsor of all Miramax Films premieres. The $300 million deal includes Coors products in 15 films during a 3-year period, along with placing the Coors logo on red carpets at openings and serving beer at Miramax parties ("Coors Scores Big," 2002).

Perhaps the newest revenue stream is providing movie rentals from the Internet. Five major Hollywood studios joined to provide a service called Movielink, which, in November 2002, allowed consumers to download movies and play them for 30 days. This would compete directly with Blockbuster and other movie rental services (Healey, 2004).

- Expenses for film production are at an all-time high. By the winter of 2004, the figure had climbed to about $103 million to produce and market a Hollywood film, on average. This is up from $39 million in 1990 (Munoz, 2004).

The most dramatic increase in the cost of making films can be traced to the rising fees of stars—even lesser known stars. In 1929, the highest paid silent film star was John Gilbert, who made $520,000 a year or about $8 million in 1997 dollars. At his peak, Clark Gable was making $208,000 the year he made *Gone With the Wind* and *Mutiny on the Bounty*. Jean Harlowe made $78,000 at her peak. When Garbo was the highest paid actress in the 1930s, she made $250,000 a picture, and in the 1940s, Barbara Stanwyck was the highest paid at $225,000 a picture (LaSalle, 1996).

The current box office mega-stars are Harrison Ford, Jim Carrey, Tom Cruise, Mel Gibson, and Sylvester Stallone, who each get about $20 million per film. Second-tier people make about half that figure; for example, Demi Moore makes $12.5 million per film, and Kurt Russell makes $10 million. Third-tier actors such as Charlie Sheen get $5 million. Unknown actors can quickly increase their fees if their early movies are successful. For example, Sandra Bullock's fee climbed from $600,000 for *Speed* to $1.2 million for *While You Were Sleeping* and now gets more than $10 million per film. Also, known actors can make a quick comeback with a successful film or two. John Travolta was down to $150,000 for *Pulp Fiction,* then bounced up to $10 million.

Big-name directors also command high fees (usually about $3 million) but not as high as big-name actors.

Scale salary for the members of the Screen Actors Guild (SAG) is $522 *a day,* which is much better than the U.S. average for salaried workers at $500 *per week* (Weinraub, 1995). However, a very small percentage of the 95,000 members of SAG work during any given day.

Hollywood studios spend a total of about $100 million annually to test their movies and to run promotional campaigns (Dutka, 2003).

Oscar awards are not always a purely aesthetic decision. There is a great deal of campaigning going on to woo the Academy's voters; it is a popularity contest, and some studios have been known to spend as much as $20 million on just one movie (Horn, 2003). That money is regarded as an investment. Films that win Academy Awards get people's attention, and people are more likely to go see them, thus increasing the studio's revenue for that film.

With costs of films rising, studios have been appointing heads who are more adept at business than art. In the early 1990s, executives and stars were showered with perks, and no expense was spared to make a film. Those days are gone as studios try to manage expenses more frugally (Eller & Bates, 1999).

- Risk: The production sector is the most risky for several reasons:

First, a Hollywood feature film takes about 18 to 24 months between the inception of the idea and the actual theatrical release. In television, it is 3 months. Therefore, there is a danger that a film might miss the changing tastes of audiences.

Second, the cost of making a feature film is very high, and it continues to escalate. The average cost of films, including their marketing, has doubled in the past 5 years. The average film now costs $50 million to make and another $50 million to market. This means that a film must gross more than $100 million at the box office to begin making money for the studio. However, the average movie makes only about $33 million.

- Concentration: Each of film industry's sectors (producers, distributors, and exhibitors) is very concentrated. Although there are many small independent producers, distributors, and exhibitors, power is concentrated in the hands of a few huge conglomerates that have diversified holdings beyond the film industry.

The film industry is dominated by seven major film studios. These seven account for 75% of all distribution.

Typically, the top 10 films each year account for one third to one half of the industry's total annual receipts. About one third of national admissions comes from nine major metropolitan areas. The 17 weeks of summer, Christmas, and Easter provide 40% to 50% of theater receipts.

The four largest film exhibition companies account for about 20% of all receipts among the nation's 26,000 movie screens. The largest exhibition chain, Carmike Cinema, controls 2,401 of these screens.

- Now with deregulation and a more complex business environment, distributors are getting back into exhibition. For example, MCA, Inc., which owns Universal Films, also owns 40% of Cineplex Odeon, a large chain of theaters. Viacom, which owns Paramount Pictures, also owns Cinamerica. In total, major movie studios now have ownership stakes in about 2,300 screens nationwide (Standard & Poor's, 1996, L19).

- The film industry has always struggled to balance art and commerce, but recently, the trend is much more toward business. For example, recent appointments of studio heads show that businesspeople rather than people with creative credentials are being selected. For example, Warner Brothers appointed Barry Meyer, a lawyer, as chairman; Universal Pictures appointed Brian Mulligan, a CPA, as cochairman; and MGM appointed Chris McGurk, who had been a senior financial analyst at PepsiCo (Eller & Bates, 1999).

# 5. The Recording Industry

## Innovation Stage

- Thomas Edison invented the original technology for recordings and playback of sound in the 1880s.

## Penetration Stage

- Technological advances have kept the industry growing and viable by continually improving the quality of the recordings and making playback more convenient.

In 1925, Joseph Maxwell invented the jukebox, which allowed recordings to compete with radio music.

In 1947, the long-playing record was marketed.

Then, in the early 1950s, the sound quality of recordings was dramatically improved with high fidelity. In 1960, 34 million units were sold, and this climbed to almost 59 million in 1970.

Records were replaced by tapes (first eight tracks, then cassettes), then with CDs (compact disks). Advances in recording techniques (digital) and playback (boom boxes, car stereos, Walkmans, MP3 players, etc.) keep people buying new equipment. And the fast turnover in music styles and recording artists keeps people buying new recordings.

## Peak Stage

- Like the book and magazine industries, the recording industry never became a dominant mass medium.

## Current Nature

- The recording industry is still growing and competing well with the other mass media. There are now about 1,300 recording and tape production companies, 125 record-processing plants, and 250 tape-duplicating plants. Each year, the industry ships about 500 million units—CDs and tapes.

- Revenue from prerecorded music sales climbed until about 1998, then flattened out at about 1.1 billion units sold for a total revenue of about $14.4 billion (Albarran, 2002).

A recording that sells 10 million copies is a huge success; however, there are only one or two recordings per year that reach this milestone.

Retailers who can't sell all the tapes and CDs return them to the recording company. The returns are then offered to club members at deep discounts. As a group, the clubs account for about 11% of all sales.

- Expenses: In the recording industry, the cost of manufacturing CDs is coming down, whereas the cost of signing artists is going up. In the early 1980s, it cost $3 to $4 to manufacture one CD, but now the cost has been reduced to less than 75 cents, including its jewel box container. The big costs are for the artists and for promotion. It now costs about $500,000 to sign a name band.

When the retail price of a CD is about $16.98, the cost to the manufacturer is about $7.54, which is itemized as follows: recording expense, $0.65; manufacturing expense, $1.25; packaging, $1.30; advertising and promotion, $2.00; artists' royalty, $1.60; freight, $0.09; and payment to musicians' trust fund, $0.65. This leaves the manufacturer with a profit of $2.94. The distributor then has expenses and a profit of $1.50, and the retailer's expenses and profit are about $5.00 (Dominick, 1999).

Producers must sell at least 300,000 to 500,000 copies of a CD before covering their costs. About 80% of all recordings lose money.

- Concentration: The record and tape industry is very concentrated, with its powerful distributors on one end and the chains of retail music stores on the other end. Distribution is dominated by six major companies: Columbia, Warner Brothers, Capital, MCA, Elektra, and Epic. These six control 99% of recording sales each year. Retailing of music is dominated by the major chains. With more than 800 outlets, Musicland StoressCorp is the largest (Albarran, 2002).

There are also thousands of independent record producers. These producers find talent, rent a recording studio to produce a recording, and get copies manufactured. Then they persuade one of the major six recording companies to distribute and market the recording. This is a high-risk endeavor because independent producers account for a very small percentage of all hit recordings.

The United States dominates the world market with a 38% world share of recording sales (Albarran, 2002).

- Record companies and groups rely on radio stations to play their songs. Between the recording companies and the radio stations are brokers called independent record promoters or "indies." Recording companies pay hundreds of millions of dollars each year to these indies, who try to get their recording companies whose recordings they represent airtime. Indies align themselves with certain radio stations and promise to provide promotional money. It's not payola strictly speaking, but it is close, and it's perfectly legal. Recording companies focus on the top 1,000 radio stations out of the 10,000 that broadcast in this country. These are the stations in the largest markets and have the largest audiences; therefore, these stations are the ones that recording companies rely on to create hits and sell their recordings. Each of those stations adds about three new recordings to its playlist each week. Indies get paid when a station adds a recording company's record to its playlist. Indies make about $3 million per week (Boehlert, 2001).

# 6. Radio

## Innovation Stage

- Radio broadcasting began in 1920, when it combined a new technology with old content forms from vaudeville and the dramatic stage.

- In 1921, there were only five AM radio stations, and only about 1% of all the households in the United States had a receiver.

## Penetration Stage

- Almost overnight, hundreds of radio stations sprang up. By 1923, there were more than 500 stations; almost half were owned by manufacturers of radio receivers who initiated the stations as a way of stimulating sales of receivers to the general public. Then, other kinds of organizations started radio stations.

- Radio had evolved from a novelty into a business as it developed the concepts of station, sponsorship through commercial advertising, and network.

- When radio began broadcasting, it received its income through the sale of home receivers. This continued to be a source of revenue to radio stations until the mid-1930s. Throughout the 1920s, stations realized that the sale of receivers would not bring in enough revenue to support the growing industry, so stations began selling advertising.

Advertising was first introduced in 1922 as a way of supporting an increasingly expensive industry. Initially, advertising was of an institutional nature, with price not being mentioned and the hard sell being avoided. More obtrusive types of advertising were not fully accepted until the late 1920s, when advertising moved toward dominance. In 1927, 20% of radio network time was sponsored, and by 1940, more than half was.

- In the 1920s, the federal government favored localism when it awarded radio licenses to local owners. The local stations were mandated to serve the needs of the communities in which they were going to broadcast. But almost from the beginning, radio broadcasters began moving away from their mandate and instead made decisions that have primarily helped their businesses to function more profitably. They have done this mostly through network affiliation and group ownership.

- Instead of generating local programming, most broadcasters have chosen to affiliate with one of the large commercial networks. These affiliates get their programming from these networks, and this programming is national in content. Network affiliation began in 1927, when 6% of available radio stations became affiliated with one of the four radio networks: ABC, CBS, MBS, and NBC. The peak period of affiliation was reached in 1947, when 97% of the country's 1,062 radio stations were affiliated with one of the four national radio networks.

## Peak Stage

- Radio reached its peak in the 1930s and 1940s. By 1936, there was an average of one receiver per household, and in 10 years, this had doubled.

- People were spending more time with radio than any other medium.

- Radio had a national orientation for both entertainment and advertising. The radio networks played a crucial role in creating and maintaining this national orientation.

## Decline Stage

- Revenues increased each year until television began taking away advertisers in the late 1940s and early 1950s. Radio hit bottom in 1955, when revenues dropped to $554 million with only 2,669 stations broadcasting.

- Radio ceased being a general national medium around 1950, when national advertisers began shifting their business to television.

## Adaptation Stage

- To survive, radio replaced its full-service, mass-oriented, family-type general entertainment format with specialized music formats designed to appeal to unique target audiences.

- Radio stations replaced their national advertising revenue with local ad revenue. Now, 80% of a station's revenue comes from local advertising. Thus, radio stations compete primarily in local markets with newspapers for advertisers.

- AM radio had a rough time in the 1970s and 1980s, when it lost a lot of its audience. But it has adapted by airing a host of syndicated talk shows beginning in the 1990s

(Rush Limbaugh, Dr. Laura Schlesinger, Don Imus, G. Gordon Liddy, etc.). FM continues to hold its audience with a variety of music formats targeted to specific audiences.

• Also, to survive the competition with television, radio became more mobile. With car radios and portable radios, people could listen to music and news anywhere—especially where they could not take a television set. Between 1950 and 1970, radio set production almost doubled, whereas the U.S. population only increased by one third.

• By the early 1960s, more than 4,000 stations were broadcasting, and revenues were up to $700 million per year. By 1980, total revenues had climbed to $3.2 billion (U.S. Bureau of the Census, 2000).

## Current Nature

• Despite the dominance of television for the past five decades, the radio industry has adapted well and is very successful. The number of radio stations has grown dramatically from about 2,000 stations in 1948 to more than 12,000 radio stations today.

• It now generates annual revenues of about $14 billion.

• Concentration: Because of the profitability of well-run radio stations and because of the limited number of stations available, large companies want to buy radio stations.

There has been a steady increase in group ownership of radio stations. In 1929, only about 3% of the country's 600 existing radio stations were group owned. By the late 1960s, the figure had climbed to about one third of all stations.

The Telecommunications Act of 1996 significantly relaxed rules on radio ownership, touching off a buying spree so that now huge conglomerates own hundreds of stations (4 companies own more than 100 stations each, and Clear Channel owns more than 1,000 stations).

In 2000 alone, 133 AM radio stations were sold for an average station price of about $3 million, up from about $500,000 in 1995; in the same year, 192 FM stations were sold at an average station price of $8.6 million, up from $2.2 million in 1995 (Albarran, 2002).

Radio is highly concentrated and is getting more so as Congress deregulates the industry in terms of the restrictions on the number of stations a single business can own. In 2004, Clear Channel Communications owned 39 TV and 1,238 radio stations.

• Now, radio stations are not likely to affiliate with national networks, or if they do affiliate, they usually only get news and features from the network. However, this does not mean that radio stations now exhibit a wide variety of programming that reflects the local needs of their communities. Instead, radio stations are likely to affiliate with a certain type of programming such as top 40, golden oldies, album-oriented rock, country and western, all news/talk, and so on. For example, most radio markets have a top 40 station, and these stations sound the same all over the country, regardless of the locale in which they broadcast. They all play the same songs on the same rotation, play the same lead-in and lead-out of the news, cover the same type of news stories with the same kind of formulas, and have the same kind of contests and promotions.

- Radio has adapted well and is thriving. It is now a mature industry with a solid future.

- The greatest competition to broadcast radio is now DARS (Digital Audio Radio Services), which began bouncing signals off satellites in 2001. These are positioned as commercial-free stations that provide multiple formats to subscribers.

# 7. Broadcast Television

## Innovation Stage

- By the 1930s, the technology had been developed to make the transmission and reception of television signals possible. The first television stations went on the air in 1941. These were commercial stations on the VHF (Very High Frequency) band.

- The first receivers were marketed in the New York City area, where the first broadcast signals were available. As stations began broadcasting in other metropolitan areas of the country, receivers were marketed in those additional areas.

- By 1948, almost 3% of all households already owned a TV receiver.

- Television broadcasting has followed the same pattern of development as radio.

- Localism: The Federal Communications Commission (FCC) attempted to reaffirm its perspective of localism as its guiding principle on licensing when it awarded television broadcasting licenses in the 1940s and 1950s. This decision required the establishment of hundreds of local stations, and the FCC had to find new spectrum space to provide these stations with their own broadcasting frequencies. As a result, the UHF band (Channels 14 through 83) was set aside for television use in addition to the already used VHF band (Channels 2 through 13).

- Commercial broadcast stations were licensed to provide service to local communities. But over the years, the FCC has done very little to ensure that the stations do, in fact, provide responsible service to their communities. Television stations have been permitted to affiliate with national networks and to buy syndicated services, both of which feature national programming.

- From the beginning, local stations affiliated with national television networks. In 1954, network affiliates were already getting 50% of their total programming from networks. Within two decades, local stations were producing only about 10% of their own programming. There are strong economic incentives for networking. Affiliates are able to share the production costs as well as the risks of a program. If something is to be produced locally, it must be inexpensive and very popular compared to the alternative program from the network. Therefore, the affiliates air most of the network programming, which is aimed at a national, not local, audience.

## Penetration Stage

- By 1950, there were 107 television stations; all of these early stations were on the VHF (Channels 2 through 13) band, and by 1953, the first UHF (Channels 14 through 83) stations went on the air. The number of stations grew to more than 500 by 1960.

- By 1953, 50% penetration was reached; that is, half of all the households in the country had a television set that could receive a signal. Television was catching on, even though few homes had much of a choice in viewing alternatives. Only one third of television households could receive as many as four channels.

## Peak Stage

- By the early 1950s, television was reaching a peak. It quickly became *the* entertainment medium, thus reducing movie attendances and radio listenership. Over time, it also became a primary source of information, thus reducing readership of newspapers and magazines. The public accepted this medium so quickly because television was seen as fulfilling the audience needs for entertainment as well as information better than any other medium.

- Advertisers, especially national advertisers, realized this shifting media preference among audiences, and they too shifted their support to television. This resulted in severe reductions in national advertising support for magazines, newspapers, and radio.

- By 1960, the average household owned at least one set; it could receive about seven channels. Television sets were turned on more than 5 hours per day in the average household. By 1980, 99.5% of all households had at least one television set, more than 90% had color sets, and over 50% had two or more sets. These household ownership rates are higher for television sets than for telephones or indoor plumbing.

- Revenue for broadcast television came primarily through one stream: advertising. So television stations and networks had to attract large audiences if they wanted a large amount of revenue. A single rating point over the course of a television series season could account for as much as $90 million.

- To maintain its peak, television had to generate the most revenue and attract the largest general audience, especially in prime time, which was from 7 to 11 P.M. each night. Unless a prime-time program could generate an audience of at least 20 million viewers every week, it was canceled. To reach the widest audience possible, programmers have adopted a policy of LOP (least objectionable programming). They need to avoid the risk of offending anyone, which would result in loss of audience or threat of governmental intervention. To determine what is least objectionable, television relied on proven formulas. This is why programming became less diversified and became more limited. When a particular program becomes very popular, programmers will try to develop similar shows in an effort to share the popularity. Because a popular show generates a great deal more revenue than an unpopular one, programmers are unwilling to take a chance on new types of shows for fear that they would be held responsible for losing money for the station or the network.

- Television networks do not produce much of their own programming; instead, they license broadcast rights from the producers. The fee to broadcast a program is not large enough to cover the producer's costs. These deficits are usually between $50,000 to $300,000 per episode. Producers hope that the series will run long enough so that they can make about 100 episodes and then sell it through syndication. A successful show like the *Cosby Show* was able to get $4 million per episode in licensing fees to television stations (Standard & Poor's, 1996, L30).

- Concentration: Concentration in station ownership was initially limited by the FCC regulations, which restricted ownership to 7 television stations, but this limit was raised to 12 stations in the 1980s and now has been raised even more. By 1995, 75% of all TV stations in the top 100 markets were licensed to multiple owners. About one quarter of these were owned by publishers of newspapers, but it is rare for a newspaper and TV station in the same market to be owned by the same company. In total, there are 210 groups that own more than 1 TV station. Twelve of these groups own 10 or more stations each (Howard, 1995).

- In the 1990s, broadcast television was in the latter days of its peak. It still had a higher reach than any other medium: TV was 88%; radio, 71%; newspapers, 56%; and magazines, 34%. There were about 1,600 broadcast television stations, and they generated revenue of more than $21 billion each year.

## Decline

- Broadcast television is now in decline.

- The networks and stations are losing viewership. Until the late 1970s, the three big television networks commanded a combined share of 95—that is, 95% of the television viewing audience at any given time was tuned into one of the three broadcast networks. By 1993, the combined share of the then four major networks (ABC, CBS, NBC, and Fox) dropped to 72 and continued to drop until in 2003, it dipped below 50. Viewers are going primarily to cable and satellite (Albarran, 2002). Also, people are spending more time watching videotapes and DVDs.

- The survival of a program depends on reaching a large audience. A show does not usually survive unless it gets at least a 10 rating.

The kind of audience is also important to a show's survival. The demographic group of women ages 18 to 49 is especially important to advertisers because they buy the most of the commonly advertised products.

- Network costs for proven shows have been escalating dramatically. When *Seinfeld* retired, NBC feared losing *ER,* so it agreed to pay $13 million per episode for *ER,* up from $2 million an episode previously (Bauder, 1998). Therefore, the producers of *ER* increased their season's income (22 episodes) from $44 million to $286 million.

## Current Nature

- There are 1,937 broadcast television stations.

- Revenue: Broadcast television generates revenues of $33.5 billion a year.

In 2003, commercial advertisers were spending about $17 billion per year on national television advertising; product placement is another form of advertising that has the advantage of occurring during the program rather than during program interruptions (James, 2003b).

Because of the expense and the risk, there are fewer independent television production studios. As of the fall of 2003, there was only one—Carsey-Werner-Mandabach, which had deep pockets from successes with *The Cosby Show* and *Roseanne.*

Up until 1995, broadcasters were prevented from owning their own shows; instead, they had to buy the rights from producers. Since 1995, they have been developing and producing their own programs. Typically, a 30-minute sitcom costs $1 million an episode to produce, and an hourlong drama costs $2.2 million per episode. In the fall of 2003, 77% of all prime-time shows were owned by the six major television networks (James, 2003a).

- The advertising on commercial television is concentrated in the hands of a few very large advertisers who can afford to buy great amounts of time each year. For example, 20 companies account for more than half of all advertising on broadcast television.

# 8. Cable Television

## Innovation Stage

- Cable television began in the 1940s as a means of delivering television signals to areas unable to receive broadcast signals because of distance or interference.

- Until the 1950s, cable systems were quite small; each had a few hundred homes as subscribers and carried only three to four broadcast signals from the closest stations. They were generally confined to mountainous areas, where people living in valleys had little or no broadcast TV reception.

- The ownership of a cable system was typically a small local company often in some related primary line of business, such as selling TV receivers. They were marginally successful as businesses.

- By 1952, there were only 70 systems, and they served a combined total of 14,000 subscribers, which represented less than 0.1% of all television households at the time.

- Growth was slow. Not until late 1950s was 1% of television households reached by cable.

## Penetration Stage

- By 1985, there were 6,600 systems serving a total of 32 million subscribers, which represented 37.7% of all television households. The 50% penetration mark was reached in early 1988.

- Cable systems are treated as natural monopolies—like utilities such as electricity and water companies. They are franchised on the local level and must therefore meet the requirements that the local community writes into the contract, such as time requirements for wiring the community, control of rates, and profit margins. Entry is controlled by economic cost, which requires capital-intensive construction and franchise requirements. However, once entry is achieved, the system typically has sole rights to the market for 10 to 15 years, and during that time, it is a monopoly.

- By 1960, there were 640 systems with a total of 650,000 subscribers, which was 1.4% of all households for an average of 1,016 subscribers per system.

- By the mid-1960s, cable began expanding into areas that already received clear broadcasting signals without help, such as the urban areas of Los Angeles and New York City.
Also, cable systems began adding channels to make their service more attractive to potential subscribers. In 1970, 3% of the systems offered more than 12 channels, and by 1976, 26% of the systems did. By the late 1960s, some cable systems were even originating programming on their own.

- Concentration: The top four firms in 1965 accounted for only about 20% of all cable subscribers.

- In the early years of cable, broadcasters welcomed cable systems as a means of extending their broadcast viewership into areas their signal could not reach.
Cable systems then began using microwave relays to bring in more distant signals, such as broadcast stations from far-away markets and also signals from some superstations such

as WTBS in Atlanta and WGN from Chicago. These new channels were in direct competition with local broadcasters, and the local broadcasters began resenting cable systems. Broadcasters began complaining that cable was receiving payment from subscribers but not giving any money to broadcasters who originated and paid for the production of the programs. Cable systems were no longer viewed by broadcasters as an expander of audiences but as direct competition.

In 1962, the FCC began to regulate the selection of programming on cable systems. The FCC decided to allow cable systems to continue to use microwave relays and bring in distant signals. But if a cable system did this, it would also have to carry all the local signals; that is, it could not ignore a local broadcast affiliate and instead bring in a station in another market in its place. During the next decade, many other regulations were added until 1972, when a period of deregulation began.

## Peak Stage

- It looks like cable television may be entering the peak stage. By 1992, cable had surpassed broadcast TV for the first time, with total revenues of more than $21 billion from a combination of subscriber fees and advertising. Subscription revenues are now about $25 billion per year, and ad revenues bring in another $4 billion.

- The number of multiple system operators (MSOs) is growing, and some of the larger ones rival the commercial television networks in terms of the size of the audience controlled through programming. With about 130,000 employees, cable now supports more people than broadcast.

- The cable industry is taking steps to secure its position as the peak mass medium by heading off future challenges by computers. The cable TV industry has linked some computer technology with its existing services to offer what is called Smart TV. Smart TV is a collection of three types of services. First, there is Interactive TV, which allows viewers to interact with the shows they are watching. Second, there is Internet TV, which lets viewers use their sets to access the Internet. Third, there is Personalized TV, which acts like a VCR.

## Current Nature

- It is now referred to as the cable and satellite TV industry; this distinguishes it from broadcast TV.

- It has 6,692 establishments, which includes 887 cable networks (which are primarily programming companies) and 5,805 establishments (which are primarily local cable operations).

- Revenue: The two primary streams of revenue for cable television are subscriptions and advertising. Most of cable's revenue comes from subscriptions. But cable is now competing with broadcast for advertising dollars and is being very successful. Cable TV advertising revenue climbed from $58 million in 1980 to $11.2 billion in 1999 (Albarran, 2002).

- Expenses: From 1998 to 2003, cable television expenses increased 40%. This large increase was traced to a combination of escalating programming costs and the industry's investments in new technology. For example, ESPN raised it charges to cable operators by 20% in each of the previous 5 years (Hofmeister, 2003).

- In 2000, there were 22 cable systems sold for an average price of $55 million per system or a cost of about $6,259 per subscriber (Albarran, 2002).

- There are no ownership limits on MSO size. In the past 30 years, the major MSOs have continued to consolidate so as to build efficient clusters. The top four MSOs (TCI, Time Warner, Continental Cablevision, and Comcast) now have a combined share of 50% of all cable subscribers (up from a 38% share just since 1993), and the top eight MSOs now have a combined 64% share. The MSOs will continue to grow by buying up smaller cable systems or by trying to put some out of business in those rare markets in which there is competition.

# 9. Computers/Internet

## Innovation

- The key innovations that are responsible for the computer becoming a mass medium are the affordable personal computer, the digitization of information, easy-to-use software, and the Internet.

- The computer as we know it was invented in the 1940s. ENIAC (Electronic Numerical Integrator and Calculator) weighed 30 tons and was several hundreds of times less powerful than the typical desktop computer of today. The first computers were very large, slow, and expensive. They were also energy hogs. Only the government and large businesses could afford to buy and use one until the 1980s, when relatively low-cost desktop personal computers began to be marketed.

- Another important innovation was the digitization of information; that is, all bits of information were reduced to a binary code. This digitization allowed for fast computations, and it also led to seamless sharing of information of all forms (data, words, sound, pictures, video, etc.) across all media.

- The Internet is a network of computer networks designed to move information around among users. It has no centralized controlling body or mechanism. It was originally set up by the Pentagon in 1969 in such a decentralized structure so as to make it resistant to breakdown by attack. A bit of information sent across the country has many alternative paths it can take, so if one path is blocked (or down), the information can take one of the other many alternatives and arrive just as quickly. The Pentagon originated the system by linking up government computers with those at universities across the country. Since that time, many other networks from all over the world have attached themselves to the Internet. Since 1975, its cost has been supported by the National Science Foundation, but now that responsibility is being turned over to businesses that want to use the Internet to advertise their products and services. Anyone with a PC, a modem, and some accessing software can get onto the Internet. Once on the Internet, people can cruise around the different parts, send e-mail to specific people, post messages on bulletin boards, enter chat rooms where interactive conversations take place on a particular topic, play games, and download information, images, or software that others have made available. These services have become very popular and are attracting new audience members constantly.

- The computer is a fundamentally different type of medium from everything that came before. All media up to this point were channels to deliver uniform, intact messages from senders. Now, with a computer, each of us can customize messages by cutting and pasting from a wide range of sources and media, then send them out for display to a particular friend, e-mail them to a great number of people simultaneously, or simply make them available on the World Wide Web, where millions of people can come and visit your messages and even download them to their own computers, where they can undertake further manipulation.

## Penetration

- Computers are now in the latter days of the penetration stage and entering into the peak. This industry has been growing rapidly at 30% per year.

- By the mid-1990s:

  There were 40 million personal computers in homes, and half of all home computers had a CD player (Maney, 1995).

  Every minute, 40 novices were logging on to the Internet for the first time.

  Every year, the number of users was doubling and had climbed to 40 million users worldwide by the mid-1990s.

  About 26% of adults in the United States (or 51 million people) had access to the Internet (Bimber, 1996).

  A new corporate or academic network was being added every 10 minutes. There were already 100,000 networks linked (Simons, 1996).

More than 97% of U.S. schools had computers—one for every 11 students, which is up from one computer for every 63 students just 10 years earlier (Intelligence Infocorp, 1996).

The World Wide Web became a popular part of the Internet. Any user can create his or her own "Web page," which is usually a billboard with graphics. Many businesses created Web pages to display their services.

The Internet became a really commercial medium. In 1995, only about $50 million was spent for online advertising in the United States out of a total of $120 billion spent on all advertising across all media. In 2004, it was projected to be $24 billion. Also, in the United States, e-commerce was about $500 billion in 2000 and was projected to be seven times that by 2004 (Albarran, 2002). This includes business to business (B2B), business to consumers (B2C), and consumer to consumer (C2C).

- This new industry was taking people and money away from other media.

A 1998 survey reports that only 38% of young people had read the newspaper the day before, whereas 69% of seniors had. Those younger than age 30 were the heaviest users of Internet news sources (Pew Research Center, 1998).

Newspapers had been losing readership, so they have been adapting to the Internet. An early adapter was the *San Jose Mercury News,* which began providing news summaries on America Online in 1994. It then created its own Web site and provided the full-text copy of their editions there, first free then for a fee (Dizard, 2000).

Satisfaction with TV was declining among children. In 1970, 38% of sixth graders said they learned a lot most of the time when they watched TV; by 1999, the figure had dropped to 29%. Furthermore, when asked which one medium they would prefer to have if they could have only one, only 13% of children said TV, whereas 33% picked computers (Rideout et al., 1999).

Some bookstores created a strong presence on the Internet to capture a slice of the $3 billion annual market in college textbooks. Some sites advertised discounts of up to 40%. However, those who conducted systematic comparisons concluded that college bookstores offer prices just as low—if not lower, on average—than the prices offered by e-bookstores (Terrell, 1999).

By 1997, the Knight Ridder news service had 32 Web sites but was losing money. The cost of the Web sites was $27 million, whereas the revenue from them was only $11 million. However, the company saw this as an investment that would pay off in the long run when more consumers log on to its sites to get their news (Dizard, 2000).

Lin and Jeffres (2001) found that each medium (newspaper, radio station, and television station) had a relatively distinctive content emphasis in their Web sites, reflecting their strength of the primary medium.

Radio stations were using the Web to complement their programming and promote their stations (Potter, 2002). Three types of information are most prevalent on those sites:

details about station events, disk jockey biographies, and contact information for the station. This is significantly different from the type of content listeners have said they desire in previous survey research.

- By the year 2000, 49% of America's households had a computer, and 89% of those computer households had a modem. Overall, 32% of America's households were considered frequent Internet users (Dizard, 2000). The primary reasons for going online were to get news/information and to use e-mail.

- Three components were establishing themselves in the computer media industry. Each created its own stream of revenue. First, there was the hardware component of PCs and peripherals. This accounted for about $100 billion per year. Second, there was software, which had sales of $86 billion in 1995. Then there was online services, which accounted for about $1 billion per year and were growing at an annual rate of 27% (Standard & Poor's, 1996, C102). Profit margins were running about 20% to 25% annually on software and about 10% to 15% on hardware (Standard & Poor's, 1996, C127).

In 1999, the computer hardware sector of the industry accounted for $229.2 billion in revenue, and the software sector accounted for an additional $199.3 billion (U.S. Bureau of the Census, 2000).

- The World Wide Web has grown to about 800 million pages (The Internet Economic Indicators, 2005). That is a great resource, but the bad news is that it is difficult for a person to get to most of it. The most comprehensive search engine today is aware of no more than 16% of the Web; most search engines are able to access less than 10%. Even if you used all the search engines, you could only get to about 42% because that is all that has been indexed (Dunn, 1999).

- Worldwide, there were more than 500 million users of the Internet as of 2000 (Albarran, 2002).

- There have been many Internet service providers (ISPs), with AOL as the largest, with a 32.5% market share (or about 22.7 million subscribers) in 2001; the next largest is MSN, with a market share of 7.2% (Albarran, 2002).

- Revenue: By 2000, the Internet was accounting for $13 billion in revenue, with about two thirds paid by consumers and the other one third by advertisers (Dizard, 2000).

- Expenses: Lots of money had to be spent to provide the infrastructure to make this new medium financially successful.

Fiber-optic cable was needed as the conduit of information into American households. Fiber-optic cable is able to carry a tremendous amount of information. Old phone lines can transmit a few pages of text per second, but a single hair-thin fiber-optic line can transmit about 5,000 pages per second. Local phone companies were spending about

$100 billion to build networks to connect all homes and buildings with fiber-optic cable—a job that is expected to be completed by 2010 (Maney, 1995).

Personnel costs are relatively high and growing. For example, the average wage of the 1.4 million people working in software services design in 1997 was $58,688; the average wage of the 1.6 million people working in hardware design, manufacture, and maintenance was $53,044. Compare these to the U.S. average wage of $22,984 across all industries (U.S. Bureau of the Census, 2000).

## Current Nature

- Clearly, the computer medium is well through the penetration stage. Whether computers grow to a peak and replace cable television as the dominant medium remains to be seen.

- There is a convergence of media driven by computers and digitization. With the newer technologies, especially digitalization, companies are becoming more defined by their content products rather than channels of distribution. For example, television networks are defining themselves much less in terms of television and more in terms of entertainment and news.

- The computer industry is very new, and there is great flux in the way companies grow quickly, get bought by larger firms, or go out of business. However, there are some trends that reveal evidence of concentration.

- E-commerce is growing dramatically. In 1997, e-commerce accounted for only about $2 billion in online retail sales; this had climbed to almost $100 billion in 2002 and is expected to reach $218 billion by 2007. Along with the increase in sales comes an increase in ads on the Web. The number of ad messages sent in 2002 was about 200 billion, and this is expected to climb to almost 600 billion by 2006 ("E-commerce," 2002).

- There are signs of concentration already in this new medium. For example, 80% of all pop-up ads were generated by just 63 companies ("E-commerce," 2002).

# Appendix B

## Immediate and Long-Term Effects of Media on Individuals

|  | *Immediate Effects* | *Long-Term Effects* |
| --- | --- | --- |
| Cognitive |  |  |
|  | Short-term learning | Learning agendas |
|  | Extensive learning | Hypermnesia |
|  | Intensive learning | Generalization |
|  | Exposing secrets |  |
| Attitudinal |  |  |
|  | Opinion creation | Sleeper effect |
|  | Opinion change | Long-term reinforcement |
|  | Inoculation | Cultivation |
|  | Immediate reinforcement | Socialization |
| Emotional |  |  |
|  | Temporary reaction | Stunting emotional growth |
|  | Mood management | Desensitization |
| Physiological |  |  |
|  | Temporary fight/flight arousal | Increasing tolerance |
|  | Temporary sexual arousal | Shifting brain activity |
| Behavioral |  |  |
|  | Attraction | Learned helplessness |
|  | Imitation | Displacement |
|  | Activation | Narcoticization |
|  | Disinhibition |  |

# Immediate Effects

## Cognitive Effects

- Cognitive effects are learning of information and retaining that information in either short-term or long-term memory. If the information is retained only in short-term memory, it will be gone and unavailable for recall within several hours. When the information is rehearsed (thinking about it repeatedly) or consciously catalogued into an existing knowledge structure, it will be retained for a far longer time.

When we encode information into our long-term memories, that learning can be intensive or extensive. These are immediate effects of the media because the encoding is done either during the exposure or shortly after.

- *Short-Term Learning.* We use the media to learn about the particular events of the day. Much of this information stays with us for several hours, and then we forget it. Also, certain advertising messages (such as jingles, sale prices, key selling appeal, and store hours) stay with us for a short period of time to allow us to act on that information, and then we forget it.

Most information is quickly forgotten unless we transfer the information from our short-term memory into our long-term memory. Think about the last time a friend told you his or her phone number. If you did not call him or her, that number was never moved from your short-term memory into your long-term memory, so it was forgotten. But if you used the number and kept using the number, it is in your long-term memory, and you can recall that number right now, even though you originally learned it many months ago.

The same is the case with all kinds of information we learn from the media. The information from the media first enters our short-term memory. We are continually clearing out the facts and images in our short-term memory to make room for the new facts and images that are constantly coming in. When we clear out our short-term memory, we select information that is important and encode it into our long-term memories; if the information is not important, we delete it. During our media exposures, very little is deemed important enough to transfer it into long-term memory; thus, almost all of what we are exposed to in the media is deleted.

- *Intensive Learning.* Intensive learning adds information to a person's existing knowledge structure; that is, people acquire another example of the same information they already have.

To illustrate, imagine that a person is following a political campaign and has built a knowledge structure about the candidates as well as their positions. The person tunes in the evening news on television and hears that one of the candidates has changed her position on an important issue. The person adds this information to his or her existing knowledge structure. This is intensive learning.

- *Extensive Learning.* In contrast, extensive learning refers to the acquisition of information on a new topic. If this information is related to an existing knowledge structure, the person can "add on" to the existing knowledge structure, thus making it broader than before. If this new information is not related to any existing knowledge structure but is still important, the person will create a new knowledge structure.

For example, a person opens the newspaper and finds out that there is going to be an election on a proposition to institute a curfew on all students on campus. The person never heard of this issue before but now has some important information on a new topic.

## Attitudinal Effects

- *Opinion Creation.* The media provide information and images that can trigger the formation of a new opinion or attitude in you. This is most likely to happen the first time you see a new television program or movie. You immediately develop an attitude about whether it is good or bad. You also immediately develop attitudes when you see a new actor or actress, read a new author, hear about a political candidate, or are exposed to a controversial issue.

Advertisers try to create positive attitudes about their product by using a process referred to as canalization. Advertisers know it is too difficult to create a brand new need in you, so they find out what needs you already have and build a "canal" in your mind between your existing needs and their product. For example, let's say you feel a high need to be popular. You see an ad where a character looking and acting like you is surrounded by the kinds of people you want to be your friends. The character is respected and admired because of drinking a certain cola or wearing a certain brand of jeans. The designer of this ad has built a psychological canal between your existing need to be popular and a particular product.

- *Opinion Change.* Media can change a person's attitudes and feelings about something. For example, after watching a teenager insult her parents and be rewarded for this by the admiration of other characters, a child could change his or her attitude that it is okay (and even desirable) to insult one's parents. Or people who watch a political debate might not just acquire new information on an issue but might also change their opinion of one of the debaters.

- *Inoculation.* Medical doctors inoculate people against disease by exposing them to a mild form of the disease so that their bodies can build up immunity. Later, when those people are exposed to that disease, they are not susceptible and do not get sick. This effect is sought by designers of media messages who want to make their audience's attitudes resistant to change.

For example, advertisers will try to inoculate their target audiences to an upcoming claim about to be made by their competitors. In this case, advertisers will design a message to belittle the upcoming claim, so that the target audience will think the claim to be false or silly. Later, when people are exposed to the competitor's claim, they will not be affected by it.

- *Immediate Reinforcement.* The media can reinforce already existing attitudes and thus make them more resistant to change. This is an especially desired effect for advertisers. It has been estimated that up to 80% of all advertising is designed not to change the attitudes or behaviors of consumers but to reinforce already existing brand loyalties and purchasing habits.

When people see an ad for a product they usually buy, they immediately feel good, and this helps to solidify their positive attitude toward the product.

## Emotional Effects

- *Temporary Reaction.* Storytellers know they must evoke our emotions to attract and hold our attention. Writers who want to tell an adventure story need to make us feel suspense, mystery, and fear. Writers of drama need to make us feel jealousy, anger, sadness, love, and happiness. Writers of comedies need to make us feel silly. The better the story, the more strongly our emotions are evoked. When the media arouse some emotions, usually those emotions dissipate shortly after the story is over.

For example, think of the relatively strong emotion of fear, as generated by a horror movie. This fear, although intense at the time, is short-lived, even with children who are more susceptible to the emotional effects of the media (Cantor, 1994). After watching a horror movie, children may look under their beds and in their closets to make sure their environment is safe and then lie awake in bed, hoping they will not be attacked (Wilson & Cantor, 1985). Although the fear can last up to several weeks with some children (Cantor, 1994), it is typically gone by the next day.

- *Mood Management.* People use the media, especially music, to manage their moods (Knobloch, 2003). People who are stressed can calm themselves down with slow music. Conversely, people who are in a lethargic mood can pep themselves up with louder, more active music.

For example, Knobloch and Zillmann (2002), in a study of university students, found that respondents used music to manage their moods; that is, the choice of music is an emotional one. People who were in a bad mood elected to listen to highly energetic-joyful music than did people in a good mood. The energetic music distracted them from their bad mood. Also, Knobloch (2003) reports that people who are preparing for a task requiring concentration are likely to choose to listen to "smoother tunes" rather than upbeat music.

# Physiological Effects

- *Temporary Fight-Flight Arousal.* We have certain physiological reactions hardwired into our brains. One of these is the fight-flight reaction when we are presented with danger. If we see a predator coming after us, the survival instinct is triggered. We must fight off the predator or run away. Our bodies get us ready for this by releasing adrenaline into our bloodstream, which increases our heart rate and blood pressure.

The media frequently present us with situations where we identify with a character who is then put in danger. Vicariously, we experience the need for survival. Our bodies automatically release adrenaline into our bloodstreams. If we stop and think about what is happening, we know that the danger is not happening to us. But still our bodies are primed for fight or flight.

- *Temporary Sexual Arousal.* Sexual arousal is also hardwired into our brains. When we see someone who is very physically attractive to us, we become sexually aroused. This arousal ensures the propagation of the human race.

The person who arouses us need not be a real person. The attraction may be to a character on a television screen or an image in a magazine—but still there are enough visual cues in these depictions to trigger a physiological response in us.

# Behavioral Effects

- *Attraction.* The media present images that attract and hold our attention. We alter our behavior to follow what attracts us.

For example, we may be flipping through the channels on our television set until we see something that attracts and holds our interest. At this point, our behavior changes; that is, we stop pushing the search button on our remote control device and keep our eyes on the screen. Perhaps we even lean forward, turn up the volume, and stop talking to other people in the room. All of these are behavioral manifestations of attraction to a message on the television screen.

- *Imitation.* Children as young as 2 have been found to imitate behaviors they see in the media (Comstock et al., 1978). In a survey of young children, 60% said they frequently copied behaviors they had seen on television (Liebert, Neale, & Davidson, 1973).

The copying need not be identical to the action seen on the screen—it can be generalized to similar actions. For example, children may watch Superman jump off a building and fly across town to rescue someone. Children will imitate this by jumping up and down with their arms outstretched as they run across the backyard. If they watch two kickboxers beat each other to death, they will imitate this by spin-jumping around, kicking, chopping their arms at each other, shouting, and grunting. Seldom will they actually hit each other. By fantasizing, the "hitting" is in their minds as they imagine they are inside the kickboxing world that they saw on television.

Usually, these imitations during play are harmless. But because so much of it is triggered by violent messages, the potential for actual physical harm is there. And once in a while, when a real weapon is available, the resulting physical harm can be very great.

• *Activation.* The media can exert a triggering effect on our behavior. For example, when watching an ad, we might jump out of our chair and rush to the store to buy the product.

Activation is different than imitation. With imitation, viewers take it upon themselves to emulate a specific behavior seen in the media. In contrast, with activation, viewers are reacting to a suggestion to do something, such as go to the store to buy an advertised product. Viewers do not see the literal behavior portrayed, so there is no pattern to imitate.

# Long-Term Effects

## Cognitive Effects

• *Learning Agendas.* By choosing certain images and themes, the media focus our attention on particular things while telling us to ignore other things. Called agenda setting, this effect was first observed in the political arena where the media were found to be very influential in telling us what to think *about* (McCombs & Shaw, 1972).

For example, the media, through a continual stream of stories about social welfare programs, are effective at telling people that this is something worth thinking about, but the media are not effective in convincing people that they should support or reject social welfare programs. The agenda-setting function of the mass media is quite powerful, especially when there is an overlap in coverage among the various media.

This agenda-setting effect is not limited to telling us what to think about politics and current events. It is much broader. It tells us what kind of music we should listen to; what kinds of people we should regard as beautiful, smart, or successful; and what kinds of events are important. By bringing certain kinds of people to our attention, the media create celebrities. The media confer status on certain people, and we continue to hear what these people have to say even when they don't have anything important to say. The noncelebrities have not been given status, so we do not hear what they have to say, even if it is something potentially important. This is the agenda-setting effect.

• *Hypermnesia.* This effect appears to be the opposite of forgetting. Instead of a person being *less* able to recall information from a message as time goes by, there are situations when people become *more* able to recall that information (Wicks, 1992).

For example, a person reads a story in a magazine about forest fires and is not able to recall many of the facts after the reading. But during the next few weeks, the television presents stories about several big forest fires in his area, and he begins to recall more of the facts from the magazine story. This is hypermnesia. It seems very strange that a person could know less immediately after reading something compared to much later. We are more used to thinking that the opposite occurs; that is, our learning is highest right after an exposure, and then our memory of those facts gradually erodes.

How is hypermnesia possible? The key to understanding hypermnesia is to recognize that when we are exposed to information, the facts are recorded somewhere in our brains. On topics where we already have a good deal of knowledge, the recording of new facts is done in a highly organized manner by cataloging them quickly and accurately in the knowledge structure that we have previously developed on that topic. When we are asked about that information, we have no trouble retrieving it. But with a topic that is new to us, we don't have a knowledge structure on that topic. The new facts may be stored haphazardly inside other knowledge structures, and this makes those facts very difficult to retrieve. As we begin to learn more about the new topic, we construct a new knowledge structure on that topic and sort through our older knowledge structures to bring all the facts on that topic together in one place. During periods of rest (such as sleep), our minds sort out the facts and move them around to where they can be more efficiently catalogued. Once all the facts on the new topic are assembled into a new knowledge structure, they are then easier to recall.

- *Generalization.* Generalization is the process of observing a few occurrences of something, perceiving a pattern that ties together those occurrences, and then inferring that the pattern reflects something more general than those occurrences. That "something more general" can be a claim about how all people behave or how things work.

For example, a person watches a local news program and hears a story about a house that was vandalized in an area near his apartment. Then he hears a story on radio that a local bank was robbed. Next he reads the newspaper and sees that there was an assault in his town last night. He has learned three facts—one from each message. But later that night, he might generalize from these three facts and draw a conclusion that crime has become a real problem in his town. This conclusion was not given to him in the media, but the media provided him with some facts that could set up his jump to this conclusion.

Let's consider another example. A person watches a situation comedy where several teenagers are very witty and joke their way out of trouble. She then watches a stand-up comedian who wins the admiration of his audience. Then she watches a romantic comedy where the characters are attracted to each other because of their shared sense of humor. She has learned facts about how these televised characters behave and the consequences of their behaviors, then generalizes to a conclusion that humor is a very useful tool that can get her whatever she wants.

The mass media have been found to stimulate many different kinds of generalizations about how much crime and violence there is in society, the structure of families, the nature of gender roles, the behavior of the elderly, and the workings of certain professions, especially the legal, law enforcement, and medical professions (Hawkins & Pingree, 1982). They also influence a person's generalized knowledge about stereotypes, especially gender, ethnicity, family, and occupational roles (Greenberg, 1982); health and nutrition (Gerbner, Morgan, & Signorielli, 1982); sexual mores (Comstock, 1982); and fashion, hair care, and facial care that generalize to an overall conception of what it means to be beautiful.

• *Exposing Secrets.* For many people, the media, especially television, serve to expose secrets about how the world works. The media do this by restructuring social arenas, according to Joshua Meyrowitz (1985), in a fascinating book titled *No Sense of Place.* Meyrowitz argues that the media affect us not through their content per se but by changing the "situational geography" of social life. Meyrowitz says that we all change the way we act depending on whether we are in public or private. When we are in public, we perform on stage in front of others, such as colleagues at work. In contrast, we have "backstage" or private behaviors that we reserve for intimates, such as very good friends or spouses. The media expose important social secrets by taking viewers into the backstage, and this is often a negative effect.

For example, Meyrowitz (1985) points out that adults used to be able to retreat to their private backstage area, which was hidden from children. While in the backstage, adults could talk about adult things (child-rearing practices, anxieties, sex, death, etc.) with each other without children being exposed. Parents could keep their shortcomings and anxieties in the backstage and thus hide from their children. Then, once parents had discussed how to handle their children, they could come onstage and take on the role of confident authority figures.

The media, especially television, expose these adult secrets to children. When children watch situation comedies on television and see parents as buffoons and when they watch talk shows and see all the problems that some adults have, children lose the belief that adults have superior wisdom and experience. It is much harder, then, for parents to establish a sense of authority over their children. Thus, Meyrowitz (1985) argues, "Children may love television because it extends their horizons of experience, because it expands their awareness of adult behavior and adult roles, and because it keeps them abreast of the latest adult attempts to control them" (p. 45).

Another example is in the political arena, where much of the president's life used to be kept backstage. Now, all of the backstage information about a president's sexual indiscretions, overeating and drinking problems, draft avoidance, previous banking practices, and so forth are brought into the foreground, and it is much harder for that person to appear presidential—that is, like a person possessing superior qualities necessary to make all the decisions he must make.

The electronic media are especially powerful at being able to destroy the place of backstage because electronic media, such as television, present "expressive" information that was once accessible only in intimate face-to-face encounters. Through TV, viewers have access to the personal expressions of people from all over the world, that is, information that was once available to only a few people. Television undermines the behavioral distinctions between foreground and background because it provides all kinds of information to all kinds of people. It leaves no secrets.

## Attitudinal Effects

- *Sleeper Effect.* This is an effect that takes a relatively long time to occur. During an exposure to a message, a person discounts the message because of a dislike for the source. But then over time, the person forgets the source, and the negative feeling about the information goes away and is replaced by a positive feeling.

To illustrate, let's say you listen to a political pundit deliver an analysis of the problem of illegal immigration in which he expresses a certain opinion. You do not like or respect the political commentator, so you do not agree with his opinion while you are viewing the show. Several weeks later, you are in an argument about illegal immigration, and you start citing many of the facts that you learned from the commentator. You also express the same opinion as the commentator did. But you have now forgotten about the commentator, who made you feel bad. All you remember is the opinion and the supporting facts, which make you feel good.

- *Reinforcement.* Although reinforcement can occur during exposure, the much stronger reinforcement effect is that which builds up over time. With each additional message that is the same or similar to all previous messages, a person's existing attitude gains greater and greater weight. Thus, over a long period of time, the attitude has gained so much weight that it is impossible to change it, no matter how powerful the arguments you use. The attitude has been reinforced so much that it is impervious to reason or counter arguments.

- *Cultivation.* There are certain messages embedded in the way stories are presented, that is, the way plots develop and the way characters are portrayed over and over. After exposure to these constant themes over the long term, people are cultivated to believe certain things.

For example, people have been cultivated to believe that the world is a mean and violent place after watching years of television, with its focus on crime in the news and on many programs. Also, after many years of exposure to ads, people have become more materialistic (Kwak, Zinkhan, & Dominick, 2002), hold more idealistic expectations about marriage (Segrin & Nabi, 2002), are more likely to distrust people in general (Shrum, 1999), and develop a "thin ideal" for body image in their characters and sports figures (Bissell & Zhou, 2004).

Some of these cultivation effects have been found to lead to behavioral changes. For example, women who have been cultivated to hold a thin body image are more likely to develop eating disorders (Bissell & Zhou, 2004). Also, a study conducted by Dartmouth University Media School reported that youngsters who watch movies in which actors smoke a lot are three times more likely to take up the habit than those exposed to less smoking on screen. It was found that 52% of adolescents who smoked said they started smoking because of seeing movie stars smoke on screen (Ross, 2003).

- *Socialization.* This is a lifelong process whereby people acquire certain attitudes and beliefs by taking from the media certain lessons and themes about society. Throughout this long-term exposure to all kinds of messages (news, ads, movies, cartoons, talk shows, etc.), we infer patterns across the individual facts, events, and character portrayals. These inferences become our beliefs about how the world is constructed.

This effect is similar to the cognitive effect of generalization. Both of these reflect the process of inference, whereby people are exposed to a few instances of something and infer general patterns from these few instances. With generalization, the inferences are about factual patterns about our society, such as the rate of crime, the proportion of women who work, the proportion of people who are on welfare, and so on. In contrast, socialization reflects on inferences about how people should interact with one another and with their social world. There are many examples of how the media gradually socialize us into believing certain things. Because this effect is so important and so subtle, I'll present several examples in detail below.

One of the themes of advertising is that material goods are what count most. Happiness is defined in terms of wealth. We are taught that problems can only be solved by buying something. Furthermore, once we buy something, our problem will be gone in a matter of seconds. Everything is commodified, and we define ourselves in terms of what we buy. We are not taught that problems are complex, that they require effort from us, and that they often take days, weeks, or even years to solve. Commercials sell products on the surface, but the more important and longer term effect is to sell an entire way of life—a way of experiencing social reality that is compatible with the needs of a mass-production, mass-consumption, capitalist society (Parenti, 1986). In a recent poll, two thirds of parents say their children define their self-worth by their possessions. More than half the parents of kids ages 2 to 17 admitted that they've bought something for their child that they disapproved of. And one in three parents are working longer hours to pay for things their children feel they need. Now, $2 billion is spent annually on marketing and advertising aimed at kids (Wride, 1999).

An advertisement does much more than provide information about its product. It also tells us what the product means. It does this by linking the product to our culture by using symbols. It also tells us what it means for us to be part of our culture. If we don't accept the message of materialism, then we are alienated from our culture. To be happy, one must own things and avail oneself of commercial services. These things improve one's life. Over time, we become obsessed with acquiring material goods and overlook the things in life that do not cost money (inner peace, harmony, strong relationships, family, respect for others, and the like).

A corollary of this is the belief that new is better and that old things wear out and/or lose their usefulness. New is better because new is improved. So your old friends are not as good as potential new ones. Your spouse is not as good as a potential new romantic attachment. Thus, we lose a sense of security because we are socialized not to believe in permanence.

Attitudes about nutrition are influenced by the mass media, especially by TV. People who say that TV is a major source of information on health and nutrition are significantly more complacent about health, are nonexercisers, and are poorly informed about health matters. Preteens who watch more TV have lower levels of nutritional knowledge. Moreover, the nutritional value of children's diets varies inversely with the amount of TV viewing. This is understandable given the world of television, where there are seldom ads for grains, fruits, or vegetables. Instead, food ads are for processed, packaged foods usually high in fat, salt, and sugar. Characters in the entertainment portions between the ads are more likely to be shown snacking instead of eating a nutritious meal. And although they rarely exercise, they are rarely overweight or out of shape.

Americans are getting fatter. Stacey Schultz (1999), writing in *U.S. News & World Report,* says that "the United States [is] now secure in its position as the fattest nation in the developed world" (p. 82). When we look at people 25 years old and older, we find that 63% of men and 55% of women are overweight. Furthermore, 18% of American adults are classified as obese, and this figure is up from 12% in 1991. Obesity is computed using a body mass index that adjusts for a person's height. For example, a woman who is 5 feet, 5 inches tall is considered overweight if she weighs 162 pounds, and she is considered obese if she weighs 186 pounds or more (Schultz, 1999).

Exposure to ads about beauty products causes adolescent girls to place more importance on beauty-related characteristics in their real-life personal roles. Also, women who watch ads of thin models can have their perceptions of their own bodies altered (Myers & Biocca, 1992). Syndicated columnist Ellen Goodman writes that advertising has given girls many new body parts to worry about:

> A glance at any teen magazine is a new anatomy lesson. Eyes are now subdivided into half a dozen distinct areas from brow to lash, each of which need to be thinned or thickened, shaved or shaded. Teeth demand brightening as well as straightening. Thighs have grown cellulite. Lips require "plumping." Arms bulge for biceps, and every unmentionable inch of the body seems to need perfume of some kind or another. (p. A9)

She likens this "evolutionary speedup" to the trend in medicine where practitioners are getting more specialized with their attention on only one part of the body. However, there is a difference between medical and beauty developments. "Medicine changed to make their patients feel better. The beauty industry changed to make their customers feel worse" (Goodman, 1997, p. A9).

Our instant access to news and entertainment provided by the media has trained us to expect instant gratification in everything. Ritzer (1993) calls this the McDonaldization of America. McDonald's hamburger stores provide everyone with food immediately for little money. Other chains include Burger King, Wendy's, Hardees, Arby's, Big Boy, Dairy Queen,

TCBY, Denny's, Sizzler, Kentucky Fried Chicken, Popeyes, Taco Bell, Chi Chi's, Pizza Hut, Domino's, Long John Silver, Baskin-Robbins, and Dunkin' Donuts. The list goes on and on.

Other nonrestaurant businesses are trying to emulate McDonald's. The vice chairman of Toys "R" Us said, "We want to be thought of as the McDonald's of toys" (Ritzer, 1993, p. 3). Other chains with these ambitions include companies in car care (Jiffy Lube, AAMCO Transmissions, Midas Muffler & Brake Shops), tax preparation (H&R Block), child care (Kinder Care), health care (Pearle Vision Centers, Nutri/System), and retailing (Walmart). All of these retailers are in business to provide us with instant gratification. And it is clear that we appreciate their services because we keep increasing their revenues each year.

Other examples of our desire for instant gratifications are ATM machines that provide us with cash 24 hours every day; FedEx, which we can use to send anything overnight; the Home Shopping Network, where it is easy to order products without having to leave one's house; and now the e-stores on the Internet, where we can buy anything and have instant shipment to our homes.

Even sex has been McDonaldized. We can experience explicit sexual situations by buying magazines and videos and calling dial-a-porn phone numbers. We can instantly engage in sex, albeit vicarious, without having to go through the trouble of meeting another human being.

The effect of all these goods and services constantly and instantly being available reinforces our desire for instant gratification. This reinforcement socializes us to make quick decisions, to think it is silly to do without, and to deal with machines rather than people.

So much is available, and it is so easy to get that we cease to think about things in much depth. For example, if there were no fast-food restaurants, you would have to plan out a week's meals, go to the grocery store, select all the elements of those meals, unpack those elements at home in some storage system, and then assemble the elements into your meals. But today, we don't have to give much thought to meals. We can drive home from work and, on impulse, stop in at a fast-food restaurant and get a fully assembled dinner in a bag.

The media foster in us a need for immediate gratification. The media themselves are so varied and available that they offer us the possibility of immediate gratification for anything we could possibly want. Also, with cable offerings of all kinds and RCDs (remote control devices), we can immediately increase our gratification. Have you ever been watching a sporting event in real life and found yourself trying to fast forward through the slow parts to get to the action? Or have you ever listened to one of your friends tell a story and wish you could push a button to speed through the boring parts to get to the "good stuff"? If so, you have been conditioned to believe that you can make time move faster.

In relationships, do you wish you could meet that "special someone" right away? Do you feel that there is something wrong with you if you haven't been swept away by love in the past several months? When you do get excited by someone, do you wish things would progress more quickly? Then, after you have developed a relationship with that "special person," have you ever then quickly become bored, wishing that someone better (or just newer) would come along to sweep you away again?

In careers, we expect very high rewards very quickly without much work. It comes as a surprise how difficult it can be to get even a mediocre job—then how much work is required to hold it. In the media, the velocity of success is very fast.

For almost 30 years, social scientists have been documenting a big decline in social connectiveness. Television has consumed more and more time of people, leaving less time for real-world activities. Now with computers and the Internet, this trend is accelerating. People who spent more time on the Internet are often found to be more lonely and depressed. Kids who spend the most time with the media (more than 10.5 hours per day) are not as content as those who spend less time (Rideout et al., 1999).

Critics of this effect say that the Internet gives lonely people a chance to connect with others through chat rooms, bulletin boards, support groups, and e-mail. Also, most people who are heavy users of the Internet say that they watch much less television (Perry, 2000).

## Emotional Effects

- *Stunting Emotional Development.* Some critics have made the argument that watching a great deal of television stunts a child's emotional development. They point out that by the time a child reaches the age of 5, he or she has been exposed to about 6,000 hours of television. The high levels of exposure to television, coupled with the extreme level of stimulation presented by television, leave viewers with no time for reflection. On television, there is a new image every 3.5 seconds on average. There are sound effects, music, laugh tracks, and constant interruptions. The pace is extremely fast, with new images replacing old, new shows replacing old. This short-circuits the natural, emotional development people need to become healthy human beings; it strangles the development of children's own voices and denies them their imaginative powers.

> Some neuro-anatomists argue that excessive TV viewing—more than four or five hours per day, seven days a week—ultimately takes a serious cognitive toll. They believe the limbic system of the brain—the mysterious, sub-cortical part of the brain that researchers designate as the image-making center—develops more slowly when a young person spends half of his or her waking life in front of the TV set. (Sanders, 1994, p. 39)

Television viewing makes people think they are experiencing emotions, but these are not real because they are not two-way; that is, there is no interaction. Viewers cannot influence the behavior of TV characters, so there is no emotional exchange. Emotions require physicality, that is, people to touch each other; TV does not provide this. Without adequate emotional development, people do not develop a sense of guilt or conscience (Sanders, 1994).

Also, TV gives so many images to viewers that viewers do not have to generate their own images; they do not practice what-if situations and thinking things through. They can't even fully process much of what they do experience on TV—there is too much. Also, viewing weakens their will. TV takes over and gives them all their excitement; people don't have to generate their own entertainment any longer (Sanders, 1994).

- *Desensitization.* Some things within the media are presented so often that we can no longer treat them with wonder or awe. Our tolerance has been increased so that those things that used to entertain us or impress us no longer do.

This is especially important with the issue of violence. Viewing TV violence leads to lowered sensitivity to aggression and violence. Among children, even watching a single violent film can make them temporarily less aware of and less concerned about aggressive acts in others. A relationship between the amount of exposure to TV violence and the willingness to use violence suggests that violence is a solution to conflict and is perceived as being effective (Liebert et al., 1973). This effect has also been found in adults who have been exposed to strong violence against women (Linz, Donnerstein, & Penrod, 1984, 1988) or even relatively mild forms of violence (Thomas, 1982).

Another form of media desensitization is a result of the superficial treatment that media give to certain issues. This superficial treatment given to subjects by the media cloaks the apathy of the audience by allowing us to feel that by knowing about a problem, we are doing something about it.

This desensitization can have positive effects in a therapeutic setting. People who fear something (such as dogs, heights, flying in airplanes) can be gradually desensitized (Dorr, 1981; Foa & Kozak, 1986; Goranson, 1970).

## Physiological Effects

- *Increasing Tolerance.* Your body builds up a resistance—or tolerance—to certain experiences. Over time, your body requires greater and greater stimulation to trigger the same physiological response in you.

For example, the first time you see a horror film, your body responds with a fight-or-flight reaction by substantially increasing your heart rate and blood pressure. As you continue to view horror films over the years, your body's reaction to these stimuli is not as strong. Your heart rate and blood pressure still increase but not as much. You are building up a higher tolerance to this type of message physiologically. In the extreme case, with massive exposure to this type of message, you might even extinguish all physiological reactions to horror.

- *Shifting Brain Activity.* Critics—such as Winn (2002), in her book *The Plug-In Drug: Television, Computers, and Family Life*—caution that television hooks children into entertainment, keeps their brains functioning at a low level, and makes them passive acceptors of the media messages as presented. Also, Marcuse (1964) argues that the mass media in America hammer the population into having a one-dimensional mind—that is, people's minds become paralyzed so that they are incapable of independent thought; they cannot criticize or oppose the messages in which they become immersed.

Healy (1990), in her book *Endangered Minds,* argues that children's minds are changing because of exposure to the visual media, especially computer games. Recent studies suggest that intensive game play actually redraws the brain's neural maps. And children who play a lot have cognitive strategies that are parallel—not sequential. This could make it more difficult for children who must learn sequential tasks such as reading or mathematical reasoning—both of which are very linear and analytical. She says that children who enter elementary school are smarter each year in some ways but are less able to handle school and its requirements. Children are less able to pay attention and to listen. This is because many children either have information overload from the constant bombardment of media messages, so they shut down when they get to school, or they have become accustomed to a level of stimulation much higher than a teacher can provide, so they become bored. Healy says that the visual media (especially television and video games) are responsible for this condition of overstimulation because those media strongly stimulate the right side of the brain while ignoring the left side. The left side of the brain is used less and develops more slowly, leading children to have trouble with reading, arithmetic, and other traditional academic subjects. Instead, the right side is stimulated by the fast-changing scenes on TV as well as video games with lots of novelty and movement. The visual media are very spatially oriented. This is especially the case with computers, which require a different form of skill. By playing computer games, children

acquire new ways of learning. They're honing special graphics and motor skills. They can process huge amounts of visual information in parallel. On a daily basis, they scope out new games, grasp the operating rules, navigate bewildering 3-D geographies, and jump through abstract mental hoops with concentration usually reserved for competitive test taking. (Gross, 1996, p. 64)

## Behavioral Effects

- *Learned Helplessness.* Television causes a decrease in persistence because viewers are learning to be helpless. This learned helplessness comes not from watching any one show or type of programming; it comes from the act of watching television itself.

- *Displacement.* The media have changed the way we spend our time. The media consume us by consuming our time. The U.S. Bureau of the Census (2000) says that the average person spends 3,391 hours with the media a year—that's 9.3 hours each day. Almost half of this time is watching television. However, only a small portion of our media exposure is exclusive of other activities. For example, while we are watching television, we might also be talking on the telephone, doing the dishes, or reading a magazine. If we were to add up all the time we spend engaging in different activities during a day, it would total more than 24 hours. Thus, the media exposure figures can be misleading if we think of that time as displacing other activities. Acknowledging this overlapping of exposure is important because it reveals something about the nature of our exposure—much of our exposure to the media does not command our full attention. The media are often only a background to other activities.

There is also a concern that exposure to the media—especially with escapist fare—will prevent people from using their time more productively. This is especially an issue with children and their schoolwork. Although the media have been found useful in stimulating interest in some topics (Schramm et al., 1961), they have not been generally found to be either a positive or a negative factor—it depends on what is exposed.

Also, there is a concern that for very young children with the television viewing habit, playtime is preempted (Singer & Singer, 1981). When TV structures a child's life, the child spends less time creatively making up his or her own games and situations.

- *Narcoticizing.* The media can be like a powerful drug. The first exposure to a new magazine, CD, TV show, and so forth can bring a rush of excitement. So we go back to it to get the same feelings again. It is habit forming. For example, people can get hooked on the media, especially computers. As early as 1995, when only 6% of households were online, there were already people showing signs of Internet addiction. These online junkies revealed a compulsion to check e-mail 20 to 30 times a day, to put the computer as a higher priority than anything else, or to spend time away from real-life important activities such as talking to spouses or kids. Therapists have already been developing 12-step plans to help these people (Vranizan, 1995).

*Internet addiction disorder* is a term coined in the mid-1990s by a psychiatrist who was seeing more and more patients who were unable to control their use of the Internet. These people typically forego sleeping, eating, and other activities to spend more time on the Internet. This includes obsessions with chat rooms, games, pornography, gambling, and shopping. Some married people have extramarital affairs online; day traders get hooked on the stock market. Estimates are that about 6% of Web users could be addicted—that is 6 million people (Yang, 2000).

When we build up a tolerance to the effect, we want more. Each time we go back, we require more from the media to get the same rush. With entertainment, we want a more outrageous story line, more attractive characters, and more visual effects. But if the media can give us only the same kinds of messages, we do not feel the rush. Over time, our expectations become very high, and we find ourselves flipping through 100 channels and saying, "There is nothing on!" What we mean by this, of course, is that TV is no longer able to exceed my expectations and to significantly arouse me in a surprising way. But we keep exposing ourselves to the TV anyway because, for many of us, it is better than not watching.

This narcoticizing effect works with news content also. At first, we are excited to find out what is happening. But, then over time, we don't want to hear the same old news. We want stories that will surprise us, so we look for more bizarre happenings, more dramatic confrontations, and more arousing debates. Our tolerance for these increases, and our expectations grow beyond what news stories can provide. We continue to watch—fearing that we will miss something important or something truly arousing.

People begin to withdraw from real life and become passive (Sayre & King, 2003). Rather than participate in life by making real friends and demonstrating for social causes, people make virtual friends in the media and watch stories about social causes to give them the sense that they are involved.

- *Disinhibition.* This is the process of gradually wearing down your inhibitions, which prevent you from behaving in certain ways.

For example, you may not like to dance in front of others, but after several months of watching dance programs, your resistance wears down, and you find yourself dancing in a club. Also, most of us have been raised to solve our problems in nonaggressive and nonviolent ways. However, after years of exposure to violent portrayals in the movies and on television, where attractive characters use violence successfully to get what they want, our aversion to using violence gradually wears down. One day, when someone steals the parking place we want, we find ourselves screaming and pounding the offender's car; our inhibitions that prevent us from behaving violently have been worn down and cannot prevent us from behaving violently.

# Appendix C

## *Media Literacy Organizations*

Center for Media Education
1511 K Street, NW, Suite 518
Washington, DC 20005
Telephone: (202) 628-2620
Fax: (202) 628-2554
Web site: www.cme.org/cme

Center for Media Literacy
4727 Wilshire Boulevard, Suite 403
Los Angeles, CA 90010
Telephone: (800) 226-9494
Fax: (213) 931-4474
Web site: www.medialit.org

Children Now
1212 Broadway, Suite 530
Oakland, CA 94612
Telephone: (510) 763-2444
Web site: www.childrennow.org

Citizens for Media Literacy
Wally Bowen
34 Wall Street, Suite 407
Asheville, NC 28801
Telephone: (704) 252-0600

Cultural Environment
   Movement
P.O. Box 31847
Philadelphia, PA 19104
Telephone: (610) 642-3061

Foundation to Improve Television
60 State Street, Suite 3400
Boston, MA 02109
Telephone: (617) 523-5520
Fax: (617) 523-4619

Media Watch
P.O. Box 618
Santa Cruz, CA 95061
Telephone: (408) 423-6355
E-mail: mwatch@cruzio.com
Web site: www.mediawatch.com

Mediascope
12711 Ventura Boulevard,
   Suite 280
Studio City, CA 91604
Telephone: (818) 508-2080
Web site: www.mediascope.org

National Association for Family
   and Community Education
Children's Television Project
P.O. Box 835
Burlington, KY 41005
Telephone: (606) 586-8333
Fax: (606) 586-8348
Web site: www.nafce.org

National Telemedia Council
120 East Wilson Street
Madison, WI 53703
Telephone: (608) 257-7712
Web site: danenet.wicip.org/ntc

Parents' Choice
119 Chestnut Street
Newton, MA 02164
Telephone: (617) 965-5913

# Consumer Groups Primarily Concerned With Advertising

Adbusters
1243 West Seventh Avenue
Vancouver, British Columbia
   V6H 1B7 Canada
Telephone: (604) 736-9401
E-mail: adbusters@adbusters.org

Children's Advertising Review Unit
Council of Better Business Bureaus
845 Third Avenue
New York, NY 10022
Telephone: (212) 705-0124

# Consumer Group Primarily Concerned With News

FAIR (Fairness and Accuracy
   in Reporting)
130 West 25th Street
New York, NY 10001
Telephone: (212) 633-6700
E-mail: fair@igc.apc.org

# Consumer Groups Primarily Concerned With TV and Movie Ratings

Classification and Rating Administration
Motion Picture Association of America, Inc.
15503 Ventura Boulevard
Encino, CA 91436-3103
Web site: www.mpaa.org

OKTV (Alternative TV Ratings)
c/o Gaffney-Livingstone
   Consultation Services
59 Griggs Road
Brookline, MA 02146
Web site: www.aacap.org
   (American Academy of Child and
   Adolescent Psychiatry)

TV Parental Guidelines
   Monitoring Board
P.O. Box 14097
Washington, DC 20004
E-mail: tvomb@usa.net
Web site: www.tvguidelines.org

# National Television Networks

ABC, Inc.
2040 Avenue of the Stars
Los Angeles, CA 90067
Telephone: (310) 557-6655
Web site: www.abc.com

CBS Entertainment
7800 Beverly Boulevard
Los Angeles, CA 90036
Telephone: (213) 460-3000
Fax: (213) 653-8266
Web site: www.channel2000.com

Fox Broadcasting Company
P.O. Box 900
Beverly Hills, CA 90213
Telephone: (310) 369-1000
Web site: www.fox.com

NBC Entertainment
3000 West Alameda
Burbank, CA 91523
Telephone: (818) 840-4404
Web site: www.nbc.com

Public Broadcasting Service
1320 Braddock Place
Alexandria, VA 22314
Telephone: (703) 739-5040
Fax: (703) 739-5295
Web site: www.pbs.org

Turner Broadcasting System
1 CNN Center
Atlanta, GA 30303
Telephone: (404) 885-4291
Web site: www.turner.com

# U.S. Governmental Agencies

Federal Communications Commission
1919 M Street, NW
Washington, DC 20554
Web site: www.fcc.gov/vchip

Federal Trade Commission
Attention: Marketing Practices
Room 238
6th Street and Pennsylvania Avenue, NW
Washington, DC 20580
Fax: (202) 326-2050

United States House of
    Representatives
Subcommittee on
    Telecommunications and Finance
2125 Rayburn Building
Washington, DC 20515
Telephone: (202) 225-2927
Web site: www.house.gov/com

United States Senate
Subcommittee on Communications
227 Hart Senate Office Building
Washington, DC 20510
Telephone: (202) 224-5184
Web site: www.senate.gov/~commerce/

# References

100 people identified in piracy raid. (2004, April 23). *Los Angeles Times,* p. C3.

Abelman, R. (1999). Preaching to the choir: Profiling TV advisory ratings users. *Journal of Broadcasting & Electronic Media, 43,* 529–550.

Ad agency women hit TV stereotypes. (1996, May 20). *Los Angeles Times,* p. 10.

Adams, D. M., & Hamm, M. E. (1989). *Media and literacy: Learning in an electronic age: Issues, ideas and teaching strategies.* Springfield, IL: Charles C Thomas.

Ader, D. R. (1995). A longitudinal study of agenda setting for the issue of environmental pollution. *Journalism & Mass Communication Quarterly, 72,* 300–311.

Albada, K. F. (2000). The public and private dialogue about the American family on television. *Journal of Communication, 50,* 79–110.

Albarran, A. B. (2002). *Media economics: Understanding markets, industries and concepts* (2nd ed.). Ames: Iowa State Press.

Allman, W. F. (1985, October). Pesticides: An unhealthy dependence? *Science, 6*(8), 14.

Altheide, D. L. (1976). *Creating reality: How TV news distorts events.* Beverly Hills, CA: Sage.

American Obesity Association. (2004, June 24). *AOA factsheets.* Retrieved July 9, 2004, from http://obesity.org/subs/fastfacts/obesity_what2.shtml

Ammons, L., Dimmick, J., & Pilotta, J. (1982). Crime news reporting in a black weekly. *Journalism Quarterly, 59,* 310–313.

Anderson, D. R., Collins, P. A., Schmitt, K. L., & Jacobvitz, R. S. (1996). Stressful life events and television viewing. *Communication Research, 23,* 243–260.

Anderson, J. A. (1983). Television literacy and the critical viewer. In J. Bryant & D. R. Anderson (Eds.), *Children's understanding of television: Research on attention and comprehension* (pp. 297–327). New York: Academic Press.

Ansolabehere, S., & Iyengar, S. (1995). *Going negative: How attack ads shrink and polarize the electorate.* New York: Free Press.

Antunes, G., & Hurley, P. (1977). The representation of criminal events in Houston's two daily newspapers. *Journalism Quarterly, 54,* 756–760.

AP Online. (2000, March 13). *Timeline of major media mergers.* Financial Section.

Arens, W. F. (1999). *Contemporary advertising* (7th ed.) Boston: Irwin McGraw-Hill.

Arndorfer, J. B. (1998, December 21). A-B looking for women via daytime TV programs. *Advertising Age, 69*(51), 8.

Association of American Publishers. (2003, May 7). March numbers show book sales still uneven. Retrieved July 23, 2004, from http://www.publishers.org/press/releases.cfm?PressRelease ArticleID=148

Austin, E. W. (1993). Exploring the effects of active parental mediation of television content. *Journal of Broadcasting & Electronic Media, 37,* 147–158.

Austin, E. W., Bolls, P., Fujioka, Y., & Engelbertson, J. (1999). How and why parents take on the tube. *Journal of Broadcasting & Electronic Media, 43,* 175–192.

Austin, E. W., & Meili, H. K. (1995). Effects of interpretations of television alcohol portrayals on children's alcohol beliefs. *Journal of Broadcasting & Electronic Media, 39,* 417–435.

Austin, E. W., & Pinkleton, B. E. (2001). The role of parental mediation in the political socialization process. *Journal of Broadcasting & Electronic Media, 45,* 221–240.

Aversa, J. (1999, May 5). Government employees get no respect on TV. *Tallahassee Democrat,* p. 3A.

Bagdikian, B. (1992). *The media monopoly* (4th ed.). Boston: Beacon.

Bagdikian, B. (2000). *The media monopoly* (6th ed.). Boston: Beacon.

Bandura, A. (1986). *Social foundations of thought and action: A social cognitive theory.* Englewood Cliffs, NJ: Prentice Hall.

Bandura, A. (1994). Social cognitive theory of mass communication. In J. Bryant & D. Zillmann (Eds.), *Media effects* (pp. 61–90). Hillsdale, NJ: Lawrence Erlbaum.

Barber, B. R. (1995). *Jihad vs. McWorld.* New York: New York Times Books.

Barner, M. R. (1999). Sex-role stereotyping in FCC-mandated children's educational television. *Journal of Broadcasting & Electronic Media, 43,* 551.

Barnet, R. J., & Cavanagh, J. (1994). *Global dreams: Imperial corporations and the new world order.* New York: Simon & Schuster.

Bartholomew, D. (2002, May 4). Bill would outlaw soda sales at schools. *Santa Barbara News-Press,* p. A3.

Baseball salaries. (n.d.). Retrieved May 7, 2004, from http://asp.usatoday.com/sports/baseball/salaries/default.aspx

Bash, A. (1997, June 10). Most parents don't use ratings to guide viewing. *USA Today,* p. 3D.

Battles, K., & Hilton-Morrow, W. (2002). Gay characters in conventional spaces: *Will and Grace* and the situation comedy genre. *Critical Studies in Media Communication, 19,* 87–106.

Bauder, D. (1998, January 15). NBC pays record price to keep *ER. Santa Barbara News-Press,* p. C3.

Bauder, D. (2000a, February 26). Fox network swears off spectacle TV—again. *Tallahassee Democrat,* p. 3E.

Bauder, D. (2000b, March 14). CBS to air two reality TV shows. *Tallahassee Democrat,* p. B1.

Bauer, R. A., & Bauer, A. (1960). America, mass society and mass media. *Journal of Social Issues, 10*(3), 3–66.

Beam, R. A. (2003). Content difference between daily newspapers with strong and weak market orientations. *Journalism & Mass Communication Quarterly, 80,* 368–390.

Becker, L. B., Kosicki, G. M., & Jones, F. (1992). Racial differences in evaluation of the mass media. *Journalism Quarterly, 69,* 124–134.

Bellamy, R. V., Jr. (1998). The evolving television sports marketplace. In L. A. Wenner (Ed.), *MediaSport* (pp. 73–87). New York: Routledge.

Bennett, W. L. (2003). *News: The politics of illusion* (5th ed.). New York: Longman.

Bettig, R. V., & Hall, J. L. (2003). *Big media, big money: Cultural texts and political economies.* Lanham, MD: Rowman & Littlefield.

Bielby, D. D., & Bielby, W. T. (2001). Audience segmentation and age stratification among television writers. *Journal of Broadcasting & Electronic Media, 45,* 391.

Bielby, D., & Bielby, W. (2002). Hollywood dreams, harsh realities: Writing for film and television. *Context, 1*(4), 21–27.

Bimber, B. (1996, December 3). Study: 51 million Americans have Internet access. *93106 Newspaper,* p. 3.

Bissell, K. L., & Zhou, P. (2004). Must-see TV or ESPN: Entertainment and sports media exposure and body-image distortion in college women. *Journal of Communication, 54*(1), 5–21.

Bloom, A. (1987). *The closing of the American mind.* New York: Simon & Schuster.

Blumer, H. (1946). Collective behavior. In A. M. Lee (Ed.), *Principles of sociology* (pp. 185–186). New York: Barnes & Noble.

Boehlert, E. (2001, March 14). Pay for play. *Salon.com Magazine. Retrieved from* http://archive.salon .com/21st/feature/1998/02/cov_11feature.html

Boswell, T. (1996, July 20). Between the commercials, waiting for the real show. *Washington Post,* p. G9.

British Broadcasting Corporation. (1972). *Violence on television: Programme content and viewer perceptions.* London: Author.

Brown, J. A. (1991). *Television "critical viewing skills" education: Major media literacy projects in the United States and selected countries.* Hillsdale, NJ: Lawrence Erlbaum.

Brown, J. A. (1998). Media literacy perspectives. *Journal of Communication, 48*(1), 44–57.

Brown, J. A. (2001). Media literacy and critical television viewing in education. In D. G. Singer & J. L. Singer (Eds.), *Handbook of children and the media* (pp. 681–697). Thousand Oaks, CA: Sage.

Brown, J. D., Childers, K. W., Bauman, K. E., & Koch, G. G. (1990). The influence of new media and family structure on young adolescents' television and radio use. *Communication Research, 17,* 65–82.

Brownfield, P. (1999, July 21). As minorities' TV presence dims, gay roles proliferate. *Los Angeles Times,* p. A1.

Bruner, J. S., Goodnow, J., & Austin, G. A. (1956). *A study of thinking.* New York: John Wiley.

Bucy, E. P., & Newhagen, J. E. (1999). The emotional appropriateness heuristic: Processing televised presidential reactions to the news. *Journal of Communication, 49*(4), 59–79.

Buerkel-Rothfuss, N. L. (1993). Background: What prior research shows. In B. S. Greenberg, J. D. Brown, & N. Buerkel-Rothfuss (Eds.), *Media, sex and the adolescent* (pp. 5–18). Cresskill, NJ: Hampton.

Busselle, R., & Crandall, H. (2002). Television viewing and perceptions about race differences in socioeconomic success. *Journal of Broadcasting & Electronic Media, 46,* 265–283.

Buzbee, S. (1995, November 2). U.S. students score poorly in American history. *Santa Barbara News-Press,* p. A3.

Bybee, C., Robinson, D., & Turow, J. (1982). Determinants of parental guidance of children's television viewing for a special subgroup: Mass media scholars. *Journal of Broadcasting, 26,* 697–710.

Cantor, J. (1994). Fright reactions to mass media. In J. Bryant & D. Zillmann (Eds.), *Media effects* (pp. 213–245). Hillsdale, NJ: Lawrence Erlbaum.

Cantor, J. (2001). The media and children's fears, anxieties, and perceptions of danger. In D. G. Singer & J. L. Singer (Eds.), *Handbook of children and the media* (pp. 207–221). Thousand Oaks, CA: Sage.

Cantor, J., & Wilson, B. J. (1984). Modifying fear responses to mass media in preschool and elementary school children. *Journal of Broadcasting, 28,* 431–443.

Cantril, H. (1947). The invasion from Mars. In T. Newcomb & E. Hartley (Eds.), *Readings in social psychology* (pp. 619–628). New York: Holt.

Cassata, M., & Skill, T. (1983). *Life on daytime television.* Norwood, NJ: Ablex.

CBS headquarters, name taken over by Westinghouse. (1997, December 2). *Santa Barbara News-Press,* p. A6.

The celebrity 100. (2004, July 5). *Forbes,* pp. 83–114.

Chew, F., & Palmer, S. (1994). Interest, the knowledge gap, and television programming. *Journal of Broadcasting & Electronic Media, 38,* 271–287.

Christianson, P. G., & Roberts, D. F. (1998). *It's not only rock & roll: Popular music in the lives of adolescents.* Cresskill, NJ: Hampton.

Coltrane, S., & Messineo, M. (2000, March). The perpetuation of subtle prejudice: Race and gender imagery in 1990s television advertising. *Sex Roles: A Journal of Research,* p. 363.

Columbia Broadcasting System. (1980). *Network prime time violence tabulations for 1978–1979 season.* New York: Author.

Combs, B., & Slovic, P. (1979). Newspaper coverage of causes of death. *Journalism Quarterly, 56,* 837–843, 849.

Comstock, G. A. (1980). *Television in America.* Beverly Hills, CA: Sage.

Comstock, G. A. (1982). Violence in television content: An overview. In D. Pearl, L. Bouthilet, & J. Lazar (Eds.), *Television and behavior: Ten years of scientific progress and implications for the eighties: Vol. II. Technical reviews* (pp. 108–125). Rockville, MD: U.S. Department of Health and Human Services.

Comstock, G. A. (1989). *The evolution of American television.* Newbury Park, CA: Sage.

Comstock, G. A., Chaffee, S., Katzman, N., McCombs, M., & Roberts, D. (1978). *Television and human behavior.* New York: Columbia University Press.

Considine, D. M. (1997). Media literacy: A compelling component of school reform and restructuring. In R. Kubey (Ed.), *Media literacy in the information age* (pp. 243–262). New Brunswick, NJ: Transaction Publishers.

Consoli, J. (1998, April 20). The 11.8-hour daily diet. *Mediweek,* pp. 8, 12.

Cooper, C. A. (1996). *Violence on television: Congressional inquiry, public criticism and industry response.* New York: University Press of America.

Cooper, R. (1993). An expanded, integrated model for determining audience exposure to television. *Journal of Broadcasting & Electronic Media, 38,* 401–418.

Coors scores big placement deal. (2002, August 13). *Santa Barbara News-Press,* p. D5.

Corder-Bolz, C. R. (1980). Mediation: The role of significant others. *Journal of Communication, 30*(3), 106–118.

Critser, G. (2004, January 25). Truth: A bitter pill for drug makers. *Los Angeles Times,* pp. M1, M2.

Croteau, D., & Hoynes, W. (1994). *By invitation only: How the media limit political debate.* Monroe, ME: Common Courage.

Croteau, D., & Hoynes, W. (2001). *The business of media: Corporate media and the public interest.* Thousand Oaks, CA: Pine Forge Press.

Currie, E. (1998). *Crime and punishment in America.* New York: Metropolitan Books.

D'Alessio, D., & Allen, M. (2000). Media bias in presidential elections: A meta-analysis. *Journal of Communication, 50,* 133–156.

Dallek, M. (2004, January 25). Primaries make voters secondary. *Los Angeles Times,* p. M2.

Daly, C., Henry, P., & Ryder, E. (2000). The structure of the magazine industry. In A. N. Greco (Ed.), *The media and entertainment industries* (pp. 26–45). Boston: Allyn & Bacon.

Davie, W. R., & Lee, J.-S. (1993). Television news technology: Do more sources mean less diversity? *Journal of Broadcasting & Electronic Media, 39,* 453–464.

Davie, W. R., & Lee, J.-S. (1995). Sex, violence, and consonance/differentiation: An analysis of local TV news values. *Journalism & Mass Communication Quarterly, 72,* 128–138.

Davies, M. M. (1997). Making media literate: Educating future media workers at the undergraduate level. In R. Kubey (Ed.), *Media literacy in the information age* (pp. 263–284). New Brunswick, NJ: Transaction Publishers.

Davis, B. (1990). Media hoaxes. *Wilson Library Bulletin, 64*(10), 139–140.

Davis, R., & Owen, D. (1998). *New media and American politics.* New York: Oxford University Press.

DeFleur, M. L., & Dennis, E. E. (1996). *Understanding mass communication: A liberal arts perspective.* Princeton, NJ: Houghton Mifflin.

Dennis, E. E. (1993, April 15). *Fighting media illiteracy: What every American needs to know and why.* Paper presented at the Roy W. Howard Public Lecture in Journalism and Mass Communication, Number 4, School of Journalism, Indiana University, Bloomington.

Desmond, R. (1997). Media literacy in the home: Acquisition versus deficit models. In R. Kubey (Ed.), *Media literacy in the information age* (pp. 323–343). New Brunswick, NJ: Transaction Publishers.

Desmond, R. J., Singer, J. L., Singer, D. G., Calam, R., & Colimore, K. (1985). Family mediation patterns and television viewing: Young children's use and grasp of the medium. *Human Communication Research, 11,* 461–480.

Diamant, A. (1994, October). Media violence. *Parents Magazine, 69*(10), 40.

Diener, E., & De Four, D. (1978). Does television violence enhance programme popularity? *Journal of Personality and Social Psychology, 36,* 333–341.

Diener, E., & Woody, L. W. (1981). TV violence and viewer liking. *Communication Research, 8,* 281–306.

Dizard, W., Jr. (2000). *Old media new media* (3rd ed.). New York: Longman.

Dominick, J. R. (1999). *The dynamics of mass communication* (6th ed.). Boston: McGraw-Hill.

Donnelly, W. J. (1986). *The confetti generation: How the new communications technology is fragmenting America.* New York: Holt.

Dorr, A. (1981). Television and affective development and functioning: Maybe this decade. *Journal of Broadcasting, 25,* 335–345.

Dorr, A., Kovaric, P., & Doubleday, C. (1989). Parent-child coviewing of television. *Journal of Broadcasting & Electronic Media, 33,* 35–51.

Douglas, W., & Olson, B. M. (1995). Beyond family structure: The family in domestic comedy. *Journal of Broadcasting & Electronic Media, 39,* 236–261.

Douglas, W., & Olson, B. M. (1996). Subversion of the American family? An examination of children and parents in television families. *Communication Research, 23,* 73–99.

Dow, B. J. (2001). Ellen, television, and the politics of gay and lesbian visibility. *Critical Studies in Media Communication, 18,* 123–132.

Doyle, G. (2002). *Understanding media economics.* London: Sage.

D'Souza, D. (1991). *Illiberal education: The politics of race and sex on campus.* New York: Free Press.

Dunn, A. (1999, July 8). Most of Web beyond scope of search sites. *Los Angeles Times,* Home Section, p. 1.

Dutka, E. (2003, August 31). Audience tests: Plot thickens. *Los Angeles Times,* p. E8.

E-commerce: The road ahead. (2002, September 30). *Newsweek,* p. 38V.

Einstein, M. (2004). *Media diversity: Economics, ownership, and the FCC.* Mahwah, NJ: Lawrence Erlbaum.

Elasmar, M., Hasegawa, K., & Brain, M. (1999). The portrayals of women in U.S. prime time television. *Journal of Broadcasting & Electronic Media, 43,* 20–34.

Eller, C. (1999, July 9). Literary manager built career by not following script. *Los Angeles Times,* pp. C1, C5.

Eller, C., & Bates, J. (1999, August 13). In Hollywood, more business than show. *Los Angeles Times,* pp. A1, A23.

Endicott, R. C. (2003, December 8). '04 pay hikes. *Advertising Age.* Retrieved May 29, 2004, from http://www.adage.com/images/random/salarysurvey03.pdf

Entman, R. M., & Rojecki, A. (2001). The black image in the White mind: Media and race in America. *CHOICE: Current Reviews for Academic Libraries, 38,* 1074.

Fabrikant, A. S. (1995, August 1). Disney to buy ABC for $19-billion. *Santa Barbara News-Press,* pp. A1, A2.

Farhi, P., & Shapiro, L. (1996, July 27). Sports as an afterthought on NBC. *The Washington Post,* pp. A1, A14.

Federal Communications Commission (FCC). (2003, June 2). Media ownership policy reexamination. Retrieved July 14, 2004, from http://www.fcc.gov/ownership

Fedler, F., & Jordan, D. (1982). How emphasis on people affects coverage of crime. *Journalism Quarterly, 59,* 474–478.

Ferguson, D. A. (1992). Channel repertoire in the presence of remote control devices, VCRs, and cable television. *Journal of Broadcasting & Electronic Media, 36,* 83–91.

Fernandez-Collado, C., Greenberg, B., Korzenny, F., & Atkin, C. (1978). Sexual intimacy and drug use in TV series. *Journal of Communication, 28*(3), 30–37.

Fewer adults reading newspapers, watching news. (1995, April 6). *Santa Barbara News-Press,* p. A5.

Fico, F., & Soffin, S. (1995). Fairness and balance of selected newspaper coverage of controversial national, state, and local issues. *Journalism & Mass Communication Quarterly, 72,* 621–633.

Fisch, S. M. (2000). A capacity model of children's comprehension of educational content on television. *Media Psychology, 2,* 63–91.

Fishman, J. M., & Marvin, C. (2003). Portrayals of violence and group difference in newspaper photographs: Nationalism and media. *Journal of Communication, 53,* 32–44.

Fishman, M. (1980). *Manufacturing the news.* Austin: University of Texas Press.

Fishoff, S. (1988, August). *Psychological research and a black hole called Hollywood.* Paper presented at the annual meeting of the American Psychological Association, Atlanta, GA.

Fiske, S. T., & Taylor, S. E. (1991). *Social cognition* (2nd ed.). New York: McGraw-Hill.

Flanigan, J. (1999, July 30). There's no defense for NFL expecting more L.A. funds. *Los Angeles Times,* pp. C1, C2.

Flanigan, J. (2003, September 7). GE's broad vision may transform media. *Los Angeles Times,* pp. C1, C4.

Foa, E. B., & Kozak, M. J. (1986). Emotional processing of fear: Exposure to corrective information. *Psychological Bulletin, 99,* 20–35.

Foehr, U. G., Rideout, V., & Miller, C. (2000). Parents and the TV ratings system: A national study. In B. S. Greenberg, L. Rampoldi-Hnilo, & D. Mastro (Eds.), *The alphabet soup of television program ratings.* Cresskill, NJ: Hampton.

Football salaries. (n.d.). Retrieved May 7, 2004, from http://asp.usatoday.com/sports/football/nfl/salaries/mediansalaries.aspx?year=2002

Fore, W. F. (1987). *Television and religion: The shaping of faith, values, and culture.* Minneapolis, MN: Augsburg.

Forgas, J. P., Brown, L. B., & Menyhart, J. (1980). Dimensions of aggression: The perception of aggressive episodes. *British Journal of Social and Clinical Psychology, 19,* 215–227.

Friedson, E. (1953). The relation of the social situation of contact to the media in mass communication. *Public Opinion Quarterly, 17,* 230–238.

Fuller, L. K. (1997). We can't duck the issue: Imbedded advertising in the motion pictures. In K. T. Frith (Ed.), *Undressing the ad: Reading culture in advertising* (pp. 109–129). New York: Peter Lang.

Gaither, C. (2004a, May 1). Online ads are Google's strength. *Los Angeles Times,* pp. C1, C8.

Gaither, C. (2004b, May 23). Can spam be canned? *Los Angeles Times,* pp. C1, C4.

Gaither, C. (2004c, June 24). Insider arrested in spam scheme. *Los Angeles Times,* pp. C1, C9.

Galician, M. L. (1986). Perceptions of good news and bad news on television. *Journalism Quarterly, 63,* 611–616.

Galloway, S. (1993, July 27). U.S. rating system: Sex before violence. *The Hollywood Reporter.*

Gardner, R. W. (1968). *Personality development at preadolescence.* Seattle: University of Washington Press.

Gellene, D. (1996, September 24). Seagram plans more TV ads for whiskey. *Los Angeles Times,* p. D2.

Gerbner, G., & Gross, L. (1976). Living with television: The violence profile. *Journal of Communication, 26*(2), 173–199.

Gerbner, G., Gross, L., Morgan, M., & Signorielli, N. (1980). The "mainstreaming" of America: Violence profile no. 11. *Journal of Communication, 30*(3), 10-29.

Gerbner, G., Gross, L., Signorielli, N., Morgan, M., & Jackson-Beeck, M. (1979). The demonstration of power: Violence profile no. 10. *Journal of Communication, 29*(3), 177–196.

Gerbner, G., Morgan, M., & Signorielli, N. (1982). Programming health portrayals: What viewers see, say and do. In D. Pearl, L. Bouthilet, & J. Lazar (Eds.), *Television and behavior: Ten years of scientific progress and implications for the eighties: Vol. II. Technical reviews* (pp. 291–307). Rockville, MD: U.S. Department of Health and Human Services.

Getter, L. (2004, May 4). Bush, Kerry awash in money. *Los Angeles Times,* pp. A1, A20.

Gilligan, C. (1993). *In a different voice.* Cambridge, MA: Harvard University Press.

Glascock, J. (2001). Gender roles on prime-time network television: Demographics and behaviors. *Journal of Broadcasting & Electronic Media, 45,* 656–669.

Goldstein, D. (1999, September 25). Biggest-grossing movies gross in other ways. *Tallahassee Democrat,* p. B1.

Goleman, D. (1995). *Emotional intelligence.* New York: Bantam.

Goodman, E. (1997, October 27). Beauty industry on a rampage. *Santa Barbara News-Press,* p. A9.

Goodwin, A., & Whannel, G. (Eds.). (1990). *Understanding television.* New York: Routledge.

Goranson, R. E. (1970). Media violence and aggressive behavior: A review of experimental research. In L. Berkowitz (Ed.), *Advances in experimental social psychology* (Vol. 5, pp. 1–31). New York: Academic Press.

Graber, D. A. (1988). *Processing the news: How people tame the information tide* (2nd ed.). New York: Longman.

Greenberg, B. S. (1982). Television and role socialization: An overview. In D. Pearl, L. Bouthilet, & J. Lazar (Eds.), *Television and behavior: Ten years of scientific progress and implications for the eighties: Vol. II. Technical reviews* (pp. 179–190). Rockville, MD: U.S. Department of Health and Human Services.

Greenberg, B. S., Edison, N., Korzenny, F., Fernandez-Collado, C., & Atkin, C. K. (1980). In B. S. Greenberg (Ed.), *Life on television: Content analysis of U.S. TV drama* (pp. 99–128). Norwood, NJ: Ablex.

Greenberg, B. S., & Rampoldi-Hnilo, L. (2001). Children and parent responses to the age-based and content-based television ratings. In D. G. Singer & J. L. Singer (Eds.), *Handbook of children and the media* (pp. 621–634). Thousand Oaks, CA: Sage.

Greenberg, B. S., Rampoldi-Hnilo, L., & Hofschire, L. (2000). Young people's responses to the age-based ratings. In B. S. Greenberg, L. Rampoldi-Hnilo, & D. Mastro (Eds.), *The alphabet soup of television program ratings.* Cresskill, NJ: Hampton.

Greenberg, B. S., Stanley, C., Siemicki, M., Heeter, C., Soderman, A., & Linsangan, R. (1993). Sex content on soaps and prime-time television series most viewed by adolescents. In B. S. Greenberg, J. D. Brown, & N. Buerkel-Rothfuss (Eds.), *Media, sex and the adolescent* (pp. 29–44). Cresskill, NJ: Hampton.

Greimel, H. (2000, February 5). Mannesmann agrees to buyout. *Tallahassee Democrat,* p. E1.

Grimm, M. (1996, June 10). Olympic grab bag. *Brandweek,* pp. 26–28, 30, 32.

Gross, L. (2001). *Up from invisibility: Lesbians, gay men and the media in America.* New York: Columbia University Press.

Gross, N. (1996, December 23). Zap! Splat! Smarts? *Newsweek,* pp. 64–71.

Grusec, J. E. (1973). Effects of co-observer evaluations on imitation: A developmental study. *Developmental Psychology, 8,* 141.

Gulbransen, S. M. (1998a, February 15). Best seller lists are numbers, power, money. *Santa Barbara News-Press,* p. D7.

Gulbransen, S. M. (1998b, March 8). The wane of the paperback revolution. *Santa Barbara News-Press,* p. D7.

Gunter, B. (1985). *Dimensions of television violence.* Aldershot, UK: Gower.

Gunter, B., Furnham, A., & Griffiths, S. (2000). Children's memory for news: A comparison of three presentation media. *Media Psychology, 2,* 93–118.

Hall, A. (2003). Reading realism: Audiences' evaluations of the reality of media texts. *Journal of Communication, 53,* 624–641.

Hancock, E. (1995, October 27). Culture cops take on sleazy TV talk shows. *Santa Barbara News-Press,* p. A1.

Harrington, C. L. (2003). Homosexuality on *All My Children:* Transforming the daytime landscape. *Journal of Broadcasting & Electronic Media, 47,* 216–235.

Hartman, T. (1999, March 22). Movie characters aren't reaping what they sow. *Tallahassee Democrat,* p. A1.

Hawkins, R. P. (1977). The dimensional structure of children's perceptions of television reality. *Communication Research, 7,* 193–226.

Hawkins, R. P., & Pingree, S. (1982). Television's influence on social reality. In D. Pearl, L. Bouthilet, & J. Lazar (Eds.), *Television and behavior: Ten years of scientific progress and implications for the eighties: Vol. II. Technical reviews* (pp. 224–247). Rockville, MD: U.S. Department of Health and Human Services.

Healey, J. (2003, October 25). Pair ordered to pay $2-million fine for spam. *Los Angeles Times,* pp. C1, C2.

Healey, J. (2004, March 7). Piracy fears limit film downloads. *Los Angeles Times,* pp. C1, C5.

Healy, J. M. (1990). *Endangered minds: Why children don't think and what we can do about it.* New York: Simon & Schuster.

Hicks, D. J. (1968). Effects of co-observer's sanctions and adult presence on imitative aggression. *Child Development, 39,* 303–309.

Himmelweit, H. (1966). Television and the child. In B. Berelson & M. Janowitz (Eds.), *Reader in public opinion and communication* (2nd ed., pp. 67–106). New York: Free Press.

Himmelweit, H., Oppenheim, A., & Vince, P. (1958). *Television and the child.* Oxford, UK: Oxford University Press.

Hirsch, E. D., Jr. (1987). *Cultural literacy: What every American needs to know.* Boston: Houghton Mifflin.

Hirsch, E. D., Jr., Kett, J. F., & Trefil, J. (1993). *The dictionary of cultural literacy* (2nd ed.). Boston: Houghton Mifflin.

Hobbs, R. (1998). The seven great debates in the media literacy movement. *Journal of Communication, 48*(1), 16–32.

Hoffner, C. (1997). Children's emotional reactions to a scary film: The role of prior outcome information and coping style. *Human Communication Research, 23,* 323–341.

Hoffner, C., & Cantor, J. (1991). Perceiving and responding to mass media characters. In J. Bryant & D. Zillmann (Eds.), *Responding to the screen* (pp. 63–101). Hillsdale, NJ: Lawrence Erlbaum.

Hofmeister, S. (1997a, February 19). $2.7-billion deal would create no. 2 radio group in U.S. *Los Angeles Times,* p. D1.

Hofmeister, S. (1997b, February 19). Seagram to buy USA Networks for $1.7-billion. *Los Angeles Times,* p. D1.

Hofmeister, S. (2003, October 25). Cable investments, sports blamed for high rates. *Los Angeles Times,* pp. C1, C2.

Hogan, M. J. (2001). Parents and other adults: Models and monitors of healthy media habits. In D. G. Singer & J. L. Singer (Eds.), *Handbook of children and the media* (pp. 663–680). Thousand Oaks, CA: Sage.

Holland, J. (1998, January 15). Internal records show tobacco firm targeted teen-agers. *Santa Barbara News-Press,* p. A2.

Hollander, B. A. (1995). The new news and the 1992 presidential campaign: Perceived vs. actual political knowledge. *Journalism & Mass Communication Quarterly, 72,* 786–798.

Hollenbeck, A., & Slaby, R. (1979). Infant visual and vocal responses to television. *Child Development, 50,* 41–45.

Holstein, W. J. (1999, September 20). MTV, meet *60 Minutes. U.S. News & World Report,* pp. 44–46.

Holstein, W. J. (2000, April 3). And then there were five. *U.S. News & World Report,* p. 46.

Hoops hype. (n.d.). Retrieved May 7, 2004, from http://www.hoopshype.com/salaries.htm

Hoover, S. M. (1988). *Mass media religion: The social sources of the electronic church.* Newbury Park, CA: Sage.

Horn, J. (2003, November 16). Oscar gold diggers. *Los Angeles Times,* pp. A1, A20.

Horowitz, D. (1996, June 24). Nowhere to hide from advertisers. *Santa Barbara News-Press,* p. B7.

Horsfield, P. G. (1984). *Religious television: The American experience.* New York: Longman.

Howard, H. H. (1995). TV station group and cross-media ownership: A 1995 update. *Journalism & Mass Communication Quarterly, 72,* 390–401.

Hudson, T. J. (1992). Consonance in depiction of violent material in television news. *Journal of Broadcasting & Electronic Media, 36,* 411–425.

Huston, A., Wright, J. C., Rice, M. L., Kerkman, D., Seigle, J., & Bremer, M. (1983, June). *Family environment and television use by preschool children.* Paper presented at the Biennial Meeting of the Society for Research on Child Development, Detroit, MI. (ERIC Document No. ED230293)

Hyde, J. (2000, March 28). Auto industry's new credo: Partner up. *Tallahassee Democrat,* p. E1.

Identify Theft Center. (2002). Facts and statistics. Retrieved May 9, 2004, from http://www.idtheft center.org/facts.shtml

Intelligence Infocorp. (1996, May 22). *Nando.net release.* La Jolla, CA: Author.

The Internet Economic Indicators. (2005). *Facts and figures.* Retrieved February 5, 2005, from http://www.internetindicators.com/facts.html

Irvine, M. (1999, November 25). Married couples are the new endangered species. *Tallahassee Democrat,* p. 6B.

Is your child safe in cyberspace? (1995, December). *USA Magazine,* pp. 28–31.

It's pretty hard to tell what's what these days. (1993, July 31). *The Washington Post,* p. A12.

Iyengar, S., & Kinder, D. (1987). *News that matters.* Chicago: University of Chicago Press.

James, M. (2003a, October 19). Indie TV studio still goes in alone. *Los Angeles Times,* pp. C1, C6.

James, M. (2003b, December 5). GE, Nielsen to follow popularity of product placement on prime-time television. *Los Angeles Times,* pp. C1, C11.

Jamieson, K. H., & Campbell, K. K. (1988). *The interplay of influence* (2nd ed.). Belmont, CA: Wadsworth.

Jamieson, K. H., & Waldman, P. (2003). *The press effect: Politicians, journalists, and the stories that shape the political world.* New York: Oxford University Press.

Jeffres, L. W. (1994). *Mass media processes* (2nd ed.). Prospect Heights, IL: Waveland.

Jensen, C. (1995). *Censored: The news that didn't make the news—and why.* New York: Four Walls Eight Windows.

Jensen, C. (1997). *20 years of censored news.* New York: Seven Stories Press.

Jensen, J., & Ross, C. (1996, July 15). Centennial Olympics open as $5 bil event of century. *Advertising Age, 67*(29), 1–2.

Jerome, R., & Bane, V. (2004, May 3). Spam I am. *People,* pp. 125–126.

Jones, J. P. (2004). *Fables, fashions, and facts about advertising: A study of 28 enduring myths.* Thousand Oaks, CA: Sage.

Jordan, A. B. (2001). Public policy and private practice: Government regulations and parental control over children's television use in the home. In D. G. Singer & J. L. Singer (Eds.), *Handbook of children and the media* (pp. 651–662). Thousand Oaks, CA: Sage.

Kagan, J., Rosman, D., Day, D., Albert, J., & Phillips, W. (1964). Information processing in the child: Significance of analytic and reflective attitudes. *Psychological Monographs, 78,* 1.

Kaiser Family Foundation. (1998, May). *Parents, children, and the television ratings system: Two Kaiser Family Foundation surveys.* Menlo Park, CA: Author.

Kaiser Family Foundation. (1999). *Parents and the V-chip.* Menlo Park, CA: Author.

Kaiser Family Foundation. (2002, Fall). *Key facts: Children and video games.* Menlo Park, CA: Author.

Kaiser Family Foundation. (2003). *Sex on TV 3.* Menlo Park, CA: Author.

Kaniss, P. (1996, December 19). Bad news: How electronic media muddle the message. *Philadelphia Inquirer,* p. A35.

Katz, E., & Gurevitch, M. (1976). *The secularization of leisure: Culture and communication in Israel.* Cambridge, MA: Harvard University Press.

Kawamoto, K. (2003). *Media and society in the digital age.* Boston: Allyn & Bacon.

Kaye, B. K., & Sapolsky, B. S. (2001). Offensive language in prime time television: Before and after content ratings. *Journal of Broadcasting & Electronic Media, 45,* 303.

Kiger, P. J. (2004, March 7). The golden age of mediocrity. *Los Angeles Times Magazine,* pp. 16–19, 32.

Kim, K., & Barnett, G. A. (1996). The determinants of international news flow: A network analysis. *Communication Research, 23,* 323–352.

King, C. M. (2000). Effects of humorous heroes and villains in violent action films. *Journal of Communication, 50*(1), 5–25.

King, P. M. (1986). Formal reasoning in adults: A review and critique. In R. A. Milnes & K. S. Kitchenor (Eds.), *Adult cognitive development: Methods and models* (pp. 1–21). New York: Praeger.

Kinkema, K. M., & Harris, J. C. (1998). MediaSport studies: Key research and emerging issues. In L. A. Wenner (Ed.), *MediaSport* (pp. 27–54). New York: Routledge.

Knobloch, S. (2003). Mood adjustment via mass communication. *Journal of Communication, 53,* 233–250.

Knobloch, S., & Zillmann, D. (2002). Mood management via the digital jukebox. *Journal of Communication, 52,* 351–366.

Koenenn, C. (1997, May 14). Let's get simple. *Los Angeles Times,* p. E1.

Kohlberg, L. (1966). Moral education in the schools: A developmental view. *School Review, 74,* 1–30.

Kohlberg, L. (1981). *The philosophy of moral development: Moral stages and the idea of justice.* New York: Harper & Row.

Koziol, R. (1989, August). *English language arts teachers' views on mass media consumption education in Maryland high schools.* Paper presented at the annual conference of the Association of Education in Journalism and Mass Communication, Washington, DC.

Krcmar, M., & Cantor, J. (1996, May). *Discussing violent television: Parents, children, and TV viewing choices.* Paper presented at the annual conference of the International Communication Association, Montreal, Canada.

Krcmar, M., & Greene, K. (1999). Predicting exposure to and uses of television violence. *Journal of Communication, 49*(3), 24–45.

Kress, G. (1992). Media literacy as cultural technology in the age of transcultural media. In C. Bazalgette, E. Bevort, & J. Savino (Eds.), *New directions: Media education worldwide* (pp. 190–202). London: British Film Institute.

Kubey, R. (1990). Television and family harmony among children, adolescents, and adults: Results from the experience of sampling method. In J. Bryant (Ed.), *Television and the American family* (pp. 73–88). Hillsdale, NJ: Lawrence Erlbaum.

Kubey, R. (1997). A rationale for media education. In R. Kubey (Ed.), *Media literacy in the information age* (pp. 15–68). New Brunswick, NJ: Transaction Publishers.

Kubey, R. (1998). Obstacles to the development of media education in the United States. *Journal of Communication, 48*(1), 58–69.

Kubey, R., Shifflet, M., Weerakkody, N., & Ukeiley, S. (1996). Demographic diversity on cable: Have the new cable channels made a difference in the representation of gender, race, and age? *Journal of Broadcasting & Electronic Media, 39,* 459–471.

Kunkel, D., Farinola, W. J. M., Farrar, K., Donnerstein, E., Bielby, E., & Swarun, L. (2002). Deciphering the V-chip: An examination of the television industry's program rating judgments. *Journal of Communication, 52*(1), 112–138.

Kwak, H., Zinkhan, G. M., & Dominick, J. R. (2002). The moderating role of gender and compulsive buying tendencies in the cultivation effects of TV shows and TV advertising: A cross cultural study between the United States and South Korea. *Media Psychology, 4,* 77–111.

Lacayo, R. (1995, June 12). Are music and movies killing America's soul? *Time,* pp. 24–30.

Lacy, S., & Blanchard, A. (2003). The impact of public ownership, profits, and competition on number of newsroom employees and starting salaries in mid-sized daily newspapers. *Journalism & Mass Communication Quarterly, 80,* 949–968.

Lacy, S., & Riffe, D. (1994). The impact of competition and group ownership on radio news. *Journalism & Mass Communication Quarterly, 71,* 583–593.

Lang, A., Potter, R. F., & Bolls, P. D. (1999). Something for nothing: Is visual encoding automatic? *Media Psychology, 1,* 145–163.

Larson, J. (1983). *Television's window on the world.* Norwood, NJ: Ablex.

LaSalle, M. (1996, July 7). Why overpaid stars aren't worth it. *Santa Barbara News-Press,* p. D9.

*L.A. Times* publisher errs, apologizes. (1999, October 31). *Tallahassee Democrat,* p. 5B.

Law, C., & Labre, M. P. (2002). Cultural standards of attractiveness: A thirty-year look at changes in male images in magazines. *Journalism & Mass Communication Quarterly, 79,* 697–711.

Lawrence, F., & Wozniak, P. (1989). Children's television viewing with family members. *Psychological Reports, 65*(2), 395–400.

The learning lag: You can't blame TV. (1996, December 2). *U.S. News & World Report,* p. 16.

Lee, K., & Light, J. (2003). Law and regulation, part I: Individual interests. In L. Shyles (Ed.), *Deciphering cyberspace: Making the most of digital communication technology* (pp. 293–322). Thousand Oaks, CA: Sage.

Lee, M., & Solomon, N. (1990). *Unreliable sources: A guide to detecting bias in news media.* New York: Carol.

Leo, J. (1996, August 19). The joys of covering press releases. *U.S. News & World Report,* p. 16.

Leo, J. (1999, September 27). And now . . . smut-see TV. *U.S. News & World Report,* p. 15.

Lewis, C. (2000, September/October). Media money. *Columbia Journalism Review,* pp. 20–27.

Lichter, L. S., & Lichter, S. R. (1983). *Prime time crime.* Washington, DC: The Media Institute.

Liebert, R. M., Neale, J. M., & Davidson, E. S. (1973). *The early window: Effects of television on children and youth.* New York: Pergamon.

Lin, C. A., & Jeffres, L. W. (2001). Comparing distinctions and similarities across websites of newspapers, radio stations, and television stations. *Journalism & Mass Communication Quarterly, 78,* 555–573.

Linz, D., Donnerstein, E., & Penrod, S. (1984). The effects of multiple exposures to filmed violence against women. *Journal of Communication, 34*(3), 130–147.

Linz, D., Donnerstein, E., & Penrod, S. (1988). Effects of long-term exposure to violent and sexually degrading depictions of women. *Journal of Personality and Social Psychology, 55*(5), 758–768.

Lippmann, W. (1922). *Public opinion.* New York: Harcourt, Brace.

Lorimer, R. (1994). *Mass communications: A comparative introduction.* Manchester, UK: Manchester University Press.

Lowry, B. (1997, September 21). TV on decline but few back U.S. regulation. *Los Angeles Times,* pp. A1, A40, A41.

Lowry, B., Jensen, E., & Braxton, G. (1999, July 20). Networks decide diversity doesn't pay. *Los Angeles Times,* p. A1.

Lowry, D. T., Nio, R. C. J., & Leitner, D. W. (2003). Setting the public fear agenda: A longitudinal analysis of network TV crime reporting, public perceptions of crime, and FBI crime statistics. *Journal of Communication, 53,* 61–73.

Lowry, D. T., & Shidler, J. A. (1995). The sound bites, the biters, and the bitten: An analysis of network TV news bias in campaign '92. *Journalism and Mass Communication Quarterly, 72,* 147–157.

Luntz, F. (2000, March). Public to press: Cool it. *Brill's Content,* pp. 74–79.

Lyall, S. (1996, November 27). Penguin's deal to buy Putnam will create major publishing force. *Santa Barbara News-Press,* p. A6.

Lyman, P., & Varian, H. R. (2003, October 27). *How much information? 2003.* Retrieved May 14, 2004, from http://www.sims.berkeley.edu/ research/ projects/ how-much-info-2003

Maddox, K. (1999, February 15). IAB: Internet advertising will reach new $2 bil for 1998. *Advertising Age, 70*(7), 34.

Makovsky, D. (1999, May 24). Getting into the ring: Wealthy American and other foreigners played a quiet role in Israel's election. *U.S. News & World Report,* p. 43.

Malamuth, N. M., & Check, J. V. P. (1980). Penile tumescence and perceptual responses to rape as a function of victim's perceived reactions. *Journal of Applied Social Psychology, 10,* 528–547.

Maney, K. (1995). *Megamedia shakeout: The inside story of the leaders and the losers in the exploding communications industry.* New York: John Wiley.

Manning, R. (1987, December 28). The selling of the Olympics. *Newsweek,* pp. 40–41.

Marcuse, H. (1964). *One-dimensional man: Studies in the ideology of advanced industrial society.* Boston: Beacon.

Mastro, D. E., & Greenberg, B. S. (2000). The portrayal of racial minorities on prime-time television. *Journal of Broadcasting & Electronic Media, 44,* 690.

Mastro, D. E., & Stern, S. R. (2003). Representations of race in television commercials: A content analysis of prime-time advertising. *Journal of Broadcasting & Electronic Media, 47,* 638–647.

Material kids are on the march. (1994, April). *NEA Today,* p. 10.

Matthews, J. (1992, April 13). To yank or not to yank? *Newsweek,* p. 59.

Maurstad, T. (1998, August 20). TV land adds 60-second sitcoms to the lineup. *Tallahassee Democrat,* p. 7D.

McCombs, M. E., & Shaw, D. (1972). The agenda setting function of the mass media. *Public Opinion Quarterly, 36,* 176–187.

McDonald, M. (2000, March 27). L.A. is their kind of town. *U.S. News & World Report,* p. 45.

McLeod, J. M., Fitzpatrick, M. A., Glynn, C. J., & Fallis, S. F. (1982). Television and social relations: Family influences and consequences for interpersonal behavior. In D. Pearl, L. Bouthilet, & J. Lazar (Eds.), *Television and behavior: Ten years of scientific progress and implications for the eighties: Vol. II. Technical reviews* (pp. 272–286). Rockville, MD: U.S. Department of Health and Human Services.

McQueen, A. (1999, November 19). Future voters come up short on knowledge of civics. *Tallahassee Democrat,* p. B1.

Meadowcroft, J., & Reeves, B. (1989). Influence of story schema development on children's attention to television. *Communication Research, 16,* 353–374.

Medrich, E. A., Roizen, J. A., Rubin, V., & Buckley, S. (1982). *The serious business of growing up: A study of children's lives outside school.* Berkeley: University of California Press.

Merli, J. (1998, October 19). Internet users not forsaking radio. *Broadcasting & Cable,* p. 59.

Messaris, P. (1994). *Visual "literacy": Image, mind, and reality.* Boulder, CO: Westview.

Messaris, P., & Kerr, D. (1984). TV-related mother-child interaction and children's perceptions of TV characters. *Journalism Quarterly, 61,* 662–666.

Metallinos, N. (1996). *Television aesthetics: Perceptual, cognitive, and compositional bases.* Mahwah, NJ: Lawrence Erlbaum.

Metropolitan Sports Facilities Commission. (n.d.). Next generation of sports facilities. Retrieved May 7, 2004, from http://www.msfc.com/nextgen.cfm

Meyrowitz, J. (1985). *No sense of place: The impact of electronic media on social behavior.* New York: Oxford University Press.

Mifflin, L. (1997, February 22). Parents give TV ratings mixed reviews. *New York Times,* p. A6.

Miller, S. (Ed.). (1989). *America's watching: 30th anniversary 1959–1989.* New York: The Roper Organization.

Mnookin, S. (2002, August 19). The tobacco sham. *Newsweek,* p. 33.

Mohr, P. J. (1979). Parental influence of children's viewing of evening television programs. *Journal of Broadcasting, 23,* 213–228.

Moody, N. M. (2002, June 16). Record industry seeking alternatives. *Santa Barbara News-Press,* pp. F1, F2.

Most valuable franchise: Yankees. (2004, April 9). *Los Angeles Times,* p. D9.

Munoz, L. (2004, March 24). Movie costs hit new high. *Los Angeles Times,* pp. E1, E4.

Music Piracy and the Audio Home Recording Act. (2002, November 20). *Duke Law and Technology Review.* Retrieved June 29, 2002, from http://www.law.duke.edu/journals/dltr/articles/2002 dltr0023.html

Myers, P. N., Jr., & Biocca, F. A. (1992). The elastic body image: The effect of television advertising and programming on body image distortions in young women. *Journal of Communication, 42*(3), 108–133.

Names & faces. (1995, September 11). *Santa Barbara News-Press,* p. B8.

Nathanson, A. I. (1999). Identifying and explaining the relationship between parental mediation and children's aggression. *Communication Research, 26,* 124–143.

Nathanson, A. I. (2001a). Mediation of children's television viewing: Working toward conceptual clarity and common understanding. In W. B. Gudykunst (Ed.), *Communication yearbook 25* (pp. 115–151). Mahwah, NJ: Lawrence Erlbaum.

Nathanson, A. I. (2001b). Parent and child perspectives on the presence and meaning of parental television mediation. *Journal of Broadcasting & Electronic Media, 45,* 201–220.

Nathanson, A. I. (2001c). Parents versus peers: Exploring the significance of peer mediation of anti-social television. *Communication Research, 28,* 251–274.

Nathanson, A. I. (2002). The unintended effects of parental mediation of television on adolescents. *Media Psychology, 4,* 207–230.

Nathanson, A. I., & Botta, R. A. (2003). Shaping the effects of television on adolescents' body image disturbance: The role of parental mediation. *Communication Research, 30,* 304–331.

Nathanson, A. I., & Cantor, J. (2000). Reducing the aggression-promoting effect of violent cartoons by increasing children's fictional involvement with the victim: A study of active mediation. *Journal of Broadcasting & Electronic Media, 44,* 94–109.

Nathanson, A. I., Eveland, W. P., Park, H.-S., & Paul, B. (2002). Perceived media influence and efficacy as predictors of caregivers' protective behaviors. *Journal of Broadcasting & Electronic Media, 46,* 385–410.

Nathanson, A. I., & Yang, M.-S. (2003). The effects of mediation content and form on children's responses to violent television. *Human Communication Research, 29*(1), 111–134.

National Football League 1999 salaries. (2000, May 23). *USA Today,* pp. 14C–15C.

National Television Violence Study (NTVS). (1996). *Scientific report.* Thousand Oaks, CA: Sage.

NBC gambles on the future. (1996, January 22). *Santa Barbara News-Press,* p. A11.

NCTV says violence on TV up 16%. (1983, March 22). *Broadcasting Magazine,* p. 63.

Nelson, J. (1995, August 8). NBC gets Olympic TV rights in coup. *Santa Barbara News-Press,* p. A12.

Neuman, W. R. (1991). *The future of the mass audience.* New York: Cambridge University Press.

Newscientist.com. (2004, March 4). Net music piracy "does not harm record sales." Retrieved June 29, 2004, from http://newscientist.com/news/news.jsp?id=ns99994831

NFL notes. (2002, December 12). *Santa Barbara News-Press,* p. C5.

NFL teams dodge salary cap. (1996, January 2). *Santa Barbara News-Press,* p. B5.

Norris, V. P. (1983). Consumer valuation of national ads. *Journalism Quarterly, 60,* 262–268.

Oliver, M. B. (1994). Portrayals of crime, race, and aggression in "reality based" police shows: A content analysis. *Journal of Broadcasting & Electronic Media, 38,* 179–192.

Oliver, M. B., & Kalyanaraman, S. (2002). Appropriate for all viewing audiences? An examination of violent and sexual portrayals in movie previews featured on video rentals. *Journal of Broadcasting & Electronic Media, 46,* 283–300.

Ostrow, R. (1996, May 6). Violent crime in U.S. fell 4% in '95, FBI says. *Los Angeles Times,* pp. A1, A11.

Ozanich, G. W., & Wirth, M. O. (1993). Media mergers and acquisitions: An overview. In A. Alexander, J. Owers, & R. Carveth (Eds.), *Media economics: Theory and practice* (pp. 115–133). Hillsdale, NJ: Lawrence Erlbaum.

Pace signs and rejoining Rams. (2003, August 27). *Los Angeles Times,* p. D10.

Parenti, M. (1986). *Inventing reality: The politics of the mass media.* New York: St. Martin's.

Patterson, T. (1980). *The mass media election.* New York: Praeger.

Penner, M. (2004, May 7). Baseball cancels plans for movie ad on bases. *Los Angeles Times,* pp. D1, D8.

Perkins, K. (1996, November 27). Statistics blur image of American family. *Santa Barbara News-Press,* pp. A1, A2.

Perry, J. (2000, February 28). Only the cyberlonely. *U.S. News & World Report,* p. 62.

Pew Internet & American Life Project. (2000, August 20). Trust and privacy online: Why Americans want to rewrite the rules. Retrieved May 9, 2004, from http://pewinternet.org/reports/reports.asp?Report=19

Pew Research Center for the People and the Press. (1998). *Internet news takes off.* Washington, DC: Author.

Picard, R. G. (1989). *Media economics: Concepts and issues.* Newbury Park, CA: Sage.

Picard, R. G. (1993). Economics of the daily newspaper industry. In A. Alexander, J. Owers, & R. Carveth (Eds.), *Media economics: Theory and practice* (pp. 181–203). Hillsdale, NJ: Lawrence Erlbaum.

Picard, R. G., Winter, J. P., McCombs, M., & Lacy, S. (Eds.). (1988). *Press concentration and monopoly: New perspectives on newspaper ownership and operation.* Norwood, NJ: Ablex.

Piette, J., & Giroux, L. (1997). The theoretical foundations of media education programs. In R. Kubey (Ed.), *Media literacy in the information age: Current perspectives, information and behavior* (Vol. 6, pp. 89–134). New Brunswick, NJ: Transaction Publishers.

Pipher, M. (1996). *The shelter of each other.* New York: Putnam.

Pizza pie in the sky. (1999, October 1). *Tallahassee Democrat,* p. B1.

Pletcher, D. (2003). *ITRC's 2003 study: Identity theft—the aftermath—2003.* Sacramento, CA: Identity Theft Research Center.

Police cars to add advertisements. (1995, July 13). *Santa Barbara News-Press,* p. A4.

Polman, D. (2003, June 1). FCC vote may prove a windfall for media giants. *Santa Barbara News-Press,* pp. B1, B2.

Pool, M. M., Koolstra, C. M., & van der Voort, R. H. A. (2003). The impact of background radio and television on high school students' homework performance. *Journal of Communication, 53,* 74–87.

Posner, M. L., & Snyder, C. R. R. (1975). Attention and cognitive control. In R. L. Solso (Ed.), *Information processing and cognition: The Loyola symposium* (pp. 55–85). Hillsdale, NJ: Lawrence Erlbaum.

Postman, N., & Powers, S. (1992). *How to watch TV news.* New York: Penguin.

Potter, R. F. (2002). Give the people what they want: A content analysis of FM radio station home pages. *Journal of Broadcasting & Electronic Media, 46,* 369–385.

Potter, W. J. (1986). Perceived reality in the cultivation hypothesis. *Journal of Broadcasting & Electronic Media, 30,* 159–174.

Potter, W. J. (1987a). Does television viewing hinder academic achievement among adolescents? *Human Communication Research, 14,* 27–46.

Potter, W. J. (1987b). News from three worlds in prestige U.S. newspapers. *Journalism Quarterly, 64,* 73–79.

Potter, W. J. (1991). Examining cultivation from a psychological perspective: Component subprocesses. *Communication Research, 18,* 77–102.

Potter, W. J. (1999). *On media violence.* Thousand Oaks, CA: Sage.

Potter, W. J. (2003). *The 11 myths of media violence.* Thousand Oaks, CA: Sage.

Potter, W. J., Pashupati, K., Pekurny, R. G., Hoffman, E., & Davis, K. (2002). Perceptions of television: A schema approach. *Media Psychology, 4,* 27–50.

Potter, W. J., & Smith, S. (2000). The context of graphic portrayals of television violence. *Journal of Broadcasting & Electronic Media, 44,* 301.

Potter, W. J., & Vaughan, M. (1997). Aggression in television entertainment: Profiles and trends. *Communication Research Reports, 14,* 116–124.

Potter, W. J., & Ware, W. (1987). An analysis of the contexts of antisocial acts on prime-time television. *Communication Research, 14,* 664–686.

Potts, R., & Sanchez, D. (1994). Television viewing and depression: No news is good news. *Journal of Broadcasting & Electronic Media, 38,* 79–90.

Preston, I. (1994). *The tangled web they weave: Truth, falsity, & advertisers.* Madison: University of Wisconsin Press.

Pritchard, D. A. (1975). Leveling-sharpening revised. *Perceptual and Motor Skills, 40,* 111–117.

Pulaski, M. A. S. (1980). *Understanding Piaget: An introduction to children's cognitive development* (Revised and expanded edition). New York: Harper & Row.

Quinn, J. B. (1996, April 1). Politics: Fable vs. fact. *Newsweek,* p. 62.

Rampoldi-Hnilo, L., & Greenberg, B. S. (2000). A poll of Latina and Caucasian mothers with 6–10 year old children. In B. S. Greenberg, L. Rampoldi-Hnilo, & D. Mastro (Eds.), *The alphabet soup of television program ratings.* Cresskill, NJ: Hampton.

Randolph, E. (1997, April 22). Journalists find little neutrality over objective reporting. *Los Angeles Times,* p. A5.

Real, M. R. (1998). MediaSport: Technology and the commodification of postmodern sport. In L. A. Wenner (Ed.), *MediaSport* (pp. 14–26). New York: Routledge.

Reid, L. N. (1979). Viewing rules as mediating factors of children's responses to commercials. *Journal of Broadcasting, 23,* 15–26.

Reid, L. N., & Frazer, C. F. (1980). Children's use of television commercials to initiate social interaction in family viewing situations. *Journal of Broadcasting, 24,* 149–158.

Reinken, T. (2003, August 19). Dome and other homes. *Los Angeles Times,* p. A10.

Rhodes, S., & Reibstein, L. (1996, July 1). Let him walk! *Newsweek,* pp. 44–45.

Rideout, V. J., Foehr, U. G., Roberts, D. F., & Brodie, M. (1999). *Kids & media @ the new millennium.* Menlo Park, CA: Kaiser Foundation.

Riggs, D. (1999, February 28). True love is alive and well, say romance book writers. *Tallahassee Democrat,* p. 3D.

Ritzer, G. (1993). *The McDonaldization of society.* Newbury Park, CA: Pine Forge Press.

Robertson, L. (2001, March). Ethically challenged. *American Journalism Review,* pp. 20–29.

Romer, D., Jamieson, K. H., & Aday, S. (2003). Television news and the cultivation of fear of crime. *Journal of Communication, 53,* 88–104.

The Roper Organization. (1981). *Sex, profanity and violence: An opinion survey about seventeen television programs.* New York: Information Office.

Roshier, B. (1981). The selection of crime news by the press. In S. Cohen & J. Young (Eds.), *The manufacture of news: Deviance, social problems and the mass media* (pp. 40–51). Beverly Hills, CA: Sage.

Ross, E. (2003, June 10). Study links movies, teen smoking. *Los Angeles Times,* pp. B1, B2.

Rothberg, D. M. (1996, June 23). Group seeks increase in foreign aid budget. *Santa Barbara News-Press,* p. F2.

Rothschild, N., & Morgan, M. (1987). Cohesion and control: Adolescents' relationships with parents as mediators of television. *Journal of Early Adolescence, 7,* 299–314.

Rubin, A. M., Perse, E. M., & Taylor, D. S. (1988). A methodological examination of cultivation. *Communication Research, 15,* 107–133.

Salomon, G. (1977). Effects of encouraging Israeli mothers to co-observe *Sesame Street* with their five-year-olds. *Child Development, 48,* 1146–1151.

Salomon, G. (1981). Introducing AIME: The assessment of children's mental involvement with television. In H. Kelley & H. Gardner (Eds.), *New directions for child development: Viewing children through television* (No. 13, pp. 89–112). San Francisco: Jossey-Bass.

Salovey, P., & Mayer, J. D. (1990). Emotional intelligence. *Imagination, Cognition, and Personality, 9,* 185–211.

Sanders, B. (1994). *A is for ox: Violence, electronic media, and the silencing of the written word.* New York: Pantheon.

Sang, F., Schmitz, B., & Tasche, K. (1992). Individuation and television coviewing in the family: Development trends in the viewing behavior of adolescents. *Journal of Broadcasting & Electronic Media, 36,* 427–441.

Sapolsky, B. S., Molitor, F., & Luque, S. (2003). Sex and violence in slasher films: Re-examining the assumptions. *Journalism & Mass Communication Quarterly, 80,* 28–38.

Sapolsky, B., & Tabarlet, J. (1990). *Sex in prime time television: 1979 vs. 1989.* Unpublished manuscript, Department of Communication, Florida State University, Tallahassee.

Sayre, S., & King, C. (2003). *Entertainment & society: Audiences, trends, and impacts.* Thousand Oaks, CA: Sage.

Scharrer, E. (2001). From wise to foolish: The portrayal of the sitcom father, 1950s–1990s. *Journal of Broadcasting & Electronic Media, 45,* 23.

Schmitt, K. (2000). *Public policy, family rules, and children's media use in the home.* Washington, DC: Annenberg Public Policy Center of the University of Pennsylvania.

Schmitt, K. L., Woolf, K. D., & Anderson, D. R. (2003). Viewing the viewers: Viewing behaviors by children and adults during television programs and commercials. *Journal of Communication, 53,* 265–281.

Schrag, R. (1990). *Taming the wild tube: A family guide to television and video.* Chapel Hill: University of North Carolina Press.

Schramm, W., Lyle, J., & Parker, E. B. (1961). *Television in the lives of our children.* Stanford, CA: Stanford University Press.

Schudson, M. (2003). *The sociology of news.* New York: Norton.

Schultz, S. (1999, November 8). Why we're fat. *U.S. News & World Report,* p. 82.

Schwartz, S. (1984, Winter). Send help before it's too late. *Parent's Choice,* p. 2.

Scribner, S., & Cole, M. (1981). *The psychology of literacy.* Cambridge, MA: Harvard University Press.

Segrin, C., & Nabi, R. (2002). Does television viewing cultivate unrealistic expectations about marriage? *Journal of Communication, 52,* 247–263.

Shoemaker, P. J. (1987). The communication of deviance. In B. Dervin (Ed.), *Progress in communication science* (Vol. 8, pp. 151–175). Norwood, NJ: Ablex.

Shoemaker, P. J., Danielian, L. H., & Brendlinger, N. (1991). Deviant acts, risky business, and US interest: The newsworthiness of world events. *Journalism Quarterly, 68,* 781–795.

Shoemaker, P. J., & Reese, S. D. (1996). *Mediating the message: Theories of influences on mass media content* (2nd ed.). White Plains, NY: Longman.

Shrum, L. J. (1999). The relationship of television viewing with attitude strength and extremity: Implications for the cultivation effect. *Media Psychology, 1,* 3–25.

Signorielli, N. (1982). Marital status in television drama: A case of reduced options. *Journal of Broadcasting, 26,* 585–597.

Signorielli, N. (1990). Television's mean and dangerous world: A continuation of the cultural indicators perspective. In N. Signorielli & M. Morgan (Eds.), *Cultivation analysis: New directions in media effects research* (pp. 85–106). Newbury Park, CA: Sage.

Signorielli, N., & Bacue, A. (1999). Recognition and respect: A content analysis of prime-time television characters across three decades. *Sex Roles, 40,* 527–544.

Signorielli, N., & Kahlenberg, S. (2001). Television's world of work in the nineties. *Journal of Broadcasting & Electronic Media, 45,* 4.

Silverblatt, A. (1995). *Media literacy: Keys to interpreting media messages.* Westport, CT: Praeger.

Simons, J. (1996, December 30). Waiting to download. *U.S. News & World Report,* p. 60.

Sinatra, R. (1986). *Visual literacy connections to thinking, reading and writing.* Springfield, IL: Charles C Thomas.

Singer, J. L., & Singer, D. G. (1981). *Television, imagination, and aggression: A study of preschoolers.* Hillsdale, NJ: Lawrence Erlbaum.

Singer, J. L., Singer, D. G., & Rapaczynski, W. S. (1984). Family patterns and television viewing as predictors of children's beliefs and aggression. *Journal of Communication, 34*(2), 73–89.

Sizer, T. R. (1995). Silences. *Daedelus, 124*(4), 77–83.

Slater, E. (2004, April 5). Technology feeds a diet of news bites. *Los Angeles Times,* p. A11.

Slater, M. D. (2003). Alienation, aggression, and sensation seeking as predictors of adolescent use of violent film, computer, and website content. *Journal of Communication, 53,* 105–121.

Slater, M. D., & Rouner, D. (2002). Entertainment-education and elaboration likelihood: Understanding the processing of narrative persuasion. *Communication Theory, 12,* 173–191.

Slattery, K. L., & Hakanen, E. A. (1994). Sensationalism versus public affairs content of local TV news: Pennsylvania revisited. *Journal of Broadcasting & Electronic Media, 38,* 205–216.

Smith, P. K., & Cowie, H. (1988). *Understanding children's development.* Oxford, UK: Basil Blackwell.

Smith, S., Lachlan, K., & Tamborini, R. (2003). Popular video games: Quantifying the presentation of violence and its context. *Journal of Broadcasting & Electronic Media, 47,* 58–77.

Smith, S. L., & Wilson, B. J. (2002). Children's comprehension of and fear reactions to television news. *Media Psychology, 4,* 1–26.

Smythe, D. W. (1954). Reality as presented on television. *Public Opinion Quarterly, 18,* 143–156.

Soley, L. C., & Reid, L. N. (1983). Satisfaction with the information value of magazine and television advertising. *Journal of Advertising, 12*(3), 27–31.

Standard & Poor's. (1996, July). *Index to surveys.* New York: Author.

Stanger, J. (1997). *Television in the home: The second annual survey of parents and children in the home* (Survey Series No. 2). Philadelphia: Annenberg Public Policy Center of the University of Pennsylvania.

Steele, J. E. (1995). Experts and the operational bias of television news: The case of the Persian Gulf War. *Journalism & Mass Communication Quarterly, 72,* 799–812.

Stern, L. (2002, April 8). Is Orwell your banker? *Newsweek,* p. 59.

Sternberg, R. J., & Berg, C. A. (1987). What are theories of adult intellectual development theories of? In C. Schooler & K. W. Schaie (Eds.), *Cognitive functioning and social structure over the life course* (pp. 3–23). Norwood, NJ: Ablex.

Stewart, L. (2004, March 24). Study criticizes school over diversity, graduation rates. *Los Angeles Times,* p. D5.

Stone, B., & Lin, J. (2002, August 19). Spamming the world. *Newsweek,* pp. 42–44.

Stoneman, Z., & Brody, G. H. (1982). An in-home investigation of maternal teaching strategies during *Sesame Street* and a popular situation comedy. *Journal of Applied Developmental Psychology, 3,* 275–284.

Strasburger, V. C., & Wilson, B. J. (2002). *Children, adolescents, & the media.* Thousand Oaks, CA: Sage.

Stroh, M. (1999, October 9). From pulp to pixel. *Tallahassee Democrat,* p. E1.

Study links teen smoking to popular ads. (1996, April 14). *Santa Barbara News-Press,* p. A2.

The super rich getting richer. (2003, September 19). *Los Angeles Times,* p. C3.

Taylor, S. E., & Howell, R. J. (1973). The ability of three-, four-, and five-year-old children to distinguish fantasy from reality. *Journal of Genetic Psychology, 122,* 315–318.

Teen drug use soars. (1996, August 21). *Asbury Park Press,* p. A1.

Terrell, K. (1999, September 20). Textbooks 101: Web offers few bargains. *U.S. News & World Report,* p. 74.

Thomas, M. H. (1982). Physiological arousal, exposure to a relatively lengthy aggressive film, and aggression behavior. *Journal of Research in Personality, 16,* 72–81.

Tuchman, G. (1978). *Making news: A study in the construction of reality.* New York: Free Press.

Tunes & 'tudes: Annual teen music survey. (2002, May 3–5). *USA Weekend,* pp. 8, 11.

Turow, J. (1992). *Media systems in society.* New York: Longman.

Tyre, P. (2002, August 5). Fighting "big fat." *Newsweek,* pp. 38, 40.

U.S. Bureau of the Census. (2000). *Statistical abstract of the United States: 1999.* Washington, DC: Department of Commerce.

U.S. Bureau of the Census. (2004). *Statistical abstract of the United States: 2003.* Washington, DC: Department of Commerce.

U.S. divorce statistics. (2002). Retrieved July 19, 2004, from http://divorcemagazine.com/statistics/statsUS.shtml

U.S. tallies consumer fraud loss at $437 million (2004, January 23). *Los Angeles Times,* p. A20.

Valkenburg, P. M., Krcmar, M., Peeters, A. L., & Marseille, N. M. (1999). "Instructive mediation," "restrictive mediation," and "social coviewing." *Journal of Broadcasting & Electronic Media, 43,* 52–66.

van der Voort, T. H. A. (1986). *Television violence: A child's-eye view.* Amsterdam: North-Holland.

van der Voort, T. H. A., Nikken, P., & van Lil, J. E. (1992). Determinants of parental guidance of children's television viewing: A Dutch replication study. *Journal of Broadcasting & Electronic Media, 36,* 61–74.

Vande Berg, L. R., & Streckfuss, D. (1992). Prime-time television's portrayal of women and the world of work: A demographic profile. *Journal of Broadcasting & Electronic Media, 36,* 195–208.

Verrier, R., & James, M. (2003, October 9). GE, Vivendi finalize NBC Universal deal. *Los Angeles Times,* pp. C1, C11.

Vranizan, M. (1995, June 5). On-line junkie hooked on his screen. *Santa Barbara News-Press,* p. A11.

Walsh, D. (1994). *Selling out America's children.* Minneapolis, MN: Fairview.

Wartella, E. (1981). The child as viewer. In M. E. Ploghoft & J. A. Anderson (Eds.), *Education for the television age* (pp. 28–17). Springfield, IL: Charles C Thomas.

Watanabe, T. (1999, July 27). The crisis facing the Good Book. *Los Angeles Times,* p. A1.

Weinraub, B. (1995, September 18). Stars' salaries skyrocketing; pressure to produce heats up demand for top talent. *New York Times,* p. C1.

Wharton, D. (1991, June 10). Let 'em eat junk? Fat chance, Solon says. *Variety,* p. 33.

What is a computer virus? (n.d.). Retrieved June 28, 2004, from http://pcsrvc.com/ardmore/VirusInf.htm

Whitman, D. (1996, December 16). I'm OK, you're not. *U.S. News & World Report,* pp. 24–30.

Whitman, D., & Loftus, M. (1996, December 16). Things are getting better? Who knew? *U.S. News & World Report,* pp. 30, 32.

Whitson, D. (1998). Circuits of promotion: Media, marketing and the globalization of sport. In L. A. Wenner (Ed.), *MediaSport* (pp. 57–72). New York: Routledge.

Wicks, R. H. (1992). Improvement over time in recall of media information: An exploratory study. *Journal of Broadcasting and Electronic Media, 36,* 287–302.

Wicks, R. H., & Souley, B. (2003). Going negative: Candidate usage of Internet Web sites during the 2000 presidential campaign. *Journalism & Mass Communication Quarterly, 80,* 128–144.

Wildavsky, B. (1999, October 11). Kids don't have the write stuff. *U.S. News & World Report,* p. 28.

Will, G. F. (1996, April 15). Civic speech gets rationed. *Newsweek,* p. 78.

Williams, T. M., Zabrack, M. L., & Joy, L. A. (1982). The portrayal of aggression on North American television. *Journal of Applied Social Psychology, 12,* 360–380.

Wilson, B. J., & Cantor, J. (1985). Developmental difference in empathy with a television protagonist's fear. *Journal of Experimental Child Psychology, 39,* 284–299.

Wilson, B. J., & Weiss, A. J. (1992). Developmental differences in children's reactions to a toy advertisement linked to a toy-based cartoon. *Journal of Broadcasting & Electronic Media, 36,* 371–394.

Windhauser, J. W., Seiter, J., & Winfree, L. T. (1990). Crime news in the Louisiana Press, 1980 vs. 1985. *Journalism Quarterly, 67,* 72–78.

Winik, L. W. (2004, March 14). How safe is your computer? *Parade,* p. 10.

Winn, M. (2002). *The plug-in drug: Television, computers, and family life.* New York: Penguin.

Witkin, H. A., & Goodenough, D. R. (1977). Field dependence and interpersonal behavior. *Psychological Bulletin, 84,* 661–689.

Wolff, M. (2003, May 26). Troubled times. *New York,* pp. 18–21.

Woodward, K. L. (1990, December 17). A time to seek. *Newsweek,* pp. 50–56.

Wride, N. (1999, August 9). Children learn to say, "Buy, buy." *Los Angeles Times,* p. E1.

Wright, J. C., Huston, A. C., Reitz, A. L., & Piemyat, S. (1994). Young children's perceptions of television reality: Determinants and developmental differences. *Developmental Psychology, 30,* 229–239.

Wulff, S. (1997). Media literacy. In W. G. Christ (Ed.), *Media education assessment handbook* (pp. 123–142). Mahwah, NJ: Lawrence Erlbaum.

Wurman, R. S. (1989). *Information anxiety.* New York: Doubleday.

Yang, D. J. (2000, January 17). Craving your next Web fix. *U.S. News & World Report,* p. 41.

Zillmann, D. (1991). Television viewing and physiological arousal. In J. Bryant & D. Zillmann (Eds.), *Responding to the screen: Reception and reaction processes* (pp. 103–133). Hillsdale, NJ: Lawrence Erlbaum.

# Index

# About the Author

**W. James Potter,** professor at the University of California at Santa Barbara, holds one PhD in Communication Studies and another in Instructional Technology. He has been teaching media courses for more than two decades in the areas of effects on individuals and society, content narratives, structure and economics of media industries, advertising, journalism, programming, and production. He was a principal investigator on the $3 million, 3-year, three-volume National Television Violence Study (1996, 1997, 1998). He has served as editor of the *Journal of Broadcasting & Electronic Media* and is the author of many journal articles and books, including the following: *On Media Violence, Theory of Media Literacy: A Cognitive Approach, The 11 Myths of Media Violence,* and *How to Publish Your Communication Research* (with Alison Alexander). He's currently editing the *Encyclopedia of Media Violence.*